T0346337

Immigration and the Constitution

Volume 3
Shark Infested Waters: Procedural Due Process in Constitutional Immigration Law

Edited with introductions by

Gabriel J. Chin
University of Cincinnati College of Law

Victor C. Romero
Pennsylvania State University, Dickinson School of Law

Michael A. Scaperlanda
University of Oklahoma College of Law

GARLAND PUBLISHING, INC.
A MEMBER OF THE TAYLOR & FRANCIS GROUP
New York & London
2000

Published in 2001 by
Garland Publishing, Inc.
29 West 35th Street
New York, NY 10001

Published in Great Britain by
Garland Publishing, Inc.
11 New Fetter Lane
London EC4 4EE

Garland is an imprint of the Taylor & Francis Group

The Library of Congress Cataloging-in-Publication Data

Immigration and the constitution / edited with introductions by
    Gabriel J. Chin, Victor C. Romero, Michael A. Scaperlanda.
        p. cm. — (Controversies in constitutional law)
    Includes bibliographical references.
    Contents: v. 1. The origins of constitutional immigration law — v.
    2. Discrimination and equality in contemporary immigration law —
    v. 3. Shark infested waters : procedural due process in constitutional
    immigration law.
        ISBN: 978-0-8153-4061-4
    1.   Emigration and immigration law—United States. 2.
    Constitutional law—United States. 3. United States—Emigration
    and immigration—Government policy. I. Chin, Gabriel J. (Gabriel
    Jackson), 1964-. II. Romero, Victor C. III. Scaperlanda, Michael A.
    IV. Series
    KF4819.A2 I4265 2000
    342.73'082—dc21   00-064646
                                             CIP

3 volume set ISBN:	0-8153-3346-3
Volume 1	0-8153-4059-1
Volume 2	0-8153-4060-5
Volume 3	0-8153-4061-3

Contents

Removal from the United States (Deportation)

Introduction

In 1950, the United States Supreme Court opined that "[w]hatever the procedure authorized by Congress is, it is due process as far as an alien denied entry is concerned."[1] This line of reasoning caused Justice Jackson to ponder whether the political branches of the government could "eject [an alien] bodily into the sea" as a constitutionally permissible means of ridding our nation of unwelcome foreigners.[2] This volume explores the contours of the procedural restrictions on Congress and the Executive as those branches of government develop and implement immigration policy.

In discussing the process values embedded in the Constitution, our main focus is on the Supreme Court's procedural due process jurisprudence for two reasons. First, our culture has tended, rightly or wrongly, to look primarily to the Supreme Court for answers of a constitutional nature. And, the Court encourages such deference to its self-proclaimed interpretative powers. For example, in 1992, the Court said that the American people's "belief in themselves as [a people desiring to live under the rule of law] is not readily separable from their understanding of the Court invested with the authority to decide their constitutional cases and speak before all others for their constitutional ideals"[3] Second, formulating process values, even more than exploring substantive values, lies at the heart of the judicial function. "Procedural due process is more elemental and less flexible than substantive due process. . . . Only the untaught layman or the charlatan lawyer can answer that procedures matter not. Severe substantive laws can be endured if they are fairly and impartially applied. Indeed, if put to the choice, one might well prefer to live under Soviet substantive law applied in good faith by our common-law procedures than under our substantive law enforced by Soviet procedural practices."[4] Apart from judicial mandate, the political branches ought to take seriously their own independent responsibility to ensure that our immigration laws coincide with our constitutional ideals, including the process values embedded in that document.[5]

Non-United States citizens stand in a myriad of often complex relationships with the United States and its inhabitants. Many, of course, have never been to the United States, have no desire to come to the United States, and have no relatives in the United States. This group is relatively uninteresting from the standpoint of the intersection of immigration and constitutional law. Others have never been to the United States or only visited briefly but have great ties to our community through family or business relationships. Does our Constitution demand certain minimal procedures before members of this group can be denied entry into the country? Still others have built up a life time's worth of relationships while in residence in the United States, acquiring a citizen spouse and having citizen children. What sort of procedural protections are they entitled to before they can be removed from the country? Or, if they are returning permanent resident aliens, are they entitled to the protections of the due process clause prior to their exclusion? Does it matter how long and for what purposes they left the country? Others have come to this country in clandestine style or have overstayed visas; are they entitled to due process before they can be removed? Are aliens facing removal entitled to the benefits of the exclusionary rule if evidence against them has been illegally obtained? Can aliens be removed by the use of secret proceedings where the government refuses to disclose all the evidence? Can aliens be detained pending a final determination of removability? Can detained aliens challenge the conditions of their confinement? Can the government expedite the removal of criminal aliens or aliens without proper documentation? These are a few of the many issues that arise under the rubric of procedural due process and immigration law.

This volume is divided into three distinct parts designed to introduce these concepts and to explore some of these questions in greater detail. Part A addresses issues related to aliens seeking visas at U.S. State Department Visa Consul Offices located outside of the United States. Part B explores the due process rights of non-citizens who present themselves — with or without visas — at our border seeking entrance. Finally, Part C looks at the rights of aliens who are present in the United States but who find themselves in removal proceedings. The materials in this volume are a combination of congressional statutes, Supreme Court cases, and law review articles.

Most aliens at or outside our borders have no judicially enforceable constitutional right to due process with regard to the decision on whether they receive a visa or whether they are permitted to enter the country. By congressional statute and administrative regulation, this group is given some minimal level of procedural protection in the course of these determinations. Only returning permanent resident aliens who have not been absent from the country for a lengthy period of time are entitled to a constitutionally grounded minimum level of process before admission may be denied. In contrast, aliens within the United States, whether here clandestinely or not and whether a permanent resident or merely a nonimmigrant, are entitled by the Constitution to some process before they can be removed from the country.

Part A consists of an article by Professor James Nafziger entitled *Review of Visa Denials by Consular Officers.*[6] An alien seeking a United States visa has no judicially established right to a minimum level of process in the course of the consular determination of whether to issue or deny the visa. In fact, it is very difficult for an alien to obtain judicial review of a visa denial by a consular official. Despite the lack of judicial interest in this area, visa processing belongs chronologically at the beginning of our journey because it is an early and crucial step in the would-be immigrant's journey. As Nafziger says, "[w]hat makes consular visa denials so distinctive is their impact on individual lives and aspirations. . . . What makes visa denials so controversial is that both administrative and judicial review of visa denials by consular officers is very limited. Courts seldom review denials, and administrative review is significantly curtailed."[7] Given the Court's lack of interest in the area, any procedural change will have to emanate from the political branches of government. After exploring the intricacies of consular processing, Nafziger recommends "a more formal review of consular discretion" to "encourage consistency and care" and to serve the "interests of fairness and legitimacy."[8]

Part B begins with two United States Supreme Court cases, *United States* ex rel. *Knauff v Shaugnessy*[9] and *Landon v. Plasencia*.[10] As the remaining stronghold of the rights/privileges doctrine, *Knauff* establishes that an alien's admission into the United States is a privilege rather than a right, and, therefore, the alien is not entitled to the protections of the Fifth Amendment's due process clause. *Landon* creates an exception for returning permanent residents. This territorial approach to due process, which grants constitutional rights to aliens in the United States while denying them to aliens knocking at our door, is explained partly by the assumption that aliens at the border lack significant ties to the United States.

Knauff illustrates the harsh limitations of a rigid territorial approach. German born Ellen Knauff served in the Royal Air Force in England during the latter part of World War II before returning to Germany where she worked as a civilian for the United States War Department. In Germany, she met and married Kurt Knauff, a United States veteran of World War II. In August of 1948, she arrived in the United States and sought admission and naturalization pursuant to the War Brides Act. After being detained for two months on Ellis Island, the Attorney General, without giving Ms. Knauff the benefit of a hearing, entered an order permanently excluding her from the United States on "the ground that her admission would be prejudicial to the interests of the United States."[11] The Supreme Court, in upholding the exclusion, held that an alien denied entry and denied a hearing to determine admissability has no access to the protections afforded by the Fifth Amendment's due process clause because the government's power to exclude is absolute.[12]

The Court's opinion in *Knauff* is, to say the least, troubling. Apart from the human drama, several legal questions are raised and not adequately answered by the Court. Among them, where does a government of limited and enumerated power obtain absolute power to exclude? Even if, as the Court suggests, this power inheres in international law concepts of sovereignty, why isn't the power to exclude restricted by the rights protecting provisions of the Constitution? And, finally, even if the federal government has the absolute power to decide the make-up of our immigrant population along racial, ethnic, political, religious, and socio-economic lines, does it necessarily follow that the government has the unfettered right to exclude allegedly undesirable aliens without providing recourse to a fair process? A sound argument can be made that Ms. Knauff and others in her position, should, at a minimum, be guaranteed the right to know the specific charges against them, to confront their accusers, to cross-examine and impeach them, and to present their own evidence and argument in rebuttal.

Fortunately for Ms. Knauff, her immigration struggle did not end in failure with the Supreme Court's decision. Instead, the battleground over Knauff's admission shifted from the judiciary to the media and Congress. After much pressure, the Attorney General reopened the case, and the Board of Immigration Appeals ultimately ordered her admission into the United States.[13] In the end, the government failed to prove that her presence in the United States created a threat to national security. The *Knauff* holding, however, remains the law, its tentacles waiting silently ready to ensnare a less fortunate victim.

The territorial absolutism of *Knauff* was modified for a limited class of non-citizens in *Landon*. In that case, the Supreme Court held that a permanent resident alien who is attempting to return to the United States after a brief absence is entitled to due process in the course of the government's effort to exclude her. In distinguishing *Knauff*, the Court reasoned that "once an alien gains admission to our country and begins to develop the ties that go with permanent residence, his constitutional status changes accordingly."[14] Citing *Mezei*, however, the Court warned that "if the permanent resident alien's absence is extended, of course, he may lose his entitlement" to due process.[15] Despite developments in due process jurisprudence over the last 50 years, *Knauff* remains the rule with *Landon* providing only a limited exception.

Part B continues with a look at the rights of detained aliens. The first piece is the United States Supreme Court's opinion in *Shaughnessy v. United States* ex rel. *Mezei*.[16] This case holds that a long time permanent resident alien who for 25 years had lived a life of "unrelieved insignificance" in the United States and who is returning after a prolonged absence is entitled to none of the procedural protections offered by the Fifth Amendment's due process clause. Therefore, upon executive determination that he was a security threat and a further determination that disclosing the evidence against him would in itself breach national security, the government was free to exclude him without a hearing and to detain him indefinitely — possibly forever — if no other country would take him.[17]

Mezei had lived in the United States for twenty-five years without becoming a citizen. After World War II, he traveled to eastern Europe supposedly to visit his ailing mother. Upon his attempted return to the United States a year and a half later, he was excluded without a hearing on national security grounds. Although the government refused to grant him a hearing, "Mezei was surely aware of the reasons why the government sought to exclude him."[18] For the twenty years prior to his departure from the United States, he had belonged to the Hungarian Working Sick Benefit and Education Society, which later became associated with the International Workers Order, which in turn was viewed by the government as a communist organization.[19] In this age of loyalty tests and anti-communist fervor, "INS officials had been instructed to give IWO members 'extra scrutiny' in immigration proceedings."[20] Having some awareness of the charges against him did Mezei little good because he had no legal recourse to a hearing where he could dispute the allegations since the Attorney General concluded that national security in this case demanded secrecy and exclusion without a hearing. With this condemnation from American authorities, no other country would take him and he remained in detention on Ellis Island. Mezei challenged this indefinite detention, arguing that it violated his substantive and procedural rights under the Constitution. Following *Knauff*, the Court sided with the government upholding his detention pending removal at some unknown time in the future.[21]

As with *Knauff*, the Supreme Court's opinion in *Mezei* proved to be an intermediate point in Mezei's attempt to return to his home in Buffalo. Although Mezei garnered less congressional support than Ellen Knauff, the Attorney General eventually relented and granted him a hearing.[22] At the hearing, the government alleged that he was excludable on three grounds: 1) past membership in the communist party, 2) conviction of a crime — petty larceny — involving moral turpitude, and 3) providing false information to the United States in order to obtain a visa.[23] Any of these allegations, if proved, could lead to Mezei's exclusion. But why the prior secrecy? As it turned out, the government's case did not require compromising national security sensitive information.

At the conclusion of the hearing, Mezei was found excludable and the Board of Immigration Appeals affirmed.[24] Although he lost the legal battle, his plea for mercy did not go unanswered and the Attorney General paroled[25] him into the United States on the conditions that he stay within 50 miles of Buffalo and not associate with communists.[26] As legal precedent, the legacy of *Mezei* lives on and was felt acutely by many Cubans who were denied entry into the United States but could not be returned to the Cuba of the 1980's.

In both *Knauff* and *Mezei*, the government had taken advantage of the absence of judicially mandated procedural protections and proceeded to exclude "undesirable" aliens without benefit of a hearing. The executive branch claim that national security counseled secrecy went unchecked by the judiciary. And, in both cases, once the facts came to light, the government's claim of national security crumbled as the evidence was brought forth. These cases illustrate the need for a check on the executive's power to unilaterally dispense with the elements of a fair hearing.

We turn from the question of confinement itself to the issues of conditions of confinement with Margaret Taylor's article, *Detained Aliens Challenging Conditions of Confinement and the Porous Border of the Plenary Power Doctrine.*[27] Taylor argues that confusion abounds in conditions of confinement cases because these cases straddle the divergent jurisprudential worlds of plenary power - marked by *The Chinese Exclusion Case*[28] — and the alien's rights tradition — marked by *Yick Wo v. Hopkins.*[29] Concluding that conditions of confinement fall outside plenary power's reach because issues of immigration are not directly involved, Taylor argues that the "courts must police the porous border between the plenary power doctrine and the alien's rights tradition," even if this leaves non-citizens without protection in the immigration context.[30]

Because arriving aliens have no procedural due process rights to any sort of hearing in the context of their request for admission, Congress can impose whatever procedures it desires. Congress grants many aliens who are not clearly entitled to enter the United States, the right to have a removal hearing before an Immigration Judge. At the hearing, the alien can be represented by an attorney, has a right to put on evidence and impeach or cross-examine the INS' evidence, and is entitled to have the hearing conducted on the record. The alien can appeal an adverse determination to the Board of Immigration Appeals with further limited appeal to an Article III court. If, however, the alien is inadmissable because of the lack of requisite entry documents, the alien is subject to expedited removal with no hearing and no judicial review.

The class of aliens most adversely affected by expedited removal provisions of the 1996 amendments to the law are asylum seekers who flee their countries of origin in fear and approach the United States with next to nothing, including documentation that would allow entry. Two of the readings in this volume explore expedited removal. Juan Osuna and Patricia Mariani's *Expedited Removal: Authorities, Implementation, and Ongoing Policy and Practice Issues,*[31] provides an overview of the expedited removal statute from the viewpoint of immigration law practice with a preliminary look at how the law functions. We have also included the expedited removal statute,[32] allowing the reader access to Congress' work directly without the filter of judicial or scholarly gloss.

Part B closes with the ever changing world of judicial review. In recent years, Congress has attempted to severely limit alien access to courts to contest adverse rulings by administrative authorities. Lenni Benson is one of many scholars and practitioners to comment on the current state of judicial review. In *The New World of Judicial Review of Removal Orders,*[33] Benson notes that the limitations placed on judicial review by the Illegal Immigration Reform and Immigrant Responsibility Act of 1996 (IIRIRA) will adversely affect both long term permanent resident aliens and relative newcomers. Instead of analyzing whether Congress has the constitutional authority to eliminate or limit judicial review of immigration decisions, Benson looks for the cracks in Congress' attempt to restrict judicial review. She concludes that "Congress has not actually eliminated all avenues of review" even though the remaining avenues "may be less the optimal." She views the writ of habeas corpus as "the ultimate escape route out of the statutory preclusions found in IIRIRA."[34]

Professor Benson's article provides a fine bridge between Part B and Part C of this volume because she explores Congress' decision to limit judicial review in removal proceeding for aliens at the border and for aliens who have already been admitted into the United States.

Part C turns to the due process issues surrounding the government's attempt to remove a non-citizen from the United States. In contrast to aliens seeking visas and aliens at our borders, aliens who are in the United States are entitled to the protections of the due process clause. Almost one hundred years ago, in the case of *Kaoru Yamataya v. Fisher (The Japanese Immigrant Case),*[35] the United States Supreme Court held that a non-citizen who had been admitted into the United States could not be deported without regard for "the fundamental principles that inhere in 'due process of law.'" Although the Court concluded, under then prevailing notions of due process, that Yamataya had received due process even though she lacked the language skills to understand the deportation hearing, the important point for our purposes is that the Court clearly established a right to due process in the deportation context. The fact that process is due does not answer the important question of what process is due.

We turn to a special subset of deportation issues to explore the question of what process is due in a given situation. Congress has recently attempted to balance the need to give an alien a fair hearing in the deportation context and the need, at times, to keep evidence confidential in the interest of national security. After giving an overview of procedural due process generally, Michael Scaperlanda, in his article, *Are We That Far Gone?: Due Process and Secret Deportation Hearings,*[36] addresses Congress' attempt to strike this balance in the context of removing alleged alien terrorists. Scaperlanda's article analyzes a bill that was pending in Congress at the time the article was written. The bill enacted in modified form is also included in this volume.[37]

We return to the Supreme Court for the two final entries in the volume and series. The 1984 case of *INS v. Lopez-Mendoza*[38] returns us to an important theme developed in Volumes I and II . Consistent with precedent, *Lopez* held that the hearing to determine whether or not to remove an alien from the country is a civil and not criminal proceeding. This understanding has had significant consequences in shaping the due process rights of aliens. In this case, the Court held that the exclusionary rule, which bars prosecutors from introducing illegally obtained evidence into the record of criminal proceedings, does not apply in the deportation context because deportation cases are civil in nature not criminal.

The judicially created exclusionary rule was the Court's attempt to deter law enforcement officers from succumbing to the temptation to violate the Fourth Amendment's prohibition against unreasonable searches and seizures.[39] "The general rule in criminal proceedings is that statements and other evidence obtained as a result of an unlawful, warrantless arrest" are excludable in that proceeding.[40] In civil proceedings, however, exclusion is not automatic. Instead, the court weighs "the likely social benefits of excluding unlawfully seized evidence against the likely costs."[41] In *Lopez*, the Court held that the cost of excluding valuable, relevant, and probative evidence from a civil deportation hearing was too high, especially given alternate avenues for curbing abusive tactics by INS officers.[42] In concluding that the cost of exclusion outweighs the deterrent benefit, the Court left the main task of policing INS agent behavior with the INS itself, ignoring many years of agent abuse and the agency's unwillingness or inability to curb such abuse.

We close the volume and the series by returning to the detention issue. In *Reno v. Flores*,[43] the Court determined that the Immigration and Naturalization Service's regulations regarding the detention of juvenile aliens violated neither substantive nor procedural due process.

As we have seen in this volume, plenary power's choke hold on immigration jurisprudence weakens, at least marginally, when the issues shift from the substantive rights of aliens to their procedural claims. Some scholars have argued that the Court's willingness to take these procedural claims seriously exposes cracks in plenary power's foundations. Other scholars disagree, arguing that the court is more willing to second guess the political branches' procedural practices as opposed to substantive practices because the Court feels more competent laboring in the procedural mines. We leave it to the reader to make his or her own judgment on the matter.

Further Reading

Cases

Mathews v. Eldridge, 424 U.S. 319 (1976).
Nishimura Ekiu v. United States, 142 U.S. 651 (1892).
Woodby v. Immigration and Naturalization Service, 385 U.S. 276 (1966).
U.S. v. Benitz-Villafuerte, 186 F.3d 651 (5th Cir. 1999).
Chi Thon Ngo v. INS, 192 F.3d 390 (3d Cir. 1999).
Palma v. Verdeyen, 676 F. 2d 100 (4th Cir. 1982).
Rodriguez-Fernandez v. Wilkinson, 654 F. 2d 1382 (10th Cir. 1981).
Tejeda-Mata v. INS, 626 F. 2d 721 (9th Cir. 1980).
Toscano-Gil v. E.M. Trominski, 210 F.3d 470, 2000 (5th Cir., 2000).

Hypolite v. *Blackman*, 57 F. Supp. 2d 128 (D. M.D. Penn. 1999).
Kiareldeen v. *Reno*, 71 F. Supp. 2d 402 (D. N.J. 1999).
Singh v. *Quarantillo*, 92 F. Supp. 2d 386 2000 (D. N.J., 2000).

Books and Articles

Alex Aleinikoff, Aliens, "Due Process, and 'Community Ties': A Response to Martin, "44 *U. Pitt. L. Rev.* 237 (1983).

Lenni Benson, "Back to the Future: Congress Attacks the Right to Judicial Review of Immigration Proceedings," 29 *Connecticut Law Review* 1411 (1997).

Lenni Benson, "By Hook or By Crook: Exploring the Legality of an INS Sting Operation," 31 *San Diego Law Rev.* 813 (1994).

Peter Billings, "A Comparative Analysis of Administrative and Adjudicative Systems for Determining Asylum Claims," 52 *Admin. L. Rev.* 253 (2000).

Michael Brady, "Asylum Adjudication: No Place for the INS," 20 *Columbia Human Rts. L. Rev.* 129 (1988).

Richard Boswell, "Rethinking Exclusion - the Rights of Cuban Refugees Facing Indefinite Detention," 17 *Vand. J. Transnat'l L Rev.*. 925 (1984).

Gabriel Chin, "Is There a Plenary Power Doctrine? A Tentative Apology and Prediction for Our Strange But Unexecptional Constitutional Immigration Law," 14 *Geo. Immig. L.J.* 257 (2000).

David Cole, "Jurisdiction and Liberty: Habeas Corpus and Due Process as Limits on Congress's Control of Federal Jurisdiction," 86 *Geo. L. J.* 2481 (1998).

Henry Friendly, "Some Kind of Hearing," 123 *U. Pa. L. Rev.* 1267 (1975).

Henry Hart, "The Power of Congress to Limit the Jurisdiction of Federal Courts: An Exercise in Dialectic," 66 *Harv. L. Rev.* 1362 (1953).

Kevin Johnson, "The Antiterrorism Act, The Immigration Reform Act, and Ideological Regulation in Immigration Laws: Important Lessons for Citizens and Noncitizens," 28 *St. Mary's L.J.* 833 (1997).

Kevin Johnson, "Responding to the 'Litigation Explosion': The Plain Meaning of Executive Branch Primacy Over Immigration," 71 *N.C. L. Rev.* 413 (1993).

Daniel Kanstroom, "Surrounding the Hole in the Doughnut: Discretion and Deference in U.S. Immigration Law," 71 *Tul. L. Rev.* 703 (1997).

Ellen R. Knauff, *The Ellen Knauff Story* (1952).

Ira Kurzban, *Immigration Law Sourcebook* (6ᵗʰ Ed. 1998).

Stephen Legomsky, *Immigration and the Judiciary: Law and Politics in Britain and America* (1987).

David Martin, "Two Cheers for Expedited Removal in the New Immigration Laws," 40 *Va. J. Int'l. L.* 673 (2000).

David Martin, "Due Process and Membership in the National Community: Political Asylum and Beyond," 44 *U. Pitt. L. Rev.* 165 (1983).

Hiroshi Motomura, "Judicial Review in Immigration Cases After AADC: Lessons From Civil Procedure," 14 *Geo. Immig. L. J.* 385 (2000).

Hiroshi Motomura, "The Curious Evolution of Immigration Law: Procedural Surrogates for Substantive Constitutional Rights," 92 *Colum. L. Rev.* 1625 (1992).

Karen Musalo, "The Expedited Removal Study: An Update as the System Completes its Second Year," 76 *Interpreter Releases* 513 (1999).

Karen Musalo, "The Expedited Removal Study: Report on the First Year of Implementation," 75 *Interpreter Releases* 973 (1998).

Gerald Neuman, "Terrorism, Selective Deportation and the First Amendment after *Reno* v. *AADC*," 14 *Geo. Immigr. L. J.* 313 (2000).

Gerald Neuman, "Habeas Corpus, Executive Detention, and the Removal of Aliens, "98 *Columbia L. Rev.* 961 (1998).

Victor Romero, "The Domestic Fourth Amendment Rights of Undocumented Immigrants: On Guitterez and the Tort Law-Immigration Law Parallel," 35 *Harvard Civil Rights-Civil Liberties Law Review* 57 (2000).

Victor Romero, Note, "Whatever Happened to the Fourth Amendment?: Undocumented Immigrants' Rights After *INS* v. *Lopez-Mendoza* and *United States* v. *Verdugo-Urquidez*," 65 S. *Cal. L. Rev.* 999 (1992).

Michael Scaperlanda, "Polishing the Tarnished Golden Door," 1993 *Wisconsin Law Review* 965.

Michael Scaperlanda, "Who is My Neighbor: An Essay on Immigrants, Welfare Reform, and the Constitution," 29 *Connecticut Law Review* 1587 (1997).

Michael Scaperlanda, "Immigration Justice: Beyond Liberal Egalitarian and Communitarian

Perspectives, LVII *Review of Social Economy* 523 (1999).

Peter Schuck and John Williams, Removing Criminal Aliens: The Pitfalls and Promises of Federalism, 22 *Harv. J. L. and Pub. Pol'y* 367 (1999).

United States General Accounting Office, *Illegal Immigration Status of Southwest Border Strategy Implementation: Report to Congressional Committees* (1999).

Paul Verkuil, A Study of Immigration Procedures, 31 *UCLA L. Rev.* 1141 (1984).

Charles D. Weisselberg, The Exclusion and Detention of Aliens: Lessons from the Livesof Ellen Knauff and Ignatz Mezei, 143 *U. Pa. L. Rev.* 933 (1995).

Leti Volpp, Court-Stripping and Class-Wide Relief: A Response to Judicial Review in Immigration Cases After AADC, 14 *Geo. Immig. L. J.* 463 (2000).

Notes

1 *United States* ex rel. *Knauff* v. *Shaughnessy*, 338 U.S. 537, 544 (1950).

2 *Shaugnessy* v. *United States* ex rel. Mezei, 345 U.S. 206, 226 (1953)(Jackson, J., dissenting).

3 *Planned Parenthood* v. *Casey*, 505 U.S.833, 868 (1992). For criticism of this approach, *see e.g.*, Michael Stokes Paulsen, "Captain James T. Kirk and the Enterprise of Constitutional Interpretation: Some Modest Proposals from the Twenty-Third Century," 59 *Alb. L. Rev.* 671, 675 (1995); and Michael Scaperlanda, "Who is My Neighbor?: An Essay on Immigrants, Welfare Reform, and the Constitution," 29 *Conn. L. Rev.* 1587 (1997).

4 *Shaugnessy* v. *United States* ex rel. Mezei, 345 U.S. 206, 224 (1953)(Jackson, J., dissenting).

5 Among the articles advocating this position, *see generally* Kevin Johnson, "Los Olvidados: Images of the Immigrant, Political Power of Noncitizens, and Immigration Law and Enforcement," 1993 *BYU L. Rev.* 1139, 1240–41 (1993); Victor Romero, "Expanding the Circle of Membership by Reconstructing the 'Alien': Lessons from Social Psychology and the 'Promise Enforcement' Cases," 32 U. *Mich. J.L. Ref.* 1 (1998); and Michael Scaperlanda, "Partial Membership: Aliens and the Constitutional Community," 81 *Iowa L. Rev.* 707, 771–773 (1996).

6 66 *Washington Law Review* 1 (1991).

7 Ibid. at 16.

8 Ibid. at 95.

9 338 U.S. 537 (1950).

10 459 U.S. 21 (1982).

11 338 U.S. at 539–540. Even though she spent two months physically within the borders of the United States, Knauff did not benefit from the constitutional due process rights afforded aliens present in the United States. For purposes of law, a person has not made an "entry" into the United States if she presents herself to immigration authorities and is awaiting adjudication of her application for admission even if the immigration authorities allow her to remain on U.S. soil pending the outcome of the adjudication. This was Ellen Knauff's status as she waited on Ellis Island for the Attorney General's decision.

12 *See id.* at 544.

13 *See* Charles Weisselberg, "The Exclusion and Detention of Aliens: Lessons from the Lives of Ellen Knauff and Ignatz Mezei," 143 *U. Penn. L. Rev.* 933 (1995).

14 459 U. S. 32 (1982).

15 *Id.* At 33.

16 345 U.S. 206 (1953).

17 *Id.* At 215.

18 Weisselberg, *supra*, at 972.

19 *Id.* at 972-73.

20 *Id.* at 973.

21 345 U.S. at 215.

22 Weisselberg, *supra*, at 971-72.

23 *See id.* at 975.

24 *See id.* at 983.

25 Parol is a tool that provides the government the flexibility to allow an alien into the country without granting them admission, which means that a paroled alien has technically not "entered" the United States and has none of the rights, including due process rights, of an alien who has been admitted. As a parolee, Mezei had no regular status in the United States and remained ineligible for permanent resident status or naturalization.

26 Weisselberg, *supra*, at 983-84.

27 22 *Hastings Const. L. Q.* 1087 (1995).

28 *Chae Chan Ping* v. *United States*, 130 U.S. 581 (1889).

29 118 U. S. 356 (1886).

30 22 *Hastings Const. L. Q.*1087, 1156 (1995).

31 *Immigration Briefings* 1 (November 1997).

32 8 U.S.C.A. §1225 (1999).

33 12 *Georgetown Immigration Law Journal* 233 (1998).

34 Ibid. at 234.

35 189 U.S. 86, 100 (1903).

36 7 *Stanford Law and Policy Review* 23 (1996).

37 8 U.S.C.A. §§ 1535, *et seq.* (1999).

38 468 U.S. 1032 (1984).

39 468 U.S. at 1041.

40 *Id.* at 1040.

41 *Id.* at 1041.

42 *Id.*

43 507 U.S. 292 (1993).

REVIEW OF VISA DENIALS
BY CONSULAR OFFICERS

James A.R. Nafziger*

Abstract: United States consular officers stationed abroad exercise enormous discretion in deciding whether to grant or deny applications for visas by foreign citizens. The process for reviewing visa denials is exceptionally limited. Federal rules and regulations and consular practices do provide for internal review of visa denials, members of Congress and the media occasionally press for review of individual cases, and the Visa Office in the Department of State issues advisory opinions from time to time on matters of both fact and law. This process is, however, inadequate for several reasons. Time and budgetary constraints generally prevent consular officers from recording reviewable explanations for denials and from undertaking comprehensive internal review of denials. Other factors limiting internal review are the absence of any provision for attorney access to the process, the refusal of the Visa Office to disclose its opinions to applicants, and a dearth of objective standards and guidance for conducting internal review of denials. By relying on ambiguous and often antiquated authority, the State Department and the courts have prevented more formal administrative review within the Department and have narrowly restricted judicial review. In doing so, courts have rendered questionable interpretations of a provision for consular discretion in the Immigration and Nationality Act and have largely ignored both the requirements of the Administrative Procedure Act and international law. The resulting nonreviewability of most visa denials is anachronistic and peculiar. Although the author's field observations indicate that consular training and decision making are of a high quality, a more formal review process would be beneficial. The availability of administrative and judicial review of visa denials would encourage greater consistency and uniformity of decisions on visa applications and better serve the interests of fairness and legitimacy. This study concludes with two sets of recommendations. The first set is of a general nature whereas the second, more detailed set takes account of alternative levels of funding for improving the review process.

* Professor of Law, Willamette University. B.A. 1962, M.A. 1969, University of Wisconsin; J.D. 1967, Harvard Law School. The author prepared an earlier version of this study as consultant to the Administrative Conference of the United States (ACUS). In that connection he gratefully acknowledges the assistance of Jeffrey S. Lubbers, Research Director; Nancy G. Miller, Staff Liaison; Richard J. Leighton, Chair, Adjudication Committee; and members of the Conference and its Adjudication Committee. The views expressed in this article are, however, the author's and do not necessarily reflect those of the Conference. The recommendations adopted by the Conference on the basis of the report were codified at 1 C.F.R. § 305.89–9 (1990).

Stephen H. Legomsky was particularly instrumental, first in suggesting that the author undertake this study and then in offering detailed comments on a first draft. The author also benefited from comments by the following individuals: Robert Donaldson, Robert Free, Robert Jucéam, Charles Stuart Kennedy, Hans A. Linde and Angelo Paparelli. The following consular officers gave generously of their time and thinking: Dianne Andruch, Anne Arries, Richard P. Bonsignore, John Brown, Jon Goodwin Edensword, Allen S. Greenberg, Steven Hardesty, Barbara Johnson, Darryl N. Johnson, Daniel F. Keller, Michael D. Kirby, Edward Kreuser, June H. Kunsman, Helen La Lime, Teresa Loar, Sylvie L. Martinez, Maurice S. Parker, Richard R. Peterson, Jerrilynn Pudschun, Rudolph Lawrence Rivera, Doreen Soler, and Phyllis S.F. Villegoureix-Ritaud. Mary Rooklidge was an indispensably careful and competent cite-checker. Any errors are the author's.

United States consulates abroad routinely shuffle passengers on Spaceship Earth by issuing or denying visas to foreign applicants. Consular decisions often have an acute impact on individuals and families. The volume of visa applications is huge. In 1988, for example, United States consulates issued 391,834 immigrant visas and 8,679,709 nonimmigrant visas,[1] figures which in a typical year would represent about 90% of all applications.[2] These figures often tell only half the story about the significance of the visa process; the other half involves the concerns of family members, prospective employers, educational institutions, and others in the United States and abroad who may have a stake in whether a foreign applicant receives a visa. Moreover, new laws often increase the number of cases subject to the exercise of consular discretion.[3] Not surprisingly, given the increasing number of

---

1. UNITED STATES DEPARTMENT OF STATE, BUREAU OF CONSULAR AFFAIRS, REPORT OF THE VISA OFFICE 1988, at 18 (1989) [hereinafter VISA REPORT].

2. See T. ALEINIKOFF & D. MARTIN, IMMIGRATION: PROCESS AND POLICY 211 (1985) (citing figures for 1983). Although the Visa Office in the State Department publishes figures on numbers of applications pending for visas and issuances, it generally does not publish figures on denials. The 10% denial rate estimated by Aleinikoff and Martin is, however, consistent with comparative information given to the author during the field study described in Section IV. The Department of Justice, in accord, estimates a 9.5% denial rate. "The annual volume of visa denials is in the neighborhood of 42,700 for immigrant visa applications and 825,000 for nonimmigrant visa applications." Letter from Robert S. Ross, Jr., Executive Assistant to the Attorney General, to Marshall J. Berger, Chairman, Administrative Conference of the United States (Oct. 13, 1989) (on file with the author).

3. For example, the Immigration Act of 1990 increases the immigration quota by approximately 35 percent. Pub. L. No. 101-649, 104 Stat. 4978. Between 1992 and 1994 the limit on allowable immigration of persons other than immediate relatives and special immigrants will increase from 490,000 to 700,000; after 1994 that limit will decline to 675,000 annually. The greatest percentage increase among preference categories is in the number of "priority," skilled and other workers. In addition, special allocations of visas will be given to foreign investors and immigrants from Hong Kong and countries that were previously deprived of historical preferences. The Act suspends deportations of some classes of aliens from four countries and lifts or modifies several grounds for exclusion. Id. For a summary of the Act, see 67 INTERPRETER RELEASES 1209 (1990). The Immigration Amendments of 1988, Pub. L. No. 100-658, 102 Stat. 3908 (1988) extend a program, which was incorporated in the Immigration Act of 1990, for increased admission of aliens from countries underrepresented in the population because of national quotas in earlier legislation. The Immigration Reform and Control Act of 1986, Pub. L. No. 99-603, 100 Stat. 3359 (1986) [hereinafter IRCA] amends the Immigration and Nationality Act of 1952, Pub. L. No. 414, 66 Stat. 163, 8 U.S.C. §§ 1101–1557 (1988) [hereinafter INA], to provide amnesty, that is, a legalized status for certain classes of undocumented aliens residing in the United States. As amnesty recipients become permanent resident aliens or citizens and seek to bring in their relatives, applications for immigrant visas are expected to increase. See, e.g., STATE, Dec. 1988, at 9. IRCA also provides that aliens who have at any time failed to maintain lawful status in the United States, other than through no fault of their own or for technical reasons, may no longer seek lawful permanent residence in the United States, but only by applying for an immigrant visa at a consular post abroad. 8 U.S.C. § 1255(a)(2). The Immigration Marriage Fraud Amendments of 1986, Pub. L. No. 99-639, 100 Stat. 3537, broaden the consul's power to exclude aliens who have obtained a visa through

persons affected, a light industry of commentary flourishes, geared in the past to the issue of excluding aliens for national security or ideological reasons.[4] The analysis that follows, however, is not specifically limited to denials of visas on such political grounds.

On a legal landscape populated with "orphan applicants," "mustangs," "munchkins," "visa shoppers," "refusal overcomes," and the notorious "consular absolutists," a colorful vocabulary adds a superficial sparkle to an otherwise sobering debate concerning global freedom of movement. The actual and prospective influx of aliens engages

---

"sham" marriages to American citizens, even if they are resident aliens returning from visits abroad, on the basis of fraud or willful misrepresentation of a material fact. Government regulations have also shifted adjustment-of-status cases from the Immigration and Naturalization Service (INS) of the Department of Justice to the consulates. *See* Paparelli & Tilner, *A Proposal for Legislation Establishing a System of Review of Visa Refusals in Selected Cases,* 65 INTERPRETER RELEASES 1027, 1031 (1988).

4. *See, e.g.,* Committee on Immigration and Nationality Law, Association of the Bar of the City of New York, *Visa Denials on Ideological Grounds: An Update,* 8 SETON HALL LEGIS. J. 249 (1985); Helton, *Reconciling the Power to Bar or Expel Aliens on Political Grounds with Fairness and the Freedoms of Speech and Association: An Analysis of Recent Legislative Proposals,* 11 FORDHAM INT'L L.J. 467 (1988); Mann, *Monopoly in the Marketplace: The Ideological Denial of Visas,* 9 LAW & POL'Y 417 (1987); Neuborne & Shapiro, *The Nylon Curtain: America's National Border and the Free Flow of Ideas,* 26 WM. & MARY L. REV. 719 (1985); Shapiro, *Ideological Exclusions: Closing the Border to Political Dissidents,* 100 HARV. L. REV. 930 (1987); Tilner, *Ideological Exclusion of Aliens: The Evolution of a Policy,* 2 GEO. IMMIGR. L. J. 1 (1987); Torrence, *Ideological Exclusions: A Prior Restraint Analysis,* 11 HASTINGS COMM. & ENT. L.J. 335 (1989); Voigt, *Visa Denials on Ideological Grounds and the First Amendment Right to Receive Information: The Case for Stricter Judicial Scrutiny,* 17 CUMB. L. REV. 139 (1986); Comment, *Ideological Exclusion, Plenary Power and the PLO,* 77 CALIF. L. REV. 831 (1989); Comment, *Immigration and the First Amendment,* 73 CALIF. L. REV. 1889 (1985); Note, *First Amendment and the Alien Exclusion Power—What Standard of Review?* 4 CARDOZO L. REV. 457 (1983); Note, *First Amendment Limitations on the Exclusion of Aliens,* 62 N.Y.U. L. REV. 149 (1987); Note, *Free Speech and the Right of Entry into the United States: Legislation to Remedy the Ideological Exclusion Provisions of the Immigration and Naturalization* [sic] *Act,* 4 AM. U.J. INT'L L. & POL'Y 443 (1989) (apparently referring to the Immigration and *Nationality* Act); Comment, *Ideological Restrictions on Immigration,* 8 U.C. DAVIS L. REV. 217 (1975); Note, *National Security Visa Denials: Delimiting the Exercise of Executive Exclusion Authority Under the Immigration and Nationality Act,* 28 VA. J. INT'L L. 711 (1988).

The Immigration Act of 1990, Pub. L. No. 101-649, 104 Stat. 4978, substantially modifies the security and foreign policy grounds for excluding aliens. Federal legislation enacted in 1987 provided that no alien who applied for a visa during 1988 could be denied one nor be excluded from admission "because of any past, current, or expected beliefs, statements, or associations which, if engaged in by a United States citizen in the United States, would be protected under the Constitution." Pub. L. 100-204, § 901, 101 Stat. 1399, 1400 (1987). In 1988 Congress extended this provision for two years, until 1991, but limited it to nonimmigrant visa applicants. Pub. L. 100-461, § 555, 102 Stat. 2268-36, 2268-37 (1988). The Immigration Act of 1990 repealed this provision and substituted a similar provision, subject to a "foreign policy" exception. Immigration Act of 1990 § 601, Pub. L. No. 101-649, 104 Stat. 4978. *See also* American Arab Anti-Discrimination Comm. v. Meese, 714 F. Supp. 1060 (C.D. Cal. 1989) (declaring certain provisions of the INA unconstitutional that have the effect of curtailing the first amendment rights within the United States of members of the Palestinian Liberation Organization (PLO)).

profound social concern about the future of the "national community"[5] and the nation's role in the global community. In the national debate, immigration often becomes an issue of defining or even preserving the body politic.

The process for reviewing consular denials of visas to foreign applicants is particularly controversial. This study will discuss the general review process, with a focus on administrative and judicial reviewability, and will offer several recommendations for improving the process.

International, constitutional, federal statutory and administrative law, as well as State Department guidelines, shape the general review process. These normative sources are interdependent. For example,

---

5. The postulation of a national community also underlies the communitarian theory of a correlation between particular rights of aliens and the strength or closeness of their attachment to the country. *See* Martin, *Due Process and Membership in the National Community: Political Asylum and Beyond,* 44 U. PITT. L. REV. 165 (1983); Schuck, *The Transformation of Immigration Law,* 84 COLUM. L. REV. 1 (1984); *cf.* Aleinikoff, *Aliens, Due Process and "Community Ties": A Response to Martin,* 44 U. PITT. L. REV. 237 (1983). For an analysis of alien exclusion issues that focuses only on the national community without considering international dimensions, see Bosniak, *Exclusion and Membership: The Dual Identity of the Undocumented Worker Under United States Law,* 1988 WIS. L. REV. 955.

Whether the immigration power should be conceptualized as a protection of membership in some kind of "national community" is controversial. *See* Aleinikoff, *Citizens, Aliens, Membership and the Constitution,* 7 CONST. COMMENTARY 9, 10, 34 (1990):

Unlinking the immigration power from theories of membership will undermine the current regime of immigration exceptionalism that has left the immigration power largely immune to the constitutional norms applied to other congressional powers. . . . We can end immigration exceptionalism by recognizing the weaknesses of earlier justifications and by resisting the siren song of membership theory.

(footnotes omitted).

Also controversial is the very reality of a national community in a functional sense relevant to immigration policy. As a matter of immigration and assimilation, it may be argued that historically the United States has been more of a mosaic than a melting pot, that is, more of a politically and economically organized mixture of lifestyle enclaves and communities, "ongoing associations of men and women with some special commitment to one another and some special sense of their common life." M. WALZER, SPHERES OF JUSTICE: A DEFENSE OF PLURALISM AND EQUALITY 62 (1983). A more complete definition of "community" is "a group of people who are socially interdependent, who participate together in discussion and decision making, and who share certain *practices* . . . . It almost always has a history and so is also a *community of memory,* defined in part by its past and its memory of its past." R. BELLAH, R. MADSEN, W. SULLIVAN, A. SWIDLER & S. TIPTON, HABITS OF THE HEART 333 (1985) (emphasis added). A "lifestyle enclave," on the other hand:

is formed by people who share some feature of private life. Members of a lifestyle enclave express their identity through shared patterns of appearance, consumption, and leisure activities, which often serve to differentiate them sharply from those with other lifestyles. They are not interdependent, do not act together politically, and do not share a history. If these things begin to appear, the enclave is on the way to becoming a community. Many of what are called communities in America are mixtures of *communities* in our strong sense and *lifestyle enclaves.*

Id. at 335 (emphasis added).

the term "review" connotes a coordinated mix of administrative and judicial review, whereas the capacity of consular discretion to affect individual rights raises issues of constitutional rights, and the extraterritorial circumstances of consular discretion engage conventional and customary international law. What follows is largely an analysis of this complex of authority, supplemented by a summary of the author's interviews in Mexico, China, Poland and the United Kingdom and his observations of on-line consular adjudications in Mexico and China. These interviews and observations are too limited to provide an empirical basis for analysis, but do reflect salient aspects of the actual process of exercising and reviewing consular discretion. The study concludes with a set of recommendations.

I. THE STATUTORY AND ADMINISTRATIVE PROCESS OF ADMITTING AND EXCLUDING ALIENS

In exercising a qualified right to admit or exclude aliens, states normally apply a mix of two systems of control. Under the *insular-Western Hemispheric* system a state relies on the gateway or front-end grant or refusal of permission to enter its territory. The *continental* (that is, the continental European) system, on the other hand, relies on residence control involving the attribution of immigration status to all resident aliens, the attachment of restrictions and other consequences to that status, and, typically, a requirement of personal identifications and work permits.[6] Exit or departure controls supplement the permit system. During the last fifty years, several changes have been occurring: a growing perception that a mixture of the two systems of control works best, a modest trend toward adoption of the continental system of residence permits, and an expanded role for international law in controlling immigration.[7]

The United States employs an insular-Western Hemispheric system of control, but also requires limited identification and registration of aliens. The United States Constitution provides no express grant of authority to control the entry of foreigners, although the commerce power and the power to establish a uniform rule of naturalization[8] bear most directly on issues of immigration. Instead, Congress has

---

6. Plender, *Recent Trends in National Immigration Control*, 35 INT'L & COMP. L.Q. 531, 535, 550–51 (1986) (the author formulates the distinction between "insular" and "continental" systems of control, the former of which is slightly modified here). *See also* Wolf, *Entry and Residence*, in THE LEGAL POSITION OF ALIENS IN NATIONAL AND INTERNATIONAL LAW 1873, 1874 (J. Frowein & T. Stein eds. 1987) [hereinafter Frowein & Stein].

7. Plender, *supra* note 6, at 535; Wolf, *supra* note 6, at 1874.

8. U.S. CONST. art. I, § 8, cls. 3–4.

relied primarily on what the courts have described as "inherent" powers to control immigration.

Whatever the constitutional premises, the Immigration and Nationality Act of 1952 (INA)[9] delegates to the Executive the authority to exclude and deport aliens according to substantive provisions for eligibility and prescribed procedures.[10] The Immigration Reform and Control Act of 1986 (IRCA),[11] among other things, establishes post-entry, continental-style procedures for verifying employment eligibility that affect citizens and aliens alike. IRCA also provides for study of the feasibility of validating social security numbers and avoiding counterfeit social security cards.

The INA imposes annual numerical limitations on alien admissions, provides detailed grounds for their exclusion and deportation, and establishes visa classes.[12] The interpretation and application of these

---

9. 8 U.S.C. §§ 1101–1557 (1988).

10. Defining immigration terminology:

"[E]xclusion" means preventing someone from entering the United States who is actually outside of the United States or is treated as being so. "Expulsion" means forcing someone out of the United States who is actually within the United States or is treated as being so. "Deportation" means the moving of someone away from the United States, after his exclusion or expulsion.

Kwong Hai Chew v. Colding, 344 U.S. 590, 596, n.4 (1953), *limited by* United States v. Verdugo Urquidez, 110 S. Ct. 1056 (1990). An alien has "entered" the United States if he or she has been lawfully admitted or has physically entered unlawfully by evading the prescribed process. *See* 8 U.S.C. § 1101(a)(13); *In re* Pierre, 14 I & N Dec. 467 (Bd. Immig. App. 1973).

The controversial and somewhat fading distinction between "exclusion" and "deportation" has important due process implications. Consular decisions to deny visas are generally nonreviewable or are subject to only very limited reviewability. An alien arriving at the border or other port of entry is, however, entitled to an exclusion proceeding if the INS detains him or her for further inquiry. In a deportation proceeding, that is, after an alien's "entry" into the United States, he or she is entitled to the formalities of due process. In an exclusion proceeding, on the other hand,

[n]otice is not required in any meaningful sense; rather, the applicant need only be informed of the issues confronting him at some point in the hearings and be given a reasonable opportunity to meet them. The rights to confrontation is not required, although depositions may be ordered if evidence is essential. Oral argument is not provided for by statute or regulation. Oral presentation of evidence is provided for, as is a limited right of cross-examination and disclosure of opposing evidence. The rights to retain counsel, to a determination on the record, and to a statement of reasons are protected, much as they are in deportation cases.

Verkuil, *A Study of Immigration Procedures,* 31 U.C.L.A. L. Rev. 1141, 1160 (1984) (footnotes omitted). *See also* Appendix B.

11. 8 U.S.C. §§ 1101–1157. The statute primarily provides for sanctions against employers of undocumented aliens, legalization (or "amnesty") of resident or previously residing undocumented aliens, a special program for agricultural workers, financial and other support for the Border Patrol, and a prohibition on adjusting the status of most undocumented aliens other than under the one-time only amnesty program.

12. INA §§ 201–03, 212, 8 U.S.C. §§ 1151–53, 1182 (as modified by the Immigration Act of 1990, Pub. L. No. 101-649, 104 Stat. 4978); 22 C.F.R. § 41.12 (1990).

quotas and grounds for exclusion have generated a vast jurisprudence that is generally beyond the scope of this study, but some examples relevant to the core discussion of reviewability will be cited.

The INA requires most persons seeking to enter the United States to obtain a visa.[13] This requirement had its origin as an emergency security measure during World War I.[14] Ordinarily, the alien must apply to a consulate in the home district, defined by the State Department, in which he or she resides.[15] An alien temporarily in the United States is considered to be a resident of the consular district of last residence abroad.[16] At the direction of the State Department or at their own discretion, consular officers may also accept visa applications from non-residents of a consular district who are "physically present" there.[17] The availability of this alternative jurisdictional basis is especially important to "orphan applicants."[18] Orphan applicants by definition cannot apply for a visa in their home district either because they fear persecution there, even though they are not technically refugees, or simply because there is no United States embassy or consular post in their home district. Applicants for nonimmigrant visas may also apply by mail to their home consular districts even if they are not physically present there, so long as they are able to waive

---

13. INA §§ 211(a), 212(a)(20)(26), 8 U.S.C. §§ 1181(a), 1182(a)(20)(26). Exceptions include temporary visitors from Canada or Mexico in possession of "border crossing card[s]," refugees, permanent resident aliens returning from visits abroad, in transit passengers, parolees, and tourists from designated countries under a pilot program established by IRCA § 313. Under the Visa Waiver Pilot Program for Certain Visitors, tourists from designated countries seeking entry for 90 days or less may conditionally receive a waiver of the visa requirements in section 212(a)(26)(B) of the INA. INA § 217, 8 U.S.C. § 1187. The Attorney General and Secretary of State jointly designate pilot program countries on the basis of low nonimmigrant visa refusal rates for nationals of those countries. INA § 217(c), 8 U.S.C. § 1187(c). Designated countries began with the United Kingdom and Japan, then France, Italy, the Netherlands, Sweden, Switzerland and West Germany. Section 201 of The Immigration Act of 1990, Pub. L. No. 101-649, 104 Stat. 4978, will revise and extend the program. *See generally* IMMIGRATION AND NATURALIZATION SERVICE, TRAVEL WITHOUT A VISA: A GUIDE FOR THE TRAVEL INDUSTRY (1988). For observations about the program, *see infra* text accompanying note 367.

14. Joint Order of the Department of State and the Department of Labor, July 26, 1917, in Laws Applicable to Immigration and Nationality 1042 (1953). *See also* Public Safety Act of June 20, 1941, ch. 209, 55 Stat. 252 (1941–42) (repealed 1948), which directed consular officers during World War II to deny a visa to any alien who sought entry into the United States to engage in activities that would endanger the public safety.

15. 22 C.F.R. §§ 41.101, 42.61. Applicants residing in Taiwan must apply to an office of the American Institute in Taiwan.

16. *Id.* § 42.61(a) (1990).

17. *Id.* §§ 41.101(a), 42.61(a).

18. Pederson, *Representing Clients Before Consular Posts in the Context of Consular Absolutism,* in II IMMIGRATION AND NATIONALITY LAW, 42ND ANNIVERSARY SYMPOSIUM OF THE AMERICAN IMMIGRATION LAWYERS ASSOCIATION 296, 314 n.6 (1988).

a personal appearance before a consular officer of the home district.[19] A visa section where an application is filed, other than in the applicant's home district, normally cables or writes the home district, if feasible, for background information.[20] In this way inter-consular communications about an applicant help detect questionable cases of visa shopping or multiple-consulate shopping.

Although the State Department does not encourage out-of-district visa shopping, it does encourage consular officers to exercise common sense in processing out-of-district applicants in order to help implement a fundamental policy of giving all aliens an opportunity to apply. State Department policy explicitly presumes that consular officers will seldom reject applicants merely on the basis of non-residence in a particular district.[21] Consular posts do not always comply with this policy, however. As an important example, the Vancouver, Canada post has at times virtually closed its doors to orphan and other non-resident alien applicants, and has barred or attempted to bar the accessibility of attorneys to the process. The post's reason seems to have been simply to avoid a backlog of applications.[22]

Related to visa or consulate-shopping is the subissue of consular officer-shopping. Within a single visa section of an embassy or consulate abroad, consular officers sometimes establish reputations for either leniency or harshness. Applicants therefore attempt to learn which officers are more apt to issue visas, and try to arrange themselves in line for an adjudication or otherwise set things up for processing by a relatively lenient officer. Rules providing for greater uniformity or consistency among officers would be a check on this localized version of visa shopping.

An "advance parole" program ensures orphan applicants and others residing in the United States a right of return after they have traveled to a third country to interview. The program thereby assures foreign authorities that, if they allow a third country national to apply for a visa in a U.S. embassy or consulate, the applicant will be able to return to the United States afterward. To be eligible for the program, an applicant must show both that he or she cannot return to the home

---

19. U.S. DEP'T OF STATE, FOREIGN AFFAIRS MANUAL, *reprinted in part in* 3 IMMIGRATION LAW AND PROCEDURE, App. J-472, note N3.1; App. J-474, note N.3 (C. Gordon & S. Mailman eds. 1990) [hereinafter FOREIGN AFFAIRS MANUAL].

20. *Id.* at App. J-473, notes PN3.2–3.5.

21. *Id.* at App. J-471, note N2.1.

22. Telephone interview with Robert A. Free, Visa Practice Committee, American Immigration Lawyers Association (Jan. 6, 1989), and documents from Mr. Free concerning a complaint to the Visa Office of the Department of State from the Washington State Chapter, American Immigration Lawyers Association (on file with the *Washington Law Review*).

district and that the third country where a consular interview based on "physical presence" is to take place will bar admission without a "guarantee" that the applicant will be allowed to reenter the United States after the interview.[23]

An alien may apply for either an immigrant visa (for permanent residency) or a nonimmigrant visa (for temporary residency). The issuance of either type of visa is subject to grounds for exclusion ("qualitative restrictions") that have been said to constitute "a magic mirror, reflecting the fears and concerns of past Congresses."[24] Intending immigrants are also subject to numerical limitations and preferences ("quantitative restrictions"), whereas nonimmigrants are generally subject to qualitative restrictions and a classification system.[25] An applicant is presumed to be an immigrant "until he establishes to the satisfaction of the consular officer"[26] entitlement to nonimmigrant status. The burden of proving eligibility for either type of visa is on the applicant.[27]

If the applicant is seeking an immigrant visa or, sometimes, a nonimmigrant visa, that person (the "beneficiary") must also be sponsored by a close relative who must be either a U.S. citizen or permanent resident alien, or an actual or potential U.S. employer. The sponsor then files a petition with the Immigration and Naturalization Service (INS) of the Department of Justice to establish either the requisite family relationship or, after acquiring labor certification, the appropriate work relationship. On approval of this petition, the INS transmits the papers to the appropriate embassy or consulate abroad as a prerequisite to the visa application.[28] Although consular officers are primarily responsible for applying grounds of exclusion, they may also redetermine the validity of the family relationship described by the applicant.[29] Because the issuance of immigrant visas per year is

---

23. Immigration and Naturalization Service (INS), Operations Instruction 212.5(c), INS Memorandum, Feb. 20, 1987 (on file with the *Washington Law Review*).

24. Lennon v. INS, 527 F.2d 187, 189 (2d Cir. 1975).

25. An immigrant may qualify as an immediate relative or special immigrant, without an annual ceiling on numbers. If not, he or she must qualify under a preference category based on a family or employment relationship with the United States. INA § 203(a)(1)–(a)(7), 8 U.S.C. § 1153(a)(1)–(a)(7) (1988) (as modified by the Immigration Act of 1990, Pub. L. No. 101-649, 104 Stat. 4978). The Act for the first time imposes a numerical limit on a nonimmigrant classification (H). *Id.* § 205.

26. INA § 214(b), 8 U.S.C. § 1184(b).

27. INA § 291, 8 U.S.C. § 1361.

28. INA § 204(a)–(b), 8 U.S.C. § 1154(a)–(b).

29. 22 C.F.R. § 42.41, 42.43 (1990).

numerically limited by law, applicants are also subject to a fairly complicated numerical control system.[30]

Consular officers have exclusive authority within the Department of State to issue or deny a visa; even the Secretary of State cannot reverse their decisions.[31] Immigrant and nonimmigrant applicants alike have the burden of proving to the satisfaction of the consular officer that they are eligible to receive a visa. Consular discretion, however, is explicitly limited. The consular officer may deny a visa only when he or she knows or has "reason to believe"[32] that the applicant is ineligible to receive a visa. "Reason to believe" requires that "a determination [be] based upon facts or circumstances which would lead a reasonable person to conclude that the applicant is ineligible."[33] Therefore, the "satisfaction of the consular officer" is defined by a reasonable person standard, according to which the officer has substantial, but limited discretion. The State Department's Foreign Affairs Manual guides, but does not control, consular discretion during the adjudication of an application for a visa. Consular officers adjudicate an application by requesting documentation and interviewing the applicant, if physical appearance has not been waived by regulatory law.[34]

An interview with the consular officer is the "most significant part of the immigrant visa issuing process."[35] Normally, the adjudication of an application for an immigrant visa is objective and formal, the family relationship or labor certification either exists or it does not, and the applicant either overcomes the grounds for exclusion or does not. The greatest number of refusals of immigrant visas involve either insufficient documentation[36] or the likelihood that the applicant will become a public charge.[37]

---

30. *See* VISA REPORT, *supra* note 1, at 123 app.

31. INA § 104(a), 8 U.S.C. § 1104(a)(1). *Cf.* Wolf, *supra* note 6, at 1876–79 (global comparison of discretion to permit or refuse entry). *But see infra* text accompanying notes 278–79 (discussing the use of para-consular assistants and Civil Service visa examiners).

32. INA § 221(g), 8 U.S.C. § 1201(g).

33. 22 C.F.R. § 40.6 (1990).

34. The consular officer may waive the requirement of a personal appearance for children under 14, foreign and international organization officials and diplomats, some temporary visitors, transits, aircraft crewmen, and otherwise in the national interest or because of an applicant's experience of hardship or other unusual circumstances. 22 C.F.R. § 41.102.

35. FOREIGN AFFAIRS MANUAL, *supra* note 19, at App. J-721, note PN6.

36. INA § 221(g), 8 U.S.C. § 1201(g). See VISA REPORT, *supra* note 1, at 110–11 for gross statistics on ineligibilities during 1988. *See also* Wildes, *Review of Visa Denials: The American Consul as 20th Century Absolute Monarch*, 26 SAN DIEGO L. REV. 887, 906 (1989).

37. INA § 212(a)(15), 8 U.S.C. § 1182(a)(15). See VISA REPORT, *supra* note 1, at 110–11 for statistics on visa denials during 1988. *See also* Wildes, *supra* note 36.

Adjudication of an application for a nonimmigrant visa, which is typically very quick, necessarily relies on a determination of an applicant's intentions and good faith, so as to ensure that the applicant will leave the United States before a visa expires.[38] In making this determination, critical factors may include family employment and financial ties at home as well as any unsuccessful previous attempts by the applicant to obtain an immigrant visa.[39] During the adjudication, a face-to-face interview between the applicant and a consular officer is critical; the applicant's documentation is of marginal importance. Most refusals of nonimmigrant visas are made under sections 221(g) and 214(b) of the INA,[40] the latter for failure to overcome the presumption that the applicant is an intending immigrant, that is, that the alien does not intend to return home from the United States upon the expiration of his or her visa. Applicants may overcome this presumption by showing family or socio-economic ties to the local community that are sufficiently strong to persuade the consular officer that their projected stays in the United States will be temporary. A nonimmigrant visa "shall be considered refused"[41] if an applicant fails to execute an application after being informed by the consular officer of a ground of ineligibility.[42]

On approval of an immigrant visa, a consular officer issues completed Forms OF-230 (Application for Immigrant Visa and Alien Registration), and OF-155A (Immigrant Visa and Alien Registration).[43] INS approval of these forms and issuance to the alien of the well-known "green card" (Alien Registration Receipt Card, Form I-551) indicate the applicant's compliance with requirements of the INA and can serve as a sort of work permit and reentry document.[44] On approval of a nonimmigrant visa, the consular officer will stamp a visa into the applicant's passport for either a single entry or multiple entries. The INS will later staple an endorsed Form I-94 (Arrival-Departure Record) into the passport.[45] Form I-94 is intended to be surrendered upon the alien's departure from the United States.

---

38. T. ALEINIKOFF & D. MARTIN, *supra* note 2, at 272.

39. C. GORDON & E. GORDON, IMMIGRATION AND NATIONALITY LAW 3-38 (student ed. 1980).

40. 8 U.S.C. §§ 1184(b), 1201(g). *See also* Wildes, *supra* note 36.

41. 22 C.F.R. § 41.121(b) (1990). The terms "refused" and "denied" are used interchangeably in this study.

42. INA § 212(a), 8 U.S.C. § 1182(a).

43. 22 C.F.R. § 42.73.

44. T. ALEINIKOFF & D. MARTIN, *supra* note 2, at 276.

45. *Id.* at 272.

Issuance of a visa is, however, no assurance of permission to enter the United States. A visa is, instead, more of a clearance to request admission by the INS at the border or other port of entry. Thus, prior to the applicant's entry, a consular officer or the Secretary of State may revoke an immigrant's visa "in his discretion."[46] Second, a "double-check" system subjects an alien to a de novo inspection and determination of admissibility by the INS at the border or other port of entry.[47] Only about three percent of all visas are cancelled, according to estimates by consular officers with whom the author spoke.

It seems strange that issuances of visas, but generally not denials, are subject to redetermination. The INS may detain any arriving alien for further inquiry if he or she does not appear "to be clearly and beyond a doubt entitled to land" in the United States. After limited exclusion proceedings, the INS may issue an exclusion order barring the alien from entry.[48] An alien can be refused entry—"kickbacked" in INS-consular jargon—for reasons that the consular officer may have overlooked, excused or could not have known. Many, if not most, "kickbacks" are seeking to enter with a nonimmigrant tourist visa. The INS might kick back an alien for a number of reasons that would have been difficult, if not impossible, to establish in the embassy or consulate: having no money or return tickets; having only one change of clothing; having drugs in a suitcase; having mostly American-label clothes, but no computerized record of previous visas (showing probability, in some circumstances, of past illegal entry); having no proof of home residence; being in possession of a driver's license issued in the United States (again, showing a sign of past undocumented residence); or even expressing intent to reside in an area characterized by the presence of undocumented aliens, coupled with other suspicious aspects. The INS records a kickback on Form I-275 (Notice of Visa Cancellation or Border Crossing Card Voidance).

The "reentry doctrine"[49] requires aliens to submit to border checks and face refusal of entry each time they travel abroad and return to the

---

46. INA § 221(i), 8 U.S.C. § 1201(i).

47. INA § 221(h), 8 U.S.C. § 1201(h).

48. INA §§ 235(b), 236, 8 U.S.C. §§ 1225(b), 1226.

49. United States *ex rel.* Volpe v. Smith, 289 U.S. 422 (1933). In Rosenberg v. Fleuti, 374 U.S. 449 (1963), the Supreme Court narrowed the doctrine to allow reentry if a trip abroad was "innocent, casual, and brief" and therefore not "meaningfully interruptive" of the alien's permanent residence in the United States. *Id.* at 461–62. Section 315(b) of IRCA amends section 244(b) of the INA, 8 U.S.C. § 1254(b), by adding the following codification of the *Fleuti* rule: "An alien shall not be considered to have failed to maintain continuous physical presence in the United States . . . if the absence . . . was brief, casual, and innocent and did not meaningfully interrupt the continuous physical presence."

United States, as if they were entering the country for the first time. In practice, few aliens with visas are excluded at the border or other port of entry.

An alien may thus be subject to exclusion by a consular officer, by an immigration inspector at the border or other port of first entry, or by an inspector when he or she attempts to reenter the United States after a trip abroad. An issue of exclusion may also arise in deportation proceedings, during an attempted adjustment of status, or in naturalization proceedings.

The INS may waive most of the grounds[50] for excluding nonimmigrants and, in exceptional circumstances, "parole"[51] them into the United States despite an unwaivable ground of exclusion. Parole may be granted, for example, to enable an alien to obtain urgent medical care, to enable the alien to appear as a witness in criminal litigation, or after an alien is detained, to provide for his or her release pending an exclusion hearing.[52] Even if a parolee is already in the United States, the law limits constitutional protections as if he or she were an excluded alien at the border.

The McGovern Amendment of 1977[53] placed a burden on the Secretary of State to overcome a presumption that a waiver of a denial under section 212(a)(28) of the INA should be granted in instances where the denial was based on membership in or affiliation with certain subversive organizations.[54] Without a waiver, this provision excluded anarchists, communists, advocates of "world communism" or "totalitarian dictatorship," violent overthrow of government or other stipulated subversive doctrines, or anyone affiliated with subversive organizations. The Amendment directed the Secretary of State to recommend to the Attorney General a waiver of ineligibility unless the Secretary certified to Congress that admission of the alien would be contrary to the security interests of the United States.[55] Subsequent

---

50. *See* INA § 212(d)(3)(A), 8 U.S.C. § 1182(d)(3)(A). The legislative history indicates the intent of Congress to admit otherwise ineligible persons "for humane reasons and for reasons of public interest." S. REP. No. 1137, 82d Cong., 2d Sess. 12 (1952). The three non-waivable provisions exclude aliens engaging in activities "prejudicial to the public interest," spies and saboteurs, and Nazi criminals. 8 U.S.C. § 1182(a)(27), (29), (33).

51. INA § 212(d)(5), 8 U.S.C. § 1182(d)(5).

52. For a good summary of this practice, see D. MARTIN, MAJOR ISSUES IN IMMIGRATION LAW 11 (1987).

53. Foreign Relations Authorization Act, Fiscal Year 1978, Pub. L. No. 95-105, § 112, 91 Stat. 848 (1977) (amending 22 U.S.C. § 2691(a) (1976)).

54. 8 U.S.C. § 1182(a)(28) (1988).

55. *See* Mann, *supra* note 4 at 420-22; Wash. Post, Apr. 15, 1989, at A8, col. 1 (denial of visas to permit two heads of state, Fidel Castro and Daniel Ortega, to speak to the American Society of Newspaper Editors).

qualifications of the McGovern Amendment and a broad interpretation of the "security interests" exception in it limited its scope somewhat, and the Immigration Act of 1990 repealed the underlying grounds for exclusion and hence the Amendment, too.[56]

II. THE REVIEW PROCESS

A. Introduction

Informal and non-reviewed decisionmaking dominates administrative process.[57] Controlling administrative discretion appropriately is often difficult. Tight constraints may inhibit bureaucratic creativity, initiative, enthusiasm for the job, and capacity to render justice in the individual case, whereas loose constraints may encourage arbitrariness and inequality.[58]

Like other government employees, consular officers make millions of decisions at the taxpayers' expense that are generally unconstrained by formal review processes. What makes consular visa denials so distinctive is their impact on individual lives and aspirations, on freedom of movement, on family reunification, on an individual's economic potential, and quite often, on the lives of American friends, relatives, and prospective employers. What makes visa denials so controversial is that both administrative and judicial review of visa denials by consular officers is very limited. Courts seldom review denials, and administrative review is significantly curtailed by section 104(a) of the INA.[59] That section provides a limited role for the Secretary of State in administering and enforcing the Act and related laws "except those powers, duties, and functions conferred upon the consular officers relating to the granting or refusal of visas."[60] An interpretation of this language that has in effect largely insulated consular denials of visas from administrative and judicial review will be discussed later;[61] it suffices here to note that this provision seems to have been designed

---

56. Immigration Act of 1990, Pub. L. No. 101-649, 104 Stat. 4978).

57. K. DAVIS, ADMINISTRATIVE LAW TEXT 88, 91 (3d ed. 1972).

58. *See* Shumavon & Hibbeln, *Administrative Discretion: Problems and Prospects,* in ADMINISTRATIVE DISCRETION AND PUBLIC POLICY IMPLEMENTATION 1–9 (Shumavon & Hibbeln eds. 1986).

59. 8 U.S.C. § 1104(a).

60. *Id.* This section *reversed* a requirement of review by the Secretary of State. *See, e.g.,* Public Safety Act of June 20, 1941, *supra* note 14 ("[I]n any case in which a diplomatic or consular officer denies a visa or other travel document under the provisions of this Act, he shall promptly refer the case to the Secretary of State for such further action as the Secretary may deem appropriate.")

61. *See infra* text accompanying notes 90–92, 97–98, 106, 127–28, 148, 160, 164, 240–41, 337–38.

rather narrowly to insulate consular discretion only from supervision by the Secretary of State, except as otherwise provided by law.

Well-defined checks on consular discretion, just as elsewhere within government, seem appropriate. To err is only human. A number of personal factors may influence an officer's exercise of discretion and help explain errors and differences among officers, including rates of visa denial. These personal factors include tenure of service, personal background, availability of time to make decisions, effect of intermediaries and peer pressure, attitudes toward management and applicants, career objectives, and the promotion system.[62] These factors may either inhibit competence or encourage compliance with policy expectations. They may also provide incentive to avoid errors, and to correct errors when they occur, to the extent that the concept of "error" makes sense in the highly discretionary context of the visa process.

If anything, the system encourages consular officers to issue rather than refuse visas in close cases, which typically involve nonimmigrant applicants. Because issuances, unlike denials, are rarely reviewed internally by supervising officers, and are therefore subject mostly to the double-check by the INS at the border or port of entry, issuing visas is relatively risk-free for career-minded consular officers.[63] They do receive reports on aliens to whom they have issued visas and who are later "kicked back" at the border by the INS, but such cases are relatively uncommon for any single consular officer. A high level of discretion may thereby tend, overall, to favor applicants.

Despite the apparently large scope of consular discretion, the law provides significant constraints. The values it serves are accountability of consular officers, uniformity or consistency of decisions among the officers and visa sections, and due process for applicants and petitioners. The law attempts to maximize these values at various levels of formality. Substantive rules confine and structure discretion[64] by identifying and attributing relative weight to various factors. The INA, its regulations, and State Department guidelines provide substantive and procedural rules, as do other textual sources, including intra-consulate rules and procedures, policy statements, findings and reasons.

---

62. *See* Study, *Consular Discretion in the Immigrant Visa-Issuing Process*, 16 SAN DIEGO L. REV. 87 (1978).

63. *Id.* at 107 (quoting one consular officer as saying, "[t]he nice thing about our job is that if you issue the visa you can't make a mistake. It is only when you refuse that you've made a mistake").

64. On confining and structuring discretion, see K. DAVIS, *supra* note 57, at 93–99.

For example, the regulations and interpretative and procedural notes to the regulations confine and structure discretion to determine whether aliens will become "public charges" after entry into the United States. This has been a particularly controversial provision of the law because it requires consular officers to make highly speculative predictions. Documents help guide the determination, however. Thus, although affidavits of support from United States citizens or resident aliens are of questionable utility, a sworn job offer from a prospective, known, and creditable employer in the United States may help establish eligibility, whereas an applicant's reliance on documentation showing expected income below the poverty guidelines will almost certainly be a disqualifier. Departmental notes encourage consular officers to elicit and consider such documentation from the applicant as proof of ownership of real estate, stocks and bonds or other property, insurance policies, posted bonds and bank deposits.[65] Although visa sections occasionally establish minimum deposits, the controlling question is not whether the applicant maintains a fixed sum on deposit, but whether, taking account of his or her total estate and income potential, the applicant can avoid becoming a public charge.[66]

A myriad of other provisions and guidelines attempts to confine and structure consular discretion. Information systems, ranging from consular files to the sophisticated Automated Visa Lookout System (AVLOS) and National Automated Immigration Lookout System (NAILS), with information on millions of aliens, assist and constrain consular discretion. Textual guidance is, however, necessarily and often deliberately so general as to invite disagreement on interpretation and construction. A more formal process of guidance and review is therefore essential.

---

65. FOREIGN AFFAIRS MANUAL, *supra* note 19, at App. J-78, note N3.

66. *Id.* at J-77, note N2.1. For example, the Visa Section Chief of one consulate explained that the impression that an applicant

must have a substantial bank account to qualify for a visa is not correct. The Immigration and Nationality Act states that all persons applying for admission to the United States are presumed to be immigrants until they prove otherwise. Applicants can overcome this presumption by demonstrating economic solvency and strong ties to their home country. One means of demonstrating solvency is with a bank account, but other factors, such as employment and strong family ties here in Mexico are equally important. In general, applicants must be able to show sufficient ties to their home country to insure that they plan to return.

Letter from Celio F. Sandate, Chief, Visa Section, Consulate General of the United States of America, Guadalajara, Mexico, to the author (June 4, 1985) (on file with the *Washington Law Review*).

In considering the alternatives for a better elaborated process, it is important to recognize that the process of reviewing consular discretion begins with an application, not with the issuance or denial of it. So defined, the review process by its very existence helps control the initial exercise of discretion by holding consular officers accountable to some extent. Moreover, key actors in the process, who are primarily interested in correcting error after the fact, may also help avoid error by their informal participation or influence before a decision is reached. These actors include supervising officers, the Visa Office in the Department of State, the Secretary of State despite section 104(a) of the INA, the INS, occasionally the Attorney General, legislators, private organizations, attorneys, the media, administrative tribunals (indirectly), and the courts.

An adequate review process should seek to maximize three values typically served by legal constraints on administrative discretion. These are accountability of consular officers, uniformity or consistency of determinations among officers and visa sections, and due process for applicants and petitioners.

B. Non-Judicial Aspects

1. Informal, Unofficial Checks

The media and private organizations, as part of an informal mechanism of review, constrain consular discretion. "Visa fixers" and other lay consultants, sometimes representing religious and other non-governmental groups, "do a thriving business and are a continuing source of irritation to consular officers."[67] Fixers are often viewed as unnecessary intermediaries who, for a fee imposed on unsophisticated applicants, waste the time of the officers. They are most visible in Mexico and other locations near their headquarters or bases of operations in the United States.

Attorneys may also play a significant role in review, particularly in helping to ensure due process and more efficient management of visa applications,[68] but their accessibility to the visa system can be a significant problem. Neither the INA nor its regulations ensure an applicant's access to counsel during consular adjudication. Thus, each visa section is free to define for itself the limits of attorney representation, including whether the attorney may enter the consular premises, be

---

67. Study, *supra* note 62, at 150.

68. The Visa Office in the State Department has acknowledged that "[i]n the sometimes complex world of visas, a good attorney can prepare a case properly, weed out 'bad' cases, and alert applicants to the risks of falsifying information." 67 INTERPRETER RELEASES 950 (1990).

present during the adjudication, be permitted to speak on behalf of the applicant, be permitted to discuss the case with the consul, or represent the applicant effectively in requesting reconsideration of a visa denial.[69]

Often, therefore, attorneys have to get their feet in the door of an embassy or consulate and then persuade the consul to allow them more extended participation in the process. This requires attorneys to devote time and energy to personal letters, telex messages, phone calls and personal visits in order to be effective participants in the process of visa issuance. Overcoming the suspicions or even hostility of consular officers may be crucial. Consular policy generally is to reply to all written communications and to return phone calls whenever time permits.

2. Congressional Inquiry

Stateside petitioners and other family members and friends of immigrant and nonimmigrant applicants routinely enlist congressional inquiries in particular cases. Typically, such official inquiries elicit prompt, though not necessarily sympathetic, responses prepared by the refusing officer and edited by a reviewing officer. Inquiries signed by members of Congress, rather than their staff members, are given special attention.[70]

3. Internal Review Procedures

By law, a consular officer who has refused to issue a visa must inform the applicant of the legal basis for the decision.[71] Similarly, after issuing a "quasi-refusal," that is, prior to filing a formal application, the consular officer must explain to a potential applicant the legal

---

69. Pederson, *supra* note 18, at 297; *supra* text accompanying note 22.

70. Study, *supra* note 62, at 109; interviews with consular officers, *infra* text in paragraph preceding note 283.

71. 22 C.F.R. §§ 41.121(b), 42.81(b) (1990). Department procedures are quite specific. The denying officer must take care not to encourage any false expectations. FOREIGN AFFAIRS MANUAL, *supra* note 19, at App. J-849, note PN1.2. The officer must be sensitive, but firm:

Some officers understandably are, or try to be, very sympathetic, but that too can create problems. If a tone of authority is not evident, the applicant may misunderstand the officer's intentions and believe the visa might still be issued. (In some societies, such a situation might be interpreted as an invitation to a bribe.)

The consular officer should aim for a measured, sympathetic but firm style which will convince the ineligible applicant that the treatment accorded was fair. The consular officer should refer to pertinent statements of the applicant, written or oral, or to a conviction, medical report, false document, previous refusal, or the like, as the basis of the refusal. The officer should then explain the law simply and clearly.

Id. at App. J-849, note PN1.1(m).

basis for an advance determination of probable ineligibility.[72] If the ground(s) cannot be overcome by the presentation of additional evidence, the principal consular officer or a designee "shall review the case without delay, record the review decision, and sign and date the prescribed form."[73] If, however, the ground(s) of ineligibility can be overcome by the presentation of additional evidence, the applicant may attempt to do so within stipulated periods of time during which the refusal is deferred.[74] If the officer or designee does not concur in the refusal, he or she may either refer the case to the Visa Office within the State Department for an advisory opinion or reverse the refusal.[75] Reference of a case to the Visa Office is largely a discretionary procedure, usually reserved by the officer for cases where correct interpretation of the law may be uncertain. The principal consular officer or designee at a particular post will usually confer with the refusing officer before overruling the latter or referring a case to the Visa Office.[76] One formal limitation in the process, however, is the lack of a requirement of notice to the applicant about a referral of his or her papers to the Visa Office, nor any requirement that the applicant be entitled to a hearing by the reviewing officer.

In the case of an immigrant visa, the applicant has yet another opportunity for review. If, within one year of a refusal, an applicant "adduces further evidence tending to overcome the ground of ineligibility on which the refusal was based, the case shall be reconsidered".[77]

---

72. 22 C.F.R. §§ 41.121(c), 42.81(c); FOREIGN AFFAIRS MANUAL, *supra* note 19, at App. J-850, note PN2.1.

73. 22 C.F.R. § 41.121(c).

74. 22 C.F.R. §§ 41.121(c), 42.81(c).

75. *Id.; see infra* text accompanying notes 80–85, 337–43 (discussing the Visa Office).

76. Department of State procedures require this consultation, as follows:

Although the regulations indicate only two possible actions for a reviewing officer who disagrees with a refusal—submission of the case to the Department or personal assumption of responsibility by reversing the refusal—the reviewing officer should discuss the case fully with the refusing officer before taking either action. The principles of good management require that the junior officer be involved in any action possible bearing on the junior officer's judgment and performance. Also, in the course of discussion the reviewing officer may become aware of additional facts which the refusing officer did not make clear in the refusal worksheet.

Most important, the junior officer will learn more about the visa function and the application of some of the more complicated laws and regulations in visa work. Ideally, any differences will be worked out in the discussion and the refusing officer, not the reviewing officer, will take whatever action is necessary. Only if there is no resolution should the reviewing officer take the actions specified in 22 CFR 42.81(c), and then only after the refusing officer has been informed what the action will be and why.

FOREIGN AFFAIRS MANUAL, *supra* note 19, at App. J-849–50, note PN1.3.

77. 22 C.F.R. § 42.81(e).

Although the integrity of this internal review process is open to question and cannot work, of course, in a one-person visa section, the possibility of reversal by a supervising officer, who may also have promotion and other personnel authority, helps confine and structure consular discretion. "A number of consular posts have demonstrated a commitment to provide meaningful review,"[78] particularly at larger posts, principally by permitting applicants or their attorneys to present additional evidence at each stage of a visa proceeding. Typically, applicants know that they can return repeatedly to present additional evidence. It is estimated that they are eventually successful in almost fifty percent of all immigrant cases after initial refusal and in sixty percent of all cases after refusal for insufficient documentation.[79]

4.   Review By the Visa Office

A principal or alternate consular officer, but not a denied applicant, may refer a case to the Visa Office in the Bureau of Consular Affairs of the State Department, or the Department itself may request a consular officer in a specific case or class of cases to submit a report on a visa refusal or refusals.[80] The Visa Office has jurisdiction to consider only substantive, not procedural issues. In some cases, this kind of limited review by the Visa Office is required by law. These cases include refusals on the ground of a sham marriage, drug trafficking, fraud or willful misrepresentation in procuring a visa or entry into the United States (under the "rule of probability") and commission of a political crime.[81]

The first step in review by the Visa Office is to consult with the consul in charge of the pertinent visa section. The particular visa applicant, who is not consulted, may not even know that the Visa Office is reviewing the case. After the Visa Office has completed its review, it issues an Advisory Opinion. This Opinion is binding on all interpretations of law so long as it complies with opinions of the Attorney General,[82] but is advisory only on factual issues.

---

78. Pederson, *supra* note 18, at 314.

79. Study, *supra* note 62, at 109, 105 n.103 & text accompanying n.104.

80. 22 C.F.R. §§ 41.121(d), 42.81(d).

81. Remarks by H. Edward Odom, Federal Bar Association, 9th Annual Immigration Seminar (May 19, 1988) [hereinafter Federal Bar Association Seminar] (on file with the *Washington Law Review*).

82. 22 C.F.R. §§ 41.121(d), 42.81(d). The issue of compliance with opinions of the Attorney General is central to the pending case of Garcia v. Baker, No. 90C2585 (N.D. Ill. May 4, 1990) (complaint on file with the *Washington Law Review*).

Consular officers generally comply with advisory opinions on matters of law,[83] but they may question an Opinion. If so, they must resubmit the case to the Department with an explanation of any proposed action that is contrary to the Opinion. Practitioners regard this process of review as fair and honest but time-consuming,[84] while many consular officers regard review by the Visa Office as either a nuisance or a means of delaying a case.[85] Advisory opinions are potentially very useful, but only marginally significant in practice today.

5. Administrative Appeals

Taking account of these procedures, it is no longer correct to conclude that "[t]he limited administrative review [of visa denials] currently available provides no independent check on consular officers"[86] or that the latter are "free from the control of a superior reviewing body."[87] The review process discussed thus far is routine and fairly well structured, helping to check errors after the fact, as Section IV indicates, and avoiding them in the first place by virtue of its very existence.

Internal administrative review and Visa Office review might seem to function in a manner that approximates more formal processes of administrative review. Possible bias inherent in the physical proximity of consular officers to their reviewing superiors, and bureaucratic unity between them, can be exaggerated by skeptics of the internal review process. Such bureaucratic unity exists in other agencies as well. For example, until 1983 special inquiry officers (or "immigration judges," as they have come to be known) were co-employees of the same unit of the Department of Justice, the INS, as that of the officers whose decisions they reviewed. Of course, intra-consular review and more formal INS processes of review are not exactly the same. Although the intra-consular process discussed thus far plays an important role, it is certainly not the equivalent of an INS review board. It

---

83. Study, *supra* note 62, at 111.

84. Remarks by Jan Pederson, Federal Bar Association Seminar, *supra* note 81. There are, of course, differences of opinions among practitioners on the process. The confidentiality of the process is particularly controversial.

85. "I always used the referral system for tactical reasons when I wanted to delay a stinking case, but never when I really wanted an informed opinion. The bureaucracy is too slow and also is too removed from the scene." Letter from Charles Stuart Kennedy, Director, Foreign Affairs Oral History Program, Georgetown University, to the author (Feb. 18, 1989) (on file with the *Washington Law Review*).

86. *Developments in the Law—Immigration Policy and the Rights of Aliens,* 96 HARV. L. REV. 1286, 1360 (1983) [hereinafter *Developments*].

87. *Hearings Before the President's Commission on Immigration and Naturalization, House Comm. on the Judiciary,* 82d Cong., 2d Sess. 1575, 1578 (1952).

lacks many of the formalities of bilateral due process and it is ad hoc. Practices among consulates vary substantially. Thus, two aliens with identical problems of eligibility for a visa but applying in different consular districts may receive dissimilar treatment. Although a lack of uniformity may be a problem even in more formal processes of administrative review, it is particularly characteristic of the intra-consular review process. Most importantly, although some immigration decisions by INS officers are not appealable administratively, most are appealable,[88] whereas there is no formal, extra-consular means for administrative review of visa denials. Even so, intra-consular review of visa denials provides *some* check on discretion.

The immunity of consular discretion from more formal administrative review is unusual within the federal government.[89] The legal basis for this deviation from the normal practice of formal administrative review is primarily a construction of section 104(a) of the INA, which precludes the Secretary of State from the administration or enforcement of "those powers, duties and functions conferred upon the consular officers relating to the granting or refusal of visas."[90] The precise legislative intent behind this language is unclear. Congress may have wished to protect the Secretary of State from complaints by foreign officials unable to obtain visas; section 104(a) enables the Secretary to disclaim responsibility for a politically delicate exclusion by explaining that he has no power to review the denial. Alternatively, Congress may have been concerned that the Department would be deluged, given the number of prospective petitioners for review. The legislative purposes are, however, mostly speculative. Probably the quoted language in section 104(a) was intended not to immunize visa determinations from review, but rather to confirm by implication the power of the Attorney General, rather than the Secretary of State, to undertake the review.[91] When the INA was enacted in 1952, Congress voted to reject an amendment to this provision that would have provided for an

---

88. T. ALEINIKOFF & D. MARTIN, *supra* note 2, at 92. *See* Appendix A (diagrams depicting avenues of administrative and judicial review under the immigration laws); MARTIN, *supra* note 52, at 104–05.

89. It is, of course, not unusual in other legal systems, but British law, by contrast, provides for both administrative appeal and judicial review of visa denials. *See* S. LEGOMSKY, *infra* note 128, at 145 n.16; UNITED KINGDOM IMMIGRANTS ADVISORY SERVICE, ANNUAL REPORT 1987–88, at 2, 19 (1989) [hereinafter cited as UKIAS REPORT].

90. 8 U.S.C. § 1104(a) (1988).

91. *See* SENATE JUD. COMM., REVISION OF IMMIGRATION AND NATIONALITY LAWS, S. REP. No. 1137, 82d Cong., 2nd Sess. 7 (1952). On the overall intent of Congress to limit reviewability to avoid administrative and judicial burdens, see SENATE JUD. COMM., THE IMMIGRATION AND NATURALIZATION SYSTEMS OF THE UNITED STATES, S. REP. No. 1515, 81st Cong., 2nd Sess. 622 (1950).

administrative board to hear appeals of visa denials. Although the amendment failed, a House committee report emphasized that the Secretary of State would have "ample authority to provide . . . for a system of cooperation between consular officers stationed abroad and the Department, so as to be able to advise and assist such officers in reaching their decision [sic] in more complex individual cases pending before them."[92]

C. Judicial Review

1. General Considerations

Courts regularly take jurisdiction to consider a wide range of immigration issues.[93] The current trend is toward exercise of jurisdiction in a wider variety of circumstances.[94]

Courts are specifically empowered to undertake habeas corpus proceedings as the "sole and exclusive remedy" for appeal of orders excluding aliens upon their arrival at the border or other port of entry

---

92. H.R. REP. No. 1365, 82d Cong., 2d. Sess. (1952), *reprinted in* 1952 U.S. CODE CONG. & ADMIN. NEWS 1653, 1688.

93. In addition to adjudications concerning deportation orders and INS orders of exclusion at the border or other port of entry,

> review proceedings can be brought to question such matters as the following: denials of visa petitions, registry, benefits under the agricultural workers program, waivers for exchange visitors, denial of parole to crewmen, and adjustment of status, denial of approval for a school qualified to accept nonimmigrant students, or withdrawal of such approval, change from one nonimmigrant status to another, denial of a labor certification, improper seizure or retention of the alien's passport, denial of extension of temporary stay, of asylum claim, claim of arbitrary, discriminatory, and unconstitutional action in bringing deportation proceeding when prosecutive discretion usually exercised to withhold deportation proceedings in similar cases, exclusion from a list of companies authorized to conduct immigration medical examinations, and breach of immigration bond.

C. GORDON & E. GORDON, *supra* note 39, at 8-40 (footnotes omitted).

94. One commentator notes:

> With limited exceptions, practically all final administrative determinations under the immigration and nationality laws are now subject to review in the courts. This was not always so. In the early days of federal immigration law enforcement, the courts maintained a reserved attitude, regarding immigration as a subject which the Constitution had committed largely to the legislative judgment of Congress. The attitudes of both Congress and the courts have changed over the last few decades and both are now more hospitable to judicial review in this field. In each of the last few years, literally hundreds of reported decisions on immigration and nationality issues have been handed down by the federal courts.

Roberts, *Judicial Review of Immigration Issues: Analysis and Forecast,* in II IMMIGRATION AND NATIONALITY LAW, 41ST ANNIVERSARY SYMPOSIUM OF THE AMERICAN IMMIGRATION LAWYERS ASSOCIATION 441 (1987).

of the United States.[95] The theory underlying habeas corpus proceedings is that anyone arriving at the border in United States territory is subject to being taken into physical custody even if that person is later released on bond, paroled, or made subject to a deportation order.[96] The formal process involves administrative review by a special inquiry officer (immigration judge), with a right of appeal. Courts have taken jurisdiction notwithstanding INA provisions that exclusion and deportation proceedings shall be "final."[97]

Judicial review of consular (as opposed to INS) discretion, however, has been very limited. Controversy about reviewing visa denials centers on an inference of judicial non-reviewability drawn from section 104(a) of the INA and questionable interpretations of the Administrative Procedure Act (APA)[98] and scattered but important judicial decisions that limit reviewability.[99] Thus, if an applicant is refused a visa, his or her rights of judicial review are extremely restricted.

2. Requirements of the Administrative Procedure Act

Section 701(a) of the APA codifies a common law presumption that the actions of governmental agencies are subject to judicial review. *Rusk v. Cort* [100] established the APA's applicability to State Department decisions, and *Brownell v. We Shung,* [101] to exclusion orders of the INS or Attorney General. In 1961 Congress expressly confirmed the latter presumption of review under then APA section 10(a) by providing in INA section 106 for review in federal district court of exclusion orders "by habeas corpus proceedings and not otherwise."[102] This provision applies only to INS exclusions after an alien presents himself at the border, so that consular discretion to deny visas before that event remains outside the express scope of INA section 106.

---

95. INA § 106(a)(9), 106(b), 8 U.S.C. § 1105(a)(9), 1105(b) (1988). Judicial review of final exclusion orders requires exhaustion of administrative remedies. INA § 106(c), 8 U.S.C. § 1105a(c).

96. 28 U.S.C. § 2241(c) (1988); INA § 106(b), 8 U.S.C. § 1105a(b). But see the requirement under the Visa Waiver Pilot Program for Certain Visitors, INA, *supra* note 13, at § 217, that eligible aliens must waive "any right to review or appeal . . . of an immigration officer's determination as to the admissibility of the alien at the port of entry into the United States." *Id.* § (b)(4)(A).

97. *See* Brownell v. We Shung, 352 U.S. 180, 185 (1956); Estep v. United States, 327 U.S. 114, 122 (1946).

98. Ch. 324, 60 Stat. 237 (1946), *repealed and replaced by* Government Organization and Employees Act, Pub. L. No. 89-554, §§ 551–59, 701–06, 80 Stat. 378 (1966), 5 U.S.C. §§ 551–59, 701–06 (1988) [hereinafter APA].

99. *See infra* text accompanying notes 123–59.

100. 369 U.S. 367 (1962).

101. 352 U.S. 180 (1956).

102. Pub. L. No. 87-301, 75 Stat. 683 (1961) (codified at 8 U.S.C. § 1105a(b)).

Under the APA there are only two exceptions to the reviewability of agency action, namely, when "(1) statutes preclude judicial review or (2) agency action is by law committed to agency discretion."[103] In order to determine judicial reviewability of visa denials under the APA, it is necessary to examine each of these two exceptions.

With reference to the first exception—when "statutes preclude judicial review"—the INA simply does not do so. Nor does any other federal legislation. Non-reviewability or limited reviewability is court-made law. It is a judicial construct, a legal fiction and, in effect, a violation of the APA. During congressional consideration of the INA, the record of debate discloses only one objection to judicial review, as opposed to several objections to consular non-reviewability.[104] During related consideration of a provision on deportation orders, both of the co-sponsors of the INA attempted to assure their colleagues that the APA applied. Although Senator McCarran opposed a specific appellate mechanism that was eventually adopted for reviewing cases other than visa denials, he did not oppose the right of appeal itself.[105]

One might infer, however, that the absence of any expression in the INA to apply the APA to visa denials implied an intent to insulate them from the APA. One might also infer that the insulation of visa denials from external administrative review under section 104 of the INA implies insulation from judicial review as well. These inferences, however, are inconsistent with the express intent of section 701(a) of the APA, that judicial review will be presumed, as a matter of the common law, except when a statute precludes review. Section 559 provides even more precisely that a "[s]ubsequent statute may not be held to supersede or modify [the Act] except to the extent that it does so expressly."[106] The INA, as "subsequent legislation," therefore cannot be properly interpreted to establish non-reviewability by implication.

In *Abbott Laboratories v. Gardner*,[107] the Supreme Court, without qualification, confirmed that the APA *presumes* judicial review unless Congress otherwise precludes it. "Exceptions from the . . . Administrative Procedure Act are not lightly to be presumed."[108] Review is precluded only if there is *clear and convincing evidence* that an Act of

---

103. 5 U.S.C. § 701.

104. 98 CONG. REC. 4431 (1952) (statement of Rep. Graham).

105. 98 CONG. REC. 4416, 5625–26, 5778–79 (1952).

106. 5 U.S.C. § 559.

107. 387 U.S. 136 (1967).

108. Marcello v. Bonds, 349 U.S. 302, 310 (1955), *quoted in* Brownell v. We Shung, 352 U.S. 180, 185 (1956).

Congress specifically prohibits it rather than simply failing to author-ize it, or that Congress by implication has clearly intended to prohibit review.[109] Congress *could have* created an exception to the APA to bar judicial review of visa denials, but never did so.

A variation on the non-reviewability-by-implication argument is that the pre-APA, common-law practice was intended to constitute an exception to section 701(a) of the APA. Accordingly, judicial non-reviewability of consular discretion to deny visas would be a special exception to the APA, despite sections 559 and 701(a), because the courts had established a common law rule of non-reviewability prior to the enactment of the APA. Therefore, one might infer that the rule was a sort of built-in common law exception to the more general com-mon law presumption of review that was later incorporated into the APA.[110] Aside from the questionability of this construction under a literal reading of sections 559 and 701(a) of the APA, Congress restated the prevailing rule requiring review without noting or incor-porating the purported exception. The only intended qualifications are the exemptions which Congress specifically provided in the statute. Congress therefore appears to have resisted the dead hand of non-reviewability.

Also, in *Abourezk v. Reagan,*[111] which addressed a challenge to a visa refusal on ideological grounds under the INA, a federal appeals court emphasized its duty to focus on questions of statutory construc-tion so as to avoid a need for constitutional construction if at all possi-ble. In applying the "cardinal principle" of *Ashwander v. Tennessee Valley Auth.,*[112] the court acknowledged a judicial duty to try to inquire "whether a construction of the statute is fairly possible by which the [constitutional] question may be avoided."[113] Thus, a sim-ple construction of the APA avoids posing any constitutional issues that might be presented by an aberrant line of common law. It would seem, therefore, that the dead hand of the pre-APA common law past ought to be ignored.

Nevertheless, section 701(a) of the APA was amended in 1976 to include language that might seem to restore the dead hand of non-reviewability. The amended language provides that "[n]othing herein

---

109. Japan Whaling Ass'n v. American Cetacean Soc'y, 478 U.S. 221, 230 n. 4 (1986); Rusk v. Cort, 369 U.S. 367, 379–380 (1962); Heikkila v. Barber, 345 U.S. 229, 237 (1953).

110. *See, e.g.,* Pena v. Kissinger, 409 F. Supp. 1182 (S.D.N.Y. 1976).

111. 785 F.2d 1043 (D.C. Cir. 1986), *aff'd per curiam,* 484 U.S. 1 (1987) (3–3 decision). For subsequent history, see City of New York v. Baker, 878 F.2d 507 (D.C. Cir. 1989).

112. 297 U.S. 288 (1936).

113. 785 F.2d at 1052 (quoting 297 U.S. at 348) (brackets in original).

28

. . . affects other limitations on judicial review or the power or duty of the court to dismiss any action or deny relief on any other appropriate legal or equitable ground."[114] The term "other limitations on judicial review" might be read to confirm the common law exception. The amendment, however, was not intended to have this effect. Instead, it is part of a larger revision of the APA to remove governmental immunity as a bar to judicial review. It was "not intended to affect or change defenses other than sovereign immunity".[115] The language quoted above therefore serves only to confirm common restrictions on judicial review, such as dismissal for lack of standing, failure to state a cause of action, or failure to exhaust administrative remedies.[116] The language of the 1976 amendment therefore does not foreclose judicial review; quite the contrary, the full amendment was intended to ensure greater accountability by opening the courts further to actions against the government.

The second statutory exception to the common law presumption of review, which was codified in section 701(a) of the APA, action "committed to agency discretion," was further elaborated in *Citizens to Preserve Overton Park Inc. v. Volpe.*[117] That decision limited the exception to situations where "there is no law to apply,"[118] either by pre-APA practice or an absence of legislative action. In *Heckler v. Chaney,*[119] the court added that the APA precluded judicial review under the second exception of section 701(a) where "the statute is drawn so that a court would have no meaningful standard against which to judge the agency's exercise of discretion."[120] The INA, however, provides specific enough requirements, together with customary international law and a long trail of jurisprudence, leaving no doubt about the existence of meaningful standards.

Just as there is no rule without a remedy, so there is no review without a plaintiff. The APA provides for standing, too. In *Association of Data Processing Service Organizations v. Camp,*[121] the Supreme Court confirmed that section 702 of the APA authorizes suit by a person who suffers a "legal wrong because of agency action or [who is] adversely affected or aggrieved by agency action within the meaning of

---

114. Act of Oct. 21, 1976, Pub. L. No. 94-574, § 702, 90 Stat. 2721, 5 U.S.C. § 702 (1988).
115. H.R. REP. No. 1656, 94th Cong., 2d Sess. 12, *reprinted in* 1976 U.S. CODE CONG. & ADMIN. NEWS 6121, 6132.
116. *Id.; see also* 2 C. KOCH, ADMINISTRATIVE LAW AND PRACTICE 217 (1985).
117. 401 U.S. 402 (1971).
118. *Id.* at 410.
119. 470 U.S. 821 (1985).
120. *Id.* at 830.
121. 397 U.S. 150 (1970).

a relevant statute."[122] In sum, although the INA does not confer a right of action to challenge a visa denial, the APA, more importantly, does.

3. Case Law to the Contrary

Because no federal statute has ever explicitly precluded judicial review of consular determinations, they are therefore subject to the APA's provisions for judicial review. There is, however, a puzzling line of cases that suggests the contrary.

Two appellate opinions of the 1920s, long before enactment of the APA, ushered in the notion that discretion exercised by consular officers in denying visas is not judicially reviewable. *United States* ex rel. *London v. Phelps*[123] cryptically observed in dicta that the court lacked "jurisdiction" to review the denial of a visa, without explaining what was meant by that term—a "gratuitous afterthought" in one commentator's words.[124] *United States* ex rel. *Ulrich v. Kellogg*[125] presumed non-reviewability and a broad consular discretion in the absence of any affirmative provisions in the 1924 Immigration Act[126] for "official review." This negative pregnant also contributed later to the interpretation of section 104(a) of the INA that infers judicial non-reviewability from a confirmation of consular authority. Thus, in the absence of any express stipulation of judicial authority, INA section 104(a) has been interpreted to preclude judicial review even though, at most, it suggests *administrative,* rather than judicial, non-reviewability.[127] None of these three bases for non-reviewability, lack of "jurisdiction," preclusively broad consular discretion, nor the absence of an affirmative authorization of judicial review, should have survived the APA.[128]

The timidity of the judicial system in these two cases is explained by the force of a "plenary power" doctrine that the Court long ago fashioned. This doctrine has been applied to require judicial deference to

---

122. 5 U.S.C. § 702 (1988).

123. 22 F.2d 288, 290 (2d Cir. 1927), *cert. denied,* 276 U.S. 630 (1928).

124. Note, *Judicial Review of Visa Denials: Reexamining Consular Nonreviewability,* 52 N.Y.U. L. REV. 1137, 1143–44 (1977).

125. 30 F.2d 984 (D.C. Cir.), *cert. denied,* 279 U.S. 868 (1929).

126. Immigration Act of 1924, ch. 190, 43 Stat. 153, 8 U.S.C. § 203 (1946 & Supp. III 1950) (repealed 1952).

127. *See* SECTION OF LITIGATION, AMERICAN BAR ASSOCIATION & AMERICAN IMMIGRATION LAWYERS ASSOCIATION, REPORT TO THE HOUSE OF DELEGATES (Feb. 1989) (report in support of a recommendation regarding amendments to legislation and regulations establishing a system for review of visa denials) (on file with the *Washington Law Review*).

128. *See* S. LEGOMSKY, IMMIGRATION AND THE JUDICIARY: LAW AND POLITICS IN BRITAIN AND AMERICA 146–49 (1987).

Congress or to executive action under congressional authority. In the Court's 1895 pronouncement of the doctrine:

> the power of Congress to exclude aliens altogether from the United States, or to prescribe the terms and conditions upon which they may come to this country, and to have its declared policy in that regard enforced exclusively through executive officers, without judicial intervention, is settled by our previous adjudications.[129]

The Court reaffirmed this plenary power of Congress in 1909 when it wrote that "over no conceivable subject is the legislative power of Congress more complete than it is [over the admission of aliens]."[130]

After these pronouncements of the plenary power doctrine, the apotheosis of Congress and the genuflection of the courts continued. Judicial decisions made clear that the powers of Congress, inherent in sovereignty, were so "plenary" as to void ordinary constitutional protection. Accordingly, Congress alone was responsible for defining and implementing first amendment, due process and other rights affecting the "privileges" of aliens. *United States* ex rel. *Knauff v. Shaughnessy*[131] and *Shaughnessy v. United States* ex rel. *Mezei*[132] established that "[w]hatever the procedure authorized by Congress is, it is due process as far as an alien denied entry is concerned."[133] "[I]t is not within the province of any court, unless expressly authorized by law, to review the determination of the political branch of the Government."[134] The remarkable result in *Mezei* was to deny reentry to an alien after a two-year visit abroad, even though he had resided in the United States for twenty-five years.

In *Galvan v. Press*,[135] a deportation case, Justice Frankfurter indicated his misgivings about the Court's refusal to place constitutional limitations on the plenary power of Congress to control immigration. "But," he wrote, "the slate is not clean. . . . Policies pertaining to the entry of aliens and their right to remain here are peculiarly concerned with the political conduct of government. . . . We are not prepared to deem ourselves wiser or more sensitive to human rights than our predecessors . . . ."[136] The full slate to which he referred included two lines of authority. First, the "yellow peril" cases of the late nineteenth and

---

129. Lem Moon Sing v. United States, 158 U.S. 538, 547 (1895), *quoted in* Kleindienst v. Mandel, 408 U.S. 753, 766 (1972).
130. Oceanic Steam Navigation Co. v. Stranahan, 214 U.S. 320, 339 (1909).
131. 338 U.S. 537 (1950).
132. 345 U.S. 206 (1953).
133. 338 U.S. at 544.
134. *Id.* at 543.
135. 347 U.S. 522 (1954).
136. *Id.* at 531.

early twentieth century[137] upheld the right of Congress to exclude entire nationalities for essentially racist reasons. Second, the somewhat mystical concept of a sovereign's inherent powers, as transmogrified into a separation-of-powers doctrine of constitutional law, has deterred many courts from reviewing the constitutionality of decisions by either of the political branches of the federal government.[138] These lines of authority help explain the inclination of the courts to view visa denials as nonreviewable *despite* the apparent policy of Congress to render them judicially reviewable under the APA.

In *Kleindienst v. Mandel,*[139] the Supreme Court indicated a limited role for the courts in reviewing visa denials. There, several Americans and a Belgian Marxist, Mandel, challenged the Attorney General's refusal to waive denial of a visa to Mr. Mandel that had been based on section 212(a)(28)(D) and (G)(v) of the INA (advocating or teaching communism).[140] The American plaintiffs claimed that the Attorney General's action violated their first amendment rights to hear lectures by Mr. Mandel in the United States. The Court, deciding in favor of the government, held that refusal to waive a visa denial was nonreviewable *if,* as here, the government had acted "on the basis of a facially legitimate and bona fide reason."[141] In *Mandel,* the reason given was the applicant's abuse of visa privileges during previous trips to the United States.

Unfortunately, *Mandel* is quite ambiguous. To be sure, the *Mandel* test seems clear: when the Executive's reasons for a waiver denial are "facially legitimate and bona fide . . . the courts will neither look behind the exercise of that discretion, nor test it by balancing its justification against the first amendment interests of those who seek personal communication with the applicant."[142] In context, however, it is unclear whether the Court considered this case to be reviewable only because it involved a first amendment issue, that is, an issue involving specially protected constitutional guarantees. It is also unclear whether reviewability is available after *Mandel* in all cases involving the exercise of executive discretion, or just those involving waiver

---

137. *See* Henkin, *The Constitution and United States Sovereignty: A Century of Chinese Exclusion and Its Progeny,* 100 HARV. L. REV. 853 (1987).

138. *See* United States v. Curtiss-Wright Export Corp., 299 U.S. 304 (1936).

139. 408 U.S. 753 (1972); *accord* Centeno v. Shultz, 817 F.2d 1212 (5th Cir. 1987), *cert. denied,* 484 U.S. 1005 (1988).

140. 8 U.S.C. § 1182(a)(28)(D), (a)(28)(G)(v) (1988).

141. 408 U.S. at 770.

142. *Id.* Fundamental rights, such as those under the first amendment, seem to provide a particularly strong rationale for judicial reviewability. Allende v. Shultz, 605 F. Supp. 1220 (D. Mass. 1985), *aff'd,* 845 F.2d 1111 (1st Cir. 1988).

denials. Finally, it is unclear whether the American plaintiffs had standing to bring the action whereas a non-resident alien alone would not have had standing. The court created two new issues: what was meant exactly by the new standard "that was remarkably deferential to the administrators,"[143] and whether an absence of any consular justification for a visa denial could withstand judicial attack.

Mandel has aroused considerable commentary, some of which has misinterpreted it to confirm the notion of judicial non-reviewability even though it clearly upheld the right to review under some circumstances. Because the decision is rather fuzzy around the edges, it leaves more questions than it resolves about the extent to which visa denials are reviewable.

Mandel, however, clearly reiterates the "plenary power" of Congress to control immigration, and thereby immunize most executive decisions from judicial scrutiny. The plenary power doctrine has gone through five historical stages:[144] (1) federal law preempts state laws excluding aliens; (2) federal exclusion statutes are justified under the commerce clause; (3) plenary power is inherent in sovereignty; (4) (shifting from issues involving an allocation of power within the federal system to the judicial role in vindicating civil rights and liberties), judicial inquiry is barred in such cases; and (5) ("the snowballing phase"), judicial inquiry is barred because the slate is not clean, so that the court is helpless to vindicate individual rights in the face of the plenary power doctrine.

Where does that leave the law today? *Mandel* has two facets. On the one hand, the opinion contributed to the snowballing effect of the plenary power doctrine by encouraging judicial abstention. Without much elaboration several lower court decisions have therefore precluded review of consular discretion.[145] Two cases merit comment because they were at least based on statutory interpretation rather than a mindless deference to an unexpressed "will" of Congress. In *Loza-Bedoya v. INS*[146] the court relied on section 221(a) of the

---

143. D. MARTIN, *supra* note 52, at 108.

144. S. LEGOMSKY, *supra* note 128, at 179–211, 217–19.

145. City of New York v. Baker, 878 F.2d 507 (D.C. Cir. 1989); Centeno v. Shultz, 817 F.2d 1212 (5th Cir. 1987), *cert. denied,* 484 U.S. 1005 (1988); Li Hing of Hong Kong, Inc. v. Levin, 800 F.2d 970 (9th Cir. 1986); Ventura-Escamilla v. INS, 647 F.2d 28, 30 (9th Cir. 1981); Rivera de Gomez v. Kissinger, 534 F.2d 518 (2d Cir.), *cert. denied,* 429 U.S. 897 (1976); Burrafato v. United States, 523 F.2d 554 (2d Cir. 1975), *cert. denied,* 424 U.S. 910 (1976); Pena v. Kissinger, 409 F. Supp. 1182 (S.D.N.Y. 1976); Hermina Sague v. United States, 416 F. Supp. 217 (D.P.R. 1976).

146. 410 F.2d 343 (9th Cir. 1969).

INA,[147] which, however, merely establishes the routine authority of consular officers to issue visas, but does not preclude review of their decisions. In *Licea-Gomez v. Pilliod,*[148] the court relied in part on section 104(a) of the INA,[149] which precludes review by the Secretary of State, even though the provision's terms do not refer to the courts.

On the other hand, *Mandel*'s "facially legitimate and bona fide reason" test has encouraged limited reviewability. After all, the courts did in fact review *Mandel* itself, and the foreign applicant was at least a nominal co-plaintiff. Thus, the plenary power doctrine may be going through a sixth stage[150] that is beginning to stall the movement of the "plenary power" snowball, or even melt it.

In *Fiallo v. Bell*[151] the Court considered the constitutionality of INA definitions of "child" and "parent"[152] that had the effect of preventing unwed fathers of citizens and illegitimate children of male citizens from relying on the blood connection to obtain immigrant visas. In view of two discriminatory distinctions, gender and legitimacy, the Court assumed its "limited judicial responsibility"[153] to review the case. The quoted language, ungenerous as it might seem, is nevertheless significant as an important counterpoint to the incantation in the same opinion of the *Stranahan* dictum ("over no conceivable subject is the legislative power of Congress more complete than it is [over the admission of aliens]").[154]

Despite *Fiallo*'s clear deference to Congress, its recognition of a "limited judicial responsibility" has been read to allow review of the constitutionality of the INA provisions upon which particular visa denials at issue were based[155] and the validity of departmental regulations structuring and confining the visa process.[156] None of these cases, however, directly addressed the issue of the reviewability of consular discretion.

Several recent cases suggest a trend toward a more direct, though still limited, review of visa denials under the APA, particularly where

---

147. INA § 221(a), 8 U.S.C. § 1201(a) (1988).

148. 193 F. Supp. 577 (N.D. Ill. 1960).

149. INA § 104(a), 8 U.S.C. § 1104(a).

150. *See* S. LEGOMSKY, *supra* note 128, at 211–17.

151. 430 U.S. 787 (1977).

152. INA § 101(b)(1)–(b)(2), 8 U.S.C. § 1101(b)(1)–(b)(2).

153. 430 U.S. at 793 n.5.

154. *Id.* at 792 (quoting Oceanic Steam Navigation Co. v. Stranahan, 214 U.S. 320, 339 (1909)).

155. *See, e.g.,* Martinez v. Bell, 468 F. Supp. 719 (S.D.N.Y. 1979).

156. *See, e.g.,* Mulligan v. Schultz [sic], 848 F.2d 655 (5th Cir. 1988); Friedberger v. Schultz [sic], 616 F. Supp. 1315 (E.D. Pa. 1985).

first amendment or other fundamental rights are implicated.[157] The question no longer is *whether* courts may review visa denial issues, but *to what extent* they may properly do so.

How far does *Mandel*'s standard of a "facially legitimate and bona fide reason" extend? What are the present contours of judicial review-ability? At the very least, the Supreme Court has indicated that the government must demonstrate a "facially legitimate and bona fide reason" for refusing to waive a visa denial, whenever a United States citizen brings action for injury to fundamental, constitutionally protected rights resulting from the government's refusal to issue a visa to a foreign applicant. Beyond that, the trail to the courthouse is rather poorly blazed. In practice, the *Mandel* standard offers an uncertain measure of constitutional protection. Some courts appear to have accepted "almost any reason the government offers,"[158] so long as it is not patently absurd, while other courts have scrutinized visa denials more carefully.[159] Section III provides further guidance along the trail to formal review.

III. AN ANALYSIS OF ARGUMENTS AGAINST REVIEW

Visa denials by consular officers are reviewable in a relatively informal manner, and in fact are regularly reviewed according to the managerial techniques and limited appellate procedures that have just been summarized. More formal and definitive procedures for reviewing visa denials, however, are severely limited. Administrative appeal, ordinarily routine in other spheres of administrative law, is limited primarily by section 104(a) of the INA,[160] and adjudication is limited primarily by. an inference drawn from section 104(a) and the plenary power doctrine despite the clear authority of the APA to the contrary.

---

157. Abourezk v. Reagan, 785 F.2d 1043, 1050–51 (D.C. Cir. 1986) (APA authorizes suit by "aggrieved" groups and individuals who suffer "injury in fact" by reason of being denied the opportunity to hear a foreign speaker who has been refused a visa), *aff'd per curiam*, 484 U.S. 1 (1987) (3–3 decision). For subsequent history of this case, see City of New York v. Baker, 878 F.2d 507 (D.C. Cir. 1989). *See also* Harvard Law School Forum v. Shultz, 633 F. Supp. 525, 528 (D. Mass.) (issue of visa denial to official of the Palestinian Liberation Organization is justiciable and plaintiffs are entitled to a preliminary injunction "to enjoin the Secretary of State from prohibiting [the PLO official] from participating in [a scheduled] debate" in the United States), *vacated without published opinion*, 852 F.2d 563 (Table) (1st Cir. 1986); Allende v. Shultz, 605 F. Supp. 1220 (D. Mass. 1985) (non-resident alien herself has "symbolic" standing and residents have actual standing to complain on first amendment grounds against refusal of visa to the alien, a prospective speaker), *aff'd*, 845 F.2d 1111 (1st Cir. 1988).

158. Note, *First Amendment Limitations on the Exclusion of Aliens*, 62 N.Y.U. L. REV. 149, 164 (1987).

159. *See* cases cited *supra* note 157.

160. 8 U.S.C. § 1104(a) (1988).

The case law does not inspire confidence that a "limited judicial responsibility" alone will serve the process very readily. Justice Frankfurter's observation that the slate is not clean offers a good description of the past and present, but a poor prescription for the future.

What is the margin for expanded reviewability within the present framework? Is the law apt to develop substantially on the basis of indirect challenges to consular discretion and the consideration of "facially legitimate and bona fide reason(s)" for visa denials? What if the slate were cleaned up? Why has Congress not mandated review? To help answer these and other questions, this section and the first portion of Section V focus on the principles and policies that have been invoked to limit reviewability and to explain the apparent reluctance of Congress to provide explicitly for review. It is essential to take account of constitutional, international legal, and practical dimensions of reviewability to define a realistic set of alternatives to guide legal development.

Although section 104(a) of the INA has been interpreted to be sufficient by itself to proscribe most administrative review outside visa sections of embassies and consulates, issues of judicial reviewability would surround administrative review even in the absence of section 104(a). Thus, if the INA were amended to provide for administrative appeals outside visa sections, the following discussion would remain relevant.

A.   Rationales for Limiting Reviewability

The two decisions during the 1920s that first struggled to articulate limitations of reviewability appear, in tandem, to have been based on three reasons: the court's lack of "jurisdiction," preclusively broad authorization by Congress of consular discretion, and the absence of affirmative authorization of judicial review.[161] Although these reasons have not been controlling in later cases, they have been influential. Each merits further consideration.

1.   Lack of Jurisdiction

Although the APA does not provide an independent basis of adjudicative jurisdiction, section 279 of the INA[162] provides for federal dis-

---

161. United States *ex rel.* Ulrich v. Kellogg, 30 F.2d 984 (D.C. Cir.), *cert. denied,* 279 U.S. 868 (1929); United States *ex rel.* London v. Phelps, 22 F.2d 288 (2d Cir. 1927), *cert. denied,* 276 U.S. 630 (1928). *See supra* text accompanying notes 123-28 (discussing *London* and *Ulrich*).

162. 8 U.S.C. § 1329.

trict court jurisdiction over all civil and criminal causes of action arising under "Title II-Immigration" of the Act, which includes the provisions for issuing and denying visas.[163] Section 104(a) of the INA should be considered irrelevant. In practice, the provision does not even seem to constrain the Department of State, through the Visa Office, from reviewing consular decisions for errors of law, nor from rendering binding opinions on points of law. If section 104 explicitly immunizes consular discretion to deny visas from the administrative supervision of the Secretary of State and yet the Visa Office supervises those decisions to a limited extent, it is difficult to argue that the provision can be used to preclude judicial review, which is not even mentioned in the section. Furthermore, the requirement that officers have "reason to believe"[164] in the ineligibility of applicants, in order to deny them visas, is premised by department regulations on a "reasonable person" standard[165] that actually invites judicial interpretation. Also, section 103(a) of the INA[166] establishes that a "determination and ruling by the Attorney General with respect to all questions of law shall be controlling" in the "administration and enforcement" of the Act. The implication is that, notwithstanding the discretion given to consular officers under section 104 of the INA vis-a-vis the Secretary of State, the Attorney General may retain competence to review. Finally, the courts ordinarily have general competence over federal questions under 28 U.S.C. § 1331.

2. Preclusively Broad Discretion of Consular Officers

The INA itself confines and structures consular discretion by its qualitative and quantitative provisions for issuing visas. Moreover, departmental regulation provides that "[a] visa can be refused only upon a ground specifically set out in the law or implementing regulations."[167] Application of such legal language and of the reasonable person standard would have little or no force without judicial review. Most importantly, the APA's insulation from judicial review of action committed to agency discretion "requires either a statutory intent to withhold review or a judicial determination that review would be impractical or improper."[168] There has been no such express intent.

---

163. Within Title II, INA § 221(g), for example, provides criteria for consular discretion to deny a visa. *See also* S. Legomsky, *supra* note 128, at 147 n.31.

164. INA § 221(g)(3), 8 U.S.C. § 1201(g)(3).

165. 22 C.F.R. § 40.6 (1990).

166. 8 U.S.C. § 1103(a).

167. 22 C.F.R. § 40.6.

168. S. Legomsky, *supra* note 128, at 148 (citing K. Davis, *supra* note 57, and other authority).

Whether review would be "impractical or improper" is a more difficult question.

3. Absence of Affirmative Authorization of Judicial Review

The APA *presumes* jurisdiction, subject to "clear and convincing evidence"[169] of any contrary intent by Congress to preclude it. The only possible evidence might be acquiescence by Congress in judicial determinations that it has not authorized review, but this is insufficient to circumvent the explicit authority of the APA.

This rationale survived the APA and influenced the interpretation of the INA that has inhibited judicial reviewability of visa denials. It is argued, mistakenly, that the courts are not authorized to review visa denials, because section 104(a) of the INA precludes direct supervision of visa denials by the Secretary of State and because the same section does not otherwise grant supervisory authority.

C. Positive International Law

International law establishes not only a customary, qualified duty to admit aliens, but certain obligations under treaties, executive agreements, and other formal instruments of international law. Some of these can be adjudicated, others lack the teeth of justiciability. Section 101(a)(17) of the INA defines the term "immigration laws" to include "all laws, conventions and treaties of the United States."[226] A complete list of these instruments lies outside the scope of the instant analysis. Some of them, however, are worth mentioning. They include the following instruments: bilateral treaties of establishment, investment treaties, and friendship, navigation and commerce treaties that provide for a mutual extension of national treatment to traders and investors; multilateral treaties, such as the United Nations Headquarters Agreement, that require access of diplomats to international organizations with headquarters in the United States; the U.S.-Mexican Joint Statement that requires cooperation in controlling the flow of undocumented aliens;[227] the Helsinki Accords[228] that prompted the McGovern Amendment and otherwise imposed obligations to facilitate family reunification and transnational marriages within the region of Europe and North America; and the Protocol to the Convention related to the Status of Refugees.[229] Important instruments that are not binding on the United States include a number of bilateral and regional agreements, particularly the European instruments on freedom of movement and labor,[230] and the treaty between the United Kingdom and China that defines the new immigration law of Hong Kong.[231] While none of these instruments obligates any state to accept particular numbers of aliens, they all impose important require-

---

226. 8 U.S.C. § 1101(a)(17) (1988).

227. Agreement on Illegal Entry of Migratory Workers, July 18, 1973, United States-Mexico, Joint Statement, 26 U.S.T. 1724, 1727–28, T.I.A.S. No. 8131.

228. Conference on Security and Co-Operation in Europe: Final Act, *reprinted in* 14 INT'L LEGAL MATERIALS 1292 (1975) [hereinafter Accords]. Although arguably not legally binding in themselves, the Accords provide a comprehensive, morally compelling expression of norms that, by influencing state behavior, may constitute *lex ferenda. See* Nafziger, *The Right of Migration Under the Helsinki Accords,* 1980 S. ILL. L.J. 395 (on state obligations under the Accords).

229. Protocol Relating to the Status of Refugees, done on Jan. 31, 1967, 19 U.S.T. 6223, T.I.A.S. No. 6577, 606 U.N.T.S. 267.

230. *See* Oellers-Frahm, *The Contribution of the Council of Europe to the Legal Position of Aliens,* in Frowein & Stein, *supra* note 6, at 1725, 1729–30; Stein & Thomsen, *The Status of the Member States' Nationals Under the Law of the European Communities,* in Frowein & Stein, *supra* note 6, at 1775, 1791–93; Plender, *supra* note 6, at 542–46.

231. Agreement on the Future of Hong Kong, Sept. 26, 1984, United Kingdom-China, art. XIV and Explanatory Notes, § XIV, Draft *reprinted in* 23 INT'L LEGAL MATERIALS 1366, 1377–78, 1388 (1984); 24 INT'L LEGAL MATERIALS 1185 (1985) (providing further information on status of the Agreement).

ments and good faith obligations to cooperate, and thereby encourage the issuance of visas under various circumstances stipulated in the instruments.

D. Practical Considerations

Although none of the justifications for non-reviewability or sharply limited reviewability of visa denials is persuasive in itself, it might be argued that taken together they at least rationalize a practice that has been fairly stable over time. Therefore, as time passes and Congress revisits the process, practical rather than doctrinal considerations are apt to be influential.

The judiciary is understandably skeptical about the weight to be given practical considerations when "fundamental rights are involved."[232] Although "[p]rocedure by presumption is always cheaper and easier than individualized determination,"[233] administrative convenience by itself is not a persuasive justification for cutting the corners of individual claims. Practical considerations are, however, highly influential in shaping legislative or administrative reform.

Several practical considerations have played an important role in forestalling legal reform. These considerations run through the general debate on reviewability as well as interpretations of the "committed to agency action" wording of the APA and other specific provisions of the law. They fall into three general categories: the freedom of consular officers to perform their functions; the feasibility of more formal, outside review; and the expectations of applicants.[234] These categories of practical considerations correspond roughly to the three basic values of review: accountability, uniformity or consistency, and due process.

1. Merits of Freeing Consular Officers from Outside Review

a. Expertise of Consular Officers

Consular officers are well trained, representing one of the most carefully selected, career-groomed corps of government, the Foreign Service. Consular officers possess high levels of competence and morale. Most officers have had special training in the visa process and are familiar with the characteristics and idiosyncracies of the local cul-

---

232. Fiallo v. Bell, 430 U.S. 787, 813 (1977).
233. Stanley v. Illinois, 405 U.S. 645, 656–57 (1972).
234. The first two of these categories are proposed and discussed in Note, *supra* note 124, at 1157–64.

ture. They generally have an experienced eye for fraud and chutzpah[235] by applicants.

On the other hand, to err is human and any exercise of discretion is potentially fallible. That is why the decisions of other agencies of government are subject to review despite their expertise. Consular interpretation of such terms as "public charges" and "reason to believe" are necessarily subjective, and guidelines are not always effective in promoting uniformity or consistency.[236] To the extent that errors are avoidable, the prospect of review would also encourage accountability. It would encourage consular officers to maintain a high level of care and commitment to applying the law correctly. Few officers would relish reversal by an outsider.

More importantly, a belt-tightening budget restricts the scope and efficacy of consular expertise. Many consulates are so financially hard-pressed that they cannot devote much time and expert judgment to a single applicant. "Batching" or group processing of applications in the same class may be necessary. On-line interviews of applicants for nonimmigrant visas average a minute or less because of severe budget constraints that spread on-line officers very thinly. Officers have little time to carefully investigate documents and employment letters and may rely heavily on income, property, and other guidelines without undertaking a more effective, case-by-case appraisal of applicants. Similarly, supervising officers often do not have enough time to review each visa denial thoroughly.[237] Spot checks or random samplings of

---

235. *See, e.g.,* Grimes, *Chutzpah by a Visa Applicant,* STATE, May 1988, at 12.

236. One study reported that:

Departmental efforts to structure consular officer discretion under the public charge provision have been minimal and sometimes confusing . . . .

The guidelines and policy statements existing under the public charge provision have met with mixed success. Some consular officers are flexible in accordance with stated policy. Others are inflexible and rely too heavily on the income poverty guidelines . . . .

The conclusion is that consular officers exercise a large amount of discretion to issue or refuse immigrant visas under the public charge provision. Major Departmental policies are contradictory, so an officer is free to rest a decision on the policy of flexibility or on the presumption of ineligibility. Either policy is acceptable. Key terms are ill-defined, so a consular officer may decide for himself what constitutes public assistance, who are dependent family members, and whether a head-of-household applicant may immigrate without his family. Indeed, two consulates [the authors visited] have opposite policies on the latter issue. Income documentation requirements are inexact, so an officer may request an extensive array of financial evidence, yet disbelieve it.

Study, *supra* note 62, at 124–25.

237. These problems have persisted for some time. *See id.* at 108, 112, 116, 148.

Typically, the refusing officer writes a few sentences explaining the grounds of ineligibility on the refusal sheet and attaches any relevant documents supporting the refusal. If an applicant is refused a visa on the ground that he is likely to become a public charge, for

denials are often the only alternative. Binding decisions on interpretations of the law by the Visa Office, congressional inquiries, and other intra-departmental processes of review, though important, are too sporadic to substitute for careful review within the consulate. Thus, budget constraints lead to a need for outside review. Internal review procedures are deficient, not because the working relationship between consular and reviewing officers is too cozy to ensure an objective review, but because too little time and money is available for a thorough review of all denials.

b. Governmental Interests

Efficient and effective management of the visa process would seem to require speed and finality, insulation of *initial* policymaking from judicial review, and uniformity or consistency of decisions.[238] These normal considerations of public administration might appear to be especially significant in the specific context of consular activity because of possible foreign policy implications of visa decisions. It is questionable, however, whether the foreign dimension of consular decisions should routinely set them apart from other types of administrative decisions, such as domestic decisions to locate state penitentiaries or nuclear power plants on the Canadian or Mexican border. In any event, review of consular determinations simply applying the INA to the facts in a particular case would not seem to involve "an initial policy determination of a kind clearly for nonjudicial discretion."[239] Nor is the need for a quick decision necessarily strong enough to overcome the need for a more deliberate, potentially correct decision. Delay of a final visa denial to allow for review is not likely to cause the kind of problem that delay of a more truly political decision, such as whether to suspend trade and tariff concessions, is apt to entail.

The need for uniformity or consistency of decisions justifies either greater regulatory control over consular discretion or review of consular decisions. Of these, the former might help alleviate the need for the latter. Regulation is direct, less costly, and potentially helpful to the consular officers in making decisions. Thus, many consular practices require greater regulation: the accessibility of attorneys or other applicant representatives to the review process; the hospitality to third-country, "orphan" applicants; the extent of pre-screening of

---

example, the consular officer might attach to the refusal sheet a copy of the applicant's job offer as evidence of inadequate income.

Id. at 108 n.124.

238. *See* Note, *supra* note 124, at 1157.

239. Baker v. Carr, 369 U.S. 186, 217 (1961).

applicants; the duration of interviews; the extent of review of visa denials by supervising officers; the capacity of denied applicants to reapply repeatedly; and the timelines for reapplications.

More uniform guidelines and regulations would assist officers in different consulates to reach consistent decisions, thus establishing uniform interpretations of national immigration policy and law. Processes should allow room for local discretion and even experimentation in some cases. Eventually, however, more uniform procedures and practices among the consulates would obviate most of the need for review.

The government has an interest not only in encouraging good exercise of consular discretion, but also in avoiding fraud and illegal migration by applicants. Ironically, the present system may encourage both by rendering an alien's status reviewable after a fraudulent or illegal entry into the United States, but not necessarily after a legitimate application and denial without illegal entry. This anomaly may encourage applicants to misrepresent or withhold information from a consular officer in the hope of getting a more formal review after illegal entry, or encourage applicants to avoid the visa process altogether. The prospect of review at the visa issuance stage might encourage prospective immigrants to do it the right way, beginning with a forthright visa application at the consulate.

2. Feasibility of More Formal, Outside Review

Whether the review process is administrative or judicial may affect its feasibility, but most of the critical arguments for or against reviewability apply in either case. Administrative and judicial review should be seen as two segments of the legal continuum. This section, however, will note whenever the type of dispute resolution might make a difference.

a. Volume of Prospective Appeals

The prospect of overburdening the State Department or clogging the courts has been cited as an important justification for non-reviewability.[240] Today, perhaps, it is *the* major practical justification, and at least partially explains INA section 104's mysterious insulation of visa denials from supervision by the Secretary of State. It has been used to support an inference against judicial review drawn from that provision. The volume of appeals is, of course, a serious consideration. Consulates issue close to a million visa denials every year. It is diffi-

---

240. S. REP. No. 1515, *supra* note 91.

cult to estimate what percentage of denied applicants would take advantage of judicial review if it were available. At a time when the federal courts are already overburdened, authorizing judicial review of all visa denials would therefore be quite risky. On the other hand, barring all judicial review seems unnecessary to avoid court congestion. Any burden to the government could be controlled to a large extent by the standard of review selected.[241]

Moreover, specialists have argued that the volume of appeals of visa denials would be small.[242] Only a small proportion of denied applicants are likely to seek judicial review. Unlike deportation cases, where aliens already in the United States may have some incentive to file frivolous court actions to obtain delay,[243] the visa applicant waiting to enter the United States has nothing to gain from delay. Further, financial costs are associated with judicial review, particularly when the alien must arrange for filing from abroad.

The likely demand for judicial review is reflected in the exclusion cases. In fiscal year 1984, for example, thousands of aliens were excluded at United States entry points. Yet, only twenty-seven aliens in that year exercised their statutory right to obtain judicial review of their exclusion orders, and only ten of these were non-asylum petitioners.[244] Significantly, these petitioners had already traveled to the United States, often at great expense. Visa applicants would seem even less likely to have actions brought on their behalf in court.

If the burden on the judicial system were still deemed to be excessive, Congress might limit the categories of visas from whose denials appeal could be taken. Thus, only family reunification cases, national security cases,[245] or cases where the applicant has a "real stake"[246] or

---

241. *See* Note, *A Case for Judicial Review of Consular Visa Decisions,* 22 STAN. J. INT'L L. 363, 373–74 (1986). *See supra* text accompanying note 91 for a discussion of the legislative intent of INA § 104(a).

242. *See, e.g.,* Paparelli & Tilner, *supra* note 3, at 1033 (noting a 13-year experience of low volume in appeals of labor certification denials).

243. Even in this instance, however, there are constraints on taking any advantage of a delay pending deportation. *See* 8 U.S.C. § 1105a(a) (1988); Haitian Refugee Center v. Smith, 676 F.2d 1023, 1032–33 (5th Cir. 1982), *overruled,* Jean v. Nelson, 727 F.2d 957 (11th Cir. 1984), *aff'd,* 472 U.S. 846 (1985).

244. Legomsky, *Forum Choices for the Review of Agency Adjudication: A Study of the Immigration Process,* 71 IOWA L. REV. 1297, 1402 (1986).

245. Note, *National Security Visa Denials, supra* note 4, at 741.

246. Bernsen, *Consular Absolutism in Visa Cases,* 63 INTERPRETER RELEASES, May 2, 1986, at 388, 391; Paparelli & Tilner, *supra* note 3, at 1032–33 (proposing review of all immigrant visa denials and nonimmigrant visa denials "except refusals to alien crewmen and aliens seeking entry merely to tour or transit the U.S. . . . review is reserved for the relatively small number of cases in which the alien has a genuine stake in gaining admission, i.e., the cases in which meaningful review is most urgent or important"; the excluded categories constitute "over 80% of all

"high stake"[247] in obtaining a visa might be reviewable. Gradual inclusion of nonimmigrant visa denials in a review process might begin with a pilot program involving a single class or two of visas, such as treaty trader and treaty investor visas. In any event, the effect of appeals on the caseload of administrative and court systems is unclear. Thus, the system-burdening factor may argue for caution, but does not require timidity in experimenting with more substantial administrative and judicial review of visa denials.

b. Adequacy of the Record

Baker v. Carr, which offers the classic formulation of the political question doctrine, recognized that access to governmental information as a practical and functional consideration, is a legitimate factor in determining justiciability of a particular issue.[248] A serious problem under present budgetary constraints is that the record available for either administrative or judicial appeal would be very limited. On-line consular officers must state reasons for visa denials,[249] but often have too little time to record much more than a citation of authority for a denial, with perhaps a few scribbled words of factual explanation. Sometimes consular notations are scarcely legible. If the issue on appeal is whether an officer has applied the law to the facts, but that officer had too little time to write up the facts or to communicate them clearly and legibly, what can an administrative appeals board or court review? With more time and resources to create a clearer, more complete record for appeal, much of this problem would dissolve. Under present budgetary circumstances, it might be unfair to sustain an appeal on the basis of an inadequate record, and yet it also seems unfair to applicants to allow the characteristic inadequacy of a consular refusal sheet to inhibit a more adequate review process.

In evaluating the adequacy of the record of a visa denial, the credibility and demeanor of applicants are often determinative factors. Although administrative tribunals seldom defer to assessments of credibility by executive officials, such assessments play a particularly important role in the visa process; by definition, applicants are generally unable to appear in the United States. Courts of law are, however, less inclined than administrative tribunals to defer to official assess-

---

nonimmigrant applications"); *see also* sources cited *supra* note 124; Baker v. Carr, 369 U.S. 186, 217 (1961); H.R. 2567, *infra* note 353, § 225(a)(4), (d)(2).

247. Martin, *Mandel, Cheng Fan Kwok, and Other Unappealing Cases: The Next Frontier of Immigration Reform,* 27 VA. J. INT'L L. 803, 812–13 (1987).

248. 369 U.S. 186, 217 (1969).

249. 22 C.F.R. §§ 41.121(b), 42.81(b) (1990).

ments of credibility and demeanor. Thus, a substitute for those assessments is required.

Voice recordings on cassette tape might substitute for the parsimonious and sometimes cryptic written records of consular adjudications. Such recordings, however, involve two problems. First, recording an adjudication could interfere with its integrity: the existence of the process itself might encourage both applicants and officers to rehearse and perform as they might not otherwise. Voice recordings do not, of course, convey live images, which are ordinarily critical in determinations of an applicant's credibility and demeanor. Videotapes would largely resolve this problem,[250] but do not appear to be politically feasible at this time because of strong opposition by the consular corps.

c. Efficacy of Discretion

The visa process necessarily relies on judgmental factors of an applicant's demeanor and credibility, as well as evolving circumstances in the local socio-economic environment. These factors argue for a relatively limited standard of review of consular discretion (as opposed to more objective issues of law and fact), such as whether a denial was "arbitrary, capricious, an abuse of discretion, or otherwise not in accordance with law."[251]

The court in *Abourezk v. Reagan*[252] adopted guidelines for determining the standard of review that the Supreme Court had previously announced in *Chevron, U.S.A. v. Natural Resources Defense Council.*[253] A court must first attempt to determine congressional intent. This analysis begins with the statute, but may include legislative history and administrative practices. Thus, past consular practices may play an important role in statutory interpretation of such open-textured terms as "public charges." If the court finds a specific intent, it enforces it regardless of the consular officer's interpretation. If, however, Congress does not appear to have had specific intent, perhaps deliberately leaving the resolution of an issue to consular discretion, "the agency's interpretation should be accorded great deference and invalidated only if it is not a 'reasonable accommodation of conflicting

---

250. Telephone interview with Angelo A. Paparelli, Member of the American Immigration Lawyers Association (AILA) Board of Governors, formerly Issue Manager for Consular Review and Vice-Chairperson, Visa Office Liaison Committee, AILA (Nov. 25, 1988) (notes on file with the *Washington Law Review*).

251. Administrative Procedure Act § 706(2)(A), 5 U.S.C. § 706(2)(A) (1988). *See infra* text accompanying notes 306–08.

252. 785 F.2d 1043 (D.C. Cir. 1986), *aff'd per curiam*, 484 U.S. 1 (1987) (3–3 decision).

253. 467 U.S. 837 (1984).

policies that were committed to the agency's care by the statute.' "[254] Despite this deference, the need for some degree of consular discretion does not bar review, either administratively or in the courts.

d. Standing of Appellants

The few visa denial cases that courts have decided might be read to limit standing to American appellants,[255] either as petitioners for an alien applicant's visa or as parties otherwise injured in fact by a visa denial, as in the case of an applicant invited to speak to an American audience. Courts have, however, included non-resident aliens, as in *Mandel,* either as actual or symbolic co-plaintiffs with citizens or permanent resident aliens. If reviewability is not limited to claims brought by citizens or permanent resident aliens, the territorial barrier might seem to pose a serious problem. How would applicants denied a visa effectively pursue a claim in the United States if the subject of their claim also denies them access to an appellate board or court? Exclusion-at-the-border cases are distinguishable in that they involve proceedings in habeas corpus "and not otherwise" under section 106(b) of the INA. That is, an alien's presence at the border gives the government theoretical "custody" over the alien. A habeas corpus action would therefore be inappropriate as a basis for review of a consular official's denial of a visa.

Limitations on the types of prospective cases subject to review would, of course, affect the issue of standing. Thus, if reviewability is limited to "high stake" cases, standing is similarly limited.

e. Confidentiality

Section 222(f) of the INA[256] provides that the "records" of the Department of State and of diplomatic and consular officers "pertaining to" the issuance or refusal of visas are to be "considered" confidential. Whether this language was intended to cover individual applicants and refusals or only statistics and other aggregate records of an office is unclear, although it may have been intended to cover both. A reasonable construction of the language in terms of foreign policy interests and sensitivities that underlie the administration of the INA might limit the scope of the protection to aggregate records. Some individual dossiers of national security significance, such as that

---

254. 785 F.2d at 1053 (quoting *Chevron,* 467 U.S. at 845).

255. *E.g.,* Fiallo v. Bell, 430 U.S. 787 (1977); Kleindienst v. Mandel, 408 U.S. 753 (1972); Ali v. INS, 661 F. Supp. 1234, 1246 (D. Mass. 1986).

256. 8 U.S.C. § 1202(f) (1988).

of Yasser Arafat, might require protection as well. Moreover, it seems reasonable to construe the language simply as a means of protecting documentation from access by unauthorized third persons. Confidentiality therefore primarily ought to protect applicants, whether or not they are more generally protected abroad by the Bill of Rights. For clarification, section 222(f) might be amended to provide for the release of records for administrative and judicial review.

A particular problem has been the nonavailability of advisory opinions by the Visa Office. The Freedom of Information Act (FOIA),[257] amending the APA, seems to require disclosure of the opinions to visa applicants,[258] but the Visa Office has invoked exemptions to FOIA to justify its refusal to inform applicants of the contents of opinions. The opinions are denominated either national security-sensitive,[259] protected by the INA,[260] or privileged as a form of intra-agency communication.[261]

Section 225(f) of the INA does allow the Secretary of State discretion, apparently as another exception to section 104(a), to make certified copies available to a court, which must "certif[y] that the information contained in such records is needed by the court in the

---

257. Pub. L. No. 90-23, § 1, 81 Stat. 54 (1967) (codified as amended at 5 U.S.C. § 552 (1988)).

258. The Court in John Doe Agency v. John Doe Corp., 110 S. Ct. 471, 475 (1989), summarized the broad scope and importance of the FOIA, as follows:

This Court repeatedly has stressed the fundamental principle of public access to Government documents that animates the FOIA. "Without question, the Act is broadly conceived. It seeks to permit access to official information long shielded unnecessarily from public view and attempts to create a judicially enforceable public right to secure such information from possibly unwilling official hands." *EPA v. Mink*, 410 U.S. 73, 80, 93 S.Ct. 827, 832, 35 L.Ed.2d 119 (1973), *superseded by statute as stated in* Phillippi v. CIA, 655 F.2d 1325 (D.C. Cir. 1976). The Act's "basic purpose reflected 'a general philosophy of full agency disclosure unless information is exempted under clearly delineated statutory language.' " *Department of Air Force v. Rose*, 425 U.S. 352, 360–61, 96 S.Ct. 1592, 1599, 48 L.Ed.2d 11 (1976), quoting S. Rep. No. 813, 89th Cong., 1st Sess., 3 (1965). "The basic purpose of FOIA is to ensure an informed citizenry, vital to the functioning of a democratic society, needed to check against corruption and to hold the governors accountable to the governed." *NLRB v. Robbins Tire & Rubber Co.*, 437 U.S. 214, 242, 98 S.Ct. 2311, 2327, 57 L.Ed.2d 159 (1978). *See also United States Department of Justice v. Reporters Committee for Freedom of the Press*, 489 U.S. 749 (1989). There are, to be sure, specific exemptions from disclosure set forth in the Act. "But these limited exemptions do not obscure the basic policy that disclosure, not secrecy, is the dominant objective of the Act." *Rose*, 425 U.S. at 361, 96 S.Ct. at 1599. Accordingly, these exemptions "must be narrowly construed." *Ibid.* Furthermore, "the burden is on the agency to sustain its action." 5 U.S.C. § 552(a)(4)(B).

259. 5 U.S.C. § 552(b)(1).

260. *Id.* § 552(b)(3). The applicable "statute" under FOIA § (b)(3) to which the Visa Office refers, is INA § 222(f), 8 U.S.C. § 1202(f); *see supra* discussion at text accompanying notes 256–57.

261. 5 U.S.C. § 552(b)(5).

interest of the ends of justice in a case pending before the court."[262] Presumably, the applicant would then have access to the record on review.

The INA contains at least one major exception to the presumption that an applicant should have access to the record. Section 235(c)[263] provides for a summary exclusionary proceeding for security reasons following an exclusion order, "without any inquiry or further inquiry by a special inquiry officer." Accordingly, the applicant may be denied access to the factual basis or procedural protections to which he or she would otherwise be entitled.[264] Summary or other in camera review proceedings may be necessary in some national security cases, but the procedure can easily be overused or abused in the absence of clearer guidelines on the scope of a national security exception to due process.

f. Costs

The cost burden on the government of improvements in the review process would, of course, depend on their scope and the extent to which some of the cost could be shifted. Financial costs are hard to estimate, but might be moderately high for an administrative review board. For example, in 1983, a bill would have provided $20 million for the first year of an administrative review system to handle appeals from refused visa applicants, with a staff of administrative law judges and an Appellate Immigration Board.[265] The Asylum Policy and Review Unit, which advised the INS to reconsider thirty-five denials and referred another thirty-five cases for reversal by officials, cost about $750,000 in its first year.[266]

User or "appeal" fees might defray the costs of providing more visa examiners and a limited administrative review board. Such fees, however, may discriminate against applicants on the basis of wealth and are not entirely consistent with the federal policy of encouraging travel to the United States. Fee waivers could be granted at least to some of the tired, the poor, and the homeless.

---

262. 8 U.S.C. § 1202(f). The State Department also makes available some information to the INS, for example, to be used in visa petition revocation proceedings. *See* United States Department of State, Cable No. 89-State-028963, 66 INTERPRETER RELEASES 149, 159 (1989) (Ref: A 84 STATE 213718 B 85 STATE 283796).

263. 8 U.S.C. § 1225(c).

264. The scope, validity, and applicability in individual cases of this extraordinary provision were incidentally at issue in Rafeedie v. INS, 880 F.2d 506 (D.C. Cir. 1989).

265. S. 2222, 97th Cong., 2d Sess., § 125 (1982).

266. N.Y. Times, Dec. 21, 1988, at A18, col. 1 (national ed.).

Another type of cost is psychological, namely, the threat and perceived nuisance that review might present to already overburdened consular officers. Nobody likes to be overruled. Moreover, little love is lost between attorneys and consular officers. The aversion of some officers to further involvement of attorneys is understandable. Still, experienced foreign service officers have minimized the psychological cost and were openminded about the possibility of a modest formalization of the review process. They acknowledged that the guidance and encouragement of greater uniformity that review could provide might make their work easier.[267]

3. Expectations of Applicants

Applicants' expectations about the issuance or denial of visas and the adequacy of the review process are of at least some relevance in considering the need for a more formal review process. If applicants do not expect review, it is arguably less necessary. If, however, they expect review and it would be reasonable, it is in the national interest to attempt to protect this country's reputation for due process. The United Kingdom, for example, provides formal administrative review of visa denials.[268]

Unfortunately, little is known about the varying expectations of different nationalities. Most British and Japanese nationals expect to get visas, whereas other Asians and Mexicans expect greater difficulty. Given the rather low rate of refusals, the majority of applicants may not be surprised. Even if they are, their expectations may be conditioned by skepticism about patterns of administrative practices and decisions of their own governments. On the other hand, an efficient and generous system of visa issuance by the local government may foster expectations of generosity or reciprocity by the United States.

IV. FIELD OBSERVATIONS AND INTERVIEWS

A. Introduction

Is there a need for changes in the review process? Theoretically, if consular officers always made the right decisions, no review would be needed. There is also a tolerable margin of error. If, however, some review is necessary, how adequate is the existing process? To recapitulate, it consists of intra-consular review; unofficial monitoring and pressuring by attorneys, the media, non-governmental organizations,

---

267. *See infra* Section IV (field observations and interview by the author).
268. S. LEGOMSKY, *supra* note 128, at 145.

and American petitioners on behalf of applicants; congressional inquiries; advisory opinions by the Visa Office, some binding, some not; departmental waiver procedures; and very limited judicial review. What would be the benefits of an expanded review process, perhaps providing applicants and petitioners greater access to administrative or judicial review? Would these benefits offset the costs?

In order to answer these questions and see the consular and informal review procedures first hand, the author conducted six sets of field observations and interviews. These took place in 1988 and 1989 at United States consular posts in Guadalajara, Mexico City, Shanghai, London, Warsaw and Krakow. The locations were selected on the basis of the relatively high volume of applications at those posts, the relative importance of all of them in the immigration process, variations among them in types of applicants, the author's ability to comprehend adjudications in Spanish at the Mexican locations, the opportunity in London to investigate a visa waiver pilot program for British tourists, and the author's already established itinerary for other purposes to the Chinese, Polish, and British locations. The author interviewed consular officers at each post; independently communicated with applicants in Guadalajara, Krakow, and Shanghai; attended visa adjudications in Guadalajara and Mexico City; and monitored four reviews of visa refusals in Shanghai. Before arrival at the two Mexican posts and Warsaw, the author sent copies of a ten-year old study of consular discretion[269] in order to indicate some questions for discussion. Subsequent discussion at the three posts centered on whether the process of visa issuance, denial, and review had changed, and, if so, how and to what extent.

The author also interviewed several practitioners during a conference on immigration law[270] and communicated with various spokespersons of the American Immigration Lawyers Association (AILA).[271] These inquiries produced a number of insights and stimu-

---

269. Study, *supra* note 62. This study consisted of interviews at consulates in Canada and Mexico and the results of a questionnaire that had been sent to consular officers. Although responses to the questionnaire were reported, there is no indication of the number or the extent of responses.

270. Federal Bar Association Seminar, *supra* note 81.

271. The author sought specific guidance on the following issues, most of which arose from an AILA study, Paparelli & Tilner, *supra* note 3: the implications for review of a lack of funding for the visa process; the feasibility of reviewing the notes of consular officers which are often hastily written under extreme time pressures; the definition of a "genuine stake," to distinguish denial cases meriting review from those not meriting review; the appropriateness and the implications for the national interest of excluding from review certain tourist and transit visa applicants; the national security and foreign policy implication of denying visas to Mexican applicants; the remoteness of a proposed administrative review board in Washington from the

lated new questions that are reflected throughout this study.[272] The summary that follows is by no means scientific, but "impressions are experience."[273]

B. General Observations of the Visa Process

Consular officers and their superiors are typically well educated, trained in the visa process, and hard-working. The Foreign Service Institute provides three levels of consular training in the visa process. The Basic Consular Course, for all first-tour officers, takes twenty-six days, about one-half of which is devoted to visa-related training. Most officers in the consular cone, or career specialization, typically as they come "off-line" into supervisory positions in their third tour of duty, voluntarily attend an Advanced Consular Course. This course lasts three to five weeks and includes a somewhat heavier concentration of training in visa processing. Finally, in a typical year the Institute conducts four overseas, regional workshops to further train and present updated procedures to both consular officers and national employees. The Institute estimates that an average of sixty to seventy officers attend these workshops each year.[274]

On-line officers, usually at lower levels of the diplomatic corps and sometimes referred to affectionately as "munchkins," neither wish nor foresee many years in such work. They do, however, view the work as important, challenging, and unequaled as an opportunity for developing language and interpersonal skills. Although on-line work is tiring, particularly during the mornings when most adjudications take place, morale is quite high.[275] Several officers talked enthusiastically about

consular exposure to local cultures; the efficiency and efficacy of having attorneys present at consular adjudications; the influence of administrative review on the objectivity of consular officers (it is much easier, if not hassle-free, for consular officers to issue visas than to deny them); cost versus benefit for aliens of delays and expenses in the administrative review process, given the opportunities simply to reapply; and the alternative of abolishing visas and relying on residence and work permits, departure controls, and other controls of aliens. *See, e.g.,* telephone interview, *supra* note 22.

272. A summary of the author's interviews in London may be found in Section V, *infra* text following note 367. Unless otherwise indicated, field notes and specific references to dates and personnel are on file with the author.

273. H. JAMES, THE ART OF FICTION (1888). Furthermore, "[t]he law is the last result of human wisdom acting upon human experience for the benefit of the public." S. Johnson, *quoted in* 1 JOHNSONIAN MISCELLANIES 223 (G. Hill ed. 1897).

274. Telephone interview with John Ratigan, Director, Consular Training, Foreign Service Institute (Jan. 5, 1989) (notes on file with the *Washington Law Review*).

275. These observations indicate considerable improvement in the twelve years since the Study, *supra* note 62, which suggested that consular officers were poorly trained and reported that "[i]n Mexico, most consular officers are disappointed and frustrated with their work." *Id.* at 137. The Study quoted one officer as stating: "[o]ur work is a farce. I think the [State]

their work and, during the author's on-line observations, appeared eager to discuss and explain their decisions. It was obvious that they took pride in developing psychological insights about the applicants, in trying to make the process as objective and scientific as possible, and in efficiently reaching decisions.

Officers work to comply with department standards of etiquette.[276] When local authorities complained about one post's "rude" treatment of applicants, the post responded as follows:

> We do process quickly because we are striving to run an efficient, cordial operation, and we want to allow everyone who shows up at the door, same day access. The fact is that we have many applicants. But we get through our line every day.[277]

This explanation reflects a general practice. The lines of applicants are often formidably long per consular officer. To get through the line, visa sections may do a limited amount of "batching" or group processing of the same class of applications. They may also pre-screen applications, particularly to determine that each applicant understands the basic process and possesses whatever documentation may be required or useful. In London, applications are generally reviewed by mail; a denied applicant may then request an interview, which typically lasts about five minutes. In Mexico City, "rovers" pass through the "barn" of waiting applicants, checking their documentation and dividing them into three groups: the fast lane of applicants who can expect to get visas within one-half hour, those with little or no possibility of success, and the "uncertains," who represent a majority of the applicants. All posts discourage excessive documentation that might lead

---

Department realizes this and that's why we don't get promoted, or enough resources, or enough manpower. It's a nothing job." *Id.* at 139.

276. For example, Department Notes provide the following guidance to consular officers:
Consular officers should make every effort to conduct visa interviews fairly and sympathetically. Any semblance of cross-examination, assumption of bad faith or entrapment must be avoided.
FOREIGN AFFAIRS MANUAL, *supra* note 19, at App. J-473, note N2 (nonimmigrants) and App. J-720, note N1 (immigrants).
(m) Convey Refusal in Sympathetic but Firm Manner—The manner in which visa applications are refused can be very important in relations between the post and the population of the host country. Consular officers must be careful not to appear insensitive.
Id. at App. J-849, note PN1.1(m).
If it appears to the consular officer that the facts involved make eventual issuance unlikely, care should be taken not to encourage the applicant to undertake useless effort and expense to reactivate the case.
Id. at App. J-849, note PN1.2. *But see supra* text accompanying note 22.
277. Office of the American Consul General, U.S. Embassy (Warsaw), Issues Affecting Work in Poland 1, August 22, 1988 [hereinafter Issues] (on file with the *Washington Law Review*).

to a paper chase. One reviewing officer indicated his preference to rely on oral rather than written evidence whenever possible because of the greater reliability of personal appearance as opposed to written, often fraudulent, documentation.

The length of applicant interviews among the posts ranged in average length from seven to fifteen minutes for immigrant visas and thirty seconds to eight minutes for nonimmigrant visas. This range can be explained partly on the basis that at the "one-minute posts" the adjudications were primarily of first-timers, whereas at the "eight-minute posts" the adjudications were primarily of repeaters or "overcomers." Most of the scores of interviews the author witnessed were handled very efficiently.

Although typically separated from each other by partitioned cubicles, on-line officers did not work in a vacuum. Supervising officers were present, making spot checks and monitoring the process. All of the supervising officers had served on-line and seemed to understand the problem of having to make quick decisions about nonimmigrant visa applicants on the basis of often skimpy documentation and nondescript personal appearances.

Consular officers made use of local employees to conduct investigations, including repeated phone calls to verify employment status of applicants for nonimmigrant visas. American nationals other than consular officers also conducted a variety of more official functions. These nationals, often spouses of diplomatic-consular officers, are generally trained on the job. As a cost measure, they interviewed most of the applicants for visas under IRCA's Special Agricultural Workers (SAW) program[278] and handled normal adjudications at another post. The use of these "para-consular assistants" or "mustangs," as they are also known, is sometimes controversial. Under the INA and departmental regulations, only consular officers may issue or refuse visas.[279] Consulates justify this apparent circumvention of regulations by explaining that the chief of the visa section or the responsible officer ultimately stands behind or overrules the decisions, so that the use of para-consular assistants is more of a clerical delegation than a delegation of responsibility. Given the time and budget constraints, however, the decisions by the mustangs can be determinative.

---

278. Determination of Agricultural Labor Shortages and Admission of Additional Special Agricultural Workers, INA § 210A, 8 U.S.C. § 1161 (1988).

279. INA § 291, 8 U.S.C. § 1361; 22 C.F.R. § 40.1(d) (1990) (definition of a "consular officer"); *id.* §§ 41.111, 41.121, 42.71, 42.81; *see also* Study, *supra* note 62, at 98, for a 10-year-old comparison of this practice.

The State Department is also experimenting with the use of civil service visa examiners to supplement consular officers in processing immigrant visa applications in Ciudad Juarez, Mexico. The border location enables the State Department to cut costs by hiring bilingual residents of El Paso to commute across the border to do the work.[280]

During adjudications, on-line and supervising officers occasionally consulted the computerized look-out systems, the Foreign Affairs Manual, and other departmental memos. The officers indicated that the Manual provides essential guidelines, but does not help them with a number of highly discretionary aspects of adjudication. One officer pointed out that she is very much on her own in drawing the proper inferences from the demeanor and other personal clues of applicants. Officers recognized that their decisions were often somewhat subjective and that mistakes were bound to happen.

The situations which may confront a consular officer during an interview are endless. What follows are just a few of the situations the author witnessed. An applicant excessively decked out from head to belt-line and wrist in tacky jewelry: is she overcompensating for limited personal circumstances or does she just like tacky jewelry? A soccer team, invited to play in a tournament against American teams, consistent with important cultural objectives of United States foreign policy: what to do when two but only two members of the team, which had been practicing for a long time together, appeared to be ineligible for nonimmigrant visas? A mother, ill with cancer, sought to visit an only daughter in the United States whom she had not seen in a year, who could not return home easily, and who had access to medical care not available to her mother at home: would the mother ever return if she received a nonimmigrant visa?

C. *Informal Statistical Analysis*

Given the need of consular officers to exercise considerable discretion, it is not surprising that the rates of refusal can vary among consular officers, even at a single post. During a sample day at one post in Mexico, five on-line officers adjudicated 630 nonimmigrant visa applications. Their individual acceptances, rejections and rates of acceptance follow:

---

280. STATE, Dec. 1988, at 9.

Officer	Acceptances	Rejections	Total	Rate/Acceptance
1	56	81	137	41%
2	22	80	102	22%
3	90	130	220	41%
4	66	55	121	55%
5	30	20	50	60%
	264	366	630	42%

The nonimmigrant acceptance rates thus varied on a single day at this one post from a low of 22% to a high of 60%. This reflects just one day at one post. Of interest, nevertheless, is both that the acceptance rates vary considerably among the officers and that the highest acceptance rate (60%) was that of the reviewing officer.

Acceptance rates, adjusted to take account of visas eventually issued to initially unsuccessful applicants, varied substantially among consular districts from a high of 99.7% for Mauritania and Naha, Japan down to a range between 48% and 84% overall, for the high-volume posts in Mexico, China, and Poland that the author visited.[281] Among the posts in Mexico, the simple and adjusted rates of acceptance for Mexico City were 81.1% and 84.1%, respectively, whereas in Guadalajara, the rates were 55.6% and 59.4%, respectively. Interestingly, the figures for other posts in Mexico tended to cluster around either the national average or the Guadalajara figure. Each of these figures reflects about the same (3–4%) adjustment to take account of "refusal overcomes," but the acceptance rates otherwise varied dramatically.

In Poland, the nonimmigrant visa acceptance rates were remarkably uniform: 48.4% in Warsaw, 50.5% in Poznan, and 50.9% in Krakow. Also remarkable is that, of the six posts visited, those in Warsaw and Krakow, only a few hours apart, had the most divergent procedures in the following respects: the required waiting period between time of refusal until eligibility for reconsideration (one year in Warsaw, on appointment in Krakow); the average length of time for an adjudication (2 minutes in Warsaw, 7–8 minutes in Krakow); and pre-screening (none in Warsaw for lack of funding, pre-screening for proper documentation in Krakow). An officer concluded flatly that such inconsistencies among the posts in Poland were "no problem." To a great extent, the uniformity of acceptance rates among the posts confirms her conclusion. The inference is that reasonable variations in procedures do not have much, if any, effect on rates of acceptance for nonimmigrant visas.

---

281. U.S. DEPARTMENT OF STATE, VISA WORKLOAD REPORT FOR FISCAL YEAR 1987.

Another inference is that, inasmuch as the rates among the three consulates in Poland are remarkably similar, they tend to verify the average rate for all three of the posts. This is not to say that mistakes do not happen—each of the posts could be making the same high percentage of mistakes, for example—but the figures do suggest that, using different personnel and procedures, the posts have semi-independently arrived at rates that, because of their similarity, validate the processes that were used. In Mexico, however, the range of acceptance rates is somewhat more divergent, perhaps because of demographic rather than administrative factors. The more prosperous and "professional" areas, such as Hermosillo and Mexico City, where trade and investment representatives and the intelligentsia tend to be concentrated, have higher rates of visa acceptances. Conversely, a higher rate of applications at the other posts came from poor, rural backgrounds. This, however, is all very impressionistic and speculative. More comprehensive figures from the field merit further analysis.

At the Shanghai post, a comparison of the issuance rates for student visas (which represent 33% of all applicants for visas) and exchange visitor visas (8% of all applicants) shows a lopsided distribution.[282] The acceptance rate for student visas is 33%, whereas the acceptance rate for exchange visitor visas is 90.4%. The author was told that most of the exchange visitor refusals (9.6%) would eventually be converted into issuances. What explains this discrepancy? Most students are more or less on their own, whereas exchange visitors have the endorsement and sometimes the sponsorship of Chinese or American institutions. Exchange visitors enjoy a presumption that, unlike students, they are likely to return home before the expiration of their visas. Thus, not surprisingly, rates of acceptance vary substantially among nonimmigrant classes, in China as elsewhere.

D. Review Process

All of the posts reported that they orally explain the bases for denials to all refused applicants. Generally, all six posts indicated that they received relatively little pressure to reverse visa denials from attorneys or members of Congress, but tried to respond promptly to them. They acknowledged that letters personally signed by members of Congress received particular attention. Although the Mexico City consulate estimated that it received an average of five congressional inquiries a day, the norm per post is closer to one inquiry per week.

---

282. Statistics were collected on-site at the consular post (notes on file with the *Washington Law Review*).

The posts experience considerably more pressures from American petitioners, sponsors, and other family members. The consulate in Krakow devotes a portion of each Tuesday and Thursday afternoon to interviews with these Americans. The officers attempt to explain the reasons for denials and offer the visitors an opportunity to present new information on behalf of Polish applicants. If a visitor is persuasive, the consulate may agree to reconsider an application. "Refusal overcomes" were treated routinely and taken seriously at all posts the author visited. One reviewing officer reported that interviews on reconsideration of immigrant denials and "overcome" attempts by immigrant and nonimmigrant applicants were never limited in time, even at his very busy post. In Warsaw, the United States Ambassador reported that applicants who had been denied tourist visas and were encouraged to reapply for work-related visas seldom did so.[283] It was unclear to the consular officers why refused applicants did not avail themselves of this opportunity. This experience suggests that a refused applicant should be required to exhaust reasonable alternatives proposed by a refusing consulate before being allowed to pursue an appeal outside the visa section of the consulate.

All four visa refusals that the author monitored were later reversed by reviewing officers. Reviewing officers reversed three of these refusals after oral clarification of factors that indicated the applicant's probable intent to depart the United States on schedule; one of the cases involved a second personal appearance by the applicant. The reviewing officer reversed the fourth refusal following production of additional documentation pertaining to the applicant's financial circumstances. The author's limited experience is certainly not definitive, but does tend to show the efficacy of the internal review process in consulates.

Consular officers generally avail themselves of the review process in the Visa Office only when required. Few consular officers viewed the Visa Office favorably; several objected to the inferior quality of regulations and dispatches prepared by the Office. Visa Office routing is largely off the consular road map. On the other hand, consulates take the required process of internal review seriously, contrary to the contention that the process is subjective, disingenuous or sloppy because of the close working and living conditions, often in isolated circumstances, between on-line and reviewing officers.[284]

---

283. *Opinions,* Polityka, Warsaw, Aug. 20, 1988, *translated in* Issues, *supra* note 277 (on file with the *Washington Law Review*).

284. Bernsen, *supra* note 246, at 389–90.

Lack of funding creates personnel shortages that may require a supervising officer to go on-line and therefore sacrifice time otherwise available for the prescribed review. Often, time is available only for spot-checking. At two of the posts visited, the internal review of denials was therefore accelerated, allowing the supervising officer time to ponder only a random sample of each on-line officer's daily set of refusals. One senior officer indicated a need for clearer, uniform standards for internal review.

None of the officers was enthusiastic about the prospect of more formal processes of administrative and judicial review, but several complained about the quality of Visa Office review under present circumstances. One officer concluded that "external review" would not be "feasible." Another officer considered more formal review to be potentially "unwieldy." One officer, emphasizing the effect more formal review of nonimmigrant refusals might have on the morale and work attitudes of on-line officers, stated that it "would turn the junior officer corps into a corps of deponents." The same officer did, however, acknowledge that more formal administrative and judicial review of *immigrant* visa denials, at least, might be feasible. Such review, he suggested, would be "cut-and-dried" and "probably not a huge burden on the government or taxpayers," although provision for such review would first need to resolve some thorny issues, such as who would be entitled to review and whether foreign applicants would have standing in court.

E. Past, Present and Future

Twelve years ago, a study of consular discretion concluded that "[b]y and large, most officers perform well under difficult circumstances. If officers misapply the law, it may be because no one corrects their errors."[285] The study made a number of recommendations, centering on improvements in management accountability. What was evident then is evident today, although the blanket speculation that errors occur because "no one" is available to correct them is questionable. In sum, consular exercise of discretion, within the time constraints, appears to be intelligent, informed and fairly well-structured and confined.

The internal review process is a good deal better today than it was ten years ago,[286] but there is room for improvement. Regulations and other dispatches prepared by the Visa Office must be improved to offer

---

285. Study, *supra* note 62, at 160.
286. Note, for example, the following observations:

better guidance to consular posts. More expanded external review, beyond Visa Office opinions, waivers of eligibility by the Secretary of State, and very limited judicial review, seems advisable. The benefit would not be the avoidance of all error nor necessarily a more efficient visa process. Instead, the benefit would be to improve the capacity of the process to overcome the three most unfortunate consequences of non-review or perfunctory review: mistakes; the appearance of a form of "consular absolutism" that is hard to justify and harmful to the visa process; and a lack of uniform decisionmaking among the consulates, that is, a failure to respond to similarly situated applicants in essentially the same way.[287] From the viewpoint of the bar:

> most consular officers are undoubtedly honorable and well-intentioned. Honor and good intentions, however, are small consolation to the alien who is mistakenly refused a visa, and to the United States citizens, residents, and entities who depend on the alien's admission. Despite a genuine need, or even a statutory entitlement, to be admitted to the United States, the alien who is denied a visa is left remediless in the face of mistaken or unlawful action by a consular official.[288]

Not only the applicants, but the visa sections, too, would benefit from a strengthened review process. Even the most competent, well-disposed consular officers might benefit from further guidance and a "second opinion."

It is not advisable, however, to provide for more extensive review, whether internal or external, without considering the cost of increased consular staffing. Funding would provide supervisors with more time and resources for internal review, making the daily, on-line routine more manageable and less hectic for consular officers and minimizing the need for external review.

V. ALTERNATIVES

What is to be done? Analysis indicates that there is room for improving the process of reviewing visa denials by consular officers. Although the current processes work reasonably well, they do not

---

Yet, this Study indicates that Departmental guidelines are often vague and ill-defined. Different consular officers and consulates interpret the law, the regulations, and the guidelines in vastly dissimilar ways. Indeed, two officers may reach opposite determinations on the same question of fact and law. The system of checking these determinations is inadequate to ensure the uniform application of the law. Review at the post is often cursory and sometimes deferred. Visa refusals occasionally pass completely unchecked. Aliens who are refused visas have little recourse.

Id. at 152.

287. *Developments, supra* note 86, at 1361.

288. Paparelli & Tilner, *supra* note 3, at 1033.

fully satisfy any of the three basic values of review, namely, accountability, uniformity or consistency, and due process. This section first considers the possibility of relying on jurisprudential developments, then considers other alternatives for improving both informal and formal stages of the review process, and concludes with a brief caveat about four uncertainties along the path to reform. These uncertainties include: the pace and extent of jurisprudential developments; more adequate funding of visa sections and the review process; the political feasibility of expanding administrative and judicial review; and statutory drafting skill.

A. Jurisprudential Developments

1. The International Legal Framework

Courts could extend the review process along a number of different lines. The first might be to establish expectations about consular discretion more squarely within the framework of international custom. The basic rule of international law, which as custom is "part of our law,"[289] establishes a qualified duty to admit aliens. Accordingly, the government may exclude aliens only if, individually or collectively, they pose serious danger to public safety, security, general welfare, or essential institutions.[290] Although this rule does not prescribe specific national means of implementation, justiciability, or enforceability by individuals, it is nevertheless significant, for it encourages states to define a proper margin of responsibility, in cooperation with other states and out of obligation to the global community. It also eliminates endless semantic debate about whether entry is a right or a privilege (to the extent that this distinction is valid anymore, entry is a qualified right), whether constitutional protections extend extraterritorially (they do insofar as consular decisions are subject to the rule), or whether Congress has plenary power, inherent in sovereignty, to exclude aliens without judicial intervention (it does not). In short, reliance on the international legal rule can bring the judiciary out of the "cataleptic trance" that the "mere mention" of the word "immigration" induces.[291]

Acknowledgment of a state's qualified duty to admit aliens may seem radical because it challenges the easy assumption that states may do as they please. The rule, however, is really quite modest. It is generally reflected in United States practice under the INA's immi-

---

289. Paquete Habana, 175 U.S. 677, 715 (1900).
290. See supra text accompanying notes 179–83.
291. Legomsky, supra note 170, at 306.

grant preference quotas and would not necessarily result in an expanded issuance of nonimmigrant visas. The rule's cutting edge would not be useful in demolishing immigration controls or in tearing a hole in the nylon, tortilla, and other curtains at the border. Instead, its cutting edge can create a greater awareness of responsibility and sense of human solidarity, and offer members of Congress and consular officers alike another tool for standardizing alien eligibility to receive visas. The rule may also assist consular officers to avoid excessively subjective determinations of ineligibility in individual cases, particularly when examining and reviewing applications for nonimmigrant visas. Whatever the difficulties may be in implementing the rule, it is incumbent on decisionmakers to try to apply it in good faith.

2. The Appropriate Standard of Judicial Review

In the words of the Supreme Court, all administrative adjudications are "to some degree judicial and to some degree political"[292] and immigration issues can be especially foreign policy-sensitive. It is clear, therefore, that the courts are expected to defer to some extent to the political branches when interpreting the INA and reviewing exercise of consular discretion under the INA. Deference, however, is a matter of degree. In reviewing consular discretion, the appropriate level of deference can be expressed in the standard for review, rather than in a rule of non-reviewability that is unnecessary and difficult to justify.

a. The Mandel Test

The intended scope of the *Mandel* test of a "facially legitimate and bona fide reason" for an immigration decision is anything but clear.[293] It can be narrowly limited, on the one hand, to waiver cases raising first amendment issues under section 212(a)(28) of the INA,[294] or it can be more broadly applied to all visa denial cases involving congressional delegation of a "conditional exercise of [the power to exclude] to the Executive."[295] Assuming a broad scope, the depth of judicial scrutiny is subject to two interpretations. According to the "superficial" test, courts defer to consular discretion so long as a result appears to be *facially* rational, that is, so long as the reasons stated for

---

292. INS v. Abudu, 485 U.S. 94, 110 (1988).
293. Shapiro, *supra* note 4, at 936; *supra* text accompanying notes 139–45.
294. 8 U.S.C. § 1182(a)(28) (1988).
295. Kleindienst v. Mandel, 408 U.S. 753, 770 (1972).

the denial on the Visa Control Card (10F-224B) bear a "reasonable relation to a proper legislative purpose [as expressed in the INA]."[296] According to this interpretation, a mere citation of the grounds for exclusion, such as "§ 214(b)" or "§ 221(g)," on the Visa Control Card is sufficient to avert court review. On the other hand, an irrational notation such as "applicant has a punk hairdo" would not in itself be sufficient.

Such a de minimis reading of the *Mandel* test, however, raises several problems. First, the Department of State itself requires thorough elaboration of the grounds for exclusion. In addition to noting the applicable INA section on the Visa Control Card, consular officers must "[i]nform the alien orally of the provision(s) of law on which the refusal is based and of any exception provided by law under which administrative relief is available."[297] The officer must also furnish a refused alien with a written explanation of the refusal, "explaining the ground(s) of ineligibility and the steps, if any, which may be taken to overcome the refusal."[298] Further, "[t]he explanation should be complete and set forth the facts which led the consular officer to determine that the cited section(s) apply to the applicant's case."[299] For example, a denial under section 221(g) of the INA on the basis of insufficient documentation requires a precise identification of the missing documents.[300]

A second problem with a de minimis reading of the *Mandel* test is that the *Mandel* court upheld the denial of a waiver of ineligibility because of a specific, departmental finding that the applicant had violated the terms of earlier visas issued to him.[301] In light of this finding, *Mandel* might be viewed as a rather innocuous decision. Finally, a superficial test of reviewability would be wholly inadequate in the majority of nonimmigrant visa denials that rely on one of the catch-all grounds—for example, sections 214(b) and 221(g) of the INA—that are barely descriptive. Thus, the *Mandel* test seems to prescribe a more than superficial scrutiny of the exercise of consular discretion, as subsequent decisions suggest. "[A] growing judicial consensus that visa denials based on an applicant's political views are not 'legitimate'

---

296. Nebbia v. New York, 291 U.S. 502, 537 (1934) (the rational basis test of constitutionality).

297. FOREIGN AFFAIRS MANUAL, *supra* note 19, at App. J-846, note PN1.1(a).

298. *Id.* at App. J-847, note PN1.1(b).

299. *Id.*

300. *Id.*

301. Kleindienst v. Mandel, 408 U.S. 753, 758–59, 769 (1972).

or 'bona fide' within a system of true expression" has emerged since *Mandel.*[302]

A preferred interpretation of the *Mandel* test would be to require deeper scrutiny by the courts.[303] To be sure, the term "facially" would seem to constrain the courts from assessing the wisdom or advisability of a denial.[304] For example, a consular officer need not justify an exclusion on the basis that the applicant "has too few assets" to avoid the likelihood of becoming a public charge after entry. On review by the courts, a finding that such an applicant was a model human being, worked hard and always turned over his earnings to his spouse would be irrelevant, as would a finding that an applicant could quickly overcome his impoverished condition.

To be "legitimate," the stated reason for a denial need only be within a margin of discretion under statutory, constitutional, and international law. This requirement overlaps the "abuse of discretion" standard. As a basis for determining "legitimacy," the "qualified duty" rule of international law could be more precisely expressed in legislation, by establishing acceptable levels of migration to the United States through a national absorptive capacity, and by providing for modification of those levels under certain circumstances. Accordingly, an alien could be excluded, for example, if those who overstay their visas become a serious problem, or the country reaches its absorptive capacity of temporary workers, or the number of elderly and infirm are straining national health and welfare support systems. The "bona fide" requirement, to whatever extent it is independently significant, calls into question only stated reasons that appear on their face to be disingenuous, vindictive, or the like.

In sum, a broad application of the *Mandel* test can be construed to comport, at least minimally, with the "abuse of discretion" test for judicial review under the APA. Preferably the courts would limit *Mandel* narrowly to a particular class of waiver denials, or relegate the text to the dustbin of bad decisions. That may not, however, be a realistic prospect, given the force of *stare decisis.*

---

302. Shapiro, *supra* note 4, at 938.

303. *See* Allende v. Shultz, 605 F. Supp. 1220 (D. Mass. 1985), *aff'd,* 845 F.2d 1111 (1st Cir. 1988). Whether a plaintiff loses on the merits according to a superficial standard or because the courts deny jurisdiction according to the plenary power doctrine might not seem to make any difference to a losing plaintiff. It may, however, "make some difference to the ultimate development of a sound body of law." T. ALEINIKOFF & D. MARTIN, *supra* note 2, at 209.

304. *See* Comment, *Immigration and the First Amendment, supra* note 4, at 1906.

b. Alternative Standards

Although consular officers are required to explain their reason(s) for applying a particular ground for exclusion, some grounds for exclusion are understandably so broad and dependent on quick judgments by consular officers that an appropriate standard of review must defer to some extent to consular discretion.[305] With respect to a few grounds, it is even appropriate to apply a wholly deferential standard of review. For example, in a few cases the exigencies of foreign policy or national security might on their facts require courts to apply the political question doctrine. Most issues of review and reviewability, however, arise out of consular determinations under open-textured provisions of the law that require the exercise of substantial discretion. A standard of review must therefore incorporate a rational relationship between a determination and evidence of ineligibility in the form of stated facts.

The most obvious alternative for reviewing consular *discretion,* as opposed to the law or facts, is the APA standard of "arbitrary, capricious, an abuse of discretion, or otherwise not in accordance with the law."[306] On review of a consular denial, a federal court could find an abuse of discretion, for example, if no evidence supports the decision or if its interpretation of the law appears to be improper or incorrect.[307] Similarly, courts have found abuse of discretion in other immigration contexts when, for example, an official failed to exercise discretion at all, failed to provide reasons for a decision, ignored relevant considerations, or departed inexplicably from normal policies.[308]

3. Standing to Complain

The law of standing cannot be made easy. It is as complex and varied as the law of who may sue to remedy what wrongs across the entire domain of law. Questions of who may sue in various settings share certain common characteristics. But to think, or pretend, that a single law of standing can be applied uniformly to all causes of action is to produce confusion, intellectual dishonesty, and chaos.[309]

---

305. U. S. COMMISSION ON CIVIL RIGHTS, THE TARNISHED GOLDEN DOOR: CIVIL RIGHTS ISSUES IN IMMIGRATION 48 (1980).

306. APA § 706, 5 U.S.C. § 706 (1988).

307. *See, e.g.,* Song Jook Suh v. Rosenberg, 437 F.2d 1098, 1102 (9th Cir. 1971) (superseded by statute as stated in Griggs v. Provident Consumer Discount Co., 459 U.S. 56 (1982)).

308. Legomsky, *Political Asylum and the Theory of Judicial Review,* 73 MINN. L. REV. 1205, 1212 (1989).

309. Fletcher, *The Structure of Standing,* 98 YALE L.J. 221, 290 (1988).

Developing a substantive framework of law and standards for review is of limited help to a refused applicant in the absence of standing to compel review. Applicants denied a visa are, by that fact, unable physically to bring an action in the United States.

In interpreting the APA, the courts have fashioned rules that would provide limited standing to American citizens to complain of injury to them resulting from denial of a visa to an alien. In *Association of Data Processing Service Organizations v. Camp,* [310] the Supreme Court applied section 702 of the APA to establish that persons have standing if they are "arguably within the zone of interests to be protected or regulated by the statute or constitutional guarantee in question"[311] and if they have suffered "injury in fact."[312] Standing, therefore, is no longer limited to those who claim an injury to legal rights; claimants need only show some kind of injury *in fact,* economic or otherwise.[313] Any American who has a strong enough relationship with an alien to file a petition for an immigrant visa on the alien's behalf would seem to be entitled to standing. Thus, all applicants in the immigrant preference categories are indirectly protected by a limited judicial reviewability of action taken on the petition filed on their behalf. In nonimmigrant cases, the post-*Mandel* line of first amendment-related decisions provides for limited standing of American citizens—relatives, prospective or actual employers, educational institutions, and so on—to complain on behalf of foreign applicants. Beyond such vicarious standing, the road to the courtroom is poorly charted.

Although non-resident aliens can bring legal action in federal and state courts, that capacity is meaningless if they are unable to obtain a visa to enter the country. The rules of standing do not explicitly protect the rights of aliens to complain about visa denials effected abroad, although *Mandel* itself and a few other cases have tacitly allowed standing to non-resident aliens, at least as symbolic parties. Archaic notions that aliens possess only a privilege and not a right to a visa, and that constitutional protections do not extend abroad, have encouraged the courts' reluctance to allow aliens standing to complain about visa denials. Courts, and others, also fear opening the floodgates to litigation if applicants are given standing to sue in such cases. These considerations explain why the limited jurisprudence generally denies standing in nonimmigrant visa denial cases unless the applicant

---

310. 397 U.S. 150 (1970).

311. *Id.* at 153.

312. *Id.* at 152; *accord* Abourezk v. Reagan, 785 F.2d. 1043, 1050 (D.C. Cir. 1986), *aff'd per curiam,* 484 U.S. 1 (1987) (3-3 decision).

313. 397 U.S. at 154.

can show a strong affiliation with the United States, such as recent residence in this country[314] or membership in a class of primarily resident plaintiffs.[315] Thus, in demonstrating the requisite connection with the United States, applicants for immigrant visas are apt to have an easier time than applicants for nonimmigrant visas.[316] Indeed, the INA's preference system for intending immigrants is based on connections that would also provide a fair and reasonable basis for standing, namely, on family reunification and the interests of American employers in foreign labor.

Mendelsohn v. Meese,[317] one of two companion cases concerning the status of the PLO Mission to the United Nations,[318] shifts the analysis of standing in a manner that is relevant to this study. In *Mendelsohn,* the court inquired whether United States citizens had standing to challenge the constitutionality of the Anti-Terrorism Act, which would allegedly deny them first amendment liberties to engage in advocacy for the PLO by closing the PLO's Permanent Observer Mission to the United Nations.

The court explicitly found the "findings of standing"[319] in *Allende* and *Abourezk* to be "unpersuasive."[320] In those cases, the court explained, the excluded aliens "had a personal stake in the outcome of the litigation;"[321] this dictum provides a basis for granting standing to any non-resident alien who can show injury in fact, resulting from denial of a visa by a consular officer. In *Mendelsohn,* by contrast, the court decided that the advocates themselves had standing, but not those whose only interest in the litigation involved their alleged "listening" rights under the first amendment.[322] The court interpreted *Mandel* to limit standing to plaintiffs who would be deprived of the "particular qualities inherent in sustained, face-to-face debate, discussion and questioning . . . . The fact that a person has a first amendment interest does not require a finding that he has standing."[323] Thus, the standing issue called for a determination not of whether the

---

314. *See, e.g.,* Estrada v. Ahrens, 296 F.2d 690 (5th Cir. 1961).

315. *See* Kleindienst v. Mandel, 408 U.S. 753 (1972) (by implication); Silva v. Bell, 605 F.2d 978 (7th Cir. 1979); Allende v. Shultz, 605 F. Supp. 1220 (D. Mass. 1985), *aff'd,* 845 F.2d 1111, 1114 n.4 (1st Cir. 1988) (non-resident alien was a "symbolic party").

316. Note, *supra* note 124, at 1154–55.

317. 695 F. Supp. 1474 (S.D.N.Y. 1988).

318. *See supra* notes 204–05.

319. 695 F. Supp. at 1479 n.5.

320. *Id.*

321. *Id.*

322. *Id.* at 1478–79.

323. *Id.* (quoting Kleindienst v. Mandel, 408 U.S. 753, 765 (1972)).

plaintiffs' "own rights of free speech are violated," but whether "the statute's very existence may cause others not before the court to refrain from constitutionally protected speech or expression."[324] *Mendelsohn,* therefore, shifts the *Mandel* analysis of standing away from a focus on vicarious injury to residents to the more immediate injury to alien applicants. Arguably, the effect of this shift could be to undermine the standing of citizens and resident aliens to complain, without establishing the standing of foreign applicants to bring an action themselves. This interpretation of the opinion, however, seems misplaced. First, the opinion acknowledges that even affected "listeners" (or, analogously, Americans deprived of the presence of aliens in exclusion cases) *might have* a "personal stake" in litigation sufficient to be entitled to standing.[325] Second, the court acknowledged that the non-resident aliens denied a visa in *Allende* and *Abourezk,* and hence others denied visas, *did* have standing by virtue of injury resulting directly from the denial.[326]

This requirement of a personal stake in the litigation is consistent with section 702 of the APA. In one or another form, the requirement might be implanted in visa review jurisprudence. Otherwise, the road to the courtroom, to whatever extent it has been charted, will remain overgrown with tangled precedent. The "injury in fact" test is otherwise difficult, if not impossible, to apply objectively,[327] and other very generalized rules of standing are likewise misleading or obfuscating.

In the absence of much constitutional authority on the issue of standing in visa denial cases, the best solution might be one of statutory and regulatory liberalization and clarification.[328] A straightforward, statutory approach to standing would then bring the analysis full circle to the jurisprudential reality of the plenary power doctrine, the political question doctrine, visas-as-privileges-not-rights, and the non-applicability of constitutional protection to non-resident aliens.

---

324. *Id.* at 1479 (quoting Broadrick v. Oklahoma, 413 U.S. 601, 612 (1973)).

325. *Id.*

326. *Id.* at 1479 n.5.

327. *See* Fletcher, *supra* note 309, at 231.

328. For example:

I do not suggest that standing decisions will become easy or noncontroversial if the suggestions made here are followed. Many will remain highly controversial, for they are often critically important decisions about which there is and sometimes can be no complete agreement. But the argument will be focused, as it should be, on the particular statutory or constitutional provision at issue. If the general structure of standing law is seen in the way suggested here, the confusion and obfuscation that have haunted standing law for the past several decades will diminish and, in time, may subside to the amount inescapably present in a legal system that makes significant changes through its judiciary.

Id. at 291.

The current articulation of these constraints is in part the product of the questionable common-law structure of standing. Because the constraints have no clear constitutional justification, Congress could enact legislation to overcome them and to provide for standing. Proposed "Immigration Exclusion and Deportation Amendments of 1987" would have provided standing to specific classes of plaintiffs in visa denial cases, based on national security grounds.[329] Any United States citizen or permanent resident alien would have had standing in a federal district court "who intends to meet in person with, or hear in person, an alien" and who has been denied that opportunity because an alien has been denied a visa.[330]

B. Internal Procedures for Review

Besides the tortuous path of jurisprudential developments, other avenues are available for extending review of consular discretion. Bureaucratic justice, reliant on administrative discretion, may at times be preferable to a more formal review process. Current evidence indicates that visa sections of consulates and embassies conform to a bureaucratic model of administrative justice.[331] That is, the consular process is active, investigatory, generally attuned and responsive to conflicting values, and accuracy-oriented. Although consular officers seek a rational basis for their determinations, however, their exercise of discretion inevitably relies to some degree on intuition, common sense and sheer experience—and mistakes can happen.

The Select Commission on Immigration and Refugee Policy, finding deficiencies in the present system of reviewing consular discretion, recommended improvements in the internal review process rather than establishment of a new administrative body within the State Department.[332] The Commission also recommended increased review by the Department of those consular operations that elicited frequent complaints or appeared to depart from established policy.[333] Thus, the Commission recommended a strengthening of limited internal and external checks on consular discretion. All denials should be carefully

---

329. H.R. 1119, 100th Cong., 1st Sess. § 2(b) (1987).

330. *Id.*

331. For a discussion of the bureaucratic model of administrative justice, see J. MASHAW, BUREAUCRATIC JUSTICE: MANAGING SOCIAL SECURITY DISABILITY CLAIMS 171–72 (1983).

332. U.S. SELECT COMMISSION ON IMMIGRATION AND REFUGEE POLICY, U.S. IMMIGRATION POLICY AND THE NATIONAL INTEREST: FINAL REPORT AND RECOMMENDATIONS 255 (1981) [hereinafter REPORT OF THE SELECT COMMISSION].

333. *Id.*

reviewed by a supervising officer. Section IV of this Article confirms the advisability of doing so.

As a further check on the process, the State Department might establish regulations or other minimum requirements for access by attorneys at each stage of decisionmaking. At a minimum, the requirements should provide for prompt response by the posts to communications from attorneys, and for some means of ensuring that attorneys and their client-applicants can conveniently meet on-site with each other. There is also a need for greater uniformity of practice among the consulates.

C. External Administrative Review (Outside the Refusing Visa Section).

No bright line divides administrative and judicial review.[334] They must be viewed together. Constituent parts of the review system are not only "incredibly complex," in the words of a veteran immigration judge,[335] but interrelated. Greater access to external administrative review can deter more disruptive, time-consuming and expensive review by the courts, and a proven track record of administrative competence could eventually encourage the courts to defer to bureaucratic justice. Such deference would occur not because of some transcendental construct of plenary legislative power or because of precedent, but because of judicial confidence in the administrative process.[336] Judicial review requires an exhaustion of administrative remedies.

Court have interpreted section 104(a) of the INA to bar administrative review outside the visa section of an embassy or consulate and thereby forestalled proposals to create a board within the Department to review visa denials.[337] In fact, however, the Visa Office, through its advisory opinions, and the Secretary of State, through his waiver authority,[338] do review denials. Eliminating this provision in section 104(a) is not a very radical step. More problematic is the design of an effective and efficient process of external administrative review.

As one alternative, the role of the Visa Office could be substantially expanded. That office issues a modest number of advisory opinions, which are binding as to questions of law but not as to questions of fact. Although a consular officer is quite likely to be the best judge of the

---

334. Legomsky, *supra* note 244, at 1299.

335. Address by William R. Robie, Chief Immigration Judge, United States Department of Justice, Federal Bar Association Seminar, *supra* note 81.

336. Verkuil, *supra* note 10, at 1206.

337. 8 U.S.C. § 1104(a) (1988); *see supra* text accompanying notes 59–61.

338. *E.g.,* 22 C.F.R. § 41.2 (1990).

facts, a process is needed to strongly discourage abuses of discretion and patterns of mistakes.

Beyond expanding the role of the Visa Office, other options include: refinement of departmental regulations and the guidelines found in the Foreign Service Manual;[339] closer monitoring of visa denials and review of field office operations and practices, as recommended by the President's Select Commission on Immigration and Refugee Policy;[340] and substantially greater use of authority to request refusal reports from embassies and consulates.[341]

Although the Visa Office flatly opposes any proposals for administrative or judicial review,[342] some form of review seems inevitable. As a start, the Visa Office might randomly sample denials, with an eye toward identifying significant departures from normal interpretations and exercises of discretion. The Department might also experiment with volume thresholds. A below-average volume of requests for advisory opinions from a particular consulate would trigger a requirement that the consulate forward all, or a random sample, of the next batch of denials. The Visa Office would then issue opinions on each of these. In view of the probability of an increased workload, it might be advisable to continue binding consular officers only on opinions of law. Finally, the Visa Office might intensify efforts to collect cases from the field, in order to issue further guidance and generally develop more uniform or consistent exercise of discretion among consulates. The Visa Office might select particularly troublesome issues, resulting in divergent determinations, for particular attention.[343] Sections 214(b) and 221(g) of the INA commend themselves for such special attention. Above all, the Visa Office should be encouraged to abandon its obdurate refusal to support or even consider proposals for administrative or judicial review.

The cloak of confidentiality should be lifted from advisory opinions.[344] Although the exemption to protect the national defense or

---

339. For historical perspective on these efforts, see U.S. COMMISSION ON CIVIL RIGHTS, *supra* note 305, at 48.

340. *See* REPORT OF THE SELECT COMMISSION, *supra* note 332, at 255.

341. *See* 22 C.F.R. §§ 41.121(d), 42.81(d) (1990).

342. *See* U.S. COMMISSION ON CIVIL RIGHTS, *supra* note 305, at 48 n.23. Cornelius D. Scully III, Head of the Office of Legislation, Regulations and Advisory Assistance in the State Department's Bureau of Consular Affairs, reiterated this opposition to any proposals for review. Telephone interviews with Cornelius D. Scully (Apr. 5 & 11, 1989) (notes on file with the *Washington Law Review*). Such opposition poses a serious obstacle in the path of reform.

343. *See* Study, *supra* note 62, at 158.

344. *See supra* text accompanying note 256.

foreign policy might remain,[345] most applicants ought to have access to advisory opinions immediately upon issuance.

As another alternative, the State Department might establish a centralized review process within the Department but outside the Visa Office.[346] As precedent, proposals to establish such a board typically cite the two-member Board of Appeals on Visa Cases during World War II. That Board reportedly handled 22,600 appeals in less than four years of operations and overturned 26% of the visa denials it

---

345. 5 U.S.C. § 552(b)(1)(A) (1988).

346. The first Board of Visa Appeals was apparently proposed in 1952 in congressional debate about the McCarran-Walter Act. *See* Study, *supra* note 62, at 158 n.462. In 1969, Senator Edward Kennedy proposed the establishment of a visa review board as follows:

Section 104 of the Immigration and Nationality Act, 8 U.S.C. § 1104 should be amended by adding at the end thereof the following new subsection:

(g)(1) There is hereby established within the Bureau of Security and Consular Affairs a Board of Visa Appeals (hereafter referred to in this subsection as the 'Board'), to be independent of the Visa Office. The Board shall consist of five members to be appointed by the Secretary of State, who shall designate one member as Chairman. The practice and procedure before the Board shall be in accordance with this subsection and, subject to paragraph (4), such regulations as the Secretary of State may prescribe.

(2) Upon petition -

(A) by any citizen of the United States claiming that an alien outside the United States is entitled to (i) a preference status by reason of a relationship to the petitioner described in paragraph (1), (4), or (5) of section 203(a), or (ii) an immediate relative status under section 201(b), or

(B) by any alien lawfully admitted for permanent residence claiming that an alien outside the United States is entitled to a preference status by reason of the relationship to the petitioner described in paragraph (2) of section 203(a), the Board shall have jurisdiction to review any determination of a United States consular officer refusing an immigration visa, or revoking an immigrant visa issued, to any such alien outside the United States who has applied for classification as a preference immigrant described in any such paragraph or as an immediate relative. Each alien shall be informed of the review procedure available under this subsection when a determination refusing or revoking an immigrant visa to him is made by a consular officer. No petition for review may be filed with the Board more than sixty days after the date of notification to an alien of the making of the determination with respect to which review is sought.

(3) Any review by the Board under this subsection shall be conducted solely upon the basis of the visa application and any other suppporting documents submitted in connection with such application by or on behalf of the alien concerned, and any other documents, materials, or information in the possession of and considered by the consular officer, together with any briefs, memoranda, or arguments submitted in writing by or on behalf of the alien. No alien, solely by virtue of a petition for review by the Board under this subsection, shall be entitled to entry or admission into the United States.

(4) The decision of the Board in each case shall be in writing and shall be communicated to the petitioner and the alien concerned. Decisions of the Board under this subsection shall be final and conclusive on all questions of law and fact relating to the issuance or revocation of a visa and shall not be subject to review by any other official, department, agency, or establishment of the United States; but, nothing in this subsection shall be construed to limit the application of section 221(d).

S. 3202, 91st Cong., 1st Sess. § 3, 115 CONG. REC. 36,967 (1969) (statement of Sen. Kennedy).

reviewed.[347] How much time did that afford for each case? On the assumption of 250 workdays per year per officer, each enjoying a two week vacation, and seven hours a day to devote to the cases, the Board had 14,000 hours at its disposal to review and write up decisions, or about thirty-seven minutes per case, going non-stop. That might clearly be inadequate for a peacetime board.

As the British experience suggests, however, the volume of appeals of visa denials might be small.[348] As assurance, some proposals for a review board would limit reviewability to denials of only certain classes of visas. The most modest alternative would draw a line between immigrant visas issued under the preference categories, which would be reviewable, and nonimmigrant visas, which would not. Presumably the family and employment interests expressed in the preference categories establish heightened individual interests, closer affiliations with the United States, and hence greater governmental interests in issuing a visa.

Distinguishing among classes of nonimmigrant visas presents difficult problems. To the extent that distinctions would be drawn not on the basis of the nature of the right but rather the government's foreign affairs interest in a particular case or category of cases, such proposals are consistent with the current ideology of reviewability. It is uncertain, however, what constitutes a strong enough governmental interest to immunize one particular class or category of visa denials, but not another. What about tourist visas? Would the government's express economic and cultural interest in promoting tourism permit tourist visa denials to be insulated from review? Would denial of a visa to a person dying of cancer to enable her to visit Disneyland be reviewable, but not a young person's desire to travel around the United States on vacation?

Ideological and non-security grounds for exclusion have posed dilemmas. One might think that denials premised on these grounds should be the most immune from review. Ironically, however, it is the very sensitive ideological and national security-oriented denials under section 212(a)(27)–(a)(29) of the INA[349] that in recent years have wound up in the courts because of volatile first amendment issues. Indeed, the proposed Immigration Exclusion and Deportation

---

347. 133 CONG. REC. E2211 (daily ed. June 2, 1987) (statement of Rep. Gonzalez).

348. On the British experience, see UKIAS REPORT, *supra* note 89, at 2; on the United States experience with administrative review and other kinds of immigration decisions, see *supra* text accompanying notes 244–47.

349. 8 U.S.C. § 1182(a)(27)–(a)(29) (as modified by the Immigration Act of 1990, Pub. L. No. 101-649, §§ 601, 603, 104 Stat. 4978).

Amendments of 1987 would have singled out national security-based denials for judicial review.[350] Clearly, individual interests must be balanced against those of the government,[351] but the weighing is not easy.

One proposal would have created a comprehensive, independent United States Immigration Board, whose final decisions would have been binding on "all administrative law judges, immigration officers, and consular officers."[352] The Gonzalez Bill[353] would have created a visa review board within the State Department. That board would have reviewed visa denials of all special immigrants, immediate relatives, preference category aliens, and a number of classes of nonimmigrants.[354] The Bill would have given the board the authority to overrule a visa denial and require the issuing officer promptly to issue the visa.[355] The Gonzalez Bill is a good point of departure for establishing a visa review board within the Department. Its somewhat narrow definition of the scope of review over nonimmigrant visa denials might seem somewhat arbitrary, but a cautionary, selective approach of this sort offers a basic orientation for exploring uncharted territory.

Perhaps the place to begin is with a pilot program involving a single class or two of nonimmigrant visas. The class of treaty traders and investors might be optimum because of a low volume of applicants, the economic importance of the visas, and the technical difficulty of interpreting and applying the law.

Section (e) of the Gonzalez Bill contains an escape clause that would enable any member of the Board, official, or employee of the federal government to refuse to disclose confidential information that in his or her judgment "would be prejudicial to the public interest, safety or security."[356] This clause could swallow the review process. Moreover, it might encourage consular officers to reverse the presumption under international law that admissions will be normal *unless* the requisite threat is apparent. Instead of having to identify a specific threat to the nation in a particular case, a consular officer would possess a wide margin of discretion to insulate denials from administrative review.

---

350. H.R. 1119, *supra* note 329, at § 2(b).

351. *See* Verkuil, *supra* note 10, at 1149.

352. Immigration Reform and Control Act of 1983, S. 529 & H.R. 1510, 98th Cong., 1st Sess. § 122a (1983); *see also* S. 3202, *supra* note 346, at § 3(g).

353. H.R. 2567, 100th Cong., 1st Sess. (1987).

354. *Id.* at § 225(a)(4).

355. *Id.* at § 225(d)(2).

356. *Id.* at § 225(e).

Whatever the precise structure or location within the government, a review board should seek to maximize the three values of accountability of consular officers, uniformity or consistency of determinations among officers and visa sections, and due process for applicants and petitioners. The British experience in allowing appeals of visa denials provides one model. The several immigration-related boards within the United States Departments of Justice and Labor offer other models.

Mathews v. Eldridge [357] established that the sufficiency of procedures under the Due Process Clause varies with the circumstances, but that courts must consider the type and magnitude of the individual's interest at stake, the risk of an erroneous deprivation of that interest as a result of a particular procedure, and the burdens and benefits of heightened procedural safeguards. The *Mathews* approach would therefore balance the government's interest in excluding classes of aliens against a visa applicant's interest in being protected against an erroneous or unfair denial.

Goldberg v. Kelly [358] lists ten minimum ingredients to satisfy the requirement of a fair hearing, administrative or judicial. The *Goldberg* menu provides a convenient, though by no means mandatory, list of procedural ingredients for a visa review board: timely and adequate notice; confrontation of adverse witnesses; oral presentation of arguments and evidence; cross-examination of adverse witnesses; disclosure to the claimant of opposing evidence; the right to retain an attorney; a determination on the record of the hearing; a statement of reasons for the determination; an indication of evidence relied on; and an impartial decisionmaker.

A visa review process outside consulates, following the model of an exclusion hearing, might include all of the above ingredients except an opportunity for cross-examination, confrontation of adverse witnesses, and oral argument. Provision might be made, however, for a well-defined range of interrogatories. Unlike an exclusion hearing, the process should provide for effective notice, but not necessarily for cross-examination. In exceptional cases involving sensitive issues of national security significance, confidential material might be presented and reviewed in camera. The refused applicant, who by definition could not enter the United States to be present in the proceedings, might be represented by a petitioner, legal counsel, or other designated representative. The applicant and local petitioner would be given

---

357. 424 U.S. 319, 334–35 (1976).
358. 397 U.S. 254, 267–71 (1970).

access to the record of consular adjudication, and the latter could present further oral evidence. The board would render a written decision. The most difficult questions relate not to the scope or procedures of the review process, but the accessibility to the process of different classes of applicants and petitioners on behalf of applicants. A first step might be a pilot review process limited to refused applicants for immigrant visas, represented by their petitioners or others, and nonimmigrant visas for treaty traders and investors. If the process operated satisfactorily, it might gradually include refused applicants for other types of nonimmigrant visas.

D. Judicial Review

From the standpoint of the State Department, a visa section, and individual consular officers, an administrative review board might seem to be preferable to judicial review. Administrative review might seem preferable, too, from a more systemic standpoint, so long as the review would "both correct errors in individual cases and enhance quality control of the system generally."[359] Nevertheless, to reconsider an appellate administrative decision, judicial review has its place.

The proposed Immigration Exclusion and Deportation Amendments of 1987[360] would have amended section 279 of the INA[361] to provide for the jurisdiction of federal district courts to review visa denials. Venue would have been proper in any district court "in which the individual resides or in which the individual intended to meet or hear the alien."[362]

Statutory provision for judicial review should require exhaustion of administrative remedies, specify the standing of at least limited classes of citizens and permanent resident aliens, confirm the qualified duty to admit aliens, and prescribe a standard for review under section 706 of the APA.[363] On issues of law, the standard should be an independent statutory interpretation. On issues of fact, courts should apply a substantial evidence test[364] that could be satisfied by reference to the consular's notations and Visa Control Card. Of the options for review of

---

359. *See* Verkuil, *supra* note 10, at 1182.

360. H.R. 1119, *supra* note 329, at § 2(b).

361. INA § 279, 8 U.S.C. § 1329 (1988) (providing for jurisdiction of the federal district courts).

362. H.R. 1119, *supra* note 329, at § 2(b).

363. 5 U.S.C. § 706 ("scope of review").

364. *See, e.g.*, Federal Power Comm'n v. Transcontinental Gas Pipe Line Corp., 423 U.S. 326, 331 (1976); Jean v. Nelson, 727 F.2d 957, 976–79 (11th Cir. 1984), *aff'd*, 472 U.S. 846 (1985); Bertrand v. Sava, 684 F.2d 204, 212–13 (2d Cir. 1982); Knoetze v. United States, 634 F.2d 207 (5th Cir. Unit B), *cert. denied*, 454 U.S. 823 (1981).

discretion, the fairly conservative "arbitrary, capricious" or "abuse of discretion" standard seems most suitable,[365] given the uncertainties *ab initio,* the geographical and political peculiarities of consular discretion, and the possibility that merely providing for reviewability would be viewed as a radical step.

If an administrative review board is established and if judicial standing is given to refused applicants, the preferred route of appeal might be a petition from an adverse ruling of the board to a court of appeals. Otherwise, a denied applicant should probably be allowed to bring an action directly in federal district court.[366] As between the two levels of federal courts, the extent and quality of the normal record available on appeal could be determinative.

E. Other Alternatives

Several other alternatives merit consideration. Although not techniques for review, these proposals would serve to limit the need for review. The State Department might consider reallocating consular personnel and adjusting their workload in order to devote more of the Department's limited resources to on-line adjudications where they are most critically needed, more extensive recordkeeping, and more thorough internal review of visa denials. Several changes would make such reallocation feasible within budgetary constraints.

A first very successful change is the pilot visa waiver program.[367] Gradually, the program could be extended to include nonimmigrant categories other than short-term tourists as well as nationals of countries other than those initially selected. The bases for country designations should be both low nonimmigrant visa refusal rates and, secondarily, high volumes of visa applications. The author's interviews at the United States Embassy in London confirm the merits of this program. During the first six months alone, consular officers issued 140,000 visas in London and 110,000 elsewhere in the United Kingdom. Less than 100 of the tourists were later denied entry by the

---

365. *See* Note, *supra* note 124, at 1168.

366. *See* Legomsky, *supra* note 244, at 1399.

367. INA § 217, 8 U.S.C. § 1187. *See supra* note 13 for a brief description of the program. Over 3.5 million persons from eight countries were admitted into the United States without visas during the first nineteen months of the program. A report by the Visa Office of the State Department has recommended a three year extension of the program, until September 30, 1994. The Visa Office concluded that the program "has successfully moved toward accomplishing both goals set by the Congress: to improve the use of United States Government resources and to encourage international travel." 67 INTERPRETER RELEASES 867 (1990). Section 201 of the Immigration Act of 1990, Pub. L. No. 101-649, 104 Stat. 4978, will revise and extend the program.

INS. This low rate of turnarounds suggests that the program relieves consular officers of administrative burdens for visa issuances, without shifting the burden onto the INS. The program has enlisted the cooperation of over 100 major air carriers. Although reports indicate that some tourists under the program have had to wait longer in line for entry at the border or other ports of entry, consular officers respond that the delays are primarily due to longer lines of tourists.

As a second administrative change, the State Department could substitute more civil service personnel within commuting distance from consular posts to conduct pre-screening and limited interviewing of applicants, thereby providing consular officers with more time for record-keeping and internal review of denials. A third change, in order to avoid time wasted on a limited number of cases raising the problem of appropriate venue for visa applications, relates to the problem of "orphan" applications. The State Department might specifically direct all visa-issuing posts to process such applications from third-country nationals, assisted by the advance parole program. Alternatively, the State Department might encourage all posts to process orphan immigrant applications, and specifically designate the following posts: Toronto, Montreal, Vancouver, Tijuana, and Ciudad Juarez. The termination of the Stateside Criteria Program in 1987, which attracted large numbers of aliens in the United States to those nearby posts to have their immigration status adjusted, has provided consular officers at those posts with more time to devote to third-country applicants.

Another alternative for reducing the need for review would eliminate preference categories for immigrant visas and substitute a point-based system whereby an applicant would receive points for various factors, such as family relationship with an American citizen or resident alien, employment potential, health, and so on. Those with the highest number of points within a world-wide quota receive priority to obtain a visa. By providing detailed guidance and confining consular discretion, a point-based system would help avoid the subjectivity of decisionmaking that is often the source of pressures for review. Systems of this sort are in effect in Australia and Canada.

A more radical alternative would experiment with gradually eliminating some classes of nonimmigrant visas altogether, while continuing to require I-94 forms as a means of monitoring and controlling exits and overstays of aliens. Visas would continue to be required for intending immigrants, although even this barrier has been questioned.[368] Such an experimental program would eliminate most of the current problems, including the issue of reviewability. It might also create new ones. If the rates for any of numerous types of violations—non-return within prescribed times for departure, unauthorized employment, failure to register or re-register, and so on—reached a sufficiently high level, the State Department could reinstitute and extend departure controls and work permits. These techniques, and the supervision by law enforcement officials they might require, would, however, raise troublesome issues of civil liberties. In the past, proposals for permits and national identification cards have not been popular.

A more conservative variation of the "no visa" approach would eliminate visas for immigrants and nonimmigrants in each of several categories—investors, fiancés, students, tourists, and so on—up to certain annual levels, at which point visas would be reinstated as a requirement for all additional nonimmigrants. Up-to-date statistical data could be maintained on the basis of oral inquiries by INS officials at the borders and other ports of entry. The data might, however, be unreliable because of multi-purpose border crossings, indeterminate purposes for particular crossings, or simply mistakes.

F. Uncertainties

The pace of jurisprudential developments will be slow. Funding of consulates has been so limited that training of officers, visa processing, record-keeping suitable for review, and internal review have been understandably restricted. It is unlikely that Congress, under continued pressure to reduce budget deficits, will provide the kind of funding needed to overcome these deficiencies quickly, or that it will readily amend the INA to enable the State Department to establish a visa review board. It is also uncertain to what extent Congress would find it politically feasible to provide for administrative or judicial review. Although the Departments of Justice, Labor and State continue to establish new immigration-related boards of review,[369] none are as

---

368. *See, e.g.*, The Wall Street Journal, Feb. 1, 1990, at A12, col. 1 ("Our own view remains that the problem is not too many immigrants, but too few. . . . Our view is, borders should be open.").

369. These include, for example, the Asylum Policy and Review Unit (Justice), *see* N.Y. Times, Dec. 21, 1988, at A18, col. 1; the Board of Alien Certification Appeals (Labor); the Exchange Visitor Waiver Review Board (State), for aliens with exchange visitor visas who petition for waivers of the two-year home country residence requirement; and the Board of Appellate Review (State), to review loss of nationality and passport determinations. Congress has also provided for review of denials of seasonal agricultural worker status, adjustment of status under IRCA's legalization program, INS determinations of unlawful employment of

ambitious as a review board that would encompass all visa classes. Finally, the capacity of Congress to draft sound legislation to provide for review is uncertain. The gestation period for preparing legislation in a politically acceptable form does not seem to make much difference. On the one hand, it took Congress ten years of drafting and redrafting in order to enact the IRCA compromise, which has serious defects.[370] On the other hand, it took all too little time for Congress to cobble together an unsuccessful revision of the framework for immigrant visas prior to The Immigration Act of 1990.[371] Taking account of these uncertainties should not deter reform, but rather encourage careful and intelligent planning.

VI. SUMMARY

United States consulates complete the processing of some ten million applications for immigrant and nonimmigrant visas each year. Approximately ninety percent are granted; ten percent are denied. Under current practice, the only official review of a consular official's denial of a visa may be by a more senior officer in the consulate or, on points of law, by the Visa Office in the State Department. The Immi-

---

aliens, and alien claims of discrimination related to IRCA. Paparelli & Tilner, *supra* note 3, at 1032.

370. *See, e.g.*, Note, *The Effect of Employer Sanctions on Employment Discrimination and Illegal Immigration*, 9 B.C. THIRD WORLD L. J. 249, 269 (1989):

The employer sanctions provision of IRCA is a costly one. The cost of the provision in increased employment discrimination far outweighs any minimal deterrent effect that the provision will have on illegal immigration. A society that has made a conscious effort to eliminate race discrimination cannot tolerate such a cost.

For a summary of a report by the United States General Accounting Office that employee sanctions in IRCA have caused widespread discrimination, see 67 INTERPRETER RELEASES, Apr. 2, 1990, at 377; *see also* Kobdish, *The Frank Amendment to the Immigration Reform and Control Act of 1986—A Labyrinth for Labor Law Litigators*, 41 Sw. L.J. 667 (1987) (IRCA's anti-discrimination provisions create a field day for attorneys); Merino, *Compromising Immigration Reform: The Creation of a Vulnerable Subclass*, 98 YALE L.J. 409 (1988) (IRCA has created a subclass of undocumented residents who are ineligible for legalization); Hernandez, *Employer Sanctions Should Go*, Christian Sci. Monitor, Apr. 10, 1990, at 18, col. 1; Suro, *False Migrant Claims: Fraud on a Huge Scale*, N.Y. Times, Nov. 12, 1989, at A1, col. 1; Armstrong, *America's Illegal Aliens: They Haven't Gone Home*, Christian Sci. Monitor, Jan. 30, 1989, at 1, col. 3; Howe, *Under the New Law, Illegal Aliens Suffer Much in Silence*, N.Y. Times, Nov. 27, 1988, at A6, col. 1; *Study Hints at Job Discrimination Against Foreign-Looking People*, N.Y. Times, Nov. 20, 1988, at A18, col. 1; Howe, *Study Says Immigration Law Is Leading to Discrimination*, N.Y. Times, Nov. 5, 1988, at A1, col. 5.

371. The bill, S. 2104, easily passed the Senate (88-4), but failed to clear the Judiciary Committee of the House. It was worked out behind closed doors and rushed through the legislative process. The bill appeared to discriminate against some family members and non-English-speaking applicants for immigrant visas. Letters from Sen. Mark O. Hatfield, Minority Chairman, Senate Appropriations Committee, to the author (Nov. 23, 1988 & Dec. 1, 1988) (on file with the *Washington Law Review*).

gration and Nationality Act has been read to preclude administrative review, and the courts, with a few exceptions, have declined to review visa denials.

Immigrant visas are available to persons with close family relationships to United States citizens and residents or with particular abilities or skills that are needed but not otherwise available in the United States. Nonimmigrant visas are available in a long list of classes, ranging from tourists to students to certain types of business personnel to diplomats.

Whatever the visa category or class, important interests are clearly at stake. These interests are not just those of the applicants themselves, but also of citizens and residents of the United States who are sponsoring the applicant or have some other interest in the applicant's presence in the United States. The interests of strengthening the global order and upholding rules of international law are also apparent. These interests warrant a close look at whether initial decisions in this important program of mass adjudication should be more fully reviewable than at present.

Over twenty years ago, Senator Edward Kennedy urged the reestablishment of a board of visa appeals to refine "the application of our belief in human dignity and equal opportunity under law."[372] Three years later, a future Legal Adviser to the Secretary of State proposed the "one small step" of establishing a Board of Visa Appeals. The Board would ensure compliance with immigration law, "upgrading the procedural protections in the visa issuing process . . . streamlining it, and render[ing] it less subject to manipulation for other foreign policy needs."[373] A visa review board is clearly an idea whose time has come, once again.

Federal law and State Department regulations give consular officers substantial discretion in adjudicating visa applications. For example, consular officials exercise absolute discretion in determining whether an applicant may be represented by an attorney or other qualified representative at the visa adjudication interview. Furthermore, although current departmental regulations require that a consular officer's denial of a visa application be reviewed by a more senior officer,[374] budgetary constraints and the high volume of applications at some

---

372. S. 3202, *supra* note 346, at 36,965.

373. Sofaer, *Judicial Control of Informal Discretionary Adjudication and Enforcement*, 72 COLUM. L. REV. 1293, 1364 n.382 (1972) (Abraham Sofaer, then a professor at Columbia University School of Law, served as Legal Adviser in the State Department during the Reagan and Bush administrations.).

374. 22 C.F.R. § 41.121(c) (1990).

posts have resulted in review of only a random sample of denials. Intra-consular review may also be a problem in single-officer posts. Consular posts send a few hundred cases a year presenting significant legal issues to the Visa Office of the State Department for an advisory opinion that is binding only with respect to legal issues. The applicant typically has no notice of this proceeding. Such review affects the results in only a small number of cases because most visa denials are based on a factual determination.

Under customary international law a state may legitimately exclude aliens only if, individually or collectively, they pose a danger to its public safety, security, general welfare, or essential institutions. Current law has, however, been interpreted to limit both administrative and judicial review of compliance with this qualified rule of law. Section 104(a) of the INA[375] is interpreted to exclude even the Secretary of State from the administration or enforcement of "those powers, duties and functions conferred upon the consular officers relating to the granting or refusal of visas." This strange provision of the law has thus been read to preclude the establishment of a more formal review mechanism within the State Department. Further, a number of judicial doctrines of varying current legitimacy have served quite consistently to limit the extent of available judicial review. It is therefore important to provide explicitly for both administrative and judicial review.

VII. RECOMMENDATIONS

Despite the high quality of consular training and decisionmaking, it is apparent that a more formal review of consular discretion would be beneficial. The availability of such review not only encourages consistency and care in the initial adjudication, but serves interests of fairness and legitimacy. A review scheme can be crafted that would keep procedure to a minimum, take account of the high volume of visa applications, and avoid over-judicializing the process.

This section offers two alternative sets of recommendations. The first provides more detailed guidance to the Department of State and Congress, whereas the second defers to a greater extent to their discretion in providing for administrative and judicial review of visa denials.

---

375. 8 U.S.C. § 1104(a) (1988).

82

A. Detailed Recommendations

The following recommendations are based on analysis of alternatives discussed in Sections III and V for improving the process of reviewing visa denials. Of the four uncertainties that were identified in Section V—the pace and extent of jurisprudential developments, the political feasibility of expanding the review process, statutory drafting skill in doing so, and funding—only the uncertainty of funding has strongly influenced the structure of these recommendations.

1. Present Level of Funding

The following recommendations could be implemented under the present level of funding, including inflationary increases, or a very modest increase in funding.

a. Reallocation of Workloads

The State Department should continue to adjust the workload of consular officers, lessening visa processing and increasing record-keeping and internal review of individual cases.

First, in order to give consular officers more time per case, the State Department should make more use of civil service personnel commuting from the United States to help process visas at consular posts along the Canadian and Mexican borders. The commuting civil servants do not require special housing or allowances and typically receive less compensation than consular officers. Appropriate amendments should be made to the departmental regulations[376] and the Foreign Affairs Manual[377] to clarify the respective roles of these personnel and the authorizing consular officers who would remain responsible for visa issuances and denials.

Second, the State Department should continue to shift consular officers from posts relieved of visa-processing responsibilities as a result of the Visa Waiver Pilot Program to other, high-intensity posts. The Department could thereby reallocate the aggregate activities of consular officers from visa processing to more extensive record keeping of adjudications and internal review of visa denials.

Finally, the State Department should specifically direct all visa-issuing posts to process orphan applications of third-country nationals, assisted by the advance parole program. The Department would thereby effectuate its regulatory mandate.[378]   Alternatively, because

---

376. *See, e.g.,* 22 C.F.R. §§ 41.121, 42.71, 42.81 (1990).

377. *See supra* note 19.

378. *See* 22 C.F.R. 42.61; FOREIGN AFFAIRS MANUAL, *supra* note 19, App. J-471, note N2.1.

the termination of the Stateside Criteria Program in 1987 has provided consular officers at the posts in Tijuana, Ciudad Juarez, Toronto, Montreal, and Vancouver with more time to devote to third-country applicants, the State Department should specifically designate those posts to process orphan immigrant applications, and encourage all other posts to do the same.

b. Representation of Applicants

The State Department should adopt a regulation ensuring attorneys meaningful access to the visa process and participation throughout the process. Providing this check on consular discretion would enhance due process; assist officers by having issues, rules, and principles articulated more formally; and thereby increase the overall fairness and efficiency of the visa process. The Department should gradually adopt uniform rules for increasing applicants' access to attorneys. At a minimum, visa sections should reply promptly to written communications from attorneys and should provide an area within each visa-issuing consulate where applicants can meet with their attorneys during the adjudication stage of the visa process. The Department should also allow attorneys to meet with responsible consular officers at least once during the course of each client's involvement in the process and to argue on behalf of the client at that time.

c. Internal Review

The State Department should expand internal review of denials within consular posts.

Initially, the Department should require consular officers to provide explicit factual and legal bases and reasons for denials. Whether or not the de minimis test of a "facially legitimate and bona fide reason" applies, departmental guidelines should require more than mere statements of determinations, citations of INA provisions under which applicants are excludable, or vague references to political considerations.

The Department should also ensure that supervising officers review all denials, rather than just a random sample of them, even if such review occasionally causes a backlog of applications. Visa denials at a single-officer post would be reviewed by the Visa Office in the State Department.

d. Visa Office Review

The State Department should expand the role of the Visa Office in the review process.

First, the Visa Office should be encouraged to require consulates or embassies registering large numbers of complaints in relation to the volume of visa applications to report to the Office. These consulates or embassies would need to send full documentation of all visa denials until the volume of complaints lessens to an acceptable level. The Office should review those denials for completeness and evidence of reasonableness.

Second, the Department should amend its regulations to remove the cloak of confidentiality from most advisory opinions. If necessary, Congress should amend section 222(f) of the INA[379] to provide explicitly for access by applicants and their attorneys to pertinent advisory opinions and consular records reviewed by the Office. Under such an amendment, only the FOIA exemption for national defense or foreign policy reasons[380] would bar access to advisory opinions.

Third, the Visa Office or the General Accounting Office (GAO) should designate one or two major controversial areas of consular discretion for special study.[381] The Office would analyze reports from visa sections of denials based on these two areas or specific statutory provisions. Based on its analysis, the Office would then prepare advisory opinions and guidelines for inclusion in the Foreign Affairs Manual.[382] This would make consular practices more uniform and consistent.

e. Judicial Reviewability

Congress and the State Department should expand the scope of judicial reviewability.

Initially, Congress should amend section 101(a)(7) of the INA[383] to provide clearly that the term "immigration laws" refers to *all* constitutionally applicable international law, not just treaties and conventions. The Department should amend its regulations to incorporate a reference to the qualified duty of the United States to admit aliens unless they pose serious danger to public safety, security, general welfare, or essential institutions of the United States.

---

379. 8 U.S.C. § 1202(f).
380. 5 U.S.C. § 552(1)(A).
381. *See e.g.,* INA §§ 214(b), 221(g), 8 U.S.C. §§ 1184(b), 1201(g).
382. *Supra* note 19.
383. 8 U.S.C. § 1101 (a)(7).

Congress should also amend the INA to provide judicial standing in federal district court, according to the normal rules of jurisdiction and venue, to all United States resident petitioners on behalf of immigrant visa applicants, to other United States residents either "with a personal stake in the litigation"[384] or under section 702 of the APA,[385] and as a pilot program to a single class of nonimmigrant visa applicants such as treaty traders and investors.

Furthermore, Congress should amend the INA to provide that a court reviewing a visa denial must comply with section 706 of the APA,[386] and adopt the following standards for review: on issues of law—independent statutory and regulatory interpretation; on issues of fact—substantial evidence; and on issues of discretion—the "abuse of discretion" standard.

f. User Fees

Congress should study the feasibility and merits of users fees to finance improvements in the process of visa issuance and review.

2. Enhanced Funding

The following recommendations are based on a higher level of funding.

a. Visa Review Board

Congress should establish a visa review board within the Department of State, perhaps independent of the Visa Office.

Specifically, Congress should eliminate the following language from section 104(a)(1) of the INA: "[E]xcept those powers, duties and functions conferred upon the consular officers relating to the granting or refusal of visas."[387] Such an amendment would remove any doubt that Congress and the Department could establish a visa review board.

Congress and the State Department should then use the Gonzalez Bill[388] as a basic framework for the board, but should limit review to immigrant visa denials and a single class or two of nonimmigrant visa denials as a pilot program. Congress and the State Department should also provide standing as set forth in recommendation 1(e) above and substantially narrow the public security and safety exception to

---

384. Mendelsohn v. Meese, 695 F. Supp. 1474, 1479 n.5 (S.D.N.Y. 1988).
385. 5 U.S.C. § 702.
386. *Id.* § 706.
387. 8 U.S.C. § 1104(a)(1).
388. *H.R.* 2567, 100th Cong., 1st Sess. (1987).

review. The minimal due process requirements for the board should include notice, oral evidence, disclosure of opposing evidence, attorney representation, determination on the record of the hearing, a written statement of reasons for the board's decision, and an impartial decisionmaker.[389]

b. Exhaustion of Remedies

As a prerequisite for judicial review of a visa denial, Congress should require applicants to exhaust administrative remedies available from the board. Congress should also provide an appeal from a decision of the proposed visa review board to the federal courts.

c. Structural Alternatives

Congress should continue to study structural alternatives to the present visa-issuing process. These alternatives, for example, include greater reliance on departure controls and information.

3. Maximum Funding

With substantially greater funding, Congress should expand the scope of the visa review board's authority to include all cases involving denials of nonimmigrant visas.

B. General Recommendations

This set of recommendations reflects a two-pronged approach to administrative review of visa denials. Its aims are to improve review at the consular level and to consider creating a level of centralized administrative review. The suggestions directed toward consular offices are intended to encourage quick, consistent, and cost-effective review that would resolve many of the issues on which review is requested. In a smaller number of cases, a more formal administrative appeal process would be needed and could be made available on a discretionary basis. This set of recommendations also urges Congress to provide specifically for judicial review.

1. Representation of Applicants

The State Department should adopt a regulation ensuring that applicants may be accompanied by an attorney or other authorized representative during the course of the visa application interview process. To the extent practicable, the State Department should take

---

389. See Appendix B.

steps to reply promptly to communications from applicants or authorized representatives, and to ensure that applicants can feasibly meet with their representatives during the application interview process.

2. Bases and Reasons for Denial

The State Department should require consular officers to provide brief but explicit statements in writing of the factual and legal bases and reasons for denying visa applications.

3. Access to Opinions

The State Department should modify its regulations to allow Visa Office advisory opinions to be made available to applicants and their authorized representatives except where national security or foreign policy reasons dictate otherwise.

4. Internal Review at Consular Posts

The State Department should either comply with its regulation requiring review within a consulate of each denial of a visa application[390] or, for reasons of cost effectiveness, examine alternative, equally effective systems to review visa denials at consular posts. Such a study should be completed in one year. In undertaking the study, the State Department should keep in mind the goal of ensuring consistency in visa adjudications, and consider possible alternatives to address exigencies created by busy consular posts. The Department could, for example, review random samples of visa denials or select certain types of denials for review, such as in visa classes involving relatively complex standards or reflecting comparatively high rates of denial.

5. Formal Administrative Review

An administrative process should be established to review all denials of immigrant visas and certain types of nonimmigrant visas to be designated by the State Department. The review process should require a written petition for review, provide for discretionary review of such petitions, and, where a petition is granted, provide for an expedited review on the paper record with some opportunity to seek leave to present additional written submissions. Congress should delete the language in section 104 of the INA that seemingly precludes the State Department from establishing an administrative entity to review con-

---

390. 22 C.F.R. § 41.12(c) (1990).

sular visa denials.[391] Upon deletion of the apparent prohibition, the State Department (or Congress) should create a suitable administrative entity within the Department to review consular visa denials. Such an administrative entity might be established either within an expanded Visa Office or as an independent visa review board.

6. *Judicial Review*

Congress should determine whether there is a need to authorize access to the courts for those adversely affected by denials of visas or certain types of them. If such a need is determined to exist, Congress should consider implementing three guidelines.

First, judicial process should be available only for questions of law, including abuse of discretion.

Second, following exhaustion of any administrative remedies, federal district courts should have jurisdiction.

Third, standing should be provided for applicants and for petitioners on behalf of applicants.

---

391. 8 U.S.C. § 1104(a).

338 U.S. 537

UNITED STATES ex rel. KNAUFF v.
SHAUGHNESSY.

No. 54.

Argued Dec. 5, 1949.

Decided Jan. 16, 1950.

Habeas corpus proceedings by the United States, on the relation of Ellen Knauff, against Edward J. Shaughnessy, Acting Director of Immigration and Naturalization, to determine the right of an alien war bride to enter the United States.

The United States Court of Appeals for the Second Circuit, 173 F.2d 599, affirmed the judgment of the District Court that the Attorney General during the national emergency had the power to bar the relatrix without a hearing, and the relatrix was granted a writ of certiorari.

The Supreme Court, in an opinion by Mr. Justice Minton, affirmed the judgment.

Mr. Justice Jackson, Mr. Justice Black and Mr. Justice Frankfurter, dissented.

1. Aliens ⊕18

Admission into the United States may not be claimed by aliens as a right but only as a privilege granted on terms prescribed by the United States government and the privilege must be exercised in conformity with the procedure provided.

2. Constitutional law ⊕62
War and national defense ⊕36

The 1941 Act empowering the President to impose additional restrictions and prohibitions on the entry into the United States during the national emergency proclaimed on May 27, 1941, and the regulations thereunder which enabled the Attorney General to deny an alien a hearing before a board of inquiry where he determined that the alien was excludable under the regulations on the basis of information of a confidential nature, the disclosure of which would be prejudicial to the public interest, are not unconstitutional delegations of legislative power. 22 U.S.C.A. § 223; Presidential Proclamation No. 2523, 55 Stat. 1696.

3. Aliens ⊕18

The exclusion of aliens is a fundamental act of sovereignty that inheres in the executive no less than in the legislative

power, and when Congress prescribes procedure for the admission of aliens it merely implements such inherent executive power.

4. Constitutional law ⊕62

The decision to admit or exclude an alien may be lawfully placed with the President, who may delegate such power to a responsible executive officer, such as the Attorney General, whose decision is conclusive.

5. Aliens ⊕54(14)

Unless expressly authorized by law no court may review the determination of the political branch of the government to exclude a given alien.

6. Constitutional law ⊕62

Congress may in broad terms authorize the executive to exclude aliens for the best interests of the country during a national emergency, since the power to exclude aliens is inherent in the executive department of Government, although Congress ordinarily prescribes the conditions on which aliens may be admitted or excluded.

7. Constitutional law ⊕62

Congress need not supply administrative officials with a specific formula for their guidance in a field where flexibility and the adaptation of congressional policy to infinitely variable conditions constitute the essence of the program.

8. Statutes ⊕184, 208, 213, 215

Standards prescribed by Congress must be read in the light of the conditions to which they are to be applied, and they derive much meaningful content from the purpose of the act, its factual background and the statutory context in which they appear.

9. Constitutional law ⊕252

The denial of entry into the United States to an alien in conformity with procedure authorized by Congress is due process, whatever the procedure may be.

10. War and national defense ⊕49

Regulations which enable the Attorney General during the national emergency of World War II to deny an alien a hearing before a board of inquiry where he determines that the alien is excludable under the regulations on the basis of information of a confidential nature, the disclosure of which will be prejudicial to the public interest, are reasonable. 22 U.S.C.A. § 223; Presidential Proclamation No. 2523, 55 Stat. 1696.

11. War and national defense ⬤49

Under later Presidential Proclamation amending and clarifying a prior proclamation regarding the exclusion of aliens during the national emergency of World War II the Attorney General was authorized to order the exclusion of aliens. Presidential Proclamation Aug. 17, 1947, No. 2850.

12. Constitutional law ⬤92

An alien had no vested right to entry which could be the subject of a prohibition against retroactive operation of regulations affecting her status.

13. War and national defense ⬤49

The War Brides Act providing for entry as nonquota immigrants of alien spouses of citizens serving in or honorably discharged from armed forces of United States during Second World War, notwithstanding statutes excluding defective aliens, Executive Orders or Presidential Proclamations issued thereunder, if otherwise admissible under immigration laws, and providing that for purpose of such act the Second World War shall be deemed to have commenced on December 7, 1941, and to have ceased on termination of hostilities as declared by the President or by a joint congressional resolution, did not affect Act of June 21, 1941, and the President's proclamations thereunder providing for exclusion of aliens by Attorney General without a hearing during the national emergency where he determined that alien was excludable under the regulations on information the disclosure of which would be prejudicial to the public interest. 22 U.S.C.A. § 223; Presidential Proclamation No. 2523, 55 Stat. 1696; Immigration Act of 1917, §§ 16, 17, as amended 8 U.S.C.A. §§ 152, 153.

14. War and national defense ⬤49

The provision in the War Brides Act that for purpose thereof the Second World War shall be deemed to have commenced on December 7, 1941, and to have ceased upon termination of hostilities, etc., was intended to define the period within which citizens must have served in the armed forces in order that their spouses and children might have the benefits of such act. Immigration Act of 1917, §§ 16, 17, as amended, 8 U.S.C.A. §§ 152, 153.

15. War and national defense ⬤49

The national emergency during which the Attorney General was authorized to exclude without a hearing an alien still exists. 22 U.S.C.A. § 223; Presidential Proclamation No. 2523, 55 Stat. 1696.

16. War and national defense ⬤49

An alien spouse of an honorably discharged member of the armed forces of the United States during the Second World War who during the national emergency had been excluded without a hearing by the Attorney General on the basis of information, the disclosure of which would be prejudicial to the public interest, was not "otherwise admissible under the immigration laws" within the War Brides Act and the decision of the Attorney General was conclusive. Immigration Act of 1917, §§ 16, 17, as amended, 8 U.S.C.A. §§ 152, 153; 22 U.S.C.A. § 223; Presidential Proclamation No. 2523, 55 Stat. 1696.

538

Mr. Gunther Jacobson, New York City, for petitioner.

Mr. Philip R. Monahan, Washington, D. C., for respondent.

539

Mr. Justice MINTON delivered the opinion of the Court.

May the United States exclude without hearing, solely upon a finding by the Attorney General that her admission would be prejudicial to the interests of the United States, the alien wife of a citizen who had served honorably in the armed forces of the United States during World War II? The District Court for the Southern District of New York held that it could, and the Court of Appeals for the Second Circuit affirmed. 173 F.2d 599. We granted certiorari to examine the question especially in the light of the War Brides Act of December 28, 1945, 8 U.S.C.A. § 232 et seq., 336 U.S. 966, 69 S.Ct. 941.

Petitioner was born in Germany in 1915. She left Germany and went to Czechoslovakia during the Hitler regime. There she was married and divorced. She went to England in 1939 as a refugee. Thereafter she served with the Royal Air Force efficiently and honorably from January 1, 1943, until May 30, 1946. She then secured civilian employment with the War Department of the United States in Germany. Her work was rated "very good" and "excellent." On February 28, 1948, with the permission of the Commanding General at Frankfurt, Germany, she married Kurt W. Knauff, a naturalized citizen of the United States. He is an honorably discharged United States Army veteran of World War II. He is, as he was at the time of his marriage, a civilian employee of the United States Army at Frankfurt, Germany.

On August 14, 1948, petitioner sought to enter the United States to be naturalized. On that day she was temporarily excluded from the United States and detained at Ellis Island. On October 6, 1948, the Assistant Commissioner of Immigration and Naturalization recommended that she be permanently excluded without a hearing on the ground that her admission would be

540

prejudicial to the interests of the United States. On the same day the Attorney General adopted this recommendation and entered a final order of exclusion. To test the right of the Attorney General to exclude her without a hearing for security reasons, *habeas corpus* proceedings were instituted in the Southern District of New York, based primarily on provisions of the War Brides Act. The District Court dismissed the writ, and the Court of Appeals affirmed.

The authority of the Attorney General to order the exclusion of aliens without a hearing flows from the Act of June 21, 1941, amending § 1 of the Act of May 22, 1918, 55 Stat. 252, 22 U.S.C. § 223, 22 U.S.C.A. § 223.[1] By the 1941 amendment it was provided that the President might, upon finding that the interests of the United States required it, impose additional restrictions and prohibitions on the entry into and departure of persons from the United States during the national emergency proclaimed May 27, 1941. Pursuant to this Act of Congress the President on November 14, 1941, issued Proclamation 2523, 55 Stat. 1696, 3 CFR, 1943 Cum.Supp., 270–272. This proclamation recited that the interests of the United States required the imposition of additional restrictions upon the entry into and

541

departure of persons from the country and authorized the promulgation of regulations jointly by the Secretary of State and the Attorney General. It was also provided that no alien should be permitted to enter the United States if it were found that such entry would be prejudicial to the interests of the United States.[2]

---

1. "When the United States is at war or during the existence of the national emergency proclaimed by the President on May 27, 1941, or as to aliens whenever there exists a state of war between, or among, two or more states, and the President shall find that the interests of the United States require that restrictions and prohibitions in addition to those provided otherwise than by this Act be imposed upon the departure of persons from and their entry into the United States, and shall make public proclamation thereof, it shall, until otherwise ordered by the President or Congress, be unlawful—

"(a) For any alien to depart from or

enter or attempt to depart from or enter the United States except under such reasonable rules, regulations, and orders, and subject to such limitations and exceptions as the President shall prescribe * * *."

2. "(3) After the effective date of the rules and regulations hereinafter authorized, no alien shall enter or attempt to enter the United States unless he is in possession of a valid unexpired permit to enter issued by the Secretary of State, or by an appropriate officer designated by the Secretary of State, or is exempted from obtaining a permit to enter in accordance

Pursuant to the authority of this proclamation the Secretary of State and the Attorney General issued regulations governing the entry into and departure of persons from the United States during the national emergency. Subparagraphs (a) to (k) of § 175.53 of these regulations specified the classes of aliens whose entry into the United States was deemed prejudicial to the public interest. Subparagraph (b) of § 175.57 provided that the Attorney General might deny an alien a hearing before a board of inquiry in special cases where he determined that the alien was excludable under the regulations on the basis of information of a confidential nature, the disclosure of which would be prejudicial to the public interest.[3]

542

It was under this regulation § 175.57(b) that petitioner was excluded by the Attorney General and denied a hearing. We are asked to pass upon the validity of this action.

[1] At the outset we wish to point out that an alien who seeks admission to this country may not do so under any claim of right. Admission of aliens to the United States is a privilege granted by the sovereign United States Government. Such privilege is granted to an alien only upon such terms as the United States shall prescribe. It must be exercised in accordance with the procedure which the United States provides. Nishimura Ekiu v. United States, 142 U.S. 651, 659, 12 S.Ct. 336, 338, 35 L.Ed. 1146; Fong Yue Ting v. United States, 149 U.S. 698, 711, 13 S.Ct. 1016, 1021, 37 L.Ed. 905.

[2, 3] Petitioner contends that the 1941 Act and the regulations thereunder are void to the extent that they contain unconstitutional delegations of legislative power. But there is no question of inappropriate delegation of legislative power involved here. The exclusion of aliens is a fundamental act of sovereignty. The right to do so stems not alone from legislative power but is inherent in the executive power to control the foreign affairs of the nation. United States v. Curtiss-Wright Export Corp., 299 U.S. 304, 57 S.Ct. 216, 81 L.Ed. 255; Fong Yue Ting v. United States, 149 U.S. 698, 713, 13 S.Ct. 1016, 1022, 37 L.Ed. 905. When Congress prescribes a procedure concerning the admissibility of aliens, it is not dealing alone with a legislative power. It is implementing an inherent executive power.

543

[4-9] Thus the decision to admit or to exclude an alien may be lawfully placed with the President, who may in turn delegate the carrying out of this function to a responsible executive officer of the sovereign, such as the Attorney General. The action of the executive officer under such authority is final and conclusive. Whatever the rule may be concerning deportation of persons who have gained entry into the United States, it is not within the province of any court, unless ex-

---

with the rules and regulations which the Secretary of State, with the concurrence of the Attorney General, is hereby authorized to prescribe in execution of these rules, regulations, and orders.

"No alien shall be permitted to enter the United States if it appears to the satisfaction of the Secretary of State that such entry would be prejudicial to the interests of the United States as provided in the rules and regulations hereinbefore authorized to be prescribed by the Secretary of State, with the concurrence of the Attorney General." 3 CFR, 1943 Cum. Supp., 271.

3. "In the case of an alien temporarily excluded by an official of the Department of Justice on the ground that he is, or

may be excludable under one or more of the categories set forth in § 175.53, no hearing by a board of special inquiry shall be held until after the case is reported to the Attorney General and such a hearing is directed by the Attorney General or his representative. In any special case the alien may be denied a hearing before a board of special inquiry and an appeal from the decision of that board if the Attorney General determines that he is excludable under one of the categories set forth in § 175.53 on the basis of information of a confidential nature, the disclosure of which would be prejudicial to the public interest." 8 CFR, 1945 Supp., § 175.57(b).

pressly authorized by law, to review the determination of the political branch of the Government to exclude a given alien. Nishimura Ekiu v. United States, 142 U.S. 651, 659-660, 12 S.Ct. 336, 338, 35 L.Ed. 1146; Fong Yue Ting v. United States, 149 U.S. 698, 713-714, 13 S.Ct. 1016, 1022, 37 L.Ed. 905; Ludecke v. Watkins, 335 U.S. 160, 68 S.Ct. 1429, 92 L.Ed. 1881. Cf. Yamataya v. Fisher, 189 U.S. 86, 101, 23 S.Ct. 611, 614, 47 L.Ed. 721. Normally Congress supplies the conditions of the privilege of entry into the United States. But because the power of exclusion of aliens is also inherent in the executive department of the sovereign, Congress may in broad terms authorize the executive to exercise the power, e. g., as was done here, for the best interests of the country during a time of national emergency. Executive officers may be entrusted with the duty of specifying the procedures for carrying out the congressional intent. What was said in Lichter v. United States, 334 U.S. 742, 785, 68 S.Ct. 1294, 1316, 92 L.Ed. 1694, is equally appropriate here:

"It is not necessary that Congress supply administrative officials with a specific formula for their guidance in a field where flexibility and the adaptation of the congressional policy to infinitely variable conditions constitute the essence of the program. * * * Standards prescribed by Congress are to be read in the light of the conditions to which they are to be applied. 'They derive much meaningful content from the purpose of the Act, its factual background and the statutory context in which they appear.'"

544

Whatever the procedure authorized by Congress is, it is due process as far as an alien denied entry is concerned. Nishimura Ekiu v. United States, supra; Ludecke v. Watkins, supra.

In the particular circumstances of the instant case the Attorney General, exercising the discretion entrusted to him by Congress and the President, concluded upon the basis of confidential information that the public interest required that petitioner be denied the privilege of entry into the United States. He denied her a hearing on the matter because, in his judgment, the disclosure of the information on which he based that opinion would itself endanger the public security.

[10-12] We find no substantial merit to petitioner's contention that the regulations were not "reasonable" as they were required to be by the 1941 Act. We think them reasonable in the circumstances of the period for which they were authorized, namely, the national emergency of World War II. Nor can we agree with petitioner's assertion that Proclamation 2523, see note 2, supra, authorized only the Secretary of State, and not the Attorney General, to order the exclusion of aliens. See Presidential Proclamation 2850 of August 17, 1949, 14 Fed.Reg. 5173, amending and clarifying Proclamation 2523. We reiterate that we are dealing here with a matter of *privilege*. Petitioner had no vested *right* of entry which could be the subject of a prohibition against retroactive operation of regulations affecting her status.

It is not disputed that the Attorney General's action was pursuant to the 8 CFR regulations heretofore discussed.[4] However, 22 U.S.C. § 223, 22 U.S.C.A. § 223,[5] authorizes these special restrictions on the entry of aliens only when the United States is at war or during the existence of the

545

national emergency proclaimed May 27, 1941, No. 2487, 50 U.S.C.A.Appendix note preceding section 1.[6] For ordinary times Congress has provided aliens with a hearing. 8 U.S.C. §§ 152, 153, 8 U.S.C.A. §§ 152, 153. And the contention of petitioner is that she is entitled to the statutory hearing because for purposes of the War Brides Act, within which she comes, the war terminated when the President proclaimed the

---

4. See note 3, supra.
5. See note 1, supra.

70 S.Ct.—20½

6. And at certain other times not material here.

cessation of hostilities.[7] She contends that the War Brides Act, applicable portions of which are set out in the margin,[8] discloses a congressional intent that special restrictions on the entry of aliens should cease to apply to war brides upon the cessation of hostilities.

[13-15] The War Brides Act provides that World War II is the period from December 7, 1941, until the proclaimed termination of hostilities. This has nothing to do with the period for which the regulations here acted under were

546

authorized. The beginning and end of the war are defined by the War Brides Act, we assume, for the purpose of ascertaining the period within which citizens must have served in the armed forces in order for their spouses and children to be entitled to the benefits of the Act. The special procedure followed in this case was authorized not only during the period of actual hostilities but during the entire war and the national emergency proclaimed May 27, 1941. The national emergency has never been terminated. Indeed, a state of war still exists. See Woods v. Cloyd W. Miller Co., 333 U.S. 138, Note 3, 68 S.Ct. 421, 422, 92 L.Ed. 596. Thus, the authority upon which the Attorney General acted remains in force. The Act of June 21, 1941, and the President's proclamations and the regulations thereunder are still a part of the immigration laws.

[16] The War Brides Act does not relieve petitioner of her alien status. Indeed, she sought admission in order to be naturalized and thus to overcome her alien status. The Act relieved her of certain physical, mental, and documentary requirements and of the quota provisions of the immigration laws. But she must, as the Act requires, still be "otherwise admissible under the immigration laws". In other words, aside from the enumerated relaxations of the immigration laws she must be treated as any other alien seeking admission. Under the immigration laws and regulations applicable to all aliens seeking entry into the United States during the national emergency, she was excluded by the Attorney General without a hearing. In such a case we have no authority to retry the determination of the Attorney General. Ludecke v. Watkins, 335 U.S. 160, 171-172, 68 S.Ct. 1429, 1434-1435, 92 L.Ed. 1881.

There is nothing in the War Brides Act or its legislative history[9] to indicate that it was the purpose of Congress,

547

by partially suspending compliance with certain requirements and the quota provisions of the immigration laws, to relax the security provisions of the immigration laws. There is no indication that Congress intended to

---

7. Proclamation 2714 of December 31, 1946, 50 U.S.C.A.Appendix, § 601 note, 3 CFR, 1946 Supp., 77.

8. "That notwithstanding any of the several clauses of section 3 of the Act of February 5, 1917, excluding physically and mentally defective aliens, and notwithstanding the documentary requirements of any of the immigration laws or regulations, Executive orders, or Presidential proclamations issued thereunder, alien spouses or alien children of United States citizens serving in, or having an honorable discharge certificate from the armed forces of the United States during the Second World War shall, if otherwise admissible under the immigration laws and if application for admission is made within three years of the effective date of this Act, be admitted to the United States * * *.

"Sec. 2. Regardless of section 9 of the Immigration Act of 1924, any alien admitted under section 1 of this Act shall be deemed to be a nonquota immigrant as defined in section 4(a) of the Immigration Act of 1924.

*   *   *   *   *   *   *

"Sec. 5. For the purpose of this Act, the Second World War shall be deemed to have commenced on December 7, 1941, and to have ceased upon the termination of hostilities as declared by the President or by a joint resolution of Congress." 59 Stat. 659, 8 U.S.C. §§ 232-236, 8 U.S.C.A. §§ 232-236.

9. See H.R.Rep. No. 1320, 79th Cong., 1st Sess. (1945); S.Rep. No. 860, 79th Cong., 1st Sess. (1945); 91 Cong.Rec. 11738, 12342 (1945).

permit members or former members of the armed forces to marry and bring into the United States aliens who the President, acting through the Attorney General in the performance of his sworn duty, found should be denied entry for security reasons. As all other aliens, petitioner had to stand the test of security. This she failed to meet. We find no legal defect in the manner of petitioner's exclusion, and the judgment is affirmed.

Affirmed.

Mr. Justice DOUGLAS and Mr. Justice CLARK took no part in the consideration or decision of this case.

Mr. Justice FRANKFURTER, dissenting.

If the essence of statutory construction is to find the thought beneath the words, the views expressed by Mr. Justice JACKSON, in which I fully concur, enforce the purpose of Congress. The contrary conclusion substantially frustrates it.

Seventy years ago began the policy of excluding mentally defective aliens from admission into the United States. Thirty years ago it became our settled policy to admit even the most desirable aliens only in accordance with the quota system. By the so-called War Brides Act Congress made inroads upon both these deeply-rooted policies. Act of December 28, 1945, 59 Stat. 659, 8 U.S.C. § 232 et seq., 8 U.S.C.A. § 232 et seq. It lifted the bar against the exclusion even of "physically and mentally defective aliens." It did this in favor of "alien spouses and alien minor children of citizen members who are serving or have served honorably in the armed forces of the United States during World War II." H.R.Rep.No.1320 and S.Rep.No.860, 79th Cong., 1st Sess. (1945).

548

This was a bounty afforded by Congress not to the alien who had become the wife of an American but to the citizen who had honorably served his country. Congress gave this bounty even though a physically or mentally defective person might thereby be added to the population of the United States. Yet it is suggested that the deepest tie that an American soldier could form may be secretly severed on the mere say-so of an official, however well-intentioned. Although five minutes of cross-examination could enable the soldier-husband to dissipate seemingly convincing information affecting the security danger of his wife, that opportunity need not be accorded. And all this, because of the literal reading of the provision of the War Brides Act that the alien spouse, though physically and mentally defective, is to be allowed to join her citizen husband "if otherwise admissible under the immigration laws". Upon that phrase is rested the whole structure of Executive regulation based on § 1 of the Act of May 22, 1918, 40 Stat. 559, as amended by the Act of June 21, 1941, 55 Stat. 252, 22 U.S.C. § 223, 22 U.S.C.A. § 223, regarding the summary exclusion, without opportunity for a hearing, of an alien whose entry the Attorney General finds inimical to the public interest.[1]

This is not the way to read such legislation. It is true also of Acts of Congress that "The letter killeth." Legislation should not be read in such a decimating spirit unless the letter of Congress is inexorable. We are reminded from time to time that in enacting legislation Congress is not engaged in a scientific process which takes account of every contingency. Its laws are not to be read as though every *i* has to be dotted and every *t*

549

crossed. The War Brides Act is legislation derived from the dominant regard which American society

1. The Attorney General is to act on information that satisfies him, but not only is there no opportunity for a hearing, but the Attorney General can lock in his own bosom the evidence that does satisfy him. 8 C.F.R. §§ 175.53, 175.57 (1949).

places upon the family. It is not to be assumed that Congress gave with a bountiful hand but allowed its bounty arbitrarily to be taken away. In framing and passing the War Brides Act, Congress was preoccupied with opening the door to wives acquired by American husbands during service in foreign lands. It opened the door on essentials—wives of American soldiers and perchance mothers of their children were not to run the gauntlet of administrative discretion in determining their physical and mental condition, and were to be deemed nonquota immigrants. Congress ought not to be made to appear to require that they incur the greater hazards of an informer's tale without any opportunity for its refutation, especially since considerations of national security, insofar as they are pertinent, can be amply protected by a hearing *in camera*. Compare Rule 46 of the Rules of Practice for Admiralty Courts during World War II, 316 U.S. 717; 328 U.S. 882, and see Haydock, *Some Evidentiary Problems Posed by Atomic Energy Security Requirements,* 61 Harv.L.Rev. 468, 482–83 (1948). An alien's opportunity of entry into the United States is of course a privilege which Congress may grant or withhold. But the crux of the problem before us is whether Congress, having extended the privilege for the benefit not of the alien but of her American husband, left wide open the opportunity ruthlessly to take away what it gave.

A regulation permitting such exclusion by the Attorney General's fiat—in the nature of things that high functionary must largely act on dossiers prepared by others—in the case of an alien claiming entry on his own account is one thing. To construe such regulation to be authorized and to apply in the case of the wife of an honorably

550

discharged American soldier is quite another thing. Had Congress spoken explicitly we would have to bow to it. Such a substantial contradiction of the congressional beneficence which is at the heart of the War Brides Act ought not to be attributed to Congress by a process of elaborate implication. Especially is this to be avoided when

to do so charges Congress with an obviously harsh purpose. Due regard for the whole body of immigration laws and policies makes it singularly appropriate in construing the War Brides Act to be heedful of the admonition that "The letter killeth."

Mr. Justice JACKSON, whom Mr. Justice BLACK and Mr. Justice FRANKFURTER join, dissenting.

I do not question the constitutional power of Congress to authorize immigration authorities to turn back from our gates any alien or class of aliens. But I do not find that Congress has authorized an abrupt and brutal exclusion of the wife of an American citizen without a hearing.

Congress held out a promise of liberalized admission to alien brides, taken unto themselves by men serving in or honorably discharged from our armed services abroad, as the Act, set forth in the Court's opinion, indicates. The petitioning husband is honorably discharged and remained in Germany as a civilian employee. Our military authorities abroad required their permission before marriage. The Army in Germany is not without a vigilant and security-conscious intelligence service. This woman was employed by our European Command and her record is not only without blemish, but is highly praised by her superiors. The marriage of this alien woman to this veteran was approved by the Commanding General at Frankfurt-on-Main.

Now this American citizen is told he cannot bring his wife to the United States, but he will not be told why.

551

He must abandon his bride to live in his own country or forsake his country to live with his bride.

So he went to court and sought a writ of *habeas corpus,* which we never tire of citing to Europe as the unanswerable evidence that our free country permits no arbitrary official detention. And the Government tells the Court that not even a court can find out why the girl is excluded. But it says we must find that Congress authorized this treatment of war brides and, even if we cannot get any reasons for it, we must say it is legal; security requires it.

Security is like liberty in that many are the crimes committed in its name. The menace to the security of this country, be it great as it may, from this girl's admission is as nothing compared to the menace to free institutions inherent in procedures of this pattern. In the name of security the police state justifies its arbitrary oppressions on evidence that is secret, because security might be prejudiced if it were brought to light in hearings. The plea that evidence of guilt must be secret is abhorrent to free men, because it provides a cloak for the malevolent, the misinformed, the meddlesome, and the corrupt to play the role of informer undetected and uncorrected. Cf. In re Oliver, 333 U. S. 257, 268, 68 S.Ct. 499, 505, 92 L.Ed. 682.

I am sure the officials here have acted from a sense of duty, with full belief in their lawful power, and no doubt upon information which, if it stood the test of trial, would justify the order of exclusion. But not even they know whether it would stand this test. And anyway, as I have said before, personal confidence in the officials involved does not excuse a judge for sanctioning a procedure that is dangerously wrong in principle. Dissent in Bowles v. United States, 319 U.S. 33, 37, 63 S.Ct. 912, 914, 87 L.Ed. 1194.

Congress will have to use more explicit language than any yet cited before I will agree that it has authorized an administrative officer to break up the family of an

552

American citizen or force him to keep his wife by becoming an exile. Likewise, it will have to be much more explicit before I can agree that it authorized a finding of serious misconduct against the wife of an American citizen without notice of charges, evidence of guilt and a chance to meet it.

I should direct the Attorney General either to produce his evidence justifying exclusion or to admit Mrs. Knauff to the country.

459 U.S. 21, 74 L.Ed.2d 21

Michael LANDON, District Director of the Immigration and Naturalization Service, Petitioner

v.

Maria Antonieta PLASENCIA.

No. 81–129.

Argued Oct. 5, 1982.

Decided Nov. 15, 1982.

Alien filed petition for writ of habeas corpus, seeking release from Immigration and Naturalization Service's exclusion order and contending that she was entitled to have the question of her admissibility litigated in a deportation proceeding where she would be entitled to procedural protections and substantive rights not available in exclusion proceedings. The United States District Court for the Central District of California vacated the INS decision, and it appealed. The Court of Appeals, Ninth Circuit, 637 F.2d 1286, affirmed, and certiorari was granted. The Supreme Court, Justice O'Connor, held that the INS had statutory authority to proceed in an exclusion hearing to determine whether respondent, a permanent resident alien who was denied admission to the United States by INS when she returned from a brief visit to Mexico that involved an attempt to smuggle aliens across the border, was attempting to "enter" the United States and whether she was excludable; nothing in the language or history of the Immigration and Nationality Act suggested that respondent's status as a permanent resident entitled her to a suspension of the exclusion hearing or required INS to proceed only through a deportation hearing.

Reversed and remanded.

Justice Marshall filed an opinion concurring in part and dissenting in part.

1. Aliens ⚌54(3)

Immigration laws create two types of proceedings in which aliens can be denied the hospitality of the United States, viz., deportation hearings and exclusion hearings; a deportation hearing is the usual means of proceeding against an alien already physically in the United States, and an exclusion hearing is the usual means of proceeding against an alien outside the United States seeking admission.

2. Aliens ⚌54(3)

An exclusion proceeding is usually held at the port of entry, while a deportation hearing is usually held near the residence of the alien within the United States.

3. Aliens ⚌54(2)

Regulations of the Attorney General require in most deportation proceedings that the alien be given seven days' notice of the charges against him, while there is no requirement of advance notice of the charges for an alien subject to exclusion proceedings. Immigration and Nationality Act, § 242(b) as amended 8 U.S.C.A. § 1252(b).

4. Aliens ⚌54.3(1)
  Habeas Corpus ⚌23

If the Immigration and Naturalization Service prevails in a deportation proceeding, the alien may appeal directly to the Court of Appeals, while the alien can challenge an exclusion order only by petition for writ of habeas corpus. Immigration and Nationality Act, § 106(a,b) as amended 8 U.S.C.A. § 1105a(a,b).

5. Aliens ⚌53.10(1, 2), 54.2(2)

Alien who loses his right to reside in the United States in a deportation hearing has a number of substantive rights not available to the alien who is denied admission in an exclusion proceeding: he can, within certain limits, designate the country of deportation, he may be able to depart voluntarily, thus avoiding both the stigma of deportation and the limitations on his selection of destination, and he can seek suspension of deportation. Immigration and Nationality Act, §§ 212(a)(16, 17), 242(b,e) 243(a), 244(e) as amended 8 U.S. C.A. §§ 1182(a)(16, 17), 1252(b,e), 1253(a), 1254(e).

6. Aliens ⬄53.10(1)

Voluntary departure for an alien who would otherwise be deported means that he will not be subject to provision of the Immigration and Nationality Act which requires aliens who have once been deported to seek prior approval of the Attorney General before reentering; there is no comparable requirement of prior approval for aliens who have been excluded and later seek again to enter. Immigration and Nationality Act, § 212(a)(16, 17) as amended 8 U.S. C.A. § 1182(a)(16, 17).

7. Aliens ⬄54(3)

Immigration and Naturalization Service had statutory authority to proceed in an exclusion hearing to determine whether respondent, a permanent resident alien who was denied admission to the United States by INS when she returned from a brief visit to Mexico that involved an attempt to smuggle aliens across the border, was attempting to "enter" the United States and whether she was excludable; nothing in the language or history of the Immigration and Nationality Act suggested that respondent's status as a permanent resident entitled her to a suspension of the exclusion hearing or required INS to proceed only through a deportation hearing. Immigration and Nationality Act, § 101 et seq. as amended 8 U.S.C.A. § 1101 et seq.

8. Aliens ⬄46

Only "entering" aliens are subject to exclusion. Immigration and Nationality Act, § 236(a) as amended 8 U.S.C.A. § 1226(a).

9. Aliens ⬄53.6(2)

An innocent, casual, and brief excursion by a resident outside this country's borders would not subject him to consequences of an "entry" on his return, but if the purpose of leaving the country is to accomplish some object which is itself contrary to some policy reflected in our immigration laws, it would appear that the interruption of residence thereby occurring would properly be regarded as meaningful. Immigration and Nationality Act,

§ 101(a)(13) as amended 8 U.S.C.A. § 1101(a)(13).

10. Aliens ⬄54(3)

It was not "circular" and "unfair" to allow the Immigration and Naturalization Service to litigate the question of "entry" in exclusion proceedings simply because that question also went to the merits of respondent's admissibility.

11. Aliens ⬄54(3)

Use of exclusion proceedings to litigate the question of "entry" by respondent did not violate either the "scope" or "spirit" of the *Fleuti* decision, in which the Supreme Court held that an "innocent, casual and brief excursion" by a resident alien outside this country's borders would not subject him to the consequences of an "entry" on his return. Immigration and Nationality Act, § 101(a)(13) as amended 8 U.S.C.A. § 1101(a)(13).

12. Aliens ⬄54.3(6)

Although respondent was entitled to due process in her exclusion hearing, the case would be remanded to the Court of Appeals to consider whether respondent was accorded due process, since the factors relevant to due process analysis had not been adequately presented to permit an assessment of the sufficiency of the hearing. U.S.C.A. Const.Amends. 5, 14.

13. Aliens ⬄39

An alien seeking initial admission to the United States requests a privilege and has no constitutional rights regarding his application, for the power to admit or exclude aliens is a sovereign prerogative.

14. Aliens ⬄3

Once an alien gains admission to the United States and begins to develop the ties that go with permanent residence, his constitutional status changes accordingly.

15. Aliens ⬄54(4)

A continuously present resident alien is entitled to a fair hearing when threatened with deportation.

16. Constitutional Law ⊗⇒252.5

Constitutional sufficiency of procedures provided in any situation varies with the circumstances, and the courts, in evaluating the procedures in any case, must consider the interest at stake for the individual, the risk of an erroneous deprivation of the interest through the procedures used as well as the probable value of additional or different procedural safeguards, and the interest of the government in using the current procedures rather than additional or different procedures.

17. Aliens ⊗⇒39, 54.3(2)

Control over matters of immigration is a sovereign prerogative, largely within the control of the executive and the legislature; the role of the judiciary is limited to determining whether the procedures meet the essential standard of fairness under the due process clause and does not extend to imposing procedures that merely displace congressional choices of policy. U.S.C.A. Const.Amends. 5, 14.

Syllabus *

Section 235 of the Immigration and Nationality Act of 1952 (Act) permits the Immigration and Naturalization Service (INS) to examine "all aliens" who seek "admission or readmission to" the United States and empowers immigration officers to take evidence concerning the privilege of any persons suspected of being an alien "to enter, reenter, pass through, or reside" in the United States, and to detain for further inquiry "every alien" who does not appear "to be clearly and beyond a doubt entitled to" enter. Under § 236(a), if an alien is so detained, the officer is directed to determine whether the alien "shall be allowed to enter or shall be excluded and deported." Following an exclusion hearing, the INS denied respondent, a permanent resident alien, admission to the United States when she returned from a brief visit to Mexico that involved an attempt to smuggle aliens

across the border. Subsequently, respondent filed a petition for a writ of habeas corpus in Federal District Court, seeking release from the exclusion order and contending that she was entitled to have the question of her admissibility litigated in a deportation proceeding where she would be entitled to procedural protections and substantive rights not available in exclusion proceedings. The District Court vacated the INS's decision, instructing it to proceed against respondent, if at all, only in deportation proceedings. The Court of Appeals affirmed.

Held:

1. The INS had statutory authority to proceed in an exclusion hearing to determine whether respondent was attempting to "enter" the United States and whether she was excludable. The language and history of the Act both clearly reflect a congressional intent that, whether or not the alien is a permanent resident, admissibility shall be determined in an exclusion hearing. Nothing in the language or history suggests that respondent's status as a permanent resident entitles her to a suspension of the exclusion hearing or requires the INS to proceed only through a deportation hearing. Pp. 325–327.

2. Contrary to the view of the Court of Appeals, it was not "circular" and "unfair" to allow the INS to litigate the question of "entry" in exclusion proceedings simply because that question also went to the merits of respondent's admissibility. Nor did the use of exclusion proceedings violate either the "scope" or "spirit" of *Rosenberg v. Fleuti,* 374 U.S. 449, 83 S.Ct. 1804, 10 L.Ed.2d 1000, where the Court held that an "innocent, casual, and brief excursion" by a resident alien outside this country's borders would not subject him to the consequences of an "entry" on his return. Pp. 327–329.

3. Although under the circumstances, respondent is entitled to due process in her exclusion hearing, the case will be remand-

|₂₂

---

* The syllabus constitutes no part of the opinion of the Court but has been prepared by the Reporter of Decisions for the convenience of the reader. See *United States v. Detroit Lumber Co.,* 200 U.S. 321, 337, 26 S.Ct. 282, 287, 50 L.Ed. 499.

ed to the Court of Appeals to consider whether she was accorded due process, because the factors relevant to due process analysis have not been adequately presented here to permit an assessment of the sufficiency of the hearing. Pp. 329–332.

9th Cir., 637 F.2d 1286, reversed and remanded.

———

Elliott Schulder, Washington, D.C., for petitioner.

Gary H. Manulkin, Los Angeles, Cal., for respondent.

———

Justice O'CONNOR delivered the opinion of the Court.

Following an exclusion hearing, the Immigration and Naturalization Service (INS) denied the respondent, a permanent resident alien, admission to the United States when she attempted to return from a brief visit abroad. Reviewing the respondent's subsequent petition for a writ of habeas corpus, the Court of Appeals vacated the decision, holding that the question whether the respondent was attempting to "enter" the United States could be litigated only in a deportation hearing and not in an exclusion hearing. Because we conclude that the INS has statutory authority to proceed in an exclusion hearing, we reverse the judgment below. We remand to allow the Court of Appeals to consider whether respondent, a permanent resident alien, was accorded due process at the exclusion hearing.

1. Section 235, as set forth in 8 U.S.C. § 1225, provides in part:

(a) "The inspection ... of aliens (including alien crewmen) seeking admission or readmission to ... the United States shall be conducted by immigration officers, except as otherwise provided in regard to special inquiry officers. All aliens arriving at ports of the United States shall be examined by one or more immigration officers at the discretion of the Attorney General and under such regulations as he may prescribe...."

(b) "Every alien ... who may not appear to the examining immigration officer at the port of arrival to be clearly and beyond a doubt entitled

|I

Respondent Maria Antonieta Plasencia, a citizen of El Salvador, entered the United States as a permanent resident alien in March 1970. She established a home in Los Angeles with her husband, a United States citizen, and their minor children. On June 27, 1975, she and her husband traveled to Tijuana, Mexico. During their brief stay in Mexico, they met with several Mexican and Salvadoran nationals and made arrangements to assist their illegal entry into the United States. She agreed to transport the aliens to Los Angeles and furnished some of the aliens with alien registration receipt cards that belonged to her children. When she and her husband attempted to cross the international border at 9:27 on the evening of June 29, 1975, an INS officer at the port of entry found six nonresident aliens in the Plasencias' car. The INS detained the respondent for further inquiry pursuant to § 235(b) of the Immigration and Nationality Act of 1952 (Act), 66 Stat. 182, as amended, 8 U.S.C. § 1101 et seq.[1] In a notice dated June 30, 1975, the INS charged her under § 212(a)(31) of the Act, 8 U.S.C. § 1182(a)(31), which provides for the exclusion of any alien seeking admission "who at any time shall have, knowingly and for gain, encouraged, induced, assisted, abetted, or aided any other alien to enter or to try to enter the United States in violation of law," and gave notice that it would hold an exclusion hearing at 11 a.m. on June 30, 1975.[2]

to land shall be detained for further inquiry to be conducted by a special inquiry officer."

2. The hearing was authorized by § 236(a), which, as set forth in 8 U.S.C. § 1226(a), provides:

"A special inquiry officer shall conduct proceedings under this section, administer oaths, present and receive evidence, and interrogate, examine, and cross-examine the alien or witnesses. He shall have authority in any case to determine whether an arriving alien who has been detained for further inquiry under section 1225 of this title shall be allowed to enter or shall be excluded and deported. The determination of such special inquiry officer shall be

An Immigration Law Judge conducted the scheduled exclusion hearing. After hearing testimony from the respondent, her husband, and three of the aliens found in the Plasencias' car, the judge found "clear, convincing and unequivocal" evidence that the respondent did "knowingly and for gain encourage, induce, assist, abet, or aid nonresident aliens" to enter or try to enter the United States in violation of law. He also found that the respondent's trip to Mexico was a "meaningful departure" from the United States and that her return to this country was therefore an "entry" within the meaning of § 101(a)(13), 8 U.S.C. § 1101(a)(13).[3] On the basis of these findings, he ordered her "excluded and deported."

After the Board of Immigration Appeals (BIA) dismissed her administrative appeal and denied her motion to reopen the proceeding, the respondent filed a petition for a writ of habeas corpus in the United States District Court, seeking release from the exclusion and deportation order. The Magistrate initially proposed a finding that, on the basis of evidence adduced at the exclusion hearing, "a meaningful departure did not occur ... and that therefore [the respondent] is entitled to a deportation hearing." After considering the Government's objections, the Magistrate declared that the Government could relitigate the question of "entry" at the deportation hearing. The District Court adopted the Magistrate's final report and recommendation and vacated the decision of the BIA,

instructing the INS to proceed against respondent, if at all, only in deportation proceedings.

The Court of Appeals for the Ninth Circuit affirmed. *Plasencia v. Sureck,* 637 F.2d 1286 (1980).

II

[1-6] The immigration laws create two types of proceedings in which aliens can be denied the hospitality of the United States: deportation hearings and exclusion hearings. See generally *Leng May Ma v. Barber,* 357 U.S. 185, 187, 78 S.Ct. 1072, 1073, 2 L.Ed.2d 1246 (1958). The deportation hearing is the usual means of proceeding against an alien already physically in the United States, and the exclusion hearing is the usual means of proceeding against an alien outside the United States seeking admission. The two types of proceedings differ in a number of ways. See generally *Maldonado-Sandoval v. INS,* 518 F.2d 278, 280 n. 3 (CA9 1975). An exclusion proceeding is usually held at the port of entry, while a deportation hearing is usually held near the residence of the alien within the United States, see 1A C. Gordon & H. Rosenfield, Immigration Law and Procedure § 5.6c (rev. ed. 1981). The regulations of the Attorney General, issued under the authority of § 242(b), 8 U.S.C. § 1252(b), require in most deportation proceedings that the alien be given seven days' notice of the charges against him, 8 CFR § 242.1(b) (1982), while there is no

---

based only on the evidence produced at the inquiry.... Proceedings before a special inquiry officer under this section shall be conducted in accordance with this section, the applicable provisions of sections 1225 and 1375(b) of this title, and such regulations as the Attorney General shall prescribe, and shall be the sole and exclusive procedure for determining admissibility of a person to the United States under the provisions of this section.... A complete record of the proceedings and of all testimony and evidence produced at such inquiry, shall be kept."

3. Section 101(a)(13), 8 U.S.C. § 1101(a)(13), defines "entry" as "any coming of an alien into the United States, from a foreign port or place or from an outlying possession, whether voluntar-

ily or otherwise, except that an alien having a lawful permanent residence in the United States shall not be regarded as making an entry into the United States for the purposes of the immigration laws if the alien proves to the satisfaction of the Attorney General that his departure to a foreign port or place or to an outlying possession was not intended or reasonably to be expected by him or his presence in a foreign port or place or in an outlying possession was not voluntary: *Provided,* That no person whose departure from the United States was occasioned by deportation proceedings, extradition, or other legal process shall be held to be entitled to such exception."

requirement of advance notice of the charges for an alien subject to exclusion proceedings. Indeed, the BIA has held that, "as long as the applicant is informed of the issues confronting him at some point in the hearing, and he is given a reasonable opportunity to meet them," no further notice is necessary. *In re Salazar*, 17 I. & N. Dec. 167, 169 (1979). Also, if the INS prevails in a deportation proceeding, the alien may appeal directly to the court of appeals, § 106(a), 75 Stat. 651, as amended, 8 U.S.C. § 1105a(a), (1976 ed. and Supp. V), while the alien can challenge an exclusion order only by a petition for a writ of habeas corpus, § 106(b), 75 Stat. 653, 8 U.S.C. § 1105a(b). Finally, the alien who loses his right to reside in the United States in a deportation hearing has a number of substantive rights not available to the alien who is denied admission in an exclusion proceeding: he can, within certain limits, designate the country of deportation, § 243(a), 8 U.S.C. § 1253(a) (1976 ed. and Supp. V); he may be able to depart voluntarily, § 244(e), 8 U.S.C. § 1254(e) (1976 ed., Supp. V), avoiding both the stigma of deportation, § 242(b), 8 U.S.C. § 1252(b) (1976 ed. and Supp. V), and the limitations on his selection of destination, § 243(a), 8 U.S.C. § 1253(a) (1976 ed. and Supp. V);[4] or |27 he |can seek suspension of deportation, § 242(e), 8 U.S.C. § 1252(e) (1976 ed. and Supp. V).

The respondent contends that she was entitled to have the question of her admissibility litigated in a deportation hearing, where she would be the beneficiary of the procedural protections and the substantive rights outlined above. Our analysis of whether she is entitled to a deportation rather than an exclusion hearing begins with the language of the Act. Section 235(a) of the Act, 8 U.S.C. § 1225(a), per-

mits the INS to examine "[a]ll aliens" who seek "admission or *readmission* to" the United States and empowers immigration officers to take evidence concerning the privilege of any person suspected of being an alien "to enter, *reenter*, pass through, or reside" in the United States. (Emphasis added.) Moreover, "every alien" who does not appear "to be clearly and beyond a doubt entitled to land shall be detained" for further inquiry. § 235(b). If an alien is so detained, the Act directs the special inquiry officer to determine whether the arriving alien "shall be allowed to enter or shall be excluded and deported." § 236(a), 8 U.S.C. § 1226(a). The proceeding before that officer, the exclusion hearing, is by statute "the sole and exclusive procedure for determining admissibility of a person to the United States ...." *Ibid.*

The Act's legislative history also emphasizes the singular role of exclusion hearings in determining whether an alien should be admitted. The Reports of both the House and Senate state:

"The special inquiry officer is empowered to determine whether an alien detained for further inquiry shall be excluded and deported or shall be allowed to enter after he has given the alien a hearing. The procedure established in the bill is made the sole and exclusive procedure for determining the admissibility of a person to the |United States." |28 S.Rep. No. 1137, 82d Cong., 2d Sess., 29 (1952); H.R.Rep. No. 1365, 82d Cong., 2d Sess., 56 (1952), U.S.Code Cong. & Admin.News 1952, p. 1653, 1711.

[7] The language and history of the Act thus clearly reflect a congressional intent that, whether or not the alien is a permanent resident, admissibility shall be determined in an exclusion hearing. Nothing in

---

4. Voluntary departure for an alien who would otherwise be deported also means that he will not be subject to § 212(a)(17), 8 U.S.C. § 1182(a)(17), which at the time of Plasencia's hearing, required aliens who had once been deported to seek prior approval of the Attorney's General before re-entering. There was no comparable requirement of prior approval for

aliens who had been excluded and sought again to enter more than one year later. § 212(a)(16), 8 U.S.C. § 1182(a)(16). The requirement of prior approval for deported aliens now applies only within five years of deportation. 95 Stat. 1612, § 212(a)(17), 8 U.S.C. § 1182(a)(17) (1976 Ed. Supp. V).

the statutory language or the legislative history suggests that the respondent's status as a permanent resident entitles her to a suspension of the exclusion hearing or requires the INS to proceed only through a deportation hearing. Under the terms of the Act, the INS properly proceeded in an exclusion hearing to determine whether respondent was attempting to "enter" the United States [5] and whether she was excludable.

III

To avoid the impact of the statute, the respondent contends, and the Court of Appeals agreed, that unless she was "entering," she was not subject to exclusion proceedings, and that prior decisions of this Court indicate that she is entitled to have the question of "entry" decided in deportation proceedings.

[8] The parties agree that only "entering" aliens are subject to exclusion. See Brief for Petitioner 19. That view accords with the language of the statute, which describes the exclusion hearing as one to determine whether the applicant "shall be allowed to *enter* or shall be excluded and deported." § 236(a), 8 U.S.C. § 1226(a) (emphasis added). But the respondent's contention that the question of entry can be determined only in deportation proceedings reflects a misconception of our decisions.

[9] In *Rosenberg v. Fleuti*, 374 U.S. 449, 83 S.Ct. 1804, 10 L.Ed.2d 1000 (1963), we faced the question whether a resident

alien's return from an afternoon trip across the border was an "entry" for immigration law purposes. The definition of that term was the same then as it is now: it means "any coming of an alien into the United States ... except that an alien having a lawful permanent residence in the United States shall not be regarded as making an entry into the United States for the purposes of the immigration laws if the alien proves to the satisfaction of the Attorney General that his departure to a foreign port or place or to an outlying possession was not intended or reasonably to be expected by him...." § 101(a)(13), 8 U.S.C. § 1101(a)(13). We held in *Fleuti* that the "intent exception" refers to an intent to depart in a "manner which can be regarded as meaningfully interruptive of the alien's permanent residence." 374 U.S. at 462, 83 S.Ct., at 1812. Thus, an "innocent, casual, and brief excursion" by a resident alien outside this country's borders would not subject him to the consequences of an "entry" on his return. *Ibid.* If, however, "the purpose of leaving the country is to accomplish some object which is itself contrary to some policy reflected in our immigration laws, it would appear that the interruption of residence thereby occurring would properly be regarded as meaningful." *Ibid.* That distinction both protects resident aliens from "unsuspected risks and unintended consequences of ... a wholly innocent action," *ibid.*, and gives effect to the language of § 101(a)(13).[6]

---

5. Apparently the practice of the INS is to determine this question in exclusion proceedings. See *In re Leal*, 15 I. & N. Dec. 477, 478–479 (BIA 1975); *In re Becerra-Miranda*, 12 I. & N. Dec. 358, 362–363 (BIA 1967).

6. Section 101(a)(13), 8 U.S.C. § 1101(a)(13), which defines "entry," was enacted in 1952 in response to the harsh results visited upon resident aliens by earlier restrictive interpretations of the term. Both the House and Senate Reports contained identical explanatory language: "Normally an entry occurs when the alien crosses the borders of the United States and makes a physical entry, and the question of whether an entry has been made is susceptible of a precise determination. However, for the purposes of

determining the effect of a subsequent entry upon the status of an alien who has previously entered the United States and resided therein, the preciseness of the term 'entry' has not been found to be as apparent. Earlier judicial constructions of the term in the immigration laws, as set forth in *Volpe v. Smith* (289 U.S. 422 [53 S.Ct. 665, 77 L.Ed. 1298] (1933)), generally held that the term 'entry' included any coming of an alien from a foreign country to the United States whether such coming be the first or a subsequent one. More recently, the courts have departed from the rigidity of that rule and have recognized that an alien does not make an entry upon his return to the United States from a foreign country where he had no intent to leave the United States (*Di Pasquale v. Karnuth*, 158

┃₃₀ ┃The Government has argued in this case that Plasencia violated the immigration laws by attempting to smuggle aliens for gain. Therefore, her departure was "meaningfully interruptive" of her residence, she was attempting an "entry," and she was subject to exclusion proceedings. And, the Government urges, under § 212(a)(31), 8 U.S.C. § 1182(a)(31), she was excludable because she had attempted to smuggle aliens for gain. Plasencia, on the other hand, argues that it would "violat[e] both the scope and spirit," Brief for Respondent 15, of *Fleuti* to permit the INS to litigate questions of "entry" in exclusion proceedings.

[10] The Court of Appeals viewed *Fleuti* as a deportation case rather than an exclusion case, 637 F.2d, at 1288, and therefore not relevant in deciding whether the question of "entry" could be determined in exclusion proceedings. For guidance on that decision, the Court of Appeals turned to *Kwong Hai Chew v. Colding*, 344 U.S. 590, 73 S.Ct. 472, 97 L.Ed. 576 (1953), which it read to hold that a resident alien re-
┃₃₁ turning from a brief trip "could not be ┃excluded without the procedural due process to which he would have been entitled had he never left the country"—*i.e.*, in this case, a deportation proceeding. 637 F.2d, at 1288. The court concluded that Plasencia was entitled to litigate her admissibility in deportation proceedings. It would be "circular" and "unfair," thought the court, to allow the INS to litigate the question of

"entry" in exclusion proceedings when that question also went to the merits of the respondent's admissibility. *Id.*, at 1288–1289.

[11] We disagree. The reasoning of *Chew* was only that a resident alien returning from a brief trip has a right to due process just as would a continuously present resident alien. It does not create a right to identical treatment for these two differently situated groups of aliens.[7] As the Ninth Circuit seemed to recognize, if the respondent here was making an "entry," she would be subject to exclusion proceedings. It is no more "circular" to allow the immigration judge in the exclusion proceeding to determine whether the alien is making an entry than it is for any court to decide that it has jurisdiction when the facts relevant to the determination of jurisdiction are also relevant to the merits. Thus, in *United States v. Sing Tuck*, 194 U.S. 161, 24 S.Ct. 621, 48 L.Ed. 917 (1904), this Court held that an immigration inspector could make a determination whether an applicant for admission was an alien or a citizen, although only aliens were subject to exclusion. Cf. *Land v. Dollar*, 330 U.S. 731, 739, 67 S.Ct. 1009, 1013, 91 L.Ed. 1209 (1947) (district court has jurisdiction to determine its jurisdiction by proceeding to a decision on the merits). Nor is it in any way "unfair" to decide the question of entry in exclusion proceedings as long as those proceedings themselves are fair. Fi-

---

F.2d 878 (C.C.A.2d 1947)), or did not leave the country voluntarily (*Delgadillo v. Carmichael*, 332 U.S. 388 [68 S.Ct. 10, 92 L.Ed. 17] (1947)). The bill defines the term "entry" as precisely as practicable, giving due recognition to the judicial precedents. Thus any coming of an alien from a foreign port or place or an outlying possession into the United States is to be considered an entry, whether voluntary or otherwise, unless the Attorney General is satisfied that the departure of the alien, other than a deportee, from this country was unintentional or was not voluntary." S.Rep. No. 1137, 82d Cong., 2d Sess., 4 (1952); H.R.Rep. No. 1365, 82d Cong., 2d Sess., 32 (1952), U.S. Code Cong. & Admin.News 1952, p. 1683.
In *Di Pasquale*, the court refused to allow a deportation that depended upon an "entry" that

occurred after an overnight train on which an alien was a passenger passed through Canada on its way from Buffalo to Detroit. In *Delgadillo*, the Court refused to define as an "entry" the return of an alien taken to Cuba to recuperate after the merchant ship on which he sailed was torpedoed in the Caribbean during World War II.

7. Indeed, we expressly declined to reach the question whether Chew himself was entitled to a deportation proceeding. We stated: "From a constitutional point of view, he is entitled to due process without regard to whether or not, for immigration purposes, he is to be treated as an entrant alien, and we do not now reach the question whether he is to be so treated." 344 U.S., at 600, 73 S.Ct., at 479.

LANDON v. PLASENCIA

nally, the use of exclusion proceedings violates neither the "scope" nor the "spirit" of *Fleuti*. As the Court of Appeals held, that case only defined "entry" and did not designate the forum for deciding questions of entry. The statutory scheme is clear: Congress intended that the determinations of both "entry" and the existence of grounds for exclusion could be made at an exclusion hearing.

IV

[12] Our determination that the respondent is not entitled to a deportation proceeding does not, however, resolve this case. In challenging her exclusion in the District Court, Plasencia argued not only that she was entitled to a deportation proceeding but also that she was denied due process in her exclusion hearing. See App. 5, ¶ 9; Record 19, 20, 23. We agree with Plasencia that under the circumstances of this case, she can invoke the Due Process Clause on returning to this country, although we do not decide the contours of the process that is due or whether the process accorded Plasencia was insufficient.

[13-15] This Court has long held that an alien seeking initial admission to the United States requests a privilege and has no constitutional rights regarding his application, for the power to admit or exclude aliens is a sovereign prerogative. See, *e.g.*, *United States ex rel. Knauff v. Shaughnessy*, 338 U.S. 537, 542, 70 S.Ct. 309, 312, 94 L.Ed. 317 (1950); *Nishimura Ekiu v. United States*, 142 U.S. 651, 659–660, 12 S.Ct. 336, 338, 35 L.Ed. 1146 (1892). Our recent decisions confirm that view. See, *e.g.*, *Fiallo v. Bell*, 430 U.S. 787, 792, 97 S.Ct. 1473, 1477, 52 L.Ed.2d 50 (1977); *Kleindienst v. Mandel*, 408 U.S. 753, 92 S.Ct. 2576, 33 L.Ed.2d 683 (1972). As we explained in *Johnson v. Eisentrager*, 339 U.S. 763, 770, 70 S.Ct. 936, 939, 94 L.Ed. 1255 (1950), however, once an alien gains admission to our country and begins to develop the ties that go with permanent residence his constitutional status changes accordingly. Our cases have frequently

suggested that a continuously present resident alien is entitled to a fair hearing when threatened with deportation, see, *e.g.*, *United States ex rel. Tisi v. Tod*, 264 U.S. 131, 133, 134, 44 S.Ct. 260, 261, 68 L.Ed. 590 (1924); *Low Wah Suey v. Backus*, 225 U.S. 460, 468, 32 S.Ct. 734, 735, 56 L.Ed. 1165 (1912) (hearing may be conclusive "when fairly conducted"); see also *Kwong Hai Chew*, 344 U.S., at 598, n. 8, 73 S.Ct., at 478, n. 8, and, although we have only rarely held that the procedures provided by the executive were inadequate, we developed the rule that a continuously present permanent resident alien has a right to due process in such a situation. See, *e.g.*, *United States ex rel. Vajtauer v. Commissioner of Immigration*, 273 U.S. 103, 106, 47 S.Ct. 302, 303, 71 L.Ed. 560 (1927); *The Japanese Immigrant Case*, 189 U.S. 86, 100–101, 23 S.Ct. 611, 614, 47 L.Ed. 721 (1903); see also *Wong Yang Sung v. McGrath*, 339 U.S. 33, 49–50, 70 S.Ct. 445, 453–54, 94 L.Ed. 616 (1950); *Bridges v. Wixon*, 326 U.S. 135, 153–154, 65 S.Ct. 1443, 1452, 89 L.Ed. 2103 (1945).

The question of the procedures due a returning resident alien arose in *Kwong Hai Chew v. Colding, supra*. There, the regulations permitted the exclusion of an arriving alien without a hearing. We interpreted those regulations not to apply to Chew, a permanent resident alien who was returning from a 5-month voyage abroad as a crewman on an American merchant ship. We reasoned that, "[f]or purposes of his constitutional right to due process, we assimilate petitioner's status to that of an alien continuously residing and physically present in the United States." 344 U.S., at 596, 73 S.Ct., at 477. Then, to avoid constitutional problems, we construed the regulation as inapplicable. Although the holding was one of regulatory interpretation, the rationale was one of constitutional law. Any doubts that *Chew* recognized constitutional rights in the resident alien returning from a brief trip abroad were dispelled by *Rosenberg v. Fleuti*, where we described *Chew* as holding "that the returning resident alien is entitled as a matter of due process to a hearing on the charges underlying any attempt to exclude him." 374 U.S., at 460, 83 S.Ct., at 1811.

If the permanent resident alien's absence is extended, of course, he may lose his entitlement to "assimilat[ion of his] status," *Kwong Hai Chew v. Colding, supra,* 344 U.S., at 596, 73 S.Ct., at 477, to that of an alien continuously residing and physically present in the United States. In *Shaughnessy v. United States ex rel. Mezei,* 345 U.S. 206, 73 S.Ct. 625, 97 L.Ed. 956 _|³⁴ (1953), this Court rejected the argument of an alien who had left the country for some 20 months that he was entitled to due process in assessing his right to admission on his return. We did not suggest that no returning resident alien has a right to due process, for we explicitly reaffirmed *Chew.* We need not now decide the scope of *Mezei;* it does not govern this case, for Plasencia was absent from the country only a few days, and the United States has conceded that she has a right to due process, see Tr. of Oral Arg. 6, 9, 14; Brief for Petitioner 9–10, 20–21.

[16, 17] The constitutional sufficiency of procedures provided in any situation, of course, varies with the circumstances. See, *e.g., Lassiter v. Department of Social Services,* 452 U.S. 18, 24–25, 101 S.Ct. 2153, 2158, 68 L.Ed.2d 640 (1981); *Greenholtz v. Nebraska Penal Inmates,* 442 U.S. 1, 12, 99 S.Ct. 2100, 2106, 60 L.Ed.2d 668 (1979); *Morrissey v. Brewer,* 408 U.S. 471, 481, 92 S.Ct. 2593, 2600, 33 L.Ed.2d 484 (1972). In evaluating the procedures in any case, the courts must consider the interest at stake for the individual, the risk of an erroneous deprivation of the interest through the procedures used as well as the probable value of additional or different procedural safeguards, and the interest of the government in using the current procedures rather than additional or different procedures. *Mathews v. Eldridge,* 424 U.S. 319, 334–335, 96 S.Ct. 893, 902–903, 47 L.Ed.2d 18 (1976). Plasencia's interest here is, without question, a weighty one. She stands to lose the

right "to stay and live and work in this land of freedom," *Bridges v. Wixon, supra,* 326 U.S., at 154, 65 S.Ct., at 1452. Further, she may lose the right to rejoin her immediate family, a right that ranks high among the interests of the individual. See, *e.g., Moore v. City of East Cleveland,* 431 U.S. 494, 499, 503–504, 97 S.Ct. 1932, 1935, 1937–1938, 52 L.Ed.2d 531 (1977) (plurality opinion); *Stanley v. Illinois,* 405 U.S. 645, 651, 92 S.Ct. 1208, 1212, 31 L.Ed.2d 551 (1972). The Government's interest in efficient administration of the immigration laws at the border also is weighty. Further, it must weigh heavily in the balance that control over matters of immigration is a sovereign prerogative, largely within the control of the Executive and the Legislature. See, *e.g., Fiallo, supra,* 430 U.S., at 792–793, 97 S.Ct., at 1477–1478; *Knauff, supra,* 338 U.S., at 542–543, 70 S.Ct., at 312; *The Japanese Immigrant Case, supra,* 189 U.S., at 97, 23 S.Ct., at 613. The role of the judiciary is limited to _|³⁵ determining whether the procedures meet the essential standard of fairness under the Due Process Clause and does not extend to imposing procedures that merely displace congressional choices of policy. Our previous discussion has shown that Congress did not intend to require the use of deportation procedures in cases such as this one. Thus, it would be improper simply to impose deportation procedures here because the reviewing court may find them preferable. Instead, the courts must evaluate the particular circumstances and determine what procedures would satisfy the minimum requirements of due process on the reentry of a permanent resident alien.

Plasencia questions three aspects of the procedures that the Government employed in depriving her of these interests. First, she contends that the Immigration Law Judge placed the burden of proof upon her. In a later proceeding in *Chew,* the Court of Appeals for the District of Columbia Circuit held, without mention of the Due Process Clause, that, under the law of the case, Chew was entitled to a hearing at which the INS was the moving party and bore the burden of proof. *Kwong Hai Chew v. Rogers*, 103 U.S.App.D.C. 228, 257 F.2d 606 (1958). The BIA has accepted that decision, and although the Act provides that the burden of proof is on the alien in an exclusion proceeding, § 291, 8 U.S.C. § 1361 (1976 ed., Supp. V), the BIA has followed the practice of placing the burden on the Government when the alien is a permanent resident alien. See, *e.g., In re Salazar*, 17 I. & N. Dec. 169; *In re Kane*, 15 I. & N. Dec. 258, 264 (BIA 1975); *In re Becerra-Miranda*, 12 I. & N. Dec. 358, 363–364, 366 (BIA 1967). There is no explicit statement of the placement of the burden of proof in the Attorney General's regulations or in the Immigration Law Judge's opinion in this case and no finding on the issue below.

Second, Plasencia contends that the notice provided her was inadequate. She apparently had less than 11 hours' notice of the charges and the hearing. The regulations do not require any advance notice of the charges against the alien in an exclusion hearing, and the BIA has held that it is sufficient that the alien have notice of the charges at the hearing, *In re Salazar, supra*, at 169. The United States has argued to us that Plasencia could have sought a continuance. It concedes, however, that there is no explicit statutory or regulatory authorization for a continuance.

Finally, Plasencia contends that she was allowed to waive her right to representation, § 292, 8 U.S.C. § 1362,[8] without a full understanding of the right or of the conse-

quences of waiving it. Through an interpreter, the Immigration Law Judge informed her at the outset of the hearing, as required by the regulations, of her right to be represented. He did not tell her of the availability of free legal counsel, but at the time of the hearing, there was no administrative requirement that he do so. 8 CFR § 236.2(a) (1975). The Attorney General has since revised the regulations to require that, when qualified free legal services are available, the immigration law judge must inform the alien of their existence and ask whether representation is desired. 44 Fed. Reg. 4654 (1979) (codified at 8 CFR § 236.-2(a) (1982)). As the United States concedes, the hearing would not comply with the current regulations. See Tr. of Oral Arg. at 11.

If the exclusion hearing is to ensure fairness, it must provide Plasencia an opportunity to present her case effectively, though at the same time it cannot impose an undue burden on the Government. It would not, however, be appropriate for us to decide now whether the new regulation on the right to notice of free legal services is of constitutional magnitude or whether the remaining procedures provided comport with the Due Process Clause. Before this Court, the parties have devoted their attention to the entitlement to a deportation hearing rather than to the sufficiency of the procedures in the exclusion hearing.[9] Whether the several hours' notice gave Plasencia a realistic opportunity to prepare her case for effective presentation in the circumstances of an exclusion hearing with-

---

8. The statute provides a right to representation without expense to the Government. § 292, 8 U.S.C. § 1362. Plasencia has not suggested that she is entitled to free counsel.

9. Thus, the question of Plasencia's entitlement to due process has been briefed and argued, is properly before us, and is sufficiently developed that we are prepared to decide it. Precisely what procedures are due, on the other hand, has not been adequately developed by the briefs or argument. The dissent undertakes to decide these questions, but, to do so, must rely heavily on an argument not raised by Plasencia: to wit,

that she was not informed at the hearing that the alleged agreement to receive compensation and the meaningfulness of her departure were critical issues. Also, the dissent fails to discuss the interests that the Government may have in employing the procedures that it did. The omission of arguments raised by the parties is quite understandable, for neither Plasencia nor the Government has yet discussed what procedures are due. Unlike the dissent, we would allow the parties to explore their respective interests and arguments in the Court of Appeals.

out counsel is a question we are not now in a position to answer. Nor has the government explained the burdens that it might face in providing more elaborate procedures. Thus, although we recognize the gravity of Plasencia's interest, the other factors relevant to due process analysis— the risk of erroneous deprivation, the efficacy of additional procedural safeguards, and the government's interest in providing no further procedures—have not been adequately presented to permit us to assess the sufficiency of the hearing. We remand to the Court of Appeals to allow the parties to explore whether Plasencia was accorded due process under all of the circumstances.

Accordingly, the judgment of the Court of Appeals is reversed, and the case is remanded for further proceedings consistent with this opinion.

It is so ordered.

Justice MARSHALL, concurring in part and dissenting in part.

I agree that the Immigration and Nationality Act permitted the INS to proceed ⎿³⁸ against respondent in an exclusion ⎿proceeding. The question then remains whether the exclusion proceeding held in this case satisfied the minimum requirements of the Due Process Clause. While I agree that the Court need not decide the precise contours of the process that would be constitutionally sufficient, I would not hesitate to decide that the process accorded Plasencia was insufficient.[1]

The Court has already set out the standards to be applied in resolving the question. Therefore, rather than just remand, I

1. Because the due process question was squarely addressed in the briefs and at oral argument, there is no doubt that the Court may now decide the issue. See *Vance v. Terrazas,* 444 U.S. 252, 258–259, n. 5, 100 S.Ct. 540, 544–545, n. 5, 62 L.Ed.2d 461 (1980), and cases cited therein. In fact, the Court has reached the threshold of deciding the constitutional question. It has identified the deficiencies in the exclusion hearing afforded Plasencia, and it has set forth the standards that it would apply to determine whether the procedures, as described, denied

would first hold that respondent was denied due process because she was not given adequate and timely notice of the charges against her and of her right to retain counsel and to present a defense.[2]

While the type of hearing required by due process depends upon a balancing of the competing interests at stake, due process requires "at a minimum ... that deprivation of life, liberty or property by adjudication be preceded by notice and opportunity for hearing." *Mullane v. Central Hanover Bank & Trust Co.,* 339 U.S. 306, 313, 70 S.Ct. 652, 656, 94 L.Ed. 865 (1950). See, *e.g., Bell v. Burson,* 402 U.S. 535, 542, 91 S.Ct. 1586, 1591, 29 L.Ed.2d 90 (1971). Permanent resident aliens who are detained upon reentry into this country clearly are entitled to adequate notice in advance of an exclusion proceeding.

⎿To satisfy due process, notice must "clari-   ⎿³⁹ fy what the charges are" in a manner adequate to apprise the individual of the basis for the government's proposed action. *Wolff v. McDonnell,* 418 U.S. 539, 564, 94 S.Ct. 2963, 2978, 41 L.Ed.2d 935 (1974). Notice must be provided sufficiently in advance of the hearing to "give the charged party a chance to marshal the facts in his defense." *Id.,* at 563, 564, 94 S.Ct., at 2978 (prisoners charged with disciplinary violations must be given "advance written notice of the claimed violation"). See, *e.g., Goldberg v. Kelly,* 397 U.S. 254, 267–268, 90 S.Ct. 1011, 1020, 25 L.Ed.2d 287 (1970) (welfare recipients must be given "timely and adequate notice detailing the reasons for a proposed termination"); *In re Gault,* 387 U.S. 1, 33, 87 S.Ct. 1428, 1446, 18

Plasencia due process. I do not see any interest to be served in declining to take the final step of applying these due process standards to the record before us, as the Court of Appeals would otherwise be required to do on remand.

2. Because Plasencia did not receive constitutionally sufficient notice, I find it unnecessary to address the other constitutional deficiencies she asserts.

L.Ed.2d 527 (1967) (juvenile must be given notice of "the specific charge or factual allegations" to be considered at delinquency hearing "at the earliest practicable time, and in any event sufficiently in advance of the hearing to permit preparation").

Respondent was not given notice sufficient to afford her a reasonable opportunity to demonstrate that she was not excludable. The Immigration Judge's decision to exclude respondent was handed down less than 24 hours after she was detained at the border on the night of June 29, 1975. By notice in English dated June 30, 1975, she was informed that a hearing would be conducted at 11 o'clock on the morning of that same day, and that the Government would seek to exclude her on the ground that she had "wilfully and knowingly aided and abetted the entry of illegal aliens into the United States in violation of the law and for gain." [3] It was not until the commencement of the hearing that she was given notice in her native language of the charges against her and of her right to retain counsel and to present evidence.

The charges against Plasencia were also inadequately explained at the hearing it-self.[4] The Immigration Judge did not explain to her that she would be entitled to remain in the ⌊country if she could demonstrate that she had not agreed to receive compensation from the aliens whom she had driven across the border.[5] Nor did the judge inform respondent that the meaningfulness of her departure was an issue at the hearing.

These procedures deprived Plasencia of a fair opportunity to show that she was not excludable under the standards set forth in the Immigration and Nationality Act. Because Plasencia was not given adequate notice of the standards for exclusion or of her right to retain counsel and present a defense, she had neither time nor opportunity to prepare a response to ⌊the Government's case. The procedures employed here virtually assured that the Government attorney would present his case without factual or legal opposition.

When a permanent resident alien's substantial interest in remaining in this country is at stake, the Due Process Clause forbids the Government to stack the deck in this fashion. Only a compelling need for truly summary action could justify this

3. It is unclear from the record whether respondent received the notice prior to the commencement of the hearing.

4. The exclusion hearing was conducted with the aid of an interpreter.

5. The principal issue of fact at the hearing was whether Plasencia had transported the six aliens "for gain." Plasencia, who was called as the Government's first witness, denied repeatedly that any of the aliens had agreed to pay her for driving them into this country. The Government's trial attorney then called three of the six aliens as witnesses. One witness, Jose Alfredo Santillana, stated unequivocally that he was picked up by the Plasencias while hitchhiking and that, without making any mention of money, they agreed to drive him to Los Angeles. A second witness, Luis Polio-Medina, testified that there had not been any talk with Plasencia at any time about payment for transportation to Los Angeles, though there "was kind of an understanding" that "some people in Los Angeles" whom he "was going to look for" would pay her a "normal amount" on his behalf. Only the third witness, Eugenia Linares-Moreno, testified

that she had an agreement to pay Plasencia for transportation into the country.

Given the weakness of the Government's evidence, Plasencia may well have been prejudiced by her inability to prepare for the hearing and to obtain counsel. The three aliens who did not testify at the hearing might have supported Plasencia's claim that she did not expect to receive financial compensation. The Immigration Judge's finding that Plasencia transported the aliens for gain must have depended on his acceptance of the testimony given by Linares-Moreno and Polio-Medina. The motives of these Government witnesses in testifying against Plasencia were open to question, since they were subject to criminal prosecution in this country. The credibility of Linares-Moreno, the Government's key witness, might also have been challenged on the grounds that she had contradicted herself on at least one key question during the course of her examination and that she had concededly lied to an INS officer by giving a false name. Vigorous cross-examination by a competent attorney might well have led the Immigration Judge to resolve the disputed issue of fact in Plasencia's favor.

one-sided proceeding. In fact, the Government's haste in proceeding against Plasencia could be explained only by its desire to avoid the minimal administrative and financial burden of providing her adequate notice and an opportunity to prepare for the hearing. Although the various other Government interests identified by the Court may be served by the exclusion of those who fail to meet the eligibility requirements set out in the Immigration and Nationality Act, they are not served by procedures that deny a permanent resident alien a fair opportunity to demonstrate that she meets those eligibility requirements.

I would therefore hold that respondent was denied due process.

345 U.S. 206

SHAUGHNESSY, District Director of Immigration and Naturalization, v. UNITED STATES ex rel. MEZEI.

No. 139.

Argued Jan. 7 and 8, 1953.

Decided March 16, 1953.

Proceedings on petition by alien detained at Ellis Island, for writ of habeas corpus. The United States District Court for the Southern District of New York, 101 F.Supp. 66, entered order sustaining writ and directing discharge on parole under specified restrictions, and both parties appealed. The Court of Appeals for the Second Circuit, 195 F.2d 964, affirmed in part and reversed in part. Certiorari was granted on petition of District Director of Immigration and Naturalization. The Supreme Court, Mr. Justice Clark, held that continued exclusion of alien, without hearing, as a bad security risk did not deprive him of any statutory or constitutional right, even though result was alien's detention at Ellis Island because of refusal of other countries to admit him.

Reversed.

Mr. Justice Black, Mr. Justice Jackson, Mr. Justice Frankfurter and Mr. Justice Douglas, dissented.

1. Courts ⚖➔383(1)

Because of serious problems in enforcement of immigration laws presented by case involving question of legality of Attorney General's continued exclusion of alien without hearing, after alien had been permanently excluded from United States on security grounds, with result that alien was stranded on Ellis Island because other countries would not take him back, Supreme Court granted certiorari.

2. Constitutional Law ⚖➔72

The power to expel or exclude aliens is a fundamental sovereign attribute to be exercised by the Government's political departments, and such power is largely immune from judicial control. 22 U.S.C.A. § 223; Proclamation No. 2523, U.S.Code Cong.Service 1941, p. 883; Emergency Powers Interim Continuation Act, § 1(40), 66 Stat. 54, 57; Joint Resolutions May 28, 1952, June 14, 1952, 66 Stat. 96, 137; Emergency Powers Continuation Act, § 1(30), 66 Stat. 330, 332.

73 S.Ct.—40

3. Aliens ⚖➔54(1)

Constitutional Law ⚖➔252

Aliens who have once entered the United States, even though illegally, may be expelled only after proceedings conforming to traditional standards of fairness as encompassed in due process of law, but alien on threshold of initial entry stands on different footing in that whatever procedure is authorized by Congress is due process as far as the alien denied entry is concerned.

4. Aliens ⚖➔54(15)

In view of fact that the action of the executive officer under procedure authorized by Congress for exclusion of aliens is final and conclusive, the Attorney General cannot be compelled by the courts to disclose the evidence underlying his determinations in an exclusion case, since it is not within province of any court, unless expressly authorized by law, to review determination of political branch of the Government. 22 U.S.C.A. § 223.

5. Constitutional Law ⚖➔68(1)

It is not within the province of any court, unless expressly authorized by law, to review the determination of the political branch of the Government.

6. Aliens ⚖➔54(15)

The courts cannot retry the determination of the Attorney General in case in which alien is excluded by Attorney General under procedure authorized by Congress. 22 U.S.C.A. § 223; Proclamation No. 2523, U.S.Code Cong.Service 1941, p. 883; Emergency Powers Interim Continuation Act, § 1(40), 66 Stat. 54, 57; Joint Resolutions May 28, 1952, June 14, 1952, 66 Stat. 96, 137; Emergency Powers Continuation Act, § 1(30), 66 Stat. 330, 332.

7. Aliens ⚖➔54(2)

Neither an alien's prior residence in United States nor his harborage on Ellis Island will transform a proceeding pursuant to which alien is denied entry into something other than an exclusion proceeding, since such harborage is not tantamount to an entry into the United States. 22 U.S.C.A. § 223; Proclamation No. 2523, U.S.Code Cong.Service 1941, p. 883;

Emergency Powers Interim Continuation Act, § 1(40), 66 Stat. 54, 57; Joint Resolutions May 28, 1952, June 14, 1952, 66 Stat. 96, 137; Emergency Powers Continuation Acts, § 1(30), 66 Stat. 330, 332.

8. Habeas Corpus ⊜23

An alien who is detained by authority of United States by reason of exclusion proceedings may test the validity of his exclusion by habeas corpus, and such right exists regardless of whether alien enjoys temporary refuge on land or remains continuously aboard ship. 22 U.S.C.A. § 223; Proclamation No. 2523, U.S.Code Cong. Service 1941, p. 883; Emergency Powers Interim Continuation Act, § 1(40), 66 Stat. 54, 57; Joint Resolutions May 28, 1952, June 14, 1952, 66 Stat. 96, 137; Emergency Powers Continuation Act, § 1(30), 66 Stat. 330, 332.

9. Aliens ⊜53

The prior residence of an alien in the United States does not preclude his exclusion after departure and attempted reentry, if alien is unqualified for admission under existing immigration laws. 22 U.S.C.A. § 223; Proclamation No. 2523, U.S. Code Cong.Service 1941, p. 883; Emergency Powers Interim Continuation Act, § 1(40), 66 Stat. 54, 57; Joint Resolutions May 28, 1952, June 14, 1952, 66 Stat. 96, 137; Emergency Powers Continuation Act, § 1(30), 66 Stat. 330, 332.

10. Constitutional Law ⊜252

A lawful resident alien may not captiously be deprived of his constitutional rights to procedural due process.

11. Aliens ⊜53

Provision of Nationality Act of 1940 pertaining to residence of aliens deems protracted absence of an alien, such as a departure from United States and residence in foreign country for period of 19 months, without prior authorization or reentry papers, to constitute a clear break in alien's continuous residence in United States. U.S.C.A.Const. Amend. 5; Nationality Act of 1940, § 307, 8 U.S.C.A. § 707; Immigration Act of 1924, §§ 2(g), 10(b, f), 8 U.S.C.A. §§ 202(g), 210(b, f).

12. Aliens ⊜53

Statute authorizing the temporary removal from ship of alien seeking entry into United States, and temporary harborage on shore, is an act of legislative grace, and bestows no additional rights on the alien, but alien is thereafter to be treated as if he had been stopped at border when attempting entry from contiguous lands. Immigration Act of 1917, §§ 15, 18, 20, as amended, 8 U.S.C.A. §§ 151, 154, 156.

13. Aliens ⊜54(6)

Resident aliens temporarily detained pending expeditious consummation of deportation proceedings may be released on bond by the Attorney General, but the Attorney General's discretion in such respect is subject to judicial review. Immigration Act of 1917, § 20, as amended, 8 U.S.C.A. § 156.

14. Aliens ⊜54(6)

The continued exclusion of alien as a bad security risk, without hearing, does not deprive alien of any statutory or constitutional right, even though refusal of other countries to accept alien results in his continued detention at Ellis Island. 22 U.S.C.A. § 223; Proclamation No. 2523, U.S.Code Cong.Service 1941, p. 883; Emergency Powers Interim Continuation Act, § 1(40), 66 Stat. 54, 57; Joint Resolutions May 28, 1952, June 14, 1952, 66 Stat. 96, 137; Emergency Powers Continuation Act, § 1(30), 66 Stat. 330, 332.

15. Constitutional Law ⊜70(1)

The right of an alien to enter the United States depends on the congressional will, and courts cannot substitute their judgment for the legislative mandate.

———•———

207

Mr. Ross L. Malone, Jr., Roswell, N. M., for petitioner.

Mr. Jack Wasserman, Washington, D. C., for respondent.

Mr. Justice CLARK delivered the opinion of the Court.

[1] This case concerns an alien immigrant permanently excluded from the United States on security grounds but stranded in his temporary haven on Ellis Island because other countries will not take him back. The issue is whether the Attorney General's continued exclusion of respondent without a hearing amounts to an unlawful detention, so that courts may admit him temporarily to the United States on bond until arrangements are made for his departure abroad. After a hearing on respondent's petition for a writ of habeas corpus, the District Court so held and authorized his temporary admission on $5,000 bond.[1] The Court of Appeals affirmed that action, but directed reconsideration of the terms of the

208

parole.[2] Accordingly, the District Court entered a modified order reducing bond to $3,000 and permitting respondent to travel and reside in Buffalo, New York. Bond was posted and respondent released. Because of resultant serious problems in the enforcement of the immigration laws, we granted certiorari. 344 U.S. 809, 73 S.Ct. 25.

Respondent's present dilemma springs from these circumstances: Though, as the District Court observed, "[t]here is a certain vagueness about [his] history", respondent seemingly was born in Gibraltar of Hungarian or Rumanian parents and lived in the United States from 1923 to 1948.[3] In May of that year he sailed for Europe, apparently to visit his dying mother in Rumania. Denied entry there, he remained in Hungary for some 19 months, due to "difficulty in securing an exit permit." Finally, armed with a quota immigration visa issued by the American Consul in Budapest, he proceeded to France and boarded the *Ile de France* in Le Havre bound for New York. Upon arrival on February 9, 1950, he was temporarily excluded from the United States by an immigration inspector acting pursuant to the Passport Act as amended and regulations thereunder. Pending disposition of his

case he was received at Ellis Island. After reviewing the evidence, the Attorney General on May 10, 1950, ordered the temporary exclusion to be made permanent without a hearing before a board of special inquiry, on the "basis of information of a confidential nature, the disclosure of which would be prejudicial to the public interest." That determination rested on a finding that respondent's entry would be prejudicial to the public interest for security reasons. But thus far all attempts to effect respondent's departure have failed: Twice he shipped

209

out to return whence he came; France and Great Britain refused him permission to land. The State Department has unsuccessfully negotiated with Hungary for his readmission. Respondent personally applied for entry to about a dozen Latin American countries but all turned him down. So in June 1951 respondent advised the Immigration and Naturalization Service that he would exert no further efforts to depart. In short, respondent sat on Ellis Island because this country shut him out and others were unwilling to take him in.

Asserting unlawful confinement on Ellis Island, he sought relief through a series of habeas corpus proceedings. After four unsuccessful efforts on respondent's part, the United States District Court for the Southern District of New York on November 9, 1951, sustained the writ. The District Judge, vexed by the problem of "an alien who has no place to go", did not question the validity of the exclusion order but deemed further "detention" after 21 months excessive and justifiable only by affirmative proof of respondent's danger to the public safety. When the Government declined to divulge such evidence, even *in camera*, the District Court directed respondent's conditional parole on bond.[4] By a divided vote, the Court of Appeals affirmed. Postulating that the power to hold could never be broader than the power to remove or shut out and that to "continue an alien's con-

---

1. 1951, 101 F.Supp. 66.

2. 2 Cir., 1952, 195 F.2d 964.

3. 101 F.Supp. at page 67.

4. 101 F.Supp. at pages 67, 70; R. 26–27.

finement beyond that moment when deportation becomes patently impossible is to deprive him of his liberty", the court found respondent's "confinement" no longer justifiable as a means of removal elsewhere, thus not authorized by statute, and in violation of due process.[5] Judge Learned Hand, dissenting, took a different view: The Attorney General's order was one of "exclusion"

210

and not "deportation"; respondent's transfer from ship to shore on Ellis Island conferred no additional rights; in fact, no alien so situated "can force us to admit him at all."[6]

[2] Courts have long recognized the power to expel or exclude aliens as a fundamental sovereign attribute exercised by the Government's political departments largely immune from judicial control. The Chinese Exclusion Case (Chae Chan Ping v. United States), 1889, 130 U.S. 581, 9 S.Ct.

623, 32 L.Ed. 1068; Fong Yue Ting v. United States, 1893, 149 U.S. 698, 13 S.Ct. 1016, 37 L.Ed. 905; United States ex rel. Knauff v. Shaughnessy, 1950, 338 U.S. 537, 70 S.Ct. 309, 94 L.Ed. 317; Harisiades v. Shaughnessy, 1952, 342 U.S. 580, 72 S.Ct. 512, 96 L.Ed. 586. In the exercise of these powers, Congress expressly authorized the President to impose additional restrictions on aliens entering or leaving the United States during periods of international tension and strife. That authorization, originally enacted in the Passport Act of 1918, continues in effect during the present emergency. Under it, the Attorney General, acting, for the President, may shut out aliens whose "entry would be prejudicial to the interests of the United States".[7] And he may exclude without a hearing when the exclusion is based on confidential information the

211

disclosure of which may be prejudicial to the public interest.[8] The At-

---

5. 195 F.2d at pages 967, 968.

6. Id., 195 F.2d at page 970.

7. Section 1 of the Act of May 22, 1918, c. 81, 40 Stat. 559, as amended by the Act of June 21, 1941, c. 210, § 1, 55 Stat. 252, 22 U.S.C. § 223, 22 U.S.C.A. § 223, provides in pertinent part:
"When the United States is at war or during the existence of the national emergency proclaimed by the President on May 27, 1941, or as to aliens whenever there exists a state of war between, or among, two or more states, and the President shall find that the interests of the United States require that restrictions and prohibitions in addition to those provided otherwise than by this Act be imposed upon the departure of persons from and their entry into the United States, and shall make public proclamation thereof, it shall, until otherwise ordered by the President or Congress, be unlawful—
"(a) For any alien to depart from or enter or attempt to depart from or enter the United States except under such reasonable rules, regulations, and orders, and subject to such limitations and exceptions as the President shall prescribe; • • •."
That authorization has been extended to cover the dates relevant in this case. 66 Stat. 54, 57, 96, 137, 330, 332. Pursuant to that authority, Presidential

Proclamation No. 2523, 6 Fed.Reg. 5821, as promulgated in 1941, U.S.Code Cong. Service 1941, p. 883, in part provided:
"No alien shall be permitted to enter the United States if it appears to the satisfaction of the Secretary of State that such entry would be prejudicial to the interests of the United States as provided in the rules and regulations hereinbefore authorized to be prescribed by the Secretary of State, with the concurrence of the Attorney General."
The Secretary of State, with the concurrence of the Attorney General, issued applicable regulations codified as Part 175 of 8 CFR. Section 175.53 defines eleven categories of aliens whose entry is "deemed prejudicial to the interests of the United States." That delegation of authority has been upheld. United States ex rel. Knauff v. Shaughnessy, 1950, 338 U.S. 537, 70 S.Ct. 309, 94 L.Ed. 317. The regulations were ratified and confirmed by Presidential Proclamation No. 2850, 14 Fed.Reg. 5173, promulgated August 17, 1949, U.S.Code Cong.Service 1949, p. 2618.

8. 8 CFR § 175.57 provides:
"§ 175.57 *Entry not permitted in special cases.* (a) Any alien, even though in possession of a permit to enter, or exempted under §§ 175.41 to 175.62, inclusive, from obtaining a permit to enter, may be excluded temporarily if at the

torney General in this case proceeded in accord with these provisions; he made the necessary determinations and barred the alien from entering the United States.

212

[3-6] It is true that aliens who have once passed through our gates, even illegally, may be expelled only after proceedings conforming to traditional standards of fairness encompassed in due process of law. The Japanese Immigrant Case (Kaoru Yamataya v. Fisher), 1903, 189 U.S. 86, 100-101, 23 S.Ct. 611, 614, 47 L.Ed. 721; Wong Yang Sung v. McGrath, 1950, 339 U.S. 33, 49-50, 70 S.Ct. 445, 453-454, 94 L.Ed. 616; Kwong Hai Chew v. Colding, 1953, 344 U.S. 590, 598, 73 S.Ct. 472, 478. But an alien on the threshold of initial entry stands on a different footing: "Whatever the procedure authorized by Congress is, it is due process as far as an alien denied entry is concerned." United States ex rel. Knauff v. Shaughnessy, supra, 338 U.S. at page 544, 70 S.Ct. at page 313; Nishimura Ekiu v. United States, 1892, 142 U.S. 651, 660, 12 S.Ct. 336, 338, 35 L.Ed. 1146. And because the action of the executive officer under such authority is final and conclusive, the Attorney General cannot be compelled to disclose the evidence underlying his determinations in an exclusion case; "it is not within the province of any court, unless expressly authorized by law, to review the determination of the political

branch of the Government". United States ex rel. Knauff v. Shaughnessy, supra, 338 U.S. at page 543, 70 S.Ct. at page 312; Nishimura Ekiu v. United States, supra, 142 U.S. at page 660, 12 S.Ct. at page 338. In a case such as this, courts cannot retry the determination of the Attorney General. United States ex rel. Knauff v. Shaughnessy, supra, 338 U.S. at page 546, 70 S.Ct. at page 314; Ludecke v. Watkins, 1948, 335 U.S. 160, 171-172, 68 S.Ct. 1429, 1434, 1435, 92 L.Ed. 1881.

213

[7-9] Neither respondent's harborage on Ellis Island nor his prior residence here transforms this into something other than an exclusion proceeding. Concededly, his movements are restrained by authority of the United States, and he may by habeas corpus test the validity of his exclusion. But that is true whether he enjoys temporary refuge on land, Nishimura Ekiu v. United States, supra, or remains continuously aboard ship. United States v. Jung Ah Lung, 1888, 124 U.S. 621, 626, 8 S.Ct. 663, 665, 31 L.Ed. 591; Chin Yow v. United States, 1908, 208 U.S. 8, 12, 28 S.Ct. 201, 202, 52 L.Ed. 369. In sum, harborage at Ellis Island is not an entry into the United States. Kaplan v. Tod, 1925, 267 U.S. 228, 230, 45 S.Ct. 257, 69 L.Ed. 585; United States v. Ju Toy, 1905, 198 U.S. 253, 263, 25 S.Ct. 644, 646, 49 L.Ed. 1040; Nishimura Ekiu v. United States, supra, 142 U.S.

---

time he applies for admission at a port of entry it appears that he is or may be excludable under one of the categories set forth in § 175.53. The official excluding the alien shall immediately report the facts to the head of his department, who will communicate such report to the Secretary of State. Any alien so temporarily excluded by an official of the Department of Justice shall not be admitted and shall be excluded and deported unless the Attorney General, after consultation with the Secretary of State, is satisfied that the admission of the alien would not be prejudicial to the interests of the United States. Any alien so temporarily excluded by any other official shall not be admitted and shall be excluded and deported unless the Secretary of State is satisfied that the admission of the alien would not be prejudicial to

* the interests of the United States.

"(b) In the case of an alien temporarily excluded by an official of the Department of Justice on the ground that he is, or may be, excludable under one or more of the categories set forth in § 175.53, no hearing by a board of special inquiry shall be held until after the case is reported to the Attorney General and such a hearing is directed by the Attorney General or his representative. In any special case the alien may be denied a hearing before a board of special inquiry and an appeal from the decision of that board if the Attorney General determines that he is excludable under one of the categories set forth in § 175.53 on the basis of information of a confidential nature, the disclosure of which would be prejudicial to the public interest."

at page 661, 12 S.Ct. at page 339. For purposes of the immigration laws, moreover, the legal incidents of an alien's entry remain unaltered whether he has been here once before or not. He is an entering alien just the same, and may be excluded if unqualified for admission under existing immigration laws. E. g., Lem Moon Sing v. United States, 1895, 158 U.S. 538, 547–548, 15 S.Ct. 967, 970–971, 39 L.Ed. 1082; United States ex rel. Polymeris v. Trudell, 1932, 284 U.S. 279, 52 S.Ct. 143, 76 L.Ed. 291.

[10] To be sure, a lawful resident alien may not captiously be deprived of his constitutional rights to procedural due process. Kwong Hai Chew v. Colding, 1953, 344 U.S. 590, 601, 73 S.Ct. 472, 479; Cf. Delgadillo v. Carmichael, 1947, 332 U.S. 388, 68 S.Ct. 10, 92 L.Ed. 17. Only the other day we held that under some circumstances temporary absence from our shores cannot constitutionally deprive a returning lawfully resident alien of his right to be heard. Kwong Hai Chew v. Colding, supra. Chew, an alien seaman admitted by an Act of Congress to permanent residence in the United States, signed articles of maritime employment as chief steward on a vessel of American registry with home port in New York City. Though cleared by the Coast Guard for his voyage, on his return from four months at sea he was "excluded" without a hearing on security grounds.

214

On the facts of that case, including reference to § 307(d) (2) of the Nationality Act of 1940, 8 U.S.C.A. § 707(d) (2), we felt justified in "assimilating" his status for constitutional purposes to that of continuously present alien residents entitled to hearings at least before an executive or administrative tribunal. Id., 344 U.S. at pages 596, 599–601, 73 S.Ct. at pages 477–480. Ac-

cordingly, to escape constitutional conflict we held the administrative regulations authorizing exclusion without hearing in certain security cases inapplicable to aliens so protected by the Fifth Amendment. Id., 344 U.S. at page 600, 73 S.Ct. at page 479.

[11] But respondent's history here drastically differs from that disclosed in Chew's case. Unlike Chew who with full security clearance and documentation pursued his vocation for four months aboard an American ship, respondent, apparently without authorization or reentry papers,[9] simply left the United States and remained behind the Iron Curtain for 19 months. Moreover, while § 307 of the 1940 Nationality Act regards maritime service such as Chew's to be continuous residence for naturalization purposes, that section deems protracted absence such as respondent's a clear break in an alien's continuous residence here.[10] In such circumstances, we have no difficulty in holding respondent an entrant alien or "assimilated to [that] status" for constitutional purposes. Id., 344 U.S. at page 599, 73 S.Ct. at page 478. That being so, the Attorney General may lawfully exclude respondent without a hearing as authorized

215

by the emergency regulations promulgated pursuant to the Passport Act. Nor need he disclose the evidence upon which that determination rests. United States ex rel. Knauff v. Shaughnessy, 1950, 338 U.S. 537, 70 S.Ct. 309, 94 L.Ed. 317.

[12] There remains the issue of respondent's continued exclusion on Ellis Island. Aliens seeking entry from contiguous lands obviously can be turned back at the border without more. United States ex rel. Polymeris v. Trudell, 1932, 284 U.S. 279, 52 S.Ct. 143, 76 L.Ed. 291. While the

---

9. See 8 U.S.C. § 210, 8 U.S.C.A. § 210. Of course, neither a reentry permit, issuable upon proof of prior lawful admission to the United States, § 210(b), nor an immigration visa entitles an otherwise inadmissible alien to entry. §§ 210(f), 202(g). An immigrant is not unaware of this; § 202(g) directs those facts to be "printed conspicuously upon every immigration

visa." For a recent study of entry procedures with recommendations, see Report of the President's Commission on Immigration and Naturalization (1953), c. 10.

10. 8 U.S.C. § 707, 8 U.S.C.A. § 707; United States v. Larsen, 2 Cir., 1947, 165 F.2d 433.

Government might keep entrants by sea aboard the vessel pending determination of their admissibility, resulting hardships to the alien and inconvenience to the carrier persuaded Congress to adopt a more generous course. By statute it authorized, in cases such as this, aliens' temporary removal from ship to shore.[11] But such temporary harborage, an act of legislative grace, bestows no additional rights. Congress meticulously specified that such shelter ashore "shall not be considered a landing" nor relieve the vessel of the duty to transport back the alien if ultimately excluded.[12] And this Court has long considered such temporary arrangements as not affecting an alien's status; he is treated as if stopped at the border. Nishimura Ekiu v. United States, 1892, 142 U.S. 651, 661–662, 12 S.Ct. 336, 339, 35 L.Ed. 1146; United States v. Ju Toy, 1905, 198 U.S. 253, 263, 25 S.Ct. 644, 646, 49 L.Ed. 1040; Kaplan v. Tod, 1925, 267 U.S. 228, 230, 45 S.Ct. 257, 69 L.Ed. 585.

[13–15] Thus we do not think that respondent's continued exclusion deprives him of any statutory or constitutional right. It is true that resident aliens temporarily detained pending expeditious consummation of deportation proceedings may be released on bond by the Attorney General whose discretion is subject to judicial review. Carlson v. Landon, 1952, 342 U.S. 524, 72 S.Ct. 525, 96 L.Ed. 547. By that procedure aliens uprooted from our midst may rejoin the
216
community until the Government effects their leave.[13] An exclusion proceeding grounded on danger to the national se-

curity, however, presents different considerations; neither the rationale nor the statutory authority for such release exists.[14] Ordinarily to admit an alien barred from entry on security grounds nullifies the very purpose of the exclusion proceeding; Congress in 1950 declined to include such authority in the statute.[15] That exclusion by the United States plus other nations inhospitality results in present hardship cannot be ignored. But, the times being what they are, Congress may well have felt that other countries ought not shift the onus to us; that an alien in respondent's position is no more ours than theirs. Whatever our individual estimate of that policy and the fears on which it rests, respondent's right to enter the United States depends on the congressional will, and courts cannot substitute their judgment for the legislative mandate. Harisiades v. Shaughnessy, 1952, 342 U.S. 580, 590–591, 72 S.Ct. 512, 519, 96 L.Ed. 586.

Reversed.

Mr. Justice BLACK, with whom Mr. Justice DOUGLAS concurs, dissenting.

Mezei came to this country in 1923 and lived as a resident alien in Buffalo, New York, for twenty-five years.
217
He made a trip to Europe in 1948 and was stopped at our shore on his return in 1950. Without charge of or conviction for any crime, he was for two years held a prisoner on Ellis Island by order of the Attorney General. Mezei sought habeas corpus in the District Court. He wanted to go to his wife and home in Buffalo. The Attorney General

11. 8 U.S.C. § 151, 8 U.S.C.A. § 151.

12. 8 U.S.C. §§ 151, 154, 8 U.S.C.A. §§ 151, 154.

13. 8 U.S.C. (Supp. V) § 156, 8 U.S.C.A. § 156. We there noted that "the problem of habeas corpus after unusual delay in *deportation hearings* is not involved in this case." 342 U.S. at page 546, 72 S.Ct. at page 537. (Emphasis added.)

14. 8 U.S.C. § 154, 8 U.S.C.A. § 154, permits temporary suspension of deportation of excluded aliens whose testimony is needed on behalf of the United States.

Manifestly respondent does not fall within that class. While the essence of that provision is retained in § 237(d) of the Immigration and Nationality Act of 1952, 66 Stat. 202, 8 U.S.C.A. § 1227(d), § 212(d) (5) of that Act, 66 Stat. 188, 8 U.S.C.A. § 1182(d) (5), vests new and broader discretion in the Attorney General. Cf. 8 U.S.C. §§ 136(p, q), 8 U.S.C. A. § 136(p, q); 8 U.S.C. (Supp. V) § 137–5(a, b), 8 U.S.C.A. § 137–5(a, b). Those provisions are not now here.

15. See S. Rep. No. 1515, 81st Cong., 2d Sess. 643–644.

defended the imprisonment by alleging that it would be dangerous to the Nation's security to let Mezei go home even temporarily on bail. Asked for proof of this, the Attorney General answered the judge that all his information was "of a confidential nature" so much so that telling any of it or even telling the names of any of his secret informers would jeopardize the safety of the Nation. Finding that Mezei's life as a resident alien in Buffalo had been "unexceptional" and that no facts had been proven to justify his continued imprisonment, the District Court granted bail. The Court of Appeals approved. Now this Court orders Mezei to leave his home and go back to his island prison to stay indefinitely, maybe for life.

Mr. Justice JACKSON forcefully points out the danger in the Court's holding that Mezei's liberty is completely at the mercy of the unreviewable discretion of the Attorney General. I join Mr. Justice JACKSON in the belief that Mezei's continued imprisonment without a hearing violates due process of law.

No society is free where government makes one person's liberty depend upon the arbitrary will of another. Dictatorships have done this since time immemorial. They do now. Russian laws of 1934 authorized the People's Commissariat to imprison, banish and exile Russian citizens as well as "foreign subjects who are socially dangerous." * Hitler's secret police were

218

given like powers. German courts were forbidden to make any inquiry whatever as to the information on which the police acted. Our Bill of Rights was written to prevent such oppressive practices. Under it this Nation has fostered and protected individual freedom. The Founders abhorred arbitrary one-man imprisonments. Their belief was—our constitu-

tional principles are—that no person of any faith, rich or poor, high or low, native or foreigner, white or colored, can have his life, liberty or property taken "without due process of law." This means to me that neither the federal police nor federal prosecutors nor any other governmental official, whatever his title, can put or keep people in prison without accountability to courts of justice. It means that individual liberty is too highly prized in this country to allow executive officials to imprison and hold people on the basis of information kept secret from courts. It means that Mezei should not be deprived of his liberty indefinitely except as the result of a fair open court hearing in which evidence is appraised by the court, not by the prosecutor.

Mr. Justice JACKSON, whom Mr. Justice FRANKFURTER joins, dissenting.

Fortunately it still is startling, in this country, to find a person held indefinitely in executive custody without accusation of crime or judicial trial. Executive imprisonment has been considered oppressive and lawless since John, at Runnymede, pledged that no free man should be imprisoned, dispossessed, outlawed, or exiled save by the judgment of his peers or by the law of the land. The judges of England developed the writ of habeas corpus largely to preserve these immunities from executive restraint.

219

Under the best tradition of Anglo-American law, courts will not deny hearing to an unconvicted prisoner just because he is an alien whose keep, in legal theory, is just outside our gates. Lord Mansfield, in the celebrated case holding that slavery was unknown to the common law of England, ran his writ of habeas corpus in favor of an alien, an African Negro slave, and against the master of a ship at anchor in the Thames.[1]

---

* Decree of the Central Executive Committee and Council of People's Commissars, U. S. S. R., 5 Nov. 1934; Collection of Laws, U. S. S. R., 1935, No. 11, Art. 84. Hazard, Materials on Soviet Law, (194), 16. See Hazard, Reforming Soviet Criminal Law, 29 Jour. Crim. Law

and Crim. 157, 168-169 (1939). See also Berman, Principles of Soviet Criminal Law, 56 Yale L.J. 803 (1947).

1. Somersett's Case, 20 How. St. Tr. 1; 2 Campbell, Lives of the Chief Justices, 418; Fiddes, Lord Mansfield and The Sommersett Case, 50 L.Q. Rev. 499.

I.

What is our case?[2]　In contemplation of law, I agree, it is that of an alien who asks admission to the country.　Concretely, however, it is that of a lawful and law-abiding inhabitant of our country for a quarter of a century, long ago admitted for permanent residence, who seeks to return home.　After a foreign visit to his aged and ailing mother that was prolonged by disturbed conditions of Eastern Europe, he obtained a visa for admission issued by our consul and returned to New York.　There the Attorney General refused to honor his documents and turned him back as a menace to this Nation's security.　This man, who seems to have led a life of unrelieved insignificance, must have been astonished to find himself suddenly putting the Government of the United States in such fear that it was afraid to tell him why it was afraid of him.　He was shipped and reshipped to France, which twice refused him landing.　Great Britain declined, and no other European country has been found willing to open its doors to him.　Twelve countries

220

of the American Hemisphere refused his applications.　Since we proclaimed him a Samson who might pull down the pillars of our temple, we should not be surprised if peoples less prosperous, less strongly established and less stable feared to take him off our timorous hands.　With something of a record as an unwanted man, neither

his efforts nor those of the United States Government any longer promise to find him an abiding place.　For nearly two years he was held in custody of the immigration authorities of the United States at Ellis Island, and if the Government has its way he seems likely to be detained indefinitely, perhaps for life, for a cause known only to the Attorney General.

Is respondent deprived of liberty?　The Government answers that he was "transferred to Ellis Island on August 1, 1950 for safekeeping," and "is not being detained in the usual sense, but is in custody solely to prevent him from gaining entry into the United States in violation of law.　He is free to depart from the United States to any country of his choice."　Government counsel ingeniously argued that Ellis Island is his "refuge" whence he is free to take leave in any direction except west.　That might mean freedom, if only he were an amphibian!　Realistically, this man is incarcerated by a combination of forces which keeps him as effectually as a prison, the dominant and proximate of these forces being the United States immigration authority.　It overworks legal fiction to say that one is free in law when by the commonest of common sense he is bound.　Despite the impeccable legal logic of the Government's argument on this point, it leads to an artificial and unreal conclusion.[3]　We must

221

regard this alien as deprived of liberty

2.　I recite facts alleged in the petition for the writ.　Since the Government declined to try the case on the merits, I think we must consider the question on well-pleaded allegations of the petition.　Petitioner might fail to make good on a hearing; the question is, must he fail without one?

3.　Mr. Justice Holmes, for the Court, said in Chin Yow v. United States, 208 U.S. 8, 12–13, 28 S.Ct. 201, 202, 52 L.Ed. 369:

"If we regard the petitioner, as in Ju Toy's Case it was said that he should be regarded, as if he had been stopped and kept at the limit of our jurisdiction (198 U.S. [253] 263, 25 S.Ct. 644, 49 L.Ed. [1040] 1044), still it would be difficult to say that he was not imprisoned,

73 S.Ct.—40½

theoretically as well as practically, when to turn him back meant that he must get into a vessel against his wish and be carried to China.　The case would not be that of a person simply prevented from going in one direction that he desired and had a right to take, all others being left open to him, a case in which the judges were not unanimous in Bird v. Jones, 7 Q.B. 742.　But we need not speculate upon niceties.　It is true that the petitioner gains no additional right of entrance by being allowed to pass the frontier in custody for the determination of his case.　But, on the question whether he is wrongly imprisoned, we must look at the actual facts.　*De facto* he is locked up until carried out of the country against his will."

ty, and the question is whether the deprivation is a denial of due process of law.

The Government on this point argues that "no alien has any constitutional right to entry into the United States"; that "the alien has only such rights as Congress sees fit to grant in exclusion proceedings"; that "the so-called detention is still merely a continuation of the exclusion which is specifically authorized ˉby Congress"; that since "the restraint is not incidental to an order [of exclusion] but is itself the effectuation of the exclusion order, there is no limit to its continuance" other than statutory, which means no limit at all. The Government all but adopts the words of one of the officials responsible for the administration of this Act who testified before a congressional committee as to an alien applicant, that "He has no rights." [4]

222

The interpretations of the Fifth Amendment's command that no person shall be deprived of life, liberty or property without due process of law, come about to this: reasonable general legislation reasonably applied to the individual. The question is whether the Government's detention of respondent is compatible with these tests of substance and procedure.

II. Substantive Due Process.

Substantively, due process of law renders what is due to a strong state as well as to a free individual. It tolerates all reasonable measures to insure the national safety, and it leaves a large, at times a potentially dangerous, latitude for executive judgment as to policies and means.[5]

After all, the pillars which support our liberties are the three branches of government, and the burden could not be carried by our own power alone. Substantive due process will always pay a high degree of deference to congressional and executive judgment, especially when they concur, as to what is reasonable policy under conditions of particular times and circumstances. Close to the maximum of respect is due from the judiciary to the political departments in policies affecting security and alien exclusion. Harisiades v. Shaughnessy, 342 U.S. 580, 72 S.Ct. 512, 96 L.Ed. 586.

Due process does not invest any alien with a right to enter the United States, nor confer on those admitted

223

the right to remain against the national will. Nothing in the Constitution requires admission or sufferance of aliens hostile to our scheme of government.

Nor do I doubt that due process of law will tolerate some impounding of an alien where it is deemed essential to the safety of the state. Even the resident, friendly alien may be subject to executive detention without bail, for a reasonable period, pending consummation of deportation arrangements. Carlson v. Landon, 342 U.S. 524, 72 S.Ct. 525, 96 L.Ed. 547. The alien enemy may be confined or his property seized and administered because hostility is assumed from his continued allegiance to a hostile state. Cf. Ludecke v. Watkins, 335 U.S. 160, 68 S.Ct. 1429, 92 L.Ed. 1881; Zittman v. McGrath, 341 U.S. 446, 71 S.Ct.

---

4. Testimony of Almanza Tripp, an immigration service official, before the Senate Subcommittee on Immigration on February 15, 1950, included the following:
"* * * Now, when we have a case of that sort, where central registry contains something derogatory of that nature, I do not believe we should make a finding of admissibility until it has been disproved. But the evidence that they had in central registry would not be sufficient for our Service to exclude by the normal board of special inquiry proceedings, because those proceedings must be conducted in a manner in which they

could not be subject to attack in a court of the United States.
"You may say that it is unfair to the applicant not to give him that protection, but you must remember that the applicant is an applicant. He has no rights * * *." (Hearings before the Subcommittee on Amendments to the Displaced Persons Act, Senate Committee on the Judiciary, 81st Cong., 1st and 2d Sessions 665.)

5. Cf. Toyosaburo Korematsu v. United States, 323 U.S. 214, 65 S.Ct. 193, 89 L.Ed. 194.

832, 95 L.Ed. 1096, and 341 U.S. 471, 71 S.Ct. 846, 95 L.Ed. 1112.

If due process will permit confinement of resident aliens friendly in fact because of imputed hostility, I should suppose one personally at war with our institutions might be confined, even though his state is not at war with us. In both cases, the underlying consideration is the power of our system of government to defend itself, and changing strategy of attack by infiltration may be met with changed tactics of defense.

Nor do I think the concept of due process so paralyzing that it forbids all detention of an alien as a preventive measure against threatened dangers and makes confinement lawful only after the injuries have been suffered. In some circumstances, even the citizen in default of bail has long been subject to federal imprisonment for security of the peace and good behavior.[6] While it is usually applied for express verbal threats, no reason is known to me why the power is not the same in the case of threats inferred by proper procedures from circumstances. The British, with whom due process is a habit, if not a written

224

constitutional dictum, permit a court in a limited class of cases to pass a "sentence of preventive detention" if satisfied that it is expedient for the protection of the public.[7]

I conclude that detention of an alien would not be inconsistent with substantive due process, provided—and this is where my dissent begins—he is accorded procedural due process of law.

III. Procedural Due Process.

Procedural fairness, if not all that originally was meant by due process of law, is at least what it most uncompromisingly requires. Procedural due process is more elemental and less flexible than substantive due process. It yields less to the times, varies less with conditions, and defers much

less to legislative judgment. Insofar as it is technical law, it must be a specialized responsibility within the competence of the judiciary on which they do not bend before political branches of the Government, as they should on matters of policy which compromise substantive law.

If it be conceded that in some way this alien could be confined, does it matter what the procedure is? Only the untaught layman or the charlatan lawyer can answer that procedures matter not. Procedural fairness and regularity are of the indispensable essence of liberty. Severe substantive laws can be endured if they are fairly and impartially applied. Indeed, if put to the choice, one might well prefer to live under Soviet substantive law applied in good faith by our common-law procedures than under our substantive law enforced by Soviet procedural practices. Let it not be overlooked that due process of law is not for the sole benefit of an accused. It is the best insurance for the Government itself against those

225

blunders which leave lasting stains on a system of justice but which are bound to occur on ex parte consideration. Cf. United States ex rel. Knauff v. Shaughnessy, 338 U.S. 537, 70 S.Ct. 309, 94 L.Ed. 317, which was a near miss, saved by further administrative and congressional hearings from perpetrating an injustice. See Knauff, The Ellen Knauff Story (New York) 1952.

Our law may, and rightly does, place more restrictions on the alien than on the citizen. But basic fairness in hearing procedures does not vary with the status of the accused. If the procedures used to judge this alien are fair and just, no good reason can be given why they should not be extended to simplify the condemnation of citizens. If they would be unfair to citizens, we cannot defend the fairness of them when applied to the more helpless and handicapped alien. This is at the root of our holdings that the resident alien must

6. 18 U.S.C. § 3043, 18 U.S.C.A. § 3043; cf. Criminal Code of New York, 66 McKinney's Consolidated Laws, c. II, § 84.

7. Criminal Justice Act, 1948, § 21(2).

be given a fair hearing to test an official claim that he is one of a deportable class. Wong Yang Sung v. McGrath, 339 U.S. 33, 70 S.Ct. 445, 94 L.Ed. 616.

The most scrupulous observance of due process, including the right to know a charge, to be confronted with the accuser, to cross-examine informers and to produce evidence in one's behalf, is especially necessary where the occasion of detention is fear of future misconduct, rather than crimes committed. Both the old proceeding by which one may be bound to keep the peace and the newer British "preventive detention" are safeguarded with full rights to judicial hearings for the accused. On the contrary, the Nazi regime in Germany installed a system of "protective custody" by which the arrested could claim no judicial or other hearing process,[8] and as a result the concentration

226

camps were populated with victims of summary executive detention for secret reasons. That is what renders Communist justice such a travesty. There are other differences, to be sure, between authoritarian procedure and common law, but differences in the process of administration make all the difference between a reign of terror and one of law. Quite unconsciously, I am sure, the Government's theory of custody for "safekeeping" without disclosure to the victim of charges, evidence, informers or reasons, even in an administrative proceeding, has unmistakable overtones of the "protective custody" of the Nazis more than of any detaining procedure known to the common law. Such a practice, once established with

the best of intentions, will drift into oppression of the disadvantaged in this country as surely as it has elsewhere. That these apprehensive surmises are not "such stuff as dreams are made on" appears from testimony of a top immigration official concerning an applicant that "He has no rights."

Because the respondent has no right of entry, does it follow that he has no rights at all? Does the power to exclude mean that exclusion may be continued or effectuated by any means which happen to seem appropriate to the authorities? It would effectuate his exclusion to eject him bodily into the sea or to set him adrift in a rowboat.

227

Would not such measures be condemned judicially as a deprivation of life without due process of law? Suppose the authorities decide to disable an alien from entry by confiscating his valuables and money. Would we not hold this a taking of property without due process of law? Here we have a case that lies between the taking of life and the taking of property; it is the taking of liberty. It seems to me that this, occurring within the United States or its territorial waters, may be done only by proceedings which meet the test of due process of law.

Exclusion of an alien without judicial hearing, of course, does not deny due process when it can be accomplished merely by turning him back on land or returning him by sea. But when indefinite confinement becomes the means of enforcing exclusion, it seems to me that due process requires that the alien be informed of its grounds

---

8. Hermann Göring, on cross-examination, made the following statements:

"* * * [T]hose who had committed some act of treason against the new state, or those who might be proved to have committed such an act, were naturally turned over to the courts. The others, however, of whom one might expect such acts, but who had not yet committed them, were taken into protective custody, and these were the people who were taken to concentration camps. * * * Likewise, if for political reasons * * * someone was taken into protective custody, that is, purely for reasons of state,

this could not be reviewed or stopped by any court." He claimed (though the claim seemed specious) that twenty-four hours after being put in concentration camps they were informed of the reasons and after forty-eight hours were allowed an attorney. "But this by no means rescinded my order that a review was not permitted by the courts of a politically necessary measure of protective custody. These people were simply to be given an opportunity of making a protest." 9 International Military Tribunal Proceedings 420–421 (March 18, 1946).

and have a fair chance to overcome them. This is the more due him when he is entrapped into leaving the other shore by reliance on a visa which the Attorney General refuses to honor.

It is evident that confinement of respondent no longer can be justified as a step in the process of turning him back to the country whence he came. Confinement is no longer ancillary to exclusion; it can now be justified only as the alternative to normal exclusion. It is an end in itself.

The Communist conspiratorial technique of infiltration poses a problem which sorely tempts the Government to resort to confinement of suspects on secret information secretly judged. I have not been one to discount the Communist evil. But my apprehensions about the security of our form of government are about equally aroused by those who refuse to recognize the dangers of Communism and those who will not see danger in anything else.

228

Congress has ample power to determine whom we will admit to our shores and by what means it will effectuate its exclusion policy. The only limitation is that it may not do so by authorizing United States officers to take without due process of law the life, the liberty or the property of an alien who has come within our jurisdiction; and that means he must meet a fair hearing with fair notice of the charges.[9]

It is inconceivable to me that this measure of simple justice and fair dealing would menace the security of this country. No one can make me believe that we are that far gone.

9. The trial court sought to reconcile due process for the individual with claims of security by suggesting that the Attorney General disclose *in camera* enough to enable a judicial determination of the legality of the confinement. The Attorney General refused. I do not know just how an *in camera* proceeding would be handled in this kind of case. If respondent, with or without counsel, were present, disclosures to them might well result in disclosures by them. If they are not allowed to be present, it is hard to see how it would answer the purpose of testing the Government's case by cross-examination or counter-evidence, which is what a hearing is for. The questions raised by the proposal need not be discussed since they do not call for decision here.

Detained Aliens Challenging Conditions of Confinement and the Porous Border of the Plenary Power Doctrine

By Margaret H. Taylor*

Table of Contents

* Associate Professor of Law, Wake Forest University School of Law. B.A., University of Texas; J.D., Yale Law School. I am grateful to participants at the immigration law professors workshop in Albuquerque, New Mexico in June 1994 for their dialogue and helpful comments. I benefitted from the additional comments of Kevin Johnson, Dan Kesselbrenner, Stephen Legomsky, Ronald Mann, David Martin, Hiroshi Motomura, J. Wilson Parker, and Michael Scaperlanda. I am particularly indebted to Lenni Benson, Vance Parker, and Ron Wright for their patient and insightful review of several drafts. My thanks also go to Laura Graham, Sean Phelan, Rebecca Perry, and Susan Bates for their research assistance.

Introduction

Jenny Flores was a teenager when she was detained by the Immigration and Naturalization Service ("INS"). Flores and other unaccompanied minors awaiting deportation proceedings were "held in detention by the INS for as long as two years in highly inappropriate conditions."[1] There were few opportunities for recreation and no educational programs.[2] The children were subjected to routine strip searches.[3] Some were forced to share sleeping quarters and bathrooms with unrelated adults of both sexes.[4]

The INS confined Godwin Imasuen for several months in local jails and municipal lock-ups not suited for long-term detention. Imasuen was transferred among as many as five such facilities each

---

1. Flores v. Meese, 934 F.2d 991, 1014 (9th Cir. 1990) (Fletcher, J., dissenting), *vacated*, 942 F.2d 1352 (9th Cir. 1991) (en banc), *rev'd sub nom.*, Reno v. Flores, 113 S. Ct. 1439 (1993).

2. *Id.*

3. The strip search policy was declared unconstitutional in Flores v. Meese, 681 F. Supp. 665 (C.D. Cal. 1988).

4. *Flores*, 934 F.2d at 1014 (Fletcher, J., dissenting); *see also* AMERICAS WATCH, BRUTALITY UNCHECKED: HUMAN RIGHTS ABUSES ALONG THE U.S. BORDER WITH MEXICO 67-75 (1992) [hereinafter BRUTALITY UNCHECKED]; AMERICAN CIVIL LIBERTIES UNION, DETENTION OF UNDOCUMENTED ALIENS 56-60 (1990) [hereinafter ACLU DETENTION REPORT] (describing the prevailing detention conditions for juvenile alien detainees). In 1987, the INS entered into a consent decree obligating it to transfer all juveniles detained more than 72 hours following arrest to "shelter care" facilities that meet certain minimum standards. Memorandum of Understanding re: Compromise of Class Action: Conditions of Detention, *Flores* (No. 85-4544-RJK) (on file with author). In later litigation, the Supreme Court refused to entertain arguments that the detention conditions for juveniles were not in compliance with this decree. *Flores*, 113 S. Ct. at 1446-47. *But see* Brief for Southwest Refugee Project, Immigrant Legal Resource Center, and the Mexican American Legal Defense and Educational Fund, As Amici Curiae in Support of Respondents, *Flores* (No. 91-905) (citing evidence of noncompliance).

week; his family and attorney were not kept informed of his whereabouts. One local holding cell was called *un vaso de agua* by INS detainees because a glass of water was all they were served for dinner.[5]

Manuel Valdés, a former Cuban diplomat seeking asylum in the United States, was confined by the INS at a detention facility run by Esmor Correctional Services Corporation in Elizabeth, New Jersey.[6] Reports of unfit detention conditions and mistreatment of detainees at Esmor were largely ignored until a riot erupted in June 1995.[7] An INS investigation, concluded after the riot, painted a shocking picture of private detention run amok at the Esmor facility, where untrained guards routinely abused detainees without oversight or intervention from INS officials.[8]

Flores, Imasuen, and Valdés are among the thousands of persons detained by the INS each year. The detention of aliens[9] has sparked litigation and controversy for over a decade. Our shifting policies to-

---

5. These allegations appear in the complaint filed in a class-action lawsuit challenging detention conditions for aliens held in the Chicago area. Imasuen v. Moyer, No. 91-C-5425, 1991 U.S. Dist. LEXIS 1449 (N.D. Ill. Aug. 27, 1991); *see also* Lizette Alvarez & Lisa Getter, *Detention: The Failed Deterrent*, MIAMI HERALD, Dec. 16, 1993, at 1A [hereinafter Alvarez & Gutter, *Detention: The Failed Deterrent*] (noting in Chicago the "INS kept detainees in barren holding cells, where they got no exercise and, at times, no food"). See *infra* notes 177-180 and accompanying text for additional discussion of the *Imasuen* litigation.

6. Robert Hanley, *Refugees Fled Woes of the World to Find Themselves Locked up in Elizabeth*, N.Y. TIMES, June 21, 1995, at A15; *see also* John Sullivan & Matthew Purdy, *In Corrections Business, Shrewdness Pays*, N.Y. TIMES, July 23, 1995, at A1; John Sullivan, *Violence at Immigration Jail Exposes Troubled Company*, N.Y. TIMES, June 20, 1995, at A1 (describing history of Esmor Correctional Services Corporation and the Elizabeth, N.J. immigration detention facility).

7. *See* Maureen Castellano, *INS to Probe Conditions at Private Jail for Aliens*, N.J. L.J., June 12, 1995, at 5 (reporting claims of inhumane treatment prompted the INS to investigate the conditions at Esmor; the investigation commenced one week before the riot); Elizabeth Llorente, *Shackled in the Land of Hope: Asylum Seekers Held for Months*, BERGEN REC., Mar. 12, 1995, at A1 (noting complaints about abuse, inedible food, and shackling of detainees).

8. *See* IMMIGRATION AND NATURALIZATION SERV., U.S. DEP'T OF JUSTICE, INTERIM REPORT: THE ELIZABETH, NEW JERSEY CONTRACT DETENTION FACILITY OPERATED BY ESMOR INC. (1995) [hereinafter INS ESMOR REPORT] (on file with author). The conditions at the Esmor facility, and the results of the INS investigation, are summarized *infra* notes 155-165 and accompanying text.

9. I use the term "alien" with some reluctance because of the pejorative connotations that this word sometimes carries. *See* Kevin R. Johnson, *A "Hard Look" at the Executive Branch's Asylum Decisions*, UTAH L. REV. 279, 281 n.5 (1991); Gerald M. Rosberg, *The Protection of Aliens from Discriminatory Treatment by the National Government*, 1977 SUP. CT. REV. 275, 303. Nevertheless, this is the term used in immigration law to describe "any person not a citizen or national of the United States." Immigration and Nationality Act of 1952 [hereinafter INA], Pub. L. No. 82-414, § 101(a)(3), 66 Stat. 163, 166, 8 U.S.C. § 1101(a)(3) (1994).

ward Haitians and Cubans seeking refuge in the United States have been at the center of this debate.[10] Most of the lawsuits filed on behalf of INS detainees have sought to secure their release or parole into the United States. Behind this first-order desire for release, however, lurks another important concern: the conditions of confinement at the detention facilities and jails where the INS detains aliens.

Alien detainees are not protected by the Eighth Amendment's prohibition against cruel and unusual punishment, as this provision applies only to prisoners incarcerated for criminal convictions.[11] Instead, aliens confined by the INS, like pretrial detainees awaiting criminal trials, must challenge the conditions of their confinement under the Due Process Clause of the Fifth Amendment.[12] Due process protection against inhumane conditions ought to be "at least as great as the Eighth Amendment protections available to a convicted prisoner."[13] For aliens seeking to enter the United States, however, any due process claim is fraught with uncertainty under the century-old "plenary power" doctrine that purports to place them "largely outside the mantle of the Due Process Clause of the Fifth Amendment."[14]

---

10. In the early 1980s, over 125,000 Cubans and several thousand Haitians seeking entry into the United States traveled in makeshift boats to Florida. Thousands were detained by the INS. *See infra* notes 70-71, 270 and accompanying text. The United States Coast Guard then began interdicting Haitians before they reached the United States shore. Haitian interdictees were, at various times, either returned to their country or held at "safe haven" camps at Guantanamo Naval Base in Cuba. *See generally* Harold Hongju Koh, *Reflections on Refoulement and Haitian Centers Council*, 35 HARV. INT'L L.J. 1 (1994) (describing litigation challenging the United States rapidly changing policy towards Haitians fleeing by boat). Cubans, on the other hand, were generally admitted to the United States until the summer of 1994, when they too were detained at Guantanamo. *See A Slow-Motion Mariel: Cubans (and Haitians) Take to Sea*, 71 INTERPRETER RELEASES 1091, 1091-92 (1994) (summarizing events leading to the recreation of detention camps on Guantanamo for Haitian and Cuban refugees).

11. Ingraham v. Wright, 430 U.S. 651, 671-72 n.40 (1977); Paul W. Schmidt, *Detention of Aliens*, 24 SAN DIEGO L. REV. 305, 321 (1987).

12. In *Bell v. Wolfish*, the Supreme Court concluded that pretrial detainees must pursue conditions claims under the Due Process Clause. 441 U.S. 520, 535 n.16 (1979). The Supreme Court has never considered the conditions claims of alien detainees, but lower courts have assumed that these claims are governed by the Due Process Clause. *See* Schmidt, *supra* note 11, at 321.

13. City of Revere v. Massachusetts Gen. Hosp., 463 U.S. 239, 244 (1983).

14. Garcia-Mir v. Meese, 788 F.2d 1446, 1450 (11th Cir.), *cert. denied sub nom.*, Ferrer-Mazorra v. Meese, 479 U.S. 889 (1986).

To someone uninitiated to the "constitutional oddity"[15] of immigration law, it may seem astonishing to suggest that aliens confined by the INS have no due process rights. Yet this suggestion has been raised time and again in leading immigration cases. The Supreme Court has staked out a role of extreme deference to the political branches' "plenary power" over immigration. This "hands off" approach dictated by the plenary power doctrine "smothers the entire field of immigration law so completely"[16] that it is unusual to find immigration cases that seriously consider constitutional claims asserted by aliens. Among the Court's most notorious plenary power decisions are those asserting that the Due Process Clause does not protect aliens seeking entry, even when they are detained within the United States.[17]

From its inception, however, the plenary power doctrine has existed alongside cases that provide constitutional protection to aliens when their claims do not relate to immigration matters. Outside of immigration law, "[a]liens, even aliens whose presence in this country is unlawful, have long been recognized as 'persons' guaranteed due process of law by the Fifth and Fourteenth Amendments."[18] Thus, aliens enjoy a full panoply of constitutional rights in criminal proceedings[19] and generally are protected from invidious discrimination by state and local authorities.[20]

This "aliens' rights" tradition contrasts sharply with the plenary power doctrine. The competing traditions are typically explained as operating in two completely separate realms. The plenary power doctrine controls "immigration law," usually defined as "the body of law governing the admission and expulsion of aliens."[21] The aliens' rights

---

15. Stephen H. Legomsky, *Immigration Law and the Principle of Plenary Congressional Power*, 1984 SUP. CT. REV. 255, 255 [hereinafter Legomsky, *Immigration Law and Plenary Power*].

16. Hiroshi Motomura, *Immigration Law After a Century of Plenary Power: Phantom Constitutional Norms and Statutory Interpretation*, 100 YALE L.J. 545, 574 (1990) [hereinafter Motomura, *Phantom Norms*].

17. Shaughnessy v. United States *ex rel.* Mezei, 345 U.S. 206, 210, 212 (1953); United States *ex rel.* Knauff v. Shaughnessy, 338 U.S. 537, 544 (1950); *see infra* notes 212-228.

18. Plyler v. Doe, 457 U.S. 202, 210 (1982).

19. Wong Wing v. United States, 163 U.S. 228, 238 (1896); United States v. Henry, 604 F.2d 908, 914 (5th Cir. 1979). *But see* United States v. Verdugo-Urquidez, 494 U.S. 259 (1990) (discussed *infra* notes 245-252 and accompanying text).

20. Graham v. Richardson, 403 U.S. 365, 371 (1971); Yick Wo v. Hopkins, 118 U.S. 356, 369 (1886). *But see infra* note 235 (discussing the "political function" exemption to this principle).

21. Motomura, *Phantom Norms, supra* note 16, at 547 (citing Legomsky, *Immigration Law and Plenary Power, supra* note 15, at 256).

tradition is said to operate outside of the realm of immigration law, when aliens bring claims that do not impinge on the "plenary" immigration power.[22] There are some notable cases withholding constitutional protection from aliens even when their claims fall outside of the immigration context.[23] Nevertheless, the aliens' rights tradition generally marks a domain where courts "t[ake] th[e] constitutional claims [of aliens] seriously, in contrast to the cavalier treatment of constitutional claims in immigration law."[24]

Only a handful of reported cases have decided the due process challenges to conditions of confinement suffered by alien detainees.[25] These cases reflect confusion over which of the two competing lines of cases—the plenary power doctrine or the aliens' rights tradition—should govern conditions claims. In *Lynch v. Cannatella*, for example, the Fifth Circuit correctly held that all alien detainees, regardless of

---

22. T. Alexander Aleinikoff, *Federal Regulation of Aliens and the Constitution*, 83 AM. J. INT'L L. 862, 865 (1989) [hereinafter Aleinikoff, *Federal Regulation*] ("Outside the immigration process, aliens receive most of the constitutional protections afforded citizens."); *see also* Motomura, *Phantom Norms, supra* note 16, at 565; Legomsky, *Immigration Law and Plenary Power, supra* note 15, at 256. For a critique of this "inside/outside" immigration law dichotomy, see Linda S. Bosniak, *Membership, Equality and the Difference that Alienage Makes*, 69 N.Y.U. L. REV. 1047, 1059-65 (1994).

23. *See Verdugo-Urquidez*, 494 U.S. at 274-75 (holding Fourth Amendment does not apply to a search by American officials of the Mexican residence of a Mexican citizen detained within the United States); Mathews v. Diaz, 426 U.S. 67, 83-84 (1976) (upholding federal law denying Medicare benefits to certain noncitizens); Flemming v. Nestor, 363 U.S. 603, 621 (1960) (upholding provision of the Social Security Act cutting off benefits to aliens deported for past membership in the Communist party). These cases are discussed *infra* notes 245-263 and accompanying text.

24. Motomura, *Phantom Norms, supra* note 16, at 566.

25. *See* Adras v. Nelson, 917 F.2d 1552, 1558 (11th Cir. 1990); Medina v. O'Neill, 838 F.2d 800 (5th Cir. 1988), *rev'g* 589 F. Supp. 1028 (S.D. Tex. 1984); Lynch v. Cannatella, 810 F.2d 1363 (5th Cir. 1987); Ortega v. Rowe, 796 F.2d 765 (5th Cir. 1986), *cert. denied*, 481 U.S. 1013 (1987); Haitian Ctrs. Council v. Sale, 823 F. Supp. 1028 (E.D.N.Y. 1993) (vacated per settlement agreement). In several other cases, courts have alluded to conditions problems at alien detention facilities, or have addressed conditions claims only tangentially in the midst of litigation challenging other aspects of INS detention. *See, e.g.*, Orantes-Hernandez v. Smith, 541 F. Supp. 351, 363-64 (C.D. Cal. 1982) (conditions of confinement discussed in conjunction with litigation seeking to end coerced departure of Salvadoran detainees); Vigile v. Sava, 535 F. Supp. 1002, 1007 (S.D.N.Y.) and Bertrand v. Sava, 535 F. Supp. 1020, 1030-31 (S.D.N.Y.) (companion cases) (noting Haitian detainees were incarcerated in "substandard" and "inadequate" facilities that constituted a "harsh environment"), *rev'd*, 684 F.2d 204, 207 n.6 (2d Cir. 1982) (characterizing district court's comments about conditions of confinement as "unsubstantiated conclusory statements made in passing"). In addition, several suits brought by alien detainees challenging conditions of confinement have settled without reported opinion. *See, e.g.*, Reno v. Flores, 113 S. Ct. 1439, 1446-47 (1993) (refusing to consider arguments that conditions were oppressive for juvenile alien detainees because similar claims had previously been settled by consent decree); Stipulation of Agreement, Lam v. Smith, No. CV-79-0795 (E.D.N.Y. filed Dec. 24, 1981).

their status under immigration law, can claim due process protection to challenge mistreatment at the hands of their captors.[26] The *Lynch* court rejected the defendants' plenary power argument that aliens on the threshold of entry "possess no constitutional rights," and instead relied upon cases from the aliens' rights tradition.[27]

Later cases, however, have suggested alien detainees who have not been formally admitted into the country have only a limited constitutional right to be free from "malicious infliction of cruel treatment" or "gross physical abuse."[28] Ironically, this standard is derived from language in *Lynch*,[29] but it is inconsistent with *Lynch*'s promise of full constitutional protection for aliens challenging conditions of confinement. No other government detainees—not even incarcerated criminals—must show "malicious infliction of cruel treatment" or "gross physical abuse" to state a constitutional violation.[30] This higher constitutional hurdle sometimes imposed on alien detainees reflects the silent influence of the plenary power doctrine on cases that should be governed by the aliens' rights tradition.

Part I of this Article provides an overview of immigration detention. Part II documents serious conditions problems at the detention facilities and state and local jails where aliens are incarcerated. Part III explains how recent litigation over the due process rights of Haitian and Cuban detainees helped to define a boundary for the plenary power doctrine, which was used by the *Lynch* court to uphold aliens' due process right to challenge the conditions of their confinement. Part IV shows how *Lynch* has been undermined by later cases that implicitly deny full due process protection to some alien detainees seeking to challenge the conditions of their confinement, much as the plenary power doctrine defeats the constitutional claims of aliens within the immigration law realm. In Part V, I conclude that courts must guard against the infiltration of the plenary power doctrine into the aliens' rights tradition, even though such vigilance might some-

---

26. *Lynch*, 810 F.2d at 1374.

27. *Id.* at 1372-73. *Accord Haitian Ctrs. Council*, 823 F. Supp at 1042.

28. Medina v. O'Neill, 838 F.2d 800, 803 (5th Cir. 1988); Adras v. Nelson, 917 F.2d 1552, 1559-60 (11th Cir. 1990); *see also* Gisbert v. United States Attorney Gen., 988 F.2d 1437, 1442, *amended on other grounds*, 997 F.2d 1122 (5th Cir. 1993); Correa v. Thornburgh, 901 F.2d 1166, 1171 n.5 (2d Cir. 1990); Xiao v. Reno, 837 F. Supp. 1506, 1550 (N.D. Cal. 1993) (dicta reiterating the "malicious infliction of cruel treatment" or "gross physical abuse" standard).

29. *Lynch*, 810 F.2d at 1374.

30. *See* Wilson v. Seiter, 501 U.S. 294, 305-06 (1991); Hudson v. McMillian, 112 S. Ct. 995, 999-1001 (1992) (rejecting similar standards as too stringent for Eighth Amendment claims); *infra* notes 330-340 and accompanying text.

times reinforce the isolation of immigration law from constitutional values.

The analysis in this Article is animated by two overarching goals. First, I want to focus attention on the conditions of confinement imposed upon alien detainees. The INS has an appalling history of detaining aliens in substandard and sometimes inhumane conditions. Despite recent efforts to improve conditions at some facilities, the INS continues to use detention to deter large influxes of potential refugees, a practice that has repeatedly created serious conditions problems. Moreover, as the recent investigation of the Esmor facility has shown, the INS also confines aliens in state and local jails and private facilities without adequate oversight. It is not surprising, then, that the agency remains embroiled in litigation over conditions of confinement.[31]

Second, I use conditions cases as a lens to examine the relationship between the plenary power doctrine and the aliens' rights tradition. Many leading commentators have argued that the plenary power doctrine should be discarded;[32] some have suggested that the doctrine is already in a state of decline.[33] But they typically have examined the impact of the plenary power doctrine only within the realm of immigration law, when aliens press claims to enter or remain in the United States.[34] From this narrow perspective, the aliens' rights tradition, to

---

31. Two class action lawsuits now pending in California challenge the conditions of confinement suffered by alien detainees. Central Am. Refugee Ctr. v. Reno, No. CV 93-4162-MRP (C.D. Cal. June 23, 1995) (order certifying class of aliens detained in the INS Los Angeles district); Kattola v. Reno, No. CV 94-4859-KN (C.D. Cal. filed May 3, 1995) (nationwide class of aliens confined by the INS in facilities across the country).

32. *See, e.g.*, Michael Scaperlanda, *Polishing the Tarnished Golden Door*, 1993 WIS. L. REV. 965, 972 [hereinafter, Scaperlanda, *Polishing the Tarnished Golden Door*]; Hiroshi Motomura, *The Curious Evolution of Immigration Law: Procedural Surrogates for Substantive Constitutional Rights*, 92 COLUM. L. REV. 1625, 1627-28 (1992) [hereinafter Motomura, *Procedural Surrogates*]; Louis Henkin, *The Constitution and United States Sovereignty: A Century of Chinese Exclusion and its Progeny*, 100 HARV. L. REV. 853, 863 (1987).

33. For a reassessment of the current state of the plenary power doctrine, see Stephen T. Legomsky, *Ten More Years of Plenary Power: Immigration, Congress, and the Courts*, 22 HASTINGS CONST. L.Q. 925 (1995) [hereinafter Legomsky, *Ten More Years*]; *see also* Motomura, *Phantom Norms*, *supra* note 16, at 549; Legomsky, *Immigration Law and Plenary Power*, *supra* note 15, at 306-07; Peter H. Schuck, *The Transformation of Immigration Law*, 84 COLUM. L. REV. 1, 90 (1984) [hereinafter Schuck, *Transformation of Immigration Law*].

34. *See, e.g.*, Legomsky, *Immigration Law and Plenary Power*, *supra* note 15, at 256 (stating that immigration law "is the sphere in which the plenary power doctrine has operated"). *But see* Scaperlanda, *Polishing the Tarnished Golden Door*, *supra* note 32, at 994-97 (arguing the plenary power doctrine has expanded beyond immigration claims to government benefits and search and seizure decisions); Bosniak, *supra* note 22, at 1065 (sug-

the extent that it is considered at all, is seen as a destabilizing force, a source of constitutional protection for aliens that may contribute to the eventual demise of the plenary power doctrine.[35] This analysis suggests that the boundary separating the plenary power doctrine from the aliens' rights tradition is slowly eroding, but only to allow the one-way migration of constitutional values into immigration law.

I contend, however, that the border between the plenary power doctrine and the aliens' rights tradition is in fact porous in both directions. And unfortunately the spillover across this porous border does not necessarily weaken the plenary power doctrine. Cases adjudicating alien detainees' challenges to conditions of confinement demonstrate how the plenary power doctrine infects decisions outside the realm of immigration law, and works to undermine the aliens' rights tradition.

I. Overview of Immigration Detention

A. Statutory Framework

The INS enjoys broad authority to detain aliens seeking entry into or awaiting expulsion from the United States. The statutory framework for detention, as does all of immigration law, distinguishes between "excludable" and "deportable" aliens. "Excludable aliens" are those seeking to enter the United States.[36] First-time applicants for admission and resident aliens seeking to re-enter the country after a trip abroad fall into this category.[37]

---

gesting the traditional analysis "tends to seriously overstate the status of aliens on the so-called 'outside'").

35. Hiroshi Motomura, for example, has argued that the aliens' rights tradition has influenced the development of immigration law by "provid[ing] the normative foundation for results at odds with strict application of the plenary power doctrine." Motomura, *Phantom Norms, supra* note 16, at 566-67. Alex Aleinikoff has made a similar argument, asserting that "cases recognizing constitutional protection for aliens outside the immigration context provide critical purchase for reorienting" immigration law. T. Alexander Aleinikoff, *Citizens, Aliens, Membership and the Constitution*, 7 CONST. COMMENTARY 9, 19 (1990) [hereinafter Aleinikoff, *Membership and the Constitution*].

36. *See* IRA J. KURZBAN, KURZBAN'S IMMIGRATION LAW SOURCEBOOK 23 (4th ed. 1994); DAVID A. MARTIN, FEDERAL JUDICIARY CTR., MAJOR ISSUES IN IMMIGRATION LAW 9-11 (1987).

37. The Immigration and Nationality Act defines an "entry" as "*any* coming of an alien into the United States, from a foreign port or place or from an outlying possession." INA § 101(a)(13), 8 U.S.C. § 1101(a)(13) (1994) (emphasis added). Under this definition, aliens lawfully residing within the United States who are returning from a trip abroad are subject to exclusion proceedings. *See* Landon v. Plasencia, 459 U.S. 21, 27-32 (1982). Lawful permanent residents, however, returning from a trip that was "innocent, casual, and brief" and not meant to be "meaningfully interruptive" of their status are deemed not to

The Immigration and Nationality Act ("INA") provides that "every alien" seeking entry "who may not appear to the examining immigration officer at the port of arrival to be clearly and beyond a doubt entitled to land *shall be detained* for further inquiry."[38] This provision appears to make detention mandatory for all aliens subject to exclusion proceedings. But a different section of the INA modifies this language by granting the Attorney General discretion to "parole" rather than detain any alien applying for admission "for emergent reasons or reasons deemed strictly in the public interest."[39] Parole allows aliens the freedom to live inside the United States while they await a final determination of their application to enter.[40]

Neither parole nor detention within the United States counts as an "entry" under immigration law.[41] Instead, under a legal fiction sometimes known as the "entry doctrine," excludable aliens are "treated as if stopped at the border," even when they are paroled or confined within the United States.[42]

The INA also provides for the detention of "deportable aliens" who, unlike excludable aliens, have already entered the United States.[43] Aliens lawfully admitted into the country can be deported for the reasons delineated in INA section 241(a).[44] Aliens who evade inspection or surreptitiously cross the border are also subject to deportation proceedings.[45] Deportable aliens may be confined pending an administrative hearing to determine their right to remain in the

---

have made a new "entry," and thus can escape application of the exclusion grounds. Rosenberg v. Fleuti, 374 U.S. 449, 461-62 (1963); *see* KURZBAN, *supra* note 36, at 25-27.

38. INA § 235(b), 8 U.S.C. § 1225(b) (1994) (emphasis added). The "further inquiry" refers to exclusion proceedings before a "special inquiry officer," now known as an immigration judge, to determine whether an alien will be admitted to the United States. *Id.*; 8 C.F.R. § 235.6 (1994). Excludable aliens can be refused permission to enter for the reasons listed in INA § 212(a), 8 U.S.C. § 1182(a) (1994).

39. INA § 212(d)(5)(A), 8 U.S.C. § 1182(d)(5)(A) (1994). The regulations governing the exercise of this parole power, codified at 8 C.F.R. § 212.5 (1994), are discussed *infra* notes 74-75.

40. *See* 2 CHARLES GORDON ET AL., IMMIGRATION LAW AND PROCEDURE § 64.01[1] (Rev. ed. 1995).

41. *See* INA § 212(d)(5)(A), 8 U.S.C. § 1182(d)(5)(A) (1994) (parole "shall not be regarded as admission"); Leng May Ma v. Barber, 357 U.S. 185, 188 (1958) (neither detention for over a year in the United States nor release on parole constitutes an "entry").

42. Shaughnessy v. United States *ex rel.* Mezei, 345 U.S. 206, 215 (1953).

43. *See* KURZBAN, *supra* note 36, at 23.

44. 8 U.S.C. § 1251(a) (1994).

45. *See generally* T. ALEXANDER ALEINIKOFF ET AL., IMMIGRATION: PROCESS AND POLICY 474-86 (3d ed. 1995) [hereinafter ALEINIKOFF ET AL., IMMIGRATION PROCESS AND POLICY]; *In re* Phelisna, 551 F. Supp. 960, 962-63 (E.D.N.Y. 1982).

country,[46] or after a final deportation order has been issued while arrangements are being made for their departure.[47]

Excludable aliens generally have fewer statutory and constitutional rights than deportable aliens.[48] This pattern holds true for aliens in detention. Deportable aliens usually are not detained unless they await expulsion for criminal conduct.[49] Aliens who are confined by the INS pending a deportation hearing are entitled to petition an immigration judge for a redetermination of their custody status.[50] Those who are subject to a final order of deportation can be held no longer than six months.[51] Additionally, aliens in deportation proceedings are entitled to claim procedural due process protection.[52] This has enabled detained deportable aliens to challenge INS practices that may impinge upon their constitutional right to fair proceedings.[53]

Excludable alien detainees do not enjoy the same protections. Detained excludable aliens, unlike deportable aliens, are not entitled

---

46. INA § 242(a)(1), 8 U.S.C. § 1252(a)(1) (1994).

47. INA § 242(c), 8 U.S.C. § 1252(c) (1994).

48. *See* ALEINIKOFF ET AL., IMMIGRATION PROCESS AND POLICY, *supra* note 45, at 475-76 (delineating differences between deportation and exclusion proceedings).

49. *See* 3 GORDON ET AL., *supra* note 40, § 72.03[4][c][iii] (during the pendency of deportation proceedings, aliens are detained only when found to be a threat to national security or a poor bail risk); *id.* § 72.08[1][b][ii] (power to order detention after final order of deportation is rarely used). The detention of aliens convicted of crimes, in order to expedite their deportation, is now a top priority for the INS. *See infra* notes 82-94 and accompanying text.

50. INA § 242(a)(1), 8 U.S.C. § 1252(a)(1) (1994); 8 C.F.R. §§ 3.19, 242.2(d) (1994); *see* 3 GORDON ET AL., *supra* note 40, § 72.03 [4][c][iii]; Janet A. Gilboy, *Setting Bail in Deportation Cases: The Role of Immigration Judges*, 24 SAN DIEGO L. REV. 347 (1987).

51. INA § 242(c), 8 U.S.C. § 1252(c) (1994); KURZBAN, *supra* note 36, at 136-37. Courts have allowed the INS to detain aliens subject to a final order of deportation for longer than six months when the alien is deemed responsible for the delay. *See* Balogun v. INS, 9 F.3d·347, 351 (5th Cir. 1993) (delay allegedly caused because alien hampered INS attempts to obtain necessary travel documents); Doherty v. Thornburgh, 943 F.2d 204, 211-12 (2d Cir. 1991) (delay caused by detainee-initiated litigation).

52. Yamataya v. Fisher (*The Japanese Immigrant Case*), 189 U.S. 86, 100-01 (1903). *See* Motomura, *Procedural Surrogates*, *supra* note 32, at 1628 (arguing this procedural due process "exception" to the plenary power doctrine often serves as a surrogate for substantive judicial review).

53. *See* Orantes-Hernandez v. Smith, 541 F. Supp. 351, 385-87 (C.D. Cal. 1982) (preliminary injunction issued on behalf of Salvadorans detained pending deportation proceedings, providing inter alia that the INS must inform class members of their right to apply for asylum and end various practices that limited detainees' access to their attorneys); Orantes-Hernandez v. Meese, 685 F. Supp. 1488, 1511-14 (C.D. Cal. 1988), *aff'd sub nom.*, Orantes-Hernandez v. Thornburgh, 919 F.2d 549 (9th Cir. 1990) (permanent injunction to same effect); Nunez v. Boldin, 537 F. Supp. 578, 587 (S.D. Tex. 1982), *appeal dismissed*, 692 F.2d 755 (5th Cir. 1982) (similar injunction); *see also* Note, *INS Transfer Policy: Interference with Detained Aliens' Due Process Right to Retain Counsel*, 100 HARV. L. REV. 2001 (1987) [hereinafter *INS Transfer Policy*].

to petition an immigration judge for release.[54] Instead, the decision to parole excludable aliens is delegated exclusively to INS officials,[55] and courts are very reluctant to overturn a denial of parole.[56] Moreover, the INA does not impose any time limit on the detention of excludable aliens; several courts have held that they can be detained indefinitely.[57] Indeed, as will be discussed below, excludable aliens are sometimes said to have "virtually no constitutional rights," even when they are detained within the United States.[58]

Excludable and deportable alien detainees are alike, however, in one important respect: they are not being incarcerated as punishment for a crime. Instead, they are held in civil confinement pending the outcome of administrative proceedings.[59] Alien detainees generally can secure their own release if they are willing to waive their right to a hearing and to abandon any claim to enter into or remain in the country. Deportable aliens can, in most circumstances, cut short their detention stay through a procedure known as "voluntary departure."[60] Excludable aliens are sometimes permitted to withdraw their applica-

---

54. *See* 2 GORDON ET AL., *supra* note 40, § 63.05[3], at 63-36.

55. The Attorney General's authority to grant parole is delegated to the INS district director in charge of the port of entry. *See id.* § 64.01[3]; 8 C.F.R. § 212.5 (1994).

56. *See* Amanullah v. Nelson, 811 F.2d 1, 9-11 (1st Cir. 1987) (district director's decision to deny parole must be upheld whenever supported by a "facially legitimate and bona fide reason"); Garcia-Mir v. Smith, 766 F.2d 1478, 1485 (11th Cir. 1985), *cert. denied*, 475 U.S. 1022 (1986) (applying same standard); Bertrand v. Sava, 684 F.2d 204, 211-13 (2d Cir. 1982) (exercise of broad discretionary power to deny parole must be viewed as "presumptively legitimate and bona fide in the absence of strong proof to the contrary").

57. *E.g.*, Barrera-Echavarria v. Rison, 44 F.3d 1441, 1445 (9th Cir. 1995); Gisbert v. United States Attorney Gen., 988 F.2d 1437, 1441-43, *amended*, 997 F.2d 1122 (5th Cir. 1993); Fernandez-Roque v. Smith, 734 F.2d 576, 582 (11th Cir. 1984). *Contra* Rodriguez-Fernandez v. Wilkinson, 654 F.2d 1382, 1389-90 (10th Cir. 1981).

58. Garcia-Mir v. Meese, 788 F.2d 1446, 1449 (11th Cir. 1986); *see infra* notes 212-228 (discussing *Knauff* and *Mezei* decisions).

59. Schmidt, *supra* note 11, at 305 (noting "the INS stands alone in its authority to incarcerate individuals who neither have been charged with, nor have been convicted of, crimes").

60. INA §§ 242(b), 244(e), 8 U.S.C. §§ 1252(b), 1254(e) (1994); *see also* 8 C.F.R. § 242.5 (1994); ALEINIKOFF ET AL., IMMIGRATION PROCESS AND POLICY, *supra* note 45, at 640-43. To be eligible for voluntary departure after the commencement of deportation proceedings, aliens must be persons of "good moral character" as defined in INA § 101(f), 8 U.S.C. § 1101(4) (1994); *see* KURZBAN, *supra* note 36, at 552-53.

tions to enter.[61] Aliens who elect these options are released from custody on the condition they leave the United States.[62]

B. The Expanded INS Detention Mission

Voluntary departure helps to allocate scarce detention resources.[63] Historically, voluntary departure operated to limit most immigration detention to short-term confinement. Most alien detainees were residents of Mexico who waived their right to a hearing and were held only a few days until transportation to the border could be arranged.[64]

Over the past two decades, however, immigration detention has been radically transformed. The average length of confinement for alien detainees has increased dramatically.[65] For many aliens, immigration detention is no longer a brief stop on the way to the border. Instead, alien detainees from all over the world[66] are now held for months, or even years, waiting for a determination of their immigra-

---

61. The INA does not explicitly provide an equivalent to voluntary departure for excludable aliens. But excludable aliens may be allowed to withdraw their application to enter if they agree to depart from the United States. Once exclusion proceedings have commenced, an immigration judge will not grant permission to withdraw unless the INS consents. *See* KURZBAN, *supra* note 36, at 67-68, 72.

62. The term "voluntary departure" is sometimes a misnomer. The desire to escape detention can be a powerful incentive to waive even valid claims; some detainees have been coerced to accept this option. *See* Orantes-Hernandez v. Meese, 685 F. Supp. 1488, 1494-97, 1505-06 (C.D. Cal. 1988), *aff'd sub nom.*, Orantes-Hernandez v. Thornburgh, 919 F.2d 549 (9th Cir. 1990) (enjoining a widespread practice of coercing detainees from El Salvador to accept voluntary departure). In addition, many aliens who elect this option do not depart, and those who leave may quickly return across the border. *See* ALEINIKOFF ET AL, IMMIGRATION PROCESS AND POLICY, *supra* note 45, at 640-43; Lizette Alvarez & Lisa Getter, *Inability to deport has fueled the influx*, MIAMI HERALD, Dec. 14, 1993, at 1A.

63. ALEINIKOFF ET AL., IMMIGRATION PROCESS AND POLICY, *supra* note 45, at 640.

64. In 1975, for example, 92% of alien detainees were residents of Mexico. Eighty-four percent of detained aliens elected voluntary departure. INS detainees spent an average of 3.2 days in confinement. IMMIGRATION AND NATURALIZATION SERV., U.S. DEP'T OF JUSTICE, FEDERAL DETENTION PLAN 1993-1997 15 (1992) [hereinafter FIVE-YEAR DETENTION PLAN].

65. Aliens confined at major INS detention facilities were being detained an average of 54 days in 1991. U.S. GEN. ACCOUNTING OFFICE, PUB. NO. GAO/GGD-92-85, IMMIGRATION CONTROL: IMMIGRATION POLICIES AFFECT INS DETENTION EFFORTS 26 (1992) [hereinafter GAO DETENTION REPORT] (field study of immigration detention). The INS reported alien detainees from countries other than Mexico ("OTMs" in INS parlance) averaged 41 days in detention in fiscal year 1991. FIVE-YEAR DETENTION PLAN, *supra* note 64, at 16.

66. The GAO field study found 73% of aliens confined in INS detention facilities were from countries other than Mexico. Alien detainees came from 92 different countries. GAO DETENTION REPORT, supra, note 65, at 24. INS statistics for the fiscal year 1991 concluded that OTMs comprised 48% of the total immigration detention population, as compared to less than 8% in 1975. FIVE-YEAR DETENTION PLAN, *supra* note 64, at 16.

tion status.[67] This transformation has been fueled by unprecedented world events and a significant expansion of the INS detention mission.

The first major shift in immigration detention policy was a controversial decision to detain virtually all excludable aliens who arrive without valid entry documents.[68] From 1954 until 1981, the vast majority of excludable aliens were paroled pending a final determination of their immigration status.[69] This policy was abandoned, however, in response to an unprecedented influx of Cubans and Haitians seeking refuge in the United States. The sudden arrival of over 125,000 Cubans in the Mariel boatlift of 1980,[70] coupled with a smaller contingent of Haitians fleeing the Duvalier regime,[71] put enormous strain on a fledgling system created to allow persons fleeing persecution in their home countries to apply for asylum within the United States.[72] Re-

---

67. *See* ACLU DETENTION REPORT, *supra* note 4, at 6-7 (at the end of 1984, 1053 aliens had been held in INS detention for over 30 days; 407 had been confined for three months or more); GAO DETENTION REPORT, supra note 65, at 29 (170 excludable aliens had been in detention over 90 days, some for almost two years); Alisa Solomon, *The Prison on Varick Street*, N.Y. TIMES, June 11, 1994, at A21 (Ethiopian Jew who claimed well-founded fear of persecution in his home country had been detained by the INS for over four years).

68. I use the term "entry documents" to refer to the visas aliens receive while still abroad and present upon initial inspection to enter the United States. Technically, however, a visa does not convey the right to enter the country. *See* INA § 221(h), 8 U.S.C. § 1201(h) (1994). Aliens with valid visas may still be excluded if they fall within the grounds listed in INA § 212(a), 8 U.S.C. § 1182(a) (1994).

69. *See* Leng May Ma v. Barber, 357 U.S. 185, 190 (1958); Louis v. Nelson, 544 F. Supp. 973, 980 n.18 (S.D. Fla. 1982), *aff'd in part and rev'd in part sub nom.*, Jean v. Nelson, 711 F.2d 1455 (11th Cir.), *vacated*, 727 F.2d 957 (11th Cir. 1984) (en banc), *aff'd as modified*, 472 U.S. 846 (1985); *see also* 1 GORDON ET AL., *supra* note 40, § 8.09[1], at 8-18.

70. *See* Mariel Cuban Parole Determinations, 52 Fed. Reg. 48, 799-802 (1987); *Louis*, 544 F. Supp. at 978-81.

71. *See* ALEINIKOFF ET AL., IMMIGRATION PROCESS AND POLICY, *supra* note 45, at 446-47; GAO DETENTION REPORT, *supra* note 65, at 36 (noting while few Haitians attempted to enter the United States in the 1970s, 15,093 Haitian migrants arrived in 1980).

72. The Refugee Act of 1980, Pub. L. No. 96-212, 94 Stat. 102, formally codified the United States' historical practice of resettling refugees, with some significant changes. First, INA § 243(h), which had granted the Attorney General *discretion* to withhold deportation for persons who would face physical persecution upon return to their home country, was transformed into a *mandatory* obligation, consistent with the international law principle of *nonrefoulement*. 8 U.S.C. § 1253(h) (1994). Second, the 1980 Act for the first time created a discretionary "asylum" status for persons already in the United States who could show they were unable or unwilling to return to their home country due to "persecution or a well-founded fear of persecution on account of race, religion, nationality, membership in a particular social group, or political opinion." INA §§ 101(a)(42)(A), 208(a), 8 U.S.C. §§ 1101(a)(42)(A), 1158(a) (1994). Within weeks after the Refugee Act was signed by President Carter, the Mariel boatlift had begun. Schuck, *Transformation of Immigration Law*, *supra* note 33, at 40. For an influential critique of the asylum adjudication system, which also explains the background of the Refugee Act of 1980, see David A. Martin,

sponding to a perception that America had "lost control of [its] borders," the Attorney General in July 1981 renounced the practice of parole and announced a new policy of detaining undocumented excludable aliens.[73]

That policy is now codified in regulations declaring that detention is the rule for aliens seeking entry who arrive without a valid visa.[74] The "parole exception" is reserved for a few narrow categories, including aliens with serious medical conditions, pregnant women, and juveniles who can be released to specific adult relatives.[75] Critics contend these regulations unfairly penalize refugees fleeing persecution in their home country, and are inconsistent with the right to apply for asylum created by the Refugee Act.[76] But the INS defends the detention of undocumented excludable aliens as a necessary deterrent to stem the flow of "illegal" immigration into the United States.[77]

The detention policy has been implemented, however, in the midst of an unanticipated volume of asylum seekers that has completely overwhelmed the asylum adjudication system. Civil war and strife in Central America, political unrest and violence in Haiti, and similar crises across the globe have sparked an enormous demand for asylum.[78] Unfortunately, the system is also clogged with frivolous

---

Reforming Asylum Adjudication: On Navigating the Coast of Bohemia, 138 PA. L. REV. 1247, 1257-66 (1990).

73. *Administration's Proposals on Immigration and Refugee Policy: Joint Hearing Before the House Subcomm. on Immigration, Refugees, and International Law and the Senate Subcomm. on Immigration and Refugee Policy*, 97th Cong., 1st Sess. 6 (1981), *quoted in Louis*, 544 F. Supp. at 980; *see also* Amanullah v. Nelson, 811 F.2d 1, 4-8 (1st Cir. 1987); Arthur C. Helton, *The Legality of Detaining Refugees in the United States*, 14 N.Y.U. REV. L. & SOC. CHANGE 353, 356-60 (1987).

74. 8 C.F.R. § 235.3(b) (1994). The regulations distinguish between two categories of aliens seeking entry. Excludable aliens who appear with fraudulent documents or no documents, or who arrive "at a place other than a designated port of entry, *shall* be detained." *Id.* (emphasis added). In contrast, aliens who arrive at a proper place with facially valid documents but who appear inadmissible for other reasons may be detained or paroled, depending on whether they are a security risk or appear likely to abscond. 8 C.F.R. § 235.3(c); *see* 1 GORDON ET AL., *supra* note 40, § 8.09[1].

75. 8 C.F.R. § 212(5)(a) (1994); *see* KURZBAN, *supra* note 36, at 61-62.

76. *See* Helton, *supra* note 73, at 367-81; Deborah M. Levy, *Detention in the Asylum Context*, 44 U. PITT. L. REV. 297, 316-28 (1983); Maurice A. Roberts, *Some Thoughts on the Wanton Detention of Aliens*, 5 GEO. IMMIGR. L.J. 225, 235 (1991).

77. This justification was repeatedly expressed when the new detention policy was adopted. *See Louis*, 544 F. Supp. at 979-80. The INS still contends the detention of undocumented excludable aliens is a deterrent to "illegal" entry, although the policy has been applied inconsistently and often toward persons with colorable asylum claims. *See* GAO DETENTION REPORT, *supra* note 65, at 35-37; *infra* note 110.

78. During the 1970s, the INS received asylum applications at a rate of between 1900 and 5800 per year. ALEINIKOFF ET AL., IMMIGRATION PROCESS AND POLICY, *supra* note 45, at 767. The number of applications skyrocketed in the 1980s. In fiscal year 1981, 61,568

claims.[79] By December 1994, asylum officers faced a staggering backlog of over 425,000 asylum applications awaiting adjudication.[80] The long wait for asylum processing has contributed to the trend toward longer detention stays for alien detainees.[81]

The second component of the expanded INS detention mission is a new emphasis on detaining "criminal aliens." The INS uses this term to describe aliens who are subject to exclusion or deportation proceedings because they have been convicted of a crime.[82] The

---

asylum cases were filed with the INS. The number of affirmative applications jumped to 101,679 in fiscal year 1989. SARAH IGNATIUS, HARVARD LAW SCH., AN ASSESSMENT OF THE ASYLUM PROCESS OF THE IMMIGRATION AND NATURALIZATION SERVICE 31-32 (1993) [hereinafter NATIONAL ASYLUM STUDY PROJECT FINAL REPORT] (tabulating INS statistics) (on file with author). In fiscal year 1994, 147,605 asylum applications were filed with the INS. *INS Finalizes Asylum Reform Regulations*, 71 INTERPRETER RELEASES 1577, 1578 (1994) [hereinafter *INS Finalizes Regulations*].

79. The INS has been receiving an increasing number of "boilerplate" applications—forms with minimal information virtually identical to hundreds of others. Some of these are prepared by unscrupulous "immigration consultants" who take advantage of unsuspecting aliens. Gregg A. Beyer, *Reforming Affirmative Asylum Processing in the United States: Challenges and Opportunities*, 9 LOY. L.A. INT'L & COMP. L.J. 43, 70 (1994); *see also INS Finalizes Regulations, supra* note 78, at 1578 (INS official estimates that 25% of new asylum applications may be "abusive"); Lizette Alvarez & Lisa Getter, *U.S. ill-equipped to weed out opportunists*, MIAMI HERALD, Dec. 15, 1993, at 1A, 22A. *But see* NATIONAL ASYLUM STUDY PROJECT FINAL REPORT, *supra* note 78, at 70 (INS erroneously returning unique applications as "boilerplate"). In the past, asylum applicants could obtain a work permit upon filing their application, so long as their claim was not "frivolous." 8 C.F.R. § 208.7 (1994). The vast majority of requests for work authorization filed with asylum claims were approved. NATIONAL ASYLUM STUDY PROJECT FINAL REPORT, *supra* note 78, at 67 (91% approved in fiscal year 1992; 83% in fiscal year 1993). The INS recently promulgated new regulations providing asylum applicants will not be eligible to apply for work authorization until 150 days after their applications are filed. 59 Fed. Reg. 62,284, 62,299 (1994) (to be codified at 8 C.F.R. § 208.7)

80. *INS Finalizes Regulations, supra* note 78; *see also* NATIONAL ASYLUM STUDY PROJECT FINAL REPORT, *supra* note 78, at 35-36 (318,800 pending cases after 11 months of fiscal year 1993). The new asylum regulations are intended to reduce this backlog by streamlining the asylum adjudication process. *INS Finalizes Regulations, supra* note 78, at 1579. *But see* Deborah Anker, *The Mischaracterized Asylum Crisis: Realities Behind Proposed Reforms*, 9 LOY. L.A. INT'L COMP. L.J. 29 (1994) (arguing misperceptions about the asylum adjudication system have fueled these procedural reforms.) The INS also plans to add more asylum officers and immigration judges to speed claims processing. Steven Greenhouse, *U.S. Moves to Halt Abuse in Political Asylum Program*, N.Y. TIMES, Dec. 3, 1994, at A8.

81. FIVE-YEAR DETENTION PLAN, *supra* note 64, at 15-17; OFFICE OF THE INSPECTOR GENERAL, U.S. DEP'T OF JUSTICE, PUB. NO. I-92-18, INSPECTION OF DETENTION FACILITIES IN THE IMMIGRATION AND NATURALIZATION SERVICE 12-14 (1993) [hereinafter INSPECTOR GENERAL DETENTION REPORT].

82. The criminal grounds for exclusion, listed in INA § 212(a)(2), include crimes "involving moral turpitude," drug offenses, and multiple criminal convictions for which the alien was sentenced to five or more years confinement. 8 U.S.C. § 1182(a)(2) (1994). Aliens who have already entered the United States can also be deported for criminal of-

"criminal alien" label has gained widespread usage but can be some-what misleading. Some "criminal aliens" have been convicted of rela-tively minor offenses, and would shed the "criminal" classification upon completion of their prison term if not for their alien status. Others are lawful permanent residents who have lived in the United States for years.[83]

Aliens who are incarcerated for criminal offenses generally can-not be deported until after they are released from prison.[84] Neverthe-less, the INS can initiate exclusion or deportation proceedings while criminal aliens are still imprisoned. Recent amendments to the INA require the INS to "begin any deportation proceedings as expedi-tiously as possible after the date of the conviction."[85] The INS is au-

---

fenses; the deportation grounds are similar but not identical to the criminal exclusion grounds. *See* INA § 241(a)(2), 8 U.S.C. § 1251(a)(2) (1994). In addition, entry without inspection is a separate ground for deportation. INA § 241(a)(1)(B), 8 U.S.C. § 1251(a)(1)(B) (1994). Thus, alien offenders who have entered illegally can be deported even if their offense is not included among the specific criminal grounds for deportation.

83. IMMIGRANTS' RIGHTS PROJECT, AMERICAN CIVIL LIBERTIES UNION, JUSTICE DE-TAINED: CONDITIONS AT THE VARICK STREET IMMIGRATION DETENTION CENTER 4 (1993) [hereinafter VARICK STREET REPORT]; *see also* Deborah Sontag, *Porous Deporta-tion System Gives Criminals Little to Fear*, N.Y. TIMES, Sept. 13, 1994, at A1; Alisa Solo-mon, *Yearning to Breathe Free*, VILLAGE VOICE, Aug. 8, 1995 at 25.

84. INA § 242(h), 8 U.S.C. § 1252(h) (1994). The United States has treaties with 34 countries providing for the voluntary transfer of alien prisoners to their home countries. But very few transfers are accomplished under these treaties. From 1987 to February 1991, only 1385 federal prisoners were returned to their home countries. *Criminal Aliens: Hear-ings on H.R. 723, H.R. 1067, H.R. 1279, H.R. 1459, H.R. 1496, H.R. 2041, H.R. 2438, H.R. 2730, H.R. 2993, H.R. 3302, H.R. 3320 (Tit. IV), H.R. 3860 (Tits. II, V, VI), H.R. 3812, and H. Con. Res. 47 Before the Subcomm. on International Law, Immigration, and Refugees of the House Judiciary Comm.*, 103d Cong., 1st Sess. 169 (1994) (testimony of Kathleen M. Hawk, Director, Federal Bureau of Prisons); *see also* Danielle Starkey, *Deporting illegal aliens convicted of felonies*, CAL. J., Oct. 1, 1993 (only seven California prisoners trans-ferred to Mexico from 1988-1993); U.S. COMM'N ON IMMIGRATION REFORM, U.S. IMMI-GRATION POLICY: RESTORING CREDIBILITY 161-62 (1994) (1994 report to Congress) (recommending increased use of treaty transfer provisions). The INS and the State of Florida have instituted a pilot program under which imprisoned deportable aliens "re-ceive[ ] clemency from prison terms in their homelands in exchange for agreeing to be deported and never to return, and to waive any pending legal challenge." *24 Criminal Aliens in Florida Deported to Free Prison Space*, N.Y. TIMES, June 30, 1994, at A20.

85. INA § 242(i), 8 U.S.C. §1252(i) (1994). The INS created its Institutional Hearing Program ("IHP") to fulfill this statutory mandate. Under this program, some deportation hearings are conducted on-site at prisons, while aliens are incarcerated. Other alien pris-oners are sent to the Oakdale, La. detention facility during the last six months of their prison term for expedited deportation hearings. *See generally Removal of Criminal and Illegal Aliens: Oversight Hearing Before the Subcomm. on Immigration and Claims of the House Judiciary Comm.* (Mar. 25, 1995), *available in* LEXIS, Legis Library, Cngtst File [hereinafter *Criminal Aliens Oversight Hearing*, Mar. 25, 1995] (testimony of T. Alexander Aleinikoff, General Counsel, Immigration and Naturalization Service) (explaining IHP program); IMMIGRATION AND NATURALIZATION SERV., U.S. DEP'T OF JUSTICE, IMMIGRA-

thorized to file a detainer to inform prison officials when an incarcerated alien is under investigation for possible deportation. Aliens subject to a detainer are taken directly into INS custody after completing their prison term.[86]

Until recently, the INS seldom deported criminal aliens immediately after their release from prison. Indeed, the agency had no way to identify aliens who had been convicted of a crime.[87] Those criminal aliens who were subject to deportation proceedings frequently were not detained, and many failed to appear for their hearings.[88]

Members of Congress, expressing outrage at this failure to deport criminal aliens, have recently catapulted this issue to the top of the agency's agenda.[89] Congress has passed several amendments to the

---

TION ACT OF 1990 REPORT ON CRIMINAL ALIENS 6-7 (1992) [hereinafter INS CRIMINAL ALIENS REPORT] (report to Congress). There are mixed reports on whether the IHP proceedings provide adequate due process protection to deportable aliens. *Compare* U.S. GEN. ACCOUNTING OFFICE, PUB. NO. GAO/GGD-90-79, CRIMINAL ALIENS: PRISON DEPORTATION HEARINGS INCLUDE OPPORTUNITIES TO CONTEST DEPORTATION 9 (1990) (concluding immigration judges at IHP hearings took necessary steps to inform aliens of their rights provided by law) *with* Jessica Ladd, *Deported to Oakdale: A Due Process Analysis of Hearings for Criminal Aliens*, IMMIGR. NEWSL. (National Immigration Project of the Nat'l Lawyers Guild, Boston, Mass.), Spring 1990, at 1 (noting serious deficiencies in deportation proceedings at Oakdale, La., aggravated by the fact that Oakdale's remote location makes it virtually impossible for detainees to obtain legal representation).

86. 8 C.F.R. § 242.2(a) (1994); *see* KURZBAN, supra note 36, at 142-144; Orozco v. INS, 911 F.2d 539, 541 n.2 (11th Cir. 1990).

87. *See* INS CRIMINAL ALIENS REPORT, *supra* note 85, at 4, 7 (noting difficulties the INS has faced in identifying criminal aliens for deportation, and conceding that "many criminal aliens are unknown to the INS, even though convicted and incarcerated"); U.S. GEN. ACCOUNTING OFFICE, PUB. NO. GAO/IMTEC-90-75, INFORMATION MANAGEMENT: IMMIGRATION AND NATURALIZATION SERVICE LACKS READY ACCESS TO ESSENTIAL DATA 4 (1990) (concluding incomplete and inaccurate information has hindered criminal alien deportation); U.S. GEN. ACCOUNTING OFFICE, GAO/GGD-88-3, CRIMINAL ALIENS: INS' ENFORCEMENT ACTIVITIES 17-30 (1987) (stating "[n]o one knows how many deportable criminal aliens exist").

88. *See generally* PERMANENT SUBCOMM. ON INVESTIGATIONS OF THE SENATE COMM. ON GOVERNMENTAL AFFAIRS, CRIMINAL ALIENS IN THE UNITED STATES, S. REP. NO. 48, 104th Cong., 1st Sess. 2, 23-24 (1995) [hereinafter SENATE CRIMINAL ALIENS REPORT] (through 1992, nearly 11,000 criminal aliens convicted of aggravated felonies failed to appear for deportation hearings; *see also* Lisa Getter & Lizette Alvarez, *Kicking out criminals*, MIAMI HERALD, Dec. 12, 1993, at 19A; Sontag, *supra* note 83, at A1.

89. The Immigration Act of 1990 required the INS to file a report with Congress documenting its efforts to increase deportation of criminal aliens. Pub. L. No. 101-649, § 510, 104 Stat. 4978 (1990) (codified at 8 U.S.C. § 1251 (1994)); *see* INS CRIMINAL ALIENS REPORT, *supra* note 85. Since then, the INS criminal alien strategy has been the subject of numerous congressional oversight hearings. *See, e.g., Criminal Aliens Oversight Hearing*, Mar. 25, 1995, *supra* note 85; *Criminal Alien Legislation: Hearing Before the Subcomm. on International Law, Immigration, and Refugees of the House Judiciary Comm.* (Feb. 23, 1994), *available in* LEXIS, Legis Library, Cngtst File; *Criminal Aliens in the United States: Hearings Before the Permanent Subcomm. on Investigations of the Senate Comm. on Gov-*

INA designed to ensure more criminal aliens are deported.[90] Among these is a requirement that the INS take all excludable and deportable aliens who have been convicted of an "aggravated felony" into custody immediately upon their release from prison.[91] Excludable aliens who have committed aggravated felonies can be paroled from immigration detention only when their home country will not accept their return and the Attorney General has determined they are not dangerous.[92] Deportable aggravated felons can be released only if they are "lawfully admitted aliens" who can demonstrate they are not a threat to the community and are likely to appear before any scheduled hearing.[93] The population of criminal aliens in immigration detention has swelled under these provisions.[94]

---

ernmental Affairs, 103d Cong., 1st Sess. 147 (1993). Congress generally has been critical of the INS criminal alien initiatives. *See* SENATE CRIMINAL ALIENS REPORT, *supra* note 88 (contending INS system of identifying and deporting criminal aliens is in disarray, despite recent reforms); *see also* Ronald J. Ostrow, *INS Assailed for Not Deporting Immigrant Criminals*, L.A. TIMES, Nov. 10, 1993, at A13.

90. For a summary of the recent "piecemeal" amendments to the INA impacting criminal aliens, see SENATE CRIMINAL ALIENS REPORT, *supra* note 88, at 10-12. Additional reforms are now pending before Congress, as part of antiterrorism and immigration reform legislation. *See generally House Republicans Introduce Bill to Rewrite Immigration Policy*, 72 INTERPRETER RELEASES 829 (1995) [hereinafter *Republicans Introduce Bill*]; *Senate Approves Anti-Terrorism Legislation, House Likely to Follow*, 72 INTERPRETER RELEASES 834 (1995).

91. INA § 236(e)(1), 8 U.S.C. § 1227(e)(1) (1994); INA § 242(a)(2)(A), 8 U.S.C. § 1252(a)(2)(A) (1994). An "aggravated felony" includes, inter alia, murder, drug and firearms trafficking offenses, money laundering, and any crime of violence or theft offense for which the term of imprisonment imposed is at least five years. INA § 101(43), 8 U.S.C. § 1101(43) (1994). The category of crimes that constitutes an "aggravated felony" is rapidly expanding as Congress continues to add new crimes to the statutory definition of this term. *See* Kenneth H. Stern, *The Noose Tightens: Trends and Developments in the Immigration Consequences of Criminal Convictions*, in 2 1995-96 Immigration and Nationality Law Handbook 305, 308 (R. Patrick Murphy et al. eds., 1995) (noting "[i]t is almost impossible to keep track of the rapidly expanding list of aggravated felonies").

92. INA §§ 236(e)(2), 243(g), 8 U.S.C. §§ 1227(e)(2), 1253(g) (1994).

93. INA § 242(a)(2)(A)-(B), 8 U.S.C. § 1252(a)(2)(A)-(B) (1994). This provision has been interpreted to establish a rebuttable presumption *against* release of lawfully admitted deportable aggravated felons. *See* 3 GORDON ET AL., *supra* note 40, § 72.03[4][c][ii]. These recent amendments have created a new category of INS detainees, "non-releasable aggravated felons," who, like the Marielito Cubans discussed *infra* notes 270-273 and accompanying text, face indefinite detention because their home country refuses to accept their return. While the number of "lifers" confined by the INS under these provisions is relatively small, a growing number of countries have refused to allow the return of their nationals who have been convicted of serious crimes within the United States. *See* Dianne Klein, *INS "Lifers" Locked Up in Limbo*, L.A. TIMES, Feb. 6, 1994, at A1.

94. GAO DETENTION REPORT, *supra* note 65, at 17.

C. Mission Impossible: Actual Detention Operations

The INS cannot, however, confine all aliens who have been convicted of a crime (or even all who have been convicted of an aggravated felony) pending deportation or exclusion proceedings.[95] The same is true for undocumented excludable aliens, who receive parole far more frequently than the governing regulations seem to contemplate.[96] In reality, the INS has the capacity to confine only a very small fraction of the aliens targeted for "mandatory" detention.

The INS now operates nine immigration detention facilities, euphemistically known as "Service Processing Centers (SPCs)."[97] An additional detention center run jointly by the INS and the Bureau of Prisons is used primarily to confine criminal aliens.[98] The INS also makes extensive use of "contract" facilities operated by private, for-profit corporations.[99] In addition, the INS obtains about twenty-five percent of its total detention capacity through ad hoc arrangements with state and local jails.[100]

---

95. SENATE CRIMINAL ALIENS REPORT, *supra* note 88, at 2, 23-24; *see also* GAO DETENTION REPORT; *supra* note 65, at 41; Alvarez & Getter, *Detention: The Failed Deterrent*, *supra* note 5, at 1A.

96. *See* Susan Freinkel, *INS May Loosen Detention Policies*, TEX. LAWYER, Feb. 17, 1992 at 4 (INS representative Duke Austin concedes the INS "can't do what the policy is—to detain exclusion cases"); *MacNeil Lehrer NewsHour* (PBS television broadcast, June 7, 1993), *available in* NEXIS, News Library, Script File (INS district director in New York explaining in June 1993, only 3-4% of inadmissible aliens arriving at Kennedy airport were detained).

97. INS Service Processing Centers are located in Aguadilla, P.R.; Boston, Mass.; El Centro, Cal.; El Paso, Tex.; Florence, Ariz.; Miami, Fla.; New York, N.Y.; Los Fresnos, Tex.; and San Pedro, Cal. The nine SPCs have a combined rated capacity of 2549 detention beds. *Containing Costs of Incarceration of Federal Prisoners and Detainees: Hearing Before the House Appropriations Comm.* (Apr. 6, 1995), *available in* LEXIS, Legis Library, Cngtst File [hereinafter *Hearing on Containing Costs*] (testimony of James A. Puleo, Executive Associate Commissioner, Immigration and Naturalization Service); *see also* IMMIGRATION AND NATURALIZATION SERV., U.S. DEP'T OF JUSTICE, DETENTION AND DEPORTATION PROGRAM 3 (June 29, 1994) [hereinafter INS DETENTION BRIEFING PAPER] (citing a rated capacity of 2238 beds) (on file with author).

98. The INS uses approximately half of the one thousand beds at the joint INS/BOP (Bureau of Prisons) facility in Oakdale, La. to house criminal aliens. INS DETENTION BRIEFING PAPER, *supra* note 97, at 3.

99. In April 1995, the INS relied on five contract facilities with a total capacity of 1095 beds. *Hearing on Containing Costs, supra* note 97 (testimony of James A. Puleo). An additional contract facility in Eloy, Ariz. contains 500 beds devoted to criminal aliens. *Id.*

100. FIVE-YEAR DETENTION PLAN, *supra* note 64, at 15, 22-23. As of March 31, 1995, about 1700 beds were being used in state and local jails. *Hearing on Containing Costs*, *supra* note 97 (testimony of James A. Puleo).

On average, the INS detains between five and six thousand excludable and deportable aliens on any given day.[101] This reflects a significant increase in detention capacity over the last two decades.[102] The agency plans to expand even more aggressively in coming years; it has proposed a forty-eight percent increase in detention bedspace for fiscal year 1996.[103]

Nevertheless, despite this rapid expansion of detention capacity, the INS reports it has been detaining significantly *fewer* aliens in recent years.[104] This anomaly is largely the result of the trend toward longer detention stays.[105] While the INS has more detention space, it now incarcerates fewer aliens because those already confined are held for much longer periods.[106]

---

101. The Detention and Deportation Division's daily population count of alien detainees fluctuated between five and six thousand for most of fiscal year 1994. Letter from Joan C. Higgins, Assistant Commissioner, Detention and Deportation Division, Immigration and Naturalization Service, to Margaret H. Taylor, Wake Forest University School of Law (n.d.), at Attachment 2 (Detention Space Status Report-FY 94) (on file with author). The daily population count rose slightly in September and October of 1994. *Id.* On October 3, 1994, for example, the INS detained 4794 aliens in its SPCs and contract facilities, and 1842 in state and local jails, for a total of 6636 detainees. *Id.* at Attachment 1 (Daily Population Report, Oct. 3, 1994); *see also* FIVE-YEAR DETENTION PLAN, *supra* note 64, at 16 (citing detention capacity of 6600 beds for fiscal year 1990); GAO DETENTION REPORT, *supra* note 65, at 37 (6259 beds for fiscal year 1992). These figures do not include all of the Marielito Cubans in INS custody, many of whom are confined in state and local jails and Bureau of Prison facilities. *See infra* notes 270-273 and accompanying text. Nor do they count the Haitian and Cuban migrants (at times as many as 40,000) who were detained in "safe haven" camps run by the U.S. military at Guantanamo Bay, Cuba in 1994. *See infra* note 142.

102. The INS has more than tripled its detention capacity since 1975 by building five SPCs and opening its contract facilities. *See* FIVE-YEAR DETENTION PLAN, *supra* note 64, at 15 (noting in 1975 the INS operated four SPCs with a total capacity of 1382 beds).

103. *Hearing on Containing Costs*, *supra* note 97 (testimony of James A. Puleo) (noting funds requested for fiscal year 1996 will provide an additional 1636 detention beds in state, local, and contract facilities, as well as 976 beds in two new INS SPCs). Some bills now pending before Congress would also authorize the INS to use closed military bases to detain aliens awaiting exclusion or deportation proceedings. *See, e.g., Republicans Introduce Bill*, *supra* note 90, at 830.

104. FIVE-YEAR DETENTION PLAN, *supra* note 64, at 15. In fiscal year 1982, the INS detained 229,135 aliens, representing approximately 24% of total apprehensions. Although the number of apprehensions increased over the next several years, both the real number and percentage of apprehended aliens who were detained dropped dramatically. In fiscal year 1991, for example, seven percent (approximately 84,000) of the 1,200,000 aliens apprehended by the INS were detained. *Id.* In fiscal year 1994 (most recent figures available), the INS detained a total of 81,707 aliens. *Hearing on Containing Costs*, *supra* note 97 (testimony of James A. Puleo).

105. *See supra* note 65.

106. FIVE-YEAR DETENTION PLAN, *supra* note 64, at 15-16. In fiscal year 1982, 92% of the aliens apprehended by the INS were from Mexico. Mexican detainees averaged less than two days in detention, while detainees from other countries were held an average of

Ironically, the new "mandates" to detain virtually all undocumented excludable aliens and aggravated felons may actually reinforce this trend. These mandates, by prohibiting the release of many detained aliens, help to create a population of long-term detainees who languish in confinement.[107] Moreover, the governing statutes and regulations do not allocate scarce detention resources in a sensible manner. While the INS purports to have a "uniform detention policy nationwide," field officers must exercise discretion to choose among competing detention priorities.[108] The result is a detention system "so random, so illogical, so arbitrary that it fails in [many] crucial missions."[109]

The controversial practice of detaining asylum seekers provides one illustration. Until recently, the INS had no guidelines to focus its detention resources on what would seem to be the logical targets: those who abuse the asylum system by filing frivolous applications. Instead, the agency sometimes used detention as a deterrent, singling out applicants from a particular country or region, such as Haiti or Central America, who often presented credible asylum claims.[110] For

---

19 days. *Id.* at 15. In fiscal year 1991, 48% of detained aliens were from countries other than Mexico; their average detention stay was 41 days. *Id.* at 16. The INS reports this increase in the average length of stay "has, of necessity, had a major adverse impact on INS detention operations." *Id.*

107. *See* Klein, *supra* note 93, at A1 (noting potential growth of the "non-releasable aggravated felon" population).

108. In July 1993, the Acting Commissioner of the INS issued a memorandum to field officers setting detention priorities, stating "[i]t is our policy to have a uniform detention policy nationwide." The memorandum noted "statutory requirements mandat[e] compulsory INS detention for some types of cases," but at the same time instructed District Directors and Chief Border Patrol Agents to "*ensure that appropriate discretion is exercised* in making custody determinations." The memorandum also explicitly conceded that "we can only apply these detention guidelines within available INS resources." Memorandum from Chris Sale, Acting Commissioner, Immigration and Naturalization Service to District Directors, et al. (July 23, 1993) (emphasis added) (on file with author). A recent investigative report on INS detention concluded "in reality, there is no [single] detention policy. There are as many policies as there are INS bosses." Alvarez & Getter, *Detention: The Failed Deterrent, supra* note 5, at 24A; *see also* Solomon, *supra* note 83, at 25.

109. Alvarez & Getter, *Detention: The Failed Deterrent, supra* note 5, at 1A.

110. *See* GAO DETENTION REPORT, supra note 65, at 35-37 (discussing "three efforts to reduce the flow of aliens entering illegally," which targeted aliens from Haiti, Central America, and China for detention); *see also* Louis v. Nelson, 544 F. Supp. 973, 979-84 (S.D. Fla. 1982) (describing new policy of detaining undocumented excludable aliens, which was intended to "regain control" of our borders and had a disproportionate impact on Haitians); Roberto Suro, *U.S. Is Renewing Border Detentions,* N.Y. TIMES, Feb. 8, 1990, at A22 (describing detention efforts in Texas to deter asylum applicants from Central America); Roberto Suro, *Despite U.S. Pledge, Detainees Languish,* WASH. POST, Dec. 20, 1994, at A3 (detention of Chinese intended to deter alien smuggling). These ad hoc detention efforts have been controversial because they have targeted aliens fleeing countries in turmoil, who

those not subject to these targeted detention efforts, only pure luck, the availability of local detention space, and the unchecked discretion of low-level officials would separate those asylum seekers who received parole from those who suffered in long-term detention.[111]

In 1992, the INS finally began interviewing detained asylum seekers to identify those with potentially valid claims for possible parole.[112] But this policy has faltered from a lack of commitment and resources.[113] Even under the current asylum pre-screening program, some applicants with a well-founded fear of persecution in their home country remain incarcerated, while others who have abused the sys-

---

often had good reason to seek protection in the United States, even if they did not fulfill the statutory definition of a refugee. *See generally* Helton, *supra* note 73, at 373-76. The use of detention as an ad hoc deterrent has also raised the specter of national origin discrimination. A panel of the Eleventh Circuit concluded that Haitians were detained because of invidious discrimination. But this decision was vacated by the en banc court on the ground that the Haitians, as excludable aliens, could not claim equal protection under the Constitution. Jean v. Nelson, 711 F.2d 1455 (11th Cir. 1983), *vacated*, 727 F.2d 957 (11th Cir. 1984).

111. *See* Alvarez & Getter, *Detention: The Failed Deterrent, supra* note 5, at 1A (describing several instances where excludable aliens were caught by seemingly arbitrary detention decisions); Diego Ribadeneira, *35 Haitians Detained in Texas*, BOSTON GLOBE, Oct. 1, 1994, at 28 (Haitians detained in Miami, where detention space was short, received parole; others similarly situated, who had previously been transferred to less-crowded facilities in Texas, would not be released); Letter from Lory Rosenberg, Director, American Immigration Law Foundation, to Dennis DeLeon, Human Rights Commissioner, City of New York 2 (Aug. 31, 1993) (citing statement by INS official in New York that aliens arriving at Kennedy Airport were confined on a "first come, first detained" basis; those arriving after spaces were filled for the day received parole) (on file with author).

112. Memorandum from Gene McNary, Commissioner, Immigration and Naturalization Service to All Regional Administrators, et al. (Apr. 20, 1992), *reprinted in* 69 INTERPRETER RELEASES 526 (1992).

113. *See generally* LAWYERS COMM. FOR HUMAN RIGHTS, DETENTION OF REFUGEES: PROBLEMS IN IMPLEMENTATION OF THE ASYLUM PRE-SCREENING OFFICER PROGRAM (1994) [hereinafter LAWYERS COMMITTEE REPORT ON APSO PROGRAM]. This study, constituting the first comprehensive assessment of the so-called "APSO" program, concluded:

[t]he program has achieved a principal objective by identifying at least some detained asylum applicants for whom detention is not warranted [,] thereby increasing the INS's ability to use its detention capability in a rational manner. However, over two years since the APSO program went into [e]ffect, there remain serious problems with its enforcement.

Id. at 9-10. Among these problems are district directors who have disregarded APSO officer recommendations to parole detained aliens and some evidence of national origin discrimination in parole decisions. *Id.* at 10-12. The report recommended the APSO program be codified in regulations. *Id.* at 18.

The INS has not issued a formal evaluation of the APSO program, but noted in its report on the Esmor detention facility in New Jersey that "a stronger APSO program" would "help the INS to make wise use of detention space while addressing humanitarian concerns raised by extended detention of credible asylum seekers." INS ESMOR REPORT, *supra* note 8, at 54. The INS Esmor report also concluded "[a] stronger APSO program will require an additional dedication of resources." *Id.*

tem (along with some aliens who have committed serious crimes) go free.[114]

There is little hope the INS can outgrow these problems by continuing to expand its detention capacity, although the agency now seems to be pursuing this rather dubious course.[115] Many critics of immigration detention have noted the grave humanitarian concerns raised by the "wanton detention of aliens," even apart from the serious problems with conditions of confinement.[116] The current program of aggressive expansion ignores these pressing issues, and still will not provide sufficient capacity to meet the "mandatory" detention requirements of the existing legal framework.[117] Moreover, some immigration reform proposals now pending before Congress would, if enacted, only increase the strain on the immigration detention system by adding additional unrealistic mandates.[118]

In the meantime, the INS remains overwhelmed by its impossible detention mission. And thousands of aliens face long-term confinement in the custody of an agency stretched beyond its capacity.

---

114. *See generally* Alvarez & Getter, *Detention: The Failed Deterrent, supra* note 5, at 1A; LAWYERS COMMITTEE REPORT ON APSO PROGRAM, *supra* note 113, at 12, 14; SENATE CRIMINAL ALIENS REPORT, *supra* note 88, at 2, 23-24.

115. *See supra* note 103 (noting INS plans to expand its detention capacity by 48% in fiscal year 1996).

116. The phrase is borrowed from Maurice Roberts, *supra* note 76; *see also* Helton, *supra* note 73; Schuck, *Transformation of Immigration Law, supra* note 33, at 68-69 (noting "[t]he prolonged incarceration of thousands of aliens, most of them innocent victims of severe economic deprivation, indiscriminate armed conflict, or intense political persecution has seared the judicial conscience as few events since the civil rights struggle of the 1950s and 1960s have done"). Professor Schuck's assessment of the judicial response to the claims of detained aliens was written before initial court victories were vacated, reversed, or undermined by later decisions. More recently, most INS detention practices (including the refusal to grant parole to excludable aliens who present pressing humanitarian concerns) have been upheld by courts employing a very deferential standard of review. *See supra* note 57; *infra* note 284.

117. Available estimates suggest, for example, approximately 20% of the federal and state prison population—about 120,000 prisoners—are deportable aliens. These figures do not take into account the increasing flow of alien offenders into the prison system. GAO DETENTION REPORT, *supra* note 65, at 38 (estimating over 72,000 aliens will be arrested yearly on felony drug charges). Even taking into account various reforms, such as the IHP and APSO programs, the GAO investigation of immigration detention concluded "[w]e do not believe that it is feasible to expand the INS detention capabilities sufficiently to solve the [agency's enforcement] problems." *Id.* at 43.

118. *Efforts to Control Illegal Immigration: Hearing Before the Subcomm. on Immigration and Claims of the House Judiciary Comm.* (June 29, 1995), *available in* LEXIS, Legis Library, Cngtst File (testimony of T. Alexander Aleinikoff, Executive Associate Commissioner, Immigration and Naturalization Service) (noting provisions in pending legislation requiring even more immigration detention would tie up INS detention space and could prevent the INS from detaining criminal aliens).

II. Conditions of Confinement at Immigration Detention Facilities

The rapid expansion of immigration detention predictably has resulted in serious problems with conditions of confinement. Although alien detainees are held in civil confinement, they sometimes are incarcerated "under conditions as severe as we apply to our worst criminals."[119] INS detention facilities, like prisons and jails across the country, too frequently do not meet minimum requirements for humane detention.

Some alien detainees also face unusually harsh conditions stemming from practices unique to immigration detention. First, deplorable conditions of confinement have resulted whenever the United States has detained large groups of potential refugees for prolonged periods to deter their fellow countrymen from seeking asylum in the United States.[120] Second, the INS confines aliens in state and local jails or private facilities without adequate oversight. Some detainees confined in these "non-Service" facilities have been subjected to abuse or inhumane detention conditions because the INS has looked the other way or has failed to make even the most basic arrangements for their care.

This section summarizes the disturbing INS record of confining aliens in substandard detention facilities,[121] focusing on conditions of

---

119. Rodriguez-Fernandez v. Wilkinson, 654 F.2d 1382, 1385 (10th Cir. 1981) (describing prevailing conditions for the Marielitos detained in overcrowded prisons in the early 1980s).

120. As was the case with the Marielito Cubans, a brief period of detention may be necessary to screen and process a large, and sometimes unexpected, volume of aliens seeking entry. But the confinement conditions suffered by Haitians, Central Americans, and the most recent wave of Cubans—groups held for much longer periods, in part to deter other asylum seekers from their home countries—demonstrate the need to develop a more humane response to so-called "immigration emergencies." *See infra* note 197 and accompanying text; *see also* U.S. COMM'N ON IMMIGRATION REFORM, *supra* note 84, at 162-74.

121. Unfortunately, the personal stories of would-be immigrants detained by the INS cannot be captured in this overview of conditions problems. Justice Brennan reminds us "it is impossible for a written opinion to convey the pernicious conditions and the pain and degradation which ordinary [persons] suffer" when they are confined in facilities that do not meet constitutional standards. Rhodes v. Chapman, 452 U.S. 337, 354 n.3 (Brennan, J., concurring) (quoting Ruiz v. Estelle, 503 F. Supp 1265, 1391 (S.D. Tex. 1980)). Several advocacy organizations (and most recently the INS itself) have issued reports that together provide a comprehensive picture of the poignant plight of INS detainees. *See* INS ESMOR REPORT, *supra* note 8; WOMEN'S COMM'N FOR REFUGEE WOMEN AND CHILDREN, A CRY FOR HELP: CHINESE WOMEN IN INS DETENTION (1995) [hereinafter CHINESE WOMEN IN DETENTION]; VARICK STREET REPORT, *supra* note 83; BRUTALITY UNCHECKED, *supra* note 4, at 54-66; MINNESOTA LAWYERS INT'L HUMAN RIGHTS & PHYSICIANS FOR HUMAN RIGHTS, HIDDEN FROM VIEW: HUMAN RIGHTS CONDITIONS IN THE KROME DETENTION

confinement and physical abuse suffered by both excludable and deportable aliens.[122] I do not contend that every example in this section unquestionably violates the Constitution, but rather that many colorable due process claims arise from the conditions of immigration detention.[123] A survey of the available evidence demonstrates serious conditions problems are endemic at alien detention facilities.[124]

CENTER (1991) [hereinafter KROME REPORT]; ACLU DETENTION REPORT, *supra* note 4; COORDINATING COMM. ON IMMIGRATION LAW, LIVES ON THE LINE: SEEKING ASYLUM IN SOUTH TEXAS 10-13 (1989) [hereinafter LIVES ON THE LINE]; LAWYERS COMM. FOR HUMAN RIGHTS, THE DETENTION OF ASYLUM SEEKERS IN THE UNITED STATES: A CRUEL AND QUESTIONABLE POLICY 22-28 (1989) [hereinafter DETENTION OF ASYLUM SEEKERS]; Lynn Marcus, *Detention Conditions in INS and Contract Facilities in the Southwest*, IMMIGR. NEWSL. (National Immigration Project of the Nat'l Lawyers Guild, Boston, Mass.), Winter 1989, at 1. For first-person stories of individual INS detainees, see LAWYERS COMM. FOR HUMAN RIGHTS & HELSINKI WATCH, MOTHER OF EXILES (1986) [hereinafter MOTHER OF EXILES]; *see also* Solomon, *supra* note 83, at 25.

122. For the most part, excludable and deportable aliens are confined together, and thus subject to the same conditions of confinement. *See* Schmidt, *supra* note 11, at 321. Mariel Cubans, however, usually are not detained in INS SPCs or contract facilities, but instead are confined in prisons or jails. FIVE-YEAR DETENTION PLAN, *supra* note 64, at 18-19. In addition, Haitians and Cubans who were interdicted and detained at "safe haven" camps at Guantanamo Naval Base inhabited a legal limbo. The government successfully argued that they could not claim even the limited statutory and constitutional protections afforded to "excludable" aliens because they were held outside the territory of the United States. *See* Cuban Am. Bar Assoc. v. Christopher, 43 F.3d 1412 (11th Cir. 1995). *But see* Haitian Ctrs. Council v. Sale, 823 F. Supp. 1028, 1041-45, (E.D.N.Y. 1993) (Haitians detained at Guantanamo can claim due process protection) (vacated per settlement agreement).

123. Under the Due Process Clause, noncriminal detainees are protected from any condition or practice amounting to "punishment" of the detainees. Bell v. Wolfish, 441 U.S. 520, 535 (1979). But allegations of mere negligence do not state a due process violation. Davidson v. Cannon, 474 U.S. 327 (1985). Courts are divided over how to apply the *Bell v. Wolfish* test, and in particular over its relationship to Eighth Amendment precedent. The Fifth Circuit, for example, has recently granted rehearing en banc for two cases raising this issue. *See infra* note 308. In general, "deliberate indifference" has become the touchstone used by many courts to assess due process claims of inadequate medical care or inhumane conditions of confinement. 1 MICHAEL MUSHLIN, RIGHTS OF PRISONERS, § 3.01, at 132 (2d ed. 1993).

This article does not undertake the task of sorting out the complex law governing due process conditions claims. Instead, I invoke the general pronouncements of *Bell*, which (with two notable exceptions discussed *infra* note 308) are still cited consistently as controlling precedent. I also draw comparisons to Eighth Amendment standards, in part because the Eighth Amendment has received considerably more attention in the Supreme Court. *See infra* notes 330-339. These well-settled touchstones are used to ascertain whether alien detainees have received a full measure of constitutional protection when challenging the conditions of their confinement. I conclude that sometimes they have not. *See infra* notes 303-328, 341-343 and accompanying text.

124. The conditions problems documented in this section are exacerbated by a related, but no less important, concern: detainees' lack of access to legal counsel. Most INS detention facilities are located in remote areas, where there is little legal help available. *See* GAO DETENTION REPORT, *supra* note 65, at 46-47; Roshan v. Smith, 615 F. Supp. 901

A. Overview of Conditions at INS Detention Facilities

The confinement conditions at INS detention facilities vary, both over time and among facilities.[125] The overall picture, however, is one of harsh detention conditions similar to—and sometimes worse than—the prevailing conditions for criminal incarceration.[126]

Severe overcrowding is a recurring source of many conditions problems. Overcrowding persisted at INS detention facilities through-

---

(D.D.C. 1985) (dismissing complaint seeking to enjoin construction of remote facility in Oakdale, La.). Moreover, various INS practices—from frequent transfers to restrictive visiting hours—have hampered detainees' ability to obtain legal representation. *See, e.g.*, Orantes-Hernandez v. Meese, 685 F. Supp 1488, 1509-11 (C.D. Cal. 1988); Nunez v. Boldin, 537 F. Supp. 578 (S.D. Tex.), *appeal dismissed*, 692 F.2d 755 (5th Cir. 1982); *INS Transfer Policy, supra* note 53. I will consider detained aliens' procedural due process challenges to these practices (as opposed to their substantive due process challenges to conditions of confinement) in a forthcoming article.

125. This section discusses detention conditions at facilities run by the INS, including the nine Service Processing Centers and the joint INS/BOP facility at Oakdale, La. I also refer on occasion to conditions at the "safe haven" camps at Guantanamo Naval Base, Cuba, which were used to hold Haitians and Cubans interdicted at sea. These camps were run by the United States military, not the INS. Nevertheless, the Guantanamo camps provide the most recent example of the deplorable conditions that have resulted whenever the United States undertakes a massive detention effort in order to deter an influx of asylum seekers. In essence, the Guantanamo camps exported offshore (and farther from public and judicial scrutiny) the same conditions problems which prevailed at detention facilities within the United States used to confine Haitians and Central Americans in the 1980s. *See infra* note 142 and accompanying text.

126. Numerous courts and scholars have compared the conditions of immigration detention to criminal imprisonment. *See, e.g.*, Rodriguez-Fernandez v. Williams, 654 F.2d 1382, 1385 (10th Cir. 1981) (Marielito Cubans confined in federal penitentiary); Helton, *supra* note 73, at 364 (conditions of immigration detention are "generally similar to prison conditions"); Schuck, *Transformation of Immigration Law, supra* note 33, at 28 n.149 ("Although the INS and the courts routinely employ the term 'detention' to describe the practice of holding aliens . . . the length of many detentions and the conditions of confinement suggest that the term 'imprisonment' more accurately depicts reality"). Others have used the analogy of concentration camps to describe immigration detention. Michael A. Olivas, *"Breaking the Law" on Principle: An Essay on Lawyers' Dilemmas, Unpopular Causes, and Legal Regimes*, 52 U. PITT. L. REV. 815, 821-22 (1991) [hereinafter Olivas, *Breaking the Law*] (comparing the "shacks, tents, and makeshift housing" used to confine alien children to the Japanese concentration camps during World War II); Puerto Rico v. Muskie, 507 F. Supp. 1035, 1043 (D.P.R.), *vacated per consent agreement sub nom.*, Marquez-Colon v. Reagan, 668 F.2d 611 (1st Cir. 1981) ("In other times and circumstances the so-called refugee facility would be referred to as a concentration camp."). Several recent reports have noted that convicted criminals sometimes fare better than civil immigration detainees. *See* VARICK STREET REPORT, supra note 83, at 29 ("Detainees who have served time for criminal offenses uniformly report that conditions at Varick Street are significantly worse than in city or state prisons where their sentences were served."); Alisa Solomon, *supra* note 83; David Stout, *Detention Jail Called Worse than Prison*, N.Y. TIMES, June 19, 1995, at B5; *Prison vs. INS Detention: Convicts have More Perks*, MIAMI HERALD, Dec. 16, 1993, at 25A [hereinafter *Prison vs. INS*]; Willa Appel, *They Did No Crime, But They're Doing Time*, NEWSDAY, Dec. 6, 1993, at 39.

out the 1980s.[127] The INS contends this problem has abated recently, in part because of funding shortfalls.[128] Nevertheless, some detention facilities at times still operate above their rated capacities.[129] Overcrowding also arises as a serious concern whenever the INS undertakes a massive ad hoc detention effort.

Soon after the new policy of detaining undocumented excludable aliens was announced in 1981, for example, the Krome detention center in Florida was filled more than three times beyond its stated capacity.[130] Over a thousand detainees (mostly Haitians) were crowded into makeshift shelters without adequate sanitation or medical care.[131] Conditions at Krome were abhorrent during this period. Untreated sewage threatened to contaminate the drinking water.[132] The Florida Health Department cited Krome for numerous health and safety violations,[133] and the state sued to close the facility because of the severe overcrowding.[134]

Similar conditions prevailed when the INS announced a sudden crackdown to detain asylum applicants at facilities in South Texas in

---

127. *See, e.g.*, Letter from Greg Leo to Sharon Hase (n.d.), *in Bureau of Prisons and the U.S. Parole Commission: Oversight Hearing Before the Subcomm. on Courts, Civil Liberties, and the Administration of Justice of the House Judiciary Comm.*, 99th Cong., 1st Sess. 148 (1995) (noting on May 31, 1984, three out of six SPCs had detainee populations exceeding stated capacity); Laurie Becklund, *Conditions Assailed: Salvadoran Men Languish in INS Center in Desert*, L.A. TIMES, Feb. 20, 1985, at B1 (El Centro, Cal. overcrowded); Liz Balmaseda, *"New" Krome a Sign of Growth in Alien Detention*, MIAMI HERALD, Mar. 12, 1985, at 4D (Krome is often "packed beyond its capacity"); Helton, *supra* note 73, at 364 ("[o]vercrowding is a recurrent problem" at SPCs); Nunez v. Boldin, 537 F. Supp. 578, 583 (S.D. Tex. 1982) (noting "crowded conditions" at Los Fresnos, Tex. facility).

128. FIVE-YEAR DETENTION PLAN, supra note 64, at 17; INSPECTOR GENERAL DETENTION REPORT, *supra* note 81, at 4.

129. *See* INSPECTOR GENERAL DETENTION REPORT, *supra* note 81, at 6 (San Pedro SPC ran "far above" its established capacity from September 1991 to April 1992); VARICK STREET REPORT, *supra* note 83, at 30 (detainees regularly sleep in library so that Varick SPC can operate at its "maximum" capacity).

130. ACLU DETENTION REPORT, *supra* note 4, at 19 (1206 Haitians detained at Krome in July 1981 when the center had a capacity of 524).

131. *Id.*

132. *Id.*

133. *See* Colon v. Carter, 507 F. Supp. 1026, 1028 (D.P.R. 1980).

134. Graham v. Smith, No. 81-1487-Civ-JE (S.D. Fla. 1981), *cited in* Louis v. Nelson, 544 F. Supp 973, 983 n.27 (S.D. Fla. 1982). This lawsuit was apparently rendered moot when Congress, in an appropriations bill, directed the Attorney General to "exercise his best efforts" to ensure no more than 525 detainees were held at Krome after March 1, 1982. *See* Pub. L. No. 97-92, § 128, 95 Stat. 1198-99 (1981). A report prepared by a human rights monitoring group in 1991, however, found Krome's population still periodically exceeded 525. KROME REPORT, *supra* note 121, at 41.

1989 and 1990.[135] This detention policy was intended to stem the flow of potential refugees from Central America.[136] The Los Fresnos SPC, designed to hold 425 detainees, was crowded with an additional 2000 aliens.[137] Predictably, deplorable conditions resulted. Detainees confined at Los Fresnos were packed into tents without access to showers or clean clothes.[138] Other detainees, including children, were confined in hastily conceived, substandard temporary facilities.[139]

Both Krome and Los Fresnos braced for a similar situation in 1994, when thousands of Haitians and Cubans again fled by boat to the United States. Krome began operating well above its stated capacity.[140] Meanwhile, Los Fresnos again prepared to house thousands of detainees. Prior experience with the Central American detention effort prompted the governor of Texas to warn federal officials that "[a]ny plans to hold detainees in tents, without adequate infrastruc-

---

135. Suro, *U.S. Is Renewing Border Detentions, supra* note 110, at A22; Richard L. Berke, *Immigration Official Warns Aliens May be Held in Jail*, N.Y. TIMES, Mar. 11, 1989, at A9; Roberto Suro, *U.S. Set to Detain Refugees in Tents Beginning Today*, N.Y. TIMES, Feb. 21, 1989, at A1 [hereinafter Suro, *U.S. Set to Detain Refugees*].

136. The INS Commissioner stated "he hoped to send a message to people seeking asylum that they face certain detention under conditions that 'won't be like the Ritz Carlton.'" Suro, *U.S. Is Renewing Border Detentions, supra*, note 110. The South Texas detention effort broke with the usual practice of the INS in that both excludable aliens who arrived without documents and deportable aliens who had already entered the United States were detained when they applied for asylum. *See* Suro, *U.S. Set to Detain Refugees, supra* note 135. Noncriminal deportable aliens usually are not subject to detention unless they present an unusual risk of absconding. *See supra* note 49.

137. BRUTALITY UNCHECKED, *supra* note 4, at 58-59; *see also* Berke, *supra* note 135, at A9. The detention effort peaked at about 3600 detainees in the spring of 1989, and was suddenly renewed again in early 1990. Suro, *U.S. Is Renewing Border Detentions, supra* note 110, at A22.

138. BRUTALITY UNCHECKED, *supra* note 4, at 58-59; *see also* Robert E. Koulish, *Systemic Deterrence Against Prospective Asylum Seekers: A Study of the South Texas Immigration Project*, 19 N.Y.U. REV. L. & SOC. CHANGE 529, 539-43 (1992) (noting serious problems with conditions of confinement and "a pattern of physical mistreatment against detainees").

139. *See* LIVES ON THE LINE, *supra* note 121, at 11 (describing conditions at various temporary facilities in South Texas, including a Red Cross shelter where "quarters were very crowded and strongly ressembled [sic] the conditions in refugee camps abroad"); Olivas, *Breaking the Law, supra* note 126, at 821-22 (children held in "shacks, tents, and makeshift housing" had "virtually no access to health care or personal counseling").

140. In August 1994, Krome confined over 600 Cubans, including 107 minors who were detained despite INS guidelines stating juveniles should be released or transferred to a juvenile shelter within 72 hours. *Attorneys Sue to Free Children*, FT. LAUDERDALE SUN-SENTINEL, Aug. 31, 1994, at 8A. The INS began paroling children from Krome on humanitarian grounds in September 1994. Lisa Ocker & Berta Delgado, *37 Cubans Win Release From Krome*, FT. LAUDERDALE SUN-SENTINEL, Sept. 16, 1994, at 1A. On October 3, 1994, the INS Daily Population Report stated Krome had a rated capacity of 200 and held 445 detainees. Letter from Joan C. Higgins, *supra* note 101, at Attachment 1.

ture, security, health, or other fundamental services would be unacceptable."[141] The Haitians and Cubans soon were interdicted at sea and sent to Guantanamo Naval Base in Cuba to face similar conditions.[142]

Even when immigration detention facilities are not overcrowded, they frequently are understaffed.[143] A chronic shortage of INS detention officers, together with the routine use of poorly trained temporary employees and contract security guards, contributes to conditions problems.[144] At the El Centro SPC, for example, detainees were forced to spend fourteen hours a day outside in the desert sun, where

---

141. *See* James Pinkerton, *S. Texas Detention Camp Ready for Influx of Cubans*, HOUSTON CHRON., Aug. 26, 1994, at A12 (quoting letter from Texas Governor Ann Richards to INS Commissioner Doris Meissner, sent by Governor Richards in response to reports that Los Fresnos had contingency plans to house up to 3500 Cuban detainees). On October 3, 1994, the Los Fresnos facility, with a rated capacity of 350, held 674 detainees. Letter from Joan C. Higgins, *supra* note 101, at Attachment 1.

142. Conditions of confinement were a constant concern, and a source of unrest, when some 40,000 Haitians and Cubans were detained at "safe haven" camps at Guantanamo during 1994. When the camps were set up, no infrastructure was in place to provide for the basic human needs of thousands of detainees. *See, e.g.,* Mireya Navarro, *Resources Strained at Guantanamo Bay*, N.Y. TIMES, Sept. 4, at A12; Patrick J. Sloyan, *Guantanamo Alert: U.S. Fears Refugees Overtaxing Navy Base*, NEWSDAY, Aug. 25, 1994, at A5; Art Pine, *Expanding Refugee Housing Poses Risks*, L.A. TIMES, Aug. 26, 1994, at A17; Joseph B. Treaster, *Guantanamo: Refugee Camps Fill With Fury*, N.Y. TIMES, Aug. 30, 1994, at A1; *Some Haitians Flee Refugee-Camp Conditions*, SAN DIEGO TRIB., July 12, 1994, at A10. Even as the military worked to improve conditions, observers reported serious deficiencies in sanitation, food distribution, and medical care. *See* Armando Valladares, *Castro Outfoxes Clinton—and Guantanamo's Detainees Pay*, WALL ST. J., Jan. 27, 1995 at A11 (human rights organization reported "lice- and mange-ridden children . . . . insufficient water and milk for infants and . . . chronic medical conditions left untreated"); Navarro, *supra* (reporting problems with food distribution); Gordon Edes, *Canseco Makes A Huge Hit To Those Left on Cuban Base*, FT. LAUDERDALE SUN-SENTINEL, Oct. 10, 1994, at 1C (noting malnutrition and "woeful sanitary conditions"); *see also* Letter from Harold Hongju Koh, Director, The Orville H. Schell, Jr. Center for International Human Rights at Yale Law School, to T. Alexander Aleinikoff, General Counsel, Immigration and Naturalization Service (July 19, 1994) (recommending numerous changes needed to improve conditions for Haitians at Guantanamo) (on file with author).

143. *See* James LeMoyne, *Florida Center Holding Aliens Is Under Inquiry*, N.Y. TIMES, May 16, 1990, at A16 (INS officials concede Krome operates "with only half the guards who are needed"); KROME REPORT, *supra* note 121, at 49; FIVE-YEAR DETENTION PLAN, *supra* note 64, at 17 ("an insufficient number of personnel" caused the INS to "underutilize" its SPCs).

144. The Varick Street facility has repeatedly been criticized for using contract guards who "time and again . . . have displayed an inability or unwillingness to perform their duties in a manner that will meet even minimal standards." VARICK STREET REPORT, *supra* note 83, at 13 (quoting internal report prepared by the New York INS district). Currently, about 40% of the detention officer staff at INS SPCs are contract employees. *Hearing on Containing Costs, supra* note 97 (testimony of James A. Puleo); *see also* KROME REPORT, *supra* note 121, at 49 (half of the Krome detention officers are temporary employees who do not undergo full INS training).

temperatures regularly exceeded one hundred degrees, simply because there were not enough security guards to supervise the air-conditioned barracks during the day.[145] And at the San Pedro SPC, the INS assigned male guards to the bathrooms and dorms of female detainees due to a shortage of female detention officers.[146]

Access to medical care is another frequently cited problem at alien detention facilities. The clinic facilities at most Service Processing Centers are generally deemed sufficient.[147] But adequate medical care is not always provided, particularly for pregnant women and detainees with psychiatric or chronic health problems.[148] Again, the problem is especially acute during ad hoc detention efforts. In 1993, a federal court condemned the deliberate refusal by the INS to provide appropriate treatment for HIV-positive Haitians detained at Guantanamo as "outrageous, callous, and reprehensible."[149]

---

145. Judith Cummings, *Aliens Staging Hunger Strike at Detention Camp*, N.Y. TIMES, June 4, 1985, at A12. This practice was discontinued in July 1985 after the INS hired additional contract guards. Detainees at El Centro are now allowed inside during parts of the day. ACLU DETENTION REPORT, *supra* note 4, at 99; BRUTALITY UNCHECKED, *supra* note 4, at 58 n.187. Other facilities in extremely hot climates, however, have also confined detainees outdoors during most of the day. ACLU DETENTION REPORT, *supra* note 4, at 107-08 (facilities in El Paso and Port Isabel, Tex.).

146. *Prison vs. INS Detention, supra* note 126, at 25A.

147. KROME REPORT, *supra* note 121, at 44-48 (Krome Public Health Service Clinic "is quite adequate and meets contemporary standards"); VARICK STREET REPORT, *supra* note 83, at 44 n.138 (independent consultant was "generally impressed" with the medical unit, but was unable to evaluate quality of treatment because site observers were not permitted to speak to obtain consent to review detainees' medical records). Five INS SPCs are medically accredited by the National Commission on Correctional Health Care. INS DETENTION BRIEFING PAPER, *supra* note 97, at 3.

148. *See* VARICK STREET REPORT, *supra* note 83, at 44-46 (detailing complaints about medical care); BRUTALITY UNCHECKED, *supra* note 4, at 59-60 (adequate care not provided for those with serious medical conditions; at most SPCs there are no psychiatric facilities); ACLU DETENTION REPORT, *supra* note 4, at 19 (pregnant women at Krome did not receive adequate nutrition). *See also* Solomon, *supra* note 83 (reporting HIV-positive detainee was unable to get prescription medicine, and detainee denied access to a walker was forced to drag himself across the floor); *Fleeing persecution, couple found new anguish*, MIAMI HERALD, Dec. 16, 1993, at 24A (San Pedro detainee did not receive adequate nutrition or medical care when she was pregnant; baby died after being born three months premature); Louis Dubose, *The Last Refuge: Asian Immigrants in Texas Jails*, TEX. OBSERVER, Apr. 24, 1992, at 1, 10 (Bayview doctors failed to diagnose AIDS-related opportunistic infection). Complaints about inadequate medical care at INS detention facilities have been raised in two class action lawsuits now pending in California. *See supra* note 31.

149. Haitian Ctrs. Council v. Sale, 823 F. Supp. 1028, 1038 (E.D.N.Y. 1993) (vacated per settlement agreement). The INS conceded medical facilities at Guantanamo were not sufficient to provide treatment for AIDS patients, yet refused to consider the recommendations of camp doctors that certain HIV-positive detainees be medically evacuated to the United States. *Id.* at 1044.

The conditions at INS detention facilities are exacerbated by the increasingly longer detention stays for alien detainees. The INS Service Processing Centers were not designed for long-term confinement.[150] At the Varick Street SPC, for example, aliens are incarcerated for months or even years in crowded "dorm" rooms designed for detention of less than one week, with no opportunity to go outdoors.[151] Programmed activities routinely provided to prison inmates under generally accepted standards for long-term detention are not available to many INS detainees.[152] The "excruciating boredom"[153] and harsh conditions of immigration detention have triggered hunger strikes and riots by detainees attempting to call attention to their plight.[154]

B. Detention Conditions at "Non-Service" Facilities

One such uprising recently succeeded in bringing both INS and public scrutiny to the conditions of confinement at "contract" detention facilities. In June 1995, violence erupted at the alien detention facility run by Esmor Correctional Services Corporation in Elizabeth, New Jersey.[155] The riot was preceded by reports of abuse and inhu-

150. KROME REPORT, *supra* note 121, at 14; VARICK STREET REPORT, *supra* note 83, at 6; BRUTALITY UNCHECKED, *supra* note 4, at 57; DETENTION OF ASYLUM SEEKERS, *supra* note 121, at 22; *Prison vs. INS Detention*, *supra* note 126, at 25A.

151. VARICK STREET REPORT, supra note 83, at 11, 32-33. The lack of outdoor exercise has long been a source of tension at Varick Street. Both New York City and the State of New York correctional standards require outdoor exercise for their detention facilities. *See id.* at 33; *see also* Solomon, *supra* note 67, at A21 (detainee at Varick Street denied access to the outdoors for over four years).

152. When an independent consultant visited the Varick Street facility, for example, the exercise room was of "poor quality," lacking equipment the INS previously agreed to provide under a settlement decree. There were no educational programs and limited work opportunities. VARICK STREET REPORT, *supra* note 83, at 34-36. The consultant concluded Varick Street failed to comply with standards for detention articulated by the American Correctional Association and INS standards for the operation of detention facilities. *Id.* at 7. *But see* KROME REPORT, *supra* note 121, at 39 (Krome recreational facilities deemed "quite adequate" in 1991).

153. VARICK STREET REPORT, *supra* note 83, at 34 (detainees commonly mentioned "sleep" as their primary activity, and their chief complaint was "nothing to do").

154. *See, e.g.*, Larry Rohter, *"Processing" for Haitians Is Time in a Rural Prison*, N.Y. TIMES, June 21, 1992, at D18 (hunger strike at Krome); James Bennet, *Illegal Aliens and Guards Hurt in Melee*, N.Y. TIMES, Dec. 30, 1991, at B9 (at least four hunger strikes in six years to protest conditions at the Varick Street SPC); Cummings, *supra* note 145, at A12 (Central American detainees stage hunger strike to protest conditions at El Centro SPC); *Haitians at 2 Detention Sites Refusing to Eat and to Talk*, N.Y. TIMES, Dec. 25, 1981, at A8.

155. Richard Perez-Pena, *Aliens' Melee Closes Center in New Jersey*, N.Y. TIMES, June 19, 1995, at A1; Elizabeth Llorente et al., *Tinderbox Explodes in Elizabeth*, BERGEN REC., June 19, 1995, at A1.

mane treatment of detainees at the Esmor facility.[156] In response to this criticism, the INS had commenced an investigation of conditions at Esmor the week before the detainee disturbance; its investigation was expanded to include inquiry into the riot.[157] The INS cancelled its New Jersey contract with Esmor after completing its investigation.[158]

In the aftermath of the riot, both the press and INS issued reports highly critical of Esmor's New Jersey facility. The INS found the low-paid Esmor guards did not receive effective supervision or even the minimal training specified in its contract.[159] Detainees were frequently subject to harassment and physical abuse as "part of a systematic methodology . . . to control the general detainee population."[160] Theft of detainee property was widespread.[161] Unfortunately, Esmor supervisors and INS personnel—both on site and at the INS District Office—turned a blind eye and ignored repeated well-founded complaints about mistreatment of alien detainees.[162]

---

156. Most notable were claims of widespread physical abuse by guards and unnecessary shackling of detainees. *See* Llorente, *supra* note 7, at A1.

157. INS ESMOR REPORT, *supra* note 8, at 1.

158. Ashley Dunn, *U.S. Inquiry Finds Detention Center Was Poorly Run*, N.Y. TIMES, July 22, 1995, at A1. Esmor still operates an alien detention facility in Seattle, Wash. *Id.*

159. The INS report noted Esmor recruited guards at the salary level of "[t]he typical warehouse guard," instead of offering the competitive wage for guards "who [are] also responsible for the welfare and security of persons." INS ESMOR REPORT, supra note 8, at 16. When the contract was awarded, the INS had ignored warnings that the salary proposed by Esmor was "unrealistic" and created a high risk Esmor could not meet the requirements of the contract. Sullivan & Purdy, *supra* note 6, at A1. Esmor indeed had trouble hiring guards and was so short-staffed that many of its employees were forced to work two consecutive eight-hour shifts. This practice was permitted since the INS contract failed to specify the number of security personnel needed to staff the facility adequately, and instead.left this decision (along with many other vital matters) to the discretion of the for-profit corporation running the facility. INS ESMOR REPORT, *supra* note 8, at 14, 33. The INS report also found Esmor put guards on duty without obtaining the requisite security clearance or providing any training. *Id.* at 16-20. This was particularly problematic since Esmor guards routinely operated without supervision from INS or Esmor personnel. *Id.* at 7, 12-13.

160. INS ESMOR REPORT, *supra* note 8, at 5.

161. *Id.* at 9. The INS report noted many Esmor detainees on the brink of deportation refused to board their outgoing flights without their funds and valuables, which had been confiscated by Esmor guards. *Id.*

162. The INS concluded its on-site personnel did not provide adequate oversight, in part because of inexperience and frequent turnover. *Id.* at 35-37. The INS claimed it was "kept in the dark" about changes in the operations at Esmor, but at the same time noted its district office did not respond to repeated complaints. *Id.* at 13, 38-39 (citing three unanswered letters from pro bono attorneys). The INS report recommended 24-hour oversight by INS personnel at contract detention facilities, noting such round-the-clock supervision "is not the current INS policy nationally for these types of contracts." *Id.* at 35.

The operation of the Esmor facility raises fundamental questions about the wisdom of delegating responsibility for detainee welfare to private, for-profit corporations.[163] The INS report traced many of the problems at Esmor to its method of contracting for private detention and to inadequate oversight at the facility.[164] Still, the agency contends Esmor was an isolated situation.[165] Yet similar problems have emerged at other private facilities. Two less-publicized disturbances at the Eloy, Arizona contract facility, for example, were linked to low pay and minimal training for contract guards, along with "shortages of food, soap, toilet paper, and other essentials."[166]

Questions of oversight also loom large when aliens are confined in state and local jails.[167] Too frequently, the INS has contracted with jails that do not provide humane conditions and adequate care for alien detainees. During the late 1970s and early 1980s, INS officials in Lubbock, Texas confined over 7000 aliens in local jails pursuant to informal, oral agreements.[168] The jails were not inspected or adequately maintained.[169] Detainees were crowded into "squalid" cells

---

163. These questions have repeatedly been raised by critics of prison privatization. *See* Ira P. Robbins, *Privatization of Corrections: Defining the Issues*, 69 JUDICATURE 325 (1986), *reprinted in* 40 VAND. L. REV. 813 (1987); James T. Gentry, Note, *The Panopticon Revisited: The Problem of Monitoring Private Prisons*, 96 YALE L.J. 353 (1986); David N. Wecht, Note, *Breaking the Code of Deference: Judicial Review of Private Prisons*, 96 YALE L.J. 815 (1986); *see also* Maureen Castellano, *Incarceration Incorporated*, N.J. L.J., July 10, 1995, at 1.

164. One prevailing criticism was that the INS statement of work, used nationwide to solicit bids for contract detention facilities, sets performance-based specifications leaving far too much discretion with the for-profit contracting entity. INS ESMOR REPORT, *supra* note 8, at 33, 60 ("a flaw in the original statement of work did not place a requirement on the contractor . . . to increase staffing proportionate to detainee levels").

165. In the wake of the Esmor disturbance, INS Commissioner Doris Meissner directed each INS District Director with jurisdiction over an SPC or contract facility to conduct a special site visit to ensure each facility was providing proper care and treatment for alien detainees. *See* Elizabeth Llorente, *Immigration Chief Orders Detention Center Visits*, BERGEN REC., June 23, 1995, at N9. She later conceded the Esmor situation "does raise for us broader issues of whether we're doing everything we can do in privatization," but stated she thought the problems at Esmor were an exception to the usual operation of contract facilities. Dunn, *supra* note 158.

166. Miriam Davidson, *Workers: Shortages Sparked Prison Riots*, ARIZ. REPUBLIC, Dec. 27, 1994, at B1.

167. About 25% of the bedspace for immigration detention is obtained through per diem contracts with local law enforcement agencies. FIVE-YEAR DETENTION PLAN, *supra* note 64, at 16. As of March 31, 1995, the INS was using about 1700 beds in state and local jails to confine aliens. *Hearing on Containing Costs, supra* note 97 (testimony of James A. Puleo).

168. Ortega v. Rowe, 796 F.2d 765, 766 (5th Cir. 1986), *cert. denied*, 481 U.S. 1013 (1987).

169. *Id.*

filled with trash. Jail officials did not provide mattresses or blankets, and detainees were forced to sleep on cardboard boxes or on the floor.[170] There was no regular supervision of aliens in detention.[171] The Fifth Circuit found that INS and local jail officials had "blindly assum[ed] away" the obligation to care for the detainees.[172]

The INS has since adopted a jail inspection program to monitor the conditions at non-Service detention facilities.[173] But this program still does not ensure minimally adequate conditions of confinement. First, state and local jails must meet only four mandatory criteria to be certified for INS use: twenty-four hour supervision; compliance with safety and emergency codes; food service; and availability of emergency medical care.[174] The mandatory criteria do not address impor-

---

170. *Id.*

171. The district court found the supervision of alien detainees to be adequate, despite the fact that no one regularly checked on detainees at any facility. In Lubbock, aliens were confined in a city jail that was closed for routine operations, with no jailer on duty. *Ortega*, No. CA-5-81-198 (N.D. Tex. July 23, 1985), *reprinted in* Appendix B to Petition for Writ of Certiorari to the United States Court of Appeals for the Fifth Circuit (Apr. 20, 1987) (No. 86-1143). "Supervision" was provided by police officers in another part of the building who were "within hearing range of the detention cells." *Id.* at 18a. At the City of Slaton jail, "supervision" was provided by a female dispatch officer within earshot who was not authorized to go back into the detention area, but was instructed to call a male officer if she heard a disturbance. *Id.* at 19a. At the Haskell jail, "supervision" was provided by the sheriff who lived upstairs. "[I]f prisoners or detainees in the jail needed help or any service they were instructed to hit a pipe which ran through the cells into the sheriff's bedroom." *Id.* at 21a.

172. *Ortega*, 796 F.2d at 768-69. The Fifth Circuit nevertheless held the "lamentable conditions" in the Lubbock area jails resulted from mere negligence that did not rise to the level of a due process violation. *Id.* The court was surely wrong in concluding "[b]lindly assuming away one's responsibilities . . . can be seen as unreasonable—nothing more" when the "responsibility" at issue is the obligation to provide adequate care for detainees in government custody. *Id.* at 769. In a case decided after *Ortega*, the Supreme Court explained "when the State takes a person into its custody and holds him there against his will, the Constitution imposes upon it a corresponding duty to assume some responsibility for his safety and general well-being." DeShaney v. Department of Social Serv., 489 U.S. 189, 199-200 (1989). For a related critique of the *Ortega* court's analysis, see *infra* note 308.

173. The INS drafted guidelines for jail inspections in December 1992, and formally initiated an inspection program in early 1983. *Ortega*, No. CA-5-81-198 (N.D. Tex. July 23, 1985); *see also* Memorandum from J. F. Salgado, Associate Commissioner of Enforcement to Regional Commissioners (Dec. 23, 1982) (on file with author). The INS issues a quarterly report on its jail inspection program, primarily noting the number of inspections completed and the number of jails yet to be inspected for each region. Under "Significant Findings," the report notes the total number of discontinued jails since February 1983. On September 30, 1994, 240 jails had been disqualified under the INS jail inspection program. Immigration and Naturalization Serv., U.S. Dep't of Justice, Non-Service Detention, Jail Inspections Report # 41 (quarter ending Sept. 30, 1994) (on file with author).

174. *See* 8 C.F.R. § 235.3(f) (1994). Despite this regulation, not all non-Service facilities used by the INS meet even these minimal standards. *See infra* note 179 (INS knowingly confined aliens at a local jail that did not feed the detainees).

tant concerns such as sanitation, adequate nutrition, and overcrowding. Second, the INS does not always execute written contracts setting minimum standards for detention conditions in the local jail.[175] As a result, serious conditions problems persist because the INS continues to "assume away" the responsibility to provide adequate care for detainees confined at non-Service facilities. [176]

In the Chicago area, for example, the INS secured detention space through informal arrangements with local jails and municipal lock-ups on a "space available" basis. As a result, some alien detainees spent months on end in a bizarre detention rotation system, where they were transferred daily among various facilities not designed for long-term confinement. The detainees often lacked toothbrushes and clean underwear; they were seldom allowed to exercise or shower. At one municipal lock-up, they were not even fed.[177]

---

175. *See* Ortega v. Rowe, 796 F.2d 765, 767 (5th Cir. 1986), *cert. denied*, 481 U.S. 1013 (1987). The INS Chicago district office did not execute written contracts with local jails, specifying the services to be provided to alien detainees until the filing of *Imasuen v. Moyer*, No. 91-C-5425, 1991 U.S. Dist. LEXIS 1449 (N.D. Ill. Aug. 27, 1991).

176. A recent report by the Women's Commission for Refugee Women and Children confirms the continuing conditions problems at some local jails used to confine INS detainees. CHINESE WOMEN IN DETENTION, supra note 121. A delegation of the Commission visited Chinese women held in the New Orleans Parish Prison and the Hancock County Justice Facility in Mississippi. The delegation was not allowed inside the New Orleans Parish Prison to view the detainees' living quarters, despite repeated requests. *Id.* at 10. Interviews with the women held there painted a grim picture of long-term detention in unsuitable facilities. The women had no access to reading materials, were not allowed to keep any personal belongings, and "reported that they lie on their beds all day staring at the ceiling." *Id.* at 9.

177. This account is based on the pleadings filed in *Imasuen*, including the uncontested affidavits of INS detainees and the sworn statements of various INS officials. *See* Statement of Material Facts in Support of Plaintiffs' Motion for Summary Judgement at 9-16 (describing detention rotation system), 21-32 (food service inadequate, and not available at one facility), 34-40 (cell conditions inadequate for long-term detention), 41-49, 50-55, 64-69 (municipal lock-ups were not required to provide personal hygiene items, clean clothing, showers, or out-of-cell recreation), *Imasuen* (No. 91-C-5425); *see also* Alvarez & Getter, *Detention: The Failed Deterrent, supra* note 5 (reporting on the Chicago detention rotation system while noting INS detainees were not fed at one holding facility).

As this article was going to press, the district court denied the plaintiffs' motion for summary judgment, and granted summary judgment for the INS on most of these claims. Memorandum Opinion and Order, Imasuen v. Moyer, No. 91-C-5425, 1995 U.S. Dist. LEXIS 12176 (N.D. Ill. Aug. 22, 1995). Much of the court's description of the "undisputed" facts forming the basis for its grant of summary judgment incorporated changes made by municipal facilities and the INS *after* the lawsuit was filed. *See id.* at *1 (noting settlement agreements resolving conditions claims were reached with the municipal defendants); *id.* at *10 (prior to 1992, detainees fed microwaved meals, but since 1992 they received hot lunches ordered from restaurants); *id.* at *13 (detainees provided outdoor recreation since 1992). As a result, the court overlooked some of the plaintiffs' key allegations, including the fact detainees were not fed at the Maybrook facility. *See id.* at *9-*12

Each of these local jails had passed INS inspection—demonstrating the remarkable shortcomings of the current minimum standards for non-Service detention and the jail inspection program. INS jail inspectors in Chicago assumed their supervisors would investigate problem reports and discontinue the use of local jails not in compliance with minimum standards. Yet various supervisors disclaimed any responsibility for deciding which jails to use, and stated that they reviewed inspection reports only to ensure the forms were filled out completely.[178] The INS continued to use substandard jails even when its own inspection reports noted serious deficiencies.[179] It was not until 1991, when a class action lawsuit was filed, that some of these problems abated.[180]

The problem of inadequate INS oversight has been particularly acute for stowaways.[181] Until recently, the INS required commercial carriers to take custody of stowaways who pressed claims for asylum pending final adjudication of their applications.[182] Some stowaways in

---

(discussion of plaintiffs' complaints about food did not mention Maybrook). The court's summary judgment also was premised on finding detainees whose hearing dates were more than one month away were transferred to appropriate long-term facilities, when the plaintiffs' factual allegations contradicted this assertion. *Compare id.* at *3 (stating long-term detainees were sent to long-term facilities) *with* Plaintiffs' Statement of Material Facts, at 10 (Plaintiff Obi was confined by the INS for five months, Plaintiff Imasuen for four months, and for much of this time they were shuttled between various short-term holding cells), *Imasuen* (No. 91-C-5425).

178. Plaintiffs' Statement of Material Facts at 16-20, *Imasuen* (No. 91-C-5425) (summarizing affidavits and deposition testimony of INS officials).

179. *Id.* at 24 (two inspection reports noted INS detainees were not being fed at one facility; additional reports noted insufficient food service at other facilities). The district court opinion granting summary judgment did not discuss these facts or consider the jail inspection program.

180. *See supra* note 177.

181. Stowaways, a "disfavored" class under the INA, are subject to immediate expulsion upon arrival. *See* INA §§ 237(a)(1), 273(d), 8 U.S.C. §§ 1227(a)(1), 1323(d) (1994), *explained in* Dia Navigation Co. v. Pomeroy, 34 F.3d 1255, 1259 (3d Cir. 1994). Stowaways who file an asylum claim, however, are entitled to a limited administrative hearing. Yui Sing Chun v. Sava, 708 F.2d 869 (2d Cir. 1983).

182. Carriers have been fighting this policy, with some success, in court and in Congress. In *Dia Navigation,* the Third Circuit concluded the INS carrier detention policy was a legislative rule, invalid because it should have been promulgated pursuant to the notice and comment provisions of the Administrative Procedure Act. 34 F.3d at 1256. A contemporaneous district court decision struck down the INS policy as inconsistent with recent amendments to the INA, which assess a "user fee" on carriers to fund, inter alia, INS detention of excludable aliens. Linea Area Nacional de Chile v. Sale, 865 F. Supp. 971 (E.D.N.Y. 1994). Despite these litigation losses, the INS was planning to promulgate regulations reiterating its rule of carrier detention when Congress interceded, passing an amendment to the INA shifting this responsibility back to the INS. *See* Michael S. Lelyveld, *INS Plans to Bypass Court, Formalize Rule on Carrier Detention of Stowaways,* J. COM., July 21, 1991, at A1; William L. Roberts, *Congress Hastily Passes Bills on Stowaways,*

private custody were shackled around the clock in run-down hotels; others were physically abused.[183] Yet the INS disclaimed *any* responsibility for monitoring the treatment of stowaways, explaining "[w]e leave [detention conditions] totally up to the carrier."[184]

Perhaps the most poignant stories, however, belong to the children confined by the INS, most often in non-Service facilities. Thousands of unaccompanied minors have been held pending deportation or exclusion proceedings, often under "highly inappropriate detention conditions."[185] It took years of litigation to win victories for these children, including an end to routine strip searches[186] and a consent decree that requires the INS to release unaccompanied minors or transfer them to a licensed juvenile care facility.[187] Still, the INS at times has ignored its obligation to detain children in appropriate and

---

J. COM., Oct. 12, 1994, at A1. This legislative victory for carriers may be short lived, as some pending immigration reform bills would again allow the INS to require carriers to take custody of stowaways. *See* Michael S. Lelyveld, *Bill Would Put Stowaways in Lines' Care*, J. COM., June 7, 1995, at B8.

183. *See* Clifford Levy, *Stowaways, Seeking Liberty, Are Caught in Limbo of Law*, N.Y. TIMES, May 17, 1994, at A2; Michael S. Lelyveld, *Shipping Firm Keeps Stowaways in Shackles*, BERGEN REC., May 12, 1994, at A1; *see also* Lynch v. Cannatella, 810 F.2d 1363, 1367 (5th Cir. 1987) (stowaways suffered "gross physical abuse" at hands of harbor officials); Medina v. O'Neill, 589 F. Supp. 1030, 1031-32 (S.D. Tex. 1984), *rev'd*, 838 F.2d 800 (5th Cir. 1988) (stowaways detained under inappropriate conditions at private security firm).

184. Lelyveld, *supra* note 183. The Third Circuit similarly noted "our attention has been directed to no set of standards, in the form of regulations or otherwise, concerning the conditions under which such aliens are detained." *Dia Navigation*, 34 F.3d at 1257.

185. Flores v. Meese, 934 F.2d 991, 1014 (9th Cir. 1990) (Fletcher, J., dissenting), *vacated*, 942 F.2d 1352 (9th Cir. 1991) (en banc). For several years, the western region of the INS refused to release unaccompanied minors, except to a parent or lawful guardian. Other adult relatives and volunteer service agencies were not allowed to take custody of alien children. Instead, unaccompanied minors were confined "for indeterminate periods, deprived of education, recreation, and visitation, commingled with adults of both sexes and subjected to strip searches with no showing of cause." *Id.* The INS settled that part of the *Flores* litigation challenging confinement conditions. *See infra* note 187. The Supreme Court ultimately upheld a modified version of the INS juvenile detention policy, which permitted release to the custody of other adult relatives. Reno v. Flores, 113 S. Ct. 1439, 1444-45 (1993).

186. The strip search policy was declared unconstitutional in Flores v. Meese, 681 F. Supp. 665 (C.D. Cal. 1988).

187. The consent decree requires the INS to act within 72 hours to release unaccompanied minors to an adult relative or to transfer them to an appropriate juvenile care facility. *See* Memorandum of Understanding re: Compromise of Class Action: Conditions of Detention, *Flores* (No. 85-4544-RJK). In 1991, INS Commissioner Gene McNary issued national guidelines that embody similar standards. Memorandum from Office of Commissioner to Regional Operations Liaison Officers et al. (Dec. 13, 1992), *reprinted in* 69 INTERPRETER RELEASES 205 (1992).

humane facilities,[188] especially in the midst of massive detention efforts. Michael Olivas has described the plight of thousands of Central American children who were traumatized by the coercive conditions of INS detention.[189] More recently, a hundred Haitian and Cuban children were confined at the overcrowded Krome SPC, in violation of INS policy,[190] while many more were held in detention camps at Guantanamo Bay.[191] The Cuban children were belatedly paroled into the United States. Some unaccompanied Haitian minors, after being detained at Guantanamo for almost a year, were forcibly repatriated back to Haiti.[192]

C. The INS Response to Conditions Problems

The INS has been slow to correct the serious problems with confinement conditions suffered by alien detainees. Too frequently, only litigation spurs the agency to action. Even then, conditions problems persist. The deplorable conditions in the Chicago area jails, for example, mirror the very problems that surfaced ten years earlier in Lubbock, Texas. And court orders and consent decrees requiring the INS to improve its treatment of alien detainees have sometimes been met with a pattern of noncompliance.[193]

---

188. *See* Brief for Southwest Refugee Project, Immigrant Legal Resource Center, and the Mexican American Legal Defense and Educational Fund, As Amici Curiae in Support of Respondents, *Flores* (No. 91-905) (citing evidence of noncompliance with *Flores* consent decree.) Troubling allegations about the detention of minors continue to emerge. In the aftermath of the Esmor disturbance, the INS discovered four juveniles who had been confined at Esmor, in violation of INS policy and the *Flores* decree. Its investigation revealed "several lapses" in the Newark district's policy of interviewing and finding placements for unaccompanied minors. INS ESMOR REPORT, *supra* note 8, at 41. In Los Angeles, the INS confined an 11-year-old girl in an office for two nights with four unknown, unrelated adult males. Central Am. Refugee Ctr. v. Reno, No. CV 93-4162-KN (C.D. Cal. June 23, 1995) (order granting motion for class certification).

189. Olivas, *Breaking the Law, supra* note 126, at 821-24.

190. Joanne Cavanaugh, *Young, Homeless, and "Hyper": Facilities Planned for Krome Kids*, MIAMI HERALD, Aug. 27, 1994, at 22A (reporting 107 children were detained at Krome despite INS policy to parole children into the community).

191. Edes, *supra* note 142, at 1C (reporting 3071 Cuban children held at Guantanamo Bay).

192. *See* David Beard, *Haitian Children Headed Out of Guantanamo*, FT. LAUDERDALE SUN-SENTINEL, June 26, 1995, at 4A; Bob Herbert, *Suffering the Children*, N.Y. TIMES, May 27, 1995, at A19 (reporting on forced repatriation of some unaccompanied Haitian children); Diego Ribadeneira, *U.S. to Ease Restrictions for Cuban Children*, BOSTON GLOBE, Dec. 3, 1994, at 2; Joanne Cavanaugh, *Children, Mothers Leaving Krome*, MIAMI HERALD, Sept. 16, 1994, at 1A (Cuban children receive humanitarian parole into the United States).

193. Orantes-Hernandez v. Meese, 685 F.2d 1488 (C.D. Cal. 1988), *aff'd*, 919 F.2d 549 (9th Cir. 1990). In *Orantes-Hernandez*, the district court issued a permanent injunction against the INS after documenting numerous instances where the INS had failed to comply

To its credit, however, the INS has recently taken some steps to improve conditions of confinement at alien detention facilities. The INS has sought voluntary accreditation for its Service Processing Centers and contract facilities, a process requiring these facilities to conform to generally accepted guidelines for long-term detention.[194] The INS has also renovated and expanded some of its SPCs.[195] Moreover, in the wake of the Esmor riot, the INS Commissioner ordered inspections of INS detention facilities to ensure they were providing adequate conditions and humane treatment for alien detainees.[196]

These efforts, while laudable, do not correct the root causes of the conditions problems at immigration detention facilities. More fundamental reforms are needed. The United States must find a more humane response to the large-scale migration of persons seeking refuge in the United States, in order to avoid the severe overcrowding and deplorable conditions inevitably resulting from massive detention efforts.[197] And as the Esmor situation has painfully illustrated, the

---

with the dictates of a preliminary injunction, requiring, inter alia, some changes in the operation of INS detention facilities. In some cases, this noncompliance was due to a "standard pattern of officially sanctioned behavior" and bad faith on the part of the INS. *Id.* at 1498, 1504. Government counsel also conceded "the agency is powerless to completely control its employees." Orantes-Hernandez v. Smith, 541 F. Supp. 351, 373 (C.D. Cal. 1982) (preliminary injunction in same litigation); *see also* Brief for Southwest Refugee Project, Immigrant Legal Resource Center, and the Mexican American Legal Defense and Educational Fund, As Amici Curiae in Support of Respondents, *Flores* (No. 91-905) (citing evidence of noncompliance with *Flores* consent decree). *Cf.* Kevin R. Johnson, *Responding to the "Litigation Explosion": The Plain Meaning of Executive Branch Privacy over Immigration*, 71 N.C. L. REV. 413, 447 (1993) (documenting the INS pattern of "overemphasizing enforcement at the expense of immigrants' rights").

194. Telephone Interview with Joan Higgins, Assistant Commissioner, Detention and Deportation, Immigration and Naturalization Service (August 2, 1994). Currently, five immigration detention facilities are medically accredited by the National Commission on Correctional Health Care. Three contract facilities and two Service Processing Centers have American Correctional Association (ACA) accreditation; the INS expected an additional facility to receive ACA accreditation in 1994. INS DETENTION BRIEFING PAPER, *supra* note 97, at 3. ACA accreditation, however, does not ensure a facility provides humane treatment to its detainees. The Esmor contract facility provides a stark example. While Esmor was accredited by ACA, the INS investigation revealed several instances where the physical plant fell short of ACA standards. INS ESMOR REPORT, *supra* note 8, at 25-26. There is also some question whether ACA standards, primarily used to judge the adequacy of prisons designed to punish criminals, are the appropriate guidelines for the civil detention of aliens awaiting deportation proceedings.

195. INS DETENTION BRIEFING PAPER, *supra* note 97, at 3.

196. Llorente, *supra* note 165, at N9.

197. *See, e.g.*, T. Alexander Aleinikoff, *From "Refugee Law" to the Law of "Coerced Migration,"* 9 LOY. L.A. INT'L & COMP. L.J. 25 (1994); Grover J. Rees, *Refugee Policy in an Age of Migration*, 9 AM. U.J. INT'L L. & POL'Y 249, 259-62 (1994); Bill Frelick, *Needed: A Comprehensive Solution for Cuban Refugees*, 72 INTERPRETER RELEASES 121 (1995); Arthur C. Helton, *Immigration Parole Power: Toward Flexible Responses to Migration*

INS must provide sustained oversight, and higher minimum standards, for the non-Service facilities used to confine aliens.

Even if these reforms were adopted, however, it is likely that serious conditions problems would still persist at alien detention facilities. Immigration detention, like criminal incarceration, is marked by a lack of adequate resources, public apathy toward conditions of confinement, and a "voteless, politically unpopular, and socially threatening" population of detainees.[198] Under these circumstances, "judicial intervention is *indispensable* if constitutional dictates—not to mention considerations of basic humanity—are to be observed."[199]

III. "Only the Most Perverse Reading of the Constitution": Due Process Protection to Challenge Conditions of Confinement

Unfortunately, courts have not always interceded when alien detainees allege unconstitutional confinement conditions. The main obstacle to these claims is the so-called "plenary power doctrine," a century of precedent mandating extreme judicial deference to Congress and the executive branch in matters involving immigration. This deference comes at the expense of aliens' constitutional rights. In short, the plenary power doctrine carves out a unique space in American public law: a realm where the Constitution does not always apply.

The rest of this Article explores the impact of the plenary power doctrine on the conditions claims of alien detainees. It would seem that "[o]nly the most perverse reading of the Constitution would deny detained aliens the right to bring constitutional challenges to the most basic conditions of their confinement."[200] Under the plenary power doctrine, however, perverse readings of the Constitution frequently prevail. I contend that the plenary power doctrine has silently and improperly infiltrated some cases adjudicating the conditions claims of aliens in immigration detention.

Emergencies, 71 INTERPRETER RELEASES 1637 (1994). The U.S. Commission on Immigration Reform, in its 1994 report to Congress, recommended that "policy approaches for handling immigration emergencies are needed to provide more effective and humane responses to such recurrent phenomena." U.S. COMM'N ON IMMIGRATION REFORM, *supra* note 84, at 174.

198. Justice Brennan identified these factors as contributing to the "pervasive neglect" of our nation's prisons in *Rhodes v. Chapman*, 452 U.S. 337, 357-58 (1981) (Brennan, J., concurring).

199. *Id.* at 354 (Brennan, J., concurring).

200. Jean v. Nelson, 472 U.S. 846, 874 (1985) (Marshall, J., dissenting).

A. The Plenary Power Doctrine

1. Foundation Cases

At the heart of the plenary power doctrine lies the belief that Congress and the executive branch must have unfettered authority to admit, exclude, or deport aliens. The doctrine has its roots in the late nineteenth century, when the Supreme Court upheld various provisions of the Chinese Exclusion Act, which embodied Congress's increasingly draconian restrictions on Chinese immigration. In the *Chinese Exclusion Case*, the Supreme Court rejected the constitutional claim of a Chinese immigrant who was excluded upon returning from a trip abroad.[201] The petitioner, a lawful permanent resident of twelve years, had obtained a certificate before he left that entitled him to re-enter the United States under then-existing law.[202] But he was stranded outside the United States when Congress, without notice, amended the Chinese Exclusion Act, declaring such certificates "void and of no effect."[203]

The Court upheld this provision, suggesting there could be no limit on congressional power to exclude aliens from the United States.[204] The Court reasoned the "power of exclusion of foreigners [is] an incident of sovereignty belonging to the Government of the United States, as a part of those sovereign powers delegated by the Constitution."[205] As such, any constitutional challenges to Congress's exercise of the exclusion power "are not questions for judicial determination."[206]

The Court soon extended this rule of judicial deference to allow Congress plenary authority to deport resident aliens from the United

---

201. Chae Chan Ping v. United States (*The Chinese Exclusion Case*), 130 U.S. 581 (1889).

202. *Id.* at 582.

203. *Id.* at 599.

204. This is the traditional interpretation of the *Chinese Exclusion Case*, bolstered by later cases that reiterate in similar terms this principle of plenary power. *See* Nishimura Ekiu v. United States, 142 U.S. 651, 659 (1892) (stating the power over admission and exclusion "belongs to the political departments of the government"); Oceanic Steam Navigation Co. v. Stranahan, 214 U.S. 320, 339 (1909) (noting "[o]ver no conceivable subject is the legislative power of Congress more complete"); United States *ex rel.* Knauff v. Shaughnessy, 338 U.S. 537, 543 (1950) (concluding "it is not within the province of any court . . . to review the determination of the political branch of the Government to exclude a given alien"). Stephen Legomsky has argued, however, that the plenary power doctrine is premised on a misreading of the *Chinese Exclusion Case*, and that the Court "never intended to preclude judicial review of all Congressional exercises of the exclusion power." STEPHEN H. LEGOMSKY, IMMIGRATION AND THE JUDICIARY 193 (1987).

205. The Chinese Exclusion Case, 130 U.S. at 609.

206. *Id.*

States. In *Fong Yue Ting v. United States*,[207] the Court refused to intercede on behalf of Chinese immigrants who were to be deported because they had failed to obtain certificates of residence, as required under additional amendments to the Chinese Exclusion Act. Aliens caught without such certificates were subject to deportation unless they could show by the testimony of "at least one credible white witness" that they were lawful residents of the United States.[208] The *Fong Yue Ting* Court upheld this provision.[209] As in the *Chinese Exclusion Case*, the Supreme Court concluded it was beyond the competence of the courts to review immigration legislation.[210]

The *Chinese Exclusion Case* and *Fong Yue Ting* seem antiquated in a modern constitutional setting. The Supreme Court's analysis was tainted by the racist backlash against Chinese laborers that motivated Congress to pass these provisions.[211] Moreover, the past one hundred years have seen a remarkable expansion of constitutional rights, which would seem to call into question many of the Supreme Court's nineteenth century pronouncements on immigration. Yet the plenary power doctrine has flourished for over a century, isolating immigration law from this constitutional revolution. Indeed, more recent Supreme Court cases embrace the plenary power doctrine in decisions with startling implications for detained aliens seeking to challenge the conditions of their confinement under the Constitution.

2. *Knauff and Mezei: Denying Due Process to Excludable Alien Detainees*

During the Cold War, the Supreme Court reaffirmed the plenary power doctrine in two cases that "come close to saying that even though the Fifth Amendment due process protection applies to all 'persons,' we simply do not regard excludable aliens as falling within

---

207. 149 U.S. 698 (1893).

208. *Id.* at 704.

209. *Id.* at 732.

210. *Id.* at 731.

211. In the *Chinese Exclusion Case*, the Supreme Court spoke approvingly of Congress's motives in passing the Chinese Exclusion Act. The Court compared Chinese immigration to a foreign invasion, concluding that "[i]t matters not in what form such aggression and encroachment come, whether from the foreign nation acting in its national character, or from vast hordes of its people crowding in upon us." The Chinese Exclusion Case, 130 U.S. at 606. In both the *Chinese Exclusion Case* and *Fong Yue Ting*, the Court suggested that Congress had reason to require corroboration of the testimony of Chinese immigrants because of the "loose notions entertained by [Chinese] witnesses of the obligation of an oath." *Id.* at 598; *Fong Yue Ting*, 149 U.S. at 730.

that category."[212] In *United States ex rel. Knauff v. Shaughnessy*,[213] the Court upheld the Attorney General's authority to exclude, without a hearing, the wife of a United States citizen. Ellen Knauff had served as a civilian employee of the United States War Department in Germany and sought to immigrate under the War Brides Act of 1945.[214] She was excluded when the Attorney General concluded, without any explanation, that her admission "would be prejudicial to the interests of the United States."[215]

Knauff had been confined on Ellis Island for over a year without being informed of the charges against her.[216] Nevertheless, the Supreme Court denied her habeas corpus petition. Relying on nineteenth century plenary power cases, the Court concluded "it is not within the province of any court . . . to review the determination of the political branch of the Government to exclude a given alien."[217] The Court's analysis was distilled in the statement "[w]hatever the procedure authorized by Congress is, it is due process as far as an alien denied entry is concerned."[218]

Three years after this decision, the Court "accomplished the improbable feat of rendering the *Knauff* outcome even more severe"[219] in *Shaughnessy v. United States ex rel. Mezei*.[220] Here the Court determined that Ignatz Mezei, the husband of a United States citizen who had lawfully resided in the United States for twenty-five years, could

---

212. David A. Martin, *Due Process and Membership in the National Community: Political Asylum and Beyond*, 44 U. PITT. L. REV. 165, 176 (1983) [hereinafter Martin, *Due Process and Membership*].

213. 338 U.S. 537 (1950).

214. *See id.* at 539-40.

215. *Id.*

216. *Id.*

217. *Id.* at 543.

218. *Id.* at 544. Charles Weisselberg recently has delved into the history of Ellen Knauff, and concludes her full story reveals the folly of such extreme judicial deference to the Attorney General's decision to exclude her summarily. Charles D. Weisselberg, *The Exclusion and Detention of Aliens: Lessons From the Lives of Ellen Knauff and Ignatz Mezei*, 143 U. PA. L. REV. 933 (1995) [hereinafter Weisselberg, *Lessons from Knauff and Mezei*]. After much public outcry, several rounds of habeas corpus litigation, and congressional hearings focused on her plight, Knauff was paroled from Ellis Island and allowed to contest the Attorney General's decision at an exclusion hearing. The hearing board upheld her exclusion, but their decision was reversed by the Board of Immigration Appeals. When she was finally afforded a hearing, Knauff was able to refute conclusively uncorroborated hearsay testimony suggesting she had passed classified information gleaned from her employment to Czech authorities. The Board of Immigration Appeals held there was no substantial evidence to support Knauff's exclusion. *See id.* at 958-64; *see also* ELLEN KNAUFF, THE ELLEN KNAUFF STORY (1952).

219. ALEINIKOFF ET AL., IMMIGRATION PROCESS AND POLICY, supra note 45, at 385.

220. 345 U.S. 206 (1953).

be excluded and detained without a hearing upon returning from a nineteen month sojourn abroad.[221] Mezei had "seem[ed] to have led a life of unrelieved insignificance"[222] until the Attorney General, deciding Mezei was a threat to national security, excluded him on the basis of confidential information.[223] He had been confined on Ellis Island for almost two years when a district court ordered his release.[224] Nevertheless, the Supreme Court, reversing the lower court's grant of habeas corpus, concluded Mezei should be "treated as if stopped at the border" for purposes of his due process claim.[225]

The majority opinion assiduously avoided any frank description of Mezei's imprisonment on Ellis Island, instead referring to his "temporary harborage" as "an act of legislative grace."[226] But the dissenting justices emphasized that upon his return to Ellis Island, Mezei could be "detained indefinitely, perhaps for life, for a cause known only to the Attorney General."[227] Still, the Supreme Court found no due process violation, repeating "[w]hatever the procedure authorized by Congress is, it is due process as far as an alien denied entry is concerned."[228]

---

221. Mezei had sailed for Europe in May 1948 to visit his dying mother in Rumania. *Id.* at 208. After being refused permission to enter Rumania, he was stranded in Hungary for 19 months because of difficulties in securing an exit visa, probably due to the "disturbed conditions of Eastern Europe" at that time. *Id* at 208; *id.* at 219 (Jackson, J., dissenting).

222. *Id.* at 219 (Jackson, J., dissenting).

223. The Attorney General refused even to divulge in camera the reasons for Mezei's exclusion. *Id.* at 209.

224. *Id.* at 220 (Jackson, J., dissenting).

225. *See Mezei*, 345 U.S. at 215. The Court concluded Mezei's detention on Ellis Island "bestow[ed] no additional rights," relying on long-standing precedent that detention does not constitute an "entry" in the United States. *Id.* at 213, 215 (citing Kaplan v. Tod, 267 U.S. 228, 230 (1925); Nishimura Ekiu v. United States, 142 U.S. 651, 661 (1892)). The Court also held Mezei's long-term residence in the United States did not confer due process protection. *Id.* at 213-14. This part of the *Mezei* Court's holding was later modified in *Landon v. Plasencia*, 459 U.S. 21, 34 (1982), in which the Court reasoned a lawful permanent resident who had been "absent from the country only a few days" was entitled to invoke procedural due process protection in exclusion proceedings. The *Plasencia* Court declined to reconsider *Mezei*, instead distinguishing the earlier opinion on its facts, emphasizing Mezei's absence from the United States had been "extended." *Id.* at 33-34.

226. *Mezei*, 345 U.S. at 215.

227. *Id.* at 220 (Jackson, J., dissenting); *see also id.* at 217 (Black, J., dissenting). Mezei had tried to no avail to find another country of refuge; at least 14 other nations had also refused to accept him. *See id.* at 219-20 (Jackson, J., dissenting).

228. *Mezei*, 345 U.S. at 212 (quoting United States *ex rel.* Knauff v. Shaughnessy, 338 U.S. 537, 544 (1950)). Mezei, like Ellen Knauff, was ultimately afforded a hearing after the Supreme Court upheld his summary exclusion. He was charged with being a member of the Communist party, based on his participation in the Hungarian Working Sick Benefit and Education Society (later a Hungarian lodge of the International Workers Order). Mezei denied that he was a member of the Communist party, but these charges were up-

This chilling statement denies due process protection to excludable aliens even when they are detained within the United States. It also marks an important distinction between aliens in exclusion and deportation proceedings, because deportable aliens can claim procedural due process protection.[229] Since "the INS intermingles deportable and excludable aliens without any distinction as to the conditions of confinement,"[230] this distinction probably does not influence the day-to-day treatment of alien detainees. But it has surfaced in some cases when *excludable* aliens bring due process challenges to their confinement conditions. *Knauff* and *Mezei* have been interposed inappropriately in litigation over detention conditions. The sweeping language in these cases has opened the door for government officials to argue that excludable aliens in their custody "possess no constitutional rights" to challenge abusive treatment or inhumane detention conditions.[231]

No court has explicitly adopted this "perverse reading" of the Constitution. In fact, some judges, in dicta or dissenting opinions, have used hypothetical examples of severe mistreatment or cruelty toward alien detainees to argue against a broad application of the plenary power doctrine.[232] These arguments find support in the aliens'

---

held by the hearing board and the Board of Immigration Appeals, based largely on the testimony of a professional witness who had testified (sometimes falsely) in several notorious loyalty cases during the Cold War. The Board of Immigration Appeals, however, also made an off-the-record recommendation that Mezei be released from Ellis Island. Four years after he was ordered excluded, Mezei was paroled into the United States. Except for an interim parole won after a fleeting victory in the lower courts, Mezei had spent much of these four years confined in the "Communist ward" on Ellis Island. Weisselberg, *Lessons From Knauff and Mezei, supra* note 218, at 970-84.

229. Yamataya v. Fisher (*The Japanese Immigrant Case*), 189 U.S. 86 (1903); *see supra* note 52.

230. Schmidt, *supra* note 11, at 321; *see supra* 122.

231. Lynch v. Cannatella, 810 F.2d 1363, 1372 (5th Cir. 1987); *accord* Haitian Ctrs. Council v. McNary, 969 F.2d 1326, 1341 (2d Cir. 1992) (rejecting government's argument that Haitians detained on Guantanamo could not claim "any protections under the due process clause . . . even if they had been subjected to physical abuse").

232. As early as 1893, a dissenting opinion in *Fong Yue Ting v. United States* rejected the majority's conclusion that Chinese immigrants were not protected by the Due Process Clause because this analysis "might have sanctioned toward [Chinese] laborers the most shocking brutality conceivable." 149 U.S. 698, 756 (1893) (Field, J., dissenting). In *Jean v. Nelson*, Justice Marshall rejected as "irrational" the notion that an excludable alien "could not invoke the Constitution to challenge the conditions of his detention." 472 U.S. 846, 874 (1985) (Marshall, J., dissenting). Justice Marshall also argued *Knauff* and *Mezei* must be read narrowly because some of the Court's language, if taken literally, would seem to allow the Attorney General to "invoke legitimate immigration goals to justify a decision to stop feeding all detained aliens." *Id.; see also* Amanullah v. Nelson, 811 F.2d 1, 9 (1st Cir. 1987) ("the mere fact that one is an excludable alien would not permit a police officer savagely to beat him"); Haitian Ctrs. Council v. Sale, 823 F. Supp. 1028, 1042 (E.D.N.Y.

rights tradition, a line of cases granting constitutional protection to aliens in an ill-defined realm "outside" of immigration law.

B.   The Aliens' Rights Tradition: Defining a Border for the Plenary Power Doctrine

1.   Foundation Cases

Like the plenary power doctrine, the aliens' rights tradition grew out of restrictive legislation against Chinese immigrants in the late nineteenth century. In *Yick Wo v. Hopkins*, decided in 1886, the Supreme Court concluded Chinese immigrants could claim equal protection to challenge the discriminatory enforcement of a municipal ordinance regulating laundries.[233] The Court held that "[t]he Fourteenth Amendment to the Constitution is not confined to the protection of citizens . . . [its] provisions are universal in their application, to all persons within the territorial jurisdiction, without regard to any differences of race, of color, or of nationality."[234] *Yick Wo* spawned a line of cases, central to the aliens' rights tradition, protecting aliens from invidious discrimination by state and local officials.[235]

Ten years after *Yick Wo*, in *Wong Wing v. United States*,[236] the Supreme Court extended constitutional protection to Chinese immigrants held in immigration detention, striking down a provision of the Chinese Exclusion Act requiring detainees to be "imprisoned at hard labor" for up to one year prior to deportation.[237] The *Wong Wing* Court reaffirmed in the strongest possible terms that Congress and the

---

1993) ("[i]f the Due Process Clause does not apply to the detainees at Guantanamo, Defendants would have discretion deliberately to starve or beat them, to deprive them of medical attention").

233.   118 U.S. 356, 373-74 (1886).

234.   *Id.* at 369.

235.   Generally, alienage classifications made by state or local governments restricting aliens' access to government benefits are subject to a heightened level of scrutiny. *See* Graham v. Richardson, 403 U.S. 365 (1971) (invalidating state statute denying welfare benefits to resident aliens). States also cannot bar aliens from ordinary trades and professions and many civil service jobs. *See* Sugarman v. Dougall, 413 U.S. 634 (1973) (invalidating statutory prohibition against employment of aliens in state competitive civil service); *In re* Griffiths, 413 U.S. 717 (1973) (invalidating state statute prohibiting resident aliens from practicing law). The Court, however, has carved out an exception to these cases, allowing state and local governments to exclude aliens from governmental positions when the restriction primarily serves a "political function." *See* Cabell v. Chavez-Salido, 454 U.S. 432, 445-46 (1982) (upholding state statute barring aliens from employment as probation officers); Foley v. Connelie, 435 U.S. 291 (1978) (police officers); Ambach v. Norwick, 441 U.S. 68 (1979) (public school teachers); *see also* Bosniak, *supra* note 22, at 1110-15 (critiquing this "political function" exception).

236.   163 U.S. 228 (1896).

237.   *Id.* at 233.

executive branch enjoy plenary power to exclude and deport aliens from the country, without interference from the judiciary.[238] The Court concluded, however, that "imprisonment at hard labor" prior to deportation moved beyond the realm of immigration regulation and into the realm of criminal law, where aliens are protected by the Constitution.[239] Other cases in the *Wong Wing* tradition extend Fifth and Sixth Amendment protection to aliens subject to criminal proceedings.[240]

Yick Wo, Wong Wing, and their progeny suggest the plenary power doctrine extends only to exercises of the sovereign power to admit, exclude, or deport aliens from the United States.[241] Later decisions support this interpretation.[242] These cases stand in stark contrast to the shocking denial of constitutional protection in immigration law. This "aliens' rights" tradition, however, has "never fully coalesced into a coherent and comprehensive body of doctrine . . . [and has] never offered a fully textured alternative to the plenary power

---

238. The Court asserted "[t]he power of Congress to exclude aliens altogether from the United States, or to prescribe the terms and conditions upon which they come to this country, and to have its declared policy in that regard enforced exclusively through executive officers, without judicial intervention, is settled by our previous adjudications." *Id.* at 233.

239. The Court explained "even aliens" were protected by the Fifth and Sixth Amendments, and thus "shall not be held to answer for a capital or other infamous crime, unless on a presentment or indictment of a grand jury, nor be deprived of life, liberty, or property without due process of law." *Id.* at 238. Thus, the Court concluded the statute before it "present[ed] a different question" from the challenges to the exclusion and deportation power raised in the *Chinese Exclusion Case* and *Fong Yue Ting. Id.* at 233.

240. *See* United States v. Casimiro-Benitez, 533 F.2d 1121 (9th Cir.), *cert. denied,* 429 U.S. 926 (1976); United States v. Henry, 604 F.2d 908 (5th Cir. 1979) (aliens in custodial interrogation entitled to Miranda warnings). *But see* United States v. Verdugo-Urquidez, 494 U.S. 259 (1990); *infra* notes 245-252 and accompanying text.

241. Stated somewhat differently, the plenary power doctrine is confined to the realm of "immigration law," which is defined as "the body of law governing the admission and expulsion of aliens." Motomura, *Phantom Norms, supra* note 16, at 547 (citing Legomsky, *Immigration Law and Plenary Power, supra* note 15, at 256).

242. In *Russian Volunteer Fleet v. United States,* 282 U.S. 481, 492 (1931), for example, the Supreme Court held aliens present in the United States are entitled to just compensation under the Takings Clause of the Fifth Amendment when the government confiscates their property. More recently the Court has stated in dicta that "an alien seeking initial admission to the United States . . . has no constitutional rights *regarding his application.*" Landon v. Plasencia, 459 U.S. 21, 32 (1982) (emphasis added). This quotation has been interpreted to mean "it is only in the admissions process that [applicants'] status as excludable aliens limits their Constitutional rights." Singh v. Nelson, 623 F. Supp. 545, 558 (S.D.N.Y. 1985); *see also* Deborah Levy, *supra* note 76, at 299 n.9 (stating "the Court in *Plasencia* acknowledged the generally accepted wisdom that an alien seeking entry lacks constitutional rights concerning his *application to enter* only. Such an appropriately limited rule leaves open the issue of constitutional rights regarding matters other than the entry application"); *see infra* notes 277-283 and accompanying text for a further explanation of this analysis.

doctrine."[243] In fact, the boundary between the plenary power doctrine and aliens' rights tradition is not easily marked, and has not always been respected even when aliens "outside" of immigration law press constitutional claims.[244]

2. Deviations from the Aliens' Rights Tradition

Several notable decisions belie the promise of *Yick Wo* and *Wong Wing*, withholding constitutional protection from aliens even when the governmental conduct at issue is not an exercise of the federal immigration power. In *United States v. Verdugo-Urquidez*, for example, the Supreme Court refused to extend Fourth Amendment protection to a nonresident alien awaiting criminal prosecution in the United States.[245] Verdugo-Urquidez sought to exclude from his criminal trial evidence obtained when federal officials searched his property in Mexico without a warrant. But the Court held the Fourth Amendment did not cover such a search, even though it was conducted while Verdugo-Urquidez was incarcerated in a United States jail.[246]

Verdugo-Urquidez relied in part on cases from the aliens' rights tradition to support his claim for constitutional protection.[247] The Supreme Court, however, adopted a very narrow reading of *Yick Wo*, *Wong Wing*, and their progeny, stating "[t]hese cases . . . establish only that aliens receive constitutional protections when they have come within the territory of the United States and developed substantial connections with this country."[248] The Court concluded that because Verdugo-Urquidez was "an alien who has had no previous significant

---

243. Motomura, *Phantom Norms, supra* note 16, at 566.

244. Rosberg, *supra* note 9, at 337. In a recent article focusing on discrimination against aliens, Linda Bosniak suggests the contrast between the plenary power doctrine and aliens' rights tradition is not so stark. She argues that distinguishing between cases falling "inside" and "outside" immigration law "can easily lead to misunderstanding because it suggests a greater uniformity on both sides of the line than is warranted." Bosniak, *supra* note 22, at 1063. I agree with this observation, and in particular with her assessment that "focusing on the difference between 'inside' and 'outside' [immigration law] tends to seriously overstate the status of aliens on the so-called 'outside.'" *Id.* Professor Bosniak's recent analysis comports with my description of a "porous border" between the plenary power doctrine and the aliens' rights tradition. *See infra* notes 341-355 and accompanying text.

245. 494 U.S. 259 (1990).

246. *Id.* at 261-62.

247. *Id.* at 270-71 (citing Wong Wing v. United States, 163 U.S. 228, 238 (1896); Yick Wo v. Hopkins, 118 U.S. 356, 369 (1886)).

248. *Id.* at 271.

voluntary connection with the United States," the aliens' rights tradition "avail[s] him not."[249]

Verdugo-Urquidez is a significant departure from *Wong Wing* and its progeny, which extended constitutional protection to aliens in criminal proceedings. Indeed, the Court's suggestion that the Constitution protects only persons who have developed "significant voluntary connections" to the "national community" reflects a recurring theme of immigration law. The plenary power doctrine is premised in part on the notion that Congress must have unfettered power to determine who will become part of our national community.[250] And one of the principle exceptions to the plenary power doctrine, which grants procedural due process protection to deportable aliens and lawful permanent residents in exclusion proceedings, reflects an understanding that persons who have developed significant ties to the United States gain constitutional rights by virtue of their connections to our community.[251] Thus, both the result and rhetoric of *Verdugo-Urquidez* echoed in immigration law, even though the alien claimant was seek-

---

249. *Id.* The *Verdugo-Urquidez* Court employed similar language when analyzing the text of the Fourth Amendment, asserting that "the people" protected by this provision are only those "who are part of [our] national community or who have otherwise developed sufficient connection with this country." 494 U.S. at 265. This analysis was criticized in Gerald L. Neuman, *Whose Constitution?*, 100 YALE L.J. 909, 984-87 (1991), and Michael Scaperlanda, *The Domestic Fourth Amendment Rights of Aliens: To What Extent Do they Survive* United States v. Verdugo-Urquidez?, 56 Mo. L. REV. 213, 240-42 (1991).

250. In the *Chinese Exclusion Case*, for example, the Supreme Court stated if Congress "considers the presence of foreigners of a different race in this country, who will not assimilate with us, to be dangerous to its peace and security . . . its determination is conclusive upon the judiciary." 130 U.S. 581, 606 (1889). This rationale—that the authority to define our national community must rest with Congress—has caused some to use the "domain of membership" as shorthand to describe cases applying the plenary power doctrine. *See* Bosniak, *supra* note 22, at 1057.

251. Three dissenting justices in *Fong Yue Ting v. United States* suggested because resident aliens have developed significant ties to the United States, they should be entitled to some measure of constitutional protection. 149 U.S. 698, 737-38 (Brewer, J., dissenting), 746 (Field, J., dissenting), 762 (Fuller, J., dissenting) (1893). Their views took hold in the *Japanese Immigrant Case*, which extended procedural due process protection to aliens in deportation proceedings. 189 U.S. 86, 100-01 (1903). This analysis reached fruition in *Landon v. Plasencia*, in which the Supreme Court carved out an exception to *Shaugnessy v. United States ex rel. Mezei*, allowing a lawful permanent resident who had been "absent from the country only a few days" to claim procedural due process protection in exclusion proceedings. 459 U.S. 21, 34 (1952); *see supra* note 242. Several commentators have explored the theory that an alien's "membership" or "ties" to the national community limit the application of the plenary power doctrine. *See, e.g.*, Martin, *Due Process and Membership*, *supra* note 212; T. Alexander Aleinikoff, *Aliens, Due Process and "Community Ties": A Response to Martin*, 44 U. PITT. L. REV. 237 (1983) [hereinafter Aleinikoff, "*Community Ties*"].

ing Fourth Amendment protection to exclude evidence from his criminal trial.[252]

A similar echo appears in the cases allowing the federal government to discriminate against aliens when administering government benefits. In *Flemming v. Nestor*, the Supreme Court upheld a provision of the Social Security Act cutting off benefits to aliens who had contributed into the Social Security system but were then deported for past membership in the Communist party.[253] The *Flemming* Court employed a highly deferential standard of scrutiny, unique to equal protection analysis, stating that the disabilities imposed on certain deported aliens would be unconstitutional "only if the statute manifests a patently arbitrary classification, utterly lacking in rational justification."[254] The dissenting justices argued the Court should not have been swayed by the challenged statute's ostensible connection to "Congress's power to regulate immigration."[255]

The Supreme Court reached a similar result in *Mathews v. Diaz*, upholding a statute denying Medicare benefits to aliens unless they had been admitted for permanent residence and had lived in the United States for at least five years.[256] The plaintiffs, aliens who were not eligible for benefits under this provision, argued in the *Yick Wo*

---

252. *Cf.* Scaperlanda, *Polishing the Tarnished Golden Door, supra* note 32, at 1000 (arguing *Verdugo-Urquidez* marks an expansion of the plenary power doctrine into the criminal rights arena).

253. 363 U.S. 603 (1960). Ephram Nestor was a lawful permanent resident of 43 years. He was deported in 1956 because he had been a member of the Communist party from 1933 to 1939. *Id.* at 605. He had a statutory right to receive Social Security benefits, in an amount determined by his contributions into the system, until Congress amended the Social Security Act to cut off benefits for those deported for membership in the Communist party. *See id.* at 608 (noting "[p]ayments under the Act are based upon the wage earner's record of earnings").

254. *Id.* at 611. Stephen Legomsky has argued that the standard applied in *Nestor* is more deferential than even the most toothless "rational basis" test, and that the Social Security Act's classification against aliens would not withstand scrutiny under traditional equal protection analysis. Stephen H. Legomsky, *Suspending the Social Security Benefits of Deported Aliens: The Insult and the Injury*, 13 SUFFOLK U. L. REV. 1235, 1248-53 (1979) [hereinafter Legomsky, *Suspending Benefits*].

255. *Flemming*, 363 U.S. at 636 (Brennan, J., dissenting). In addition to rejecting Nestor's equal protection claim, the Court concluded the provision cutting off benefits to certain deported aliens did not impose "punishment" in violation of the Constitution. The Court relied in part on the fact that "deportation has been held to be not punishment, but an exercise of the plenary power of Congress to fix the conditions under which aliens are to be permitted to enter and remain in this country." *Id.* at 616 (citing Fong Yue Ting v. United States, 149 U.S. 698, 730 (1893)). The dissenting justices pointedly noted the plenary power to control immigration was not implicated by Nestor's suit seeking reinstatement of Social Security benefits. *Id.* at 636 (Brennan, J., dissenting).

256. 426 U.S. 67, 69 (1976).

tradition that the federal government could not discriminate based on alienage when setting eligibility requirements for welfare programs.

The *Mathews* Court began its analysis with a resounding endorsement of the aliens' rights tradition, concluding every alien, "even one whose presence in this country is unlawful, involuntary, or transitory, is entitled to . . . constitutional protection under the Fifth and Fourteenth Amendments."[257] But the Court soon shifted to the language of plenary power, repeatedly stressing that the judiciary must defer to the political branches "broad power over naturalization and immigration."[258] Ultimately the plenary power approach prevailed: the *Mathews* Court concluded that alienage restrictions on federal benefits were a legitimate part of "the business of the political branches of the Federal Government . . . to regulate the conditions of entry and residence of aliens."[259]

The conflicting language in *Mathews* has led to discordant interpretations of the opinion. Some commentators focus on the Supreme Court's initial reaffirmation of the aliens' rights tradition, and emphasize that *Mathews'* language can serve as a stepping stone toward eventual integration of aliens into the constitutional tradition.[260] Others stress that the alien plaintiffs lost after the *Mathews* Court expressly invoked the plenary power doctrine, and argue that the Supreme Court improperly transformed a case about eligibility for government benefits into an issue of immigration regulation.[261]

The *Mathews* decision illustrates just how difficult it can be to define the boundary that separates the aliens' rights tradition from the plenary power doctrine.[262] In the *Yick Wo-Wong Wing* line of cases,

---

257. *Id.* at 77 (citing Wong Wing v. United States, 163 U.S. 228, 238 (1893)).

258. *Id.* at 79-80.

259. *Id.* at 84.

260. A recent commentary by Hiroshi Motomura expresses this view. Professor Motomura concludes that even though the alien plaintiffs in *Mathews* did not prevail, "the contrast with the total judicial deference in the plenary power cases is striking." Hiroshi Motomura, *Immigration and Alienage, Federalism and Proposition 187*, 35 VA. J. INT'L L. 201, 210 (1995). He suggests the rhetoric in *Mathews* may be more important than its result, noting language from the decision provided a "key building block" for later decisions expanding the aliens' rights tradition. *Id.* (citing Plyler v. Doe, 457 U.S. 202, 210 (1982)). At the same time, however, the plenary power rhetoric that also pervades the *Mathews* opinion has played a key role in recent immigration decisions reaffirming the plenary power doctrine. *See* Fiallo v. Bell, 430 U.S. 787 (1977) (citing *Mathews*, 426 U.S. at 80-82 to uphold discriminatory admission criteria against equal protection challenge).

261. *See* Bosniak, *supra* note 22, at 1065-67; Scaperlanda, *Polishing the Tarnished Golden Door*, *supra* note 32, at 995-96.

262. *Cf.* Bosniak, *supra* note 22, at 1066-67 (noting "the line separating 'inside' from 'outside' [immigration law] is not pre-ordained but rather is subject to dispute").

the Court emphasized that not all claims pressed by aliens are governed by the plenary power doctrine. But cases like *Verdugo-Urquidez*, *Flemming*, and *Mathews* send a contradictory message. Several commentators have noted these latter decisions suggest *any* federal action against aliens is inextricably linked to the power to control immigration, and thus must be reviewed with extreme judicial deference.[263]

The Supreme Court has not explicitly acknowledged its occasional departures from the aliens' rights tradition. Nor has it provided consistent guidance on how to determine when aliens are entitled to protection under the Constitution. Thus, the lower courts have been saddled with the task of adjudicating the constitutional claims of aliens on inconsistent precedent, most recently in decisions adjudicating the due process claims of Haitians and Cubans seeking parole from immigration detention. These claims have forced courts to consider anew the scope of the *Knauff* and *Mezei* decisions. While the *holdings* of recent lower court cases continue to deny due process protection to excludable aliens, their *reasoning* helps to mark the sometimes elusive boundary between the plenary power doctrine and the aliens' rights tradition.

C. The 1980s Detention Litigation: Revisiting the Due Process Rights of Excludable Alien Detainees

As the Cold War subsided, there was little occasion for courts to reconsider the holdings of *Knauff* and *Mezei*. Indeed, soon after *Mezei* was decided, summary exclusion fell into disfavor.[264] The detention of excludable aliens also became rare; the government closed Ellis Island and began paroling virtually all applicants for entry while

---

263. *See* Aleinikoff, *Federal Regulation, supra* note 22, at 869 ("courts have wrongly assumed that every federal regulation based on *alienage* is necessarily sustainable as an exercise of the *immigration* power") (emphasis added); Legomsky, *Suspending Benefits, supra* note 254, at 1264 ("Whatever merit there might be to the view that immigration regulation should generate unusual judicial restraint, no reason is readily perceivable for requiring a similar result with respect to all federal regulation of aliens."); Rosberg, *supra* note 9, at 325 ("the government's legitimate interest in flexibility [to fashion immigration policy] does not require immunity from careful judicial scrutiny for every piece of federal legislation that has some bearing on aliens or immigration"); *see also* Scaperlanda, *Polishing the Tarnished Golden Door, supra* note 32, at 994-1000 (arguing that *Mathews* and *Verdugo-Urquidez* mark an expansion of the plenary power doctrine to cases outside of the immigration context).

264. Although now codified in statute, the summary exclusion proceedings of *Knauff* and *Mezei* are invoked far less frequently today than in the Cold War era. *See* INA § 235(c), 8 U.S.C. § 1225(c) (1994); ALEINIKOFF ET AL., IMMIGRATION PROCESS AND POLICY, *supra* note 45, at 402.

they awaited an administrative hearing.[265] The Supreme Court continued to cite *Knauff* and *Mezei* for the general proposition that the judiciary cannot intercede in immigration decisions,[266] and the two cases spawned a cottage industry of academic criticism.[267] But the broad assertion that excludable aliens have no due process rights, and the suggestion they might be detained indefinitely, were seldom at issue for almost three decades.

Beginning in 1980, however, the due process rights of excludable aliens in detention became a critical concern on two litigation fronts. Thousands of Haitians seeking asylum were confined under the new policy, announced in 1981, targeting undocumented excludable aliens for immigration detention.[268] Haitian detainees claimed their incarceration was the result of national origin discrimination, in violation of the equal protection component of the Due Process Clause.[269]

In addition, while most of the Cubans arriving in the Mariel boatlift of 1980 were paroled into the United States, a small percentage with criminal records were excluded. When Cuba refused to accept their return, they were confined by the INS.[270] To their ranks were soon added excludable Marielitos whose initial parole was revoked when they committed crimes within the United States.[271] The INS

---

265. *See* Leng May Ma v. Barber, 357 U.S. 185, 190 (1958); Louis v. Nelson, 544 F. Supp. 973, 980 n.18 (S.D. Fla. 1982), *aff'd in part and rev'd in part sub nom.*, Jean v. Nelson, 711 F.2d 144 (11th Cir. 1983), *vacated*, 727 F.2d 957 (11th Cir. 1984) (en banc), *aff'd as modified*, 472 U.S. 846 (1985).

266. *E.g.*, Landon v. Plasencia, 459 U.S. 21, 34 (1981); Fiallo v. Bell, 430 U.S. 787, 792 (1977); Kleindienst v. Mandel, 408 U.S. 753, 766 n.6 (1972).

267. *See, e.g.*, Aleinikoff, *"Community Ties," supra* note 251, at 237-39; Henry Hart, *The Power of Congress to Limit the Jurisdiction of Federal Courts: An Exercise in Dialectic*, 66 HARV. L. REV. 1362, 1389-96 (1953); Martin, *Due Process and Membership, supra* note 212, at 173-80; Schuck, *Transformation of Immigration Law, supra* note 33, at 20-21.

268. *Louis*, 544 F. Supp. at 1000.

269. There was in fact significant evidence of discriminatory enforcement of the policy of detention for undocumented excludable aliens. Government memoranda deliberating on the new detention policy were captioned "Haitian Program." *Jean*, 711 F.2d at 1468. A memorandum sent by the Attorney General to the President acknowledged "[d]etention could create an appearance of 'concentration camps' filled largely by blacks." *Louis*, 544 F. Supp. at 980 n.19. A panel of the Eleventh Circuit, in an opinion ultimately vacated by the en banc court, found "ample unrebutted evidence that [the detained Haitians] were denied equal protection of the laws." *Jean*, 711 F.2d at 1509.

270. *See* James LeMoyne, *Most Who Left Mariel Sailed to New Life, a Few to Limbo*, N.Y. TIMES, Apr. 15, 1990, at A1; *What Happened to the Marielitos?*, N.Y. TIMES, Nov. 25, 1987, at B6 (flow chart summarizing the status of Marielitos, stating 103,000 were released immediately and 22,000 were initially detained); Paul L. Montgomery, *1774 People Without a Country: Cuban Refugees Sit in U.S. Jails*, N.Y. TIMES, Dec. 7, 1980, at A1 (1774 of those initially detained were still confined by the INS in December 1980).

271. LeMoyne, *supra* note 143; Ronald Smothers, *Their Crimes Vary, but Most Cubans Are Serving Sentences of Frustration*, N.Y. TIMES, Nov. 30, 1987, at B11.

continues to confine thousands of Marielitos with criminal records.[272] Many face uncertainty as to whether they will ever be released.[273] Like Ignatz Mezei, they have argued the Due Process Clause does not countenance indefinite detention by executive fiat, even for aliens who technically have not yet "entered" the United States.

The due process claims of Marielito Cubans and Haitians triggered a fresh examination of *Knauff* and *Mezei*. The issues were starkly presented: Can Marielito Cubans who have committed crimes be incarcerated indefinitely? Can Haitians who claim invidious discrimination be confined without recourse to the Constitution? Initially, the Marielito and Haitian detainees met with some success in litigation seeking parole.[274] But most appellate courts have since concluded *Knauff* and *Mezei* preclude even these poignant due process claims.[275] The linchpin of these decisions is a determination that parole from immigration detention is intimately linked to the admissions process, and hence to broader immigration policy. As such, most

---

272. Generally, the INS revokes the parole of Marielitos who have been convicted of crimes in the United States, issues detainers while they are serving out their criminal sentence, and then takes them into custody at the end of their prison term. Most are then ordered excluded after a hearing before an immigration judge. The INS reported 2151 Marielitos in custody as of May 1, 1992. Detainers had been placed on another 2300 Marielitos serving prison sentences. FIVE-YEAR DETENTION PLAN, *supra* note 64, at 18. Because of a history of riots by Marielito detainees, protesting the resumption of flights returning them to Cuba, Marielitos are usually confined in Bureau of Prison facilities. *Id.* at 19.

273. The prospects for the eventual return of excluded incarcerated Marielitos to Cuba are "dependent on the uncertainties of diplomacy between two feuding and mutually suspicious nations." ALEINIKOFF ET AL., IMMIGRATION PROCESS AND POLICY, *supra* note 45, at 447. Cuba has only sporadically agreed to accept the return of some Marielitos. The INS reviews annually the files of detained Marielitos to determine if they are eligible for supervised parole. The current procedures for this review are set out in the Cuban Review Plan, codified at 8 C.F.R. § 212.12-.13 (1994). This review provides a personal interview for detainees who are not recommended for parole, but does not include procedures for a more formal adversarial hearing. *Id.* § 212.12(d)(4)(ii); *see generally* ALEINIKOFF ET AL., IMMIGRATION PROCESS AND POLICY, *supra* note 45, at 445-52, 465-73 (detailing litigation and policy developments for Marielito Cuban detainees); Barrera-Echavarria v. Rison, 44 F.3d 1441 (9th Cir. 1995) (refusing to order release for excluded Marielito Cuban with criminal record who had been detained since 1985).

274. *See* Louis v. Nelson, 544 F. Supp. 973, 993-97, 1002-04 (S.D. Fla. 1982) (concluding the INS promulgation of the new policy of detention for undocumented excludable aliens violated the Administrative Procedure Act, and ordering Haitians released on parole), *aff'd in part and rev'd in part sub nom.*, Jean v. Nelson, 711 F.2d 144 (11th Cir. 1983), *vacated*, 727 F.2d 957 (11th Cir. 1984) (en banc), *aff'd as modified*, 472 U.S. 846 (1985); Rodriguez-Fernandez v. Wilkinson, 654 F.2d 1382 (10th Cir. 1981) (concluding the INA does not authorize the indefinite detention of excludable aliens, and ordering release of Marielito Cuban who was confined in federal prison).

275. *See infra* note 284.

courts have reasoned that the plenary power doctrine must govern these claims.

Jean v. Nelson, the Haitian class action litigation, provides the most prominent example of this analysis.[276] Initially, a panel of the Eleventh Circuit emphasized that the Haitian plaintiffs did not claim a constitutional right to be admitted to the United States. Rather, at issue was "a right to be considered for parole in a nondiscriminatory fashion."[277] The panel therefore concluded the Haitians' claims did not relate to the political branches' authority over immigration, and should be governed by the aliens' rights tradition.[278] Finding strong evidence of "selective and discriminatory enforcement" of the new detention policy, the court determined the Haitian detainees should be paroled.[279]

Sitting en banc, the Eleventh Circuit vacated the panel opinion. The full court adopted the same framework for analysis: "whether the grant or denial of parole is an integral part of the admissions process."[280] Unlike the panel, the en banc court concluded the plenary power doctrine defeated the Haitians' equal protection claim.[281] The court reasoned special deference was warranted because a judicial order to parole excludable alien detainees "would ultimately result in our losing control over our borders."[282] As such, the plenary power doctrine must govern these claims. Applying *Mezei*, the court held "the Haitian plaintiffs in this case *cannot claim equal protection rights under the Fifth Amendment*, even with regard to challenging the Executive's exercise of its parole discretion."[283]

Jean v. Nelson marked an unfortunate turning point in the continuing litigation over the due process rights of excludable aliens. For the most part, later cases have adopted the analysis of the *Jean* en

---

276. In *Jean*, the Supreme Court granted certiorari to decide the pressing question of whether excludable Haitian detainees could raise an equal protection challenge, via the Due Process Clause, to the allegedly discriminatory denial of their parole applications. 472 U.S. at 849. The Court decided the case by interpreting the governing regulations to preclude national origin discrimination in parole decisions. *Id.* at 857. The Court therefore refused to reach the constitutional question on prudential grounds. *See id.* at 854. Nevertheless, the opinions below remain an influential analysis of the due process rights of excludable alien detainees. *See also supra* notes 69-70 and accompanying text (background of *Jean*).

277. *Jean*, 711 F.2d at 1484.
278. *Id.* at 1483-1505, 1509.
279. *Id.*
280. *Jean*, 727 F.2d at 971.
281. *Id.* at 975.
282. *Id.*
283. *Id.* at 970 (emphasis added).

banc court, and continue to deny due process protection to excludable alien detainees seeking parole.[284] These cases have reinvigorated the *Knauff* and *Mezei* decisions in the post-Cold War era. Their impact is felt most keenly by Marielito criminals whose parole has been revoked by the INS. Many have been incarcerated long past the end of their criminal sentence, and face continued indefinite confinement.[285]

Nevertheless, while the *Jean* en banc court applied *Knauff* and *Mezei* to deny due process protection to excludable alien detainees seeking parole, it also recognized an important limitation to the plenary power doctrine. The court summarized its opinion as a "simple and straightforward" holding that excludable aliens cannot claim equal protection to "challenge the decisions of executive officials *with regard to their applications for admission, asylum, or parole.*"[286] At the same time, the court explicitly recognized "aliens can raise constitutional challenges ... outside the context of entry or admission, when the plenary authority of the political branches is not implicated."[287] Thus, because its analysis centered on the *Yick Wo-Wong Wing* boundary of the plenary power doctrine, *Jean* was also a reaffirmation of the aliens' rights tradition.

D.   *Lynch v. Cannatella*: Due Process Protection to Challenge Conditions of Confinement

Some cases have recognized that this boundary should protect even excludable alien detainees from the incursion of the plenary power doctrine when they seek due process protection to challenge the conditions of their confinement. In *Haitian Centers Council v. Sale*, for example, the court held the conditions of confinement at segregated camps used to confine HIV-positive Haitians violated due

---

284. *See, e.g.*, Barrera-Echavarria v. Rison, 44 F.3d 1441 (9th Cir. 1995); Gisbert v. United States Attorney Gen., 988 F.2d 1437, 1441-43 (5th Cir. 1993); Alvarez-Mendez v. Stock, 941 F.2d 956, 962-63 (9th Cir. 1991), *cert. denied*, 113 S. Ct. 127 (1992); Amanullah v. Nelson, 811 F.2d 1, 8-9 (1st Cir. 1987); Fernandez-Roque v. Smith, 734 F.2d 576, 582 (11th Cir. 1984). For a summary of the "consensus view" that "excludable aliens are outside the Constitution's mantle, possessing no constitutional rights with respect to their detention," see Cruz-Elias v. United States Attorney Gen., 870 F. Supp. 692 (E.D. Va. 1994). The *Cruz-Elias* case collects both the academic commentary and cases discussing the constitutional rights of excludable aliens detained by the INS. *Id.* at 693-98.

285. *See, e.g.*, Barrera-Echavarria v. Rison, 21 F.3d 314 (9th Cir. 1994) (granting writ of habeas corpus for Marielito) (concluding "[t]he practice of administratively imprisoning persons indefinitely is not a process tolerable in use against any person in any corner of our country"), *vacated*, 44 F.3d 1441 (9th Cir. 1995) (en banc) (holding continued detention "is constitutional under *Mezei*").

286. *Jean*, 727 F.2d at 984 (emphasis added).

287. *Id.* at 972.

185

process, condemning the "squalid and prison-like" camps and the government's deliberate refusal to provide adequate medical care.[288] In dicta, the court rejected the argument that the Haitians confined at Guantanamo could not claim any protection under the Constitution to challenge even the most egregious mistreatment by their captors.[289]

The same analysis was the explicit holding of the Fifth Circuit in *Lynch v. Cannatella*.[290] The *Lynch* plaintiffs were stowaways who claimed they were severely mistreated while in the custody of the New Orleans harbor police.[291] The harbor police officers, sued for damages in their individual capacities, asserted qualified immunity against these charges.[292]

Government officials claiming qualified immunity must show "their conduct does not violate *clearly established* statutory or constitutional rights of which a reasonable person would have known."[293] In *Lynch*, the stowaways' captors relied on the plenary power doctrine to establish their qualified immunity defense.[294] They argued that since *Jean v. Nelson* and its progeny had stated excludable aliens were not entitled to due process protection, the stowaways did not have a "clearly established" constitutional right—or indeed *any* constitu-

---

288. 823 F. Supp. 1028, 1042 (E.D.N.Y. 1993) (vacated per settlement agreement).

289. *Id.* (stating "[i]f the Due Process Clause does not apply to the detainees at Guantanamo, Defendants would have discretion deliberately to starve or beat them, [or] to deprive them of medical attention"). Similar dicta appeared in a Second Circuit opinion earlier in this litigation. Haitian Ctrs. Council v. McNary, 969 F.2d 1326, 1341-42 (2d. Cir. 1992) (affirming district court's grant of a preliminary injunction in the face of assertions by government attorneys that the detained Haitians would not be protected by the Due Process Clause "even if they had been subjected to physical abuse").

290. 810 F.2d 1363 (5th Cir. 1987).

291. Fourteen stowaways were transferred from the barge they had boarded directly into the custody of the New Orleans harbor police. Two others jumped ship, were retrieved by the Coast Guard, and spent two days in INS custody before they were delivered to the harbor police. *Lynch*, 810 F.2d at 1367. The stowaways claimed during 10 days of detention they were denied minimal physical comforts such as heat, adequate toilet facilities, and proper bedding; were hosed down with a fire hose when they refused to take cold showers; and in some cases were beaten by harbor police officers. They further alleged they were drugged and locked in a steel container lashed insecurely to the deck of a barge for the return trip to Jamaica, until the barge was intercepted by federal officials. *Id.* at 1367-68.

292. *Id.* at 1372, 1374.

293. Harlow v. Fitzgerald, 457 U.S. 800, 818 (1982) (emphasis added).

294. Surprisingly, the *Lynch* court never used the term "plenary power doctrine." Nevertheless, the *Lynch* court framed its analysis as an inquiry into whether the limited constitutional protection afforded to excludable aliens within immigration law also precluded challenges to their treatment while in custody. 810 F.2d at 1373-74.

tional right—to be protected from abuse or mistreatment while in custody.[295]

In response to this argument, the Fifth Circuit conceded that excludable aliens' "right to be free from purposeful physical abuse . . . has never been explicitly examined by the courts."[296] The court recognized excludable aliens had limited constitutional rights "with regard to immigration and deportation proceedings," but ultimately concluded this precedent "does not limit the right of excludable aliens detained within United States territory to humane treatment."[297] The *Lynch* court also focused on the underlying justification for the plenary power doctrine: "the overriding concern that the United States, as a sovereign, maintain its right to self-determination."[298] The court emphasized the sovereignty of the United States would not be undermined if the stowaways were entitled to challenge the conditions of their confinement, explaining "we cannot conceive of any national interests that would justify the *malicious infliction of cruel treatment* on a person in United States territory simply because that person is an excludable alien."[299] Thus, the court held "whatever due process rights excludable aliens may be denied by virtue of their status, they are entitled under the Due Process Clauses of the Fifth and Fourteenth Amendments to be free of *gross physical abuse* at the hands of state or federal officials."[300]

IV. The Porous Border of the Plenary Power Doctrine

Lynch invoked the boundary of the plenary power doctrine—first articulated in *Yick Wo* and *Wong Wing* and reinvigorated by the Eleventh Circuit in *Jean v. Nelson*—to conclude alien detainees' claims of

---

295. *Lynch*, 810 F.2d at 1372. The defendants relied on Garcia-Mir v. Meese, 788 F.2d. 1446 (11th Cir. 1986), which held that Marielito Cubans seeking parole could not claim due process protection, to argue that excludable aliens "have virtually no constitutional rights." *Lynch*, 810 F.2d at 1372 (quoting *Garcia-Mir*, 788 F.2d at 1449).

296. *Id.* at 1372.

297. *Id.* at 1373 (citing Jean v. Nelson, 727 F.2d 957, 969 (11th Cir. 1984 (en banc)).

298. *Id.*

299. *Id.* at 1374 (emphasis added).

300. *Id.* (emphasis added). The court then remanded to allow the plaintiffs further opportunity to develop their claims. *Id.* at 1377. The *Lynch* court accepted the plaintiffs' allegations as true when reviewing the district court's refusal to grant summary judgment on the individual defendants' qualified immunity defense. Nevertheless, the court found some of the allegations in the complaint were "patently inadequate to state a claim of constitutional dimension." *Id.* at 1376. On remand, the plaintiffs' attorney failed to comply with instructions to file an amended complaint. The district court then dismissed all remaining claims with prejudice. Lynch v. Cannatella, 122 F.R.D. 195 (E.D. La.), *aff'd*, 860 F.2d 651 (5th Cir. 1988).

mistreatment should be adjudicated under the aliens' rights tradition.[301] Standing alone, *Lynch* proclaims that regardless of their status under immigration law, excludable aliens can claim due process protection to challenge the conditions of their confinement.[302] But later

---

301. The *Lynch* court did not consider an additional argument that is sometimes invoked to dilute, or even circumvent, the plenary power doctrine. Some courts and commentators have suggested the plenary power doctrine applies with most force to *congressional* action, and should not insulate executive conduct from judicial review. *See, e.g.*, Louis v. Nelson, 544 F. Supp. 973, 998 (S.D. Fla. 1982) ("[i]t is important to note that the actions challenged herein are not congressional"). *Cf.* Johnson, *supra* note 193, at 497 (arguing "the INS' long record of heavy-handed enforcement tactics" should weigh against employing the usual rules of judicial deference to agency action.); Legomsky, *Immigration Law and Plenary Power, supra* note 15, at 255 (leading article considering principle of plenary *congressional* power).

But what initially appears to be a fairly simple distinction between congressional and executive action raises a host of issues, beyond the scope of this article, yet to be fully explored. The argument that only Congress should be accorded deference in immigration matters is undermined by leading plenary power cases upholding executive branch action. *See, e.g.*, Kleindienst v. Mandel, 408 U.S. 753, 770 (1972) (when the executive refuses to waive an exclusion ground "on the basis of a facially legitimate and bona fide reason, the courts will [not] look behind the exercise of that discretion"). Moreover, it is not always easy to separate congressional and executive authority. For example, one of the most infamous articulations of the principle of plenary power comes from the Supreme Court's decision in *United States ex rel. Knauff v. Shaughnessy*, where the Court concluded "[w]hatever the procedure authorized by *Congress* is, it is due process as far as an alien denied entry is concerned." 338 U.S. 537, 544 (1950) (emphasis added). But Ellen Knauff was challenging the Attorney General's decision to exclude her without a hearing, a decision made under regulations promulgated pursuant to a presidential proclamation, which in turn was authorized by a war time statute permitting the President to "impose additional restrictions and prohibitions on the entry into and departure of persons from the United States" during an (already declared) national emergency. Only in the loosest sense did the challenged conduct "flow" from *Congress's* exercise of the federal immigration power. *Id.* at 540. Finally, the executive branch acts in a myriad of ways to enforce our immigration laws, and proponents of the executive/congressional distinction have not yet sorted out what acts and which actors should be insulated from plenary power deference. *Compare* Orantes-Hernandez v. Smith, 541 F. Supp. 351, 365 (C.D. Cal. 1982) ("[a]lthough the Court recognizes the great deference owed to Congress and the President in the immigration field, the deference owed to the INS is more circumscribed") *with* Jean v. Nelson, 727 F.2d 957, 970 (11th Cir. 1984) (en banc) (excludable aliens cannot claim equal protection to challenge discretionary parole decisions made by INS officials) *and* Pena v. Kissenger, 409 F.2d 1182 (S.D.N.Y. 1976) (stating well-settled rule that denials of visa applications by consular officials overseas are insulated from judicial review).

My own view is that the source of the challenged action—whether an act of Congress, a regulation issued by the INS, or a discretionary decision by an official in the field—can be a relevant factor when deciding whether, and with how much force, plenary power deference should apply. The congressional/executive distinction, however, is sometimes employed as a rather inexact surrogate for the inquiry that properly occupied center stage in *Lynch*: whether the challenged action is an exercise of the power to control immigration.

302. Other commentators have similarly suggested that *Lynch* is a vindication of the aliens' rights tradition. *See* Motomura, *Phantom Norms, supra* note 16, at 586 n.215 (placing *Lynch* among those cases "in the spirit of" *Wong Wing* and *Yick Wo*); ALEINIKOFF ET AL., IMMIGRATION PROCESS AND POLICY, *supra* note 45, at 465 (contrasting *Lynch* with

cases, focusing only on *Lynch*'s memorable language, have suggested that excludable aliens *must* show "malicious infliction of cruel treatment" or "gross physical abuse" to state a viable due process claim.

A.   "Malicious Infliction of Cruel Treatment" or "Gross Physical Abuse": Betraying the Promise of *Lynch v. Cannatella*

Medina v. O'Neill marked the first step away from the holding of *Lynch*.[303] In *Medina*, sixteen stowaways in the custody of a private security firm were detained together twenty-four hours a day in a single cell designed to hold six people. After two days of detention, the aliens attempted to escape.[304] One alien was killed and another wounded during this attempt when a shotgun being used by a guard to prod the detainees accidentally discharged.[305]

The stowaways sued INS officials, seeking both injunctive relief and damages.[306] The Fifth Circuit reversed a district court ruling in their favor on several grounds. The court held, contrary to the lower court's analysis, that the INS did not have a statutory duty to arrange for the detention of stowaways in appropriate facilities.[307] The Fifth Circuit also concluded the allegations against INS officials were no more than claims of negligence, insufficient to state a due process violation.[308]

---

cases rejecting excludable aliens' due process claims seeking parole from immigration detention).

303.   838 F.2d 800 (5th Cir. 1988), *rev'g* 589 F. Supp. 1028 (S.D. Tex. 1984).

304.   *Medina*, 589 F. Supp. at 1031 n.7.

305.   *Medina*, 838 F.2d at 801.

306.   *Medina*, 589 F. Supp. at 1034.

307.   *Medina*, 838 F.2d at 802.

308.   *Id.* at 803. The *Medina* court, following *Ortega v. Rowe*, 796 F.2d 765, 767-69 (5th Cir. 1986), held that the district court incorrectly relied upon *Bell v. Wolfish*, 441 U.S. 520 (1979), the leading Supreme Court decision delineating the analysis to be used when pretrial detainees bring due process challenges to the conditions of their confinement. *Id.* Under *Bell*, pretrial detainees are protected from any mistreatment "amount[ing] to punishment of the detainee." *Bell*, 441 U.S. at 535. Both *Medina* and *Ortega* concluded the *Bell* "punishment" standard was significantly undermined by later Supreme Court cases holding simple negligence did not amount to a due process violation. *Medina*, 838 F.2d at 803 (concluding "the Supreme Court has shifted ground since *Bell*"); *Ortega*, 796 F.2d at 767-69 (asserting the later Supreme Court decisions "render much of *Bell*'s language surplusage"). But *Medina* and *Ortega* appear to stand alone in explicitly questioning the continued vitality of *Bell*. The Fifth Circuit, while currently embroiled in disagreement over scope of due process protection afforded to pretrial detainees, continues to cite *Bell* consistently as the controlling precedent for due process conditions claims. *See* Grawbowski v. Jackson County Pub. Defenders Office, 47 F.3d 1386, 1395 (5th Cir. 1995), *reh'g en banc granted*, 1995 U.S. App. LEXIS 5999 (5th Cir. Mar. 14, 1995); Hare v. City of Corinth, 36 F.3d 412, 415 (5th Cir. 1994), *reh'g en banc granted*, 1994 U.S. App. LEXIS 34475 (5th Cir. Dec. 8, 1994). *Medina* and *Ortega*'s rejection of *Bell* apparently has not spread to other

In addition, the *Medina* court invoked *Lynch* to consider "the substantive due process rights of excludable aliens."[309] After quoting *Lynch*'s statements that no national interest would justify "malicious infliction of cruel treatment" and that excludable aliens were surely entitled to be free from "gross physical abuse," the *Medina* court concluded: "[t]he stowaways [in this case] alleged neither that cruel treatment was maliciously inflicted upon them nor that they suffered gross physical abuse. They stated no claim for violation of due process rights."[310]

This brief analysis seems to convert the factual allegations in *Lynch* into a threshold standard for all excludable alien detainees, blurring the distinction between specific allegations of misconduct found sufficient to defeat qualified immunity and the full scope of due process protection. The court did not rest its decision solely on this ground.[311] Still, instead of considering *Lynch*'s careful explanation of the proper scope of the plenary power doctrine, the *Medina* court suggested "malicious infliction of cruel treatment" or "gross physical abuse" were prerequisites for excludable aliens to state a due process violation.

A similar misreading of *Lynch* appears in *Adras v. Nelson*, an Eleventh Circuit decision adjudicating residual claims left unresolved in the *Jean v. Nelson* litigation.[312] In addition to asserting various damage claims for alleged unlawful detention,[313] the Haitian plaintiffs in *Adras* also challenged the conditions of confinement at the Krome SPC where they were confined in the early 1980s.[314] The *Adras* court readily rejected the bulk of the plaintiffs claims as precluded by the plenary power doctrine and discretionary function exception to the Federal Tort Claims Act.[315] The court also concluded INS officials were protected by qualified immunity, even against the plaintiffs' alle-

---

cases. *See also supra* note 172 (critiquing *Ortega* court's application of the negligence bar to due process liability).

309. *Medina*, 838 F.2d at 803.

310. *Id.* Because the *Medina* court concluded the plaintiffs' allegations did not state a due process violation, it found it unnecessary to consider the defendants' qualified immunity argument. *Id.* at 802.

311. *See supra* notes 307-308.

312. 917 F.2d 1552 (11th Cir. 1990).

313. The damage claims for unlawful detention were primarily asserted under the Federal Torts Claims Act ("FTCA"). *See id.* at 1555. The plaintiffs also sought damages under *Bivens v. Six Unknown Fed. Narcotics Agents*, 403 U.S. 388 (1971). *Id.* at 1557.

314. Krome was severely overcrowded, with numerous attendant conditions problems, during this time period. *See supra* notes 130-134 and accompanying text.

315. *Adras*, 917 F.2d at 1556-59. The court relied on *Jean v. Nelson* to conclude the detention of the Haitian plaintiffs was not unlawful, and also held that the defendants were

gations of unconstitutional conditions of confinement.[316] The *Adras* court found no conflict between its ruling and *Lynch*'s refusal to grant qualified immunity because "[t]here is no allegation [by the *Adras* plaintiffs] of 'gross physical abuse' and malicious infliction of harm by INS agents."[317]

Adras appears to be unique in its grant of qualified immunity to government officials in the face of a complaint stating the plaintiffs suffered "severe overcrowding, insufficient nourishment, inadequate medical treatment and other conditions of ill-treatment arising from inadequate facilities and care."[318] The Fifth Circuit, rejecting a qualified immunity defense asserted by local jail officials who failed to provide reasonable medical treatment to a pretrial detainee, has pointedly noted that "[a] constitutional right to minimally adequate care and treatment is not a novel proposition."[319] Yet the *Adras* court granted qualified immunity even for claims of severe overcrowding and inadequate medical care because the court "f[ou]nd no complaint here approaching the 'gross' physical abuse outlined in *Lynch*."[320]

Thus *Adras*, like *Medina*, extracted language from *Lynch* to set an unusually high threshold for excludable aliens seeking to challenge the conditions of their confinement. It appears that the *Lynch* court selected the phrases "malicious infliction of cruel treatment" and "gross physical abuse" to emphasize the audacity of the argument that

---

shielded from liability under the "discretionary function" exception of the FTCA. *See id.* at 1557.

The *Adras* plaintiffs apparently also pursued the challenge to the conditions of their confinement as an FTCA claim. *Id.* at 1559. The FTCA seldom provides an adequate remedy for federal detainees challenging conditions of confinement. Detainees in federal custody can recover damages under the FTCA only for claims (such as negligence in providing medical care) stating a cause of action recognized under state tort law. 28 U.S.C. § 1346(b) (1994). The FTCA does not provide relief for all deprivations of constitutional rights. *See* Muniz v. United States, 374 U.S. 150 (1962); Carlson v. Green, 446 U.S. 14 (1980). Also, because the FTCA reaches only the negligence of "employee[s] of the Government," and does not impose liability on any "contractor with the United States," federal detainees held in local jails or contract facilities cannot bring FTCA claims to challenge their treatment in these facilities. *See* 28 U.S.C. §§ 1346(b), 2761 (1994); Logue v. United States, 412 U.S. 521 (1972).

316. *Adras*, 917 F.2d at 1557-59.

317. *Id.* at 1559 (quoting Lynch v. Cannatella, 810 F.2d 1363, 1374 (5th Cir. 1987)).

318. *Id.* (quoting Plaintiffs' Second Amended Complaint).

319. Colle v. Brazos, 981 F.2d 237, 246 (5th Cir. 1993); *see also* Thompson v. City of Los Angeles, 885 F.2d 1439, 1448 (9th Cir. 1989) (reversing summary judgment in favor of the defendant county jail on claim that the failure to provide pretrial detainee with bed or mattress violated due process); Lyons v. Powell, 838 F.2d 28, 31 (1st Cir. 1988) (due process claim may be stated when detainee was confined with a cellmate for 22-23 hours per day and forced to sleep on a floor mattress).

320. *Adras*, 917 F.2d at 1559.

excludable alien detainees do not have a "clearly established" constitutional right to be free from such serious mistreatment.[321] In contrast, *Medina* and *Adras* suggest excludable aliens seeking to challenge the conditions of their confinement *must* allege abuse of at least this severity to state a viable due process claim.[322]

The *Medina* and *Adras* courts did not seem to be conscious of this marked shift from *Lynch*'s original analysis. Instead, the "malicious infliction of cruel treatment" or "gross physical abuse" standard evolved silently, largely within the context of adjudicating individual defendants' assertions of qualified immunity.[323] As such, it might be seen as a by-product of the many limitations on damage claims against governmental entities and government officials, which would not impact claims for injunctive relief.[324]

There are hints, however, that "malicious infliction of cruel treatment" or "gross physical abuse" may take root in a broader array of cases as a prerequisite for excludable aliens to establish a constitutional violation. Indeed, dicta in later opinions suggests that this interpretation has already overtaken the *Lynch* court's original analysis. In *Gisbert v. United States Attorney General*, for example, the Fifth Circuit rejected an argument by Marielito Cuban detainees that *Lynch* supported their claim of substantive due process protection to challenge their indefinite confinement. The court cautioned its holding in *Lynch* should be read very narrowly, explaining that *Lynch* created a "gross physical abuse exception" to the general principle that excluda-

---

321. *See* Lynch, 810 F.2d at 1374. The court was incredulous the defendants would claim qualified immunity in the face of allegations that they had denied the stowaways proper shelter and access to toilets, and had hosed them down with fire hoses, slamming the detainees against their cell walls. *Id.* at 1367. The court noted, for example, "[i]f the arguments advanced by the harbor police defendants were sound, the Constitution would not have protected the stowaways from torture or summary execution." *Id.* at 1375.

322. Medina v. O'Neill, 838 F.2d 800, 803 (5th Cir. 1988); *Adras*, 917 F.2d at 1559-60.

323. In *Lynch*, *Medina*, and *Adras*, the plaintiffs sought both injunctive relief and damages from government officials sued in their individual capacities. The *Medina* court did not reach the qualified immunity issue, concluding that because the plaintiffs had "alleged neither that cruel treatment was inflicted upon them nor that they suffered gross physical abuse" they had failed to state a due process claim. 838 F.2d at 803. In *Lynch* and *Adras*, however, the phrases "malicious infliction of cruel treatment" and "gross physical abuse" played a critical (albeit dramatically different) role in the courts' qualified immunity analysis. *Lynch*, 810 F.2d at 1374; *Adras*, 917 F.2d at 1559-60.

324. Qualified immunity is but one of a host of doctrines that limit the damage liability of governments and their employees. *See generally* PETER H. SCHUCK, SUING GOVERNMENT: CITIZEN REMEDIES FOR OFFICIAL WRONGS 203-07 (1983) (summarizing various "complex and to some degree unsettled" liability and immunity doctrines).

ble aliens have no due process rights in immigration proceedings.[325] Similarly, the Second Circuit, citing *Lynch*, has asserted that excludable aliens enjoy "little or no" due process protection "[o]ther than protection against gross physical abuse."[326] And a federal district court has read *Lynch*, as "narrow[ed]" by *Gisbert*, to hold that "an alien's substantive due process right to humane treatment while in INS detention is *limited* to the right to be free from 'gross physical abuse.'"[327]

Thus it appears the central lesson of *Lynch*—that excludable aliens can claim full due process protection to challenge their treatment while in custody—may be supplanted by a requirement that they must allege deliberate cruelty or severe physical abuse to overcome a qualified immunity defense, or even to state a viable claim. This requirement has not been imposed on pretrial detainees.[328] The "malicious infliction of cruel treatment" and "gross physical abuse" of *Medina* and *Adras* is also notable for its departure from the analysis used by the Supreme Court to adjudicate the conditions claims of convicted prisoners.

B. A Comparison to Eighth Amendment Standards

Pretrial detainees, and others in civil confinement, ought to enjoy due process protection against inhumane detention conditions "at least as great as the Eighth Amendment protection available to a convicted prisoner."[329] *Medina* and *Adras*, however, do not provide this

---

325. 988 F.2d 1437, 1442 (5th Cir.), *amended on other grounds*, 997 F.2d 1122 (5th Cir. 1993).

326. Correa v. Thornburgh, 901 F.2d 1166, 1171 n.5 (2d Cir. 1990). *Correa* has been cited in later decisions reiterating the "other than protection against gross physical abuse" language. *See* Haitian Ctrs. Council v. McNary, 969 F.2d 1326, 1349 (2d Cir. 1992) (Mahoney, J., dissenting) (rejecting grant of due process protection to excludable aliens); Mejia-Ruiz v. INS, 871 F. Supp. 159, 164 (E.D.N.Y. 1994).

327. Xiao v. Reno, 837 F. Supp. 1506, 1550 (N.D. Cal. 1993) (emphasis added).

328. *See supra* note 319. A search of computer databases reveals that *Lynch, Medina, Adras*, and the later cases explicitly citing to these decisions are the only federal court cases containing either the phrase "malicious infliction of cruel treatment" or "gross physical abuse." The only exception is *Swenson v. Stidham*, where the Supreme Court used the phrase "gross physical abuse" when describing a criminal defendant's claim he had been coerced by police to confess to a crime. 409 U.S. 224, 225 (1972).

329. City of Revere v. Massachusetts Gen. Hosp., 463 U.S. 239, 244 (1983) (citing Bell v. Wolfish, 441 U.S. 520, 545 (1979)). Pretrial detainees are protected against any condition or practice that amounts to "punishment," while incarcerated criminals must show "cruel or unusual punishment" to establish that the conditions of their confinement violate the Constitution. *Bell*, 441 U.S. at 535 n.16. Thus, conditions constituting "cruel and unusual" punishment under the Eighth Amendment a fortiori should also amount to a due process violation. Hare v. City of Corinth, 36 F.2d 412, 415-16 (5th Cir. 1994), *reh'g en*

heightened protection to excludable alien detainees. To the contrary, the "malicious infliction of cruel treatment" or "gross physical abuse" standard echoes requirements that the Supreme Court has rejected as too stringent even for convicted prisoners challenging detention conditions under the Eighth Amendment.

In *Wilson v. Seiter*, for example, the Supreme Court held prisoners must prove a "culpable state of mind" on the part of prison officials in order to establish an Eighth Amendment violation.[330] This subjective component of the Eighth Amendment must be satisfied even when prisoners allege widespread, systemic problems with conditions of confinement. Yet the *Wilson* Court concluded that prisoners challenging overall detention conditions do not have to prove government officials acted "maliciously and sadistically for the very purpose of causing harm," thus rejecting a standard that mirrors the "malicious infliction of cruel treatment" language in *Medina* and *Adras*.[331] The *Wilson* Court explicitly stated this "very high state of mind . . . does not apply to prison conditions cases."[332] Instead, "deliberate indifference"—a term meaning "something less than acts or omissions for the very purpose of causing harm"—is the appropriate subjective standard for most conditions claims.[333]

The Eighth Amendment also has an objective component. In *Hudson v. McMillian*, the Supreme Court rejected the Fifth Circuit's attempt to transform this component into a standard requiring a threshold showing of a "significant injury" to state an Eighth Amendment claim.[334] Instead, the Court reiterated that the objective component of the Eighth Amendment is a contextual standard drawing its meaning from "the evolving standards of decency that mark the pro-

---

banc granted, 1994 U.S. App. LEXIS 34475 (5th Cir. 1994); Matzker v. Herr, 748 F.2d 1142, 1146 (7th Cir. 1984). *But see* 1 MUSHLIN, *supra* note 123, § 3.01, at 132 (arguing "[i]t is doubtful whether there is a practical difference between the application of these two standards").

330. 501 U.S. 294 (1991).

331. *Wilson*, 501 U.S. at 302 (quoting Johnson v. Glick, 481 F.2d 1028, 1033 (2d Cir. 1973), *cited in* Whitley v. Albers, 475 U.S. 312, 320-21 (1986)). The Court had previously adopted this heightened subjective standard for emergency situations involving prison disturbances. *Whitley*, 475 U.S. at 320-21.

332. *Wilson*, 501 U.S. at 302-03.

333. Farmer v. Brennan, 114 S. Ct. 1970 (1994); *Wilson*, 501 U.S. at 302-03.

334. 503 U.S. 1, 5 (1992). In *Hudson*, an inmate who had been beaten by prison guards suffered bruises and swelling on his face, mouth, and lip. The blows also loosened the prisoner's teeth and cracked his dental plate. The Fifth Circuit concluded the guards' use of force was "clearly excessive and occasioned unnecessary and wanton infliction of pain," but held the prisoner could not prevail on his Eighth Amendment claim because he had suffered only "minor" injuries. *Id.* at 4-5.

gress of a maturing society."[335] The *Hudson* Court concluded that "[w]hen prison officials maliciously and sadistically use force to cause harm, contemporary standards of decency are always violated . . . whether or not significant injury is evident."[336]

The *Medina* and *Adras* courts' emphasis on *"gross"* physical abuse seems inconsistent with *Hudson*'s holding that the use of excessive force raises a colorable Eighth Amendment claim, even when it does not cause a particularly serious or lasting physical injury. Moreover, other Supreme Court cases make clear that many types of harm—including inadequate medical care,[337] serious overcrowding,[338] and even prolonged exposure to unreasonably high levels of environmental tobacco smoke[339]—can constitute "cruel and unusual punishment." Yet dicta in the immigration detention context suggests "an alien's substantive due process right to humane treatment while in INS detention is *limited* to the right to be free from 'gross physical abuse.'"[340] This standard would leave alien detainees without protection from many types of inhumane treatment that are prohibited by the Eighth Amendment.

C. The Silent Influence of the Plenary Power Doctrine

It appears, therefore, that excludable aliens challenging the conditions of their confinement have been cut off from the usual framework for analyzing conditions claims under the Constitution. The Supreme Court has held that neither malicious treatment for the very purpose of causing harm nor physical abuse resulting in significant injury are necessary to show "cruel and unusual punishment" under the Eighth Amendment. But the conditions claims of excludable aliens have on occasion been dismissed outright or rejected on qualified immunity grounds for failing to allege "malicious infliction of cruel treatment" or "gross physical abuse." This standard has developed in

---

335. *Id.* at 8-9 (quoting Rhodes v. Chapman, 452 U.S. 337, 346 (1981); Trop v. Dulles, 356 U.S. 86, 101 (1958) (plurality opinion)).

336. *Id.* at 9.

337. Estelle v. Gamble, 429 U.S. 97, 104 (1976).

338. *See* Rhodes v. Chapman, 452 U.S. 337, 356 (1981) (Brennan, J., concurring) (discussing numerous lower court rulings where overcrowding was held unconstitutional).

339. Helling v. McKinney, 113 S. Ct. 2475, 2481 (1993).

340. Xiao v. Reno, 837 F. Supp. 1506, 1550 (N.D. Cal. 1993) (quoting Lynch v. Cannatella, 810 F.2d 1363, 1374 (5th Cir. 1987), as explained in Gisbert v. United States Attorney Gen., 988 F.2d 1437, 1442 (5th Cir. 1993)) (emphasis added); *see also* Correa v. Thornburgh, 901 F.2d 1166, 1171 n.5 (dicta suggesting excludable aliens enjoy "little or no" due process protection "[o]ther than protection against gross physical abuse").

isolation; it has been imposed only upon excludable alien detainees.[341] And it is all the more unusual since it has been applied to due process claims, where civil detainees are supposed to receive greater constitutional protection than the Eighth Amendment affords convicted prisoners. In short, excludable aliens seeking to challenge the conditions of their confinement have at times been granted significantly less than a full measure of due process rights.

Under the Eleventh Circuit's analysis in *Jean v. Nelson*, however, conditions claims should fall beyond the reach of the plenary power doctrine. Indeed, *Lynch v. Cannatella*—the source of the "malicious infliction of cruel treatment" or "gross physical abuse" language—recognized that *Jean* "does not limit the right of excludable aliens detained within United States territory to humane treatment."[342] *Medina* and *Adras* misconstrued the holding in *Lynch*, and instead allowed plenary power analysis to infect their adjudication of conditions claims. In this respect, they resemble *United States v. Verdugo-Urquidez, Flemming v. Nestor*, and *Mathews v. Diaz*—cases where the Supreme Court applied plenary power deference reflexively to any constitutional challenge pressed by aliens, even when their claims were not linked to the federal government's power to control immigration.[343]

What is striking about *Lynch* and its progeny, however, is the *unconscious* evolution of the "malicious infliction of cruel treatment" or "gross physical abuse" standard. *Verdugo-Urquidez, Mathews*, and to a lesser extent *Flemming* all reflect a deliberate choice between the plenary power doctrine and the aliens' rights tradition.[344] In contrast,

---

341. *See supra* notes 319, 328.

342. 810 F.2d at 1373.

343. *See supra* notes 245-263 and accompanying text.

344. In *Verdugo-Urquidez*, the Supreme Court explicitly rejected the alien respondent's arguments from *Yick Wo-Wong Wing* line of cases in the aliens' rights tradition, concluding "[r]espondent is an alien who has had no previous significant voluntary connection with the United States, so these cases avail him not." 494 U.S. at 271; *see supra* notes 245-252 and accompanying text. In *Mathews v. Diaz*, the Court at first invoked the language of the aliens' rights tradition but ultimately was swayed by the plenary power argument that Congress's denial of Medicaid benefits to aliens was an exercise of its "broad power over naturalization and immigration." 426 U.S. at 77, 79-80; *see supra* notes 256-262 and accompanying text. The competition between the plenary power doctrine and the aliens' right tradition was less overt in *Flemming v. Nestor*, where the alien plaintiffs' "most insistently pressed constitutional objections" centered on whether the termination of Social Security benefits constituted legislative "punishment" without judicial trial. 363 U.S. 602, 612-13 (1960). Still, the Court relied in part on plenary power cases stating deportation is not "punishment" under the Constitution, a move that was challenged by the dissenting justices who argued "the Court cannot rest [its] decision . . . on Congress' power to regu-

the *Medina* court simply seized on language in *Lynch* and incorrectly assumed that protection from "malicious infliction of cruel treatment" or "gross physical abuse" was all that the Constitution provided excludable aliens. Similarly, the *Adras* court overlooked the distinction between the Haitian plaintiffs' claims of unlawful detention, which under *Jean* should be governed by the plenary power doctrine, and their challenges to the conditions of confinement. Instead, the court allowed the plenary power doctrine to pervade its entire opinion. These analytical errors have since spread, at least in dicta, to other cases.[345] In short order, *Lynch*'s careful analysis, which was protective of the due process rights of excludable alien detainees outside of the immigration context, has silently evolved into a standard limiting their due process rights even to challenge the conditions of their confinement.

This silent spread of the plenary power doctrine might be seen as the mirror image of a similarly subtle flow of constitutional values *into* the immigration law realm. Hiroshi Motomura has convincingly argued that "phantom constitutional norms" sometimes spill across the boundary isolating immigration law from the rest of public law, and thus contribute to the gradual erosion of the plenary power doctrine.[346] These "phantom norms," which are derived from the aliens' rights tradition, influence the interpretation of immigration statutes, "produc[ing] results that are much more sympathetic to aliens" than a plenary power analysis would suggest.[347] In essence, Professor Motomura argues that the process of statutory interpretation can serve as a vehicle to smuggle constitutional protection for aliens into the immigration law realm. He and others suggest only a crumbling and soon-to-be defunct barrier separates aliens from full integration into "the people" protected by the Constitution.[348]

But this focus on an eroding plenary power doctrine, which until recently has dominated immigration law scholarship, overlooks the polluting effect of the plenary power doctrine *outside* the immigration

---

late immigration." *Id.* at 616; *id.* at 636 (Brennan, J., dissenting); *see supra* note 255; *see also* Legomsky, *Suspending Benefits, supra* note 254, at 1264.

345. *See supra* notes 325-327 and accompanying text.

346. Motomura, *Phantom Norms, supra* note 16, at 547-50, 564-75.

347. *Id.* at 564.

348. *Id.* at 549 (citing a "widely accepted view . . . that the doctrine is in some state of decline"); Schuck, *supra* note 33, at 90. Stephen Legomsky's essay for this symposium issue, which argues the current trend seems to point toward the emergence of a "restricted plenary power doctrine—a new 'PPD-lite,'" is in a similar vein. Legomsky, *Ten More Years, supra* note 33, at 936-37.

law realm.[349] The traditional analysis of the relationship between the plenary power doctrine and the aliens' rights tradition depicts only a one-way flow of constitutional norms into the immigration law realm. In fact, the border is porous in both directions. The cases adjudicating the conditions claims of excludable alien detainees illustrate a second silent migration: the influence of the plenary power doctrine also spills out beyond the boundary of immigration law.

V.   Conclusion: Policing the Porous Border

To stop this leaching, courts must police the porous border between the plenary power doctrine and the aliens' rights tradition. Such vigilance, however, may come with a price: it can reinforce the barrier separating aliens from the Constitution whenever they press immigration law claims. A strong boundary between the plenary power doctrine and the aliens' rights tradition may, in some cases, be used to defeat aliens' constitutional claims.

Jean v. Nelson illustrates this point. The Eleventh Circuit framed its analysis of the due process rights of Haitian detainees seeking parole as a choice between the plenary power doctrine and the aliens' rights tradition. The court distilled a standard for making this choice: "whether the grant or denial of parole is an integral part of the admissions process."[350] *Jean* clarified the scope of the plenary power doctrine and the aliens' rights tradition, but ultimately concluded excludable aliens seeking parole could not claim due process protection.

While many have criticized this result, *Jean* at least asked the correct question: whether granting aliens constitutional protection will impinge on the political branches' authority to control immigration.[351] This same analysis enabled the *Lynch* court to decide what others had

---

349. *Cf.* Scaperlanda, *Polishing the Tarnished Golden Door*, *supra* note 32, at 994-1000; Bosniak, *supra* note 22, at 1059-68.

350. *Jean v. Nelson*, 727 F.2d 957, 971 (11th Cir. 1984) (en banc), *vacating* 711 F.2d 1455 (11th Cir. 1983).

351. *Jean*'s ruling that excludable Haitian detainees seeking parole cannot claim equal protection rights under the Fifth Amendment, even in the face of strong evidence of national origin discrimination, is not the inevitable result of this analysis. The panel opinion, vacated by the en banc court, applied the same test but concluded that the Haitian plaintiffs' claim of "a right to be considered for parole in a nondiscriminatory fashion" did not implicate the political branches plenary power over immigration, and thus should be governed by the aliens' rights tradition. 711 F.2d at 1484. The panel went on to find "ample unrebutted evidence that the plaintiffs were denied equal protection." *Id.* at 1509; *see supra* notes 276-287 and accompanying text (discussing the *Jean* panel and en banc opinions).

only suggested in dicta: despite the sweeping language of *Knauff* and *Mezei*, the plenary power doctrine does not reach the due process conditions claims of alien detainees.

The different results in *Jean* and *Lynch* show that the porous border between the plenary power doctrine and aliens' rights tradition lies in neutral territory. Insisting that courts respect this boundary does not automatically advantage either of the two competing traditions. The outcome depends on whether the challenged governmental conduct is inextricably linked to an exercise of the immigration power.

But emphasizing the border between the plenary power doctrine and the aliens' rights tradition does cause a subtle shift in analysis. A common pattern in immigration cases is to consider first whether alien claimants "deserve" constitutional protection—based on whether they have "entered" the country or have developed significant ties to the United States.[352] When courts make an explicit choice between the plenary power doctrine and the aliens' rights tradition, however, the focus shifts to the nature of the governmental power at issue. Courts are then deciding whether there is a reason to stand back and allow the government especially wide latitude to treat aliens differently under the Constitution. I believe that if courts routinely considered the constitutional claims of aliens from this perspective, instead of reflexively (or unconsciously) invoking plenary power precedent, it could weaken the plenary power doctrine.

Nevertheless, some might argue that fortifying the border between the plenary power doctrine and the aliens' rights tradition will only impede the flow of constitutional values into the immigration law realm. It hardly seems advantageous to aliens to reinforce the very barrier isolating them "in the backwaters of constitutional jurisprudence."[353] But even as norms derived from the aliens' rights tradition occasionally seep into the realm of immigration law, I suspect that there is at least as much spillover in the opposite direction. *Medina* and *Adras* illustrate the unsettling stealth and ease with which the plenary power doctrine can overshadow the aliens' rights tradition.

Moreover, the plenary power doctrine is the stronger of these competing traditions, more firmly entrenched in the body of law governing the constitutional rights of aliens. Despite a wealth of academic criticism and litigation aimed at reform, the plenary power doctrine remains the central tenet of immigration law. The aliens'

---

352. *See supra* notes 242, 251.
353. Aleinikoff, *Membership and the Constitution, supra* note 35, at 9.

rights tradition has not developed into a doctrine of equal stature.[354] I conclude that so long as the plenary power doctrine "smothers the entire field of immigration law,"[355] courts must be vigilant in policing its porous border. Otherwise, the "perverse readings of the Constitution" that mark immigration law will continue to seep out to infect claims—like the conditions claims of alien detainees—where aliens should be granted full constitutional protection.

---

354. *See* Bosniak, *supra* note 22, at 1004 (noting "wholly apart from questions of admission, expulsion, and naturalization, the law continues to treat alienage as the rightful basis for less favorable treatment of persons in a variety of contexts, notwithstanding the *Yick Wo* tradition").

355. Motomura, *Phantom Norms*, *supra* note 16, at 574.

IMMIGRATION BRIEFINGS®

Published by the Editors of *INTERPRETER RELEASES*

Practical Analysis of Immigration and Nationality Issues

EXPEDITED REMOVAL: AUTHORITIES, IMPLEMENTATION, AND ONGOING POLICY AND PRACTICE ISSUES

by

JUAN P. OSUNA and PATRICIA MARIANI

MORE THAN SIX MONTHS have passed since the Immigration and Naturalization Service (INS or Service) began implementing the "expedited removal" system at U.S. ports of entry. This system, created by the Illegal Immigration Reform and Immigrant Responsibility Act of 1996 (IIRIRA),[1] gives INS inspectors a powerful tool to deny admission to aliens arriving in the U.S. with improper or fraudulent documentation. Even before the IIRIRA became law, attorneys and advocacy organizations warned that expedited removal would likely inflict serious harm on bona fide refugees and persons with relatively minor defects in their travel documents.

In recent months, INS regulations and policy directives have addressed a number of questions about expedited removal. The INS should be commended for trying to implement expedited removal in an intelligent and humane manner, under the tight deadline set by Congress. Nevertheless, substantial problems remain in the expedited removal system — and need to be addressed before more legitimate refugees are subjected to the harsh effects of the expedited removal process.

This month's BRIEFING focuses on the implementation of expedited removal since the system took effect on April 1, 1997. The BRIEFING outlines the statutory and regulatory authorities for expedited removal, and analyzes the effects of expedited removal on particular classes of aliens, including unaccompanied minors and persons who claim permanent resident status. The BRIEFING considers the new importance of withdrawing applications for admission to avoid the long-term consequences of expedited removal. The new detention responsibilities that accompany the expedited removal system also are discussed. Finally, the BRIEFING offers practical insights on how expedited removal has functioned so far.

The Issue In Brief

THE STATUTE
* Expedited Removal in Brief
* Administrative and Judicial Review
* Application of Expedited Removal to Other Aliens

INS IMPLEMENTATION OF EXPEDITED REMOVAL
* The Inspection Process Under Expedited Removal
* Withdrawing the Application for Admission
* Review of Claims to Permanent Resident, Refugee, or Asylee Status
* The Credible Fear Interview
* Special Guidelines for Unaccompanied Minors
* Application of Expedited Removal to Aliens in the U.S.

DETENTION AND EXPEDITED REMOVAL

HOW IS EXPEDITED REMOVAL WORKING?
* INS Statistics
* Practice Issues

CONCLUSION

Juan P. Osuna is the Managing Editor of INTERPRETER RELEASES and the Executive Editor of IMMIGRATION BRIEFINGS. Patricia Mariani is the Editor of IMMIGRATION BRIEFINGS. This BRIEFING updates and expands an article to be published in Practice Under the IIRAIRA One Year Later (R. Patrick Murphy ed., AILA 1997).

THE STATUTE

• Expedited Removal in Brief

The expedited removal system has substantially altered the treatment of certain aliens deemed inadmissible to the U.S. Before the IIRIRA, aliens arriving at a port of entry with invalid documents were eligible for a hearing before an immigration judge (IJ) to determine their admissibility. They were also eligible for both administrative and judicial review of the IJ's decision.

The expedited removal system changed that process. Now, aliens arriving at U.S. ports of entry who are found inadmissible under the grounds of inadmissibility set forth at INA § 212(a)(6)(C) (misrepresentation) or INA § 212(a)(7) (no valid documentation) are subject to expedited removal.[2] Aliens affected by this new system include those who arrive with fraudulent documents or with no documents, as well as aliens who, either by fraud or willful misrepresentation seek to procure admission to the U.S. The stakes are high for these arriving aliens — an alien ordered removed under expedited removal is inadmissible to the U.S. for five years, unless the Attorney General agrees to an earlier admission.

The statute outlines how the expedited removal process is supposed to work. An immigration officer at the port of entry screens each member of the affected class of arriving aliens to determine whether the alien intends to apply for asylum or fears persecution. If the officer finds that the alien does not intend to apply for asylum or does not fear persecution, the statute provides that the immigration officer must order the alien to be removed summarily from the U.S.[3]

If an alien indicates that he or she wishes to apply for asylum or fears persecution, the immigration officer must refer the alien to an asylum officer to determine whether he or she has a "credible fear" of persecution. The law provides that the interview may be conducted at the port of entry, or at another place designated by the INS. It also permits the alien to consult a representative before the interview, if the alien can locate such a representative. This consultation must be at no expense to the government and must not delay the process unreasonably. Moreover, the INS must provide information concerning the credible fear interview to aliens who may be eligible.[4]

According to the INA, as amended by the IIRIRA, a "credible fear of persecution" means that, taking into account the alien's statements in support of her or his claim and other facts known to the officer, "there is a significant possibility" that the alien could establish eligibility for asylum under INA § 208.[5] The statute also clarifies the meaning of the phrase "asylum officer." As used in the expedited removal context, an asylum officer is an immigration officer who: (i) has had professional training in country conditions, asylum law, and interview techniques comparable to that provided to full-time adjudicators of asylum applications under INA § 208; and (ii) is supervised by an officer who meets the training conditions described above in (i), and has had substantial experience adjudicating applications under INA § 208.[6]

If the asylum officer determines, during the credible fear interview, that the alien does not have a credible fear of persecution, the officer must order the alien removed from the U.S. without further hearing or review.[7] The asylum officer must prepare a written record of her or his decision, setting out a summary of the material facts as stated by the applicant, any additional facts relied upon by the officer, and the officer's analysis of why, in light of the facts, the alien has not established a credible fear of persecution.[8] The statute also requires that a copy of the officer's interview notes be attached to the summary.

Upon the alien's request, a determination that the alien does not have a credible fear of persecution is subject to review by an IJ. This review must include an opportunity for the alien to be heard and questioned by

Immigration Briefings (ISSN 0897–6708) is published monthly and copyrighted © 1997. Subscriptions: $366. Executive Editor: Juan P. Osuna. Editor: Patricia Mariani. Published by Federal Publications Inc., 1120 20th Street, NW, Suite 500 South, Washington, DC 20036–3484. Telephone: (202) 337–7000, (800) 922–4330; facsimile: (202) 659–2233, (800) 292–4330; Internet address: http://www.fedpub.com/immigration. Periodicals postage paid at Washington, DC and at additional mailing offices. Postmaster: Send address changes to Immigration Briefings, Suite 500 South, 1120 20th Street, NW, Washington, DC 20036–3484. Printed on recycled paper.

the IJ, either in person or by telephone or a video/ telephone connection. Under the IIRIRA, the IJ's review must be concluded "as expeditiously as possible, to the maximum extent practicable within 24 hours, but in no case later than 7 days" after the asylum officer's finding of no credible fear.[9] The law also requires that any alien requesting review of a negative credible fear determination be detained, pending the IJ's decision. If the IJ finds that the alien has no credible fear, the alien's detention lasts until he or she is removed.[10]

The process differs considerably if the asylum officer finds that the alien has established a credible fear of persecution. The statute provides that if the alien can establish a credible fear, the alien "shall be detained for further consideration of the application for asylum."[11] As noted below, INS regulations have interpreted this provision to mean that the alien will be referred to full-fledged removal proceedings under INA § 240, in which the claim for asylum will be adjudicated.

• **Administrative and Judicial Review**
The IIRIRA permits only extremely limited administrative review of any orders in the expedited removal context. Except for allowing an alien to request that an IJ review a negative credible fear determination, the statute provides that an expedited removal order is not subject to administrative appeal. The only exceptions are for an alien who claims under oath (or under penalty of perjury under 28 USC § 1746) to have been admitted previously for permanent residence, or to have been admitted as a refugee under INA § 207, or granted asylum under INA § 208. The alien must first have been warned of the penalties for making a false claim to permanent resident, refugee, or asylee status.[12]

Judicial review of the expedited removal process is also sharply circumscribed. The IIRIRA explicitly provides that no court has jurisdiction to review: (i) an individual determination, or to entertain any other cause or claim arising from the implementation or operation of an expedited removal order; (ii) a decision by the Attorney General to invoke the expedited removal provisions; (iii) the application of expedited removal to individual aliens, including credible fear determinations; and (iv) procedures and policies adopted by the Attorney General to implement expedited removal.[13]

Moreover, the law makes clear that "without regard to the nature of the action or claim and without regard to the identity of the party or parties bringing the action," no court may: (i) enter declaratory, injunctive, or other equitable relief in any action pertaining to an order to exclude an alien under expedited removal (except in habeas corpus proceedings as discussed below), or (ii) certify a class under Rule 23 of the Federal Rules of Civil Procedure in any action challenging expedited removal for which judicial review is authorized.[14] In addition, the statute provides that in any action brought against an alien under INA § 275(a) (improper entry or misrepresentation and concealment of facts) or INA § 276 (reentry of removed alien), no court has jurisdiction to hear any collateral claim attacking the validity of an expedited removal order.[15]

Whatever judicial review of expedited removal is available is set forth in INA § 242(e). Under that section, judicial review of an individual expedited removal order is available only by habeas corpus and is limited to determinations of whether the petitioner: (i) is an alien, (ii) was ordered removed under the expedited removal process, and (iii) can prove, by a preponderance of the evidence, that he or she is a lawful permanent resident, has been admitted as a refugee, or granted asylum.[16] If the alien makes the requisite showing, the court may order only that the petitioner receive a removal hearing under INA § 240.[17] In addition, the statute provides that in determining whether an alien was ordered removed pursuant to expedited removal, the court's inquiry is limited to whether the order was in fact issued and whether it relates to the particular individual. The court may not review "whether the alien is actually inadmissible or entitled to any relief from removal."[18]

The IIRIRA also specifically addresses jurisdiction over challenges to the validity of the expedited removal system. The law states that judicial review of the implementation of expedited removal is available in the U.S. District Court for the District of Columbia and must be filed within 60 days after the date that the challenged section, regulation, directive, guideline, or procedure is first implemented.[19] The statute also limits challenges to the validity of the system to whether the section, or any regulation issued to implement it, is constitutional and whether a regulation or written directive, policy guideline, or procedure issued by the Attorney General to implement the process is in violation of law.[20]

Finally, the IIRIRA contains a provision calling on the federal courts, including the district courts, the courts of appeals, and the Supreme Court, to "advance on the docket and to expedite to the greatest extent possible" any case pertaining to expedited removal.[21]

- **Application of Expedited Removal to Other Aliens**

The IIRIRA does not limit the application of expedited removal procedures to arriving aliens. Under the INA, as amended by the IIRIRA, the Attorney General may apply expedited removal to any alien who: (i) has not been admitted or paroled into the U.S., and (ii) cannot affirmatively show an immigration officer that he or she has been physically present in the U.S. continuously for the two-year period immediately preceding the date of the determination of inadmissibility.[22]

This provision thus gives the INS the authority to apply expedited removal procedures to persons who entered without inspection (EWI) and have been in the U.S. for less than two years. For this reason, it is a potentially sweeping authority, which could affect thousands of individuals. As discussed below, however, the INS has so far elected not to invoke this authority, in part because of the administrative headaches that would be entailed.[23]

INS IMPLEMENTATION OF EXPEDITED REMOVAL

In March 1997, the INS and the Executive Office for Immigration Review (EOIR) published interim regulations implementing many sections of the IIRIRA, including the expedited removal provisions.[24] Further guidance is contained in a March 31, 1997 policy memorandum issued by then INS Deputy Commissioner Chris Sale (Sale Memorandum).[25] While the regulations and policy memorandum to some extent codify and restate the statutory language, they also provide important guidance on some issues relating to expedited removal.

- **The Inspection Process Under Expedited Removal**[26]

A passenger who arrives at a port of entry first has contact with the INS when he or she presents travel documents to the INS officer stationed in an immigration booth. Primary inspection is usually a brief process, at which entry documents are examined and basic questions are asked to determine admissibility. If the "primary" inspector thinks that the documents may not be in order, the inspector has the passenger escorted to a "secondary" inspector, who conducts a more thorough examination of the alien.[27] Many of those who are unable to persuade the secondary inspector of their admissibility to the U.S. may depart voluntarily or be detained for further proceedings.[28] Aliens who are inadmissible because of

INA § 212(a)(6)(C) or INA § 212(a)(7), however, are subject to expedited removal.

A secondary inspector can issue a final order of expedited removal. It is therefore important that an arriving alien understand the significance of the secondary inspection interview. In drafting its regulations, however, the INS rejected proposals by advocates that all arriving aliens be provided with information concerning asylum. In the preamble to the regulations, the INS set forth its position in detail:

To understand the Service position on this issue, one must understand the general inspection process. All persons entering the United States at ports of entry undergo primary inspection. U.S. citizens are exempt from the inspection process, but must nevertheless undergo an examination to determine entitlement to exemption from inspection. In [fiscal year (FY)] 96, the Service conducted more than 475 million primary inspections. During the primary inspection stage, the immigration officer literally has only a few seconds to examine documents, run basic lookout queries, and ask pertinent questions to determine admissibility and issue relevant entry documents. At most land border ports of entry, primary inspection duties are shared with U.S. Customs inspectors, who are cross-designated to perform primary immigration inspections. If there appear to be discrepancies in documents presented or answers given, or if there are any other problems, questions, or suspicions that cannot be resolved within the exceedingly brief period allowed for primary inspection, the person must be referred to a secondary inspection procedure, where a more thorough inquiry may be conducted. In addition, aliens are often referred to secondary inspection for routine matters, such as processing immigration documents and responding to inquiries. While millions of aliens (almost 10 million in FY 96) are referred to secondary inspection each year for many reasons, approximately 90 percent of these aliens are ultimately admitted to the United States in a very short period of time once they have been interviewed and have established their admissibility.

The secondary officer often does not know if an alien is likely to be removed under the expedited removal process until he or she has questioned the alien. Congress, in drafting the expedited removal provisions, chose to include both section 212(a)(6)(C) and 212(a)(7) of the Act as the applicable grounds of inadmissibility. The common perception is that most expedited removal cases will involve obvious fraudulent documents, or aliens arriving with no documents at all. This is not necessarily the type of case that most frequently falls within the provisions of sections 212(a)(6)(C) and (7) of the Act. Section 212(a)(6)(C) of the Act includes "any alien who, by fraud or willfully misrepresenting a material fact, seeks to procure (or has sought to procure or has procured) a visa, other documentation, or admission into the United States or other benefit provided under this Act . . . ," as well as aliens who falsely represent themselves to be citizens of the United States. In addition to the presentation of fraudulent documents, the falsity of which may not be verified until a thorough examination has been conducted, the fraud and misrepresentation referenced in this section may include falsehoods told by the alien concerning his or her admission or other misrepresentations told to Government officials now or in the past.

Section 212(a)(7) of the Act, in addition to covering a lack of valid documents (including expired or incorrect visas or passports), also encompasses the alien "who is not in possession of a valid unexpired immigrant visa." Under immigration law, aliens who cannot establish entitlement to one of the nonimmigrant categories contained in the Act are presumed to be immigrants, and, if not in possession of a valid immigrant visa, are inadmissible under section 212(a)(7) of the Act. The majority of the aliens currently found inadmissible to the United States fall into this category and will now be subject to expedited removal. Again, inadmissibility under this ground often cannot be determined until the secondary inspector has thoroughly questioned the alien.

To fully advise, prior to any secondary questioning, nearly all aliens referred to secondary inspection of the expedited removal procedures and of the possibility of requesting asylum would needlessly delay the millions of aliens who are ultimately found admissible

after secondary questioning. For almost all of these people, asylum, fear of persecution, or fear of return is not an issue.[29]

According to the INS regulations, the secondary inspector must read all of the information contained in INS Form I–867A ("Record of Sworn Statement in Proceedings Under Section 235(b)(1) of the Act") to the alien.[30] The disclosure includes the following paragraph:

> U.S. law provides protection to certain persons who face persecution, harm or torture upon return to their home country. If you fear or have a concern about being removed from the United States or about being sent home, you should tell me so during this interview because you may not have another chance. You will have the opportunity to speak privately and confidentially to another officer about your fear and concern. That officer will determine if you should remain in the United States and not be removed because of that fear.[31]

INS regulations also require the creation of an official file to document expedited removal cases. In addition to reading the information to the alien on Form I–867A, the inspector must record the alien's responses to the inspector's questions on INS Form I–867B ("Jurat for Record of Sworn Statement in Proceedings under Section 235(b)(1) of the Act"), and must obtain the alien's signature on the form.[32] The inspector must advise the alien of the charges against her or him on INS Form I–860 ("Notice and Order of Expedited Removal"), and the alien must be given the opportunity to respond. After obtaining a supervisor's concurrence, which must include a review of the sworn statement and any of the alien's answers and statements,[33] the inspector must serve the alien with Form I–860, thereby ordering her or him removed.[34]

The regulations prohibit INS officers from charging any aliens in the expedited removal process with any additional grounds of inadmissibility other than those in INA § 212(a)(6)(C) or INA § 212(a)(7). If a person appears inadmissible on any other grounds of inadmissibility, he or she must be referred to regular removal proceedings before an IJ under INA § 240.[35]

Even with the INS's efforts to incorporate protections for refugees, the expedited removal process presents some serious problems, and many worry about the system's potential harm to legitimate asylum seekers. Despite pleas from advocates that arriving aliens be given an opportunity to rest before the secondary inspection,[36] the INS usually ushers arriving aliens immediately into the waiting area for secondary inspections.[37] An alien who has relatives or friends in the U.S. is not permitted to telephone them before the interview. Similarly, the alien is not permitted to call a legal services provider.

Problems also exist with regard to language barriers. The INS regulations state that "interpretative assistance" will be used if necessary,[38] but offer no guidance on who may serve as interpreters, or what their legal and ethical obligations, with respect to the information they obtain, may be.[39]

On the positive side, the INS is providing its officers with additional training on the special issues that arise in expedited removal. This instruction includes sensitivity training for its secondary inspectors, to enable them to recognize at least some of the nonverbal indications that a person may have been subjected to persecution.[40] The Sale Memorandum cautions that inspectors "should consider verbal as well as non-verbal cues given by the alien."[41]

• **Withdrawing the Application for Admission**
In its regulations, the INS expressly recognizes that some aliens at ports of entry who would otherwise be subject to expedited removal may be allowed to withdraw their applications for admission to the U.S.[42]

INS inspectors have always had the administrative authority to permit aliens to withdraw their applications for admission, a process that essentially allows an alien to abandon her or his visit to the U.S. and return to the alien's home country.[43] Traditionally, inspectors have allowed such withdrawals to spare the government the time and expense of formal exclusion proceedings. The number of persons who withdraw their applications each year is substantial. In FY 1996, according to the INS, 994,633 aliens withdrew their applications during the inspections process.[44] Only 25,529 aliens continued their cases before an IJ.[45]

With expedited removal, withdrawal of applications has taken on a new importance. Ironically, what previously was a tool of convenience for the government

now may be a crucial safety valve for an alien who otherwise would be subject to expedited removal — and thereby a five-year bar on admissibility to the U.S. In addition, an alien who has been subjected to expedited removal may have that fact come back to haunt her or him, for example, when applying for a visa at a U.S. consulate at a later date.

> *With expedited removal, withdrawal of applications has taken on a new importance. Ironically, what previously was a tool of convenience for the government now may be a crucial safety valve for an alien who otherwise would be subject to expedited removal — and thereby a five-year bar on admissibility to the U.S.*

It is noteworthy, however, that withdrawal of applications for admission is a matter of discretion for the INS; the alien has no inherent right to withdrawal. The regulations allow, but do not require, inspectors to permit withdrawal and then only in situations where the alien intends, and is able, to depart immediately.[46] In the preamble to the March 1997 regulations, the INS noted:

> Permission to withdraw an application for admission is solely at the discretion of the Attorney General and is not a right of the alien, a premise that has been consistently upheld by the BIA.[47] Only the Attorney General may decide whether to pursue removal charges against an alien who has violated the immigration laws. Withdrawal of application for admission is only one of several discretionary options that may be considered by the Service once the facts of the case are known, and so will not automatically be offered to all aliens subject to expedited removal.[48]

In the preamble to the regulations, the INS also provided some clues as to how inspectors should exercise their discretion to allow withdrawal of an admission application. The Service agreed with commenters that "aliens who may be inadvertently or unintentionally in violation of the immigration laws should not be subject to the harsh consequences of a formal removal order."[49] In the Sale Memorandum, the INS added that officers may allow an alien to withdraw her or his application for admission in cases "where a lack of proper documents is the result of inadvertent error, misinformation, or where no fraud was intended (e.g., an expired nonimmigrant visa)."[50]

A liberal policy allowing withdrawals in appropriate cases would comport with congressional intent. Sen. Alan K. Simpson, the chief sponsor of expedited removal, explained that the purpose of the process is to target "aliens who enter without inspection, or with fraudulent documents, and those who board a plane with documents, then dispose of them, and upon entry fraudulently claim asylum."[51]

- **Review of Claims to Permanent Resident, Refugee, or Asylee Status**

The INS regulations provide a process by which inspectors handle claims to lawful permanent resident, refugee, or asylee status. Under the regulations, if an applicant for admission who is subject to expedited removal claims to be a permanent resident, or to have been admitted as a refugee or asylee, the inspector must attempt to verify the claim, through a check of INS systems and other means. In the case of an alien whose status cannot be verified, the alien must be allowed to make a statement, under penalty of perjury, regarding her or his status.[52] The officer must then issue an expedited order of removal and refer the alien to the IJ for review of the order.[53]

In contrast, the regulations provide that if the alien's claim to permanent residence is verified, the examining immigration officer cannot issue an expedited removal order, and instead must determine whether the alien is considered to be making an application for admission. If the alien appears inadmissible, the immigration officer may initiate regular removal proceedings against the alien under INA § 240.[54] Similar provisions apply to aliens whose status as a refugee or asylee is verified.[55]

- **The Credible Fear Interview**

If a secondary inspector encounters an alien in expedited removal who expresses a credible fear of persecution or an intent to apply for asylum, the INS regulations require the officer to stop questioning the alien and to refer her or him for a credible fear interview.[56] The officer must provide the individual with INS Form M–444 ("Information About Credible Fear Interview"). The referral information must delineate: (i) the purpose of the referral and the credible fear interview; (ii) the right to consult with other persons before the interview; (iii) the right to request a review by an IJ of the asylum officer's credible fear determination; and (iv) the consequences of failing to establish a credible fear of persecution.[57]

The regulations require the asylum officer to conduct the credible fear interview in a "nonadversarial manner, separate and apart from the general public."[58] The INS is conducting most credible fear interviews at INS detention facilities near major airports, striking a

middle ground between advocates who urged that the interviews be conducted at INS asylum offices and others, including members of Congress, who argued that the interviews be conducted at the airports themselves.[59] It is the responsibility of the detention or deportation officer to notify the appropriate asylum office when an alien subject to expedited removal requires a credible fear interview, and whether that alien requires an interpreter or other special considerations.[60]

The regulations offer little clarification of the IIRIRA's vague references to "asylum officers." The INS has indicated that it will generally attempt to assign "full-time asylum officers" to credible fear interviews.[61] As some observers have pointed out, however, this could mean a newly trained asylum officer on her or his first day of "full-time" work.[62] The INS initially designated a team of 45 asylum officers to conduct all credible fear interviews. INS officials have stated, however, that eventually the Service plans to involve all asylum officers in the process.

The alien may consult with a person of her or his choosing before the credible fear interview, and may present evidence at the interview. The INS is normally giving aliens 48 hours in which to contact such persons.[63] Also, the Service usually is providing aliens with a list of pro bono legal services, as well as access to a telephone. Echoing the statutory language, however, the regulations specify that such consultation must be at no expense to the government and may not "unreasonably delay" the process.[64] Accordingly, the INS does allow aliens to make telephone calls at its expense and does not provide aliens with petty cash to make the telephone calls.[65]

The person with whom the alien chooses to consult may be present at the interview, and may be permitted, "in the discretion of the asylum officer," to present a statement at the end of the interview.[66] If necessary, the asylum officer must arrange for the services of an interpreter in conducting the interview. The interpreter may not be a representative of the alien's country of nationality.

Language and interpretation issues have presented particular problems at the credible fear stage. As noted below, many advocates believe that inadequate language interpretation may be the biggest problem with the credible fear process to surface so far.[67]

Upon the conclusion of the credible fear interview, the asylum officer must create a written record of her or his decision, including a summary of the material facts as stated by the applicant, any additional facts the officer has relied upon in making the credible fear determination, and a statement of the officer's determination of whether the alien has established a credible fear of persecution.[68] The decision does not become final, however, until it is reviewed by a supervisory asylum officer.

If the alien is found to have a credible fear of persecution, the asylum officer must inform the alien of this decision and issue an INS Form I-862 ("Notice to Appear"), for consideration of the asylum claim in INA § 240 proceedings.[69] If the alien is found not to have a credible fear, the asylum officer must provide the alien with a written notice of the decision and inquire whether the alien wants to have an IJ review the negative decision, using INS Form I-869 ("Record of Negative Credible Fear Finding and Request for Review by Immigration Judge"). If the alien requests such review, the asylum officer must serve her or him with INS Form I-863 ("Notice of Referral to Immigration Judge").[70]

If the IJ agrees with the asylum officer that the alien does not have a credible fear of persecution, the case is returned to the INS for removal of the alien. In contrast, if the IJ finds that the alien has a credible fear, the IJ must vacate the order of the asylum officer. The INS then may initiate INA § 240 removal proceedings, during which time the alien may file an asylum application.[71]

- **Special Guidelines for Unaccompanied Minors**

In August 1997, the INS established special procedures relating to the expedited removal process for persons under the age of 18. These guidelines for minors were set forth in an August 21, 1997 policy memorandum from the INS Office of Programs.[72]

The August 21 memorandum states that, whenever appropriate, the INS should permit unaccompanied minors to withdraw their application for admission rather than placing them in formal removal proceedings. Before permitting a minor to withdraw her or his application for admission, however, the INS inspector must be satisfied either that the minor is capable of understanding the withdrawal process, or that a responsible adult is aware of the actions taken and of the minor's impending return.[73]

These guidelines also state that when deciding whether to permit a minor to withdraw an application for admission, INS officers must try to determine whether the minor has a fear of persecution or of returning to her

or his country. If the minor indicates a fear of persecution or an intention to apply for asylum — or if there is any doubt on those issues, especially in the case of a country with known human rights abuses or where turmoil exists — the minor should be placed in removal proceedings under INA § 240.[74]

The August 21 memorandum provides that if a decision is made to pursue formal removal charges against the unaccompanied minor, normally he or she should be placed in INA § 240 removal proceedings rather than in expedited removal proceedings. Because an alien minor is considered likely to become a public charge, he or she will be charged with being inadmissible under both INA § 212(a)(7)(A)(i)(I) and INA § 212(a)(4) (public charge). Under certain circumstances, however, an unaccompanied minor may be placed in expedited removal proceedings, if he or she has: (i) in the presence of an INS officer, engaged in criminal activity that would qualify as an aggravated felony if committed by an adult; (ii) been convicted or adjudicated delinquent of an aggravated felony within the U.S. or another country, and the inspecting officer has confirmation of that order; or (iii) previously been formally removed, excluded, or deported from the U.S. If an unaccompanied minor is placed in expedited removal proceedings, the removal order must be reviewed and approved by the district director or deputy district director, in addition to the normal supervisory approval required of all expedited removal cases.[75]

- **Application of Expedited Removal to Aliens in the U.S.**

As noted above, the IIRIRA allows the Attorney General, in her or his discretion, to apply expedited removal to EWI aliens who have been present in the U.S. for less than two years. In publishing the current implementing regulations, the INS confirmed that, for the moment, it will not apply expedited removal to such aliens, but may do so in the future. For now, the INS will apply expedited removal only to "arriving aliens," as defined in the regulations.

The Service cautioned, however, that it reserves the right to expand the coverage of expedited removal. The INS emphasized that:

a proposed expansion of the expedited removal procedures may occur at any time and may be driven either by specific situations such as a sudden influx of illegal aliens motivated by political or economic unrest or other events or by a general need to increase the effectiveness of enforcement operations at one or more locations.[76]

DETENTION AND EXPEDITED REMOVAL.[77]

By its very nature, the expedited removal process carries with it additional detention mandates. Most aliens subject to the process face almost continuous detention, even at the credible fear interview stage.

As discussed above, arriving aliens without valid entry documents who claim permanent resident, refugee, or asylee status, but whose claim cannot be verified by the INS inspector, will be ordered removed and then referred to an IJ for review of the expedited removal order. The INS regulations provide that such persons "shall be detained pending review of the expedited removal order," and that parole will be permitted only when it is "required to meet a medical emergency or is necessary for a legitimate law enforcement objective."[78]

Similarly, with regard to aliens referred to a credible fear interview, INA § 235(b)(1)(B)(ii) states that "if the officer determines at the time of the interview that an alien has a credible fear of persecution . . . the alien shall be detained for further consideration of the application for asylum." Aliens who are interviewed by an asylum officer and are found not to have a credible fear of persecution will be ordered removed, subject to a review by a supervisory officer and, if requested by the applicant, a review by an IJ.[79] The law requires that these individuals also be detained pending a final determination of a credible fear of persecution and, if found not to have such fear, until removed.

Taking the cue from the statutory language, the regulations make clear that asylum applicants who arrive without valid documents almost certainly will be detained during the expedited removal process.[80] The regulations specify that an arriving alien whose inadmissibility is being considered under expedited removal or who has been ordered removed may be paroled out of detention only "to meet a medical emergency or [when parole] is necessary for a legitimate law enforcement objective."[81] The same limitation applies while a credible fear determination by an asylum officer is pending.[82]

Arriving aliens who establish a credible fear of persecution and who are placed in INA § 240 removal proceedings are to be detained.[83] The regulations further specify that parole of such aliens may only be considered in accordance with the parole provisions of 8 CFR § 212.5(a). Unfortunately, as one commentator has observed, this parole provision simply incorporates by reference existing parole considerations, without any recognition that more liberal release criteria should apply to asylum applicants who have already demonstrated a "significant possibility" that they will prevail on their claims.[84]

There is a danger that once asylum applicants have been transferred to a detention facility they will remain incarcerated even after they have demonstrated the plausibility of their claims. Attorneys point to the INS's five-year old, but largely dormant, asylum pre-screening officer (APSO) program as an illustration of the problem. The APSO program was established in 1992 as an informal program to interview excludable detainees and identify those with potentially valid asylum claims for possible parole from detention.[85] APSO, however, has not functioned effectively as an informal program because often individual INS offices never schedule screening interviews, or INS district directors never act upon parole recommendations.

The INS is considering a plan to "revitalize" the APSO program. Advocates are encouraging the Service to adopt the presumption contained in the APSO program that arriving aliens who establish a credible fear of persecution in an interview with an asylum officer should not be detained absent specific countervailing factors, such as a likelihood that the applicant poses a security risk or will abscond.[86] The bipartisan Commission on Immigration Reform (Immigration Commission) endorsed this view in June 1997. In a report recommending refugee and asylum policy changes, the Immigration Commission expressed concern about the expedited removal system and its potential for harming legitimate asylum seekers.[87] Moreover, the Immigration Commission noted that detaining asylum seekers who have shown an initial likelihood of eligibility for asylum, by passing the credible fear test, "is not a good use of scarce detention resources." Indeed, the public interest is best served, the Immigration Commission stated, if such individuals are released from detention.[88]

HOW IS EXPEDITED REMOVAL WORKING?

- **INS Statistics**
  Since the implementation of expedited removal on April 1, 1997, the INS has been tracking the system closely. In a series of briefings for attorneys and advocacy organizations over the past few months, INS officials have released statistics and other information about the system.[89]

INS officials have noted that only a tiny fraction of the nearly 500 million persons inspected each year at U.S. ports of entry are being subjected to expedited removal procedures. According to the INS, as of the end of August 1997, 18,273 individuals had been subjected to expedited removal. Earlier in the year, about 1,200 individuals per week were being subjected to expedited removal.[90]

The INS reported in July 1997 that of the cases of persons arriving at the 25 largest land, sea, and air ports of entry involving aliens subject to expedited removal, approximately 5% had been referred by INS inspectors for a credible fear hearing before an asylum officer. Of the cases involving airport arrivals only, about 20% of the aliens subject to expedited removal had been referred for a credible fear hearing. The vast majority (80%) of the total number of cases referred had met the credible fear standard. Overall, there were 400 to 500 credible fear interviews in the first three months of expedited removal.[91] In addition, as of July 1997, about 33% of the persons inadmissible under expedited removal had been permitted to withdraw their applications for admission.

The vast majority of aliens placed in expedited removal are nationals of Mexico. Of the aliens referred for a credible fear interview, the two largest groups have been Chinese and Sri Lankan nationals. Overall, nationals of more than 60 countries have been referred for credible fear interviews. As of July 1997, of those individuals found to have a credible fear, 20% had been released from detention pursuant to the APSO program.

Attorneys and commentators have focused on certain problems in the first six months of the implementation of expedited removal. One of these involves language translation at the credible fear interview. At the interview, according to INS officials, if the asylum officer is fluent in the applicant's native language, he or she will proceed in that language. Otherwise, the INS will use an interpreter from a language services company. The INS has used, among others, AT&T and Berlitz for such purposes.

Another problem is the lack of monitoring of the secondary inspection process. Attorneys have argued that the INS should allow independent organizations to perform such monitoring. The INS continues to insist that it cannot allow attorneys to monitor secondary inspection. The Service, however, is considering an arrangement by which the United Nations High Commissioner for Refugees (UNHCR) may have an official present during secondary inspection.

- **Practice Issues**

The expedited removal system is a radically new approach to INS inspections, and, for this reason, it has presented special challenges to both the Service and practitioners. While the statistics cited above offer an overview of how the system is working, getting a handle on the impact the new procedures are having on individuals going through the system has been difficult, in part because information regarding secondary inspection is scarce. Nevertheless, through information gleaned from the INS, as well as from individuals who have gone through the process, some attorneys have assembled enough material to offer some preliminary insights and practical tips for practitioners representing an alien at a credible fear interview.[92] A summary of this information follows.[93]

With regard to secondary inspections, there have been some accounts of aliens being forced to wait for hours before an inspector can examine them. Some aliens have reported being shackled to a bench for more than 12 hours — often without food.[94] There have also been instances of aliens who are referred to a credible fear interview, but do not receive INS Form M–444 and the required list of legal services.[95] Attorneys report that it is even less likely that such aliens will receive copies of the INS Form I–867A/B statement. In a few cases, the responsible INS detention or deportation officer has neglected to notify the appropriate asylum office that an alien needs a credible fear interview, thus leaving the individual waiting in detention for days or even weeks.

Eighty percent of credible fear interviews are being held at INS detention facilities near five cities: Miami (usually at the Krome detention facility), Los Angeles, San Francisco, New York, and Newark. Sometimes aliens are held for a few days at a local jail before they are transported to the INS detention facility for the interview. Once at the detention facility, an asylum officer will usually conduct an "orientation" with the individual 24 hours after arrival, at which time the officer explains what happens during the credible fear interview. Attorneys should advise their clients to ask for a copy of INS Form I–867A/B if they have not received one.[96] Attorneys should also brief the individual thoroughly before the interview, so that he or she knows what to emphasize at the interview.

There have been instances where attorneys have had problems obtaining access to clients before the credible fear interview. Attorneys frequently have been forced to wait one to three hours before being allowed to see their clients. There have even been reports of detainees at some facilities being forced to choose between visiting with their attorney or eating lunch, because such visits often occur in the middle of the day. Not surprisingly, persons represented by counsel at the credible fear interview stand a much higher chance of receiving a favorable determination.[97]

Credible fear interviews apparently vary widely in scope and detail, depending on the asylum officer conducting the interview. Some officers allow the alien to tell her or his story in narrative fashion and interject with questions where appropriate. Others prefer asking the individual a series of questions. The latter approach may be more common nationwide. At least one attorney feels that while asking "boilerplate" questions may be a way for the INS to ensure quality control of the interviews, the method may not provide enough flexibility to elicit relevant information from the alien.[98] The length of credible fear interviews varies substantially, ranging from 45 minutes in some locations to four hours in others.

Applicants are supposed to receive copies of the asylum officer's airport notes at the credible fear interview. Attorneys report, however, that the asylum officer's airport notes are not always given to applicants. In at least one facility, pro se applicants are never provided with the notes, and they are told that they can only obtain them if an attorney requests them.[99]

The role of the attorney at the interview also varies. Some asylum officers allow attorneys to ask the alien questions at the end of the interview. Others allow the attorney merely to suggest lines of questioning. An attorney representing a person at a credible fear interview should make a closing statement, and try to obtain a copy of the Form I–867A/B and available evidence. Also, attorneys may be able to have a negative credible fear decision changed to a positive decision, and will find it easier to do so before the asylum officer makes the decision formally, rather than after. Attorneys should also counsel clients to ask for IJ review of a negative decision.

By most accounts, perhaps the most serious problem at the credible fear stage is the need for language interpretation for aliens who do not speak English. Poor interpretation is the biggest threat to asylum seekers, one attorney noted, because it has a direct impact on their credibility at the interview.[100] There have been a number of instances where an alien's statement of a

material fact was translated erroneously, and had it not been detected, that error likely would have contributed to a negative credible fear determination. It is fair to assume that in other cases such errors were not detected, and individuals who had a credible fear of persecution were improperly removed.

Finally, attorneys should be particularly vigilant when representing clients at the credible fear stage who are basing their fear of persecution on emerging areas of asylum law. Examples include persons who base their claims on their gender or on being tortured abroad. These areas of the law are still evolving and, as such, represent a challenge to asylum seekers and attorneys, as well as to the INS.[101] Asylum officers conducting credible fear interviews may be less willing to listen to a claim based on these grounds than those founded on the traditional grounds, because many may be seeing such a claim for the first time. While the INS has instructed its officers to be aware that such cases may be presented, attorneys may need to intervene in situations where a claim based on torture or gender is not receiving appropriate consideration.

CONCLUSION

In creating the expedited removal system, Congress handed the INS a significant enforcement tool. The challenge for the Service is to implement the system in a humanitarian and compassionate manner that protects legitimate asylum seekers from being returned to countries where they might be persecuted. The challenge for attorneys is to monitor the implementation of the system carefully, and to bring problems to the attention of the INS and, if necessary, to the courts and Congress.

The future of expedited removal is unclear. Significant changes are unlikely anytime soon, because the program is only a few months old. Changes farther down the road are not out of the question, however. One of the primary supporters of expedited removal in Congress, Sen. Orrin Hatch (R–Utah), pledged in 1996 to revisit expedited removal if the system did not protect persons fleeing persecution.[102]

Several factors could determine the ultimate fate of the system in the coming months. A number of lawsuits brought by, among others, the American Immigration Lawyers Association (AILA) and the American Civil Liberties Union (ACLU), could affect expedited removal. The litigation is challenging alleged harm inflicted by the system on both asylum seekers and on legitimate visa holders. The AILA lawsuit, for example, is challenging the expedited removal proceedings as they are being applied to: (i) nonimmigrant visa holders with facially valid visas; (ii) parolees; iii) juveniles; (iv) lawful permanent residents; (v) U.S. citizens; and (vi) persons otherwise eligible for admission to the U.S.[103] The ACLU litigation is focusing on harm to legitimate asylum seekers.

It remains to be seen whether the plaintiffs in those lawsuits will succeed in striking down portions of the expedited removal system. For the moment, attorneys and advocacy organizations are concentrating on monitoring the implementation of the system, to ensure that the IIRIRA's experiment in enforcement does not become an unforgiving barrier for legitimate travelers, and a nightmare for refugees.

References

1   Illegal Immigration Reform and Immigrant Responsibility Act of 1996 (IIRIRA), Pub. L. No. 104–208, 110 Stat. 3009 (enacted as Division C of the Omnibus Appropriations Act of 1996), *reported on and reproduced in* 73 Interpreter Releases 1317, 1327, 1360 (Oct. 7, 1996).

2   INA § 235(b)(1)(A)(i), as amended by IIRIRA § 302. The INS wrote a new definition of "arriving aliens" for purposes of the IIRIRA. *See* 8 CFR § 1.1(q).

3   The statute carved out one exception from the summary exclusion process. The law provides that an alien who is a native or citizen of a country in the Western Hemisphere with which the U.S. does not have diplomatic relations is exempt from the expedited removal process. In essence, this provides an exception for Cubans. INA § 235(b)(1)(F).

4   INA § 235(b)(1)(B)(iv).

5   INA § 235(b)(1)(B)(v). One commentator has observed that a "significant possibility" should not be read to mean anything more stringent than the "one in 10" test for a well-founded fear of persecution set forth by the U.S. Supreme Court 10 years ago in *INS v. Cardoza-Fonseca*, 480 U.S. 421 (1987). *See* Daniel C. Horne, *Summary Exclusion/ Expedited Removal, in* Introducing the 1996 Immigration Reform Act: AILA's New Law Handbook 30, 34 (R. Patrick Murphy et al. eds., 1996) [hereinafter Horne, AILA Handbook].

6   INA § 235(b)(1)(E). This definition of an asylum officer stops short of requiring that credible fear interviews be conducted by full-fledged asylum officers from the INS's asylum officer corps. If Congress had wanted to require this, it could have said so explicitly. Instead, the statute merely requires the interviewing officers to have training "comparable" to that of asylum officers, and to be supervised by officers with "substantial experience." The law does not define these terms.

7   INA § 235(b)(1)(B)(iii)(I)–(II).

8   The purpose of the credible fear interview is not to hold a complete asylum interview, but rather to determine whether the aliens will be allowed to proceed to an asylum hearing. *See* Horne, AILA Handbook, *supra* note 5, at 34.

9   INA § 235(b)(1)(B)(iii)(III).

10   INA § 235(b)(1)(B)(iii)(IV).

11   INA § 235(b)(1)(B)(ii).

12   INA § 235(b)(1)(C).

13   INA § 242(a)(2)(A).

14   INA § 242(e)(1). For a detailed discussion of judicial review under the IIRIRA, see Lucas Guttentag, *The 1996 Immigration Act: Federal Court Jurisdiction — Statutory Restrictions and Constitutional Rights*, 74 Interpreter Releases 245, 252 (Feb. 10, 1997).

15   INA § 235(b)(1)(D).

16   INA § 242(e)(2).

17   INA § 242(e)(4).

18   INA § 242(e)(5).

19   INA § 242(e)(3)(A)–(B). Any appeal taken from the court's order must be filed within 30 days of the order. INA § 242(e)(C).

20   INA § 242(e)(3)(A)(ii).

21   INA § 242(e)(3)(E).

22   INA § 235(b)(1)(A)(iii).

23   *See* 74 Interpreter Releases 489, 492 (Mar. 24, 1997).

24   62 Fed. Reg. 10,312–95 (Mar. 6, 1997), *reported on and reproduced in* 74 Interpreter Releases 353, 368 (Mar. 10, 1997).

25   Office of the Deputy Commissioner, Memorandum on Implementation of Expedited Removal (Mar. 31, 1997), *reported on and reproduced in* 74 Interpreter Releases 633, 646 (Apr. 21, 1997) [hereinafter Sale Memorandum]. The Sale Memorandum is in the process of being incorporated into Chapter 17 of the INS's Inspector's Field Manual (IFM), which eventually will replace the INS Operations Instructions. Another INS memorandum setting forth information collection responsibilities for ports of entry is reported on and reproduced in 74 Interpreter Releases 747, 765 (May 5, 1997).

26   For a detailed discussion of the expedited removal process, the potential problems that can arise, and suggestions for improving the process, see Philip G. Schrag & Michele R. Pistone, *Asylum Changes and Expedited Removal*, *in* Understanding the 1996 Immigration Act 2–8 (Juan P. Osuna ed., Federal Publications Inc., 1997).

27   *See* Daniel C. Horne & L. Ari Weitzhandler, *Asylum Law After the Illegal Immigration Reform and Immigrant Responsibility Act*, 97–4 Immigration Briefings 13 (Apr. 1997) [hereinafter Horne & Weitzhandler, Immigration Briefings].

28   According to the INS, almost ten million secondary inspections are held annually. All but 900,000 of these inspections result in the immediate admission to the U.S. of the person being inspected. The remaining 900,000 persons return voluntarily or are put into proceedings (which, until expedited removal took effect on April 1, 1997, were always conducted by an IJ). Of the 900,000 persons, 7,000 are not cleared promptly for admission by the secondary inspector. *See* Schrag & Pistone, *supra* note 26, at 2–8.

29   62 Fed. Reg. 10,312, 10,318 (Mar. 6, 1997) (preamble).

30   8 CFR § 235.3(b)(2)(i). INS Form I–867A/B is reproduced as Appendix I in Horne & Weitzhandler, Immigration Briefings, *supra* note 27, at 23–24.

31   INS Form I–867A ("Record of Sworn Statement in Proceedings under Section 235(b)(1) of the Act"), *reproduced in* Horne & Weitzhandler, Immigration Briefings, *supra* note 27, at 23.

32   8 CFR § 235.3(b)(2). The regulations do not indicate what happens if an individual refuses to sign the I–867B.

33   The supervisory review must be carried out at least at the second line supervisor level. 8 CFR § 235(b)(7).

34   8 CFR § 235.3(b)(2).

35   8 CFR § 235.3(b)(3).

36   Schrag & Pistone, *supra* note 26, at 2–9.

37   62 Fed. Reg. 10,312, 10,319 (Mar. 6, 1997) (preamble).

38   8 CFR § 235.3(b)(2)(i).

39   Schrag & Pistone, *supra* note 26, at 2–9.

40   *Id.* at 2–11.

41   Sale Memorandum, *supra* note 25, at 3.

42   The regulations reflect the language of the IIRIRA, which explicitly allows the Attorney General to permit an alien to withdraw the application for admission. *See* INA § 235(a)(4).

43   *See generally* Sam Bernsen, *Withdrawal of Applications for Admission*, 71 Interpreter Releases 441 (Apr. 4, 1994).

44   Immigration and Naturalization Service, U.S. Dep't of Justice, 1996 Statistical Yearbook of the Immigration and Naturalization Service 170 (1997).

45   *Id.*

46   8 CFR § 235.4(a).

47   *See, e.g., Matter of Vargas-Molina*, 13 I&N Dec. 651 (BIA 1971) (an applicant for admission may not withdraw her or his application as a matter of right, without regard to whether the application is made at a land port, and without regard to whether the IJ has entered a decision); *Matter of Gutierrez*, 19 I&N Dec. 562 (BIA 1988) (an IJ may permit an alien in exclusion proceedings to withdraw her or his application for admission, if "justice may best be served" by permitting withdrawal and if the alien possesses both the intent and the means to depart immediately from the U.S.). The BIA also noted in *Gutierrez* that "[i]t was never contemplated that the withdrawal of an application for admission would become a nonstatutory form of 'relief' from excludability which an applicant could apply for after excludability became apparent." *Id.*

48   62 Fed. Reg. 10,312–13 (Mar. 6, 1997).

49   *Id.* at 10,313.

50   Sale Memorandum, *supra* note 25, at 2. *See also* 74 Interpreter Releases 489, 492–93 (Mar. 24, 1997).

51   142 Cong. Rec. S4467 (daily ed. May 1, 1996) (statement of Sen. Simpson), *quoted in* Horne & Weitzhandler, Immigration Briefings, *supra* note 27, at 12.

52   8 CFR § 235.3(b)(5)(i).

53   *Id.*

54   8 CFR § 235.3(b)(5)(ii).

55   In the course of drafting the regulations, the INS received comments pointing out that neither the IIRIRA nor the proposed regulations explicitly provide for review of expedited removal orders of aliens claiming to be U.S. citizens. In response to these comments, the INS noted that each year there are about 35,000 false claims to U.S. citizenship made at ports of entry. Nevertheless, the INS, "[t]o provide an additional level of review and safeguard against a mistaken determination," instituted the same procedures for persons claiming U.S. citizenship as those for persons claiming permanent resident, refugee, or asylee status. 62 Fed. Reg. 10,312, 10,315 (Mar. 6, 1997) (preamble).

56   Note that the INS's March 31 policy memorandum requires inspectors to ask the alien enough follow-up questions to ascertain the general nature of the alien's fear or claim. Sale Memorandum, *supra* note 25, at 3. The memorandum, however, also instructs inspectors to "err on the side of caution and apply the criteria generously, referring to the asylum officer any questionable cases." *Id.*

57   8 CFR § 235.3(b)(4)(i).

58   8 CFR § 208.30(b).

59   Schrag & Pistone, *supra* note 26, at 2–12. In the preamble to the March regulations, the INS notes that in cases where the port of entry is not near a detention facility, it may hold the alien in a local or county jail. 62 Fed. Reg. 10,312, 10,319–20 (Mar. 6, 1997) (preamble).

60   Sale Memorandum, *supra* note 25, at 3. The Sale Memorandum also notes that if there is insufficient detention space at a port of entry, as a "last resort" the alien may be required to wait in Canada or Mexico pending a final determination. *Id.* at 4.

61   62 Fed. Reg. 443, 447 (Jan. 3, 1997) (preamble).

62   Schrag & Pistone, *supra* note 26, at 2–13.

63   62 Fed. Reg. 10,312, 10,320 (Mar. 6, 1997) (preamble).

64   Neither the IIRIRA nor the regulations define what constitutes an "unreasonable delay."

65   62 Fed. Reg. 10,312, 10,320 (Mar. 6, 1997) (preamble).

66   8 CFR § 208.30(b). The regulations provide special procedures for alien stowaways. *Id.*

67   Early on, at least one commentator observed that perhaps the most glaring oversight in the credible fear process is inadequate provision for interpreters. As a result, "Congress has risked making a mockery of a process already fraught with complexities and inconsistencies." Horne, AILA Handbook, *supra* note 5, at 33.

68   8 CFR § 208.30(b).

69   *Id.*

70   *Id.*

71   *Id.*

72   INS, Office of Programs, Memorandum on Unaccompanied Minors Subject to Expedited Removal (HQINS 50/5.12 96Act.054) (Aug. 21, 1997), *reported on and reproduced in* 74 Interpreter Releases 1367, 1377 (Sept. 8, 1997). The contents of the August 21 memorandum will also be incorporated into Chapter 17 of the IFM.

73   *Id.*

74   *Id.*

75   *Id.*

76   62 Fed. Reg. 10,312, 10,314 (Mar. 6, 1997).

77   This section is adapted from Margaret H. Taylor, *Detention and Related Issues, in* Understanding the 1996 Immigration Act 5–1 (Juan P. Osuna ed., Federal Publications Inc., 1997).

78   8 CFR § 235.3(b)(5)(i).

79   8 CFR § 235.3(b)(7).

80   Taylor, *supra* note 77, at 5–3.

81   8 CFR § 235.3(b)(2)(iii). *See also* Sale Memorandum, *supra* note 25, at 3.

82 8 CFR § 235.3(b)(4)(ii).

83 8 CFR § 235.3(c). The preamble to the interim regulation explains that the regulation was amended "to clarify that aliens found to have a credible fear will be subject to the generally applicable detention and parole standards contained in the Act." 62 Fed. Reg. 10,312, 10,320 (Mar. 6, 1997).

84 Taylor, *supra* note 77, at 5–4.

85 *See* 69 Interpreter Releases 503 (Apr. 27, 1992).

86 Taylor, *supra* note 77, at 5–4. Preliminary assessments of the expedited removal system have confirmed the inconsistent application of the APSO program. While in some locations, such as New Jersey, the INS is allowing release under APSO of persons who establish credible fear, in others, the Service is not releasing such persons.

87 The Immigration Commission also questioned the need for expedited removal, because during the last two years, the INS has been able to control asylum abuse at ports of entry. U.S. Commission on Immigration Reform, U.S. Refugee Policy: Taking Leadership 29 (1997), *reported on in* 74 Interpreter Releases 957–58 (June 16, 1997).

88 *Id.*

89 *See, e.g.,* 74 Interpreter Releases 1101 (July 21, 1997).

90 *See also* L.A. Times, July 10, 1997, at A1.

91 In addition, according to Charles Wheeler, an attorney with the Catholic Legal Immigration Network, Inc., in San Francisco, a Freedom of Information Act (FOIA) request revealed that from April 4 to July 2, 1997, 84 IJ reviews of negative credible fear determinations had been requested. The IJs affirmed the asylum officers' determination in 61 cases, and vacated it in 13, with ten cases still pending, as of July 1997. 74 Interpreter Releases 1101–02 (July 21, 1997).

92 Among those who recently expressed concerns about the lack of monitoring of secondary inspection was Sen. Edward M. Kennedy (D–Mass.). In a July 3, 1997 letter to the INS, Sen. Kennedy noted that "[i]t is in the best interests of the INS to show the public that true asylum seekers are not being returned to their countries of persecution or torture, and that the expedited removal process is working effectively." Letter from Sen. Edward M. Kennedy to the Director of the Policy Directives and Instructions Branch, Immigration and Naturalization Service (July 3, 1997) (on file with Immigration Briefings), *reported on in* 74 Interpreter Releases 1101–02 (July 21, 1997). This cannot happen, Sen. Kennedy said, unless independent outside organizations are allowed to ob-

serve the expedited removal process, especially at the secondary inspection stage. *Id.* Another problem Sen. Kennedy identified was that some IJs have not allowed counsel to represent asylum seekers actively on appeal from negative credible fear determinations. Sen. Kennedy urged the INS to amend the regulations to allow representation of asylum seekers at this stage. *Id.*

93 This information was provided in part by attorneys Mary McClenahan, of Newark, New Jersey, and Charles Wheeler, of San Francisco, California, both with the Catholic Legal Immigration Network, Inc., and Carol Wolchok, with the American Bar Association, in Washington, D.C. The authors gratefully acknowledge their assistance.

94 Telephone Interview with Mary McClenahan, Attorney, Catholic Legal Immigration Network (October 17, 1997) [hereinafter McClenahan Interview]. In at least one case, an asylum seeker was shackled to a bench for 24 hours.

95 The INS has translated the M–444 into 13 languages, but attorneys report that only the English version of the form is given to many aliens. *Id.* The legal services list is also only provided in English. *Id.*

96 *Id.*

97 *See* 74 Interpreter Releases 1101, 1103 (July 21, 1997).

98 McClenahan Interview, *supra* note 94.

99 Charles Wheeler & Mary McClenahan, Memorandum to Interested Persons on Credible Fear and Expedited Removal 3 (Oct. 29, 1997) (copy on file with Immigration Briefings).

100 *Id.*

101 *See, e.g.,* Elisa C. Massimino, *Relief From Deportation Under Article 3 of the United Nations Convention Against Torture, in* 2 American Immigration Lawyers Association 1997–98 Immigration and Nationality Handbook (R. Patrick Murphy et al. eds., 1997); Karen Musalo, *The Developing Jurisprudence of Gender-Based Claims, in* 2 American Immigration Lawyers Association 1997–98 Immigration and Nationality Handbook (R. Patrick Murphy et al. eds., 1997).

102 142 Cong. Rec. S11491 (daily ed. Sept. 27, 1996) (statement of Sen. Orrin Hatch).

103 *American Immigration Lawyers Association v. Reno,* No. 97–1229 (EGS) (D.D.C. filed May 30, 1997).

§ 1225. Inspection by immigration officers; expedited removal of inadmissible arriving aliens; referral for hearing

(a) Inspection

(1) Aliens treated as applicants for admission

An alien present in the United States who has not been admitted or who arrives in the United States (whether or not at a designated port of arrival and including an alien who is brought to the United States after having been interdicted in international or United States waters) shall be deemed for purposes of this chapter an applicant for admission.

(2) Stowaways

An arriving alien who is a stowaway is not eligible to apply for admission or to be admitted and shall be ordered removed upon inspection by an immigration officer. Upon such inspection if the alien indicates an intention to apply for asylum under section 1158 of this title or a fear of persecution, the officer shall refer the alien for an interview under subsection (b)(1)(B) of this section. A stowaway may apply for asylum only if the stowaway is found to have a credible fear of persecution under subsection (b)(1)(B) of this section. In no case may a stowaway be considered an applicant for admission or eligible for a hearing under section 1229a of this title.

(3) Inspection

All aliens (including alien crewmen) who are applicants for admission or otherwise seeking admission or readmission to or transit through the United States shall be inspected by immigration officers.

(4) Withdrawal of application for admission

An alien applying for admission may, in the discretion of the Attorney General and at any time, be permitted to withdraw the application for admission and depart immediately from the United States.

(5) Statements

An applicant for admission may be required to state under oath any information sought by an immigration officer regarding the purposes and intentions of the applicant in seeking admission to the United States, including the applicant's intended length of stay and whether the applicant intends to remain permanently or become a United States citizen, and whether the applicant is inadmissible.

(b) Inspection of applicants for admission

(1) Inspection of aliens arriving in the United States and certain other aliens who have not been admitted or paroled

(A) Screening

(i) In general

If an immigration officer determines that an alien (other than an alien described in subparagraph (F)) who is arriving in the United States or is described in clause (iii) is inadmissible under section 1182(a)(6)(C) or 1182(a)(7) of this title, the officer shall order the alien removed from the United States without further hearing or review unless the alien indicates either an intention to apply for asylum under section 1158 of this title or a fear of persecution.

(ii) Claims for asylum

If an immigration officer determines that an alien (other than an alien described in subparagraph (F)) who is arriving in the United States or is described in clause (iii) is inadmissible under section 1182(a)(6)(C) or 1182(a)(7) of this title and the alien indicates either an intention to apply for asylum under section 1158 of this title or a fear of persecution, the officer shall refer the alien for an interview by an asylum officer under subparagraph (B).

(iii) Application to certain other aliens

(I) In general

The Attorney General may apply clauses (i) and (ii) of this subparagraph to any or all aliens described in subclause (II) as designated by the Attorney General. Such designation shall be in the sole and unreviewable discretion of the Attorney General and may be modified at any time.

(II) Aliens described

An alien described in this clause is an alien who is not described in subparagraph (F), who has not been admitted or paroled into the United States, and who has not affirmatively shown, to the satisfaction of an immigration officer, that the alien has been physically present in the United States continuously for the 2–year period immediately prior to the date of the determination of inadmissibility under this subparagraph.

(B) Asylum interviews

(i) Conduct by asylum officers

An asylum officer shall conduct interviews of aliens referred under subparagraph (A)(ii), either at a port of entry or at such other place designated by the Attorney General.

(ii) Referral of certain aliens

If the officer determines at the time of the interview that an alien has a credible fear of persecution (within the meaning of clause (v)), the alien shall be detained for further consideration of the application for asylum.

(iii) Removal without further review if no credible fear of persecution

(I) In general

Subject to subclause (III), if the officer determines that an alien does not have a credible fear of persecution, the officer shall order the alien removed from the United States without further hearing or review.

(II) Record of determination

The officer shall prepare a written record of a determination under subclause (I). Such record shall include a summary of the material facts as stated by the applicant, such additional facts (if any) relied upon by the officer, and the officer's analysis of why, in the light of such facts, the alien has not established a credible fear of persecution. A copy of the officer's interview notes shall be attached to the written summary.

(III) Review of determination

The Attorney General shall provide by regulation and upon the alien's request for prompt review by an immigration judge of a determination under subclause (I) that the alien does not have a credible fear of persecution. Such review shall include an opportunity for the alien to be heard and questioned by the immigration judge, either in person or by telephonic or video connection. Review shall be concluded as expeditiously as possible, to the maximum extent practicable within 24 hours, but in no case later than 7 days after the date of the determination under subclause (I).

(IV) Mandatory detention

Any alien subject to the procedures under this clause shall be detained pending a final determination of credible fear of persecution and, if found not to have such a fear, until removed.

(iv) Information about interviews

The Attorney General shall provide information concerning the asylum interview described in this subparagraph to aliens who may be eligible. An alien who is eligible for such interview may consult with a person or persons of the alien's choosing prior to the interview or any review thereof, according to regulations prescribed by the Attorney General. Such consultation shall be at no expense to the Government and shall not unreasonably delay the process.

(v) Credible fear of persecution defined

For purposes of this subparagraph, the term "credible fear of persecution" means that there is a significant possibility, taking into account the credibility of the statements made by the alien in support of the alien's claim and such other facts as are known to the officer, that the alien could establish eligibility for asylum under section 1158 of this title.

(C) Limitation on administrative review

Except as provided in subparagraph (B)(iii)(III), a removal order entered in accordance with subparagraph (A)(i) or (B)(iii)(I) is not subject to administrative appeal, except that the Attorney General shall provide by regulation for prompt review of such an order under subparagraph (A)(i) against an alien who claims under oath, or as permitted under penalty of perjury under section 1746 of Title 28, after having been warned of the penalties for falsely making such claim under such conditions, to have been lawfully admitted for permanent residence, to have been admitted as a refugee under section 1157 of this title, or to have been granted asylum under section 1158 of this title.

(D) Limit on collateral attacks

In any action brought against an alien under section 1325(a) of this title or section 1326 of this title, the court shall not have jurisdiction to hear any claim attacking the validity of an order of removal entered under subparagraph (A)(i) or (B)(iii).

(E) Asylum officer defined

As used in this paragraph, the term "asylum officer" means an immigration officer who—

(i) has had professional training in country conditions, asylum law, and interview techniques comparable to that provided to full-time adjudicators of applications under section 1158 of this title, and

(ii) is supervised by an officer who meets the condition described in clause (i) and has had substantial experience adjudicating asylum applications.

(F) Exception

Subparagraph (A) shall not apply to an alien who is a native or citizen of a country in the Western Hemisphere with whose government the United States does not have full diplomatic relations and who arrives by aircraft at a port of entry.

(2) Inspection of other aliens

(A) In general

Subject to subparagraphs (B) and (C), in the case of an alien who is an applicant for admission, if the examining immigration officer determines that an alien seeking admission is not clearly and beyond a doubt entitled to be admitted, the alien shall be detained for a proceeding under section 1229a of this title.

(B) Exception

Subparagraph (A) shall not apply to an alien—
   (i) who is a crewman,
   (ii) to whom paragraph (1) applies, or
   (iii) who is a stowaway.

(C) Treatment of aliens arriving from contiguous territory

In the case of an alien described in subparagraph (A) who is arriving on land (whether or not at a designated port of arrival) from a foreign territory contiguous to the United States, the Attorney General may return the alien to that territory pending a proceeding under section 1229a of this title.

(3) Challenge of decision

The decision of the examining immigration officer, if favorable to the admission of any alien, shall be subject to challenge by any other immigration officer and such challenge shall operate to take the alien whose privilege to be admitted is so challenged, before an immigration judge for a proceeding under section 1229a of this title.

(c) Removal of aliens inadmissible on security and related grounds

(1) Removal without further hearing

If an immigration officer or an immigration judge suspects that an arriving alien may be inadmissible under subparagraph (A) (other than clause (ii)), (B), or (C) of section 1182(a)(3) of this title, the officer or judge shall—

   (A) order the alien removed, subject to review under paragraph (2);

   (B) report the order of removal to the Attorney General; and

   (C) not conduct any further inquiry or hearing until ordered by the Attorney General.

(2) Review of order

(A) The Attorney General shall review orders issued under paragraph (1).

(B) If the Attorney General—

(i) is satisfied on the basis of confidential information that the alien is inadmissible under subparagraph (A) (other than clause (ii)), (B), or (C) of section 1182(a)(3) of this title, and

(ii) after consulting with appropriate security agencies of the United States Government, concludes that disclosure of the information would be prejudicial to the public interest, safety, or security,

the Attorney General may order the alien removed without further inquiry or hearing by an immigration judge.

(C) If the Attorney General does not order the removal of the alien under subparagraph (B), the Attorney General shall specify the further inquiry or hearing that shall be conducted in the case.

(3) Submission of statement and information

The alien or the alien's representative may submit a written statement and additional information for consideration by the Attorney General.

(d) Authority relating to inspections

(1) Authority to search conveyances

Immigration officers are authorized to board and search any vessel, aircraft, railway car, or other conveyance or vehicle in which they believe aliens are being brought into the United States.

(2) Authority to order detention and delivery of arriving aliens

Immigration officers are authorized to order an owner, agent, master, commanding officer, person in charge, purser, or consignee of a vessel or aircraft bringing an alien (except an alien crewmember) to the United States—

(A) to detain the alien on the vessel or at the airport of arrival, and

(B) to deliver the alien to an immigration officer for inspection or to a medical officer for examination.

(3) Administration of oath and consideration of evidence

The Attorney General and any immigration officer shall have power to administer oaths and to take and consider evidence of or from any person touching the privilege of any alien or person he believes or suspects to be an alien to enter, reenter, transit through, or reside in the United States or concerning any matter which is material and relevant to the enforcement of this chapter and the administration of the Service.

(4) Subpoena authority

(A) The Attorney General and any immigration officer shall have power to require by subpoena the attendance and testimony of witnesses before immigration officers and the production of books, papers, and documents relating to the privilege of any person to enter, reenter, reside in, or pass through the United States or concerning any matter which is material and relevant to the enforcement of this chapter and the administration of the Service, and to that end may invoke the aid of any court of the United States.

(B) Any United States district court within the jurisdiction of which investigations or inquiries are being conducted by an immigration officer may, in the event of neglect or refusal to respond to a subpoena issued under this paragraph or refusal to testify before an immigration officer, issue an order requiring such persons to appear before an immigration officer, produce books, papers, and documents if demanded, and testify, and any failure to obey such order of the court may be punished by the court as a contempt thereof.

(June 27, 1952, c. 477, Title II, ch. 4, § 235, 66 Stat. 198; Nov. 29, 1990, Pub.L. 101–649, Title VI, § 603(a)(11), 104 Stat. 5083; Apr. 24, 1996, Pub.L. 104–132, Title IV, §§ 422(a), 423(b), 110 Stat. 1270, 1272; Sept. 30, 1996, Pub.L. 104–208, Div. C, Title III, §§ 302(a), 308(d)(5), 371(b)(4), 110 Stat. 3009–579, 3009–619, 3009–645.)

HISTORICAL AND STATUTORY NOTES

Revision Notes and Legislative Reports

1952 Acts. House Report No. 1365 and Conference Report No. 2096, see 1952 U.S. Code Cong. and Adm. News, p. 1653.

1990 Acts. House Report No. 101–723(Parts I and II), House Conference Report No. 101–955, and Statement by President, see 1990 U.S. Code Cong. and Adm. News, p. 6710.

1996 Acts. Senate Report No. 104–179 and House Conference Report No. 104–518, see 1996 U.S. Code Cong. and Adm. News, p. 924.

Amendments

1996 Amendments. Pub.L. 104–208, § 302(a), amended section generally, substituting provisions relating to inspection of aliens, expedited removal of inadmissible arriving aliens, and referral for hearing, including general inspection provisions and inspection of applicants for admission, removal of aliens inadmissible on security and related grounds,

and authority relating to inspections, for provisions relating to inspection by immigration officials, including powers of officers, detention for further inquiry, challenge of favorable decision, temporary exclusion, permanent exclusion by Attorney General, and collateral attacks on orders of exclusion, special exclusion, or deportation.

Pub.L. 104–208, § 371(b)(4), substituted "immigration judges" for "special inquiry officers" and "immigration judge" for "special inquiry officer" wherever appearing.

Subsec. (b). Pub.L. 104–132, § 422(a), which amended subsec. (b) generally, was repealed by section 308(d)(5) of Div. C of Pub.L. 104–208, which provided in part that this chapter was to be applied as if section 422 of Pub.L. 104–132 had never been enacted.

Subsec. (d). Pub.L. 104–132, § 423(b), added subsec. (d).

THE NEW WORLD OF JUDICIAL REVIEW
OF REMOVAL ORDERS

LENNI B. BENSON*

I. CONGRESS LIMITS JUDICIAL REVIEW OF IMMIGRATION PROCEEDINGS

In many respects the changes created by the Illegal Immigration Reform and Immigrant Responsibility Act of 1996 ("IIRIRA") dramatically alter immigration law.[1] The legislation contains major doctrinal alterations such as the attempt to eliminate the "entry doctrine" which would allow the INS to treat "illegal" entrants as if they were first time applicants for admission.[2] Yet perhaps the most important change is the Congressional attempt to eliminate or severely curtail judicial review of immigration decisions. The ability of Congress to insulate administrative decisions from federal court review is an important issue in administrative law, but it is particularly disturbing in the context of the removal of noncitizens because of the impact on the individual's life. Many of the people now statutorily prevented from seeking recourse to the judiciary are long-term lawful permanent residents of the United States. Yet even the newcomer may have his or her life irretrievably affected by the decision of an INS inspector. As this new law is beginning to be implemented, many are critical of the unchecked power

---

* Associate Professor of Law, New York Law School. This article was prepared with the assistance of Lisa Schatz and Martin Bloor, students at New York Law School. The author also wishes to thank Lucas Guttentag, Dan Kesselbrenner, Gerald Neuman, Stephen Yale-Loehr, R. Patrick Murphy, Gary Endelman, Michael Botein, Peter Schuck, Kathleen Sullivan and Steven Clark. The author has assisted in the preparation of amicus briefs on the issue of habeas jurisdiction in several of the cases discussed in this article. This article is adapted from an article which first appeared in the 1997 annual conference proceedings of the American Immigration Lawyer's Association. Copyright © 1997 by the American Immigration Lawyers Association. Portions reprinted with permission from 1997-98 IMMIGRATION AND NATIONALITY LAW Volume II—Advanced Practice 32-59.

1. The Anti-terrorism and Effective Death Penalty Act attempted to eliminate all judicial review for aliens who were deportable due to criminal activity. *See* Antiterrorism and Effective Death Penalty Act of 1996, Pub. L. No. 104-132, 110 Stat. 1214 (1996) [hereinafter AEDPA]. The Illegal Immigration Reform and Immigrant Responsibility Act of 1996 supersedes the provisions of AEDPA. *See* Illegal Immigration Reform and Immigrant Responsibility Act of 1996, Div. C, Omnibus Appropriations Act of 1996 (H.R. 3610), Pub. L. No. 104-208, 110 Stat. 3009 (1996) (corrected in a technical corrections bill, Pub. L. No. 104-302, 110 Stat. 3656 (Oct. 11, 1996)) [hereinafter IIRIRA]. This article is scheduled for publication in the Spring of 1998. There will still be many cases which require careful analysis of the preexisting statute, AEDPA, and the transitional provisions of IIRIRA. As a general rule, these earlier statutes should be scrutinized in any case in which the INS commenced the removal proceeding prior to April 1, 1996. For an excellent discussion of the transitional provisions, *see* Lucas Guttentag, *The 1996 Immigration Act: Federal Court Jurisdiction—Statutory Restrictions and Constitutional Rights*, 74 INTERP. REL. 245-60 (Feb. 10, 1997).

2. *See, e.g.*, Stanley Mailman, *"Admission" and "Unlawful Presence" in the New IIRIRA Lexicon*, 2 IMMIGRATION AND NATIONALITY LAW HANDBOOK 1 (1997-98).

225

Congress appears to have conferred upon the INS.[3] And given the scope and importance of these changes, understanding judicial review of administrative immigration decisions is much like exploring an unknown territory or a "new world."[4] Many of the issues raised by this legislation will require reexamination of fundamental constitutional principals such as the scope and power of Congress to eliminate federal court jurisdiction,[5] the constitutional requirement of judicial review, and the nature of the constitutional guarantee of the writ of habeas corpus.

This article will describe the statutes which create the "new world"of judicial review of removal orders, but it does not answer the pure question of whether or not Congress has the power to eliminate all federal court jurisdiction.[6] The main reason that I do not address this important question is that I believe Congress has not actually eliminated all avenues of review. The forms of review remaining may be less than optimal, but some form of review exists primarily in the form of a writ of habeas corpus. In a šense, habeas corpus is the ultimate escape route out of the statutory preclusions found in IIRIRA. This article will also briefly mention some of the strategies necessary to preserve issues for judicial review and to maximize the likelihood of review. Although administrative appeals are not addressed here, most

---

3. Anthony Lewis has written several articles on the Op-Ed page of the NEW YORK TIMES. *See, e.g.,* Anthony Lewis, *Is This America?*, N.Y. TIMES, Aug.18, 1997, at A19; *Kafka in America*, N.Y. TIMES, Sept. 26, 1997, at A27; *Mr. Smith Tells a Tale*, N.Y. TIMES, Mar. 10, 1997, at A15. Congressman Lamar Smith has responded to Mr. Lewis' critique by blaming the way in which the INS has implemented the statute: "It's not the fault of the laws .... It's the fault of the INS." Anthony Lewis, *A Generous Country*, N.Y. TIMES, Dec. 22, 1997, at A27. Yet the INS has little discretion in many of the situations because Congress has mandated specific exclusions or actions.

4. I put the phrase "new world" in quotes, for in reality, jurisdictional limits are a time-honored tradition in immigration legislation. Congress has a long history of attempting to make the administrative determinations in immigration proceedings "final" and not subject to judicial review. The system of judicial review which allowed for petitions for review to courts of appeal and writs of habeas corpus in other circumstances has only been part of the Immigration and Nationality Act, 8 U.S.C. § 1101 *et seq.* (1997)[hereinafter INA] since 1961. Further, I use the term ironically, for as I will explain, much of what these new statutory preclusions do is return us to early forms of judicial review.

5. *Marbury v. Madison*, 5 U.S. (1 Cranch) 137 (1803), is usually cited for the principle that although Congress may create and enact legislation with the executive, it is for the courts to rule on the constitutional validity of the law. Few may recall that in that famous opinion, Justice Marshall ultimately found that the Supreme Court lacked original jurisdiction to consider the mandamus petition brought against the chief executive. The attacks on judicial review in IIRIRA begin with limits on federal court jurisdiction, and if a court lacks jurisdiction it may not be able to exercise the review function. Of course, it is unclear whether Congress has the ability to eliminate all federal court jurisdiction. The debate is excellently presented in the famous law review article by Henry Hart, *The Power of Congress to Limit the Jurisdiction of Federal Courts: An Exercise in Dialectic,* 66 HARV. L. REV. 1362 (1953). That article was inspired in part by the immigration cases which upheld the ability of Congress to exclude aliens who allegedly posed a national security risk without a hearing. *See* Shaughnessey v. United States *ex rel.* Mezei, 345 U.S. 206 (1953). *See also* United States *ex rel.* Knauff v. Shaughnessey, 338 U. S. 537 (1950).

6. This article will also not address the specific motivation of Congress in limiting judicial review or the history of other Congressional attempts to curtail or eliminate federal court jurisdiction. For example, Congress apparently believed that judicial review was delaying removals. Yet by my estimates fewer than 2 percent of all cases were ever appealed. I discuss these motivations, legislative history, and the volume of appeals, *in* Lenni B. Benson, *Back to the Future: Congress Attacks the Right to Judicial Review of Immigration Proceedings,* 29 CONN. L. REV. 1411, 1439-43 (1997).

cases will be resolved in immigration court proceedings and the subsequent appeal to the Board of Immigration Appeals ("BIA").[7]

II. PETITIONS FOR REVIEW—THE EXPRESS PROVISIONS OF JUDICIAL REVIEW IN THE INA

In adopting the new Immigration and Nationality Act ("INA") section 242, Congress preserved judicial review of final orders of removal with several important exceptions. The statute purports to eliminate judicial review if the case involves certain disfavored classes of removable noncitizens, or where the case arises in a specific procedural context such as expedited removal or an in absentia proceeding. Even where judicial review is generally preserved, the statute attempts to isolate from judicial review certain portions of a final order of removal such as the decision to grant discretionary relief from removal. Notwithstanding these important limitations and exceptions, in the "general case," the noncitizen may obtain judicial review by filing a petition for review in the court of appeals. This preserves much of the prior practice under former section 106. Roughly speaking, just as IIRIRA created a single consolidated removal procedure, the statute eliminates the distinctions between judicial review of exclusion orders and deportation orders.[8]

---

7. Frankly, the appeal to the Board of Immigration Appeals [hereinafter BIA] is now (and really always was) one of the most important stages in an immigration case. *See* 8 C.F.R. § 3.1(b) (defining the appellate jurisdiction of the BIA, as amended in the interim regulations effective Apr. 1, 1997, 62 Fed. Reg. 10311-10295 (Mar. 6, 1997)). (All future citations to the regulations include any relevant interim regulations). BIA review may not be available for noncitizens placed in expedited removal proceedings pursuant to INA § 235, 8 U.S.C. § 1225. These proceedings are discussed in section III.A below. Note that this regulation states that there is no administrative appeal which solely seeks to challenge the length of the grant of voluntary departure. *See* 8 C.F.R. § 3.1(b)(2), (3). The interim regulations relocated the former ban on administrative appeal of an in absentia order formerly found in this section in 8 C.F.R. § 240.53. The proper procedure in an in absentia case is to first file a motion to reopen seeking rescission of the in absentia order of removal. 8 C.F.R. § 3.23(b)(4)(ii). In absentia orders and judicial review are discussed in section III.C. below.

There is an automatic stay prohibiting removal for most aliens pending review of the removal order before the BIA. There is no automatic stay for motions to reopen or reconsider except for motions to rescind in absentia orders under 8 C.F.R. § 3.23. IIRIRA appears to create an exception to the stay of removal pending the initial removal hearing for "arriving aliens" seeking admission from a contiguous territory. *See* INA § 235(b)(2)(C), 8 U.S.C. § 1225(b)(2)(C). The statute contemplates that the alien may wait in that contiguous territory during the administrative adjudication. 8 C.F.R. § 3.4 provides that departure of aliens other than "arriving aliens" is a withdrawal of the appeal. *See* the discussion of the effect of departure in section V.D.2 below.

For more on administrative appeals, *see* "Administrative Review" *in* IRA KURZBAN, KURZBAN'S IMMIGRATION LAW SOURCEBOOK (5th ed. 1995). *See generally,* Theodore Ruthizer, *Administrative Appeals of Immigration Decisions: A Practitioner's Guide,* 88-1 IMMIGRATION BRIEFINGS (Jan. 1988), for a discussion of the variety of administrative appeals available and the special jurisdiction of the agency appellate units.

8. A noncitizen had to file a writ of habeas corpus in federal district court to seek judicial review of an exclusion order. The jurisdictional basis of this writ was expressly found in former INA § 106(a)(10).

A. Review of a Final Order

The petition for review is only of a "final order" of removal.[9] In the general case, the alien may seek judicial review of a final order of removal by filing an appeal called a "petition for review" in the United States circuit court of appeals.[10] The procedure for petitions for review is generally found in the Hobbs Act.[11] The noncitizen is the "petitioner" and the Attorney General becomes the "respondent."[12] The petition for review must be served on the Attorney General and on the officer or employee of the INS in charge of the district in which the final order of removal under new INA § 240 was entered.[13]

A petition for review of an order of removal must contain a copy of the final administrative order—the decision of the BIA. In addition, the petition must identify whether a court has previously upheld the validity of that administrative order, and if so, the petition must identify which court, the date of the court's ruling, and the type of proceeding.[14]

B. Where is the Petition for Review Filed?

IIRIRA altered the prior rules governing the venue for petitions for review. Previously, the noncitizen might file the petition for review in the circuit court of appeals where the immigration proceedings were completed, *or* in the circuit where he maintained a residence.[15] Now a noncitizen's residence is irrelevant. Venue is proper only where the immigration proceedings were completed. In all cases, unless the noncitizen can obtain a change of venue,[16] the INS will be able to select the venue by commencing proceedings in that

---

9. The definition of a final order of removal is not set out in the statute or regulations. There is a partial definition in 8 C.F.R. § 3.39 which concerns finality of orders of removal. But as will be discussed below, if an agency action can be described as outside the scope of a final order of removal, the limitations of INA § 242, 8 U.S.C. § 1252 might not apply. *See* section II.F.

10. INA § 242(b)(2), 8 U.S.C. § 1252(b)(2).

11. 28 U.S.C. §§ 2341-51. The only change that IIRIRA made was to exempt out of the Hobbs Act the provision which allowed the taking of additional evidence, 28 U.S.C. § 2347(c). *See* INA § 242(a)(1), 8 U.S.C. § 1252(a)(1). This section was used to allow the court of appeals to suspend the adjudication of the petition for review where a motion to reopen was pending. Litigants might look to other authority for staying the petition for review such as the All Writs Act, 28 U.S.C. § 1651, or the general ability of appellate courts to order a remand.

12. The terminology can be confusing because in the past, in deportation proceedings the alien was called the "respondent," since she was responding to an order to show cause (OSC) why she should not be removed from the United States. IIRIRA § 239 now refers to a "notice to appear" rather than an order to show cause. The interim regulations retain the practice of referring to the alien in removal proceedings as "respondent." *See* 8 C.F.R. § 3.13 (regarding the charging document) and § 3.15 (regarding the contents of the charging document).

13. IIRIRA § 306(a)(2); amended INA § 242(b)(3)(A), 8 U.S.C. § 1252(b)(3)(A). Service is made on the District Director.

14. IIRIRA § 306(A)(2); amended INA § 242(c), 8 U.S.C. § 1252(c).

15. Former INA § 106(a)(2).

16. The regulations governing change of venue in the immigration court are found in 8 C.F.R. § 3.20(b). The immigration judge may grant a change of venue for good cause upon motion by one of the parties, but only after the other party has notice of the motion and an opportunity to respond. Recent cases discussing judicial review of a denial of change of venue are: *Maldonado-Perez v. INS*, 865 F.2d 328 (D.C. Cir. 1989) (finding no abuse of discretion where alien had two months notice of schedule hearing before

jurisdiction. IIRIRA also provides for increased use of detention,[17] and as the INS has the power to select the detention site, the INS has the power to select the ultimate jurisdiction for the appeal. Again, unless the alien is able to obtain a change of venue at the commencement of the immigration proceeding, detention will increase the ability of the INS to forum shop and choose those circuit courts of appeals where precedent is in the government's favor. The substantive interpretation of the immigration law may vary in significant ways in a variety of federal circuits.[18]

C. When is the Petition for Review Filed?

IIRIRA requires that a petition to review a final order of removal must be filed no later than thirty days after the date of the final order.[19] Note that this is a significant change from the previous rule under the INA, which required that petitions for review to the circuit court of appeals be filed within ninety days of issuance of the BIA's decision (thirty days in the case of an aggravated felon) or sixty days if the administrative order was issued following in absentia proceedings.[20] This change is but one of many aimed at expediting the judicial review process.

In an unusual provision, the statute specifies the briefing schedule for the respondent. The respondent must serve and file the opening brief in connection with the petition for judicial review no later than forty days after the date on which the administrative record is available, and may serve and file a reply brief no later than fourteen days after service of the government's brief.[21] In addition, the court of appeals may not extend these deadlines except when counsel files a motion demonstrating "good cause."[22] If the noncitizen fails to file a brief within the statutorily defined periods, the court shall dismiss the appeal unless a manifest injustice would result.[23] Notably, the new requirements do not impose statutory deadlines on the government's

---

requesting venue change), and *Portillo Barres v. INS*, 856 F.2d 89 (9th Cir. 1988) (finding abuse of discretion where denial of change of venue interfered with right to produce evidence).

17. *See* Margaret Taylor, *The 1996 Immigration Act: Detention and Related Issues*, 74 INTERP. REL. 209 (Feb. 3, 1997).

18. For example, in the past, the circuit courts varied widely in interpreting the term "lawful residence" in INA § 212(c), 8 U.S.C. § 1182(c). Some circuits allowed the client to continue to accrue time toward the seven-year requirement notwithstanding the commencement of proceedings, and other circuits cut off the lawful residence with the service of the OSC. Congress mooted these particular differences by repealing INA § 212(c), 8 U.S.C. § 1282(c) altogether and clarifying the calculation of the residency requirement in new INA § 240A, 8 U.S.C. § 1229b. Obviously new differences between circuit decisions will arise as other aspects of the new law are interpreted.

19. IIRIRA§ 306(a)(2); amended INA § 242(b)(1), 8 U.S.C. § 1252(b)(1).

20. Former INA § 106(a)(1); former INA § 242B(c)(4), 8 U.S.C. § 1252B(c)(4).

21. IIRIRA § 306(a)(2); amended INA § 242(b)(3)(C), 8 U.S.C. § 1252(b)(3)(C).

22. The term "good cause" is not a new concept in general civil procedure. Lawyers might look for analogous terms and case law interpreting the FEDERAL RULES OF CIVIL PROCEDURE.

23. The meaning of "manifest injustice" is not clear except that it appears to set a higher standard than the traditional showing of "good cause."

submission of briefs.[24]

D. *Stay of Removal*

IIRIRA eliminates the automatic stay of removal upon service of a petition for review but still contemplates a court-ordered stay.[25] Prior to IIRIRA, an automatic stay of deportation attached once notice of the filing of a petition for review had been served on the district director of the INS district in which the clerk of the court of appeals was located, except in the case of aggravated felons.[26] As the new law removes the automatic stay in all petitions for review, it is of the utmost necessity to file a request for a stay of the order of removal pending the court's decision on the petition for review. In some cases, the INS may be statutorily barred from executing the order of removal, such as in any case where the "alien's life or freedom would be threatened in that country because of the alien's race, religion, nationality, membership in a particular social group, or political opinion."[27] This is the international law obligation of *non-refoulement,* formerly known as "withholding of deportation."

Given that the issuance of a stay is now discretionary, attorneys should file a memorandum of law listing any statutory bars to removal, explaining the hardship to the alien and the merits of the issues on appeal with any stay request.[28] Although the court of appeals will not lose its jurisdiction to consider the appeal if the noncitizen is removed,[29] there are, of course, other substantial harms to the noncitizen. Further, if the noncitizen ultimately prevails and is successful in reversing the order of removal, the government should bear the expense of returning the noncitizen to the United States.[30]

E. *New Limits on the Standard of Review in Petitions for Review*

1. *Scope*

IIRIRA limits the scope or standard of review in those situations where the INA expressly provides for judicial review.[31] But not all issues of the

---

24. This obvious inequity may result in due process and equal protection challenges to the statutory provisions.

25. IIRIRA § 306(a)(2); amended INA § 242(b)(3)(B), 8 U.S.C. § 1252(b)(3)(B). Judicial review of the denial of stays of removal which might be issued by administrative officers are not discussed here.

26. Former INA § 106(a)(3). Aggravated felons could seek a discretionary stay under the prior law.

27. INA § 241(b)(3), 8 U.S.C. § 1251(b)(3). *Nonrefoulement* or withholding of deportation was formerly found in INA § 243(h), 8 U.S.C. § 1253(h). To qualify for withholding, the alien must establish a "clear probability" of harm. *See* Stevic v. INS, 467 U.S. 407 (1984).

28. *See* De Leon v. INS, No. 97-70127 (9th Cir. May 22, 1997) (detailing procedure for discretionary stays).

29. Under the prior statutory scheme, departure could trigger the loss of jurisdiction. *See* former INA § 106(c).

30. Singh v. Waters, 87 F.3d 346 (9th Cir. 1996) (ordering INS to return alien after unlawful departure, impliedly at INS expense).

31. This article does not discuss judicial review of claims of U.S. nationality or the appropriate standard of review in those cases. *See* INA § 242(b)(5)(B), 8 U.S.C. § 1252(b)(5)(B). *See also* CHARLES

appropriate reviewing standard are addressed in the INA. For example, if an alien is raising a due process or other constitutional challenge, the court of appeals will consider this challenge on a *de novo* basis.[32]

The statute repeats a standard axiom that the courts of appeals shall rule on petitions for review based solely upon the administrative record on which the order of removal is based.[33] But the most important implication of this requirement is that attorneys do everything they can to present a full record for review. If necessary, the attorney should consider filing a motion to reopen to augment the record with additional evidence.

The second change that IIRIRA made was to state that the administrative findings of fact are conclusive unless "any reasonable adjudicator would be compelled to conclude to the contrary."[34] Is this a new tougher standard? I submit that it is simply a new way of saying the same thing Congress wrote in former INA § 106. The language in the former INA § 106 provided "that the Attorney General's findings of fact, if supported by reasonable, substantial, and probative evidence on the record considered as a whole, shall be conclusive." In *Woodby v. INS*, the Supreme Court interpreted this language in the former INA § 106 and found that this language only governed the scope of review and did not alter the requirement that the finding of deportability had to be based on "clear, unequivocal, and convincing evidence."[35] But most interestingly, the *Woodby* decision quotes the legislative history surrounding the adoption of section 106 as establishing that "reasonable, substantial, and probative evidence" meant "where the decision rests upon evidence of such a nature that it cannot be said that a reasonable person might not have reached the conclusion which was reached, the case may not be reversed."[36] So it appears that the new language is

---

GORDON, STANLEY MAILMAN & STEPHEN YALE-LOEHR, 3 IMMIGRATION LAW AND PROCEDURE § 81.12 ("Determination of Claims to American Citizenship") (rev. ed. 1997) [hereinafter GORDON, MAILMAN & YALE-LOEHR].

32. *See, e.g.*, Anwar v. INS, 107 F.3d 339 (5th Cir. 1997) (granting *de novo* review of due process allegation and retention of jurisdiction to consider constitutional questions notwithstanding jurisdictional bar in AEDPA).

33. INA § 242(b)(4)(A), 8 U.S.C. § 1252(b)(4)(A). As noted previously, IIRIRA specifically bars the courts of appeals from taking additional evidence pursuant to 28 U.S.C. § 2347(c). This statutory provisions had been used by courts of appeals to remand to the INS for consideration of additional evidence. Litigants will have to find alternative statutory authority to seek remand for additional evidence. Perhaps the All Writs Act, 28 U.S.C. § 1651, could be used to stay the petition for review when a remand is necessary in the interest of justice or otherwise necessitated by due process. *See* Michael v. INS, 48 F.3d 657 (2d Cir. 1996) (pre-IIRIRA case granting a stay pending BIA adjudication of a motion to reopen).

34. INA § 242(b)(4)(B), 8 U.S.C. § 1252(b)(4)(B). The reason that Congress must expressly state the scope of review is that where the INA is silent, the provisions of review in the Administrative Procedure Act, 5 U.S.C. § 703 [hereinafter APA] apply. Such was the result in *Wong Yang Sung v. McGrath*, 339 U.S. 33 (1950), until Congress expressly exempted deportation proceedings from the APA.

35. Woodby v. INS, 385 U.S. 276 (1966). Note that the *Woodby* court set this standard notwithstanding the former statute INA § 242(b)(4), 8 U.S.C. § 1252(b)(4), which provided that no decision of deportability shall be valid unless it is based upon reasonable, substantial, and probative evidence. This is the same standard of deportability under the new INA § 240(c)(3)(A), 8 U.S.C. § 1230(c)(3)(A). Therefore the *Woodby* standard of clear, unequivocal, and convincing evidence should remain the ultimate burden of proof. If *Woodby* is read as a constitutional decision then the burden could not be altered by Congress.

36. *Woodby*, 385 U.S. at 284.

simply a return to what Congress thought they had said in 1961 with the adoption of former INA § 106.

The standard of review for decisions concerning admission is phrased differently. IIRIRA provides that a decision that an alien is not eligible for admission to the United States is conclusive unless "manifestly contrary to law."[37] Perhaps a decision could be manifestly contrary to law if it was not supported by "some evidence."[38] Alternatively, if the decision is wrong as a matter of law, it is also "manifestly contrary to law." This phrase was also used by the Supreme Court in *INS v. Elias-Zacharias*,[39] and yet it did not apparently alter the standard of review applied in lower court cases following this decision. Congress may have intended a more deferential standard of review, but in essence, "manifestly contrary to law" may be no different than the standard of review previously used.

The appropriate standard of review for issues of law is *de novo* review. The leading case in administrative law is *Chevron U.S.A., Inc. v. Natural Resources Defense Council*,[40] where the Supreme Court required that reviewing courts give great deference to agency interpretation of the statutes the agency implements. But deference does not mean that courts fail to exercise *de novo* review. Even after *Chevron*, the Supreme Court has refused to defer to an erroneous INS interpretation of its own statutes.[41]

2. Discretionary Relief

In one of the most important changes, INA § 242 specifically attempts to preclude judicial review of any discretionary decision by the Attorney General except for the grant of asylum.[42] Although no formal statistics are available, my own calculations establish that the vast majority of immigration cases involved review of a discretionary form of relief.[43]

The statute provides that no court shall have jurisdiction to review "any judgment regarding the granting of relief under INA sections 212(h), 212(i), 240A, 240B, or 245."[44] The petition for review may still seek review of

---

37. INA § 242(b)(4)(C), 8 U.S.C. § 1252(b)(4)(C). If the case concerns asylum as relief the statute provides that the decision on asylum shall be conclusive unless it is both manifestly contrary to law and an abuse of discretion. *See* INA § 242(b)(4)(D), 8 U.S.C. § 1252(b)(4)(D).

38. It must be noted that some early immigration cases upheld exclusion orders where "any evidence" supported the decision. *See* Gerald L. Neuman, *The Constitutional Requirement of "Some Evidence*," 25 SAN DIEGO L. REV. 633, 637-41 (1988) (discussing these cases).

39. 502 U.S. 478 (1992).

40. 467 U.S. 837 (1984).

41. INS v. Cardozo-Fonseca, 480 U.S. 421 (1987).

42. INA § 242(a)(2)(B)(ii), 8 U.S.C. § 1252(a)(2)(B)(ii). As previously mentioned, there are specific limits on judicial review in the asylum context found in INA § 208, 8 U.S.C. § 1158 itself.

43. *See* Benson, *supra* note 6, at 1439-43.

44. Amended INA § 242(a)(2)(B)(i), 8 U.S.C. § 1252(a)(2)(B)(i). Outside of the context of a petition for review of a final order of removal, it may be that some of these forms of discretionary relief might still be subject to review in other administrative contexts. But as was discussed above in considering the example adjustment of status before the District Director, some of the relief and waiver sections carry their own independent prohibitions on judicial review.

statutory eligibility for such relief, if not review of the aspect of the decision committed to the discretion of the Attorney General. For example, consider cancellation of removal in INA § 240A. The applicant for cancellation must establish that she meets the statutory criteria for cancellation. One of the criteria is continuous residence for ten years. This is a legal determination. This interpretation which distinguishes between statutory eligibility and discretionary action was affirmed in *Kalaw v. INS*.[45] Another element is "exceptional and extremely unusual hardship" to a relative upon removal. Unfortunately, the court in *Kalaw* held that the determination of whether the alien has met her burden of proving hardship is a discretionary determination and thus, is unreviewable.[46] In my view, the standard of "exceptional and extreme hardship," is a legal issue, although it is one delegated to the Attorney General.[47] The statute says that the finding of "hardship" should be "in the opinion of the Attorney General." But it does not say "in the discretion of the Attorney General," and therefore, when the BIA is rendering an opinion as to hardship, it is defining a legal term. The agency's interpretation of the statutory criteria should remain reviewable.[48]

Further, when Congress uses different language in different parts of the statute, courts should view these differences as deliberate. If you compare INA § 242(a)(2)(B)(ii) with other provisions of the INA, you will find that where Congress wanted to preclude all review, they specifically said so. For example, in section 212(d)(12)(a), Congress precluded review of "a decision of the Attorney General to grant or deny a wavier under this paragraph." This language is much stronger than that found in section 242(a)(2)(B)(ii). Thus, if Congress intended to preclude all review, including statutory eligibility, it should have just done so with stronger language, as it had in other provisions of the Act.[49]

Unfortunately, although review of the statutory eligibility may be obtained, the review may be but an academic exercise. The immigration judge or the BIA may render decisions that simply rely on a denial of relief as an exercise of discretion and assume the noncitizen established statutory eligibility.[50] Moreover, if the alien were to convince a court that she met the

---

45. *See* 133 F.3d 1147 (9th Cir. 1997). *Kalaw* is a case decided under the transitional rules and interprets the former INA § 244 which concerned "suspension of deportation" not the new, similar form of relief found in new INA § 240A, 8 U.S.C. § 1229b(a), "Cancellation of Removal." The petitioners in *Kalaw* have filed a motion for rehearing.

46. *Kalaw*, 133 F.3d 1147 (9th Cir. 1997).

47. The statute specifically states: "that the alien has established, in the opinion of the Attorney General, that deportation would result in an extreme and exceptional hardship . . . ." INA § 240A(b)(1)(D), 8 U.S.C. § 1229b(b)(1)(D).

48. As the statute specifically reserves the finding of "hardship" to the "opinion" of the Attorney General, the standard of review would obviously be extremely deferential but that does not insulate it from all review. *But cf.* INA § 208(b)(2)(D), 8 U.S.C. § 1158(b)(2)(D) (stating that "there shall be no judicial review" of a determination of the Attorney General that a noncitizen is removable for "terrorist activity").

49. *See* STEPHEN LEGOMSKY, IMMIGRATION AND REFUGEE LAW AND POLICY 623 (1997).

50. The INS might even deny cases without determining whether the threshold statutory requirements were met. *See* Rios-Pineda v. INS, 471 U.S. 444, 449 (1985).

statutory elements, the court would simply remand, leaving the issue of discretion to the BIA.

Another argument to preserve judicial review in this context may be made based on the use of the phrase "granting of relief" in section 242(a)(2)(B)(i). This phrase might be construed to allow judicial review where the petitioner is *denied* relief.[51] This construction could be read as a statutory codification of the practice that existed under the former section 106, where the alien could appeal the denial of relief, but the government was bound by the grant of relief by the BIA.[52]

F. *Defining the Scope of a Final Order*

Some matters, such as the appeal of a denial of a visa petition, have traditionally been interpreted as outside the scope of a deportation or exclusion hearing, and thus might also continue to be outside the scope of a removal hearing.[53] In IIRIRA, Congress included several subsections which are designed to prevent preemptive judicial review,[54] to combine all of the issues for review into a single case,[55] and to foreclose other avenues of review.[56] Whether these subsections will be effective in reaching those goals will certainly be a matter of future litigation.

---

51.   Lucas Guttentag makes this argument in *Federal Court Jurisdiction After the 1996 Act: Statutory Restrictions and Constitutional Rights, supra* note 1.

52.   The government could seek to overturn the BIA decision by *de novo* review before the Attorney General. *See* 8 C.F.R. § 3.1(h)(iii). The most recent example of this type of review is found in the Attorney General's reversal of the BIA in *Matter of Soriano*, BIA Int. Dec. 3289 (1996) (*see* Op. Att'y Gen. Feb. 21, 1997).

53.   The leading case is *Cheng Fan Kwok v. INS*, 392 U.S. 206 (1968). *See* further discussion in section IV.

54.   INA § 242(b)(9), 8 U.S.C. § 1252(b)(9) provides:

Consolidation of issues for judicial review. Judicial review of all questions of law and fact, including interpretation and application of constitutional and statutory provisions, arising from any action taken or proceeding brought to remove an alien from the United States under this title shall be available only in judicial review of a final order under this section.

This section appears to be designed to prevent aliens from seeking declaratory judgments or injunctions in advance of removal proceedings. *See, e.g.,* Massieu v. Reno, 91 F.3d 416 (3d Cir. 1996) (finding that former INA § 106 precluded the district court, in advance of the deportation hearing, from declaring a ground of deportability unconstitutional because the statute contemplated only review from final orders of deportation). *See also* American-Arab Anti-Discrimination Committee v. Reno, 119 F.3d 1367, 1373 (9th Cir. 1997) (discussing the relationship between sections 242(b)(9), 242(g), and 242(f) and preserving jurisdiction to hear constitutional challenge).

55.   INA § 242(b)(6), 8 U.S.C. § 1252(b)(6) provides:

Consolidation with review of motions to reopen or reconsider—When a petitioner seeks review of an order under this section, any review sought of a motion to reopen or reconsider the order shall be consolidated with the review of the order.

See the discussion of this type of consolidation in the next paragraph of the accompanying text.

56.   INA § 242(g), 8 U.S.C. § 1252(g) provides:

Except as provided in this section and notwithstanding any other provision of law, no court shall have jurisdiction to hear any cause or claim by or on behalf of any alien arising from the decision or action by the Attorney General to commence proceedings, adjudicate cases, or execute removal orders against any alien under this Act.

The consolidation provision in section 242(b)(6) is aimed at the situation where a noncitizen is seeking not only judicial review of the final order, but additionally wishes to pursue a motion to reopen. In 1995 the U.S. Supreme Court, interpreting the former INA § 106, concluded that the filing of a motion to reopen did not affect the finality of the decision of the BIA.[57] Consequently, the Court ruled that the time period for the petition for review was not tolled by the filing of a motion to reopen or reconsider.[58] IIRIRA appears to follow the same approach and is similar enough to the former section 106 that attorneys should not assume that the thirty-day period to file the petition for review is tolled by any other application or filing. Therefore, the petition for review should be filed within thirty days even if the noncitizen may also be filing a motion to reopen with the BIA.

This interpretation means that the noncitizen might have one petition for review appealing the order of removal, and then a second petition seeking review of the denial of a motion to reopen or reconsider. The statute seeks to avoid that inefficient result by ordering consolidation. Ideally, the statute contemplates review of both the order and any motions to reconsider or reopen at the same time.[59] But the ideal may be impossible to achieve in all cases. The statute now allows the filing of a motion to reopen within 90 days of the final order. There are possible exceptions to the 90-day limit such as the exception allowing an application of political asylum due to changed country conditions.[60] Theoretically, the court of appeals might have ruled on the petition of review by the time the motion to reopen is filed. In that situation, if the BIA denied the motion to reopen, the noncitizen should file a second petition for review seeking review of that denial, which is a separate final order. The government will undoubtedly oppose the second petition for review, but to deny review when the statute and regulations grant express authority to file the motion to reopen would be to deny the express grant of statutory review in INA § 242 of all final orders.[61]

The more dramatic provisions, popularly labeled the "catch-all" subsections, are found in sections 242(b)(9) and 242(g). These subsections aim at eliminating judicial review outside the scheme of section 242 and its express provisions. The scope of the preclusive effect of these subsections is analyzed below, following a discussion of why noncitizens have been able to use the

---

57. Stone v. INS, 514 U.S. 386 (1995).
58. *Id.*
59. *See* INA § 242(b)(6), 8 U.S.C. § 1252(b)(6). A similar consolidation clause also appeared in the former INA § 106. *See* Akrap v. INS, 966 F.2d 267 (7th Cir. 1992) (holding that the former provision does not remove the ability to file a petition for review of a final order denying the motion to reopen).
60. INA § 208, 8 U.S.C. § 1158. *See also* 8 C.F.R. § 3.2 (regulation concerning reopening before the BIA) and § 3.23 (regulation concerning reopening before the immigration judge).
61. If the noncitizen was ultimately found to have been foreclosed from a petition for review on her motion to reopen, the alien may seek judicial review in habeas corpus proceedings under 28 U.S.C. § 2241. *See* the discussion of habeas jurisdiction which follows in section V. *See, e.g.,* Chow v. INS, 113 F.3d 659 (7th Cir. 1997) (finding authority in IIRIRA that denials of motions to reopen are final orders usually subject to judicial review).

Administrative Procedure Act ("APA") and other grants of federal jurisdiction to review actions of the INS.

III.   THE EXPRESS LIMITATIONS ON JUDICIAL REVIEW IN THE INA

For several disfavored groups, Congress eliminates the express right of judicial review under the INA. The new statute expressly prohibits judicial review of (1) expedited removal orders[62] (except for habeas corpus petitions by aliens asserting lawful permanent resident status);[63] (2) denials from certain forms of discretionary relief;[64] (3) orders of removal against certain criminal aliens;[65] and (4) medical certification.[66] This section will explore some of these express prohibitions and analyze the scope of the preclusion. Yet, removing the express grant of judicial review under the INA does not necessarily eliminate all jurisdiction to review the agency action. In section IV, this article will explore the forms of jurisdiction which might remain notwithstanding the limits found in section 242.

A.   *Expedited Removal*

Congress has enacted an expedited removal process for aliens arriving in the United States where an immigration officer believes they are inadmissible under INA § 212(a)(6) or (7).[67] Therefore, an INS officer at the port of entry has unrestricted authority to order an alien removed if the officer determines that the alien lacks documentation, does not have the proper documentation, or has made a misrepresentation in attempting to enter the United States. Only three classes of aliens may derail the expedited procedure: lawful permanent residents, aliens who hold refugee or asylee status, and those who convince the inspector that they intend to apply for asylum or indicate a credible fear of persecution. Additionally, people who make a claim to citizenship are given limited administrative review.[68]

---

62.   INA § 235(b)(1), 8 U.S.C. § 1225(b)(1). Congress has also allowed the INS to invoke expedited removal procedures in cases where the alien entered without inspection within the last two years immediately prior to the commencement of removal proceedings. In essence, this change is seeking to overcome the traditional entry doctrine. *See* Mailman, *supra* note 2.63.

63.   INA § 242(e)(2), 8 U.S.C. § 1252(e)(2). Apparently, U.S. citizens could also use this habeas petition to challenge alienage.

64.   INA § 242(a)(2)(B), 8 U.S.C. § 1252(a)(2)(B). *See* discussion in section III.D.

65.   INA § 242(a)(2)(C), 8 U.S.C. § 1252(a)(2)(C).

66.   INA § 242(a)(3), 8 U.S.C. § 1252(a)(3), referencing INA § 240(c)(1)(B), 8 U.S.C. § 1252(c)(1)(B).

67.   Amended INA § 235(b)(1)(A), 8 U.S.C. § 1225(b)(1)(A). If an alien is removed under the expedited removal process, the alien is barred from reentering the United States for five years. *See* INA § 212(a)(9)(A)(i), 8 U.S.C. § 1182(a)(9)(A)(i). *See also* Michele Pistone & Phil Schrag, *The 1996 Act: Asylum and Expedited Removal—What the INS Should Do*, 73 INTERP. REL. 1565-80 (Nov. 11, 1996). *See also* Philip G. Schrag & Michele R. Pistone, *The New Asylum Rule: Not Yet a Model of Fair Procedure*, 11 GEO. IMMIGR. L.J. 267 (1997).

68.   Under the regulations, a person making a claim of U.S. citizenship which is not verifiable by the admission officer will be referred to an immigration judge for a review of the expedited removal order. There is no further administrative review of the immigration judge determination that the person is not a citizen. People who wish to challenge the INS determination of citizenship in an expedited removal proceeding should file in federal district court using the provisions of the Declaratory Judgment Act, 28

For the first two classes, lawful permanent residents and asylee or refugees, the statute contains two separate provisions which appear to take the case out of the expedited process. First, in INA § 235, the statute provides that the Attorney General may design regulations which will allow those aliens who claim lawful permanent resident, asylee, or refugee status to also have some administrative review of the expedited removal.[69] The INS has proposed that in these cases where the INS database does not verify the claim to such status, the alien will be given only review of the expedited removal before an immigration judge.[70] If the INS can verify the claim to lawful permanent resident, asylee, or refugee status, the admission officer may admit the alien or refer the alien for a regular removal hearing under section 240.[71]

If the immigration judge does not find that the alien was previously admitted as a lawful permanent resident, INA § 242(e)(4)(2) provides that lawful permanent residents may also file a special habeas petition in federal district court.[72] In this habeas petition, the alien must establish her status as a lawful permanent resident. If the federal district court agrees that she holds that permanent resident status, she is entitled to further administrative review as described in INA § 235. The lawful permanent resident appears to be entitled to a remand for a full hearing under INA § 240.[73]

U.S.C. § 2201, *et seq.*, and habeas corpus jurisdiction under 28 U.S.C. § 2241. Prior to IIRIRA, INA § 360, 8 U.S.C. § 1503 had not permitted a declaratory judgment challenge if the issue of citizenship arose in connection with "any exclusion proceeding." In a "housekeeping" provision of IIRIRA directed at conforming the new term of "removal," Congress amended INA § 360 to refer to "removal" proceedings. INA § 360 does not refer to "expedited removal." Congress appears to have failed to realize that citizenship claims might be made in expedited removal proceedings. On its face, the limits of INA § 360 do not apply. The absence of discussion of citizenship claims in INA § 235, 8 U.S.C. § 1225 might be a basis to argue that citizenship claims must be heard in regular INA § 240, 8 U.S.C. § 1230 hearings. However, the INS disagrees and the interim regulations provide for an extraordinarily streamlined administrative process with review only before an immigration judge. *See* 8 C.F.R. § 235.3(b)(5)(iv). Further, section 360 seems to be specifically contradicted in INA § 242(b)(5), 8 U.S.C. § 1252(b)(5), which provides for judicial review of citizenship claims in the court of appeals, and if a fact finding hearing is required, for remand to the federal district court. *See* INA § 242(b)(5)(B), 8 U.S.C. § 1252(b)(5)(B). As harsh as it may seem, in 1905 the Supreme Court ruled that Congress could bar judicial review of claims of citizenship made in an exclusion proceeding. *See* United States v. Ju Toy, 198 U.S. 253 (1905). *Cf.* Ng Fung Ho v. White, 259 U.S. 276 (1922) (finding judicial hearing required for persons making a citizenship claim inside the United States). For excellent material on citizenship claims, see Gary Endelman, *How to Prevent Loss of Citizenship*, 89-11 & 89-12, IMMIGRATION BRIEFINGS (1989).

69. INA § 235(b)(1)(C), 8 U.S.C. § 1225(b)(1)(C).
70. *See* 8 C.F.R. § 235.3(b)(5)(i) and (iv).
71. *See* 8 C.F.R. § 235.3(b)(5)(ii) and (iii).
72. INA § 242(e)(2), 8 U.S.C. § 1252(e)(2). This section provides that the habeas proceeding is limited to the following questions: (A) whether the petitioner is an alien, (B) whether the petitioner was ordered removed under [INA § 235], and (C) whether the petitioner can prove by a preponderance of the evidence that the petitioner is an alien lawfully admitted for permanent residence and is entitled to such further inquiry as prescribed by the Attorney General pursuant to INA § 235(b)(1)(C), 8 U.S.C. § 1225(b)(1)(C). But in reading this section with INA § 242(e)(4), 8 U.S.C. § 1252(e)(4), it may be that asylees and refugees may also use the habeas procedure and that all three classes are entitled to a remand for a full removal hearing under INA § 240 rather than only a form of administrative review.
73. INA § 242(e)(4), 8 U.S.C. § 1252(e)(4). There is a contradiction in the statute which in INA § 242(e)(2), 8 U.S.C. § 1252(e)(2) says the lawful permanent resident is entitled to judicial review of his or her lawful status, but INA § 242(e)(4), 8 U.S.C. § 1252(e)(4) says that lawful permanent residents, asylees and refugees are limited to a remand for full removal hearings under INA § 240, 8 U.S.C. § 1229a.

In the case of an alien who indicates an intention to apply for asylum, the inspector refers the case to an asylum officer for an interview.[74] That officer must determine if the alien has presented a "credible fear of persecution."[75] If the asylum officer agrees that the claim is credible, the alien will then be entitled to pursue her claim for asylum through the regular removal procedures. If the asylum officer rejects the claim of persecution, the alien is given a chance to have an immigration judge review her claim.[76] Only if the immigration judge finds the claim credible will the alien be referred for a regular removal hearing.[77] There is no appeal to the BIA from the immigration judge's review of credible fear, but an alien could potentially seek habeas review as discussed below.

Congress has clearly tried to insulate the expedited removal provisions from judicial review. First, the statute establishes a scheme that would limit judicial review of the statute and regulations within the first sixty days of implementation.[78] The statute also tries to bar injunctions, declaratory or equitable relief, and the use of class actions to challenge the validity of the law.[79] The statute does not expressly bar the use of the writ of habeas corpus under 28 U.S.C. § 2241. Although it may be difficult to get access to the client and to file a writ of habeas corpus before the alien is summarily removed, it may be that this avenue of judicial review remains open.[80]

A habeas challenge to an order of expedited removal was brought in *Li v. Eddy*.[81] Meng Li, a Chinese businesswoman, was placed in expedited removal when the admission officer challenged her facially valid business visitor visa and ordered her removed for using a fraudulent document under section 212(a)(6). It appears that the admission officer saw a record in an INS

---

74. *See* 8 C.F.R. § 235.3(b)(4). The admission officer must refer the alien for asylum officer interview. The alien may be detained pending the interview by the asylum officer but parole is possible. *Id.*

75. INA § 235(b)(1)(B)(v), 8 U.S.C. § 1225(b)(1)(B)(v) defines "credible fear of persecution" as a

significant possibility, taking into account the credibility of the statements made by the alien in support of the alien's claim and such other facts as are known to the officer, that the alien could establish eligibility for asylum under section [208] of this title.

76. INA§ 235(b)(1)(B)(iii)(III), 8 U.S.C. § 1225(b)(1)(B)(iii)(III). The immigration judge review may take place in person, by telephone, or by video conference. *See also* 8 C.F.R. § 3.25(c).

77. *See* 8 C.F.R. § 208.30(f)(2). Note that stowaways are treated differently and their credible claim would be filed immediately before the reviewing immigration judge. 8 C.F.R. § 208.30(f)(3).

78. INA § 242(e)(3)(B), 8 U.S.C. § 1252(e)(3)(B). AILA and the ACLU have filed a suit in the D.C. Circuit Court of Appeals. AILA v. Reno, 1997 WL 161944 (D.D.C. Mar. 31, 1997) (challenging expedited removal generally); Wood v. Reno, No. 97-CV001229, (D.D.C. Mar. 27, 1997) (challenging the application of expedited removal to those persons with facially valid visas, with grants of parole and others who might have exemptions from normal visa requirements). *See also* Liberians United v. Reno, No. 97-CV001237 (D.D.C. Mar. 1997) (challenging expedited removal as it applies to asylum seekers).

79. INA § 242(e)(1), 8 U.S.C. § 1252(e)(1).

80. Perhaps the airlines, who will be forced to bear the cost of removing the noncitizens, will file the writ of habeas corpus on behalf of the noncitizens. There is precedent for the involvement of transportation companies. *See* U.S. Lines v. Watkins, 170 F.2d 998 (2d Cir. 1948).

81. 1997 U.S. Dist. LEXIS 14431 (D. Alaska 1997). This case is on appeal to the Ninth Circuit. Margaret Stock, Ms. Li's attorney, was able to overcome the difficulty of gaining access to Ms. Li in time to file the habeas petition because due to a misinterpretation, the INS thought that she was applying for asylum and she was detained in a prison in the city of Anchorage.

computer that reflected that a U.S. employer had filed a nonimmigrant H-1B petition on Ms. Li's behalf which would have authorized her to work in the United States. Ms. Li had not accepted the U.S. employment and was seeking entry as a business visitor on behalf of her employer in China. The admission inspector did not believe her and must have thought she was seeking to avoid obtaining the H1-B visa stamp.[82]

The district court denied the writ of habeas corpus finding that section 242(e) eliminated the court's jurisdiction. The district court found that the provisions for habeas corpus in INA § 235(e)(2) are specific and control over 28 U.S.C. § 2241, thus severely limiting the scope of review in habeas. Meng Li has appealed to the Ninth Circuit Court of Appeals. The government takes the position that both *United States ex rel. Knauff v. Shaughnessey*[83] and *Shaughnessey v. United States ex rel. Mezei*[84] establish that noncitizens who have not yet been admitted are not entitled to judicial review. Although *Knauff* held that a non-citizen at the border had no right to review the government's denial of entry, her challenge to the procedures was still allowed to be heard and the case can be read as requiring that the INS, at minimum, provide the applicant for admission the procedures which Congress had prescribed.[85] Historically, an excluded non-citizen was able to challenge her detention in habeas corpus.[86]

Ms. Li is arguing that her right to judicial review is protected by a guarantee of procedural due process. In 1982, in *Landon v. Plasencia*,[87] the Supreme Court found that a returning lawful permanent resident was entitled to procedures which protected her due process interests even if she was making her claim in an exclusion hearing at the border. Justice O'Connor found that the exclusion procedures should be reviewed under the balancing test set forth in *Mathews v. Eldridge*.[88] Although *Plasencia* deals with a returning lawful permanent resident who briefly left the country, *Matthews* could be used as a benchmark for evaluating the expedited removal procedures.

Ms. Li is also arguing that section 242(e) is unconstitutional as it suspends the writ of habeas corpus. That statute requires that all challenges to the expedited removal process be filed within sixty days of the implementation of the law.[89] The statute also requires filing in the D.C. Circuit court of

---

82. Telephone interview with Margaret Stock, Esq., attorney for Meng Li (July 21, 1997).
83. 338 U S. 537 (1950).
84. 345 U.S. 206 (1953).
85. Ellen Knauff was excluded under a special provision concerning national security. It might be possible to limit the case to that unique factual scenario and to an interpretation of the specific statute involved.
86. *See* Benson, *supra* note 6, section II (discussing the history of judicial review in immigration cases).
87. 459 U.S. 21 (1982).
88. 424 U.S. 319 (1976).
89. The statutory provision became effective April 1, 1997, and the INS began implementing the statute on that date.

appeals.[90] If section 242(e) is read as a limit on habeas corpus, it would be in direct conflict with the Suspension Clause of the Constitution.[91] Alternatively, litigants might want to argue that the statutory scheme practically eliminates habeas corpus because of the inability of the alien to get access to counsel and to the courts. It may be that a court would find that the statutory scheme has thus removed or suspended habeas corpus and therefore the statute is unconstitutional.

B. *Aliens with Certain Criminal Convictions*

The limitations on judicial review for aliens convicted of crimes is consistent with other changes Congress has made which are targeted at the removal of criminal aliens.[92] Even relatively minor criminal offenses can trigger one of the bars or preclusions to federal court review of a removal order. The statutory provision in INA § 242(a)(2)(C) states that:

> notwithstanding any other provision of law, no court shall have jurisdiction to review any final order of removal against an alien who is removable by reasons of having committed a criminal offense covered [in various sections of the INA].[93]

For example, conviction for minor drug possession would fall within the definition of section 237(2)(B), conviction relating to a controlled substance, and a final order of deportation on this ground would be foreclosed from judicial review.

Does this statute prevent a federal court from exercising its jurisdiction to determine if the noncitizen is within one of the classes of criminals described in section 242(a)(2)(C)? There appears to be a split of authority with the majority of the circuit courts of appeals finding that they have jurisdiction to determine whether the bar applies.[94]

---

90. Ms. Li has tried to join *Wood v. Reno*, CA 97 CV00597 (U.S.D.C. D.C. filed Mar. 27, 1997) which was filed to challenge the expedited removal system. The government has taken the position that she is precluded from joining the suit because sixty days has elapsed since the passage of the statute.

91. U.S. CONST. art. I, § 9, cl. 2.

92. There are other provisions of IIRIRA which would expedite the removal process for certain noncitizens convicted of aggravated felonies, section 238(b) or those ordered removed as part of the judicial criminal proceeding, section 238(c)(3)(A)(i). *See* Benson, *supra* note 6, at 1447-48 (discussing these provisions).

93. The remainder of INA § 242(a)(2)(C), 8 U.S.C. § 1252(a)(2)(C) references criminal related sections of the INA and reads:

> ... section [212](a)(2)[criminal grounds of inadmissibility] or [237](a)(2)(A)(iii) [aggravated felonies defined in § 101(a)(43)], B [controlled substances], C [certain firearm offenses] or D [convictions relating to sabotage] or any offense covered by section [237](a)(2)(A)(ii) [multiple criminal convictions] for which both predicate offenses are, without regard to their date of commission, otherwise covered by section [237](a)(2)(A)(i)[certain crimes of moral turpitude].

The brackets are descriptive only.

94. *See, e.g.,* Choeum v. INS, 129 F.3d 29 (1st Cir. 1997) (review of the order of removal to determine if conviction was one which would preclude review); Anwar v. INS, 116 F.3d 140, 141-44 (5th Cir. 1997);

Does this statute prevent federal court review of the finding of removability itself? The Tenth Circuit Court of Appeals has held that Congress meant to preclude judicial review of both the finding of removability and to any forms of relief.[95] The Seventh Circuit has developed two possible exceptions to the preclusions. The most significant is discussed in *Yang v. INS*,[96] where Judge Easterbrook said that the agency's findings alone will not support a preclusion of judicial review:

> Whether Yang is an alien deportable by reason of certain crimes is open to review, although the answer "yes" brings proceedings to an end. We think it highly unlikely that Congress meant to enable the Attorney General to expel an alien with a clean record just by stating that the person is a criminal, without any opportunity for judicial review of a claim of mistaken identity or political vendetta.[97]

The Seventh Circuit Court of Appeals has also created a limited exception to preclusion of all review where the noncitizen can show that he or she was "mouse-trapped" into conceding deportability, and relied on relief from removal or judicial review of the denial of relief, which had since been eliminated.[98] Where a noncitizen can articulate a colorable defense to removal, the Seventh Circuit Court of Appeals would not apply the preclusion statutes retroactively and preclude judicial review.[99] Obviously, this defense will be short-lived and limited to cases where the bars to jurisdiction are applied retroactively.

C. In Absentia Proceedings

Congress did not remove all judicial review of in absentia orders, but placed numerous obstacles to administratively overturning an in absentia order and narrowed the scope of review of the administrative action. Former INA § 242B, concerning the conduct of deportation proceedings, was stricken in its entirety by section 308(b)(6) of IIRIRA and incorporated into amended INA § 240. In general,

> any alien who, after written notice required under paragraph (1) or (2) of section 239(a) has been provided to the alien or the alien's counsel of record, does not attend a proceeding under this section, shall be ordered removed in absentia.[100]

Coronado-Durazo v. INS, 108 F.3d 210 (9th Cir. 1996), *petition for reh'g denied and new opinion substituted*, 123 F.3d 1322 (9th Cir. 1997). *But cf.* Berehe v. INS, 114 F.3d 159 (10th Cir. 1997).

95. *See Berehe, supra* note 94.
96. 109 F.3d 1185 (7th Cir. 1997) (interpreting AEDPA provisions).
97. *Yang,* 109 F.3d at 1192.
98. *See* Reyes-Hernandez v. INS, 89 F.3d 490 (7th Cir. 1996) (interpreting AEDPA preclusion of review). *See also* Arevalo-Lopez v. INS, 104 F.3d 100 (7th Cir. 1997).
99. *Id.* at 492-93.
100. INA § 240(b)(5)(A), 8 U.S.C. § 1250(b)(5)(A).

The government must establish by clear, unequivocal, and convincing evidence that the statutory written notice describing the consequences of failure to appear was actually provided to the alien or the alien's counsel of record.[101]

IIRIRA imposes a limitation on the availability of discretionary relief for failure to appear.[102] Consequently, any alien against whom a final order of removal is entered in absentia (unless there was a failure to provide the notice or if exceptional circumstances are demonstrated), is precluded from relief under INA §§ 240A, 240B, 245, 248, or 249 for a period of ten years after the date of the entry of the final order of removal.[103] Thus the motion to rescind an in absentia order will be of great importance.

In absentia orders may be rescinded only by the filing of a motion to reopen.[104] In cases where the alien received the required notice, section 240 requires the motion to reopen to be filed within 180 days after the date of the order of removal.[105] The alien must demonstrate that the failure to appear was because of (1) "exceptional circumstances," such as serious illness of the alien or serious illness or death of the spouse, child, or parent of the alien;[106] (2) that the alien did not receive proper notice;[107] or (3) that the alien was in federal or state custody and did not appear through no fault of the alien.[108] The filing of the motion to reopen shall stay the removal of the alien pending disposition of the motion by the immigration judge.[109] This is the only provision in the regulations which creates an automatic stay with the filing of a motion to reopen.

The motion to reopen seeking rescission may be appealed to the BIA. If the BIA denies the motion to reopen seeking rescission, the alien then files a petition for review under INA § 242. Congress limited the scope of judicial review in these cases to (i) the validity of the notice provided to the alien; (ii) the reasons for the alien's not attending the proceedings; and (iii) whether or

---

101. *Id. See also* 8 C.F.R. § 3.26.
102. IIRIRA § 304; amended INA § 240(b)(7), 8 U.S.C. § 1250(b)(7).
103. *Id.*
104. *See* INA § 240(b)(5)(C), 8 U.S.C. § 1250(b)(5)(C).
105. *Id.* If the alien never received the statutory notice, the 180-day limit is ineffective. 8 C.F.R. § 3.23(4). Although the regulations are not clear on this point, I believe that the 180-day limit is also inapplicable to motions to reopen to rescind where the alien is reopening to seek asylum or withholding of removal under INA § 241(b)(3), 8 U.S.C. § 1251(b)(3), provided that the application is based on a change in country conditions. *See* 8 C.F.R. § 3.3(4)(i) and (ii). But even in a case where the alien might have received notice or is not seeking asylum, she might still try to reopen her case. She should file the untimely motion, explaining the good cause for the delay and exhaust all administrative process before seeking judicial review. In my view, the alien may file a petition for review under INA § 242, notwithstanding the passage of 180 days. If the petition is dismissed, the alien might seek further judicial review in habeas proceedings. The regulations governing reopening are found at 8 C.F.R. § 3.23.
106. INA § 240(b)(5)(c)(i), 8 U.S.C. § 1250(b)(5)(c)(i), and INA § 240(e)(1), 8 U.S.C. § 1250(e)(1). *See also* 8 C.F.R. § 3.23(b)(4)(iii) (suggesting that exceptional circumstances beyond the control of the alien include but are not limited to such examples as "serious illness of the alien or serious illness or death of an immediate relative of the alien, but not including less compelling circumstances").
107. INA § 240(b)(5)(C)(ii), 8 U.S.C. § 1250(b)(5)(C)(ii).
108. *Id.*
109. INA § 240(b)(5)(C), 8 U.S.C. § 1250(b)(5)(C).

not the alien is removable.[110] Notwithstanding this express limitation, the alien should also be able to challenge the sufficiency of the evidence submitted by the INS to establish deportability.[111]

D. Miscellaneous Additional Restrictions on Judicial Review

IIRIRA provides new provisions and amendments regarding district court challenges to the Immigration and Naturalization Service and Executive Office for Immigration Review policies and practices. First, IIRIRA amends INA § 279 to provide for federal district court jurisdiction only in claims by the United States.[112] This amendment applies only to cases filed after September 30, 1996.[113] Second, as of April 1, 1997, IIRIRA precludes courts (except the Supreme Court) from issuing injunctions except in individual cases against "the operation" of the provisions in sections 231-244 of the amended INA.[114] Section 242(f)(2) states that:

> no court shall enjoin the removal of any alien pursuant to a final order under this section unless the alien shows by clear and convincing evidence that the entry or execution . . . is prohibited as a matter of law.

However, the limitation on injunctions does not preclude the filing of class action suits, and the prohibition against enjoining *removal* orders should not apply to orders of *deportation* or *exclusion*, since those are not issued "under this section" of the amended INA. Finally, IIRIRA § 377 denies jurisdiction over legalization claims filed under INA § 245A, enacted by the Immigration Reform and Control Act of 1986 ("IRCA"), unless the petitioner in fact filed a legalization application or attempted to file a complete application and fee with an INS legalization officer before May 5, 1988, and the application was refused. The Ninth Circuit upheld the constitutionality of section 377 on April 30, 1997, and dismissed the class action challenge.[115]

IV. IMPLIED OR DEFAULT GRANTS OF JURISDICTION OUTSIDE OF THE INA

Judicial review of final orders of removal is a special variant of the general issue concerning the power of Congress to limit judicial review of agency

---

110.   INA § 240(b)(5)(D), 8 U.S.C. § 1250(b)(5)(D).

111.   The requirement that a deportation order is supported by some evidence is a constitutional requirement. *See* Gerald L. Neuman, *The Constitutional Requirement of "Some Evidence,"* 25 SAN DIEGO L. REV. 631 (1988).

112.   IIRIRA § 381, amending INA § 279. Section 279 formerly conferred jurisdiction on the federal district courts over "all causes, civil and criminal, arising under any of the provisions" of title II, encompassing former INA §§ 201-93.

113.   IIRIRA § 381(b).

114.   INA § 242(f), 8 U.S.C. § 1252(f).

115.   *See* Catholic Soc. Serv. v. Reno, 1997 WL 209158 (9th Cir. Apr. 30, 1997).

action.[116] The decisions, regulations, and actions of the INS are generally governed by the terms of the Administrative Procedure Act ("APA").[117] The APA allows for judicial review except where review is specifically prohibited in another statute,[118] and even then courts have preserved jurisdiction to consider constitutional challenges.[119] Courts will read the provisions of IIRIRA as carving out special limits on APA review. But many courts read these limitations on review very carefully.[120]

To understand the breadth of the exceptions to APA review, it becomes critical to examine the exact scope of administrative action which comes within the phrase "final order of removal." The prior statutory scheme for judicial review of deportation and exclusion orders expressly stated that the statute set forth the "sole and exclusive" procedure for judicial review of all final orders of deportation.[121]

---

116. *See* Richard Fallon, *Of Legislative Courts, Administrative Agencies, and Article III*, 101 HARV. L. REV. 915 (1988).

117. From 1946 to the 1961 adoption of former INA § 106, the APA and the Federal Declaratory Judgment Act governed all immigration matters. *See* Brownell v. Shung, 352 U.S. 180 (1956). *See also* Shaughnessey v. Pedreiro, 349 U.S. 48 (1955). Section 106 only removed APA review from those decisions within the scope of section 106.

118. *See* 5 U.S.C. § 702. But the APA does not contain a general grant of jurisdiction itself. *See* Califano v. Sanders, 430 U.S. 99 (1977). To obtain APA review, most litigants will turn to 28 U.S.C. § 1331 which provides: "The district courts shall have original jurisdiction of all civil actions arising under the Constitution, laws, or treaties of the United States." *See, e.g.*, El Rescate Legal Serv., Inc. v. Executive Office of Immigration Review, 959 F.2d 742 (9th Cir. 1992) (upholding section 1331 jurisdiction to challenge systematic problems with translations in immigration court); Montes v. Thornburgh, 919 F.2d 531 (9th Cir. 1990) (allowing section 1331 jurisdiction to challenge action of an individual immigration judge who refused to accept documents); and Jean v. Nelson, 727 F.2d 957 (11th Cir. 1984) (*en banc*), *aff'd*, 472 U.S. 846 (1985) (using section 1331 to challenge failure to give notice of the right to apply for asylum, although no discussion of jurisdiction at Supreme Court).

In the past, some litigants used the grant of jurisdiction contained in INA § 279, 8 U.S.C. § 1329 which gave federal district court power to hear cases arising under a subchapter of the INA. IIRIRA amended INA § 279 to make it clear that this section can only be used by the government to initiate proceedings. *See, e.g.*, Chen Chaun-Fa v. Kiley, 459 F. Supp.762 (S.D.N.Y. 1978) (refusing to exercise jurisdiction under section 279 because the issue was not within subchapter II of the INA and finding that Congress intended to limit 28 U.S.C. § 1331 through the language of section 279). *Cf.* Yim Tong Chung v. Smith, 640 F. Supp. 1065 (S.D.N.Y. 1986) (finding no jurisdiction under section 279 or 28 U.S.C. § 1331); Martinez v. Bell, 468 F. Supp. 719 (S.D.N.Y. 1979) (finding section 279 can limit the grant of federal question jurisdiction). Given that Congress has now made clear that section 279 is only a grant of jurisdiction to the U.S. government, perhaps courts would be willing to reconsider whether this section should truly be read as an implied limit on private litigants ability to use the general grant of jurisdiction in 28 U.S.C. § 1331.

The Declaratory Judgment Act, 28 U.S.C. § 2201, may not independently confer subject matter jurisdiction. *See* Skelly Oil Co. v. Phillips Petroleum Co., 339 U.S. 667 (1950). *See also* Robertson v. Attorney General, 957 F.Supp. 1035 (N.D. Ill. 1997) (discussing subject matter jurisdiction under declaratory judgment and mandamus statutes, 28 U.S.C. § 1361). For a discussion of the Declaratory Judgment Act and proceedings under the APA, *see* GORDON, MAILMAN & YALE-LOEHR, *supra* note 31, § 81.05.119.

119. *See, e.g.*, Webster v. Doe, 486 U.S. 592 (1988) (preserving judicial review of constitutional challenge to administrative action); Lindahl v. Office of Personnel Mgm't, 470 U.S. 768 (1985) (preserving review of the legality of administrative decisions); Johnson v. Robinson, 415 U.S. 361 (1974).

120. A classic example of judicial protection of the power to review administrative action is found in *Shaughnessey v. Pedreiro, supra* note 116, where the Supreme Court refused to apply a literal reading to the language of the INA which made deportation orders "final." At least where the Supreme Court found that Congress had not clearly "intended" to bar all review, some form of judicial review remained.

121. Former INA § 106(a).

Yet where the Supreme Court found the government action was not part of the "final order," the limits of the former section 106 did not apply.[122] The reasoning of *Cheng Fan Kwok* provides a clear illustration of the narrow statutory interpretation the Supreme Court traditionally has applied to language aimed at restricting judicial review of administrative action. Scholars have critiqued *Cheng* and recognized that it created a hole in the unified design which had sought to restrict all judicial review to the former section 106 procedures.[123]

It is unclear if Congress has plugged the hole created by *Cheng Fan Kwok,* although Congress appears to have tried to design two subsections of section 242 to do just that. The language of the new statute varies from former section 106 by setting forth exclusive procedures for review of removal orders and for other types of decisions and actions under the INA. In an important subsection of the new statute, Congress tries to consolidate review of all "questions of law or fact . . . arising from any action taken . . . to remove an alien from the United States . . . shall be available only in judicial review of a final order under this section."[124] In another section, Congress tries to eliminate other forms of litigation by providing that:

> notwithstanding any other provision of law, no court shall have jurisdiction to hear any cause or claim by or on behalf of any alien arising from the decision or action by the Attorney General to commence proceedings, adjudicate cases, or execute removal orders against any alien under this chapter.[125]

But all of INA § 242 is concerned with review of matters within the scope of a *final order of removal.* The reference to "adjudicate cases" arises in the context of the entire provision which is captioned "Judicial Review of Orders of Removal."

To avoid the court-stripping effect of section 242(g), the early cases have used a variety of strategies. Some have primarily relied upon the strategy of *Cheng Fan Kwok*, finding that the issue is outside of the scope of a final order

---

122.   *See* Cheng Fan Kwok v. INS, 392 U.S. 206 (1968).

123.   David Martin, *Cheng Fan Kwok and Other Unappealing Cases: The Next Frontier of Immigration Reform*, 27 VA. J. INT'L L. 803 (1987).

124.   INA § 242(b)(9), 8 U.S.C. § 1252(b)(9). This is similar to the provisions concerning judicial review in cases filed under the "amnesty" or "seasonal agricultural worker" provisions of the Immigration Reform and Control Act of 1986 [hereinafter IRCA]. *Cf.* INA §§ 245A, 210, 8 U.S.C. §§ 1255, 1160. For example, section 210(3) provided that "[t]here shall be judicial review of such a denial only in the judicial review of an order of exclusion or deportation under section 106." The same language appeared in INA § 245A(f)(4), 8 U.S.C. § 1255(f)(4) for amnesty cases. Note that in *Reno v. Catholic Soc. Serv.*, 509 U.S. 43 (1993), the Court used the ripeness doctrine, not the literal language of the statute, to avoid deciding a challenge to the regulations governing the amnesty program. *See* section III.D, concerning Congressional elimination of federal court jurisdiction in some pending class actions concerning the amnesty program.

125.   INA § 242(g), 8 U.S.C. § 1252(g). *See* Rodriguez v. Wallis, No. 96-3518-Civ. Davis (S.D. Fla. Jan. 29, 1997) (finding that bond determinations are outside the scope of the actions covered by section 242(g)).

of removal and therefore that Congress did not intend to remove the court's jurisdiction.[126] Others have also applied the doctrine that even where Congress has generally removed jurisdiction, courts will retain jurisdiction to consider constitutional issues.[127] A few courts have found that Congressional intention to foreclose all review is clearly stated in section 242(g).[128] Undoubtedly, litigation will have to determine the ability of INA § 242 to block all arguments for jurisdiction, especially those based on alternative theories of jurisdiction such as the general grant of federal question jurisdiction, or preservation of jurisdiction to consider constitutional claims.

As an illustration of how these new sections may interact, consider the issue of challenging an INS District Director's denial of adjustment of status.[129] In some circuits, the courts of appeal have held that the denial of an application for adjustment of status pending before a District Director was not within the scope of review of an order of deportation.[130] Therefore, the noncitizen might have challenged the action of the District Director under the general federal question jurisdiction provided in 28 U.S.C. § 1331[131] and the provision of the APA, 5 U.S.C. § 702, which contemplates judicial review of administrative actions.

How will this type of INS action be treated in the future? Certainly, the noncitizen can still argue that the denial of adjustment by the District Director is not within the scope of a final order of removal and assert that it is not "an action taken to remove" the alien within the scope of INA § 242(b)(9). The provision found in INA § 242(a)(2)(B)(i) concerning review of adjustment of status would appear to only concern the application for adjustment of

---

126. *See, e.g.*, Wang Zong Xiao v. Reno, 963 F. Supp. 874 (N.D.Cal. 1997) (application for travel documents is outside the scope of section 242(g)); Thomas v. INS, 975 F. Supp. 840 (W.D. La. 1997) (challenges to the conditions of custody are not within the scope of section 242(g)).

127. *See, e.g.*, American-Arab Antidiscrimination Comm. v. Reno, 119 F.3d 1367 (9th Cir. 1997).

128. *See, e.g.*, Auguste v. Attorney General, 118 F.3d 723 (11th Cir. 1997) (rejecting review of denial of a stay of removal for a person who used the visa waiver program to enter the United States and had also as a condition of that admission waived rights to review); Ramallo v. Reno, 114 F.3d 1210 (D.C.Cir. 1997) (finding that section 242(g) precluded review of an alleged contract with the Department of Justice to suspend removal proceedings).

129. There is no administrative appeal of the District Director's decision although the application for INA § 245, 8 U.S.C. § 1255 adjustment may be renewed, in most cases, in a removal proceedings if one is begun by the INS. *See* 8 C.F.R. § 242.2(a)(5). Denial of adjustment of status before the immigration judge is within the scope of a final order of removal and may not be reviewable due to the bar on review of discretionary relief found in INA § 242 (a)(2)(B)(i), 8 U.S.C. § 1252(a)(2)(B)(i). Note that the language of INA § 242(a)(2)(b), 8 U.S.C. § 1252(a)(2)(b) refers to the "grant" of relief and perhaps might be read as a limitation on government appeals of grants of relief. Further, the issue of statutory eligibility for INA § 245, 8 U.S.C. § 1255 relief should also still be reviewable.

130. *See, e.g.*, Shahla v. INS, 749 F.2d 561 (9th Cir. 1984); Karim v. N.Y. Dist. Office of the INS, 1998 U.S. Dist. LEXIS 21917 (S.D.N.Y. Feb. 13, 1998) (pre-IIRIRA case); and Ijoma v. INS, 854 F. Supp. 612 (D. Neb. 1993).

131. In some cases the alien relied on INA § 279, 8 U.S.C. § 1329 which allowed district courts to hear matters governed by subchapter II of the INA which would include the application for adjustment of status which is governed by INA § 245, 8 U.S.C. § 1255. As noted previously, Congress amended INA § 279 to expressly limit the grant of jurisdiction for use solely by the U.S. government.

status made in a removal proceeding. The provision which follows in INA § 242(a)(2)(B)(ii) is the most difficult to overcome. This subsection states:

> (B) Denials of Discretionary Relief
> Notwithstanding any other provision of law, no court shall have jurisdiction to review ... (ii) any other decision or action of the Attorney General the authority for which is specified under this title to be within the discretion of the Attorney General, other than the granting of relief under section [208](a).[132]

Again, one can argue that this subsection cannot apply to decisions which are not part of orders of removal because INA § 242 concerns limits on review of orders of removal, not general review of all INS action. Another argument is that this subsection, INA § 242(a)(2)(B)(ii), only concerns those specific actions which are expressly "in the discretion of the Attorney General" and within the scope of title II of the INA.[133] Adjustment of status is within Title II but INA § 245 uses different language. It reads "in his discretion and under such regulations as he may prescribe."[134] This difference in language and the reference to a source of authority, the regulations, which are outside of the scope of Title II, may lead a court to conclude that this bar on judicial review was not meant to preclude APA review of the District Director's actions in adjustment of status cases.

Similarly the catch-all barrier in INA § 242(g), which bars review whenever the Attorney General "adjudicates cases" under the INA, should also be limited to the context of removal proceedings as this catch-all bar is still but a subsection of the review of removal orders.[135] If Congress had meant to bar judicial review of administrative decisions concerning adjustment of status not arising in the context of a removal proceeding, they should have amended INA § 245 itself. This they did not do.[136] Courts will need to

---

132. INA § 242(a)(2)(B)(ii), 8 U.S.C. § 1252(a)(2)(B)(ii).
133. This argument was made by Lucas Guttentag, *supra* note 1, at 250-51.
134. INA § 245(a), 8 U.S.C. § 1255(a).
135. If INA § 242, 8 U.S.C. § 1252 is read to bar review of the District Director's decision concerning adjustment of status, then it might be seen as one of the exceptions to judicial review contemplated in APA § 702. Although it is also beyond the scope of this article to consider how the new statute might limit litigation which seeks to raise challenges such as the failure to promulgate or improper promulgation of regulations, or a claim that the regulation was contrary to the statutory authority, the catch-all provision does not directly contradict such suits which are brought pursuant to the APA and federal question jurisdiction. *See, e.g.,* McNary v. Haitian Refugee Cent., Inc., 498 U.S. 479 (1991) (upholding a challenge to the SAW program notwithstanding the judicial review limitations as challenge alleged a pattern and practice of violation of constitutional rights and did not seek to adjudicate individual rights). *See also* Rodriguez v. Wallis, No. 96-3518 Civ. Davis (S.D. Fla. Jan. 29, 1997) (interpreting section 242(g) narrowly and holding it does not govern bond determinations).
136. Note that this failure to amend INA § 245, 8 U.S.C. § 1255 is in contrast to other provisions of IIRIRA which contain their own limitations on judicial review. *See, e.g.,* INA § 208(a)(3), 8 U.S.C. § 1158 (a)(3) (precluding review of the INS determination of exceptions to the ability to file a claim for asylum); INA § 208(b)(2)(D), 8 U.S.C. § 1158(a)(3)(B) (limiting review of the INS characterization of an asylum applicant as a terrorist).

carefully consider whether or not various provisions of IIRIRA have actually limited APA review and lawyers should not assume that blanket declarations in INA § 242 will have completely blocked review.

Further, even if Congress may have believed that the statute successfully eliminated all judicial review for the disfavored groups, or blocked access to APA review, in reality, the elimination of the petition for review jurisdiction has instead revitalized the default jurisdiction for review residing in the writ of habeas corpus under 28 U.S.C. § 2241.[137] Habeas jurisdiction exists because of the way in which an order of removal must be executed. Eventually, the alien must be apprehended or seized. The custodial aspect of removal, both actual and constructive, provides the factual predicate necessary to support habeas corpus jurisdiction.

V. AVAILABILITY OF HABEAS CORPUS

A. *Constitutional Right of Alien to Seek Habeas Review*

In the beginning, there was the writ of habeas corpus. Until 1961 and the adoption of the first provisions for judicial review in the INA itself,[138] most aliens obtained judicial review of immigration matters through the writ of habeas corpus. In *Heikkila v. Barber,*[139] the Court discussed the history of judicial review of immigration orders. Although the 1891 and 1917 Immigration Acts had intended to preclude judicial review "to the fullest extent permitted under the Constitution," courts continued to review the legality of deportation and exclusion orders in habeas corpus proceedings.[140] Although habeas corpus jurisdiction was not expressly granted in the immigration laws at that time, the *Heikkila* Court held that the Constitution guarantees, as a constitutional minimum, habeas corpus review. The *Heikkila* opinion recounts many Supreme Court and lower court decisions involving review of deportation and exclusion orders issued under the 1891 and 1917 Acts despite language which sought to make the agency action final.[141]

---

137. The APA also contemplates use of the writ of habeas corpus but the APA provision is not an express grant of jurisdiction. *See* 5 U.S.C. § 703. *See also* discussion of the APA in text and *supra* note 115. Of course the writ of habeas corpus is also protected by the U.S. CONST. art. I, § 9, cl. 2. In one instance, IIRIRA creates a special form of habeas for lawful permanent residents and asylees who are challenging expedited removal under INA § 235. *See* INA § 242(e)(2), 8 U.S.C. § 1252(e)(2).

138. Former section 106 was created in 1961. This section specifically referred to habeas corpus as the form of review for exclusion orders and whenever an alien was in the custody of the INS. Under the former statute, an alien in deportation proceedings could file a petition for review and if she lost that petition, file a writ of habeas corpus once the INS moved to execute the final order of deportation. In cases where the alien did not have a stay of deportation, the writ of habeas corpus was filed under section 106(a)(10) to prevent the removal of the alien even while the petition for review was awaiting adjudication.

139. 345 U.S. 229 (1953) (considering the availability of habeas corpus review for aliens facing exclusion or deportation).

140. *Id.* at 235 (noting aliens historically have been able to "attack a deportation order" by habeas corpus).

141. For history of immigration statutes and "finality" *see* GORDON, MAILMAN & YALE-LOEHR, *supra* note 31, § 81.01. *See also* LUCY E. SALYER, LAWS HARSH AS TIGERS: CHINESE IMMIGRANTS AND THE

B. Statutory Authority for Habeas Review

The statutory authority for the writ of habeas corpus is found in 28 U.S.C. § 2241. Section 2241 provides for jurisdiction to grant writs of habeas corpus for persons "in custody in violation of the Constitution or laws ... of the United States" and for persons "in custody under or by color of the authority of the United States."[142] Neither IIRIRA nor the AEDPA expressly amended 28 U.S.C. § 2241, and the Supreme Court has consistently held that habeas corpus jurisdiction cannot be amended or repealed absent express language.[143] In litigation concerning the elimination of judicial review for aggravated felons and certain other aliens convicted of crimes under the provisions of the AEDPA,[144] the government conceded in several cases and numerous courts ruled that although the language of AEDPA eliminated the writ of habeas corpus provision which had formerly lodged in the INA, the statute had not eliminated the writ of habeas corpus pursuant to 28 U.S.C. § 2241.[145] These courts preserved the writ of habeas corpus even in the face of a statutory section which expressly barred review by stating that "any final order of deportation ... shall not be reviewable by any court."[146] Similarly, the broad sweeping language in IIRIRA is also ineffective to remove all forms of judicial review.[147] Nevertheless, Judge Easterbrook of the Seventh

---

SHAPING OF MODERN IMMIGRATION LAW (1995); Benson, *supra* note 6, at 1429-30 (discussing the *Heikkila* decision).

142. 28 U.S.C. § 2241(c)(1), (3).

143. *See* Felker v. Turpin, 518 U.S. 651 (1996) (holding that under the well established "clear statement" rule, section 2241 jurisdiction cannot be repealed by "implication").

144. Pub. L. No. 104-132, 110 Stat. 1214 (1996).

145. Former section 106(a)(10) which provided for habeas review of aliens "in custody" was modified in AEDPA § 440(a). Of course all of former INA § 106 was removed in IIRIRA. The main AEDPA decisions are: Salazar-Haro v. INS, 95 F.3d 309 (3d Cir. 1996), *cert. denied*, 117 S.Ct. 1842 (1997); Mendez-Rosas v. INS, 87 F.3d 672 (5th Cir. 1996), *cert. denied*, 117 S. Ct. 694 (1997); Anwar v INS, 116 F.3d 140 (5th Cir 1997) (finding that notwithstanding section 440a the court had jurisdiction over constitutional issues); Williams v. INS, 114 F.3d 82 (5th Cir. 1997) (finding that some opportunity to apply for habeas relief remains; however, does not define the scope); Mansour v. INS, 123 F.3d 423 (6th Cir. 1997) (finding AEDPA's limits on review constitutional because of the continued availability of habeas review); Figueroa-Rubio v. INS, 108 F.3d 110 (8th Cir. 1997); Arevalo-Lopez v. INS, 104 F.3d 100 (7th Cir. 1997); Chow v. INS, 113 F.3d 659 (7th Cir. 1997) (upholding judicial review limits and not deciding what type of habeas jurisdiction exists); Yang v. INS, 109 F.3d 1185 (7th Cir. 1997) (acknowledging habeas corpus but limits the types of claims); Duldulao v. INS, 90 F.3d 396 (9th Cir. 1996) (acknowledging preservation of habeas review although issue was not before the court); Fernandez v. INS, 113 F.3d 1151 (10th Cir. 1997) (dismissing petition for review but finding that habeas exists for "substantial" constitutional errors); Boston-Bollers v. INS, 106 F.3d 352 (11th Cir. 1997) (per curiam); Kolster v. INS, 101 F.3d 785 (1st Cir. 1996) (finding some form of habeas review remains notwithstanding express prohibition in section 440a of AEDPA); Hincapie-Nieto v. INS, 92 F.3d 27 (2d Cir. 1996) (referring to 28 U.S.C. § 2241). Following the Ninth Circuit decision dismissing his petition for review, Mr. Duldulao sought habeas review in the federal district court in Hawaii. *See* Duldulao v. Reno, 958 F. Supp. 476 (D. Haw. 1997) (allowing habeas under 28 U.S.C. § 2241 but limiting the scope of review available and denying the petition). *See also* Yesil v. Reno, 958 F. Supp. 828 (S.D.N.Y. 1997) (granting habeas under 28 U.S.C. § 2241 for aggravated felony); Eltayeb v. Ingham, 950 F. Supp. 95 (S.D.N.Y. 1997) (habeas jurisdiction for aggravated felony); Mbiya v. INS, 930 F. Supp. 609 (N.D. Ga. 1996) (habeas review). The scope of review in habeas corpus is discussed in section V.D.4 of this article.

146. AEDPA § 440(a).

147. *See* Szilagyi v. INS, 131 F.3d 148 (9th Cir. 1997) (finding habeas remained under section 2241 for constitutional claims); United States v. Zadvydas, 986 F. Supp. 1011 (E.D. La. 1997) (finding that 28

Circuit found in *Yang v. INS*[148] that section 242(a) of the IIRIRA does, in fact, preclude review under 28 U.S.C. § 2241. According to Judge Easterbrook, "effective April 1, 1997, § 306(a) of [IIRIRA] abolishes even review under § 2241, leaving only the constitutional writ unaided by statute."[149] In striking contrast to Judge Easterbrook's opinion in *Yang*,[150] Judge Weinstein of the Eastern District of New York not only found that statutory habeas continued to be available under 28 U.S.C. § 2241, but also that it could be used to challenge the agency's interpretation of the statute.[151] Although the petitioner in *Mojica v. Reno* raised constitutional issues regarding the retroactive application of AEDPA to his application for section 212(c) relief, Judge Weinstein ultimately found, on statutory grounds, that the Attorney General had misinterpreted the statute in her decision in *Matter of Soriano*.[152] Another New York judge, this time in the Southern District, also disagreed with Judge Easterbrook's analysis. Judge Chin held in *Yesil v. Reno*[153] that statutory habeas was still available to the petitioner. Judge Chin did not define the exact scope of statutory habeas available, but held that the allegation of an erroneous statuory violation depriving a long-term resident of any possibility of relief from deportation could constitute a due process violation, thus presenting a constitutional claim that clearly supports statutory habeas review.[154]

In *U.S. ex rel. Morgan v. McElroy*,[155] Judge Sprizzo of the Southern District of New York distinguished *Mojica* and *Yesil*,[156] and held that 28 U.S.C. § 2241 was no longer available after the passage of IIRIRA. According to Judge Sprizzo, the new section 242(g) effectively bars all review of claims arising from the "action or decision of the Attorney General

---

U.S.C. § 2241 remained despite the limits of IIRIRA codified in section 242(g)); Jurado-Gutierrez v. Green, 977 F. Supp. 1089 (D. Col. 1997) (finding habeas corpus remained to adjudicate constitutional claims; appeal pending in the 10th Circuit); Padilla v. Caplinger, 1997 WL 564008 (E.D. La. Sept. 5, 1997) (finding that habeas corpus remained under art. 1, § 9, cl. 2 of the Constitution for constitutional claims, but finding that the petitioner failed to raise a colorable constitutional claim). *But see* U.S. *ex rel.* Morgan v. McElroy, 981 F. Supp. 873 (S.D.N.Y. 1997) (finding that section 242 barred all review, including habeas except as provided in the INA).

148. 109 F. 3d 1185 (7th Cir. 1997).

149. *Id.* at 1195. I believe that Judge Easterbrook's evaluation of the impact of section 242 on the availability of habeas corpus must be viewed as dicta because he was ruling on a case governed by AEDPA and the issue was not properly before the Court.

150. *See also* Sandoval v. Reno, 1997 U.S. Dist. LEXIS 20976 (E.D. Pa. Dec. 30, 1997) (exercising habeas jurisdiction under section 2241, finding miscarriage of justice based on a legal error); Jurado-Gutierrez v. Green, 1997 U.S. Dist. LEXIS 15057 (D. Col. Sept. 29, 1997) (finding review was available under section 2241 to review colorable, substantial constitutional violations).

151. *See* Mojica v. Reno, 970 F. Supp. 130 (E.D.N.Y. 1997).

152. 1997 WL 159795 (Feb. 21, 1997) (Op. Att'y Gen.) (reversing the vacated decision by the BIA, Int. Dec. 3289 (BIA 1996)). Judge Weinstein's opinion has been appealed to the Second Circuit, and oral arguments were presented on January 21, 1998.

153. 985 F. Supp. 828 (S.D.N.Y. 1997).

154. This case is also on appeal to the Second Circuit Court of Appeals. Oral argument was consolidated with the appeal in *Mojica* and heard on January 21, 1998.

155. 1997 WL 736512 (S.D.N.Y. Nov. 24, 1997).

156. Judge Sprizzo distinguishes the cases by stating that they were interpreting the provisions of AEDPA and were not considering the effect of the new section 242(g).

to commence proceedings . . . ." In this particular case, the court character-ized the denial of adjustment of status as within the preclusion intended by section 242(g). Judge Sprizzo took the position that the only form of habeas corpus review available to aliens is that which is set forth in the INA itself.[157] He noted that even if there is some form of habeas corpus guaranteed by the Constitution, the merits of the peitioner's claim do not rise to a constitutional level.[158]

The conflict between these decisions reflects the failure of the statutory reforms to adequately address the role of habeas corpus review in immigra-tion cases. The confusion about the jurisdictional basis for habeas is closely connected with issues surrounding the appropriate scope of habeas review, which is discussed below in section D.4.

On the very day that this article was going to print, the First Circuit Court of Appeals ruled in *Goncalves v. Reno*, 1998 WL 236799 (1st Cir. May 15, 1998) that nothing in the recent immigration legislation had specifically amended 28 U.S. C. § 2241 and therefore, District Courts had habeas corpus jurisdiction to review immigration matters. The First Circuit also found that habeas review included jurisdiction to consider challenges to the agency's statutory interpretations.

C. *Constitutional Grant of Habeas Review*

If IIRIRA could be read to eliminate the statutory right to a writ of habeas corpus, the right to habeas should be available as a matter of constitutional right. The writ of habeas corpus is guaranteed by the Constitution and cannot be suspended except where "in Cases of Rebellion or Invasion the Public Safety may require it."[159] One circuit court has referred to a "free standing" power in the federal courts to hear a constitutional writ of habeas corpus.[160]

However, if IIRIRA is read as blocking the statutory basis for habeas corpus jurisdiction then we must ask: What federal court has jurisdiction to hear constitutional claims of habeas corpus? The government might argue that Congress must expressly create a grant of federal court jurisdiction for the court to be able to hear the writ.[161] My own view is that if IIRIRA is read

---

157. *See, e.g.,* INA § 242(e), 8 U.S.C. § 1252(e). This section limits habeas to determinations of whether the petitioner is an alien, whether the petitioner was ordered removed under INA § 235 (b)(1), 8 U.S.C. § 1225(b)(1) and whether the petitioner is a lawful resident, refugee or asylee. In *Li v. Eddy*, 1997 U.S. Dist. LEXIS 14431 (D. Alaska July 2, 1997), the court held that the determination of whether the petitioner was ordered removed under the provision of INA § 235(b)(1), 8 U.S.C. § 1225(b)(1) does not include a "good faith" determination. Therefore the court may not determine if section 235(b)(1) is being used as a pretext. This rasies the question of whether this limited form of habeas review could be deemed a *pro se* violation of the Suspension Clause of the Constitution. In limiting review to a point of essentially no review at all, Congress has, arguably, suspended the writ of habeas corpus in violation of the Constitution.

158. *Id.*

159. U.S. CONST. art. I, § 9, cl. 2.

160. *See* Kolster v. INS, 101 F.3d 785, 790-91 n.4 (1st Cir. 1996).

161. *See Ex parte* Bollman, 8 U.S. (4 Cranch) 75, 100-01 (1807) (discussing, in dicta, limits on the Supreme Court's original jurisdiction to grant a writ of habeas corpus and implying that the writ can only be issued by a court which is expressly granted jurisdiction).

to repeal the statutory basis for habeas, then this reading constitutes a suspension of the writ of habeas corpus and the statute is unconstitutional.[162]

D. *Procedural Considerations in Habeas Corpus*

1. *Venue and Personal Jurisdiction*

This is another complex area in habeas litigation. The federal statutes do not specify the precise venue. Rather, courts have interpreted the statutes to require that the petition be filed in the jurisdiction where the officer has custody over the person seeking the writ.[163] The appropriate venue is where the alien is in the custody of the INS. But where is an alien in custody? And who is the custodian, the District Director or the Attorney General? In a recent habeas case under 28 U.S.C. § 2241, the federal district court ruled that venue was appropriate in the Southern District of New York where the alien was residing.[164] This same case also addressed the issue of whether the court had personal jurisdiction over the District Director in Oakdale, Louisiana. The government had opposed the writ on the ground that the Southern District of New York lacked personal jurisdiction. The court ruled that actions of the District Director in New York in requesting that the alien surrender for deportation were sufficient to allow the assertion of personal jurisdiction over the Oakdale, Louisiana District Director.[165]

2. *Custody and Effect of Departure*

In the past, most habeas cases named the District Director as the officer having custody over the alien. In a few recent cases, courts have accepted jurisdiction over the Attorney General.[166] Some courts required actual custody of the alien before the writ could be issued. In cases interpreting the former section 106(a)(10), the custody determination may have been more

---

162. A theoretical argument to avoid reading the statute as a suspension would be to read it as eliminating federal court jurisdiction but allowing state courts to hear writ of habeas corpus claims. However, in *Tarble's Case*, 80 U.S. (13 Wall.) 397 (1872), the Supreme Court held that no state court has the power to release an individual from federal custody. Section 242 also seems to intend exclusive federal court jurisdiction to review immigration cases, although the exclusivity language is only used to head a subsection which in itself precludes review. *See* INA § 242(g), 8 U.S.C. § 1252(g).

163. *See, e.g.*, Braden v. 30th Judicial Cir. Ct. Ky., 410 U.S. 484 (1973) (reviewing of a state criminal conviction). The statute says that the writ should be "directed to the person having custody of the person detained." 28 U.S.C. § 2243.

164. Yesil v. Reno, 958 F.Supp. 828, *mot. to reconsider denied*, 973 F. Supp. 372 (S.D.N.Y. 1997).

165. *Id.*

166. *See, e.g.*, Nwankwo v. Reno, 828 F. Supp. 171 (E.D.N.Y. 1993) (finding that the Attorney General was appropriate officer where writ presented solely questions of law and did not require production of the alien); Yesil v. Reno, *et al.*, *supra* note 83, (holding that the court had personal jurisdiction in New York over the district director from Oakdale). In *Nwankwo*, the alien was in detention in Oakdale awaiting deportation. He had originally begun detention for a criminal conviction and sentence issued by the Eastern District. The court treated his request as a writ of habeas corpus challenging his continued detention in excess of six months after an order of deportation. The former section INA § 242(c) was repealed in IIRIRA. The court also noted that the Western District of Louisiana had been flooded with habeas filings "as a result of lengthy delays in processing detainees for deportation." 828 F. Supp. at 174. Many practitioners choose to name both the District Director and the Attorney General.

rigidly defined because habeas review was allowed in addition to the other forms of review once the alien was placed in custody.[167] Other courts have recognized that the alien can show a form of constructive custody due to restraints on her liberty.[168]

In the former judicial review statute, if an alien had departed the country or was legally removed from the country, the courts lost jurisdiction.[169] The new statute is silent on the effect of departure. If we look to cases decided before the 1961 judicial review provisions, we find some cases that allowed the court to continue to exercise habeas jurisdiction even after removal of the alien but the habeas had begun before the removal.[170] In a recent case, the Ninth Circuit held that the district court had habeas jurisdiction nine months after the alien had been deported because the removal was unlawful.[171] The better practice will be to assume that you must file the writ of habeas corpus *before* the INS removes the alien.

3. Habeas and Order to Show Cause Proceedings

There are two routes for the courts and the government to respond to a writ of habeas corpus. In the first, the government must produce the alien and respond immediately by establishing the lawfulness of the detention. In the second, the government may request that the court issue an order to show cause which will allow for motions and argument before the alien must be

---

167. U.S. *ex rel.* Marcello v. District Director, INS, 634 F.2d 964 (5th Cir.) *cert. denied*, 452 U.S. 917 (1981) (requiring actual custody although alien was only under order of supervision and habeas review allowed). The Fifth Circuit may have read in a strict custody requirement because the court was trying to understand why Congress allowed both a petition for review and habeas jurisdiction to review deportation orders under the former INA § 106. The Fifth Circuit coupled a strict custody requirement with a broad scope of review in habeas to reconcile the "streamlining" goals of Congress in adopting section 106 in 1961. *See* El-Youssef v. Meese, 678 F. Supp. 1508, 1513-16 (D. Kan. 1988) (addressing the scope of review in habeas corpus under former section 106).

168. *See, e.g.,* Galaviz-Medina v. Wooten and U.S. Immigration Review Bd. of Appeals, 27 F.3d 487 (10th Cir. 1994) (finding custody where alien was held in state prison pursuant to an INS detainer and an outstanding final order of deportation; but case was interpreting former section 106(a)(10)). The law concerning writs of habeas corpus evolves like any other body of law. The modern trend has been to recognize general constraints on liberty as sufficient to create habeas corpus jurisdiction. *See generally,* JAMES S. LIEBMAN & RANDY HERTZ, FEDERAL HABEAS CORPUS PRACTICE AND PROCEDURE, § 8.2(b)(1004). *See* Hensley v. Municipal Court, 411 U.S. 345 (1973) (finding release pending trial was sufficient constraint); Jones v. Cunningham, 371 U.S. 236 (1963) (finding state release on parole was sufficient restraint on liberty to justify habeas review). The government will undoubtedly try to establish a very strict custody requirement to narrow the ability of aliens to seek judicial review and even to avoid review. Even if the alien has been removed, theoretically habeas jurisdiction should still be available especially now that the provision which terminated jurisdiction upon the departure of the alien has been repealed. *See, e.g.,* Singh v. Waters, 87 F.3d 346 (9th Cir. 1996) (unlawful deportation equaled continuing restraint on alien and thus court had habeas jurisdiction, interpreting former INA § 106).

169. Former INA § 106(c).

170. *See, e.g., Ex parte* Endo, 323 U.S. 283 (1944) (allowing continued habeas); *Ex parte* Catanzaro, 138 F.2d 100 (3d Cir. 1943) (allowing continued habeas). *See* cases cited in GORDON, MAILMAN & YALE-LOEHR, *supra* note 31, § 81.04[2][c] fn. 4. For cases which held that the habeas had to begin before the removal of the alien, *see* Terrado v. Moyer, 820 F.2d 920 (7th Cir. 1987); U.S. *ex rel.* Smith v. Warden of Philadelphia City Prison, 87 F. Supp. 339 (E.D. Pa. 1949) *aff'd per curiam*, 181 F.2d 847 (2d Cir. 1950).

171. Singh v. Waters, 87 F.3d 346 (9th Cir. 1996). *See also* Mendez v. INS, 563 F.2d 956 (9th Cir. 1977) (creating the unlawful deportation exception to loss of jurisdiction under the former section 106). Not every circuit agreed with the *Mendez* exception.

released or produced. The alien must contravene the government's assertions in the response in a pleading known as a "traverse." Any government allegation not contravened in the traverse is deemed to be true.

4. *Scope of Review*

The exact scope of review under a writ of habeas corpus is debated.[172] Prior to the 1961 judicial review provisions, the writ was used in a wide variety of circumstances and the standard of review varied with the allegations of illegality in the seizure of the alien. The changes created by IIRIRA have returned the courts to the pre-1961 habeas jurisprudence. In these early habeas cases, courts were willing to hear constitutional challenges such as an attack on the immigration law itself or on the procedure afforded under the statutes.[173] But habeas was also used to hear non-constitutional claims such as the appropriateness of the agency interpretation of the statute or challenges to the sufficiency of the evidence presented in the administrative hearing.[174] As this article was going to print, the First Circuit Court of Appeals concluded in *Goncalves v. Reno*, 1998 WL 236799 (1st Cir. May 15, 1998) that habeas review included review of pure statutory or legal issues such as the failure to exercise discretion. The case left open the issue of whether habeas could be used to review decisions made in the exercise of agency discretion. (See note 17.)

Unfortunately, in some recent federal court decisions, the district courts concluded that the appropriate standard for review was whether the case presented a "miscarriage of justice"[175] or "grave constitutional error."[176] These courts appear to have accepted the government's argument that habeas review could not be an equal substitute for the direct review which Congress

---

172. The scope of review depends in part on whether the habeas petition is based on 28 U.S.C. § 2241 or whether it is a pure constitutional habeas. For a discussion of some of the distinction between constitutional habeas and habeas under section 2241, *see* Benson, *supra* note 6, at 1465-78.

173. *See* Yamataya v. Fisher, 189 U.S. 86 (1903) (hearing challenges to the grant of plenary power to the inspection officer in the 1891 immigration laws).

174. For challenges to the interpretation of the statute *see* Haw Tan v. Phelan, 333 U.S. 6 (1948) (rejecting executive's interpretation of multiple criminal conviction deportation provision); Delgadillo v. Carmichael, 332 U.S. 388 (1947) (rejecting executive's interpretation of "entry"); Kessler v. Strecker, 307 U.S. 22 (1939) (rejecting executive's interpretation of ideological deportation provision); Mahler v. Eby, 264 U.S. 32 (1924) (rejecting executive's interpretation of findings necessary for deportation after conviction under espionage act); Gegiow v. Uhl, 239 U.S. 3 (1915) (rejecting executive's broad interpretation of public charge exclusion provision). *See also* Kwong Hai Chew v. Colding, 344 U.S. 590 (1953) (rejecting executive's interpretation of procedural regulation); Wong Yang Sung v. McGrath, 339 U.S. 908 (1950) (rejecting executive's interpretation of APA procedural requirements). For cases dealing with the sufficency of evidence, *see* Ex Parte Fierstein, 41 F.2d 53 (9th Cir. 1930) (finding no evidence); Maltez v. Nagle, 27 F.2d 835 (9th Cir. 1928) (unfair procedure); United States *ex rel.* Vajtauer v. Commissioner, 273 U.S. 103 (1927); Tang Tun v. Edsell, 223 U.S. 673 (1912); Chin Yow v. United States, 208 U.S. 8 (1908). *See also* Gerald L. Neuman, *The Constitutional Requirement of "Some Evidence,"* 25 SAN DIEGO L. REV. 631, 637-41 (1988).

175. *See* Eltayeb v. Ingham, 950 F. Supp. 95 (S.D.N.Y. 1997); Mbyia v. INS, 930 F. Supp. 609 (N.D. Ga. 1996). In *Eltayeb*, the court recites a miscarriage of justice standard, yet appears to conduct a form of review analogous to abuse of discretion review.

176. *See* Duldulao v. Reno, 958 F. Supp. 476 (D. Haw. 1997).

eliminated in the AEDPA. But even with the adoption of the "miscarriage of justice or grave constitutional error" standard, the district courts have applied a varied interpretation of the types of claims which can fall within the scope of that phrase. In *Yesil* the district court granted a writ of habeas corpus in a case where the alien alleged the INS had improperly interpreted his length of lawful residence for statutory eligibility for the section 212(c) waiver.[177] Judge Chin found that this allegation of incorrect statutory interpretation amounted to a due process violation.[178] In contrast, in *Eltayeb*,[179] the court said it would only conduct review for a miscarriage of justice but appeared to conduct a form of "abuse of discretion" review.[180] In *Duldulao*,[181] the district court judge held that a claim of abuse of discretion in denying section 212(c) relief did not present any constitutional claims, nor did it represent a miscarriage of justice and the habeas corpus petition was denied.[182]

The obvious result of these decisions is that litigants will now endeavor to present a habeas petition which articulates constitutional claims.[183] Of course, not every case will contain a strong constitutional claim, but where it is possible to fashion a legitimate allegation of a constitutional violation, attorneys will do so to support the court's exercise of jurisdiction.[184] The unintended result may be that some judges, in an effort to overturn abusive discretionary actions or erroneous statutory interpretations, may couch their decisions in constitutional terms and create new constitutional rights for aliens in general.[185]

5. Appellate Review of Habeas Corpus

The decision of the U.S. district court in granting or denying the writ of habeas corpus may be appealed to the circuit court of appeals pursuant to 28 U.S.C. § 2253. The decision of the court of appeals may be appealed to the U.S. Supreme Court via the writ of certiorari. The Supreme Court also has original jurisdiction to consider a writ of habeas corpus under 28 U.S.C. § 2241.

---

177. 985 F.Supp. 828 (S.D.N.Y. 1997).

178. *Id.*

179. *See* Eltayeb v. Ingham, 950 F.Supp. 95 (S.D.N.Y. 1997).

180. *Id.*

181. Duldulao v. Reno, 958 F.Supp. 476 (D. Haw. 1997).

182. *Id.* The district court also rejected Mr. Duldulao's objection to the admission of hearsay evidence, finding that in the "instant case," the evidence did not present a Fifth Amendment due process claim. *Id.* at 481.

183. *See, e.g.,* Chow v. INS, 113 F.3d 659 (7th Cir. 1997) (reading Chow's claims as presenting a due process challenge to the nature of the deportation hearing itself and suggesting habeas review would be available but not deciding the jurisdictional authority for habeas).

184. *See* Lenni Benson, *Surviving to Fight Another Day: Preserving Issues for Appeal,* 1995-1996 IMMIGRATION AND NATIONALITY LAW HANDBOOK 353-66 VOL. II (AILA 1995). In that article I discuss how to preserve constitutional claims in administrative hearings before an agency not empowered to rule directly on such claims.

185. For a discussion of the "constitutionalization" of immigration law *see* Benson, *supra* note 6, at 1484-94.

VI. CONCLUSION

The attacks on judicial review of removal orders represents an extraordinary assertion of Congressional power to control the jurisdiction of the federal courts and of its power over aliens. Although both of these powers have been called "plenary," the central issue remains whether our constitution will allow Congress to empower the INS with unfettered discretion to both interpret and implement the immigration laws.

Although Congress has the power to define the vessel for judicial review and to streamline the procedures, it cannot constitutionally eliminate the vessel altogether. The right to habeas corpus review and to review of constitutional claims will reshape the contours of immigration practice and raise the stakes of litigation.

KAORU YAMATAYA, *Appt.*,
v.

THOMAS M. FISHER, Immigrant and Chinese Inspector.

Aliens—exclusion of paupers—effect of treaty with Japan—deportation after entry—review by habeas corpus.

1. Japanese subjects who are "paupers or persons likely to become a public charge," and are therefore forbidden to enter the United States by the immigration act of March 3, 1891 (26 Stat. at L. 1085, chap. 551, U. S. Comp. Stat. 1901, p. 1294), are not given such right of entry by the provision of the treaty of March 21, 1895, with Japan, that the citizens or subjects of each of the two countries shall have "full liberty to enter, travel, or reside in any part of the territories of the other country,"—especially since such treaty expressly excepts from its operation any ordinance or regulation relating to "police and public security."

2. Aliens of the excluded class are not protected from deportation by the executive officers of the government, because they have effected an entry into the United States, in view of the power given the Secretary of the Treasury by the act of October 19, 1888, chap. 1210 (25 Stat. at L. 566, U. S. Comp. Stat. 1901, p. 1294), if satisfied that an immigrant has been allowed to land contrary to law, to cause his deportation at any time within a year after the landing, which power was again substantially conferred by the provision of the act of March 3, 1891, chap. 551, § 11, that an alien immigrant may be sent out of the country, "as provided by law," at any time within a year after his illegal entry into the United States.

3. Executive officers of the United States government were not invested, by the provisions of the acts of October 19, 1888, chap. 1210, and March 3, 1891, chap. 551, for the deportation of aliens of excluded classes within a year after their illegal entry, with the power arbitrarily to deport an alien who has entered the country and has become subject in all respects to its jurisdiction and a part of its population, without giving him an opportunity to be heard upon the question involving his right to be and remain in the United States.

4. Federal courts will not intervene by habeas corpus to prevent the deportation by the executive officers of the government, under the authority of the acts of October 19, 1888, chap. 1210, and March 3, 1891, chap. 551, of an alien found to be one of the excluded class where such alien had notice, though not a formal one, of the investigation instituted for the purpose of ascertaining whether she was legally in the United States, and was not denied an opportunity to be heard, although she pleads a want of knowledge of the English language preventing her from understanding the nature and import of the questions propounded to her, and that the investigation made was a "pretended" one, and that she did not at the time know that it had reference to her deportation.

[No. 171.]

Argued February 24, 1903. Decided April 6, 1903.

ON APPEAL from the District Court of the United States for the District of

Washington to review a decree dismissing a writ of habeas corpus to inquire into the detention of an alien immigrant under a warrant from the Secretary of the Treasury requiring her deportation. *Affirmed.*

The facts are stated in the opinion.

Messrs. **Vere Goldthwaite**, *Harold Preston*, and *Walter A. Keene* for appellant.

Assistant Attorney General **Hoyt** for appellee.

Mr. Justice **Harlan** delivered the opinion of the court:

* This case presents some questions arising under the act of Congress relating to the exclusion of certain classes of alien immigrants.

On the 11th day of July, 1901, appellant, a subject of Japan, landed at the port of Seattle, Washington; and on or about July 15th, 1901, the appellee, an immigrant inspector of the United States, having instituted an investigation into the circumstances of her entering the United States, decided that she came here in violation of law, in that she was a pauper and a person likely to become a public charge,— aliens of that class being excluded altogether from this country by the act of March 3d, 1891 (26 Stat. at L. 1085, chap. 551, U. S. Comp. Stat. 1901, p. 1294).

The evidence obtained by the inspector was transmitted to the Secretary of the Treasury, who, under date of July 23d, 1901, issued a warrant addressed to the immigrant inspector at Seattle, reciting that the appellant had come into the United States contrary to the provisions of the above act of 1891, and ordering that she be taken into custody and returned to Japan at the expense of the vessel importing her.

The inspector being about to execute this warrant, an application was presented in behalf of the appellant to the district court of the United States for the district of Washington, northern division, for a writ of habeas corpus. The application alleged that the imprisonment of the petitioner was unlawful, and that she did not come here in violation of the act of 1891, or of any other law of the United States relating to the exclusion of aliens.

The writ having been issued, a return was made by the inspector, stating that he had found upon due investigation and the admissions of the appellant that she was a pauper and a person likely to become a public charge, and had " surreptitiously, clandestinely, unlawfully, and without any authority come into the United States;" that, " in pursuance of said testimony, admissions of the petitioner, Kaoru Yamataya, evidence, facts, and circumstances," he had decided that she had no right to be within the territory of the United States, and was a proper person for deportation; all which he reported to the proper officers of the government, who confirmed his decision, and thereupon the Secretary of the Treasury issued his warrant, requiring the deportation of the appellant. That warrant was produced and made part of the return.

The return of the inspector was traversed, the traverse admitting that the inspector had investigated the case of the petitioner, and had made a finding that she had illegally come into this country, but alleging that the investigation was a "pretended" and an inadequate one; that she did not understand the English language, and did not know at the time that such investigation was with a view to her deportation from the country; and that the investigation was carried on without her having the assistance of counsel or friends, or an opportunity to show that she was not a pauper or likely to become a public charge. The traverse alleged that the petitioner was not in the United States in violation of law.

A demurrer to the traverse was sustained, the writ of habeas corpus was dismissed, and the appellant was remanded to the custody of the inspector. From that order the present appeal was prosecuted.

It will conduce to a clear understanding of the questions to be determined if we recall certain legislation of Congress relating to the exclusion of aliens from the United States, and to the treaty of 1894 between Japan and the United States.

By the deficiency appropriation act of October 19th, 1888, chap. 1210, it was provided that the act of February 23d, 1887, chap. 220, amendatory of the act prohibiting the importation and immigration of foreigners and aliens under contract or agreement to perform labor in the United States, its territories, and the District of Columbia (24 Stat. at L. 414, U. S. Comp. Stat. 1901, p. 1292), be so amended "as to authorize the Secretary of the Treasury, in case he shall be satisfied that an immigrant has been allowed to land contrary to the prohibition of that law, to cause such immigrant, within the period of one year after landing or entry, to be taken into custody and returned to the country from whence he came, at the expense of the owner of the importing vessel, or, if he entered from an adjoining country, at the expense of the person previously contracting for the services." 25 Stat. at L. 566 (U. S. Comp. Stat. 1901, p. 1294).

By the 1st section of the act of Congress of March 3d, 1891, chap. 551, amendatory of the various acts relating to immigration and importation of aliens under contract or agreement to perform labor, it was provided: "That the following classes of aliens shall be excluded from admission into the United States, in accordance with the existing acts regulating immigration, other than those concerning Chinese laborers: All idiots, insane persons, paupers, or persons likely to become a public charge, persons suffering from a loathsome or a dangerous contagious disease, persons who have been convicted of a felony or other infamous crime or misdemeanor involving moral turpitude, polygamists, and also any person whose ticket or passage is paid for with the money of another or who is assisted by others to come, unless it is affirmatively and satisfactorily shown, on special inquiry, that such person does not belong to one of the foregoing excluded classes, or to the class of contract laborers excluded by the act of February twenty-sixth, eighteen hundred and eighty-five [23 Stat. at L. 332, chap. 164, U. S. Comp. Stat. 1901, p. 1290]. . . ." 26 Stat. at L. 1084 (U. S. Comp. Stat. 1901, p. 1294).

By the 8th section of that act it was provided: "That upon the arrival by water at any place within the United States of any alien immigrants it shall be the duty of the commanding officer and the agents of the steam or sailing vessel by which they came to report the name, nationality, last residence, and destination of every such alien, before any of them are landed, to the proper inspection officers, who shall thereupon go or send competent assistants on board such vessel and there inspect all such aliens, or the inspection officers may order a temporary removal of such aliens for examination at a designated time and place, and then and there detain them until a thorough inspection is made. . . . The inspection officers and their assistants shall have power to administer oaths, and to take and consider testimony touching the right of any such aliens to enter the United States, all of which shall be entered of record. During such inspection, after temporary removal, the superintendent shall cause such aliens to be properly housed, fed, and cared for, and also, in his discretion, such as are delayed in proceeding to their destination after inspection. All decisions made by the inspection officers or their assistants touching the right of any alien to land, when adverse to such right, shall be final unless appeal be taken to the superintendent of immigration, whose action shall be subject to review by the Secretary of the Treasury. It shall be the duty of the aforesaid officers and agents of such vessel to adopt due precautions to prevent the landing of any alien immigrant at any place or time other than that designated by the inspection officers, and any such officer or agent or person in charge of such vessel who shall, either knowingly or negligently, land or permit to land any alien immigrant at any place or time other than that designated by the inspection officers, shall be deemed guilty of a misdemeanor and punished by a fine not exceeding one thousand dollars, or by imprisonment for a term not exceeding one year, or by both such fine and imprisonment." 26 Stat. at L. 1085 (U. S. Comp. Stat. 1901, p. 1298).

By the 10th section it is provided that "all aliens who may unlawfully come to the United States shall, if practicable, be immediately sent back on the vessel by which they were brought in."

The 11th section of the same act provided: "That any alien who shall come into the United States in violation of law may be returned as by law provided, at any time within one year thereafter, at the expense of the person or persons, vessel, transportation company, or corporation bringing such alien into the United States, and, if that cannot be done, then at the expense of the United States; and any alien who becomes a public charge within one year after his arrival in the United States, from causes existing prior to his landing therein, shall be deemed to have come in violation of law, and shall be returned as aforesaid." 26 Stat. at L. 1086 (U. S. Comp. Stat. 1901, p. 1299).

In the sundry civil appropriation act of August 18th, 1894, chap. 301, was the following provision: "In every case where an alien is excluded from admission into the United States under any law or treaty now existing or hereafter made, the decision of the appropriate immigration or customs officers, if adverse to the admission of such alien, shall be final, unless reversed on appeal to the Secretary of the Treasury." 28 Stat. at L. 372, 390 (U. S. Comp. Stat. 1901, p. 1303).

Then came the treaty between the United States and the Empire of Japan, concluded November 23d, 1894, and proclaimed March 21st, 1895, and which, by its terms, was to go into operation July 17th, 1899. By the 1st article of that treaty it was provided: "The citizens or subjects of each of the two high contracting parties shall have full liberty to enter, travel, or reside in any part of the territories of the other contracting party, and shall enjoy full and perfect protection for their persons and property." 29 Stat. at L. 848. But by the 2d article it was declared: "It is, however, understood that the stipulations contained in this and the preceding article do not in any way affect the laws, ordinances, and regulations with regard to trade, the immigration of laborers, police and public security, which are in force or which may hereafter be enacted in either of the two countries." 29 Stat. at L. 849.

1. From the above acts of Congress it appears that among the aliens forbidden to enter the United States are those, of whatever country, who are "paupers or persons likely to become a public charge." We are of opinion that aliens of that class have not been given by the treaty with Japan full liberty to enter or reside in the United States; for that instrument expressly excepts from its operation any ordinance or regulation relating to "police and public security." A statute excluding paupers or persons likely to become a public charge is manifestly one of police and public security. Aside from that specific exception, we should not be inclined to hold that the provision in the treaty with Japan, that the citizens or subjects of each of the two counties should have "full liberty to enter, travel, or reside in any part of the territories of the other contracting party," has any reference to that class, in either country, who, from their habits or condition, are ordinarily or properly the object of police regulations designed to protect the general public against contact with dangerous or improper persons.

2. The constitutionality of the legislation in question, in its general aspects, is no longer open to discussion in this court. That Congress may exclude aliens of a particular race from the United States; prescribe the terms and conditions upon which certain classes of aliens may come to this country; establish regulations for sending out of the country such aliens as come here in violation of law; and commit the enforcement of such provisions, conditions, and regulations exclusively to executive officers, without judicial intervention,—are principles firmly established by the decisions of this court. Nishimura Ekiu v. United States, 142 U. S. 651, 35 L. ed. 1146, 12 Sup. Ct. Rep. 336; Fong Yue Ting v. United States, 149 U. S. 698, 37 L. ed. 905, 13 Sup. Ct. Rep. 1016; Lem Moon Sing v. United States, 158 U. S. 538, 39 L. ed. 1082, 15 Sup. Ct. Rep. 967; Wong Wing v. United States, 163 U. S. 228, 41 L. ed. 140, 16 Sup. Ct. Rep. 977; Fok Yung Yo v. United States, 185 U. S. 296, 305, 46 L. ed. 917, 921, 22 Sup. Ct. Rep. 686, 690.

In Nishimura Ekiu's Case the court said: "The supervision of the admission of aliens into the United States may be intrusted by Congress either to the Department of State, having the general management of foreign relations, or to the Department of the Treasury, charged with the enforcement of the laws regulating foreign commerce; and Congress has often passed acts forbidding the immigration of particular classes of foreigners, and has committed the execution of these acts to the Secretary of the Treasury, to collectors of customs, and to inspectors acting under their authority." After observing that Congress, if it saw fit, could authorize the courts to investigate and ascertain the facts on which depended the right of the alien to land, this court proceeded: "But, on the other hand, the final determination of those facts may be intrusted by Congress to executive officers; and in such a case, as in all others in which a statute gives a discretionary power to an officer, to be exercised by him upon his own opinion of certain facts, he is made the sole and exclusive judge of the existence of those facts, and no other tribunal, unless expressly authorized by law to do so, is at liberty to re-examine or controvert the sufficiency of the evidence on which he acted. Martin v. Mott, 12 Wheat. 19, 31, 6 L. ed. 537, 541; Philadelphia & T. R. Co. v. Stimpson, 14 Pet. 448, 458, 10 L. ed. 535, 540; Benson v. McMahon, 127 U. S. 457, 32 L. ed. 234, 8 Sup. Ct. Rep. 1240; Re Oteiza y Cortes, 136 U. S. 330, sub nom. Oteiza y Cortes v. Jacobus, 34 L. ed. 464, 10 Sup. Ct. Rep. 1031. It is not within the province of the judiciary to order that foreigners who have never been naturalized, nor acquired any domicil or residence within the United States, nor even been admitted into the country pursuant to law, shall be permitted to enter, in opposition to the constitutional and lawful measures of the legislative and executive branches of the national government. As to such persons, the decisions of executive or administrative officers, acting within powers expressly conferred by Congress, are due process of law. Den ex dem. Murray v. Ho-

boken Land & Improv. Co. 18 How. 272, 15 L. ed. 372; *Hilton* v. *Merritt,* 110 U. S. 97, 28 L. ed. 83, 3 Sup. Ct. Rep. 548."

In *Lem Moon Sing's Case* it was said: " The power of Congress to exclude aliens altogether from the United States, or to prescribe the terms and conditions upon which they may come to this country, and to have its declared policy in that regard enforced exclusively through executive officers, without judicial intervention, is settled by our previous adjudications." And in *Fok Yung Yo's Case,* the latest one in this court, it was said: " Congressional action has placed the final determination of the right of admission in executive officers, without judicial*intervention, and this has been for many years the recognized and declared policy of the country."

What was the extent of the authority of the executive officers of the government over the petitioner after she landed? As has been seen, the Secretary of the Treasury, under the above act of October 19th, 1888, chap. 1210, was authorized, within one year after an alien of the excluded class entered the country, to cause him to be taken into custody and returned to the country whence he came. Substantially the same power was conferred by the act of March 3d, 1891, chap. 551, by the 11th section of which it is provided that the alien immigrant may be sent out of the country, "as provided by law," at any time within the year after his illegally coming into the United States. Taking all its enactments together, it is clear that Congress did not intend that the mere admission of an alien, or his mere entering the country, should place him at all times thereafter entirely beyond the control or authority of the executive officers of the government. On the contrary, if the Secretary of the Treasury became satisfied that the immigrant had been allowed to land contrary to the prohibition of that law, then he could at any time within a year after the landing cause the immigrant to be taken into custody and deported. The immigrant must be taken to have entered subject to the condition that he might be sent out of the country by order of the proper executive officer if, within a year, he was found to have been wrongfully admitted into, or had illegally entered, the United States. These were substantially the views expressed by the circuit court of appeals for the ninth circuit in *United States* v. *Yamasaka,* 40 C. C. A. 454, 100 Fed. 404.

It is contended, however, that in respect of an alien who has already landed it is consistent with the acts of Congress that he may be deported without previous notice of any purpose to deport him, and without any opportunity on his part to show by competent evidence before the executive officers charged with the execution of the acts of Congress, that he is not here in violation of law; that the deportation of an alien without provision for such a notice and for an opportunity to be heard *was inconsistent with the due process of law required by the 5th Amendment of the Constitution.

Leaving on one side the question whether an alien can rightfully invoke the due process clause of the Constitution who has entered the country clandestinely, and who has been here for too brief a period to have become, in any real sense, a part of our population, before his right to remain is disputed, we have to say that the rigid construction of the acts of Congress suggested by the appellant are not justified. Those acts do not necessarily exclude opportunity to the immigrant to be heard, when such opportunity is of right. It was held in *Den ex dem. Murray* v. *Hoboken Land & Improv. Co.* 18 How. 272, 280, 281, 283, 15 L. ed. 372, 376, 377, that "though ' due process of law ' generally implies and includes *actor, reus, judex,* regular allegations, opportunity to answer and a trial according to some settled course of judicial proceedings, . . . yet this is not universally true;" and "that though, generally, both public and private wrongs are redressed through judicial action, there are more summary extra-judicial remedies for both." Hence, it was decided in that case to be consistent with due process of law for Congress to provide summary means to compel revenue officers — and, in case of default, their sureties — to pay such balances of the public money as might be in their hands. Now, it has been settled that the power to exclude or expel aliens belonged to the political department of the government, and that the order of an executive officer invested with the power to determine finally the facts upon which an alien's right to enter this country, or remain in it, depended, was " due process of law, and no other tribunal, unless expressly authorized to do so, was at liberty to re-examine the evidence on which he acted, or to controvert its sufficiency." *Nishimura Ekiu* v. *United States,* 142 U. S. 651, 659, 35 L. ed. 1146, 1149, 12 Sup. Ct. Rep. 336; *Fong Yue Ting* v. *United States,* 149 U. S. 698, 713, 37 L. ed. 905, 913, 13 Sup. Ct. Rep. 1016; *Lem Moon Sing* v. *United States,* 158 U. S. 538, 547, 39 L. ed. 1082, 1085, 15 Sup. Ct. Rep. 967. But this court has never held, nor must we now be understood as holding, that administrative officers, when executing the provisions of a statute involving the liberty of persons, may disregard the fundamental principles that inhere in " due process of law " as understood at the time of the adoption of the Constitution. *One of these principles is that no person shall be deprived of his liberty without opportunity, at some time, to be heard, before such officers, in respect of the matters upon which that liberty depends,— not necessarily an opportunity upon a regular, set occasion, and according to the forms of judicial procedure, but one that will secure the prompt, vigorous action contemplated by Congress, and at the same time be appropriate to the nature of the case upon which such officers are required to act. Therefore, it is not competent for the Secretary of the Treasury or any executive officer, at any time within the year limited by the statute, arbitrarily to cause an alien who has entered the country, and has become subject in all respects to its jurisdiction, and a part of its population, although alleged to be illegally here, to be taken into custody and deported without giving him all opportunity to be heard upon the questions involving his right to be and remain in the United States. No such arbitrary power can exist where the principles involved in due process of law are recognized.

This is the reasonable construction of the acts of Congress here in question, and they need not be otherwise interpreted. In the case of all acts of Congress, such interpretation ought to be adopted, without doing violence to the import of the words used, will bring them into harmony with the Constitution. An act of Congress must be taken to be constitutional unless the contrary plainly and palpably appears. The words here used do not require an interpretation that would invest executive or administrative officers with the absolute, arbitrary power implied in the contention of the appellant. Besides, the record now before us shows that the appellant had notice, although not a formal one, of the investigation instituted for the purpose of ascertaining whether she was illegally in this country. The traverse to the return made by the immigration inspector shows upon its face that she was before that officer pending the investigation of her right to be in the United States, and made answers to questions propounded to her. It is true that she pleads a want of knowledge of our language; that she did not understand the nature and import of the questions propounded to her; that the investigation made was a "pretended" one; and that she did not, at the time, know that the investigation had reference to her being deported from the country. These considerations cannot justify the intervention of the courts. They could have been presented to the officer having primary control of such a case, as well as upon an appeal to the Secretary of the Treasury, who had power to order another investigation if that course was demanded by law or by the ends of justice. It is not to be assumed that either would have refused a second or fuller investigation, if a proper application and showing for one had been made by or for the appellant. Whether further investigation should have been ordered was for the officers charged with the execution of the statutes to determine. Their action in that regard is not subject to judicial review. Suffice it to say, it does not appear that appellant was denied an opportunity to be heard. And as no appeal was taken to the Secretary from the decision of the immigration inspector, that decision was final and conclusive. If the appellant's want of knowledge of the English language put her at some disadvantage in the investigation conducted by that officer, that was her misfortune, and constitutes no reason, under the acts of Congress, or under any rule of law, for the intervention of the court by habeas corpus. We perceive no ground for such intervention,— none for the contention that due process of law was denied to appellant.

The judgment is affirmed.

Mr. Justice **Brewer** and Mr. Justice **Peckham** dissented.

Are We That Far Gone?: Due Process and Secret Deportation Proceedings[1]

by

Michael Scaperlanda

The Oklahoma City and World Trade Center bombings, coupled with a resurgent anti-immigration sentiment, have led to renewed debate concerning the removal of "undesirable" aliens from the United States. The Comprehensive Terrorism Prevention Act of 1995 ("Terrorism Bill"),[2] contains provisions for partially secret *ex parte* deportation hearings and several bills introduced during the 104th Congress would curtail judicial review of deportation hearings.[3] In addition to these proposed procedural reforms, the nation is rethinking its substantive immigration policy.[4] By distinguishing the roles of procedure and substance in the implementation of our immigration policy, this article will accentuate the desirability of sound procedural safeguards. The Terrorism Bill's deportation mechanism provides a concrete backdrop for this discussion because it represents a model of sensitive balancing by policymakers attempting to reconcile the competing interests of the individual alien and the national community.

> *The Terrorism Bill ... attempt[s] to reconcile the competing interests of the individual alien and the national community.*

Michael Scaperlanda is a professor of law at the University of Oklahoma College of Law, where he specializes in administrative, constitutional and immigration law. He is a past chair of the American Immigration Lawyers Association's Law Professors Committee and received his B.A. (Economics) and his J.D. from the University of Texas.

THE PROCEDURE — SUBSTANCE DICHOTOMY

The history of U.S. immigration law reflects a paradox in public policy. Our professed faith in a "golden door" through which the world's downtrodden can pass on their journey to a new and better life continues to manifest itself in extremely generous immigration and asylum laws. Simultaneously, fear and prejudice have limited access to immigration and naturalization in ways that seem antithetical to our fundamental commitments to equality and justice.[5] For much of our nation's history, Congress' naturalization scheme read "Whites Only."[6] For example, the infamous Chinese Exclusion Laws prevented a longtime resident of the United States from returning home after a trip to China,[7] and the red scare of the McCarthy era led to the deportation of many long-term resident aliens who had relatively insignificant ties to the communist movement.[8]

Restrictive immigration legislation reflects the national mood at various points in our history. For example, several anti-Chinese laws enacted in the latter part of the nineteenth century reflected a national view strikingly captured by Justice Field's characterization of the Chinese as "a different race ... who will not assimilate with us."[9] Justice Brewer, who would have protected Chinese laborers from deportation, bluntly referred to them as "the obnoxious Chinese."[10] Today, economic despair, national security concerns, and racial anxiety bring us once again to the brink of enacting

263

nativist legislation.[11] At the state level, California's Proposition 187, which passed by a 59% to 41% margin,[12] excludes undocumented aliens from public schools, public health care, and public social services.[13] At a national level, Congress is considering several immigration reform bills, including some that would place a moratorium on immigration.[14]

As we chart a more restrictive course during the next few years, it is worthwhile to mine our immigration history for nuggets that might prove valuable in the contemporary debate. A small part of this history reveals that the citizenry, through elected representatives, is ultimately responsible for substantive immigration policy; the Supreme Court refuses to participate in the debate. In contrast, the Court does at times evaluate the procedures chosen to effectuate these substantive value choices. For instance, over a century ago and as part of its comprehensive plan to limit the Chinese population in the United States, Congress made both the substantive choice that Chinese citizens unlawfully in the United States would face a year of imprisonment at hard labor before being deported, and the procedural choice that the executive department, acting alone, could administer this policy upon summary hearing.[15] The Supreme Court deferred to Congress' substantive policy choices, but scrutinized the legislature's procedural choices.[16]

This section briefly examines the underlying rationale for judicial deference to the political departments' substantive immigration policy as contrasted with the Court's greater willingness to scrutinize Congress' procedural choices.

PLENARY CONGRESSIONAL POWER

The development of substantive immigration law is distinguished by a lack of judicial involvement in the interbranch dialogue that usually occurs when Congress' policy choices arguably conflict with established constitutional norms. "For reasons long recognized as valid, the responsibility for regulating the relationship between the United States and our alien visitors has been committed to the political branches of the Federal Government. Over no conceivable subject is the legislative power of Congress more complete."[17] "The reasons that preclude judicial review of political questions also dictate a narrow standard of review of decisions made by the Congress or the President in the area of immigration and naturalization."[18] In the immigration field, this judicial deference is known as the plenary power doctrine.[19]

Kleindienst v. Mandel,[20] an instance of ideological exclusion, serves as a useful example. Ernest Mandel, a Belgian journalist and self-described "revolutionary Marxist," received an invitation from American academics to speak in the United States, but the U.S. government

refused to issue a nonimmigrant visa because of his political beliefs.[21] The academics filed suit to test the exclusion, contending that the government had violated their First Amendment right to hear Mandel.

Although it explicitly recognized the legitimacy of this constitutional claim, the Court denied relief without engaging in its usual searching inquiry. The Court even refused to balance the government's interest against the academics' first amendment claims.[22] The academics lost because:

> In accord with ancient principles of the international law of nation-states, . . . the power to exclude aliens is "inherent in sovereignty, necessary for maintaining normal international relations and defending the country against foreign encroachments and dangers — a power to be exercised exclusively by the political branches of government." . . . The Court without exception has sustained Congress' plenary power to make rules for the admission of aliens and to exclude those who possess those characteristics which Congress has forbidden.[23]

In my opinion, the Court's refusal to provide a check on Congress' substantive immigration policy flows from its belief that citizens, through their elective representatives, possess the ultimate responsibility for determining the composition of the national community.[24] The Court has, however, taken a more active role in monitoring the political departments' procedural choices.

PROCEDURAL LIMITATIONS

Since plenary power's genesis in the late nineteenth century, the Court has continued to judge and develop the procedural mechanisms by which Congress' immigration policy is implemented.[25] This role is confined to ensuring that the "procedures meet the essential standard of fairness under the Due Process Clause and does not extend to imposing procedures that merely displace congressional" policy choices.[26]

For the most part, a noncitizen's right to procedural due process depends on her location; if she is within the territory of the United States, she is entitled to due process, but if she is considered outside United States territory, she has no process rights.

Two executive attempts to remove aliens from the country on *ex parte* evidence illustrate the scope of judicial review. In both cases, the Attorney General entered final orders of exclusion without granting a hearing because the exclusions were based on "confidential information the disclosure of which may be prejudicial to the public interest."[27] In these cases, the

Court claimed to rely almost exclusively on the location of the alien, although the rulings appear difficult to reconcile.[28]

The first case, *Kwong Hai Chew v. Colding,*[29] involved the government's attempt to bar a permanent resident alien from reentering the United States to return to his home and citizen spouse. The noncitizen, a seaman, sought to return to the United States following a lengthy voyage on a merchant vessel of United States registry. The Attorney General permanently excluded him from the United States without a hearing or even notice of the "nature and cause of any accusations against him."[30]

The critical issue for the court was the noncitizen's position in relation to the government; should the government consider him outside the country (an alien subject to exclusion) or inside (an alien subject to deportation). The Court recognized that aliens within U.S. borders are "persons" protected by the Constitution, including the due process clause of the Fifth Amendment. Prior to their deportation, such aliens are thus "entitled to notice of the nature of the charge and a hearing . . . . Although Congress may prescribe conditions for his expulsion and deportation, not even Congress may expel him without allowing him a fair opportunity to be heard."[31]

The Court skirted the constitutional due process issue, holding the *ex parte* exclusion procedures inapplicable to Kwong Hai Chew because his status was that of a person within the United States.[32] Location mattered; as someone considered within the United States, he was entitled to due process.

In contrast, the Court in *Shaughnessy v. United States ex rel. Mezei*[33] rejected a noncitizen's claim to due process even though he faced indefinite detention on Ellis Island pending removal to a third country. Mezei, a permanent resident alien who had resided in the United States for a quarter of a century, had made a 21-month trip abroad. Upon his attempted return, the government permanently excluded him and refused to reveal its evidence of excludability, even *in camera*, to a United States District Court Judge.

The Supreme Court rejected Mezei's due process claim, holding that the constitutional guarantee of due process did not extend to an alien at the border (a legal fiction because of his actual physical presence on U.S. soil). "Whatever the procedure authorized by Congress is, it is due process as far as an alien denied entry is concerned."[34] Therefore, the Attorney General's permanent exclusion order based on undisclosed evidence sealed Mezei's fate. *Kwong Hai Chew* was distinguished because Mezei's absence from the country was much longer than Kwong Hai Chew's, and Mezei had not obtained reentry papers prior to his departure.

Today, both noncitizens in the United States and permanent resident aliens who seek to reenter after a brief absence benefit from the constitutional guarantee that their liberty interest in remaining in (or returning to) the United States will not be denied without due process of law. Therefore, although remaining silent on substantive immigration issues, the Court now demonstrates a willingness to ensure that the federal government applies its general immigration policy to a particular noncitizen in a manner that reduces the risk of an erroneous decision. An individual is most vulnerable when she is singled out and the power of the government is brought to bear on her. Procedural safeguards are thus necessary to ensure that the substantive law is administered fairly — not arbitrarily — with respect to the specific individual.[35] With this brief overview of the procedure/substance dichotomy in immigration law, we now turn to the current policy debate concerning the procedures for removal of suspected alien terrorists.

TERRORIST REMOVAL PROCEDURES

On February 10, 1995, President Clinton transmitted to Congress his Omnibus Counterterrorism Act of 1995. His cover letter stated that:

> [one] of the most significant provisions of the bill will . . . provide a workable mechanism, utilizing U.S. District Court Judges appointed by the Chief Justice, to deport expeditiously alien terrorists without risking the disclosure of national security information or techniques.[36]

In the wake of the Oklahoma City bombing, Clinton renewed his call for passage of anti-terrorist legislation: "The tragic bombing of the Murrah Federal Building in Oklahoma City on April 19th . . . makes clear the need to enhance the Federal Government's ability to investigate, prosecute, and punish terrorist activity."[37]

To deport suspected terrorists without compromising due process, lawmakers have proposed an elaborate procedural scheme (special removal procedures) enhancing some procedural safeguards in deportation while significantly curtailing another. Procedural enhancements include: (1) the deportation decision will be made by an Article III judge appointed by the Chief Justice of the United States Supreme Court; (2) the alien will be entitled to counsel, including court-appointed counsel for aliens financially unable to secure their own; and (3) the alien will be allowed to appeal the deportation order directly to the Court of Appeals for the District of Columbia, sitting *en banc.*[38]

The procedural compromise, and it looms large, denies the alien the right to know all of the evidence against him and consequently the right to cross-examine

265

witnesses or officials about that evidence. When the special removal procedure is utilized, "the judge shall authorize the introduction *in camera* and *ex parte* of any evidence for which the Attorney General determines that public disclosure would pose a risk to the national security of the United States because it would disclose classified information."[39] The alien is entitled only to an unclassified summary of the evidence.[40]

The government can only utilize this special removal procedure when the judge finds probable cause to believe that: (1) "the Attorney General or Deputy Attorney General has approved of the proceeding"; (2) the suspected terrorist is in the United States; and (3) removing the alien from the United States by regular deportation proceedings "would pose a risk to the national security of the United States because such proceedings would disclose classified information."[41]

During debate on the Senate floor, Senator Hatch, in summarizing the procedures, characterized the Terrorism Bill as "just and fair." He said these measures are warranted:

> to give our law enforcement and courts the tools they need to quickly remove alien terrorists from within our midst without jeopardizing ... national security or the lives of law enforcement personnel .... The success of our counter-terrorism efforts depends on the effective use of classified information used to infiltrate foreign terrorist groups. We cannot afford to turn over these secrets in open court, jeopardizing both the future success of these programs and the lives of those who carry them out.[42]

Hatch reminded the opposition that deportation is not a criminal proceeding: "[T]he result will simply be the removal of these aliens from U.S. soil — that is all."[43]

Senator Biden spoke against the measure. He recognized that "the Oklahoma City bombing and earlier bombing of the World Trade Center demonstrate clearly that the United States must respond seriously to those, whether foreign or domestic, who kill and seek to make their point through killings and mass killings of Americans."[44] Biden would not, however, have the United States fight foreign terrorism with deportation upon secret evidence. He succinctly stated the dangers inherently lurking in the use of such procedures:

> We have never had such a procedure ... in America, where someone can bring a charge against an individual, go into Federal court, have the prosecutor meet alone with the judge and say:

> "Judge, these are all the horrible things that the defendant did. We're not going to tell the defendant what evidence there is that he did these horrible things .... We're not going to let the defendant's lawyer answer these questions. You and me judge — me, the prosecutor; you, the judge — let's deport him in a secret hearing, using secret evidence. Let's walk out of this courtroom, out of your chambers ... and say, 'OK, Smedlap, you're deported. We find you're a terrorist. You're out of here.'"

> And Smedlap looks and says, "Hey, tell me who said I was a terrorist. How do you know that?" We say, "Oh, no, we can't tell you. We know you did it, and we can't tell you how we know."

> Now I think that is about as un-American as it gets.

> Now what we will hear is — and I think the President is dead wrong on this — but what we will hear is, "Well, look, these folks are not American citizens. They are not entitled to the same privileges as American citizens in a courtroom."

> Well, that is technically true. But, my lord, I do not want to be part of anything that establishes that kind of Star Chamber proceeding. Technically, they may be right; philosophically, it is dead wrong.[45]

Is Biden correct? Are secret deportation proceedings repugnant to core American values? Or do these provisions reflect a careful, delicate and searching balancing of competing interests in line with our constitutional due process traditions? In other words, do these special removal procedures provide the requisite procedural fairness?

I will frame and discuss the question as a constitutional law issue, which, given our constitutional history, places the judiciary at center stage. This choice reflects reality, not desire — I believe strongly that legislators and the President, as persons who take an oath of fidelity to the Constitution (not to the Court) and who form our national political community, should all take the Constitution seriously.[46] For the nation's lawmakers, this duty takes on special importance; they should not enact legislation that they believe violates the fundamental commitments reflected in our founding document. It is vitally important that policymakers, as well as the courts, reconcile our laws — including the one at issue here — with our fundamental law. In the next section, I analyze the special removal procedures against our constitutional norms.

REMOVAL PROCEDURES: CONSTITUTIONAL?

I will approach the question of constitutionality at two levels: the interest-balancing approach utilized by the judiciary to determine the process due and Judge Henry Friendly's reflections on the attributes of a fair hearing.

INTEREST BALANCING

In *Landon v. Plasencia*,[47] the Court held that a permanent resident alien who seeks to return to the United States after a brief absence is entitled to due process. In determining the process due, the Court employed the balancing test it had adopted in *Mathews v. Eldridge*:

> In evaluating the procedures in any case, the courts must consider the interest at stake for the individual, the risk of an erroneous deprivation of the interest through the procedures used as well as the probable value of additional or different procedural safeguards, and the interest of the government in using the current procedures rather than additional or different procedures.[48]

If we look to the Court as a guide, we discover that it seeks accuracy in the administrative determination tempered by the realization that "procedural requirements entail the expenditure of limited resources, [so] that at some point the benefit to individuals from an additional safeguard is substantially outweighed by the cost of providing such protection."[49] Judge Friendly provides a framework within which to conduct this balancing to ensure that balancing does not "lead to the anomalous result that an individual will have a clear due process right to no process."[50]

ELEMENTS OF A FAIR HEARING

In descending order of importance, Friendly lists the attributes of a fair hearing as (1) "an unbiased tribunal," (2) "notice of proposed action and grounds asserted for it," (3) "an opportunity to present reasons why the proposed action should not be taken," (4) the right "to call witnesses," (5) the right "to know the evidence against one," (6) the right "to have the decision based only on the evidence presented," (7) the right to counsel, (8) "the making of a record," (9) a "statement of reasons" for action to be taken, (10) a proceeding open to the public, and (11) judicial review.[51] Friendly would not consider these elements separately; "if an agency chooses to go

further than is constitutionally demanded with respect to one item, this may afford good reason for diminishing or even eliminating another."[52] Similarly, Redish and Marshall conclude that an unbiased independent adjudicator is *the* necessary procedure to ensure that the values underlying the command of procedural due process are met.[53]

Employing the *Mathews* balancing test and informed by Friendly's rank ordering of procedural possibilities, we turn now to an analysis of the special removal procedures, looking first to the individual's interest, then to the accuracy of given procedures, and finally to the government's interests.

INTEREST OF THE SUSPECTED TERRORIST

We need not dwell long here; an alien's interest or potential interest in deportation is great. The special removal procedures could be utilized to deport a permanent resident alien who has built a life here and literally knows nothing of her country of origin. Imagine a fifty-five-year-old who came to this country fifty years ago from Eastern Europe and has never returned. In the intervening half century, she married a citizen, raised citizen children, established intimate relationships in her community, and built her own business. In short, she has much to lose if deported.

Her problem may be compounded by the scarlet letter she has to bear. Having been adjudged a terrorist, she may be unable to gain admittance to any other country, forcing her to take a place alongside Mezei's ghost as an indefinite guest at a governmental detention facility.

ACCURACY

Any student of our immigration history ought to find the prospect of secret immigration proceedings cause for grave concern. We need look no further than *Knauff* and *Mezei* to fully appreciate the mischief occasioned by secret immigration proceedings. In both cases, the aliens were excluded from the United States on the basis of secret information (which, the government successfully argued, could not be revealed without compromising the public interest) allegedly indicating that entry of these aliens into the United States would constitute a breach of national security.

In the end and after much publicity, both Knauff and Mezei were granted full hearings and allowed to return to the United States. Knauff was admitted by order of the Board of Immigration Appeals, and Mezei was paroled into the United States on order of the Attorney General.[54] And, as Charles Weisselberg demonstrates in his illuminating study of these two cases, the government's double national security claims (entry would breach security and telling you why would also breach security) turned out to be rather tenuous.

With respect to Knauff, the Board of Immigration Appeals concluded that "there was no substantial evidence that Knauff gave secret information to the Czechoslovakian authorities, nor was there evidence to support any inference that Knauff would engage in subversive activities if admitted to the United States. Uncorroborated hearsay" is not enough to support the exclusion.[55]

In contrast, some of the claims against Mezei were substantiated and did provide a basis for exclusion, but they did not amount to a national security threat which would warrant an indefinite and possibly life-long detention without a hearing. When the government was forced to disclose its charges, it alleged that Mezei was excludable on the following grounds: (1) he was a member of the Communist Party for at least some time between 1929 and 1945;[56] (2) he was convicted of a crime involving moral turpitude (petty larceny); and (3) he gave false information to Hungarian consular officers in order to obtain an immigrant visa.[57]

In hindsight, *Knauff* and *Mezei* may well be considered travesties of justice — the low water marks of American procedure. But on what grounds? Was procedural fairness denied by the failure to disclose the evidence against Knauff and Mezei and give them each a chance to rebut or cross-examine? In both cases, the procedural deficiencies went much farther.

Knauff and *Mezei* deserve scorn from anyone who, like Justice Jackson, believes that "[p]rocedural fairness and regularity are the indispensable essence of liberty" because the United States denied these two individuals each element of procedural fairness listed by Judge Friendly.[58] No unbiased and independent adjudicator sat in check of the executive's exercise of power. Although informed of the proposed actions, the excluded aliens were not informed of the specific grounds for the action. Since no hearing was held, no opportunity existed to argue in favor of admission, to call witnesses, to know the evidence, to have a decision on the record, to have meaningful use of counsel, to have a record made, to have an open proceeding, or to have meaningful judicial review.

The special removal procedures now contemplated by Congress and the President represent a far more complex and nuanced attempt to effectuate the government's legitimate interest in maintaining national security. The statute and regulations relied upon in *Knauff* and *Mezei* did not even have the pretense of an attempt to balance the competing interests of individual and nation; the policymakers simply took a sledgehammer to the problem, completely obliterating the individual alien's interests. The special removal procedures of the

Terrorism Bill, however, reflect a carefully crafted attempt to reconcile the competing interests. They take away procedural protection where deemed necessary in the interest of national security but mitigate the damage in two ways: by placing an independent check on the executive's assertion of security interests and by providing the alien with other added procedural safeguards.

Congress increased the level of adjudicatory independence for terrorist deportation. Unlike the typical deportation case, which is heard by a quasi-independent immigration judge with appeal to the Board of Immigration Appeals (another quasi-independent body), the suspected terrorist has her case heard outside of the Justice Department by a life-tenured Article III judge appointed by the Chief Justice, with appeal to the United States Court of Appeals for the District of Columbia sitting *en banc*. Adjudicatory independence places a "meaningful check on the Attorney General's decision" to seek *ex parte* and *in camera* deportation proceedings.[59] Although the judge does not have to agree with the Attorney General's conclusion that regular deportation hearings would compromise national security by disclosing classified information, the judge must independently conclude that "there is probable cause to believe" that this compromise of security would occur. As Judge Friendly has commented, "there is wisdom in recognizing that the further the tribunal is removed from the agency and thus from any suspicion of bias, the less may be the need for other procedural safeguards."[60]

Providing the alien with a judge-approved "unclassified summary of the specific [classified] evidence," enhances — albeit imperfectly — the ability of the alien to defend herself against the charges, especially given the statutory assurance that the alien will have the assistance of counsel. And, as is the case in all other deportation proceedings, the order of deportability will only issue on a finding that the Attorney General met her case by clear and convincing evidence.[61]

This second element of the *Mathews* balancing test attempts to assess the risk of error and the probable change in that risk if other procedures are used. At one level, it is certainly true that the risk of error is greater, maybe even much greater, when a person is denied access to the full raw evidence against him, leaving him incapable of testing the integrity of that evidence by cross-examination and rebuttal.[62] At another level though, it is not entirely clear that the risk of error would be reduced if we were to treat terrorist deportations in the same fashion as other deportation proceedings. Although regular deportation procedure requires the government to fully disclose its evidence, it also allows the deportation decision to be made by a Justice Department official with review by other Justice Department officials. We can assume that these independent administrative adjudicators would act in good faith and in an unbiased fashion, but they still lack the degree of independence of a life-tenured judge. Additionally, suspected alien terrorists without financial means under regular deportation procedures do not have access to counsel. I lack the critical tools necessary to determine whether the risk of an erroneous deprivation would be reduced by utilizing the normal deportation procedures in terrorist deportations; suffice it to say that I do not think the answer is self-evident.

THE GOVERNMENT'S INTEREST: NATIONAL SECURITY
The government's interest, like the alien's, weighs heavy. In prepared testimony before the House Judiciary Committee, William O. Studeman, Acting Director of Intelligence, articulated the national interest:

[In combating terrorism it is] even more crucial that the United States obtain the close and continual cooperation of other countries. One of the best ways to ensure this cooperation is to protect the information that these countries share with us about terrorists. Foreign governments simply will not confide in us if we cannot keep their secrets.

One goal of [the Terrorism Bill] is to provide a mechanism to do just that by protecting classified information in special removal hearings for alien terrorists. The objective is to permit the court to consider classified information as evidence without risking the compromise of sensitive intelligence sources and methods for foreign government information.[63]

The proposed Omnibus Counterterrorism Act of 1995,[64] which also contains special removal procedures for alien terrorists, supports the intelligence community's concerns. Section 3 of the bill sets out several legislative findings supporting Congress' proposed action, including:

Law enforcement officials have been hindered in using current immigration law to deport alien terrorists because the law fails to provide procedures to protect classified intelligence sources and information. Moreover, a few high ranking members of terrorist organizations have been naturalized as United States citizens because denial of such naturalizations would have necessitated public disclosure of highly classified sources and methods. Furthermore, deportation hearings frequently extend over several years, thus hampering the expeditious removal of aliens engaging in terrorist activity.

Present immigration law is inadequate to protect the United States from terrorist attacks by certain aliens. New procedures are needed to permit expeditious removal of alien terrorists from the United States, thereby reducing the threat that such aliens pose to the national security and other vital interests of the United States.[65]

Suppose that Biden's Smedlap has lived a life of "unrelieved insignificance"[66] until one day the United States government receives concrete evidence that he is a member of a pro-nationalist Russian terrorist group dedicated to undermining the government of Boris Yeltsin through all means available, including kidnapping, bombing, and sabotage. The United States obtains this information from British Intelligence, which has personnel who have infiltrated this terrorist organization.

Without the ability to use classified information as evidence in the deportation of terrorists, the executive branch is placed on the horns of a most difficult dilemma: it can disclose the evidence and deport, alienating the British in the process, compromising British agents in the field, and possibly compromising British intelligence techniques, or it can refuse to disclose the evidence and knowingly harbor a terrorist.

CONCLUSION: THE SPECIAL REMOVAL PROCEDURES AS A MODEL IN BALANCING
Banishing someone from their community and home should never be undertaken lightly. And, to sanction such action without allowing the person to know and test the integrity of the evidence against him should cause every legislator, the President, and all Americans to shudder from the realization that important procedural safeguards have been cast aside. Our sorrow and fear at the loss of innocence precipitated by terrorism's arrival on our shores should not paralyze our resolve. If Congress believes that our liberties can best be safeguarded by adjusting the deportation procedures for suspected terrorists, it can do so within the flexible parameters of the due process clause. "Like any other constitutional provision, due process can be subordinated to some extraordinarily pressing governmental need. As Justice Goldberg put it, 'while the Constitution protects against invasions of individual rights, it is not a suicide pact.'"[67]

The special removal provisions do not, however, subordinate due process to compelling national security concerns. In a more limited and carefully crafted fashion, Congress chose to subordinate one procedure to the peace and security of the nation. Instead of a wholesale scrapping of procedural safeguards, as happened in *Knauff* and *Mezei*, Congress followed Judge Friendly's advice by

269

replacing the lost procedure with other powerful reinforcements.

To answer the question posed in the title — no, we are not that far gone. In fact, we should congratulate the policymakers for a fine job of balancing the important interests present when the United States seeks to deport a suspected terrorist. Deportation of noncitizens who are perceived as national security threats is a recurring theme in our nation's history. In fact, our first national immigration law, the unpopular Alien Act of 1798, allowed the executive to expel dangerous aliens from the United States.[46] In all likelihood, our national desire to deport "dangerous" noncitizens will continue with the call to legislative action that is prominent in times of crisis or tragedy. Hopefully, the special removal procedures will serve as a model for future policymakers when they are called upon to implement our constitutional due process norms in the face of grave national or international dangers.

NOTES

[1] Justice Jackson twice denounced the use of secret exclusion hearings. *See* Shaughnessy v. United States *ex rel.* Mezei, 345 U.S. 206, 218 (1953) (Jackson, J., dissenting); and United States *ex rel.* Knauff v. Shaughnessy, 338 U.S. 537, 550 (1950) (Jackson, J., dissenting). In *Mezei*, he concluded, "[i]t is inconceivable to me that this measure of simple justice and fair dealing [a fair hearing with fair notice of the charges] would menace the security of this country. No one can make me believe that we are that far gone." *Mezei*, 345 U.S. at 228.

[2] 735, 104th Cong., 1st Sess. (1995) (passed by the Senate).

[3] *See, e.g.*, S. 269, 104th Cong., 1st Sess. (1995).

[4] *See, e.g.*, H.R. 373, 104th Cong., 1st Sess. (1995) (proposing an immigration moratorium; narrowing the scope of both family-sponsored and employment-based immigration categories; decreasing family-sponsored immigration from a minimum of 226,000 to 10,000 per year and employment-based immigration from 140,000 to 5,000 per year; and eliminating visas for the diversity immigrant category); H.R. 4, 104th Cong., 1st Sess. § 500 (1995) (passed by the House) ([as] part of comprehensive welfare reform, immigration provisions severely restrict permanent resident alien eligibility under several welfare programs and authorize states to follow suit); and H.R. 605, 104th Cong., 1st Sess. (1995) (requiring certain legal aliens to reside in the United States for five consecutive years to be eligible for preferential public housing and rental assistance).

[5] *See generally* Kevin R. Johnson, *Public Benefits and Immigration: The Intersection of Immigration Status, Ethnicity, Gender, and Class*, 42 UCLA L. REV. 1509, 1519-28 (1995) (describing the historical fear that aliens would consume too many public resources).

[6] The first Congress declared that only "free white person[s]" were eligible for citizenship. *See* Act of Mar. 26, 1790, ch. 3, § 1, 1 Stat. 103. This "only 'free whites' need apply" rule was whittled away over the years. *See* Act of July 16, 1870, ch. 254, § 7, 16 Stat. 256 (aliens of African nativity or descent eligible for naturalization); Act of Oct. 14, 1940, ch. 876, § 303, 54 Stat. 1137, 1140 ("races indigenous to the Western Hemisphere" eligible for naturalization); Act of Dec. 17, 1943, ch. 344, § 1, 57 Stat. 600, 601 (aliens of Chinese origins eligible for naturalization); and § 3, 60 Stat. 416 (1946) ("races indigenous to India" and Filipinos eligible for naturalization). In 1952, Congress ended its racially discriminatory naturalization policies. *See* Act of June 27, 1952, ch. 477, § 311, 66 Stat. 163, 239, codified as amended at 8 U.S.C.A. § 1422 (West Supp. 1995). The 1952 repeal primarily benefited Japanese immigrants, who at that time were the largest group of aliens living in the United States but ineligible for citizenship. *Cf.* Oyama v. California, 332 U.S. 633 (1948) (concerning a Japanese farmer ineligible for naturalization). *See generally* 4 CHARLES GORDON & STANLEY MAILMAN, IMMIGRATION LAW AND PROCEDURE § 15.12 (1990); Charles Gordon, *The Racial Barrier to American Citizenship*, 93 U. PA. L. REV. 237 (1945).

[7] *See* Chae Chan Ping v. United States (The Chinese Exclusion Case), 130 U.S. 581 (1889). Chae Chan Ping, a Chinese citizen, had lived and worked in California for 12 years prior to his return to China in 1887. *Id.* at 582.

[8] *See* Harisaides v. Shaughnessy, 342 U.S. 580, 581-83 (1952); and Galvan v. Press, 347 U.S. 522, 523 (1954). The four defendants in *Harisaides* and *Galvan* had a collective 142-year presence in the United States, with each defendant residing here for over 30 years. One defendant had been associated with the Communist Party for only six years, his membership having ceased 17 years prior to his deportation.

[9] *Chae Chan Ping*, 130 U.S. at 606.

[10] Fong Yue Ting v. United States, 149 U.S. 698, 743 (1893) (Brewer, J., dissenting).

[11] *Cf.* Kevin R. Johnson, *Fear of an Alien Nation? Race, Immigration, and Immigrants*, STAN. L. & POL'Y REV., Summer 1996, at 111.

[12] California Secretary of State, Statement of Vote, November 8, 1994 at 115 (1994).

[13] Proposition 187's provisions are scattered throughout California's statutes. *See, e.g.*, CAL. EDUC. CODE §§ 48215, 66010.8 (West Supp. 1995); CAL. HEALTH & SAFETY CODE §130 (West Supp. 1995); CAL. WELF. & INST. CODE §10001.5 (West Supp. 1995).

[14] *See* note 4, *supra*.

[15] Act of May 5, 1892, ch. 60, § 4, 27 Stat. 25 ("[A]ny such Chinese person . . . adjudged to be not lawfully entitled to be or remain in the United States shall be imprisoned at hard labor for a period of not exceeding one year and thereafter removed from the United States."). "[S]uch imprisonment is to be adjudged against the accused by a justice, judge, or commissioner, upon a summary hearing." Wong Wing v. United States, 163 U.S. 228, 236 (1896).

[16] Compare Fong Yue Ting v. United States, 149 U.S. 698, 731 (1893) ("The question whether, and upon what conditions, these aliens shall be permitted to remain within the United States being one to be determined by the political departments of the government, the judicial department cannot properly express an opinion upon the wisdom, the policy or the justice of the measures enacted by Congress . . .") with Wong Wing, 163 U.S. at 237 (holding that Congress cannot promote its immigration policy by criminal punishment without providing "for a judicial trial to establish the guilt of the accused").

[17] Reno v. Flores, 113 S. Ct. 1439, 1449 (1993) (citations and internal quotations omitted).

[18] Fiallo v. Bell, 430 U.S. 787, 796 (1977) (citations and internal quotations omitted). But see American-Arab Anti-Discrimination Committee v. Reno, 70 F.3d 1045, 1065 (9th Cir. 1995) (instead of deferring to Congress' judgment with respect to the grounds for deportation as the plenary power doctrine would require, the court concluded that "[w]e find no merit in the Government's argument that the broad authority of the political branches over immigration matters justifies limited First Amendment protection for aliens at deportation").

[19] See, e.g., Louis Henkin, The Constitution and the United States Sovereignty: A Century of Chinese Exclusion and Its Progeny, 100 HARV. L. REV. 853, 859 (1987); Stephen H. Legomsky, Immigration Law and The Principle of Plenary Congressional Power, 1984 SUP. CT. REV. 255 (1984); Hiroshi Motomura, Immigration Law After a Century of Plenary Power: Phantom Constitutional Norms and Statutory Interpretation, 100 YALE L.J. 545, 547 (1990); Michael Scaperlanda, Polishing the Tarnished Golden Door, 1993 WISC. L. REV. 965, 967 (1993); Margaret Taylor, Alien Detainees Challenging Conditions of Confinement and the Porous Border of the Plenary Power Doctrine 22 HASTINGS CONST. L.Q. 928 (1995).

[20] 408 U.S. 753 (1972).

[21] Id.

[22] See id. at 770.

[23] Id. at 765-66. Plenary power also applies in the context of deportation. See Fong Yue Ting v. United States, 149 U.S. 698, 707 (1893) ("The right of a nation to expel or deport

foreigners . . . rests upon the same grounds, and is as absolute and unqualified as the right to prohibit and prevent their entrance into the country."). Several academics have criticized the plenary power doctrine, which has "been taken to mean that there are no constitutional limitations on the power of Congress to regulate immigration." Louis Henkin, supra note 19, at 859 (1987). Professor Nafziger has convincingly challenged the international law foundations of the plenary power doctrine. See James A. Nafziger, The General Admission of Aliens Under International Law, 77 AM. U. J. INT'L. L. & POL'Y 804 (1983) (arguing that international law never permitted unbounded sovereign discretion in matters of admission, exclusion, and expulsion of noncitizens). In a previous article, I argued that even if international law once provided a reasonable basis upon which to build these inherent sovereign powers, it no longer does in light of emerging international human rights norms. See Scaperlanda, supra note 19, at 965.

[24] See Michael Scaperlanda, Partial Membership: Aliens and the Constitutional Community (forthcoming in the Iowa Law Review).

[25] See, e.g., Yamataya v. Fisher (The Japanese Immigrant Case), 189 U.S. 86, 100 (1903) (conceding that the political branches possessed unfettered power over substantive immigration policy, the Court said that "we have never held, nor must we now be understood as holding," that government officials can dispense with due process, including the right to a fair hearing in a deportation proceeding).

[26] Landon v. Plasencia, 459 U.S. 21, 34-35 (1982).

[27] Shaughnessy v. United States ex rel. Mezei, 345 U.S. 206, 210 (1953). Accord Kwong Hai Chew v. Colding, 344 U.S. 590, 595 (1953). Congress had delegated to the executive the authority to prohibit, during international tension and strife, alien admission that would prejudice United States interests. See Mezei, 345 U.S. at 210. Pursuant to this authority, the executive promulgated regulations authorizing the Attorney General to "deny an alien a hearing . . . where he determined that the alien was excludable . . . on the basis of information of a confidential nature, the disclosure of which would be prejudicial to the public interest." United States ex rel. Knauff v. Shaughnessy, 338 U.S. 537, 541 (1950).

[28] This territorial approach to the guarantee of due process has come under considerable attack by legal scholars. See, e.g., David A. Martin, Due Process and Membership in the National Community: Political Asylum and Beyond, 44 U. PITT. L. REV. 165, 176 (1983) (the territorial approach reflected in "[t]he Knauff-Mezei doctrine comes close to saying that even though the fifth amendment due process protection applies to 'persons,' we simply do not regard excludable aliens as falling within that category").

[29] Kwong Hai Chew, 344 U.S. at 595.

[30] *Id.*

[31] *Id.* at 597-98.

[32] *Id.* at 596. Although the Court's analysis relied on statutory grounds, it has since come to be recognized as constitutional law. *See* Landon v. Plasencia, 459 U.S. 21, 33 (1982). In *Landon,* the Court specifically recognized that permanent resident aliens who are only briefly absent from the country are entitled to due process prior to a determination of exclusion. *Id.* at 32-33.

[33] 345 U.S. 206 (1950).

[34] *Id.* at 212 (quoting United States *ex rel.* Knauff v. Shaughnessy, 338 U.S. 537, 544 (1950)).

[35] As Professor Rubin stated: "[W]hen the state focuses its power upon an individual, that person is potentially subject to all the abuses which arbitrary, resentful, or corrupt state agents may inflict." Edward L. Rubin, *Generalizing the Trial Model of Procedural Due Process: A New Basis for the Right to Treatment,* 17 HARV. C.R.-C.L. L. REV. 61, 71 (1982). For purposes of discussing due process in the administrative state, a distinction between the due process accorded an individual when an agency acts in an enforcement role, targeting a specific individual and in a legislative/policymaking role, targeting a broad group of people, can be traced back to Londoner v. Denver, 210 U.S. 373 (1908) (landowners entitled to a hearing upon the assessment of fee for paving done on adjacent streets) and Bi-Metallic Inv. Co. v. State Bd. of Equalization, 239 U.S. 441 (1915) (no right to a hearing on question of increase in the valuation of property citywide). *See, e.g.,* 2 KENNETH C. DAVIS & RICHARD J. PIERCE, JR., ADMINISTRATIVE LAW TREATISE § 9.2, at 9 (1994) ("When ... government singles out an individual for adverse action, the political process provides little protection. Individuals singled out for adverse action can be protected only by forcing the government to use a decisionmaking process that ensures fairness to the individual."); Michael Scaperlanda, *Judicial Solecism Repeated: An Analysis of the Oklahoma Supreme Court's Refusal to Recognize the Adjudicative Nature of Particularized Ratemaking,* 47 OKLA. L. REV. 601, 611-14 (1995).

[36] 141 CONG. REC. S2493-01, S2398 (February 10, 1995) (letter from President Clinton to Congress on the Omnibus Counterterrorism Act of 1995).

[37] 141 CONG. REC. S7597 (May 26, 1995) (letter from President Clinton to Senator Robert Dole).

[38] *See* S. 735, 104th Cong., 1st Sess., § 503 (1995) (passed by the Senate).

[39] *Id.* at § 503(e)(C)(5).

[40] *Id.*

[41] *Id.* at § 503(a)-(d).

[42] 141 CONG. REC. S7480 (daily ed. May 25, 1995) (remarks of Sen. Hatch).

[43] *Id.* Hatch is correct in this characterization; the Court has always considered deportation as a civil matter. *See, e.g.,* Fong Yue Ting v. United States, 149 U.S. 698, 730 (1893). Dissenting justices have vigorously disputed this conclusion. Justice Field, the author of the majority opinion in *Chae Chin Ping,* dissented in *Fong Yue Ting* because deportation is punishment "beyond all reason in its severity ... It is cruel and unusual. As to its cruelty, nothing can exceed forcible deportation from a country of one's residence, and the breaking up of all the relations ... there contracted." *Id.* at 759 (Field, J., dissenting). *See generally* Michael Scaperlanda, *Thurgood Marshall and the Legacy of Dissent in Federal Alienage Cases,* 8 GEO. IMMIGR. L.J. 1 (1994) (exploring a century of dissent from plenary power).

[44] 141 CONG. REC. S7484 (daily ed. May 25, 1995) (remarks of Sen. Biden).

[45] *Id.*

[46] *See* Scaperlanda, *supra* note 19, at 1028-32. *See also* CASS R. SUNSTEIN, THE PARTIAL CONSTITUTION 350 (1994) (calling for "nonjudicial actors — Congress, the President, state officials, ordinary citizens — to engage in deliberation about the meaning of the Constitution's broad guarantees"); Wayne D. Moore, *Reconceiving Interpretative Autonomy: Insights From the Virginia and Kentucky Resolutions,* 11 CONST. COMM. 315, 315 (1994) ("It is necessary ... to move beyond widespread preoccupation with the Constitution's *judicial* interpretation and enforcement).

[47] 459 U.S. 21 (1982).

[48] *Id.* at 34 (paraphrasing *Mathews,* 424 U.S. 219, 334-35 (1976)). The *Mathews* balancing approach has many critics. *See, e.g.,* JERRY L. MASHAW, DUE PROCESS IN THE ADMINISTRATIVE STATE 32 (1985) (arguing "that the basic methodology of administrative due process adjudication has gone awry"); Martin H. Redish and Lawrence C. Marshall, *Adjudicatory Independence and the Values of Procedural Due Process,* 95 YALE L.J. 455, 474 (1986) ("the indeterminacy of *Mathews'* balancing test threatens to undermine wholly the viability of the guarantee").

[49] Henry J. Friendly, "*Some Kind of Hearing,*" 123 U. PA. L. REV. 1267, 1276 (1975).

[50] Redish & Marshall, *supra* note 48, at 472.

32

[51] Friendly, *supra* note 49, at 1279-95.

[52] *Id.* at 1279.

[53] Redish & Marshall, *supra* note 48, at 475.

[54] Charles D. Weisselberg, *The Exclusion and Detention of Aliens: Lessons from the Lives of Ellen Knauff and Ignatz Mezei*, 143 U. PA. L. REV. 933, 964, 984 (1995).

[55] *Id.* at 963-64.

[56] This allegation was "proved" by an unreliable professional witness, the protection of whose identity can hardly be justified on national security grounds. *Id.* at 980.

[57] *Id.* at 975.

[58] Shaughnessy v. United States ex rel. Mezei, 345 U.S. 206, 224 (Jackson, J., dissenting).

[59] *Cf.* Weisselberg, *supra* note 54, at 1024.

[60] Friendly, *supra* note 49, at 1279. *See also* Redish & Marshall, *supra* note 48, at 475. ("It is our position that the participation of an independent adjudicator is such an essential safeguard, and may be the only one . . . . [W]e shall demonstrate that, under certain circumstances, the values of due process might arguably be safeguarded absent [other] specific procedural protections.").

[61] If the court does not approve the unclassified summary, the special removal proceedings will terminate "unless the court, . . . after reviewing the classified information *in camera* and *ex parte* issues written findings that

   (i) the alien's continued presence in the United States would likely cause

    (I) serious and irreparable harm to the national security; or

    (II) death or serious bodily injury to any person; and

   (ii) provision of either the classified information or an unclassified summary that meets the [statutory] standard . . . would likely cause

    (I) serious and irreparable harm to the national security; or

    (II) death or serious bodily injury to any person; and

   (iii) the unclassified summary prepared by the Justice Department is adequate to allow the alien to prepare a defense."

S. 735, 104th Cong., 1st Sess. § 503(e)(6)(E) (1995).

[62] One recent Ninth Circuit opinion inferred that full disclosure of the evidence against a noncitizen lies at "the core of constitutional due process," concluding that "use of undisclosed information in adjudications should be presumptively

unconstitutional." American-Arab Anti-Discrimination Comm. v. Reno, 70 F.3d 1045, 1070 (1995). It is beyond the scope of this essay to tackle this opinion point by point. Although there are factual and legal distinctions that might distinguish that case from anything that might arise under the special removal procedures, I will assume for the sake of argument that those differences are of minimal relevance. The real differences between the court's views and my own, are, I think, philosophical. These differences are underscored by the court's *Mathews* balancing. With respect to the individual aliens' interest we agree: the alien has a strong liberty interest in remaining in the United States. *See id.* at 1069. This is where our agreement ends. In a summary fashion, the court concludes that a hearing held upon partially secret evidence is "inherently unfair because of the enormous risk of error." *Id.* at 1069-70. Here, the court follows what I perceive to be the prevalent view — fairness demands complete disclosure of evidence used against an alien in an immigration proceeding. In fact, this was my unexamined view when I started this project. My intent is to question that assumption. Procedural fairness derives from a flexible aggregate of safeguards, which cannot accurately be viewed in isolation from each other. The court also assigns a much lower value to the government's claimed interest than I would: "If the Government chooses not to reveal its information in order to protect its sources, the *only risk it faces* is that attendant to tolerance of [the aliens'] presence so long as they do not engage in deportable activities." *Id.* at 1070 (emphasis added). The risk is much larger than the court suggests. If the secret evidence portion of the Terrorism Bill were struck down under the due process clause, the Government, if it chose not to reveal its information, would face the risk of tolerating the alien's presence even though he or she is deportable as a terrorist.

[63] *International Terrorism, 1995: Hearing on H.R. 896 Before the House Judiciary Committee*, 104th Cong., 1st Sess. (1995) (statement of William O. Studeman, Acting Director, Central Intelligence).

[64] H.R. 896, 104th Cong., 1st Sess. (1995).

[65] *Id.* at § 3(a)(21), (22).

[66] This is Justice Jackson's phrase characterizing Ignatz Mezei's life. Shaughnessy v. United States *ex rel.* Mezei, 345 U.S. 206, 219 (Jackson, J., dissenting).

[67] Redish & Marshall, *supra* note 48, at 475 n.85 (quoting Kennedy v. Mendoza-Martinez, 372 U.S. 144, 160 (1963)). *See also* Friendly, *supra* note 49, at 1286 ("[D]enial of cross-examination . . . suppression of the names of witnesses and consequent serious curtailment of the right to know the evidence against one . . . should be permitted . . . if the dangers of disclosure are exceedingly grave.").

[68] Act of June 25, 1798, 1 Stat. 570 (1798).

SUBCHAPTER V—ALIEN TERRORIST REMOVAL PROCEDURES

§ 1531. Definitions

As used in this subchapter—

(1) the term "alien terrorist" means any alien described in section 1227(a)(4)(B) of this title;

(2) the term "classified information" has the same meaning as in section 1(a) of the Classified Information Procedures Act (18 U.S.C. App.);

(3) the term "national security" has the same meaning as in section 1(b) of the Classified Information Procedures Act (18 U.S.C. App.);

(4) the term "removal court" means the court described in section 1532 of this title;

(5) the term "removal hearing" means the hearing described in section 1534 of this title;

(6) the term "removal proceeding" means a proceeding under this subchapter; and

(7) the term "special attorney" means an attorney who is on the panel established under section 1532(e) of this title.

(June 27, 1952, c. 477, Title V, § 501, as added Apr. 24, 1996, Pub.L. 104–132, Title IV, § 401(a), 110 Stat. 1258, and amended Sept. 30, 1996, Pub.L. 104–208, Div. C, Title III, §§ 308(g)(1), 354(a)(5), 110 Stat. 3009–622, 3009–643.)

HISTORICAL AND STATUTORY NOTES

Revision Notes and Legislative Reports
1996 Acts. Senate Report No. 104–179 and House Conference Report No. 104–518, see 1996 U.S. Code Cong. and Adm. News, p. 924.

References in Text
Section 1(a) of the Classified Information Procedures Act, referred to in par. (2), is section 1(a) of Pub.L. 96–456, Oct. 15, 1980, 94 Stat. 2025, as amended, which is classified to Appendix 3 to Title 18, Crimes and Criminal Procedure.

Section 1(b) of the Classified Information Procedures Act, referred to in par. (3), is section 1(b) of Pub.L. 96–456, Oct. 15, 1980, 94 Stat. 2025, as amended, which is classified to Appendix 3 to Title 18, Crimes and Criminal Procedure.

Amendments
1996 Amendments. Par. (1). Pub.L. 104–208, § 308(g)(1), substituted "1227(a)94)(B)" for "1251(a)(4)(B)".

Par. (7). Pub.L. 104–208, § 354(a)(5), added par. (7).

Effective Dates
1996 Acts. Amendment by section 308 of Div. C of Pub.L. 104–208 effective, with certain exceptions and subject to certain transitional rules, on the first day of the first month beginning more than 180 days after Sept. 30, 1996, see section 309 of Div. C of Pub.L. 104–208, set out as a note under section 1101 of this title.

Amendment by section 354(a)(5) of Div. C of Pub.L. 104–208 effective as if included in enactment of Pub.L. 104–132, Title IV, Subtitle A, § 401, Apr. 24, 1996, 110 Stat. 1258, see section 358 of Div. C of Pub.L. 104–208, set out as a note under section 1182 of this title.

Section effective Apr. 24, 1996 and applicable to all aliens without regard to date of entry or attempted entry into United States, see section 401(f) of Pub.L.

104–132, set out as a note under section 1105a of this title.

Severability of Provisions

If any provision of Division C of Pub.L. 104–208 or the application of such provision to any person or circumstances is held to be unconstitutional, the remainder of Division C of Pub.L. 104–208 and the application of the provisions of Division C of Pub.L. 104–208 to any person or circumstance not to be affected thereby, see section 1(e) of Pub.L. 104–208, set out as a note under section 1101 of this title.

WESTLAW ELECTRONIC RESEARCH

See WESTLAW guide following the Explanation pages of this volume.

§ 1532.   Establishment of removal court

(a) Designation of judges

The Chief Justice of the United States shall publicly designate 5 district court judges from 5 of the United States judicial circuits who shall constitute a court that shall have jurisdiction to conduct all removal proceedings. The Chief Justice may, in the Chief Justice's discretion, designate the same judges under this section as are designated pursuant to section 103(a) of the Foreign Intelligence Surveillance Act of 1978 (50 U.S.C. 1803(a)).

(b) Terms

Each judge designated under subsection (a) of this section shall serve for a term of 5 years and shall be eligible for redesignation, except that of the members first designated—

(1) 1 member shall serve for a term of 1 year;

(2) 1 member shall serve for a term of 2 years;

(3) 1 member shall serve for a term of 3 years; and

(4) 1 member shall serve for a term of 4 years.

(c) Chief judge

(1) Designation

The Chief Justice shall publicly designate one of the judges of the removal court to be the chief judge of the removal court.

(2) Responsibilities

The chief judge shall—

(A) promulgate rules to facilitate the functioning of the removal court; and

(B) assign the consideration of cases to the various judges on the removal court.

(d) Expeditious and confidential nature of proceedings

The provisions of section 103(c) of the Foreign Intelligence Surveillance Act of 1978 (50 U.S.C. 1803(c)) shall apply to removal proceedings in the same manner as they apply to proceedings under that Act [50 U.S.C.A. § 1801 et seq.].

(e) Establishment of panel of special attorneys

The removal court shall provide for the designation of a panel of attorneys each of whom—

(1) has a security clearance which affords the attorney access to classified information, and

(2) has agreed to represent permanent resident aliens with respect to classified information under section 1534(e)(3) of this title in accordance with (and subject to the penalties under) this subchapter.

(June 27, 1952, c. 477, Title V, § 502, as added Apr. 24, 1996, Pub.L. 104–132, Title IV, § 401(a), 110 Stat. 1259, and amended Sept. 30, 1996, Pub.L. 104–208, Div. C, Title III, § 354(a)(4), 110 Stat. 3009–643.)

HISTORICAL AND STATUTORY NOTES

Revision Notes and Legislative Reports
1996 Acts. Senate Report No. 104–179 and House Conference Report No. 104–518, see 1996 U.S. Code Cong. and Adm. News, p. 924.

References in Text
The Foreign Intelligence Surveillance Act of 1978 and that Act, referred to in subsecs. (a) and (d), is Pub.L. 95–511, Oct. 25, 1978, 92 Stat. 1783, as amended, which is classified principally to chapter 36 (section 1801 et seq.) of Title 50, War and National Defense. Section 103(a) and (c) of such Act is classified to section 1803(a) and (c), respectively, of Title 50. For complete classification of this Act to the Code, see Short Title note set out under section 1801 of Title 50 and Tables.

Amendments
1996 Amendments. Subsec. (e). Pub.L. 104–208, § 354(a)(4), added subsec. (e).

Effective Dates
1996 Acts. Amendment by section 354(a)(4) of Div. C of Pub.L. 104–208

effective as if included in enactment of Pub.L. 104–132, Title IV, Subtitle A, § 401, Apr. 24, 1996, see section 358 of Div. C of Pub.L. 104–208, set out as a note under section 1182 of this title.

Section effective Apr. 24, 1996 and applicable to all aliens without regard to date of entry or attempted entry into United States, see section 401(f) of Pub.L. 104–132, set out as a note under section 1105a of this title.

Severability of Provisions
If any provision of Division C of Pub.L. 104–208 or the application of such provision to any person or circumstances is held to be unconstitutional, the remainder of Division C of Pub.L. 104–208 and the application of the provisions of Division C of Pub.L. 104–208 to any person or circumstance not to be affected thereby, see section 1(e) of Pub.L. 104–208, set out as a note under section 1101 of this title.

LIBRARY REFERENCES

American Digest System
    Courts ⊙70.

Encyclopedias
    C.J.S. Courts § 123.

WESTLAW ELECTRONIC RESEARCH

Courts cases: 106k[add key number]
See WESTLAW guide following the Explanation pages of this volume.

§ 1533.   Removal court procedure

(a) Application

(1) In general

In any case in which the Attorney General has classified information that an alien is an alien terrorist, the Attorney General may seek removal of the alien under this subchapter by filing an application with the removal court that contains—

(A) the identity of the attorney in the Department of Justice making the application;

(B) a certification by the Attorney General or the Deputy Attorney General that the application satisfies the criteria and requirements of this section;

(C) the identity of the alien for whom authorization for the removal proceeding is sought; and

(D) a statement of the facts and circumstances relied on by the Department of Justice to establish probable cause that—

(i) the alien is an alien terrorist;

(ii) the alien is physically present in the United States; and

(iii) with respect to such alien, removal under subchapter II of this chapter would pose a risk to the national security of the United States.

(2) Filing

An application under this section shall be submitted ex parte and in camera, and shall be filed under seal with the removal court.

(b) Right to dismiss

The Attorney General may dismiss a removal action under this subchapter at any stage of the proceeding.

(c) Consideration of application

(1) Basis for decision

In determining whether to grant an application under this section, a single judge of the removal court may consider, ex parte and in camera, in addition to the information contained in the application—

(A) other information, including classified information, presented under oath or affirmation; and

(B) testimony received in any hearing on the application, of which a verbatim record shall be kept.

(2) Approval of order

The judge shall issue an order granting the application, if the judge finds that there is probable cause to believe that—

(A) the alien who is the subject of the application has been correctly identified and is an alien terrorist present in the United States; and

(B) removal under subchapter II of this chapter would pose a risk to the national security of the United States.

(3) Denial of order

If the judge denies the order requested in the application, the judge shall prepare a written statement of the reasons for the denial, taking all necessary precautions not to disclose any classified information contained in the Government's application.

(d) Exclusive provisions

If an order is issued under this section granting an application, the rights of the alien regarding removal and expulsion shall be governed solely by this subchapter, and except as they are specifically referenced in this subchapter, no other provisions of this chapter shall be applicable.

(June 27, 1952, c. 477, Title V, § 503, as added Apr. 24, 1996, Pub.L. 104–132, Title IV, § 401(a), 110 Stat. 1259.)

HISTORICAL AND STATUTORY NOTES

Revision Notes and Legislative Reports
1996 Acts. Senate Report No. 104-179 and House Conference Report No. 104-518, see 1996 U.S. Code Cong. and Adm. News, p. 924.

References in Text
This chapter, referred to in subsec. (d), was in the original, "this Act", meaning Act June 27, 1952, c. 477, 66 Stat. 163, as amended, known as the Immigration and Nationality Act, which is classified princi-

pally to this chapter. For complete classification of this Act to the Code, see Tables.

Effective Dates
1996 Acts. Section effective Apr. 24, 1996 and applicable to all aliens without regard to date of entry or attempted entry into United States, see section 401(f) of Pub.L. 104–132, set out as a note under section 1105a of this title.

LIBRARY REFERENCES

American Digest System
Aliens ⊕52 to 54.3.

Encyclopedias
C.J.S. Aliens §§ 70, 71, 75, 77 to 79, 81, 82, 84 to 87, 92, 97 to 102, 109, 111, 114, 116, 118 to 130, 134, 136, 138, 139, 142, 143, 145 to 148, 151 to 153, 156 to 159, 161 to 163, 165 to 175, 177 to 184, 186 to 191, 193 to 195, 197, 198, 200 to 203, 205 to 207, 210, 211, 217, 218, 220 to 233, 235, 236.

§ 1534. Removal hearing

(a) In general

(1) Expeditious hearing

In any case in which an application for an order is approved under section 1533(c)(2) of this title, a removal hearing shall be conducted under this section as expeditiously as practicable for the purpose of determining whether the alien to whom the order pertains should be removed from the United States on the grounds that the alien is an alien terrorist.

(2) Public hearing

The removal hearing shall be open to the public.

(b) Notice

An alien who is the subject of a removal hearing under this subchapter shall be given reasonable notice of—

(1) the nature of the charges against the alien, including a general account of the basis for the charges; and

(2) the time and place at which the hearing will be held.

(c) Rights in hearing

(1) Right of counsel

The alien shall have a right to be present at such hearing and to be represented by counsel. Any alien financially unable to obtain counsel shall be entitled to have counsel assigned to represent the alien. Such counsel shall be appointed by the judge pursuant to the plan for furnishing representation for any person financially unable to obtain adequate representation for the district in which the hearing is conducted, as provided for in section 3006A of Title 18. All provisions of that section shall apply and, for purposes of determining the maximum amount of compensation, the matter shall be treated as if a felony was charged.

(2) Introduction of evidence

Subject to the limitations in subsection (e) of this section, the alien shall have a reasonable opportunity to introduce evidence on the alien's own behalf.

(3) Examination of witnesses

Subject to the limitations in subsection (e) of this section, the alien shall have a reasonable opportunity to examine the evidence against the alien and to cross-examine any witness.

(4) Record

A verbatim record of the proceedings and of all testimony and evidence offered or produced at such a hearing shall be kept.

(5) Removal decision based on evidence at hearing

The decision of the judge regarding removal shall be based only on that evidence introduced at the removal hearing.

(d) Subpoenas

(1) Request

At any time prior to the conclusion of the removal hearing, either the alien or the Department of Justice may request the judge to issue a subpoena for the presence of a named witness (which subpoena may also command the person to whom it is directed to produce books, papers, documents, or other objects designated therein) upon a satisfactory showing that the presence of the witness is necessary for the determination of any material matter. Such a request may be made ex parte except that the judge shall inform the Department of Justice of any request for a subpoena by the alien for a witness or material if compliance with such a subpoena would reveal classified evidence or the source of that evidence. The Department of Justice shall be given a reasonable opportunity to oppose the issuance of such a subpoena.

(2) Payment for attendance

If an application for a subpoena by the alien also makes a showing that the alien is financially unable to pay for the attendance of a witness so requested, the court may order the costs incurred by the process and the fees of the witness so subpoenaed to be paid from funds appropriated for the enforcement of subchapter II of this chapter.

(3) Nationwide service

A subpoena under this subsection may be served anywhere in the United States.

(4) Witness fees

A witness subpoenaed under this subsection shall receive the same fees and expenses as a witness subpoenaed in connection with a civil proceeding in a court of the United States.

(5) No access to classified information

Nothing in this subsection is intended to allow an alien to have access to classified information.

(e) Discovery

(1) In general

For purposes of this subchapter—

(A) the Government is authorized to use in a removal proceedings [1] the fruits of electronic surveillance and unconsented physical searches authorized under the Foreign Intelligence Surveillance Act of 1978 (50 U.S.C. 1801 et seq.) without regard to subsections (c), (e), (f), (g), and (h) of section 106 of that Act [50 U.S.C.A. § 1806(c), (e), (f), (g), (h)] and discovery of information derived pursuant to such Act, or otherwise collected for national security purposes, shall not be authorized if disclosure would present a risk to the national security of the United States;

(B) an alien subject to removal under this subchapter shall not be entitled to suppress evidence that the alien alleges was unlawfully obtained; and

(C) section 3504 of Title 18, and section 1806(c) of Title 50, shall not apply if the Attorney General determines that public disclosure would pose a risk to the national security of the United States because it would disclose classified information or otherwise threaten the integrity of a pending investigation.

(2) Protective orders

Nothing in this subchapter shall prevent the United States from seeking protective orders and from asserting privileges ordinarily available to the United States to protect against the disclosure of classified information, including the invocation of the military and State secrets privileges.

(3) Treatment of classified information

(A) Use

The judge shall examine, ex parte and in camera, any evidence for which the Attorney General determines that public disclosure would pose a risk to the national security of the United States or to the security of any individual because it would disclose classified information and neither the alien nor the public shall be informed of such evidence or its sources other than through reference to the summary provided pursuant to this paragraph. Notwithstanding the previous sentence, the Department of Justice may, in its discretion and, in the case of classified information, after coordination with the originating agency, elect to introduce such evidence in open session.

(B) Submission

With respect to such information, the Government shall submit to the removal court an unclassified summary of the specific evidence that does not pose that risk.

(C) Approval

Not later than 15 days after submission, the judge shall approve the summary if the judge finds that it is sufficient to enable the alien to prepare a defense. The Government shall deliver to the alien a copy of the unclassified summary approved under this subparagraph.

(D) Disapproval

(i) In general

If an unclassified summary is not approved by the removal court under subparagraph (C), the Government shall be afforded 15 days to correct the deficiencies identified by the court and submit a revised unclassified summary.

(ii) Revised summary

If the revised unclassified summary is not approved by the court within 15 days of its submission pursuant to subparagraph (C), the removal hearing shall be terminated unless the judge makes the findings under clause (iii).

(iii) Findings

The findings described in this clause are, with respect to an alien, that—

(I) the continued presence of the alien in the United States would likely cause serious and irreparable harm to the national security or death or serious bodily injury to any person, and

(II) the provision of the summary would likely cause serious and irreparable harm to the national security or death or serious bodily injury to any person.

(E) Continuation of hearing without summary

If a judge makes the findings described in subparagraph (D)(iii)—

(I) if the alien involved is an alien lawfully admitted for permanent residence, the procedures described in subparagraph (F) shall apply; and

(ii) in all cases the special removal hearing shall continue, the Department of Justice shall cause to be delivered to the alien a statement that no summary is possible, and the classified information submitted in camera and ex parte may be used pursuant to this paragraph.

(F) Special procedures for access and challenges to classified information by special attorneys in case of lawful permanent aliens

(i) In general

The procedures described in this subparagraph are that the judge (under rules of the removal court) shall designate a special attorney to assist the alien—

(I) by reviewing in camera the classified information on behalf of the alien, and

(II) by challenging through an in camera proceeding the veracity of the evidence contained in the classified information.

(ii) Restrictions on disclosure

A special attorney receiving classified information under clause (i)—

(I) shall not disclose the information to the alien or to any other attorney representing the alien, and

(II) who discloses such information in violation of subclause (I) shall be subject to a fine under Title 18, imprisoned for not less than 10 years nor more than 25 years, or both.

(f) Arguments

Following the receipt of evidence, the Government and the alien shall be given fair opportunity to present argument as to whether the evidence is sufficient to justify the removal of the alien. The Government shall open the argument. The alien shall be permitted to reply. The Government shall then be permitted to reply in rebuttal. The judge may allow any part of the argument that refers to evidence received in camera and ex parte to be heard in camera and ex parte.

(g) Burden of proof

In the hearing, it is the Government's burden to prove, by the preponderance of the evidence, that the alien is subject to removal because the alien is an alien terrorist.

(h) Rules of evidence

The Federal Rules of Evidence shall not apply in a removal hearing.

(i) Determination of deportation

If the judge, after considering the evidence on the record as a whole, finds that the Government has met its burden, the judge shall order the alien removed and detained pending removal from the United States. If the alien was released pending the removal hearing, the judge shall order the Attorney General to take the alien into custody.

(j) Written order

At the time of issuing a decision as to whether the alien shall be removed, the judge shall prepare a written order containing a statement of facts found and conclusions of law. Any portion of the order that would reveal the substance or source of information received in camera and ex parte pursuant to subsection (e) of this section shall not be made available to the alien or the public.

(k) No right to ancillary relief

At no time shall the judge consider or provide for relief from removal based on—

(1) asylum under section 1158 of this title;

(2) by [1] withholding of removal under section 1227(b)(3) of this title;

(3) cancellation of removal under section 1229b of this title;

(4) voluntary departure under section 1254a(e)[2] of this title;

(5) adjustment of status under section 1255 of this title; or

(6) registry under section 1259 of this title.

(June 27, 1952, c. 477, Title V, § 504, as added Apr. 24, 1996, Pub.L. 104–132, Title IV, § 401(a), 110 Stat. 1260, and amended Sept. 30, 1996, Pub.L. 104–208, Div. C, Title III, §§ 308(g)(7)(B), (8)(B), 354(a)(1), (2), (b), 357, 110 Stat. 3009–623, 3009–624, 3009–641, 3009–642, 3009–643, 3009–644.)

[1] So in original.

[2] See References in Text note below.

HISTORICAL AND STATUTORY NOTES

Revision Notes and Legislative Reports

1996 Acts. Senate Report No. 104–179 and House Conference Report No. 104–518, see 1996 U.S. Code Cong. and Adm. News, p. 924.

References in Text

The Foreign Intelligence Surveillance Act of 1978 and such Act, referred to in subsec. (e)(1)(A), is Pub.L. 95–511, Oct. 25, 1978, 92 Stat. 1783, as amended, which is classified principally to chapter 36 (section 1801 et seq.) of Title 50, War and National Defense. Subsections (c), (e), (f), (g), and (h) of section 106 of that Act are classified to subsecs. (c), (e), (f), (g), and (h), respectively, of section 1806 of Title 50. For complete classification of this Act to the Code, see Short Title note set out under 1801 of Title 50 and Tables.

The Federal Rules of Evidence, referred to in subsec. (h), are set out in Title 28, Judiciary and Judicial Procedure.

Section 1254a(e) of this title, referred to in subsec. (k)(4), was in the original a reference to "section 244(e)", meaning section 244(e) of act June 27, 1952, which was classified to section 1254(e) of this title. Pub.L. 104–208, div. C, title III, § 308(b)(7), Sept. 30, 1996, 110 Stat. 3009–615, repealed section 244 and renumbered section 244a as section 244, which is classified to section 1254a of this title. For provisions relating to voluntary departure, see section 1229c of this title.

Amendments

1996 Amendments. Subsec. (e)(1)(A). Pub.L. 104–208, § 354(b)(1)(A), added provision relating to use of fruits of electronic surveillance and unconsented physical searches and substituted reference to 50 USCA § 1801 et seq. for reference to 50 USCA § 1806(c) and (e) to (h).

Subsec. (e)(3)(A). Pub.L. 104–208, § 354(b)(1)(B), added provisions relating to informing of evidence or its sources and to introduction in open session.

Subsec. (e)(3)(D)(ii). Pub.L. 104–208, § 354(a)(1)(A), added provision relating to findings under cl. (iii).

Subsec. (e)(3)(D)(iii). Pub.L. 104–208, § 354(a)(1)(B), added cl. (iii).

Subsec. (e)(3)(E), (F). Pub.L. 104–208, § 354(a)(2), added subpars. (E) and (F).

Subsec. (f). Pub.L. 104–208, § 354(b)(2), added provisions relating to in camera and ex parte proceedings.

Subsec. (j). Pub.L. 104–208, § 354(b)(3), added provision relating to not making available certain portions of order.

Subsec. (k)(2). Pub.L. 104–208, § 308(g)(7)(B), substituted "by withholding of removal under section 1227(b)(3) of this title" for "withholding of deportation under section 1253(h) of this title".

Subsec. (k)(3). Pub.L. 104–208, § 308(g)(8)(B), substituted "cancellation of removal under section 1229b" for "suspension of deportation under subsection (a) or (e) of section 1254".

Subsec. (k)(4) to (6). Pub.L. 104–208, § 357, added par. (4). Former pars. (4) and (5) were redesignated (5) and (6), respectively.

Effective Dates

1996 Acts. Amendment by section 308 of Div. C of Pub.L. 104–208 effective, with certain exceptions and subject to certain transitional rules, on the first day of the first month beginning more than 180 days after Sept. 30, 1996, see section 309 of Div. C of Pub.L. 104–208, set out as a note under section 1101 of this title.

Amendment by section 357 of Div. C of Pub.L. 104–208 effective as if included in enactment of Pub.L. 104–132, Title IV, Subtitle A, Apr. 24, 1996, 110 Stat. 1258, see section 358 of Div. C of Pub.L. 104–208, set out as a note under section 1182 of this title.

Section effective Apr. 24, 1996 and applicable to all aliens without regard to date of entry or attempted entry into United States, see section 401(f) of Pub.L. 104–132, set out as a note under section 1105a of this title.

Severability of Provisions

If any provision of Division C of Pub.L. 104–208 or the application of such provision to any person or circumstances is held to be unconstitutional, the remainder of Division C of Pub.L. 104–208 and the application of the provisions of Division C of Pub.L. 104–208 to any person or circumstance not to be affected thereby, see section 1(e) of Pub.L. 104–208, set out as a note under section 1101 of this title.

§ 1535. Appeals

(a) Appeal of denial of application for removal proceedings

(1) In general

The Attorney General may seek a review of the denial of an order sought in an application filed pursuant to section 1533 of this title. The appeal shall be filed in the United States Court of Appeals for the District of Columbia Circuit by notice of appeal filed not later than 20 days after the date of such denial.

(2) Record on appeal

The entire record of the proceeding shall be transmitted to the Court of Appeals under seal, and the Court of Appeals shall hear the matter ex parte.

(3) Standard of review

The Court of Appeals shall—

(A) review questions of law de novo; and

(B) set aside a finding of fact only if such finding was clearly erroneous.

(b) Appeal of determination regarding summary of classified information

(1) In general

The United States may take an interlocutory appeal to the United States Court of Appeals for the District of Columbia Circuit of—

(A) any determination by the judge pursuant to section 1534(e)(3) of this title; or

(B) the refusal of the court to make the findings permitted by section 1534(e)(3) of this title.

(2) Record

In any interlocutory appeal taken pursuant to this subsection, the entire record, including any proposed order of the judge, any classified information and the summary of evidence, shall be transmitted to the Court of Appeals. The classified information shall be transmitted under seal. A verbatim record of such appeal shall be kept under seal in the event of any other judicial review.

(c) Appeal of decision in hearing

(1) In general

Subject to paragraph (2), the decision of the judge after a removal hearing may be appealed by either the alien or the Attorney General to the United States Court of Appeals for the District of Columbia Circuit by notice of appeal filed not later than 20 days after the date on which the order is issued. The order shall not be enforced during the pendency of an appeal under this subsection.

(2) Automatic appeals in cases of permanent resident aliens in which no summary provided

(A) In general

Unless the alien waives the right to a review under this paragraph, in any case involving an alien lawfully admitted for permanent residence who is denied a written summary of classified information under section 1534(e)(3) of this title and with respect to which the procedures described in section 1534(e)(3)(F) of this title apply, any order issued by the judge shall be reviewed by the Court of Appeals for the District of Columbia Circuit.

(B) Use of special attorney

With respect to any issue relating to classified information that arises in such review, the alien shall be represented only by the special attorney designated under section 1534(e)(3)(F)(i) of this title on behalf of the alien.

(3) Transmittal of record

In an appeal or review to the Court of Appeals pursuant to this subsection—

(A) the entire record shall be transmitted to the Court of Appeals; and

(B) information received in camera and ex parte, and any portion of the order that would reveal the substance or source of such information, shall be transmitted under seal.

(4) Expedited appellate proceeding

In an appeal or review to the Court of Appeals under this subsection—

> **(A)** the appeal or review shall be heard as expeditiously as practicable and the court may dispense with full briefing and hear the matter solely on the record of the judge of the removal court and on such briefs or motions as the court may require to be filed by the parties;

> **(B)** the Court of Appeals shall issue an opinion not later than 60 days after the date of the issuance of the final order of the district court;

> **(C)** the court shall review all questions of law de novo; and

> **(D)** a finding of fact shall be accorded deference by the reviewing court and shall not be set aside unless such finding was clearly erroneous, except that in the case of a review under paragraph (2) in which an alien lawfully admitted for permanent residence was denied a written summary of classified information under section 1534(c)(3)[1] of this title, the Court of Appeals shall review questions of fact de novo.

(d) Certiorari

Following a decision by the Court of Appeals pursuant to subsection (c) of this section, the alien or the Attorney General may petition the Supreme Court for a writ of certiorari. In any such case, any information transmitted to the Court of Appeals under seal shall, if such information is also submitted to the Supreme Court, be transmitted under seal. Any order of removal shall not be stayed pending disposition of a writ of certiorari, except as provided by the Court of Appeals or a Justice of the Supreme Court.

(e) Appeal of detention order

(1) In general

Sections 3145 through 3148 of Title 18, pertaining to review and appeal of a release or detention order, penalties for failure to appear, penalties for an offense committed while on release, and sanctions for violation of a release condition shall apply to an alien to whom section 1537(b)(1) of this title applies. In applying the previous sentence—

> **(A)** for purposes of section 3145 of Title 18 an appeal shall be taken to the United States Court of Appeals for the District of Columbia Circuit; and

(B) for purposes of section 3146 of Title 18 the alien shall be considered released in connection with a charge of an offense punishable by life imprisonment.

(2) No review of continued detention

The determinations and actions of the Attorney General pursuant to section 1537(b)(2)(C) of this title shall not be subject to judicial review, including application for a writ of habeas corpus, except for a claim by the alien that continued detention violates the alien's rights under the Constitution. Jurisdiction over any such challenge shall lie exclusively in the United States Court of Appeals for the District of Columbia Circuit.

(June 27, 1952, c. 477, Title V, § 505, as added Apr. 24, 1996, Pub.L. 104–132, Title IV, § 401(a), 110 Stat. 1263, and amended Sept. 30, 1996, Pub.L. 104–208, Div. C, Title III, § 354(a)(3), 110 Stat. 3009–642.)

¹ So in original. Probably should be "1534(e)(3)".

HISTORICAL AND STATUTORY NOTES

Revision Notes and Legislative Reports

1996 Acts. Senate Report No. 104–179 and House Conference Report No. 104–518, see 1996 U.S. Code Cong. and Adm. News, p. 924.

Amendments

1996 Amendments. Subsec. (c)(1). Pub.L. 104–208, § 354(a)(3)(A), inserted reference to par. (2).

Subsec. (c)(3)(D). Pub.L. 104–208, § 354(a)(3)(B), added provisions relating to exception for certain cases under par. (2).

Subsec. (c)(2) to (4). Pub.L. 104–208, § 354(a)(3)(C), (D), added par. (2). Former pars. (2) and (3) were redesignated pars. (3) and (4), respectively.

Effective Dates

1996 Acts. Amendment by section 354(a)(3) of Div. C of Pub.L. 104–208 effective as if included in enactment of Pub.L. 104–132, Title IV, Subtitle A, Apr. 24, 1996, 110 Stat. 1258, see section 358 of Div. C of Pub.L. 104–208, set out as a note under section 1182 of this title.

Section effective Apr. 24, 1996 and applicable to all aliens without regard to date of entry or attempted entry into United States, see section 401(f) of Pub.L. 104–132, set out as a note under section 1105a of this title.

Severability of Provisions

If any provision of Division C of Pub.L. 104–208 or the application of such provision to any person or circumstances is held to be unconstitutional, the remainder of Division C of Pub.L. 104–208 and the application of the provisions of Division C of Pub.L. 104–208 to any person or circumstance not to be affected thereby, see section 1(e) of Pub.L. 104–208, set out as a note under section 1101 of this title.

References to Order of Removal Deemed to Include Order of Exclusion and Deportation

For purposes of this chapter, any reference in law to an order of removal is deemed to include a reference to an order of exclusion and deportation or an order of deportation, see section 309(d)(2) of Pub.L. 104–208, set out in an Effective Date of 1996 Amendments note under section 1101 of this title.

LIBRARY REFERENCES

American Digest System
Aliens ⬤⇒54.3.

Encyclopedias
C.J.S. Aliens §§ 128 to 130, 225 to 233.

§ 1536. Custody and release pending removal hearing

(a) Upon filing application

(1) In general

Subject to paragraphs (2) and (3), the Attorney General may—

(A) take into custody any alien with respect to whom an application under section 1533 of this title has been filed; and

(B) retain such an alien in custody in accordance with the procedures authorized by this subchapter.

(2) Special rules for permanent resident aliens

(A) Release hearing

An alien lawfully admitted for permanent residence shall be entitled to a release hearing before the judge assigned to hear the removal hearing. Such an alien shall be detained pending the removal hearing, unless the alien demonstrates to the court that the alien—

(i) is a person lawfully admitted for permanent residence in the United States;

(ii) if released upon such terms and conditions as the court may prescribe (including the posting of any monetary amount), is not likely to flee; and

(iii) will not endanger national security, or the safety of any person or the community, if released.

(B) Information considered

The judge may consider classified information submitted in camera and ex parte in making a determination whether to release an alien pending the removal hearing.

(3) Release if order denied and no review sought

(A) In general

Subject to subparagraph (B), if a judge of the removal court denies the order sought in an application filed pursuant to section 1533 of this title, and the Attorney General does not seek review of such denial, the alien shall be released from custody.

(B) Application of regular procedures

Subparagraph (A) shall not prevent the arrest and detention of the alien pursuant to subchapter II of this chapter.

(b) Conditional release if order denied and review sought

(1) In general

If a judge of the removal court denies the order sought in an application filed pursuant to section 1533 of this title and the Attorney General seeks review of such denial, the judge shall release the alien from custody subject to the least restrictive condition, or combination of conditions, of release described in section 3142(b) and clauses (i) through (xiv) of section 3142(c)(1)(B) of Title 18, that—

(A) will reasonably assure the appearance of the alien at any future proceeding pursuant to this subchapter; and

(B) will not endanger the safety of any other person or the community.

(2) No release for certain aliens

If the judge finds no such condition or combination of conditions, as described in paragraph (1), the alien shall remain in custody until the completion of any appeal authorized by this subchapter.

(June 27, 1952, c. 477, Title V, § 506, as added Apr. 24, 1996, Pub.L. 104–132, Title IV, § 401(a), 110 Stat. 1265.)

HISTORICAL AND STATUTORY NOTES

Revision Notes and Legislative Reports
  1996 Acts. Senate Report No. 104–179 and House Conference Report No. 104–518, see 1996 U.S. Code Cong. and Adm. News, p. 924.

Effective Dates
  1996 Acts. Section effective Apr. 24, 1996 and applicable to all aliens without regard to date of entry or attempted entry into United States, see section 401(f) of Pub.L. 104–132, set out as a note under section 1105a of this title.

LIBRARY REFERENCES

American Digest System
  Aliens ☞53.9.

Encyclopedias
  C.J.S. Aliens §§ 84 to 87, 170, 197, 198.

WESTLAW ELECTRONIC RESEARCH

Aliens cases: 24k[add key number]
See WESTLAW guide following the Explanation pages of this volume.

§ 1537.   Custody and release after removal hearing

(a) Release

(1) In general

Subject to paragraph (2), if the judge decides that an alien should not be removed, the alien shall be released from custody.

(2) Custody pending appeal

If the Attorney General takes an appeal from such decision, the alien shall remain in custody, subject to the provisions of section 3142 of Title 18.

(b) Custody and removal

(1) Custody

If the judge decides that an alien shall be removed, the alien shall be detained pending the outcome of any appeal. After the conclusion of any judicial review thereof which affirms the removal order, the Attorney General shall retain the alien in custody and remove the alien to a country specified under paragraph (2).

(2) Removal

(A) In general

The removal of an alien shall be to any country which the alien shall designate if such designation does not, in the judgment of the Attorney General, in consultation with the Secretary of State, impair the obligation of the United States under any treaty (including a treaty pertaining to extradition) or otherwise adversely affect the foreign policy of the United States.

(B) Alternate countries

If the alien refuses to designate a country to which the alien wishes to be removed or if the Attorney General, in consultation with the Secretary of State, determines that removal of the alien to the country so designated would impair a treaty obligation or adversely affect United States foreign policy, the Attorney General shall cause the alien to be removed to any country willing to receive such alien.

(C) Continued detention

If no country is willing to receive such an alien, the Attorney General may, notwithstanding any other provision of law, retain the alien in custody. The Attorney General, in coordination with the Secretary of State, shall make periodic efforts to reach agreement with other countries to accept such an alien and at least every 6 months shall provide to the attorney representing the alien at the removal hearing a written report on the Attorney General's efforts. Any alien in custody pursuant to this subparagraph shall be released from custody solely at the discretion of the Attorney General and subject to such conditions as the Attorney General shall deem appropriate.

(D) Fingerprinting

Before an alien is removed from the United States pursuant to this subsection, or pursuant to an order of removal because such alien is inadmissible under section 1182(a)(3)(B) of this title, the alien shall be photographed and fingerprinted, and shall be advised of the provisions of section 1326(b) of this title.

(c) Continued detention pending trial

(1) Delay in removal

The Attorney General may hold in abeyance the removal of an alien who has been ordered removed, pursuant to this subchapter, to allow the trial of such alien on any Federal or State criminal charge and the service of any sentence of confinement resulting from such a trial.

(2) Maintenance of custody

Pending the commencement of any service of a sentence of confinement by an alien described in paragraph (1), such an alien shall remain in the custody of the Attorney General, unless the Attorney General determines that temporary release of the alien to the custody of State authorities for confinement in a State facility is appropriate and would not endanger national security or public safety.

(3) Subsequent removal

Following the completion of a sentence of confinement by an alien described in paragraph (1), or following the completion of State criminal proceedings which do not result in a sentence of confinement of an alien released to the custody of State authorities pursuant to paragraph (2), such an alien shall be returned to the custody of the Attorney General who shall proceed to the removal of the alien under this subchapter.

(d) Application of certain provisions relating to escape of prisoners

For purposes of sections 751 and 752 of Title 18, an alien in the custody of the Attorney General pursuant to this subchapter shall be subject to the penalties provided by those sections in relation to a person committed to the custody of the Attorney General by virtue of an arrest on a charge of a felony.

(e) Rights of aliens in custody

(1) Family and attorney visits

An alien in the custody of the Attorney General pursuant to this subchapter shall be given reasonable opportunity, as determined by the Attorney General, to communicate with and receive visits from members of the alien's family, and to contact, retain, and communicate with an attorney.

(2) Diplomatic contact

An alien in the custody of the Attorney General pursuant to this subchapter shall have the right to contact an appropriate diplomatic or consular official of the alien's country of citizenship or nationality or of any country providing representation services therefore. The Attorney General shall notify the appropriate embassy, mission, or consular office of the alien's detention.

(June 27, 1952, c. 477, Title V, § 507, as added Apr. 24, 1996, Pub.L. 104–132, Title IV, § 401(a), 110 Stat. 1266, and amended Sept. 30, 1996, Pub.L. 104–208, Div. C, Title III, § 308(d)(4)(Q), 110 Stat. 3009–619.)

HISTORICAL AND STATUTORY NOTES

Revision Notes and Legislative Reports
1996 Acts. Senate Report No. 104–179 and House Conference Report No. 104–518, see 1996 U.S. Code Cong. and Adm. News, p. 924.

Amendments
1996 Amendments. Subsec. (b)(2)(D). Pub.L. 104–208, § 308(d)(4)(Q), substituted "removal because such alien is inadmissible" for "exclusion because such alien is excludable".

Effective Dates
1996 Acts. Amendment by section 308 of Div. C of Pub.L. 104–208 effective, with certain exceptions and subject to certain transitional rules, on the first day of the first month beginning more than 180 days after Sept. 30, 1996, see section 309 of Div. C of Pub.L. 104–208, set out as a note under section 1101 of this title.

Section effective Apr. 24, 1996 and applicable to all aliens without regard to date of entry or attempted entry into United States, see section 401(f) of Pub.L. 104–132, set out as a note under section 1105a of this title.

Severability of Provisions
If any provision of Division C of Pub.L. 104–208 or the application of such provision to any person or circumstances is held to be unconstitutional, the remainder of Division C of Pub.L. 104–208 and the application of the provisions of Division C of Pub.L. 104–208 to any person or circumstance not to be affected thereby, see section 1(e) of Pub.L. 104–208, set out as a note under section 1101 of this title.

References to Order of Removal Deemed to Include Order of Exclusion and Deportation
For purposes of this chapter, any reference in law to an order of removal is

deemed to include a reference to an order of exclusion and deportation or an order of deportation, see section 309(d)(2) of Pub.L. 104–208, set out in an Effective Date of 1996 Amendments note under section 1101 of this title.

LIBRARY REFERENCES

American Digest System
Aliens ☞53.9.

Encyclopedias
C.J.S. Aliens §§ 84 to 87, 170, 197, 198.

WESTLAW ELECTRONIC RESEARCH

Aliens cases: 24k[add key number]
See WESTLAW guide following the Explanation pages of this volume.

468 U.S. 1032, 82 L.Ed.2d 778

⌐₁₀₃₂IMMIGRATION AND NATURALIZA-
TION SERVICE, Petitioner

v.

Adan LOPEZ–MENDOZA et al.

No. 83–491.

Argued April 18, 1984.

Decided July 5, 1984.

Aliens petitioned for review of orders
of the Board of Immigration Appeals dismissing their appeals from deportation orders. The Court of Appeals, 705 F.2d 1059,
reversed one order of deportation and vacated the second order of deportation, ordering latter case remanded. Certiorari
was granted. The Supreme Court, Justice
O'Connor, held that: (1) mere fact of illegal
arrest had no bearing on subsequent deportation proceeding against alien who had
objected only to fact that he had been
summoned to a deportation hearing following unlawful arrest, but had entered no
objection to receipt in evidence of admission, after arrest, of illegal entry into country, and (2) exclusionary rule would not
apply in civil deportation hearing to require
that admission of illegal entry by alien
after allegedly unlawful arrest be excluded
from evidence.

Reversed.

Justices Brennan, White, Marshall and
Stevens dissented and filed opinions.

1. Aliens ⚖══53

A deportation proceeding is a purely
civil action to determine eligibility to remain in country, not to punish unlawful
entry, though entering or remaining unlawfully in country is itself a crime. Immigration and Nationality Act, §§ 262, 266, 275,
8 U.S.C.A. §§ 1302, 1306, 1325.

2. Aliens ⚖══54.1(3)

Deportation hearing looks prospectively to alien's right to remain in country in
future; past conduct is relevant only insofar as it may shed light on alien's right to
remain. Immigration and Nationality Act,
§§ 241, 242(b), 8 U.S.C.A. §§ 1251, 1252(b).

3. Aliens ⚖══53

Consistent with civil nature of a deportation proceeding, various protections that
apply in context of a criminal trial do not
apply in a deportation hearing.

4. Aliens ⚖══54(1)

A deportation hearing is intended to
provide a streamlined determination of eligibility to remain in country, and nothing
more; purpose of deportation is not to punish past transgressions but rather to put an
end to a continuing violation of the immigration laws.

5. Criminal Law ⚖══394.4(9)

The "body" or identity of a defendant
or respondent in a criminal or civil proceeding is never itself suppressible as a fruit of
an unlawful arrest, even if it is conceded
that an unlawful arrest, search, or interrogation occurred.

6. Forfeitures ⚖══4

Forfeiture proceedings directed
against contraband or other forfeitable
property are not precluded by fact that
seizure may have resulted from an unlawful arrest, search, or interrogation.

7. Aliens ⚖══53.1

Mere fact of illegal arrest had no bearing on subsequent deportation proceeding
against alien who had objected only to fact
that he had been summoned to a deportation hearing following unlawful arrest, but
had entered no objection to receipt in evidence of admission, after arrest, of illegal
entry into country.

8. Criminal Law ⚖══394.4(9), 412.1(3)

General rule in criminal proceeding is
that statements and other evidence obtained as a result of an unlawful, warrantless arrest are suppressible if link between
evidence and unlawful conduct is not too
attenuated.

9. Aliens ⚖══54.1(2, 3)

Since person and identity of alien are
not themselves suppressible as fruit of an
illegal arrest, Immigration and Naturalization Service must prove only alienage in a
deportation proceeding and that will sometimes be possible using evidence gathered
independently of, or sufficiently attenuated
from, original arrest.

10. Aliens ⚖══54.1(3)

Exclusionary rule does not apply in
civil deportation hearings held by the Immigration and Naturalization Service.

11. Aliens ⬤=54.1(3)

Exclusionary rule would not apply in civil deportation hearing to require that admission of illegal entry by alien after allegedly unlawful arrest be excluded from evidence.

12. Aliens ⬤=54.1(3)

Evidence derived from illegal but peaceful arrests by Immigration and Naturalization Service officers need not be suppressed in a civil deportation hearing held by the INS. (Per Justice O'Connor with three Justices concurring.)

Syllabus *

Respondent Mexican citizens were ordered deported by an Immigration Judge. Respondent Lopez-Mendoza unsuccessfully objected to being summoned to the deportation hearing following his allegedly unlawful arrest by an Immigration and Naturalization Service (INS) agent, but he did not object to the receipt in evidence of his admission, after the arrest, of illegal entry into this country. Respondent Sandoval-Sanchez, who also admitted his illegal entry after being arrested by an INS agent, unsuccessfully objected to the evidence of his admission offered at the deportation proceeding, contending that it should have been suppressed as the fruit of an unlawful arrest. The Board of Immigration Appeals (BIA) affirmed the deportation orders. The Court of Appeals reversed respondent Sandoval-Sanchez' deportation order, holding that his detention by INS agents violated the Fourth Amendment, that his admission of illegal entry was the product of this detention, and that the exclusionary rule barred its use in a deportation proceeding. The court vacated respondent Lopez-Mendoza's deportation order and remanded his case to the BIA to determine whether the Fourth Amendment had been violated in the course of his arrest.

Held:

1. A deportation proceeding is a purely civil action to determine a person's eligibility to remain in this country. The purpose of deportation is not to punish past transgressions but rather to put an end to

a continuing violation of the immigration laws. Consistent with the civil nature of a deportation proceeding, various protections that apply in the context of a criminal trial do not apply in a deportation hearing. P. 3483.

2. The "body" or identity of a defendant in a criminal or civil proceeding is never itself suppressible as the fruit of an unlawful arrest, even if it is conceded that an unlawful arrest, search, or interrogation occurred. On this basis alone, the Court of Appeals' decision as to respondent Lopez-Mendoza must be reversed, since he objected only to being summoned to his deportation hearing after an allegedly unlawful arrest and did not object to the evidence offered against him. The mere fact of an illegal arrest has no bearing on a subsequent deportation hearing. Pp. 3483-3484.

⌐₁₀₃₃3. The exclusionary rule does not apply in a deportation proceeding; hence, the rule does not apply so as to require that respondent Sandoval-Sanchez' admission of illegal entry after his allegedly unlawful arrest be excluded from evidence at his deportation hearing. Under the balancing test applied in *United States v. Janis,* 428 U.S. 433, 96 S.Ct. 3021, 49 L.Ed.2d 1046, whereby the likely social benefits of excluding unlawfully obtained evidence are weighed against the likely costs, the balance comes out against applying the exclusionary rule in civil deportation proceedings. Several factors significantly reduce the likely deterrent value of the rule in such proceedings. First, regardless of how the arrest of an illegal alien is effected, deportation will still be possible when evidence not derived directly from the arrest is sufficient to support deportation. Second, based on statistics indicating that over 97.7 percent of illegal aliens agree to voluntary deportation without a formal hearing, every INS agent knows that it is unlikely that any particular arrestee will end up challenging the lawfulness of his arrest in a formal deportation hearing. Third, the INS has its own comprehensive scheme for deterring Fourth Amendment violations by

---

* The syllabus constitutes no part of the opinion of the Court but has been prepared by the Reporter of Decisions for the convenience of the reader. See *United States v. Detroit Lumber Co.,* 200 U.S. 321, 337, 26 S.Ct. 282, 287, 50 L.Ed. 499.

its agents. And finally, the deterrent value of the exclusionary rule in deportation proceedings is undermined by the availability of alternative remedies for INS practices that might violate Fourth Amendment rights. As to the social costs of applying the exclusionary rule in deportation proceedings, they would be high. In particular, the application of the rule in cases such as respondent Sandoval-Sanchez' would compel the courts to release from custody persons who would then immediately resume their commission of a crime through their continuing, unlawful presence in this country, and would unduly complicate the INS's deliberately simple deportation hearing system. Pp. 3484–3489.

705 F.2d 1059 (CA9 1983), reversed.

Andrew L. Frey, Washington, D.C., for petitioner.

⌊₁₀₃₄Mary L. Heen, New York City, for respondent.

Justice O'CONNOR announced the judgment of the Court and delivered the opinion of the Court with respect to Parts I, II, III, and IV, and an opinion with respect to Part V, in which Justice BLACKMUN, Justice POWELL, and Justice REHNQUIST joined.**

This litigation requires us to decide whether an admission of unlawful presence in this country made subsequent to an allegedly unlawful arrest must be excluded as evidence in a civil deportation hearing. We hold that the exclusionary rule need not be applied in such a proceeding.

I

Respondents Adan Lopez-Mendoza and Elias Sandoval-Sanchez, both citizens of Mexico, were summoned to separate deportation proceedings in California and Washington, and both were ordered deported. They challenged the regularity of those proceedings on grounds related to the lawfulness of their respective arrests by officials of the Immigration and Naturalization Service (INS). On administrative appeal the Board of Immigration Appeals (BIA), an agency of the Department of Justice, affirmed the deportation orders.

** THE CHIEF JUSTICE joins all but Part V of

The Court of Appeals for the Ninth Circuit, sitting en banc, reversed Sandoval-Sanchez' deportation order and vacated and remanded Lopez-Mendoza's deportation order. 705 F.2d 1059 (1983). It ruled that Sandoval-Sanchez' admission of his illegal presence in this country was the fruit of an unlawful arrest, and that the exclusionary rule applied in a deportation proceeding. Lopez-Mendoza's deportation order was vacated and his case remanded to the BIA to ⌊₁₀₃₅determine whether the Fourth Amendment had been violated in the course of his arrest. We granted certiorari, 464 U.S. 1037, 104 S.Ct. 697, 79 L.Ed.2d 163 (1984).

A

Respondent Lopez-Mendoza was arrested in 1976 by INS agents at his place of employment, a transmission repair shop in San Mateo, Cal. Responding to a tip, INS investigators arrived at the shop shortly before 8 a.m. The agents had not sought a warrant to search the premises or to arrest any of its occupants. The proprietor of the shop firmly refused to allow the agents to interview his employees during working hours. Nevertheless, while one agent engaged the proprietor in conversation another entered the shop and approached Lopez-Mendoza. In response to the agent's questioning, Lopez-Mendoza gave his name and indicated that he was from Mexico with no close family ties in the United States. The agent then placed him under arrest. Lopez-Mendoza underwent further questioning at INS offices, where he admitted he was born in Mexico, was still a citizen of Mexico, and had entered this country without inspection by immigration authorities. Based on his answers, the agents prepared a "Record of Deportable Alien" (Form I-213), and an affidavit which Lopez-Mendoza executed, admitting his Mexican nationality and his illegal entry into this country.

A hearing was held before an Immigration Judge. Lopez-Mendoza's counsel moved to terminate the proceeding on the ground that Lopez-Mendoza had been arrested illegally. The judge ruled that the legality of the arrest was not relevant to the deportation proceeding and therefore declined to rule on the legality of Lopez-

this opinion.

Mendoza's arrest. *Matter of Lopez-Mendoza*, No. A22 452 208 (INS, Dec. 21, 1977), reprinted in App. to Pet. for Cert. 97a. The Form I–213 and the affidavit executed by Lopez-Mendoza were received into evidence without objection from Lopez-Mendoza. On the basis of this evidence the Immigration Judge found Lopez-Mendoza₁₀₃₆ deportable. Lopez-Mendoza was granted the option of voluntary departure.

The BIA dismissed Lopez-Mendoza's appeal. It noted that "[t]he mere fact of an illegal arrest has no bearing on a subsequent deportation proceeding," *In re Lopez-Mendoza*, No. A22 452 208 (BIA, Sept. 19, 1979), reprinted in App. to Pet. for Cert. 100a, 102a, and observed that Lopez-Mendoza had not objected to the admission into evidence of Form I–213 and the affidavit he had executed. *Id.*, at 103a. The BIA also noted that the exclusionary rule is not applied to redress the injury to the privacy of the search victim, and that the BIA had previously concluded that application of the rule in deportation proceedings to deter unlawful INS conduct was inappropriate. *Matter of Sandoval*, 17 I. & N. Dec. 70 (BIA 1979).

The Court of Appeals vacated the order of deportation and remanded for a determination whether Lopez-Mendoza's Fourth Amendment rights had been violated when he was arrested.

B

Respondent Sandoval-Sanchez (who is not the same individual who was involved in *Matter of Sandoval, supra*) was arrested in 1977 at his place of employment, a potato processing plant in Pasco, Wash. INS Agent Bower and other officers went to the plant, with the permission of its personnel manager, to check for illegal aliens. During a change in shift, officers stationed themselves at the exits while Bower and a uniformed Border Patrol agent entered the plant. They went to the lunchroom and identified themselves as immigration officers. Many people in the room rose and headed for the exits or milled around; others in the plant left their equipment and started running; still others who were entering the plant turned around and started walking back out. The two officers eventually stationed themselves at

the main entrance to the plant and looked for passing employees who averted their heads, avoided eye contact, or tried to hide ₁₀₃₇themselves in a group. Those individuals were addressed with innocuous questions in English. Any who could not respond in English and who otherwise aroused Agent Bower's suspicions were questioned in Spanish as to their right to be in the United States.

Respondent Sandoval-Sanchez was in a line of workers entering the plant. Sandoval-Sanchez testified that he did not realize that immigration officers were checking people entering the plant, but that he did see standing at the plant entrance a man in uniform who appeared to be a police officer. Agent Bower testified that it was probable that he, not his partner, had questioned Sandoval-Sanchez at the plant, but that he could not be absolutely positive. The employee he thought he remembered as Sandoval-Sanchez had been "very evasive," had averted his head, turned around, and walked away when he saw Agent Bower. App. 137, 138. Bower was certain that no one was questioned about his status unless his actions had given the agents reason to believe that he was an undocumented alien.

Thirty-seven employees, including Sandoval-Sanchez, were briefly detained at the plant and then taken to the county jail. About one-third immediately availed themselves of the option of voluntary departure and were put on a bus to Mexico. Sandoval-Sanchez exercised his right to a deportation hearing. Sandoval-Sanchez was then questioned further, and Agent Bower recorded Sandoval-Sanchez' admission of unlawful entry. Sandoval-Sanchez contends he was not aware that he had a right to remain silent.

At his deportation hearing Sandoval-Sanchez contended that the evidence offered by the INS should be suppressed as the fruit of an unlawful arrest. The Immigration Judge considered and rejected Sandoval-Sanchez' claim that he had been illegally arrested, but ruled in the alternative that the legality of the arrest was not relevant to the deportation hearing. *Matter of Sandoval-Sanchez*, No. A22 346 925

₁₀₃₈(INS, Oct. 7, 1977), reprinted in App. to Pet. for Cert. 104a. Based on the written record of Sandoval-Sanchez' admissions the Immigration Judge found him deportable and granted him voluntary departure. The BIA dismissed Sandoval-Sanchez' appeal. *In re Sandoval-Sanchez*, No. A22 346 925 (BIA, Feb. 21, 1980). It concluded that the circumstances of the arrest had not affected the voluntariness of his recorded admission, and again declined to invoke the exclusionary rule, relying on its earlier decision in *Matter of Sandoval, supra.*

On appeal the Court of Appeals concluded that Sandoval-Sanchez' detention by the immigration officers violated the Fourth Amendment, that the statements he made were a product of that detention, and that the exclusionary rule barred their use in a deportation hearing. The deportation order against Sandoval-Sanchez was accordingly reversed.

II

[1, 2] A deportation proceeding is a purely civil action to determine eligibility to remain in this country, not to punish an unlawful entry, though entering or remaining unlawfully in this country is itself a crime. 8 U.S.C. §§ 1302, 1306, 1325. The deportation hearing looks prospectively to the respondent's right to remain in this country in the future. Past conduct is relevant only insofar as it may shed light on the respondent's right to remain. See 8 U.S.C. §§ 1251, 1252(b); *Bugajewitz v. Adams*, 228 U.S. 585, 591, 33 S.Ct. 607, 608, 57 L.Ed. 978 (1913); *Fong Yue Ting v. United States*, 149 U.S. 698, 730, 13 S.Ct. 1016, 1028, 37 L.Ed. 905 (1893).

[3, 4] A deportation hearing is held before an immigration judge. The judge's sole power is to order deportation; the judge cannot adjudicate guilt or punish the respondent for any crime related to unlawful entry into or presence in this country. Consistent with the civil nature of the proceeding, various protections that apply in the context of a criminal trial do not apply in a deportation hearing. The respondent must be given "a reasonable opportunity to be present at [the] proceeding," but if the respondent fails to avail himself₁₀₃₉of that opportunity the hearing may proceed in his absence. 8 U.S.C. § 1252(b). In many deportation cases the INS must show only identity and alienage; the burden then shifts to the respondent to prove the time, place, and manner of his entry. See 8 U.S.C. § 1361; *Matter of Sandoval*, 17 I. & N.Dec. 70 (BIA 1979). A decision of deportability need be based only on "reasonable, substantial, and probative evidence," 8 U.S.C. § 1252(b)(4). The BIA for its part has required only "clear, unequivocal and convincing" evidence of the respondent's deportability, not proof beyond a reasonable doubt. 8 CFR § 242.14(a) (1984). The Courts of Appeals have held, for example that the absence of *Miranda* warnings does not render an otherwise voluntary statement by the respondent inadmissible in a deportation case. *Navia-Duran v. INS*, 568 F.2d 803, 808 (CA1 1977); *Avila-Gallegos v. INS*, 525 F.2d 666, 667 (CA2 1975); *Chavez-Raya v. INS*, 519 F.2d 397, 399–401 (CA7 1975). See also *Abel v. United States*, 362 U.S. 217, 236–237, 80 S.Ct. 683, 696, 4 L.Ed.2d 668 (1960) (search permitted incidental to an arrest pursuant to an administrative warrant issued by the INS); *Galvan v. Press*, 347 U.S. 522, 531, 74 S.Ct. 737, 742, 98 L.Ed. 911 (1954) (*Ex Post Facto* Clause has no application to deportation); *Carlson v. Landon*, 342 U.S. 524, 544–546, 72 S.Ct. 525, 536–537, 96 L.Ed. 547 (1952) (Eighth Amendment does not require bail to be granted in certain deportation cases); *United States ex rel. Bilokumsky v. Tod*, 263 U.S. 149, 157, 44 S.Ct. 54, 57, 68 L.Ed. 221 (1923) (involuntary confessions admissible at deportation hearing). In short, a deportation hearing is intended to provide a streamlined determination of eligibility to remain in this country, nothing more. The purpose of deportation is not to punish past transgressions but rather to put an end to a continuing violation of the immigration laws.

III

[5, 6] The "body" or identity of a defendant or respondent in a criminal or civil proceeding is never itself suppressible as a fruit of an unlawful arrest, even if it is conceded that an unlawful arrest, search,

or interrogation occurred. See *Ger͵stein* 1040 *v. Pugh,* 420 U.S. 103, 119, 95 S.Ct. 854, 865, 43 L.Ed.2d 54 (1975); *Frisbie v. Collins,* 342 U.S. 519, 522, 72 S.Ct. 509, 511, 96 L.Ed. 541 (1952); *United States ex rel. Bilokumsky v. Tod, supra,* 263 U.S., at 158, 44 S.Ct., at 57. A similar rule applies in forfeiture proceedings directed against contraband or forfeitable property. See, *e.g., United States v. Eighty-Eight Thousand, Five Hundred Dollars,* 671 F.2d 293 (CA8 1982); *United States v. One (1) 1971 Harley-Davidson Motorcycle,* 508 F.2d 351 (CA9 1974); *United States v. One 1965 Buick,* 397 F.2d 782 (CA6 1968).

[7] On this basis alone the Court of Appeals' decision as to respondent Lopez-Mendoza must be reversed. At his deportation hearing Lopez-Mendoza objected only to the fact that he had been summoned to a deportation hearing following an unlawful arrest; he entered no objection to the evidence offered against him. The BIA correctly ruled that "[t]he mere fact of an illegal arrest has no bearing on a subsequent deportation proceeding." [1] *In re Lopez-Mendoza,* No. A22452208 (BIA, Sept. 19, 1979, reprinted in App. to Pet. for Cert. 102a.

IV

[8] Respondent Sandoval-Sanchez has a more substantial claim. He objected not to his compelled presence at a deportation proceeding, but to evidence offered at that

1. The Court of Appeals brushed over Lopez-Mendoza's failure to object to the evidence in an apparently unsettled footnote of its decision. The Court of Appeals was initially of the view that a motion to terminate a proceeding on the ground that the arrest of the respondent was unlawful is, "for all practical purposes," the same as a motion to suppress evidence as the fruit of an unlawful arrest. Slip opinion, at 1765, n. 1 (Apr. 25, 1983). In the bound report of its opinion, however, the Court of Appeals takes a somewhat different view, stating in a revised version of the same footnote that "the only reasonable way to interpret the motion to terminate is as one that includes both a motion to suppress and a motion to dismiss." 705 F.2d 1059, 1060, n. 1 (1983).

proceeding. The general rule in a criminal proceeding is that statements and other evidence obtained as a result of an unlawful, warrantless arrest are suppressible if the link between the ⌊1041⌋evidence and the unlawful conduct is not too attenuated. *Wong Sun v. United States,* 371 U.S. 471, 83 S.Ct. 407, 9 L.Ed.2d 441 (1963). The reach of the exclusionary rule beyond the context of a criminal prosecution, however, is less clear. Although this Court has once stated in dictum that "[i]t may be assumed that evidence obtained by the [Labor] Department through an illegal search and seizure cannot be made the basis of a finding in deportation proceedings," *United States ex rel. Bilokumsky v. Tod, supra,* 263 U.S., at 155, 44 S.Ct., at 56, the Court has never squarely addressed the question before. Lower court decisions dealing with this question are sparse.[2]

In *United States v. Janis,* 428 U.S. 433, 96 S.Ct. 3021, 49 L.Ed.2d 1046 (1976), this Court set forth a framework for deciding in what types of proceeding application of the exclusionary rule is appropriate. Imprecise as the exercise may be, the Court recognized in *Janis* that there is no choice but to weigh the likely social benefits of excluding unlawfully seized evidence against the likely costs. On the benefit side of the balance "the 'prime purpose' of the [exclusionary] rule, if not the sole one, 'is to deter future unlawful police conduct.' " *Id.,* at 446, 96 S.Ct., at 3028, quoting *United States v. Calandra,* 414 U.S. 338, 347, 94 S.Ct. 613, 619, 38 L.Ed.2d 561

2. In *United States v. Wong Quong Wong,* 94 F. 832 (Vt.1899), a District Judge excluded letters seized from the appellant in a civil deportation proceeding. In *Ex parte Jackson,* 263 F. 110 (Mont.), appeal dism'd *sub nom. Andrews v. Jackson,* 267 F. 1022 (CA9 1920), another District Judge granted habeas corpus relief on the ground that papers and pamphlets used against the habeas petitioner in a deportation proceeding had been unlawfully seized. *Wong Chung Che v. INS,* 565 F.2d 166 (CA1 1977), held that papers obtained by INS agents in an unlawful search are inadmissible in deportation proceedings.

(1974). On the cost side there is the loss of often probative evidence and all of the secondary costs that flow from the less accurate or more cumbersome adjudication that therefore occurs.

At stake in *Janis* was application of the exclusionary rule in a federal civil tax assessment proceeding following the unlawful seizure of evidence by state, not federal, officials. The Court noted at the outset that "[i]n the complex and turbulent₁₀₄₂ history of the rule, the Court never has applied it to exclude evidence from a civil proceeding, federal or state." 428 U.S., at 447, 96 S.Ct., at 3029 (footnote omitted). Two factors in *Janis* suggested that the deterrence value of the exclusionary rule in the context of that case was slight. First, the state law enforcement officials were already "punished" by the exclusion of the evidence in the state criminal trial as a result of the same conduct. *Id.*, at 448, 96 S.Ct., at 3029. Second, the evidence was also excludable in any federal criminal trial that might be held. Both factors suggested that further application of the exclusionary rule in the federal civil proceeding would contribute little more to the deterrence of unlawful conduct by state officials. On the cost side of the balance, *Janis* focused simply on the loss of "concededly relevant and reliable evidence." *Id.*, at 447, 96 S.Ct., at 3029. The Court concluded that, on balance, this cost outweighed the likely social benefits achievable through application of the exclusionary rule in the federal civil proceeding.

While it seems likely that the deterrence value of applying the exclusionary rule in deportation proceedings would be higher than it was in *Janis*, it is also quite clear that the social costs would be very much greater as well. Applying the *Janis* balancing test to the benefits and costs of excluding concededly reliable evidence from a deportation proceeding, we therefore reach the same conclusion as in *Janis*.

The likely deterrence value of the exclusionary rule in deportation proceedings is difficult to assess. On the one hand, a civil deportation proceeding is a civil complement to a possible criminal prosecution, and to this extent it resembles the civil proceeding under review in *Janis*. The INS does not suggest that the exclusionary rule should not continue to apply in criminal proceedings against an alien who unlawfully enters or remains in this country, and the prospect of losing evidence that might otherwise be used in a criminal prosecution undoubtedly supplies some residual deterrent to unlawful conduct by INS officials. But it must be acknowledged ₁₀₄₃that only a very small percentage of arrests of aliens are intended or expected to lead to criminal prosecutions. Thus the arresting officer's primary objective, in practice, will be to use evidence in the civil deportation proceeding. Moreover, here, in contrast to *Janis*, the agency officials who effect the unlawful arrest are the same officials who subsequently bring the deportation action. As recognized in *Janis*, the exclusionary rule is likely to be most effective when applied to such "intrasovereign" violations.

[9] Nonetheless, several other factors significantly reduce the likely deterrent value of the exclusionary rule in a civil deportation proceeding. First, regardless of how the arrest is effected, deportation will still be possible when evidence not derived directly from the arrest is sufficient to support deportation. As the BIA has recognized, in many deportation proceedings "the sole matters necessary for the Government to establish are the respondent's identity and alienage—at which point the burden shifts to the respondent to prove the time, place and manner of entry." *Matter of Sandoval,* 17 I. & N. Dec., at 79. Since the person and identity of the respondent are not themselves suppressible, see *supra*, at 3485, the INS must prove only alienage, and that will sometimes be possible using evidence gathered independently of, or sufficiently attenuated from, the original arrest. See *Matter of Sandoval, supra,* at 79; see, *e.g., Avila-Gallegos v. INS*, 525 F.2d 666 (CA2 1975). The INS's task is simplified in this regard by

the civil nature of the proceeding. As Justice Brandeis stated: "Silence is often evidence of the most persuasive character.... [T]here is no rule of law which prohibits officers charged with the administration of the immigration law from drawing an inference from the silence of one who is called upon to speak.... A person arrested on the preliminary warrant is not protected by a presumption of citizenship comparable to the presumption of innocence in a criminal case. There is no provision which forbids drawing an adverse inference from the fact of standing₁₀₄₄ mute." *United States ex rel. Bilokumsky v. Tod*, 263 U.S., at 153–154, 44 S.Ct., at 55–56.

The second factor is a practical one. In the course of a year the average INS agent arrests almost 500 illegal aliens. Brief for Petitioner 38. Over 97.5% apparently agree to voluntary deportation without a formal hearing. 705 F.2d, at 1071, n. 17. Among the remainder who do request a formal hearing (apparently a dozen or so in all, per officer, per year) very few challenge the circumstances of their arrests. As noted by the Court of Appeals, "the BIA was able to find only two reported immigration cases since 1899 in which the [exclusionary] rule was applied to bar unlawfully seized evidence, only one other case in which the rule's application was specifically addressed, and fewer than fifty BIA proceedings since 1952 in which a Fourth Amendment challenge to the introduction of evidence was even raised." *Id.,* at 1071. Every INS agent knows, therefore, that it is highly unlikely that any particular arrestee will end up challenging the lawfulness of his arrest in a formal deportation proceeding. When an occasional challenge is brought, the consequences from the point of view of the officer's overall arrest and deportation record will be trivial. In these circumstances, the arresting officer is most unlikely to shape his conduct in anticipation of the exclusion of evidence at a formal deportation hearing.

Third, and perhaps most important, the INS has its own comprehensive scheme for deterring Fourth Amendment violations by

its officers. Most arrests of illegal aliens away from the border occur during farm, factory, or other workplace surveys. Large numbers of illegal aliens are often arrested at one time, and conditions are understandably chaotic. See Brief for Petitioner in *INS v. Delgado,* O.T.1983, No. 82–1271, pp. 3–5. To safeguard the rights of those who are lawfully present at inspected workplaces the INS has developed rules restricting stop, interrogation, and arrest practices. *Id.,* at 7, n. 7, 32–40, and n. 25. These ₁₀₄₅regulations require that no one be detained without reasonable suspicion of illegal alienage, and that no one be arrested unless there is an admission of illegal alienage or other strong evidence thereof. New immigration officers receive instruction and examination in Fourth Amendment law, and others receive periodic refresher courses in law. Brief for Petitioner 39–40. Evidence seized through intentionally unlawful conduct is excluded by Department of Justice policy from the proceeding for which it was obtained. See Memorandum from Benjamin R. Civiletti to Heads of Offices, Boards, Bureaus and Divisions, Violations of Search and Seizure Law (Jan. 16, 1981). The INS also has in place a procedure for investigating and punishing immigration officers who commit Fourth Amendment violations. See Office of General Counsel, INS, U.S. Dept. of Justice, The Law of Arrest, Search, and Seizure for Immigration Officers 35 (Jan. 1983). The INS's attention to Fourth Amendment interests cannot guarantee that constitutional violations will not occur, but it does reduce the likely deterrent value of the exclusionary rule. Deterrence must be measured at the margin.

Finally, the deterrent value of the exclusionary rule in deportation proceedings is undermined by the availability of alternative remedies for institutional practices by the INS that might violate Fourth Amendment rights. The INS is a single agency, under central federal control, and engaged in operations of broad scope but highly repetitive character. The possibility of declaratory relief against the agency thus offers a means for challenging the validity of INS practices, when standing requirements for bringing such an action can be met. Cf. *INS v. Delgado*, 466 U.S. 210, 104 S.Ct. 1758, 80 L.Ed.2d 247 (1984).

Respondents contend that retention of the exclusionary rule is necessary to safeguard the Fourth Amendment rights of ethnic Americans, particularly the Hispanic-Americans lawfully in this country. We recognize that respondents raise here legitimate and important concerns. But application of the exclusionary rule to civil deportation proceedings [1046]can be justified only if the rule is likely to add significant protection to these Fourth Amendment rights. The exclusionary rule provides no remedy for completed wrongs; those lawfully in this country can be interested in its application only insofar as it may serve as an effective deterrent to future INS misconduct. For the reasons we have discussed we conclude that application of the rule in INS civil deportation proceedings, as in the circumstances discussed in *Janis*, "is unlikely to provide significant, much less substantial, additional deterrence." 428 U.S., at 458, 96 S.Ct., at 3034. Important as it is to protect the Fourth Amendment rights of all persons, there is no convincing indication that application of the exclusionary rule in civil deportation proceedings will contribute materially to that end.

On the other side of the scale, the social costs of applying the exclusionary rule in deportation proceedings are both unusual and significant. The first cost is one that is unique to continuing violations of the law. Applying the exclusionary rule in pro-

ceedings that are intended not to punish past transgressions but to prevent their continuance or renewal would require the courts to close their eyes to ongoing violations of the law. This Court has never before accepted costs of this character in applying the exclusionary rule.

Presumably no one would argue that the exclusionary rule should be invoked to prevent an agency from ordering corrective action at a leaking hazardous waste dump if the evidence underlying the order had been improperly obtained, or to compel police to return contraband explosives or drugs to their owner if the contraband had been unlawfully seized. On the rare occasions that it has considered costs of this type the Court has firmly indicated that the exclusionary rule does not extend this far. See *United States v. Jeffers*, 342 U.S. 48, 54, 72 S.Ct. 93, 96, 96 L.Ed. 59 (1951); *Trupiano v. United States*, 334 U.S. 699, 710, 68 S.Ct. 1229, 1234, 92 L.Ed. 1663 (1948). The rationale for these holdings is not difficult to find. "Both *Trupiano* and *Jeffers* concerned objects the possession of which, without more, constitutes a crime. The repossession[1047] of such *per se* contraband by Jeffers and Trupiano would have subjected them to criminal penalties. The return of the contraband would clearly have frustrated the express public policy against the possession of such objects." *One 1958 Plymouth Sedan v. Pennsylvania*, 380 U.S. 693, 699, 85 S.Ct. 1246, 1250, 14 L.Ed.2d 170 (1965) (footnote omitted). Precisely the same can be said here. Sandoval-Sanchez is a person whose unregistered presence in this country, without more, constitutes a crime.[3] His release

---

3. Sandoval-Sanchez was arrested on June 23, 1977. His deportation hearing was held on October 7, 1977. By that time he was under a duty to apply for registration as an alien. A failure to do so plainly constituted a continuing crime. 8 U.S.C. §§ 1302, 1306. Sandoval-Sanchez was not, of course, prosecuted for this crime, and we do not know whether or not he did make the required application. But it is safe to assume that the exclusionary rule would never be at issue in a deportation proceeding brought against an alien who entered the country unlaw-

fully and then voluntarily admitted to his unlawful presence in an application for registration.

Sandoval-Sanchez was also not prosecuted for his initial illegal entry into this country, an independent crime under 8 U.S.C. § 1325. We need not decide whether or not remaining in this country following an illegal entry is a continuing or a completed crime under § 1325. The question is academic, of course, since in either event the unlawful entry remains both

---

within our borders would immediately subject him to criminal penalties. His release would clearly frustrate the express public policy against an alien's unregistered presence in this country. Even the objective of deterring Fourth Amendment violations should not require such a result. The constable's blunder may allow the criminal to go free, but we have never suggested that it allows the criminal to continue in the commission of an ongoing crime. When the crime in question involves unlawful presence in this country, the criminal may go free, but he should not go free within our borders.[4]

⌊1048Other factors also weigh against applying the exclusionary rule in deportation proceedings. The INS currently operates a deliberately simple deportation hearing system, streamlined to permit the quick resolution of very large numbers of deportation actions, and it is against this backdrop that the costs of the exclusionary rule must be assessed. The costs of applying the exclusionary rule, like the benefits, must be measured at the margin.

The average immigration judge handles about six deportation hearings per day. Brief for Petitioner 27, n. 16. Neither the hearing officers nor the attorneys participating in those hearings are likely to be well versed in the intricacies of Fourth Amendment law. The prospect of even occasional invocation of the exclusionary rule might significantly change and complicate the character of these proceedings. The BIA has described the practical problems as follows:

"Absent the applicability of the exclusionary rule, questions relating to deportability routinely involve simple factual allegations and matters of proof. When Fourth Amendment issues are raised at

deportation hearings, the result is a diversion of attention from the main issues which those proceedings were created to resolve, both in terms of the expertise of the administrative decision makers and of the structure of the forum to accommodate inquiries into search and seizure questions. The result frequently seems to be a long, confused record in which the issues are not clearly defined and in which there is voluminous testimony . . . . The ensuing delays and inordinate amount of time spent on such cases at all levels has an adverse impact on the effective administration₁₀₄₉ of the immigration laws. . . . This is particularly true in a proceeding where delay may be the only 'defense' available and where problems already exist with the use of dilatory tactics." *Matter of Sandoval*, 17 I. & N., at 80 (footnote omitted).

This sober assessment of the exclusionary rule's likely costs, by the agency that would have to administer the rule in at least the administrative tiers of its application, cannot be brushed off lightly.

The BIA's concerns are reinforced by the staggering dimension of the problem that the INS confronts. Immigration officers apprehend over one million deportable aliens in this country every year. *Id.*, at 85. A single agent may arrest many illegal aliens every day. Although the investigatory burden does not justify the commission of constitutional violations, the officers cannot be expected to compile elaborate, contemporaneous, written reports detailing the circumstances of every arrest. At present an officer simply completes a "Record of Deportable Alien" that is introduced to prove the INS's case at the deportation hearing; the officer rarely must at-

punishable and continuing grounds for deportation. See 8 U.S.C. § 1251(a)(2).

4. Similarly, in *Sure-Tan, Inc. v. NLRB*, 467 U.S. 883, 104 S.Ct. 2803, 81 L.Ed.2d 732 (1984), the Court concluded that an employer can be guilty of an unfair labor practice in his dealings with an alien notwithstanding the alien's illegal presence in this country. Retrospective sanctions against the employer may accordingly be im-

posed by the National Labor Relations Board to further the public policy against unfair labor practices. But while he maintains the status of an illegal alien, the employee is plainly not entitled to the prospective relief—reinstatement and continued employment—that probably would be granted to other victims of similar unfair labor practices.

tend the hearing. Fourth Amendment suppression hearings would undoubtedly require considerably more, and the likely burden on the administration of the immigration laws would be correspondingly severe.

Finally, the INS advances the credible argument that applying the exclusionary rule to deportation proceedings might well result in the suppression of large amounts of information that had been obtained entirely lawfully. INS arrests occur in crowded and confused circumstances. Though the INS agents are instructed to follow procedures that adequately protect Fourth Amendment interests, agents will usually be able to testify only to the fact that they followed INS rules. The demand for a precise account of exactly what happened in each particular arrest would plainly preclude mass arrests, even when the INS is confronted, ⌊1050⌋as it often is, with massed numbers of ascertainably illegal aliens, and even when the arrests can be and are conducted in full compliance with all Fourth Amendment requirements.

[10, 11] In these circumstances we are persuaded that the *Janis* balance between costs and benefits comes out against applying the exclusionary rule in civil deportation hearings held by the INS. By all appearances the INS has already taken sensible and reasonable steps to deter Fourth Amendment violations by its officers, and this makes the likely additional deterrent value of the exclusionary rule small. The costs of applying the exclusionary rule in the context of civil deportation hearings are high. In particular, application of the exclusionary rule in cases such as Sandoval-Sanchez', would compel the courts to release from custody persons who would then immediately resume their commission of a crime through their continuing, unlawful presence in this country.

"There comes a point at which courts, consistent with their duty to administer the law, cannot continue to create barriers to law enforcement in the pursuit of a supervisory role that is properly the duty of the Executive and Legislative Branches." *United States v. Janis,* 428 U.S., at 459, 96 S.Ct., at 3034. That point has been reached here.

V

[12] We do not condone any violations of the Fourth Amendment that may have occurred in the arrests of respondents Lopez-Mendoza or Sandoval-Sanchez. Moreover, no challenge is raised here to the INS's own internal regulations. Cf. *INS v. Delgado,* 466 U.S. 210, 104 S.Ct. 1758, 80 L.Ed.2d 247 (1984). Our conclusions concerning the exclusionary rule's value might change, if there developed good reason to believe that Fourth Amendment violations by INS officers were widespread. Cf. *United States v. Leon,* 468 U.S. 897, 928, 104 S.Ct. 3405, 3424, 82 L.Ed.2d 677 (BLACKMUN, J., concurring). Finally, we do not deal here with egregious violations of Fourth Amendment or other liberties that might transgress notions of fundamental fairness and undermine ⌊1051⌋the probative value of the evidence obtained.[5] Cf. *Rochin v. California,* 342 U.S. 165, 72 S.Ct. 205, 96 L.Ed. 183 (1952). At issue here is the exclusion of credible evidence gathered in connection with peaceful arrests by INS officers. We hold that evidence derived from such arrests need not be suppressed in an INS civil deportation hearing.

The judgment of the Court of Appeals is therefore

Reversed.

---

5. We note that subsequent to its decision in *Matter of Sandoval,* 17 I. & N. Dec. 70 (1979), the BIA held that evidence will be excluded if the circumstances surrounding a particular arrest and interrogation would render use of the evidence obtained thereby "fundamentally unfair" and in violation of due process requirements of the Fifth Amendment. *Matter of Toro,* 17 I. & N. Dec. 340, 343 (1980). See also *Matter of Garcia,* 17 I. & N. Dec. 319, 321 (BIA 1980) (suppression of admission of alienage obtained after request for counsel had been repeatedly refused); *Matter of Ramira-Cordova,* No. A21 095 659 (Feb. 21, 1980) (suppression of evidence obtained as a result of a night-time warrantless entry into the aliens' residence).

Justice BRENNAN, dissenting.

I fully agree with Justice WHITE that under the analysis developed by the Court in such cases as *United States v. Janis*, 428 U.S. 433, 96 S.Ct. 3021, 49 L.Ed.2d 1046 (1976), and *United States v. Calandra*, 414 U.S. 338, 94 S.Ct. 613, 38 L.Ed.2d 561 (1974), the exclusionary rule must apply in civil deportation proceedings. However, for the reasons set forth today in my dissenting opinion in *United States v. Leon*, *ante*, 468 U.S. 897, 104 S.Ct. 3405, 82 L.Ed.2d 677, I believe the basis for the exclusionary rule does not derive from its effectiveness as a deterrent, but is instead found in the requirements of the Fourth Amendment itself. My view of the exclusionary rule would, of course, require affirmance of the Court of Appeals. In this case, federal law enforcement officers arrested respondents Sandoval-Sanchez and Lopez-Mendoza in violation of their Fourth Amendment rights. The subsequent admission of any evidence secured pursuant to these unlawful arrests ⌊1052in civil deportation proceedings would, in my view, also infringe those rights. The Government of the United States bears an obligation to obey the Fourth Amendment; that obligation is not lifted simply because the law enforcement officers . were agents of the Immigration and Naturalization Service, nor because the evidence obtained by those officers was to be used in civil deportation proceedings.

Justice WHITE, dissenting.

The Court today holds that the exclusionary rule does not apply in civil deportation proceedings. Because I believe that the conclusion of the majority is based upon an incorrect assessment of the costs and benefits of applying the rule in such proceedings, I respectfully dissent.[1]

The paradigmatic case in which the exclusionary rule is applied is when the prosecutor seeks to use evidence illegally obtained by law enforcement officials in his case-in-chief in a criminal trial. In other classes of cases, the rule is applicable only when the likelihood of deterring the unwanted conduct outweighs the societal costs imposed by exclusion of relevant evidence. *United States v. Janis*, 428 U.S. 433, 454, 96 S.Ct. 3021, 3032, 49 L.Ed.2d 1046 (1976). Thus, the Court has, in a number of situations, refused to extend the exclusionary rule to proceedings other than the criminal trial itself. For example, in *Stone v. Powell*, 428 U.S. 465, 96 S.Ct. 3037, 49 L.Ed.2d 1067 (1976), the Court held that the deterrent effect of the rule would not be reduced by refusing to allow a state prisoner to litigate a Fourth Amendment claim in federal habeas corpus proceedings if he was afforded a full and fair opportunity to litigate it in state court. Similarly, in *United*⌊1053 *States v. Calandra*, 414 U.S. 338, 351, 94 S.Ct. 613, 621, 38 L.Ed.2d 561 (1974), we concluded that "[a]ny incremental deterrent effect which might be achieved by extending the rule to grand jury proceedings is uncertain at best." And in *United States v. Janis*, *supra*, we declined to extend the exclusionary rule to bar the introduction in a federal civil proceeding of evidence unconstitutionally seized by a state law enforcement officer. In all of these cases it was unquestioned that the illegally seized evidence would not be admissible in the case-in-chief of the proceeding for which the evidence was gathered; only its collateral use was permitted.

Civil deportation proceedings are in no sense "collateral." The majority correctly acknowledges that the "primary objective" of the INS agent is "to use evidence in the civil deportation proceeding" and that "the agency officials who effect the unlawful

---

1. I also question the Court's finding that Lopez-Mendoza failed to object to admission of the evidence. *Ante*, at 3485, and n. 1. The Court of Appeals held that he had made a proper objection, 705 F.2d 1059, 1060, n. 1 (CA9 1983), and the INS did not seek review of that conclusion.

Brief for Petitioner 8, n. 8. Moreover, the fact that changes in an opinion are made between the time of the slip opinion and the bound volume has never before been considered evidence that the holding of a case is "unsettled." See *ante*, at 3484, n. 1.

arrest are the same officials who subsequently bring the deportation action." *Ante*, at 3485. The Immigration and Naturalization Service likewise concedes that INS agents are "in the business of conducting searches for and seizures of illegal aliens for the purpose of bringing about their deportation." Brief for Petitioner 37. Thus, unlike the the situation in *Janis*, the conduct challenged here falls within "the offending officer's zone of primary interest." 428 U.S., at 458, 96 S.Ct., at 3034. The majority nonetheless concludes that application of the rule in such proceedings is unlikely to provide significant deterrence. Because INS agents are law enforcement officials whose mission is closely analogous to that of police officers and because civil deportation proceedings are to INS agents what criminal trials are to police officers, I cannot agree with that assessment.

The exclusionary rule rests on the Court's belief that exclusion has a sufficient deterrent effect to justify its imposition, and the Court has not abandoned the rule. As long as that is the case, there is no principled basis for distinguishing between the deterrent effect of the rule in criminal cases and in civil deportation proceedings. The majority attempts to justify the distinction by asserting that deportation will still [1054]be possible when evidence not derived from the illegal search or seizure is independently sufficient. *Ante*, at 3485–3486. However, that is no less true in criminal cases. The suppression of some evidence does not bar prosecution for the crime, and in many cases even though some evidence is suppressed a conviction will nonetheless be obtained.

The majority also suggests that the fact that most aliens elect voluntary departure dilutes the deterrent effect of the exclu-

sionary rule, because the infrequency of challenges to admission of evidence will mean that "the consequences from the point of view of the officer's overall arrest and deportation record will be trivial." *Ante*, at 3486. It is true that a majority of apprehended aliens elect voluntary departure, while a lesser number go through civil deportation proceedings and a still smaller number are criminally prosecuted. However, that fact no more diminishes the importance of the exclusionary sanction than the fact that many criminal defendants plead guilty dilutes the rule's deterrent effect in criminal cases. The possibility of exclusion of evidence quite obviously plays a part in the decision whether to contest either civil deportation or criminal prosecution. Moreover, in concentrating on the incentives under which the individual agent operates to the exclusion of the incentives under which the agency as a whole operates neglects the "systemic" deterrent effect that may lead the agency to adopt policies and procedures that conform to Fourth Amendment standards. See, *e.g., Dunaway v. New York*, 442 U.S. 200, 221, 99 S.Ct. 2248, 2261, 60 L.Ed.2d 824 (1979) (STEVENS, J., concurring).

The majority believes "perhaps most important" the fact that the INS has a "comprehensive scheme" in place for deterring Fourth Amendment violations by punishing agents who commit such violations, but it points to not a single instance in which that scheme has been invoked.[2] *Ante*, at [1055]3486. Also, immigration officers are instructed and examined in Fourth Amendment law, and it is suggested that this education is another reason why the exclusionary rule is unnecessary. *Ibid.* A contrary lesson could be discerned from the existence of these programs, however, when it is recalled that they were instituted

---

2. The INS suggests that its disciplinary rules are "not mere paper procedures" and that over a period of four years 20 officers were suspended or terminated for misconduct toward aliens. Brief for Petitioner 45, n. 28. The INS does not

assert, however, that any of these officers were disciplined for Fourth Amendment violations, and it appears that the 11 officers who were terminated were terminated for rape or assault. See Brief for Respondents 60, n. 42.

during "a legal regime in which the cases and commentators uniformly sanctioned the invocation of the rule in deportation proceedings." 705 F.2d 1059, 1071 (CA9 1983). Thus, rather than supporting a conclusion that the exclusionary rule is unnecessary, the existence of these programs instead suggests that the exclusionary rule has created incentives for the agency to ensure that its officers follow the dictates of the Constitution. Since the deterrent function of the rule is furthered if it alters either "the behavior of individual law enforcement officers or the policies of their departments," *United States v. Leon,* 468 U.S., at 918, 104 S.Ct., at 3419, it seems likely that it was the rule's deterrent effect that led to the programs to which the Court now points for its assertion that the rule would have no deterrent effect.

The suggestion that alternative remedies, such as civil suits, provide adequate protection is unrealistic. Contrary to the situation in criminal cases, once the Government has improperly obtained evidence against an illegal alien, he is removed from the country and is therefore in no position to file civil actions in federal courts. Moreover, those who are legally in the country but are nonetheless subjected to illegal searches and seizures are likely to be poor and uneducated, and many will not speak English. It is doubtful that the threat of civil suits by these persons will strike fear into the hearts of those who enforce the Nation's immigration laws.

It is also my belief that the majority exaggerates the costs associated with applying the exclusionary rule in this context. Evidence obtained through violation of the Fourth Amendment is not automatically suppressed, and any inquiry [1056]into the burdens associated with application of the exclusionary rule must take that fact into account. In *United States v. Leon,* 468

U.S. 897, 104 S.Ct. 3405, 82 L.Ed.2d 677, we have held that the exclusionary rule is not applicable when officers are acting in objective good faith. Thus, if the agents neither knew nor should have known that they were acting contrary to the dictates of the Fourth Amendment, evidence will not be suppressed even if it is held that their conduct was illegal.

As is noted, *ante,* at 3489, n. 5, the BIA has already held that evidence will be suppressed if it results from egregious violations of constitutional standards. Thus, the mechanism for dealing with suppression motions exists and is utilized, significantly decreasing the force of the majority's predictions of dire consequences flowing from "even occasional invocation of the exclusionary rule." *Ante,* at 3488. Although the standard currently utilized by the BIA may not be precisely coextensive with the good-faith exception, any incremental increase in the amount of evidence that is suppressed through application of *Leon* is unlikely to be significant. Likewise, any difference that may exist between the two standards is unlikely to increase significantly the number of suppression motions filed.

Contrary to the view of the majority, it is not the case that Sandoval-Sanchez' "unregistered presence in this country, without more, constitutes a crime." *Ante,* at 3487. Section 275 of the Immigration and Nationality Act makes it a crime to enter the United States illegally. 8 U.S.C. § 1325.[3] The first offense constitutes a misdemeanor, and subsequent offenses constitute felonies. *Ibid.* Those few cases that have construed this statute have held that a violation takes [1057]place at the time of entry and that the statute does not describe a continuing offense. *Gonzales v. City of Peoria,* 722 F.2d 468, 473–474 (CA9 1983);

---

3. Section 275 provides in part:
"Any alien who (1) enters the United States at any time or place other than as designated by immigration officers, or (2) eludes examination

or inspection by immigration officers, or (3) obtains entry to the United States by a willfully false or misleading representation ... shall be guilty of a [crime] ...." 8 U.S.C. § 1325.

United States v. Rincon-Jimenez, 595 F.2d 1192, 1194 (CA9 1979). Although this Court has not construed the statute, it has suggested in dictum that this interpretation is correct, *United States v. Cores*, 356 U.S. 405, 408, n. 6, 78 S.Ct. 875, 878, n. 6, 2 L.Ed.2d 873 (1958), and it is relatively clear that such an interpretation is most consistent with the statutory language. Therefore, it is simply not the case that suppressing evidence in deportation proceedings will "allo[w] the criminal to continue in the commission of an ongoing crime." *Ante*, at 3488. It is true that some courts have construed § 276 of the Act, 8 U.S.C. § 1326, which applies to aliens previously deported who enter or are found in the United States, to describe a continuing offense.[4] *United States v. Bruno*, 328 F.Supp. 815 (WD Mo.1971); *United States v. Alvarado-Soto*, 120 F.Supp. 848 (SD Cal. 1954); *United States v. Rincon-Jimenez, supra* (dictum). But see *United States v. DiSantillo*, 615 F.2d 128 (CA3 1980). In such cases, however, the Government will have a record of the prior deportation and will have little need for any evidence that might be suppressed through application of the exclusionary rule. See *United States v. Pineda-Chinchilla*, 712 F.2d 942 (CA5 1983) (illegality of arrest does not bar introduction of INS records to demonstrate prior deportation) cert. denied, 464 U.S. 964, 104 S.Ct. 402, 78 L.Ed.2d 343 (1983).

Although the majority relies on the registration provisions of 8 U.S.C. §§ 1302 and 1306 for its "continuing crime" argument, those provisions provide little support for the general ₁₀₅₈rule laid down that the exclusionary rule does not apply in civil deportation proceedings. First, § 1302 requires that aliens register within 30 days of entry into the country. Thus, for the first 30 days failure to register is not a crime. Second, § 1306 provides that only *willful*

failure to register is a misdemeanor. Therefore, "unregistered presence in this country, without more," *ante*, at 3487, does not constitute a crime; rather, unregistered presence plus willfulness must be shown. There is no finding that Sandoval-Sanchez willfully failed to register, which is a necessary predicate to the conclusion that he is engaged in a continuing crime. Third, only aliens 14 years of age or older are required to register; those under 14 years of age are to be registered by their parents or guardian. By the majority's reasoning, therefore, perhaps the exclusionary rule should apply in proceedings to deport children under 14, since their failure to register does not constitute a crime.

Application of the rule, we are told, will also seriously interfere with the "streamlined" nature of deportation hearings because "[n]either the hearing officers nor the attorneys participating in those hearings are likely to be well versed in the intricacies of Fourth Amendment law." *Ante*, at 3488. Yet the majority deprecates the deterrent benefit of the exclusionary rule in part on the ground that immigration officers receive a thorough education in Fourth Amendment law. *Ante*, at 3488. The implication that hearing officers should defer to law enforcement officers' superior understanding of constitutional principles is startling indeed.

Prior to the decision of the Board of Immigration Appeals in *Matter of Sandoval*, 17 I. & N. Dec. 70 (1979), neither the Board nor any court had held that the exclusionary rule did not apply in civil deportation proceedings. 705 F.2d at 1071. The Board in *Sandoval* noted that there were "fewer than fifty" BIA proceedings since 1952 in which motions had been made to suppress evidence on Fourth Amendment ₁₀₅₉grounds. This is so despite the

---

4. Section 276 provides in part:
   "Any alien who—
   "(1) has been arrested and deported or excluded and deported, and thereafter

"(2) enters, attempts to enter, or is at any time found in, the United States ... shall be guilty of a felony." 8 U.S.C. § 1326.

fact that "immigration law practitioners have been informed by the major treatise in their field that the exclusionary rule was available to clients facing deportation. See 1A C. Gordon and H. Rosenfield, Immigration Law and Procedure § 5.2c at 5–31 (rev. ed. 1980)." 705 F.2d, at 1071. The suggestion that "[t]he prospect of even occasional invocation of the exclusionary rule might significantly change and complicate the character of these proceedings," *ante*, at 3488, is thus difficult to credit. The simple fact is that prior to 1979 the exclusionary rule was available in civil deportation proceedings, and there is no indication that it significantly interfered with the ability of the INS to function.

Finally, the majority suggests that application of the exclusionary rule might well result in the suppression of large amounts of information legally obtained because of the "crowded and confused circumstances" surrounding mass arrests. *Ante*, at 3489. The result would be that INS agents would have to keep a "precise account of exactly what happened in each particular arrest," which would be impractical considering the "massed numbers of ascertainably illegal aliens." *Ante*, at 3489. Rather than constituting a rejection of the application of the exclusionary rule in civil deportation proceedings, however, this argument amounts to a rejection of the application of the Fourth Amendment to the activities of INS agents. If the pandemonium attending immigration arrests is so great that violations of the Fourth Amendment cannot be ascertained for the purpose of applying the exclusionary rule, there is no reason to think that such violations can be ascertained for purposes of civil suits or internal disciplinary proceedings, both of which are proceedings that the majority suggests provide adequate deterrence against Fourth Amendment violations. The Court may be willing to throw up its hands in dismay because it is administratively inconvenient to determine whether ⌊1060constitutional rights have been violated, but we neglect our duty when we subordinate constitution-

al rights to expediency in such a manner. Particularly is this so when, as here, there is but a weak showing that administrative efficiency will be seriously compromised.

In sum, I believe that the costs and benefits of applying the exclusionary rule in civil deportation proceedings do not differ in any significant way from the costs and benefits of applying the rule in ordinary criminal proceedings. Unless the exclusionary rule is to be wholly done away with and the Court's belief that it has deterrent effects abandoned, it should be applied in deportation proceedings when evidence has been obtained by deliberate violations of the Fourth Amendment or by conduct a reasonably competent officer would know is contrary to the Constitution. Accordingly, I dissent.

Justice MARSHALL, dissenting.

I agree with Justice WHITE that application to this case of the mode of analysis embodied in the decisions of the Court in *United States v. Janis*, 428 U.S. 433, 96 S.Ct. 3021, 49 L.Ed.2d 1046 (1976), and *United States v. Calandra*, 414 U.S. 338, 94 S.Ct. 613, 38 L.Ed.2d 561 (1974), compels the conclusion that the exclusionary rule should apply in civil deportation proceedings. *Ante*, at 3490–3491. However, I continue to believe that that mode of analysis fails to reflect the constitutionally mandated character of the exclusionary rule. See *United States v. Leon*, 468 U.S., at 931–938, 104 S.Ct., at 3431–3435 (BRENNAN, J., joined by MARSHALL, J., dissenting); *United States v. Janis, supra*, at 460, 96 S.Ct., at 3035 (BRENNAN, J., joined by MARSHALL, J., dissenting). In my view, a sufficient reason for excluding from civil deportation proceedings evidence obtained in violation of the Fourth Amendment is that there is no other way to achieve "the twin goals of enabling the judiciary to avoid the taint of partnership in official lawlessness and of assuring the people—all potential victims of unlawful government conduct—that the government would not profit from its lawless behavior, thus minimizing the risk of seriously undermining ₗ₁₀₆₁popular trust in government." *United States v. Calandra, supra,* at 357, 94 S.Ct., at 624 (BRENNAN, J., joined by MARSHALL, J., dissenting).

Justice STEVENS, dissenting.

Because the Court has not yet held that the rule of *United States v. Leon,* 468 U.S. 897, 104 S.Ct. 3405, 82 L.Ed.2d 677 has any application to warrantless searches, I do not join the portion of Justice WHITE's opinion that relies on that case. I do, however, agree with the remainder of his dissenting opinion.

507 U.S. 292, 123 L.Ed.2d 1

⌊292⌋Janet RENO, Attorney General, et al., Petitioners

v.

Jenny Lisette FLORES et al.

No. 91–905.

Argued Oct. 13, 1992.

Decided March 23, 1993.

Class of juvenile aliens, who had been detained on suspicion of being deportable, brought suit challenging Immigration and Naturalization Service (INS) regulation governing release of detained alien juveniles. The United States District Court for the Central District of California, Kelleher, J., 681 F.Supp. 665, granted summary judgment to aliens. After initially reversing and remanding, 934 F.2d 991, rehearing en banc was ordered, and the Court of Appeals for the Ninth Circuit, 942 F.2d 1352, affirmed decision of district court. Certiorari was granted. The Supreme Court, Justice Scalia, held that: (1) regulation permitting detained juvenile aliens to be released only to their parents, close relatives, or legal guardians, except in unusual and compelling circumstances, does not facially violate substantive due process; (2) INS procedures do not deny juvenile aliens procedural due process; and (3) regulation is within scope of Attorney General's statutory discretion to continue custody over arrested aliens.

Judgment of Court of Appeals reversed and remanded.

Justice O'Connor filed concurring opinion, in which Justice Souter joined.

Justice Stevens filed dissenting opinion, in which Justice Blackmun joined.

1. Aliens ⬤⟞53.9

Attorney General has broad discretion to determine whether and on what terms alien arrested on suspicion of being deportable should be released pending deportation hearing. Immigration and Nationality Act,

§ 242(a)(1, 2), as amended, 8 U.S.C.A. § 1252(a)(1, 2).

2. Administrative Law and Procedure ⬤⟞391

To prevail in facial challenge to regulation which has not been applied, party challenging regulation must establish that no set of circumstances exist under which regulation would be valid; such is true as to both constitutional and statutory challenges.

3. Federal Courts ⬤⟞460

Juvenile aliens would not be permitted to reopen settled claims, regarding conditions of confinement pending determination of whether they were deportable, on petition for certiorari challenging validity of regulations under which they were confined.

4. Aliens ⬤⟞40, 53.9

Constitutional Law ⬤⟞274.3

Regulation permitting juvenile aliens, who are detained on suspicion of being deportable, to be released only to parents, close relatives, or legal guardians, except in unusual and compelling circumstances, does not involve a "fundamental" right and is rationally related to government's interest in preserving and promoting welfare of detained juveniles, and thus does not violate substantive due process. U.S.C.A. Const.Amends. 5, 14.

See publication Words and Phrases for other judicial constructions and definitions.

5. Constitutional Law ⬤⟞251

Substantive due process analysis must begin with careful description of asserted right, for doctrine of judicial self-restraint requires Supreme Court to exercise utmost care whenever it is asked to break new ground in such field. U.S.C.A. Const. Amends. 5, 14.

6. Constitutional Law ⬤⟞255(4)

Where juvenile has no available parent, close relative, or legal guardian, where government does not intend to punish child, and where conditions of governmental custody are decent and humane, custody of juvenile does not violate substantive due process; it is rationally connected to governmental interest in preserving and promoting welfare of child, and is not punitive, since it is not excessive in relation to that valid purpose. U.S.C.A. Const.Amends. 5, 14.

7. Aliens ☞53.9

Constitutional Law ☞274.3

If institutional custody of juvenile aliens suspected of being deportable does not violate substantive due process in itself, despite availability of responsible private custodians, it does not become unconstitutional simply because it is shown to be less desirable than some other arrangement for particular child; although best interests of child is proper and feasible criterion for making decision as to which of two parents will be accorded custody, it is not the sole criterion, much less the sole constitutional criterion, for other, less narrowly channeled judgments involving children, where their interests conflict in various degrees with interests of others. U.S.C.A. Const.Amends. 5, 14.

8. Guardian and Ward ☞29

Parent and Child ☞2(3.1)

Best interests of child is not the legal standard that governs parents' or guardians' exercise of custody: so long as certain minimum requirements of child care are met, interests of child may be subordinated to interests of other children, or indeed even to interests of parents or guardians themselves.

9. Constitutional Law ☞255(4)

"The best interests of the child" is not absolute and exclusive constitutional criterion, for substantive due process purposes, for government's exercise of custodial responsibilities that it undertakes, which must be reconciled with many other responsibilities, and thus, child care institutions operated by state in exercise of its parens patriae authority are not constitutionally required to be funded at such level as to provide best

schooling or best health care, nor does Constitution require state to substitute, whenever possible, private nonadoptive custody for institutional care.

10. Aliens ☞53.9

Constitutional Law ☞274.3

Substantive due process requires that substantive standards be met when government holds in custody juvenile aliens suspected of being deportable, and juveniles' fundamental rights must not be impaired, but decision to go beyond those requirements, giving one or another of child's additional interests priority over other concerns that compete for public funds and administrative attention, is policy judgment rather than constitutional imperative. U.S.C.A. Const.Amends. 5, 14.

11. Constitutional Law ☞251, 318(1)

Impairment of interest less than fundamental demands no more than a "reasonable fit" between governmental purpose and means chosen to advance that purpose, to satisfy substantive due process; this standard leaves ample room for agency to decide that administrative factors favor using one means rather than another. U.S.C.A. Const. Amends. 5, 14.

12. Aliens ☞53.9, 54(3.1)

Constitutional Law ☞274.3

Juvenile aliens detained on suspicion of being deportable, on basis that there is no parent, close relative, or guardian to whom they can be released, have no substantive due process right to hearing to determine whether private placement would be better, so long as institutional custody is "good enough," which it is, assuming compliance with requirements of consent decree.

13. Aliens ☞53.9

Constitutional Law ☞274.3

Immigration and Naturalization Service (INS) policy of releasing juvenile aliens suspected of being deportable only to close relatives or guardians, absent unusual circumstances, but releasing aliens with close relatives or legal guardians does not violate "equal protection guaranty" of the Fifth Amendment; distinction in the releasing of alien juveniles with close relatives or legal guardians is justified by tradition of reposing custody in close relatives and legal guardians, while the difference between citizens and aliens is adequate to support distinction allowing release to unrelated adults those juveniles detained pending federal delinquency proceedings. 18 U.S.C.A. § 5034; Immigration and Nationality Act, § 242(a), as amended, 8 U.S.C.A. § 1252(a); U.S.C.A. Const.Amend. 5.

14. Aliens ⊙=53.9

Constitutional Law ⊙=274.3

Procedures under Immigration and Naturalization Service (INS) regulation permitting release of juvenile aliens, who have been detained on suspicion of being deportable, only to parents, close relatives, or legal guardians, except in unusual and compelling circumstances, do not violate procedural due process, even though INS is not required to determine in each case that detention by INS would better serve juvenile's interest than release to some "responsible adult"; juveniles have right to hearing before immigration judge, although there is no provision for automatic review by immigration judge of initial deportability and custody determinations. U.S.C.A. Const.Amends. 5, 14.

15. Aliens ⊙=54(1)

Constitutional Law ⊙=274.3

Fifth Amendment entitles aliens to due process of law in deportation proceedings. U.S.C.A Const.Amend. 5.

16. Aliens ⊙=44, 53.9

Immigration and Naturalization Service (INS) regulation permitting juvenile aliens, who have been detained by the INS on suspicion of being deportable, to be released only to their parents, close relatives, or legal guardians, except in unusual and compelling circumstances, is within the scope of the Attorney General's statutory discretion to continue custody over arrested aliens. Immigration and Nationality Act, § 242(a)(1), as amended, 8 U.S.C.A. § 1252(a)(1).

17. Aliens ⊙=53.9

Immigration and Nationalization Service (INS) regulation permitting juvenile aliens, who have been detained by the INS on suspicion of being deportable, to be released only to their parents, close relatives, or legal guardians provides for sufficient level of individualized determination to satisfy requirements of statute granting Attorney General discretion to continue custody over arrested aliens, by requiring INS to make determinations as to whether there is reason to believe that alien is deportable, whether alien is juvenile, availability of a relative or legal guardian, and whether case is so exceptional as to require consideration of release to someone else. Immigration and Nationality Act, § 242(a)(1), as amended, 8 U.S.C.A. § 1252(a)(1).

18. Aliens ⊙=44, 53.9

Immigration and Naturalization Service (INS) regulation permitting juvenile aliens, who have been detained on suspicion of being deportable, to be released only to their parents, close relatives, or legal guardians does not permit juvenile to be detained indefinitely, in violation of statutory authority granted Attorney General; custody is inherently limited by pending deportation hearing, which must be concluded with reasonable dispatch to avoid habeas corpus. Immigration and Nationality Act, § 242(a)(1), as amended, 8 U.S.C.A. § 1252(a)(1).

Syllabus *

Respondents are a class of alien juveniles arrested by the Immigration and Naturalization Service (INS) on suspicion of being deportable, and then detained pending deportation hearings pursuant to a regulation,

---

* The syllabus constitutes no part of the opinion of the Court but has been prepared by the Reporter of Decisions for the convenience of the reader.

See *United States v. Detroit Lumber Co.*, 200 U.S. 321, 337, 26 S.Ct. 282, 287, 50 L.Ed. 499.

promulgated in 1988 and codified at 8 CFR § 242.24, which provides for the release of detained minors only to their parents, close relatives, or legal guardians, except in unusual and compelling circumstances. An immigration judge will review the initial deportability and custody determinations upon request by the juvenile. § 242.2(d). Pursuant to a consent decree entered earlier in the litigation, juveniles who are not released must be placed in juvenile care facilities that meet or exceed state licensing requirements for the provision of services to dependent children. Respondents contend that they have a right under the Constitution and immigration laws to be routinely released into the custody of other "responsible adults." The District Court invalidated the regulatory scheme on unspecified due process grounds, ordering that "responsible adult part[ies]" be added to the list of persons to whom a juvenile must be released and requiring that a hearing before an immigration judge be held automatically, whether or not the juvenile requests it. The Court of Appeals, en banc, affirmed.

Held:

1. Because this is a facial challenge to the regulation, respondents must establish that no set of circumstances exists under which the regulation would be valid. *United States v. Salerno,* 481 U.S. 739, 745, 107 S.Ct. 2095, 2100, 95 L.Ed.2d 697. Pp. 1446–1447.

2. Regulation 242.24, on its face, does not violate the Due Process Clause. Pp. 1447–1451.

(a) The regulation does not deprive respondents of "substantive due process." The substantive right asserted by respondents is properly described as the right of a child who has no available parent, close relative, or legal guardian, and for whom the government is responsible, to be placed in the custody of a private custodian rather than of a government-operated or government-selected child-care institution. That novel claim cannot be considered " 'so rooted in the traditions and conscience of our people as to be

ranked as fundamental.' " *United |₂₉₃States v. Salerno, supra,* at 751, 107 S.Ct. at 2103. It is therefore sufficient that the regulation is rationally connected to the government's interest in preserving and promoting the welfare of detained juveniles, and is not punitive since it is not excessive in relation to that valid purpose. Nor does each unaccompanied juvenile have a substantive right to an individualized hearing on whether private placement would be in his "best interests." Governmental custody must meet minimum standards, as the consent decree indicates it does here, but the decision to exceed those standards is a policy judgment, not a constitutional imperative. Any remaining constitutional doubts are eliminated by the fact that almost all respondents are aliens suspected of being deportable, a class that can be detained, and over which Congress has granted the Attorney General broad discretion regarding detention. 8 U.S.C. § 1252(a)(1). Pp. 1447–1449.

(b) Existing INS procedures provide alien juveniles with "procedural due process." Respondents' demand for an individualized custody hearing for each detained alien juvenile is merely the "substantive due process" argument recast in procedural terms. Nor are the procedures faulty because they do not require automatic review by an immigration judge of initial deportability and custody determinations. In the context of this facial challenge, providing the *right* to review suffices. It has not been shown that all of the juveniles detained are too young or ignorant to exercise that right; any waiver of a hearing is revocable; and there is no evidence of excessive delay in holding hearings when requested. Pp. 1449–1451.

3. The regulation does not exceed the scope of the Attorney General's discretion to continue custody over arrested aliens under 8 U.S.C. § 1252(a)(1). It rationally pursues a purpose that is lawful for the INS to seek, striking a balance between the INS's concern that the juveniles' welfare will not permit their release to just any adult and the INS's

assessment that it has neither the expertise nor the resources to conduct home studies for individualized placements. The list of approved custodians reflects the traditional view that parents and close relatives are competent custodians, and otherwise defers to the States' proficiency in the field of child custody. The regulation is not motivated by administrative convenience; its use of presumptions and generic rules is reasonable; and the period of detention that may result is limited by the pending deportation hearing, which must be concluded with reasonable dispatch to avoid habeas corpus. Pp. 1451–1454.

942 F.2d 1352 (CA9 1991), reversed and remanded.

SCALIA, J., delivered the opinion of the Court, in which REHNQUIST, C.J., and WHITE, O'CONNOR, KENNEDY, SOUTER, and THOMAS, JJ., |₂₉₄joined. O'CONNOR, J., filed a concurring opinion, in which SOUTER, J., joined, *post*, p. 1454. STEVENS, J., filed a dissenting opinion, in which BLACKMUN, J., joined, *post*, pp. 1456–1457.

Maureen E. Mahoney, for petitioners.

Carlos Holguin, for respondents.

Justice SCALIA delivered the opinion of the Court.

Over the past decade, the Immigration and Naturalization Service (INS or Service) has arrested increasing numbers of alien juveniles who are not accompanied by their parents or other related adults. Respondents, a class of alien juveniles so arrested and held in INS custody pending their deportation hearings, contend that the Constitution and immigration laws require them to be released into the custody of "responsible adults."

I

[1] Congress has given the Attorney General broad discretion to determine whether, and on what terms, an alien arrested on suspicion of being deportable should be released pending |₂₉₅the deportation hearing.[1] The Board of Immigration Appeals has stated that "[a]n alien generally . . . should not be detained or required to post bond except on a finding that he is a threat to the national security . . . or that he is a poor bail risk." *Matter of Patel,* 15 I. & N. Dec. 666 (1976); cf. *INS v. National Center for Immigrants' Rights, Inc. (NCIR),* 502 U.S. 183, 112 S.Ct. 551, 116 L.Ed.2d 546 (1991) (upholding INS regulation imposing conditions upon release). In the case of arrested alien *juveniles,* however, the INS cannot simply send them off into the night on bond or recognizance. The parties to the present suit agree that the Service must assure itself that someone will care for those minors pending resolution of their deportation proceedings. That is easily done when the juvenile's parents have also been detained and the family can be released together; it becomes complicated when the juvenile is arrested alone, *i.e.,* unaccompanied by a parent, guardian, or other related adult. This problem is a serious one, since the INS arrests thousands of alien juveniles each year (more than 8,500 in 1990 alone)— as many as 70% of them unaccompanied. Brief for Petitioners 8. Most of these minors are boys in their mid-teens, but perhaps 15% are girls and the same percentage 14 years of age or younger. See *id.,* at 9, n. 12; App. to Pet. for Cert. 177a.

---

1. Title 8 U.S.C. § 1252(a)(1), 66 Stat. 208, as amended, provides:

"[A]ny such alien taken into custody may, in the discretion of the Attorney General and pending such final determination of deportability, (A) be continued in custody; or (B) be released under bond . . . containing such conditions as the Attor-

ney General may prescribe; or (C) be released on conditional parole. But such bond or parole . . . may be revoked at any time by the Attorney General, in his discretion. . . . ."

The Attorney General's discretion to release aliens convicted of aggravated felonies is narrower. See 8 U.S.C. § 1252(a)(2) (1988 ed., Supp. III).

For a number of years the problem was apparently dealt with on a regional and ad hoc basis, with some INS offices releasing unaccompanied alien juveniles not only to their parents but also to a range of other adults and organizations. ₋₂₉₆In 1984, responding to the increased flow of unaccompanied juvenile aliens into California, the INS Western Regional Office adopted a policy of limiting the release of detained minors to " 'a parent or lawful guardian,' " except in " 'unusual and extraordinary cases,' " when the juvenile could be released to " 'a responsible individual who agrees to provide care and be responsible for the welfare and well being of the child.' " See *Flores v. Meese*, 934 F.2d 991, 994 (CA9 1990) (quoting policy), vacated, 942 F.2d 1352 (CA9 1991) (en banc).

In July of the following year, the four respondents filed an action in the District Court for the Central District of California on behalf of a class, later certified by the court, consisting of all aliens under the age of 18 who are detained by the INS Western Region because "a parent or legal guardian fails to personally appear to take custody of them." App. 29. The complaint raised seven claims, the first two challenging the Western Region release policy (on constitutional, statutory, and international law grounds), and the final five challenging the conditions of the juveniles' detention.

The District Court granted the INS partial summary judgment on the statutory and international law challenges to the release policy, and in late 1987 approved a consent decree that settled all claims regarding the detention conditions. The court then turned to the constitutional challenges to the release policy, and granted respondents partial summary judgment on their equal protection claim that the INS had no rational basis for treating alien minors in deportation proceedings differently from alien minors in exclusion proceedings[2] (whom INS regulations permitted to be paroled, in some circum-

stances, to persons other than parents and legal guardians, including other relatives and "friends," see 8 CFR § 212.5(a)(2)(ii) (1987)). This prompted the INS to initiate ₋₂₉₇notice-and-comment rulemaking "to codify Service policy regarding detention and release of juvenile aliens and to provide a single policy for juveniles in both deportation and exclusion proceedings." 52 Fed.Reg. 38245 (1987). The District Court agreed to defer consideration of respondents' due process claims until the regulation was promulgated.

The uniform deportation-exclusion rule finally adopted, published on May 17, 1988, see Detention and Release of Juveniles, 53 Fed. Reg. 17449 (codified as to deportation at 8 CFR § 242.24 (1992)), expanded the possibilities for release somewhat beyond the Western Region policy, but not as far as many commenters had suggested. It provides that alien juveniles "shall be released, in order of preference, to: (i) a parent; (ii) a legal guardian; or (iii) an adult relative (brother, sister, aunt, uncle, grandparent) who are [*sic*] not presently in INS detention," unless the INS determines that "the detention of such juvenile is required to secure his timely appearance before the Service or the immigration court or to ensure the juvenile's safety or that of others." 8 CFR § 242.24(b)(1) (1992). If the only listed individuals are in INS detention, the Service will consider simultaneous release of the juvenile and custodian "on a discretionary case-by-case basis." § 242.24(b)(2). A parent or legal guardian who is in INS custody or outside the United States may also, by sworn affidavit, designate another person as capable and willing to care for the child, provided that person "execute[s] an agreement to care for the juvenile and to ensure the juvenile's presence at all future proceedings." § 242.24(b)(3). Finally, in "unusual and compelling circumstances and in the discretion of the [INS] district

---

2. Exclusion proceedings, which are not at issue in the present case, involve aliens apprehended before "entering" the United States, as that term

is used in the immigration laws. See *Leng May Ma v. Barber*, 357 U.S. 185, 187, 78 S.Ct. 1072, 1073, 2 L.Ed.2d 1246 (1958).

director or chief patrol agent," juveniles may be released to other adults who execute a care and attendance agreement. § 242.24(b)(4).

If the juvenile is *not* released under the foregoing provision, the regulation requires a designated INS official, the "Juvenile Coordinator," to locate "suitable placement . . . in a facility designated for the occupancy of juveniles." $\lfloor_{298}$§ 242.24(c). The Service may briefly hold the minor in an "INS detention facility having separate accommodations for juveniles," § 242.24(d), but under the terms of the consent decree resolving respondents' conditions-of-detention claims, the INS must within 72 hours of arrest place alien juveniles in a facility that meets or exceeds the standards established by the Alien Minors Care Program of the Community Relations Service (CRS), Department of Justice, 52 Fed. Reg. 15569 (1987). See Memorandum of Understanding Re Compromise of Class Action: Conditions of Detention, *Flores v. Meese*, No. 85–4544–RJK (Px) (CD Cal., Nov. 30, 1987) (incorporating the CRS notice and program description), reprinted in App. to Pet. for Cert. 148a–205a (hereinafter Juvenile Care Agreement).

Juveniles placed in these facilities are deemed to be in INS detention "because of issues of payment and authorization of medical care." 53 Fed.Reg., at 17449. "Legal custody" rather·than "detention" more accurately describes the reality of the arrangement, however, since these are not correctional institutions but facilities that meet "state licensing requirements for the provision of shelter care, foster care, group care, and related services to dependent children," Juvenile Care Agreement 176a, and are operated "in an open type of setting without a need for extraordinary security measures," *id.*, at 173a. The facilities must provide, in accordance with "applicable state child welfare statutes and generally accepted child welfare standards, practices, principles and procedures," *id.*, at 157a, an extensive list of services, including physical care and maintenance, individual and group counseling, edu-

cation, recreation and leisure-time activities, family reunification services, and access to religious services, visitors, and legal assistance, *id.*, at 159a, 178a–185a.

Although the regulation replaced the Western Region release policy that had been the focus of respondents' constitutional claims, respondents decided to maintain the litigation as a challenge to the new rule. Just a week after the regulation$_{299}$ took effect, in a brief, unpublished order that referred only to unspecified "due process grounds," the District Court granted summary judgment to respondents and invalidated the regulatory scheme in three important respects. *Flores v. Meese*, No. CV 85–4544–RJK (Px) (CD Cal., May 25, 1988), App. to Pet. for Cert. 146a. First, the court ordered the INS to release "any minor otherwise eligible for release . . . to his parents, guardian, custodian, conservator, *or other responsible adult party.*" *Ibid.* (emphasis added). Second, the order dispensed with the regulation's requirement that unrelated custodians formally agree to *care for* the juvenile, 8 CFR §§ 242.24(b)(3) and (4) (1992), in addition to ensuring his attendance at future proceedings. Finally, the District Court rewrote the related INS regulations that provide for an initial determination of prima facie deportability and release conditions before an INS examiner, see § 287.3, with review by an immigration judge upon the alien's request, see § 242.2(d). It decreed instead that an immigration-judge hearing on probable cause and release restrictions should be provided "forthwith" after arrest, whether or not the juvenile requests it. App. to Pet. for Cert. 146a.

A divided panel of the Court of Appeals reversed. *Flores v. Meese*, 934 F.2d 991 (CA9 1990). The Ninth Circuit voted to rehear the case and selected an 11–judge en banc court. See Ninth Circuit Rule 35–3. That court vacated the panel opinion and affirmed the District Court order "in all respects." *Flores v. Meese*, 942 F.2d 1352, 1365 (1991). One judge dissented in part, see *id.*, at 1372–1377 (opinion of Rymer, J.), and four *in toto*, see *id.*, at 1377–1385 (opinion of Wallace, C.J.). We granted certiorari. 503 U.S. 905, 112 S.Ct. 1261, 117 L.Ed.2d 490 (1992).

II

Respondents make three principal attacks upon INS regulation 242.24. First, they assert that alien juveniles suspected of being deportable have a "fundamental" right to "freedom from physical restraint," Brief for Respondents 16, ⌊300and it is therefore a denial of "substantive due process" to detain them, since the Service cannot prove that it is pursuing an important governmental interest in a manner narrowly tailored to minimize the restraint on liberty. Second, respondents argue that the regulation violates "procedural due process," because it does not require the Service to determine, with regard to *each individual* detained juvenile who lacks an approved custodian, whether his best interests lie in remaining in INS custody or in release to some other "responsible adult." Finally, respondents contend that even if the INS regulation infringes no constitutional rights, it exceeds the Attorney General's authority under 8 U.S.C. § 1252(a)(1). We find it economic to discuss the objections in that order, though we of course reach the constitutional issues only because we conclude that the respondents' statutory argument fails.[3]

[2] Before proceeding further, however, we make two important observations. First, this is a facial challenge to INS regulation 242.24. Respondents do not challenge its application in a particular instance; it had not yet been applied in a particular in-

stance—because it was not yet in existence—when their suit was brought (directed at the 1984 Western Region release policy), and it had been in effect only a week when the District Court issued the judgment invalidating it. We have before us no findings of fact, indeed no record, concerning the INS's interpretation of the regulation or the ⌊301history of its enforcement. We have only the regulation itself and the statement of basis and purpose that accompanied its promulgation. To prevail in such a facial challenge, respondents "must establish that no set of circumstances exists under which the [regulation] would be valid." *United States v. Salerno,* 481 U.S. 739, 745, 107 S.Ct. 2095, 2100, 95 L.Ed.2d 697 (1987). That is true as to both the constitutional challenges, see *Schall v. Martin,* 467 U.S. 253, 268, n. 18, 104 S.Ct. 2403, 2412 n. 18, 81 L.Ed.2d 207 (1984), and the statutory challenge, see *NCIR,* 502 U.S., at 188, 112 S.Ct., at 555.

[3] The second point is related. Respondents spend much time, and their *amici* even more, condemning the conditions under which some alien juveniles are held, alleging that the conditions are so severe as to belie the Service's stated reasons for retaining custody—leading, presumably, to the conclusion that the retention of custody is an unconstitutional infliction of punishment without trial. See *Salerno, supra,* 481 U.S., at 746–748, 107 S.Ct. at 2101–2102; *Wong Wing v. United States,* 163 U.S. 228, 237, 16 S.Ct. 977, 981, 41 L.Ed. 140 (1896). But whatever those conditions might have been when this litigation began, they are now (at least in the Western Region, where all members of the respondents' class are held) presumably in compliance with the extensive requirements

3. The District Court and all three judges on the Court of Appeals panel held in favor of the INS on this statutory claim, see *Flores v. Meese,* 934 F.2d 991, 995, 997–1002 (CA9 1991); *id.*, at 1015 (Fletcher, J., dissenting); the en banc court (curiously) did not address the claim, proceeding immediately to find the rule unconstitutional. Although respondents did not cross-petition for certiorari on the statutory issue, they may legiti-

mately defend their judgment on any ground properly raised below. See *Washington v. Confederated Bands and Tribes of Yakima Nation,* 439 U.S. 463, 476, n. 20, 99 S.Ct. 740, 749 n. 20, 58 L.Ed.2d 740 (1979). The INS does not object to our considering the issue, and we do so in order to avoid deciding constitutional questions unnecessarily. See *Jean v. Nelson,* 472 U.S. 846, 854, 105 S.Ct. 2992, 2997, 86 L.Ed.2d 664 (1985).

set forth in the Juvenile Care Agreement that settled respondents' claims regarding detention conditions, see *supra*, at 1445. The settlement agreement entitles respondents to enforce compliance with those requirements in the District Court, see Juvenile Care Agreement 148a–149a, which they acknowledge they have not done, Tr. of Oral Arg. 43. We will disregard the effort to reopen those settled claims by alleging, for purposes of the challenges to the regulation, that the detention conditions are other than what the consent decree says they must be.

III

[4, 5] Respondents' "substantive due process" claim relies upon our line of cases which interprets the Fifth and Fourteenth Amendments' guarantee of "due process of law" to include |302a substantive component, which forbids the government to infringe certain "fundamental" liberty interests *at all*, no matter what process is provided, unless the infringement is narrowly tailored to serve a compelling state interest. See, *e.g., Collins v. Harker Heights*, 503 U.S. 115, 125, 112 S.Ct. 1061, 1068, 117 L.Ed.2d 261 (1992); *Salerno, supra*, 481 U.S., at 746, 107 S.Ct., at 2101; *Bowers v. Hardwick*, 478 U.S. 186, 191, 106 S.Ct. 2841, 2844, 92 L.Ed.2d 140 (1986). "Substantive due process" analysis must begin with a careful description of the asserted right, for "[t]he doctrine of judicial self-restraint requires us to exercise the utmost care whenever we are asked to break new ground in this field." *Collins, supra*, 503 U.S., at 125, 112 S.Ct., at 1068; see *Bowers v. Hardwick, supra*, 478 U.S., at 194–195, 106 S.Ct., at 2846. The "freedom from physical restraint" invoked by respondents is not at issue in this case. Surely not in the sense of shackles, chains, or barred cells, given the Juvenile Care Agreement. Nor even in the sense of a right to come and go at will, since, as we have said elsewhere, "juveniles, unlike adults, are always in some form of custody," *Schall*, 467 U.S., at 265, 104 S.Ct., at 2410, and where the custody of the parent or legal guardian fails, the government may (indeed, we have said *must*) either exercise custody itself or appoint someone else to do so. *Ibid.* Nor is the right asserted the right of a child to be released from all other custody into the custody of its parents, legal guardian, or even close relatives: The challenged regulation requires such release when it is sought. Rather, the right at issue is the alleged right of a child who has no available parent, close relative, or legal guardian, and for whom the government is responsible, to be placed in the custody of a willing-and-able private custodian rather than of a government-operated or government-selected child-care institution.

[6] If there exists a fundamental right to be released into what respondents inaccurately call a "non-custodial setting," Brief for Respondents 18, we see no reason why it would apply only in the context of government custody incidentally acquired in the course of law enforcement. It would presumably apply to state custody over orphans and abandoned |303children as well, giving federal law and federal courts a major new role in the management of state orphanages and other child-care institutions. Cf. *Ankenbrandt v. Richards*, 504 U.S. 689, 703–704, 112 S.Ct. 2206, 2215, 119 L.Ed.2d 468 (1992). We are unaware, however, that any court—aside from the courts below—has ever held that a child has a constitutional right not to be placed in a decent and humane custodial institution if there is available a responsible person unwilling to become the child's legal guardian but willing to undertake temporary legal custody. The mere novelty of such a claim is reason enough to doubt that "substantive due process" sustains it; the alleged right certainly cannot be considered " 'so rooted in the traditions and conscience of our people as to be ranked as fundamental.' " *Salerno, supra*, 481 U.S., at 751, 107 S.Ct., at 2103 (quoting *Snyder v. Massachusetts*, 291 U.S. 97, 105, 54 S.Ct. 330, 332, 78 L.Ed. 674

(1934)). Where a juvenile has no available parent, close relative, or legal guardian, where the government does not intend to punish the child, and where the conditions of governmental custody are decent and humane, such custody surely does not violate the Constitution. It is rationally connected to a governmental interest in "preserving and promoting the welfare of the child," *Santosky v. Kramer*, 455 U.S. 745, 766, 102 S.Ct. 1388, 1401, 71 L.Ed.2d 599 (1982), and is not punitive since it is not excessive in relation to that valid purpose. See *Schall, supra*, 467 U.S., at 269, 104 S.Ct., at 2412.

[7, 8] Although respondents generally argue for the categorical right of private placement discussed above, at some points they assert a somewhat more limited constitutional right: the right to an individualized hearing on whether private placement would be in the child's "best interests"—followed by private placement if the answer is in the affirmative. It seems to us, however, that if institutional custody (despite the availability of responsible private custodians) is not unconstitutional in itself, it does not become so simply because it is shown to be less desirable than some other arrangement for the particular child. "The best interests of the child," a venerable phrase familiar from divorce proceedings, is a |₃₀₄proper and feasible criterion for making the decision as to which of two parents will be accorded custody. But it is not traditionally the sole criterion— much less the sole *constitutional* criterion— for other, less narrowly channeled judgments involving children, where their interests conflict in varying degrees with the interests of others. Even if it were shown, for example, that a particular couple desirous of adopting a child would *best* provide for the child's welfare, the child would nonetheless not be removed from the custody of its parents so long as they were providing for the child *adequately*. See *Quilloin v. Walcott*, 434 U.S. 246, 255, 98 S.Ct. 549, 555, 54 L.Ed.2d 511 (1978). Similarly, "the best interests of the child" is not the legal standard that governs parents' or guardians' exercise of

their custody: So long as certain minimum requirements of child care are met, the interests of the child may be subordinated to the interests of other children, or indeed even to the interests of the parents or guardians themselves. See, *e.g.*, *R.C.N. v. State*, 141 Ga.App. 490, 491, 233 S.E.2d 866, 867 (1977).

[9, 10] "The best interests of the child" is likewise not an absolute and exclusive constitutional criterion for the government's exercise of the custodial responsibilities that it undertakes, which must be reconciled with many other responsibilities. Thus, child-care institutions operated by the State in the exercise of its *parens patriae* authority, see *Schall, supra*, 467 U.S., at 265, 104 S.Ct., at 2410, are not constitutionally required to be funded at such a level as to provide the *best* schooling or the *best* health care available; nor does the Constitution require them to substitute, wherever possible, private nonadoptive custody for institutional care. And the same principle applies, we think, to the governmental responsibility at issue here, that of retaining or transferring custody over a child who has come within the Federal Government's control, when the parents or guardians of that child are nonexistent or unavailable. Minimum standards must be met, and the child's fundamental rights must not be impaired; but the decision to go beyond₃₀₅ those requirements—to give one or another of the child's additional interests priority over other concerns that compete for public funds and administrative attention—is a policy judgment rather than a constitutional imperative.

[11, 12] Respondents' "best interests" argument is, in essence, a demand that the INS program be narrowly tailored to minimize the denial of release into private custody. But narrow tailoring is required only when fundamental rights are involved. The impairment of a lesser interest (here, the alleged interest in being released into the custody of strangers) demands no more than a

"reasonable fit" between governmental purpose (here, protecting the welfare of the juveniles who have come into the Government's custody) and the means chosen to advance that purpose. This leaves ample room for an agency to decide, as the INS has, that administrative factors such as lack of child-placement expertise favor using one means rather than another. There is, in short, no constitutional need for a hearing to determine whether private placement would be better, so long as institutional custody is (as we readily find it to be, assuming compliance with the requirements of the consent decree) good enough.

If we harbored any doubts as to the constitutionality of institutional custody over unaccompanied juveniles, they would surely be eliminated as to those juveniles (concededly the overwhelming majority of all involved here) who are aliens. "For reasons long recognized as valid, the responsibility for regulating the relationship between the United States and our alien visitors has been committed to the political branches of the Federal Government." *Mathews v. Diaz,* 426 U.S. 67, 81, 96 S.Ct. 1883, 1892, 48 L.Ed.2d 478 (1976). " '[O]ver no conceivable subject is the legislative power of Congress more complete.' " *Fiallo v. Bell,* 430 U.S. 787, 792, 97 S.Ct. 1473, 1478, 52 L.Ed.2d 50 (1977) (quoting *Oceanic Steam Navigation Co. v. Stranahan,* 214 U.S. 320, 339, 29 S.Ct. 671, 676, 53 L.Ed. 1013 (1909)). Thus, "in the exercise of its broad power over immigration and naturalization, 'Congress regularly makes $_{306}$rules that would be unacceptable if applied to citizens.' " 430 U.S., at 792, 97 S.Ct., at 1478 (quoting *Mathews v. Diaz, supra,* 426 U.S., at 79–80, 96 S.Ct., at 1891). Respondents do not dispute that Congress has the authority to detain aliens suspected of entering the country illegally pending their deportation hearings, see *Carlson v. Landon,* 342 U.S. 524, 538, 72 S.Ct. 525, 533, 96 L.Ed. 547 (1952); *Wong Wing v. United States,* 163 U.S., at 235, 16 S.Ct., at 980. And in enacting the precursor to 8 U.S.C. § 1252(a), Congress eliminated any presumption of release pending deportation, commit-

ting that determination to the discretion of the Attorney General. See *Carlson v. Landon, supra,* 342 U.S., at 538–540, 72 S.Ct., at 533–534. Of course, the INS regulation must still meet the (unexacting) standard of rationally advancing some legitimate governmental purpose—which it does, as we shall discuss later in connection with the statutory challenge.

[13] Respondents also argue, in a footnote, that the INS release policy violates the "equal protection guarantee" of the Fifth Amendment because of the disparate treatment evident in (1) releasing alien juveniles with close relatives or legal guardians but detaining those without, and (2) releasing to unrelated adults juveniles detained pending federal delinquency proceedings, see 18 U.S.C. § 5034, but detaining unaccompanied alien juveniles pending deportation proceedings. The tradition of reposing custody in close relatives and legal guardians is in our view sufficient to support the former distinction; and the difference between citizens and aliens is adequate to support the latter.

IV

[14, 15] We turn now from the claim that the INS cannot deprive respondents of their asserted liberty interest *at all,* to the "procedural due process" claim that the Service cannot do so on the basis of the procedures it provides. It is well established that the Fifth Amendment entitles aliens to due process of law in deportation proceedings. See *The Japanese Immigrant Case,* 189 U.S. 86, 100–101, 23 S.Ct. 611, 614, 47 L.Ed. 721 (1903). To determine whether these alien juveniles have received it here, we must $_{307}$first review in some detail the procedures the INS has employed.

Though a procedure for obtaining warrants to arrest named individuals is available, see 8 U.S.C. § 1252(a)(1); 8 CFR § 242.2(c)(1) (1992), the deportation process ordinarily begins with a warrantless arrest by an INS officer who has reason to believe that the arrestee "is in the United States in violation of any [immigration] law or regulation and is likely to escape before a warrant can be obtained," 8 U.S.C. § 1357(a)(2). Arrested aliens are almost always offered the choice of departing the country voluntarily, 8 U.S.C. § 1252(b) (1988 ed., Supp. III); 8 CFR § 242.5 (1992), and as many as 98% of them take that course. See *INS v. Lopez–Mendoza,* 468 U.S. 1032, 1044, 104 S.Ct. 3479, 3486, 82 L.Ed.2d 778 (1984). Before the Service seeks execution of a voluntary departure form by a *juvenile,* however, the juvenile "must in fact communicate with either a parent, adult relative, friend, or with an organization found on the free legal services list." 8 CFR § 242.24(g) (1992).[4] If the juvenile does not seek voluntary departure, he must be brought before an INS examining officer within 24 hours of his arrest. § 287.3; see 8 U.S.C. § 1357(a)(2). The examining officer is a member of the Service's enforcement staff, but must be someone other than the arresting officer (unless no other qualified examiner is readily available). 8 CFR § 287.3 (1992). If the examiner determines that "there is prima facie evidence establishing that the arrested alien is in the United States in violation of the immigration laws," *ibid.,* a formal deportation proceeding is initiated through the issuance of an order to show cause, § 242.1, and within 24 hours the decision is made whether to continue the alien juvenile in custody or release him, § 287.3.

|308The INS notifies the alien of the commencement of a deportation proceeding and of the decision as to custody by serving him with a Form I–221S (reprinted in App. to Brief for Petitioners 7a–8a) which, pursuant to the Immigration Act of 1990, 8 U.S.C. § 1252b(a)(3)(A) (1988 ed., Supp. III), must be in English and Spanish. The front of this form notifies the alien of the allegations against him and the date of his deportation hearing. The back contains a section enti-

tled "NOTICE OF CUSTODY DETERMINATION," in which the INS officer checks a box indicating whether the alien will be detained in the custody of the Service, released on recognizance, or released under bond. Beneath these boxes, the form states: "You may request the Immigration Judge to redetermine this decision." See 8 CFR § 242.2(c)(2) (1992). (The immigration judge is a quasi-judicial officer in the Executive Office for Immigration Review, a division separated from the Service's enforcement staff. § 3.10.) The alien must check either a box stating "I do" or a box stating "[I] do not request a redetermination by an Immigration Judge of the custody decision," and must then sign and date this section of the form. If the alien requests a hearing and is dissatisfied with the outcome, he may obtain further review by the Board of Immigration Appeals, § 242.2(d); § 3.1(b)(7), and by the federal courts, see, *e.g., Carlson v. Landon, supra,* 342 U.S., at 529, 531, 72 S.Ct., at 528, 529.

Respondents contend that this procedural system is unconstitutional because it does not require the Service to determine in the case of each individual alien juvenile that detention in INS custody would better serve his interests than release to some other "responsible adult." This is just the "substantive due process" argument recast in "procedural due process" terms, and we reject it for the same reasons.

The District Court and the en banc Court of Appeals concluded that the INS procedures are faulty because they do not provide for *automatic* review by an immigration judge of the initial deportability and custody determinations. See|309942 F.2d, at 1364. We disagree. At least insofar as this facial challenge is concerned, due process is satisfied by giving the detained alien juveniles the *right* to a hearing before an immigration

---

4. Alien juveniles from Canada and Mexico must be offered the opportunity to make a telephone call but need not in fact do so, see 8 CFR § 242.24(g) (1992); the United States has treaty obligations to notify diplomatic or consular officers of those countries whenever their nationals are detained, see § 242.2(g).

judge. It has not been shown that all of them are too young or too ignorant to exercise that right when the form asking them to assert or waive it is presented. Most are 16 or 17 years old and will have been in telephone contact with a responsible adult outside the INS—sometimes a legal services attorney. The waiver, moreover, is revocable: The alien may request a judicial redetermination at any time later in the deportation process. See 8 CFR § 242.2(d) (1992); *Matter of Uluocha,* Interim Dec. 3124 (BIA 1989). We have held that juveniles are capable of "knowingly and intelligently" waiving their right against self-incrimination in criminal cases. See *Fare v. Michael C.,* 442 U.S. 707, 724–727, 99 S.Ct. 2560, 2571–2573, 61 L.Ed.2d 197 (1979); see also *United States v. Saucedo–Velasquez,* 843 F.2d 832, 835 (CA5 1988) (applying *Fare* to alien juvenile). The alleged right to redetermination of prehearing custody status in deportation cases is surely no more significant.

Respondents point out that the regulations do not set a time period within which the immigration-judge hearing, if requested, must be held. But we will not assume, on this facial challenge, that an excessive delay will invariably ensue—particularly since there is no evidence of such delay, even in isolated instances. Cf. *Matter of Chirinos,* 16 I. & N. Dec. 276 (BIA 1977).

V

[16] Respondents contend that the regulation goes beyond the scope of the Attorney General's discretion to continue custody over arrested aliens under 8 U.S.C. § 1252(a)(1). That contention must be rejected if the regulation has a " 'reasonable foundation,' " *Carlson v. Landon,* 342 U.S., at 541, 72 S.Ct., at 534, that is, if it rationally pursues a purpose that it is lawful for the INS to seek. See

also *NCIR,* 502 U.S., at 194, 112 S.Ct., at 558–559. We think that it does.

|310The statement of basis and purpose accompanying promulgation of regulation 242.24, in addressing the question "as to whose custody the juvenile should be released," began with the dual propositions that "concern for the welfare of the juvenile will not permit release to just any adult" and that "the Service has neither the expertise nor the resources to conduct home studies for placement of each juvenile released." Detention and Release of Juveniles, 53 Fed. Reg. 17449 (1988). The INS decided to "strik[e] a balance" by defining a list of presumptively appropriate custodians while maintaining the discretion of local INS directors to release detained minors to other custodians in "unusual and compelling circumstances." *Ibid.* The list begins with parents, whom our society and this Court's jurisprudence have always presumed to be the preferred and primary custodians of their minor children. See *Parham v. J.R.,* 442 U.S. 584, 602–603, 99 S.Ct. 2493, 2504, 61 L.Ed.2d 101 (1979). The list extends to other close blood relatives, whose protective relationship with children our society has also traditionally respected. See *Moore v. East Cleveland,* 431 U.S. 494, 97 S.Ct. 1932, 52 L.Ed.2d 531 (1977); cf. *Village of Belle Terre v. Boraas,* 416 U.S. 1, 94 S.Ct. 1536, 39 L.Ed.2d 797 (1974). And finally, the list includes persons given legal guardianship by the States, which we have said possess "special proficiency" in the field of domestic relations, including child custody. *Ankenbrandt v. Richards,* 504 U.S., at 704, 112 S.Ct., at 2215. When neither parent, close relative, or state-appointed guardian is immediately available,[5] the INS will normally keep legal custody of the juvenile, place him in a government-supervised and state-licensed shelter-care |311facility, and continue searching

---

5. The regulation also provides for release to any person designated by a juvenile's parent or guardian as "capable and willing to care for the juvenile's well-being." 8 CFR § 242.24(b)(3) (1992). "[To] ensur[e] that the INS is actually receiving the wishes of the parent or guardian," 53 Fed.Reg. 17450 (1988), the designation must be in the form of a sworn affidavit executed before an immigration or consular officer.

for a relative or guardian, although release to others is possible in unusual cases.[6]

Respondents object that this scheme is motivated purely by "administrative convenience," a charge echoed by the dissent, see, e.g., post, at 1456–1457. This fails to grasp the distinction between administrative convenience (or, to speak less pejoratively, administrative efficiency) as the *purpose* of a policy—for example, a policy of not considering late-filed objections—and administrative efficiency as the reason for selecting one means of achieving a purpose over another. Only the latter is at issue here. The requisite statement of basis and purpose published by the INS upon promulgation of regulation 242.24 declares that the purpose of the rule is to protect "the welfare of the juvenile," 53 Fed.Reg. 17449 (1988), and there is no basis for calling that false. (Respondents' contention that the real purpose was to save money imputes not merely mendacity but irrationality, since respondents point out that detention in shelter-care facilities is more expensive than release.) Because the regulation involves no deprivation of a "fundamental" right, the Service was not compelled to ig-

nore the costs and difficulty of alternative means of advancing its declared goal. Cf. Stanley⌐ 312ν. Illinois, 405 U.S. 645, 656–657, 92 S.Ct. 1208, 1215, 31 L.Ed.2d 551 (1972). It is impossible to contradict the Service's assessment that it lacks the "expertise," and is not "qualified," to do individualized child-placement studies, 53 Fed.Reg. 17449 (1988), and the right alleged here provides no basis for this Court to impose upon what is essentially a law enforcement agency the obligation to expend its limited resources in developing such expertise and qualification.[7] That reordering of priorities is for Congress—which has shown, we may say, no inclination to shrink from the task. See, e.g., 8 U.S.C. § 1154(c) (requiring INS to determine if applicants for immigration are involved in "sham" marriages). We do not hold, as the dissent contends, that "minimizing administrative costs" is adequate justification for the Service's detention of juveniles, post, at 1457; but we do hold that a detention program justified by the need to protect the welfare of juveniles is not constitutionally required to give custody to strangers if that entails the expenditure of administrative effort and resources that the Service is unwill-

---

6. The dissent maintains that, in making custody decisions, the INS cannot rely on "[c]ategorical distinctions between cousins and uncles, or between relatives and godparents or other responsible persons," because "[d]ue process demands more, far more." Post, at 1469. Acceptance of such a proposition would revolutionize much of our family law. Categorical distinctions between relatives and nonrelatives, and between relatives of varying degree of affinity, have always played a predominant role in determining child custody and in innumerable other aspects of domestic relations. The dissent asserts, however, that it would prohibit such distinctions only for the purpose of "prefer[ring] *detention* [by which it means institutional detention] to *release*," and accuses us of "mischaracteriz[ing] the issue" in suggesting otherwise. Post, at 1469, n. 29. It seems to us that the dissent mischaracterizes the issue. The INS uses the categorical distinction between relatives and nonrelatives not to deny release, but to determine which potential custodians will be accepted without the safeguard of state-decreed guardianship.

7. By referring unrelated persons seeking custody to state guardianship procedures, the INS is essentially drawing upon resources and expertise that are already in place. Respondents' objection to this is puzzling, in light of their assertion that the States generally view unrelated adults as appropriate custodians. See post, at 1459, n. 7 (STEVENS, J., dissenting) (collecting state statutes). If that is so, one wonders why the individuals and organizations respondents allege are eager to accept custody do not rush to state court, have themselves appointed legal guardians (temporary or permanent, the States have procedures for both), and then obtain the juveniles' release under the terms of the regulation. Respondents and their *amici* do maintain that becoming a guardian can be difficult, but the problems they identify—delays in processing, the need to ensure that existing parental rights are not infringed, the "bureaucratic gauntlet"— would be no less significant were the INS to duplicate existing state procedures.

ing to commit.[8]

[17] ₗ₃₁₃Respondents also contend that the INS regulation violates the statute because it relies upon a "blanket" presumption of the unsuitability of custodians other than parents, close relatives, and guardians. We have stated that, at least in certain contexts, the Attorney General's exercise of discretion under § 1252(a)(1) requires "some level of individualized determination." *NCIR,* 502 U.S., at 194, 112 S.Ct., at 558–559; see also *Carlson v. Landon,* 342 U.S., at 538, 72 S.Ct., at 533. But as *NCIR* itself demonstrates, this does not mean that the Service must forswear use of reasonable presumptions and generic rules. See 502 U.S., at 196, n. 11, 112 S.Ct., at 559 n. 11; cf. *Heckler v. Campbell,* 461 U.S. 458, 467, 103 S.Ct. 1952, 1957, 76 L.Ed.2d 66 (1983). In the case of each detained alien juvenile, the INS makes those determinations that are specific to the individual and necessary to accurate application of the regulation: Is there reason to believe the alien deportable? Is the alien under 18 years of age? Does the alien have an available₃₁₄ adult relative or legal guardian? Is the alien's case so exceptional as to require consideration of release to someone else? The particularization and individuation need go no further than this.[9]

[18] Finally, respondents claim that the regulation is an abuse of discretion because it permits the INS, once having determined that an alien juvenile lacks an available relative or legal guardian, to hold the juvenile in detention indefinitely. That is not so. The period of custody is inherently limited by the pending deportation hearing, which must be concluded with "reasonable dispatch" to avoid habeas corpus. 8 U.S.C. § 1252(a)(1);

---

8. We certainly agree with the dissent that this case must be decided in accordance with "indications of congressional policy," *post,* at 1464. The most pertinent indication, however, is not, as the dissent believes, the federal statute governing detention of juveniles pending delinquency proceedings, 18 U.S.C. § 5034, but the statute under which the Attorney General is here acting, 8 U.S.C. § 1252(a)(1). That grants the Attorney General *discretion* to determine when temporary detention pending deportation proceedings is appropriate, and makes her exercise of that discretion "presumptively correct and unassailable except for abuse." *Carlson v. Landon,* 342 U.S. 524, 540, 72 S.Ct. 525, 534, 96 L.Ed. 547 (1952). We assuredly cannot say that the decision to rely on universally accepted presumptions as to the custodial competence of parents and close relatives, and to defer to the expertise of the States regarding the capabilities of other potential custodians, is an abuse of this broad discretion simply because it does not track policies applicable outside the immigration field. See *NCIR,* 502 U.S. 183, 193–194, 112 S.Ct. 551, 558, 116 L.Ed.2d 546 (1991). Moreover, reliance upon the States to determine guardianship is quite in accord with what Congress has directed in other immigration contexts. See 8 U.S.C. § 1154(d) (INS may not approve immigration petition for an alien juvenile orphan being adopted unless "a valid home-study has been favorably recommended by an agency of the State of the child's proposed residence, or by an agency authorized by that State to conduct such a study"); § 1522(d)(2)(B)(ii) (for refugee children unac-

companied by parents or close relatives, INS shall "attempt to arrange ... placement under the laws of the States"); see also 45 CFR § 400.113 (1992) (providing support payments under § 1522 until the refugee juvenile is placed with a parent or with another adult "to whom legal custody and/or guardianship is granted under State law").

9. The dissent would mandate fully individualized custody determinations for two reasons. First, because it reads *Carlson v. Landon,* as holding that the Attorney General may not employ "mere presumptions" in exercising her discretion. *Post,* at 1465–1466. But it was only the *dissenters* in *Carlson* who took such a restrictive view. See 342 U.S., at 558–559, 563–564, 568, 72 S.Ct., at 543, 546, 548 (Frankfurter, J., dissenting). Second, because it believes that § 1252(a) must be interpreted to require individualized hearings in order to avoid " 'constitutional doubts.' " *Post,* at 1464 (quoting *United States v. Witkovich,* 353 U.S. 194, 199, 77 S.Ct. 779, 782, 1 L.Ed.2d 765 (1957)); see *post,* at 1466–1467. The "constitutional doubts" argument has been the last refuge of many an interpretive lost cause. Statutes should be interpreted to avoid *serious* constitutional doubts, *Witkovich, supra,* at 202, 77 S.Ct., at 783, not to eliminate all possible contentions that the statute *might* be unconstitutional. We entertain no serious doubt that the Constitution does not require any more individuation than the regulation provides, see *supra,* at 1447–1448, 1450–1451, and thus find no need to supplement the text of § 1252(a).

cf. *U.S. v. Salerno,* 481 U.S., at 747, 107 S.Ct., at 2101 (noting time limits placed on pretrial detention by the Speedy Trial Act). It is expected that alien juveniles will remain in INS custody an average of only 30 days. See Juvenile Care Agreement 178a. There is no evidence that alien juveniles are being held for undue periods pursuant to regulation 242.24, or that habeas corpus is insufficient to remedy particular abuses.[10] And the reasonableness of the ⌐315Service's negative assessment of putative custodians who fail to obtain legal guardianship would seem, if anything, to increase as time goes by.

*　　*　　*

We think the INS policy now in place is a reasonable response to the difficult problems presented when the Service arrests unaccompanied alien juveniles. It may well be that other policies would be even better, but "we are [not] a legislature charged with formulating public policy." *Schall v. Martin,* 467 U.S., at 281, 104 S.Ct., at 2419. On its face, INS regulation 242.24 accords with both the Constitution and the relevant statute.

The judgment of the Court of Appeals is reversed, and the case is remanded for further proceedings consistent with this opinion.

It is so ordered.

Justice O'CONNOR, with whom Justice SOUTER joins, concurring.

I join the Court's opinion and write separately simply to clarify that in my view these children have a constitutionally protected interest in freedom from institutional confinement. That interest lies within the core of the Due Process Clause, and the Court today does not hold otherwise. Rather, we reverse the decision of the Court of Appeals because the INS program challenged here, on its face, complies with the requirements of due process.

"Freedom from bodily restraint has always been at the core of the liberty protected by the Due Process Clause from arbitrary governmental action." *Foucha v. Louisiana,* 504 U.S. 71, 80, 112 S.Ct. 1780, 1785, 118 L.Ed.2d 437 (1992). "Freedom from bodily restraint" means more than freedom from handcuffs, straitjackets, or detention cells. A person's core liberty interest is also implicated when she is confined in a prison, a mental hospital, or some other form of custodial institution, even if the conditions of confinement are liberal. This is clear beyond cavil, at least ⌐316where adults are concerned. "In the substantive due process analysis, it is the State's affirmative act of restraining the individual's freedom to act on his own behalf—through incarceration, institutionalization, or other similar restraint of personal liberty—which is the 'deprivation of liberty' triggering the protections of the Due Process Clause...." *DeShaney v. Winnebago County Dept. of Social Services,* 489 U.S. 189, 200, 109 S.Ct. 998, 1006, 103 L.Ed.2d 249 (1989). The institutionalization of an adult by the government triggers heightened, substantive due process scrutiny. There must be a "sufficiently compelling" governmental interest to justify such action, usually a punitive interest in imprisoning the convicted criminal or a regulatory interest in forestalling danger to the community. *United States v. Salerno,* 481 U.S. 739, 748, 107 S.Ct. 2095, 2102, 95 L.Ed.2d 697 (1987); see *Foucha, supra,* 504 U.S., at 80–81, 112 S.Ct., at 1785–1786.

Children, too, have a core liberty interest in remaining free from institutional confinement. In this respect, a child's constitutional "[f]reedom from bodily restraint" is no narrower than an adult's. Beginning with *In re Gault,* 387 U.S. 1, 87 S.Ct. 1428, 18 L.Ed.2d 527 (1967), we consistently have rejected the

---

10. The dissent's citation of a single deposition from 1986, *post,* at 1458, and n. 6, is hardly proof that "excessive delay" will result in the "typical" case, *post,* at 1459, under regulation 242.24, which was not promulgated until mid-1988.

assertion that "a child, unlike an adult, has a right 'not to liberty but to custody.' " *Id.,* at 17, 87 S.Ct., at 1438. *Gault* held that a child in delinquency proceedings must be provided various procedural due process protections (notice of charges, right to counsel, right of confrontation and cross-examination, privilege against self-incrimination) when those proceedings may result in the child's institutional confinement. As we explained:

> "Ultimately, however, we confront the reality of . . . the Juvenile Court process. . . . A boy is charged with misconduct. The boy is committed to an institution where he may be restrained of liberty for years. It is of no constitutional consequence—and of limited practical meaning—that the institution to which he is committed is called an Industrial School. The fact of the matter is that, however euphemistic the title, a 'receiving home' |₃₁₇or an 'industrial school' for juveniles is an institution of confinement in which the child is incarcerated for a greater or lesser time. His world becomes a building with whitewashed walls, regimented routine and institutional hours. Instead of mother and father and sisters and brothers and friends and classmates, his world is peopled by guards, custodians, [and] state employees. . . ." *Id.,* at 27, 87 S.Ct., at 1443 (footnote and internal quotation marks omitted).

See also *In re Winship,* 397 U.S. 358, 90 S.Ct. 1068, 25 L.Ed.2d 368 (1970) (proof-beyond-reasonable-doubt standard applies to delinquency proceedings); *Breed v. Jones,* 421 U.S. 519, 95 S.Ct. 1779, 44 L.Ed.2d 346 (1975) (double jeopardy protection applies to delinquency proceedings); *Parham v. J.R.,* 442 U.S. 584, 99 S.Ct. 2493, 61 L.Ed.2d 101 (1979) (proceedings to commit child to mental hospital must satisfy procedural due process).

Our decision in *Schall v. Martin,* 467 U.S. 253, 104 S.Ct. 2403, 81 L.Ed.2d 207 (1984), makes clear that children have a protected liberty interest in "freedom from institutional

restraints," *id.,* at 265, 104 S.Ct. at 2410, even absent the stigma of being labeled "delinquent," see *Breed, supra,* 421 U.S., at 529, 95 S.Ct., at 1785, or "mentally ill," see *Parham, supra,* 442 U.S., at 600–601, 99 S.Ct., at 2503. In *Schall,* we upheld a New York statute authorizing pretrial detention of dangerous juveniles, but only after analyzing the statute at length to ensure that it complied with substantive and procedural due process. We recognized that children "are assumed to be subject to the control of their parents, and if parental control falters, the State must play its part as *parens patriae.* " 467 U.S., at 265, 104 S.Ct., at 2410. But this *parens patriae* purpose was seen simply as a plausible *justification* for state action implicating the child's protected liberty interest, not as a limitation on the scope of due process protection. See *ibid.* Significantly, *Schall* was essentially a facial challenge, as is this case, and New York's policy was to detain some juveniles in "open facilit[ies] in the community . . . without locks, bars, or security officers where the child receives schooling and counseling and has access to recreational facilities." *Id.,* at 271, 104 S.Ct., at 2413. A |₃₁₈child's placement in this kind of governmental institution is hardly the same as handcuffing her, or confining her to a cell, yet it must still satisfy heightened constitutional scrutiny.

It may seem odd that institutional placement as such, even where conditions are decent and humane and where the child has no less authority to make personal choices than she would have in a family setting, nonetheless implicates the Due Process Clause. The answer, I think, is this. Institutionalization is a decisive and unusual event. "The consequences of an erroneous commitment decision are more tragic where children are involved. [C]hildhood is a particularly vulnerable time of life and children erroneously institutionalized during their formative years may bear the scars for the rest of their lives." *Parham, supra,* 442 U.S., at 627–628, 99 S.Ct., at 2517 (footnotes omitted) (opinion of Brennan, J.). Just as it is true that "[i]n our society liberty [for adults] is the norm, and detention prior to trial or without trial is the carefully limited exception," *Salerno, supra,* 481 U.S., at 755, 107 S.Ct., at 2105, so too, in our society, children normally grow up in families, not in governmental institutions. To be sure, government's failure to take custody of a child whose family is unable to care for her may also effect harm. But the purpose of heightened scrutiny is not to prevent government from placing children in an institutional setting, where necessary. Rather, judicial review ensures that government acts in this sensitive area with the requisite care.

In sum, this case does not concern the scope of the Due Process Clause. We are not deciding whether the constitutional concept of "liberty" extends to some hitherto unprotected aspect of personal well-being, see, *e.g., Collins v. Harker Heights,* 503 U.S. 115, 112 S.Ct. 1061, 117 L.Ed.2d 261 (1992); *Michael H. v. Gerald D.,* 491 U.S. 110, 109 S.Ct. 2333, 105 L.Ed.2d 91 (1989); *Bowers v. Hardwick,* 478 U.S. 186, 106 S.Ct. 2841, 92 L.Ed.2d 140 (1986), but rather whether a governmental decision implicating a squarely protected liberty interest comports with substantive and procedural due process. See *ante,* at 1446–1449 |₃₁₉(substantive due process scrutiny); *ante,* at 1449–1451 (procedural due process scrutiny). Specifically, the absence of available parents, close relatives, or legal guardians to care for respondents does not vitiate their constitutional interest in freedom from institutional confinement. It does not place that interest outside the core of the Due Process Clause. Rather, combined with the Juvenile Care Agreement, the fact that the normal forms of custody have faltered explains why the INS program facially challenged here survives heightened, substantive due process scrutiny. "Where a juvenile has no available parent, close relative, or legal guardian, where the government does not intend to punish the child, and where the conditions of governmental custody are decent and humane, such custody

surely does not violate the Constitution. It is rationally connected to a governmental interest in 'preserving and promoting the welfare of the child,' *Santosky v. Kramer,* 455 U.S. 745, 766 [102 S.Ct. 1388, 1401, 71 L.Ed.2d 599] (1982), and is not punitive since it is not excessive in relation to that valid purpose." *Ante,* at 1448. Because this is a facial challenge, the Court rightly focuses on the Juvenile Care Agreement. It is proper to presume that the conditions of confinement are no longer " 'most disturbing,' " *Flores v. Meese,* 942 F.2d 1352, 1358 (CA9 1991) (en banc) (quoting *Flores v. Meese,* 934 F.2d 991, 1014 (CA9 1990) (Fletcher, J., dissenting)), and that the purposes of confinement are no longer the troublesome ones of lack of resources and expertise published in the Federal Register, see 53 Fed.Reg. 17449 (1988), but rather the plainly legitimate purposes associated with the Government's concern for the welfare of the minors. With those presumptions in place, "the terms and conditions of confinement ... are in fact compatible with [legitimate] purposes," *Schall, supra,* 467 U.S., at 269, 104 S.Ct., at 2412, and the Court finds that the INS program conforms with the Due Process Clause. On this understanding, I join the opinion of the Court.

|₃₂₀Justice STEVENS, with whom Justice BLACKMUN joins, dissenting.

The Court devotes considerable attention to debunking the notion that "the best interests of the child" is an "absolute and exclusive" criterion for the Government's exercise of the custodial responsibilities that it undertakes. *Ante,* at 1448. The Court reasons that as long as the conditions of detention are "good enough," *ante,* at 1449, the Immigration and Naturalization Service (INS or Agency) is perfectly justified in declining to expend administrative effort and resources to minimize such detention. *Ante,* at 1449, 1451–1452.

As I will explain, I disagree with that proposition, for in my view, an agency's interest in minimizing administrative costs is a patently inadequate justification for the detention of harmless children, even when the conditions of detention are "good enough." [1] What is most curious about the Court's analysis, however, is that the INS *itself* vigorously denies that its policy is motivated even in part by a desire to avoid the administrative burden of placing these children in the care of "other responsible adults." Reply Brief for Petitioners 4. That is, while the Court goes out of its way to attack "the best interest of the child" as a criterion for judging the INS detention policy, it is precisely that interest that the INS invokes as the sole basis for its refusal to release these children to "other responsible adults":

> "[T]he articulated basis for the detention is that it furthers the government's interest in ensuring the welfare of the juveniles in its custody....
>
> "[Respondents] argu[e] that INS's interest in furthering juvenile welfare does not in fact support the policy |₃₂₁because INS has a 'blanket' policy that requires detention without any factual showing that detention is necessary to ensure respondents' welfare.... That argument, however, represents nothing more than a policy disagreement, because it criticizes INS for failing to pursue a view of juvenile welfare that INS has not adopted, namely the view held by respondent: that it is better for alien juveniles to be released to unrelated adults than to be cared for in suitable, government-monitored juvenile-care facilities, except in those cases where the government has knowledge that the particular adult seeking custody is unfit. The policy adopted by INS, reflecting the traditional view of our polity that parents and guardians are the most reliable custodians for juveniles, is that it is inappropriate to release alien juveniles—whose troubled background and lack of familiarity with our

society and culture, give them particularized needs not commonly shared by domestic juveniles—to adults who are not their parents or guardians." *Id.,* at 4–5 (internal citations, emphasis, and quotation marks omitted).

Possibly because of the implausibility of the INS' claim that it has made a reasonable judgment that detention in government-controlled or government-sponsored facilities is "better" or more "appropriate" for these children than release to independent *responsible* adults, the Court reaches out to justify the INS policy on a ground not only not argued, but expressly disavowed by the INS, that is, the tug of "other concerns that compete for public funds and administrative attention," *ante,* at 1448. I cannot share my colleagues' eagerness for that aggressive tack in a case involving a substantial deprivation of liberty. Instead, I will begin where the INS asks us to begin, with its assertion that its policy is justified by its interest in protecting the welfare of these children. As I will explain, the INS' decision to detain these juveniles despite the existence of responsible |₃₂₂adults willing and able to assume custody of them is contrary to federal policy, is belied by years of experience with both citizen and alien juveniles, and finds no support whatsoever in the administrative proceedings that led to the promulgation of the Agency's regulation. I will then turn to the Court's statutory and constitutional analysis and explain why this ill-conceived and ill-considered regulation is neither authorized by § 242(a) of the Immigration and Nationality Act nor consistent with fundamental notions of due process of law.

At the outset, it is important to emphasize two critical points. First, this case involves the institutional detention of juveniles who

---

1. Though the concurring Justices join the Court's opinion, they too seem to reject the notion that the fact that "other concerns ... compete for public funds and administrative attention," *ante,*

at 1448, is a sufficient justification for the INS' policy of refusing to make individualized determinations as to whether these juveniles should be detained. *Ante,* at 1456 (concurring opinion).

pose no risk of flight and no threat of harm to themselves or to others. They are children who have responsible third parties available to receive and care for them; many, perhaps most, of them will never be deported.[2] It makes little difference that juveniles, unlike adults, are always in some form of custody, for detention in an institution pursuant to the regulation is vastly different from release to a responsible person—whether a cousin,[3] a godparent, a friend, or a charitable organization—willing to assume responsibility for the juvenile for the time the child would otherwise be detained.[4] In many ways the difference is |₃₂₃comparable to the difference between imprisonment and probation or parole. Both conditions can be described as "legal custody," but the constitutional dimensions of individual "liberty" identify the great divide that separates the two. See *Morrissey v. Brewer*, 408 U.S. 471, 482, 92 S.Ct. 2593, 2600, 33 L.Ed.2d 484 (1972). The same is true regarding the allegedly improved conditions of confinement—a proposition, incidentally, that is disputed by several *amici*

curiae.[5] The fact that the present conditions may satisfy standards appropriate for incarcerated juvenile offenders does not detract in the slightest from the basic proposition that this is a case about the wholesale detention of children who do not pose a risk of flight, and who are not a threat to either themselves or the community.

Second, the period of detention is indefinite, and has, on occasion, approached one year.[6] In its statement of policy |₃₂₄governing proposed contracts with private institutions that may assume physical (though not legal) custody of these minors, the INS stated that the duration of the confinement "is anticipated to be approximately thirty (30) days; however, due to the variables and uncertainties inherent in each case, [r]ecipients must design programs which are able to provide a combination of short term and long term care." Juvenile Care Agreement 178a. The INS rule itself imposes no time limit on the period of detention. The only limit is the statutory right to seek a writ

2. See Tr. of Oral Arg. 55 (statement by counsel for petitioners).

3. The Court assumes that the rule allows release to any "close relative," *ante,* at 1447. The assumption is incorrect for two reasons: The close character of a family relationship is determined by much more than the degree of affinity; moreover, contrary to the traditional view expressed in *Moore v. East Cleveland,* 431 U.S. 494, 504, 97 S.Ct. 1932, 1938, 52 L.Ed.2d 531 (1977), the INS rule excludes cousins.

4. The difference is readily apparent even from the face of the allegedly benign Memorandum of Understanding Re Compromise of Class Action: Conditions of Detention, reprinted in App. to Pet. for Cert. 148a–205a (Juvenile Care Agreement), upon which the Court so heavily relies to sustain this regulation. To say that a juvenile care facility under the agreement is to be operated " 'in an open type of setting without a need for *extraordinary* security measures,' " *ante,* at 1445 (quoting Juvenile Care Agreement 173a) (emphasis added), suggests that the facility has some *standard* level of security designed to ensure that children do not leave. That notion is reinforced by the very next sentence in the agreement: "However, [r]ecipients are required to design programs and strategies to discourage runaways and prevent the unauthorized absence of minors in care." *Ibid.*

Indeed, the very definition of the word "detention" in the American Bar Association's Juvenile Justice Standards reflects the fact that it still constitutes detention even if a juvenile is placed in a facility that is "decent and humane," *ante,* at 1448:
"The definition of detention in this standard includes every facility used by the state to house juveniles during the interim period. Whether it gives the appearance of the worst sort of jail, or a comfortable and pleasant home, the facility is classified as 'detention' if it is not the juvenile's usual place of abode." Institute of Judicial Administration, American Bar Association, Juvenile Justice Standards: Standards Relating to Interim Status 45 (1980) (citing Wald, "Pretrial Detention for Juveniles," in Pursuing Justice for the Child 119, 120 (Rosenheim ed. 1976)).
The point cannot be overemphasized. The legal formalism that children are always in someone else's custody should not obscure the fact that "[i]nstitutionalization," as Justice O'CONNOR explains, "is a decisive and unusual event." *Ante,* at 1455 (concurring opinion).

5. See Brief for Southwest Refugee Rights Project et al. as *Amici Curiae* 20–33.

6. See Deposition of Kim Carter Hedrick, INS Detention Center Director–Manager (CD Cal., June 27, 1986), p. 68.

of habeas corpus on the basis of a "conclusive showing" that the Attorney General is not processing the deportation proceeding "with such reasonable dispatch as may be warranted by the particular facts and circumstances in the case...." 8 U.S.C. § 1252(a)(1). Because examples of protracted deportation proceedings are so common, the potential for a lengthy period of confinement is always present. The fact that an excessive delay may not "invariably ensue," *ante*, at 1451, provides small comfort to the typical detainee.

I

The Court glosses over the history of this litigation, but that history speaks mountains about the bona fides of the Government's asserted justification for its regulation, and

demonstrates the complete lack of support, in either evidence or experience, for the Government's contention that detaining alien juveniles when there are "other responsible parties" willing to assume care somehow protects the interests of these children.

The case was filed as a class action in response to a policy change adopted in 1984 by the Western Regional Office of the INS. Prior to that change, the relevant policy in the Western Region had conformed to the practice followed by the INS in the rest of the country, and also followed by federal magistrates throughout the country in the administration of § 504 of the Juvenile Justice and Delinquency Prevention₃₂₅ Act of 1974. Consistently with the consensus expressed in a number of recommended standards for the treatment of juveniles,[7] that

---

7. See, *e.g.*, U.S. Dept. of Health, Education, and Welfare, Model Acts for Family Courts and State–Local Children's Programs 24 (1975) ("[W]ith all possible speed" the child should be released to "parents, guardian, custodian, or other suitable person able and willing to provide supervision and care"); U.S. Dept. of Justice, National Advisory Committee for Juvenile Justice and Delinquency Prevention, Standards for the Administration of Juvenile Justice 299 (1980) (a juvenile subject to the jurisdiction of the family court "should be placed in a foster home or shelter facility only when ... there is no person willing and able to provide supervision and care"); National Advisory Commission on Criminal Justice Standards and Goals, Corrections 267 (1973) ("Detention should be used only where the juvenile has no parent, guardian, custodian, or other person able to provide supervision and care"); Institute of Judicial Administration, American Bar Association, Standards Relating to Noncriminal Misbehavior 41, 42 (1982) ("If the juvenile consents," he should be released "to the parent, custodian, relative, or other responsible person as soon as practicable").

State law from across the country regarding the disposition of juveniles who come into state custody is consistent with these standards. See, *e.g.*, Ala.Code § 12–15–62 (1986) (allowing release to custody of "a parent, guardian, custodian or any other person who the court deems proper"); Conn.Gen.Stat. § 46b–133 (1986) (allowing release to "parent or parents, guardian or some other suitable person or agency"); D.C.Code Ann. § 16–2310 (1989) (allowing re-

lease to "parent, guardian, custodian, or other person or agency able to provide supervision and care for him"); Idaho Code § 16–1811.1(c) (Supp.1992) (allowing release to custody of "parent or other responsible adult"); Iowa Code § 232.19(2) (1987) (release to "parent, guardian, custodian, responsible adult relative, or other adult approved by the court"); Ky.Rev.Stat.Ann. § 610.200 (Michie 1990) (release to custody of "relative, guardian, person exercising custodial control or supervision or other responsible person"); Me.Rev.Stat.Ann., Tit. 15, § 3203–A (Supp.1992) (release to "legal custodian or other suitable person"); Md.Cts. & Jud.Proc.Code Ann. § 3–814(b)(1) (1989) (release to "parents, guardian, or custodian or to any other person designated by the court"); Mass.Gen.Laws § 119:67 (1969) (release to "parent, guardian or any other reputable person"); Minn.Stat. § 260.171 (1992) (release to "parent, guardian, custodian, or other suitable person"); Miss.Code Ann. § 43–21–301(4) (Supp.1992) (release to "any person or agency"); Neb.Rev.Stat. § 43–253 (1988) (release to "parent, guardian, relative, or other responsible person"); Nev.Rev.Stat. § 62.170 (1991) (release to "parent or other responsible adult"); N.H.Rev.Stat.Ann. § 169–B:14 (1990) (release to relative, friend, foster home, group home, crisis home, or shelter-care facility); S.C.Code Ann. § 20–7–600 (Supp.1992) (release to "parent, a responsible adult, a responsible agent of a court-approved foster home, group home, facility, or program"); S.D. Codified Laws § 26–7A–89 (1992) (release to probation officer or any other suitable person appointed by the court); Tex.Fam.Code Ann. § 52.02 (Supp.1993) (release to "parent, guardian, custodian of the

statute authorizes the release of a juvenile |₃₂₆charged with an offense "to his parents, guardian, custodian, or *other responsible party (including, but not limited to, the director of a shelter-care facility)* upon their promise to bring such juvenile before the appropriate court when requested by such court unless the magistrate determines, after hearing, at which the juvenile is represented by counsel, that the detention of such juvenile is required to secure his timely appearance before the appropriate court or to insure his safety or that of others." 18 U.S.C. § 5034 (emphasis added).[8] There is no evidence in the record of this litigation that any release by the INS, or by a federal magistrate, to an "other responsible party" ever resulted in any harm to a juvenile. Thus, nationwide experience prior to 1984 discloses no evidence of any demonstrated need for a change in INS policy.

Nevertheless, in 1984 the Western Region of the INS adopted a separate policy for minors in deportation proceedings, but not for exclusion proceedings. The policy provided that minors would be released only to a parent or lawful guardian, except " 'in unusual and extraordinary cases, at the

|₃₂₇discretion of a District Director or Chief Patrol Agent.' " *Flores v. Messe,* 942 F.2d 1352, 1355 (CA9 1991). The regional Commissioner explained that the policy was " 'necessary to assure that the minor's welfare and safety is [*sic*] maintained and that the agency is protected against possible legal liability.' " *Flores v. Meese,* 934 F.2d 991, 994 (CA9 1990), vacated, 942 F.2d 1352 (CA9 1991) (en banc). As the Court of Appeals noted, the Commissioner "did not cite any instances of harm which had befallen children released to unrelated adults, nor did he make any reference to suits that had been filed against the INS arising out of allegedly improper releases." 942 F.2d, at 1355.[9]

The complete absence of evidence of any need for the policy change is not the only reason for questioning the bona fides of the Commissioner's expressed interest in the welfare of alien minors as an explanation for his new policy. It is equally significant that at the time the new policy was adopted the conditions of confinement were admittedly "deplorable." [10] How a responsible administrator could possibly |₃₂₈conclude that the practice of commingling harmless children

child, or other responsible adult"); Utah Code Ann. § 78–3a–29(3)(a) (1992) (release to "parent or other responsible adult").

8. As enacted in 1938, the Federal Juvenile Delinquency Act authorized a committing magistrate to release a juvenile "upon his own recognizance or that of some responsible person. . . . Such juvenile shall not be committed to a jail or other similar institution, unless in the opinion of the marshal it appears that such commitment is necessary to secure the custody of the juvenile or to insure his safety or that of others." § 5, 52 Stat. 765. The "responsible person" alternative has been a part of our law ever since.

9. The court added: "It has remained undisputed throughout this proceeding that the blanket detention policy is not necessary to ensure the attendance of children at deportation hearings." 942 F.2d, at 1355. Although the Commissioner's expressed concern about possible legal liability may well have been genuine, in view of the fact that the policy change occurred prior to our decision in *DeShaney v. Winnebago County Dept. of Social Services,* 489 U.S. 189, 109 S.Ct. 998,

103 L.Ed.2d 249 (1989), the Court of Appeals was surely correct in observing that "governmental agencies face far greater exposure to liability by maintaining a special custodial relationship than by releasing children from the constraints of governmental custody." 942 F.2d, at 1363. Even if that were not true, the Agency's selfish interest in avoiding potential liability would be manifestly insufficient to justify its wholesale deprivation of a core liberty interest. In this Court, petitioners have prudently avoided any reliance on what may have been the true explanation for the genesis of this litigation.

10. In response to respondents' argument in their brief in opposition to the petition for certiorari that the unsatisfactory character of the INS detention facilities justified the injunction entered by the District Court, the INS asserted that "these deplorable conditions were addressed and remedied during earlier proceedings in this case. . . ." Reply to Brief in Opposition 3. If the deplorable conditions prevailed when the litigation began, we must assume that the Western Regional Commissioner was familiar with them when he adopted his allegedly benevolent policy.

with adults of the opposite sex [11] in detention centers protected by barbed-wire fences,[12] without providing them with education, recreation, or visitation,[13] while subjecting them to arbitrary strip searches,[14] would be in their best interests is most difficult to comprehend.

The evidence relating to the period after 1984 only increases the doubt concerning the true motive for the policy adopted in the Western Region. First, as had been true before 1984, the absence of any indication of a need for such a policy in any other part of the country persisted. Moreover, there is evidence in the record that in the Western Region when undocumented parents came to claim their children, they were immediately arrested and deportation proceedings were instituted against them. 934 F.2d, at 1023 (Fletcher, J., dissenting). Even if the detention of children might |₃₂₉serve a rational enforcement purpose that played a part in the original decisional process, that possibility can only add to the Government's burden of trying to establish its legitimacy.

After this litigation was commenced, the District Court enjoined the enforcement of the new policy because there was no rational basis for the disparate treatment of juveniles in deportation and exclusion proceedings. That injunction prompted the INS to promulgate the nationwide rule that is now at issue.[15] Significantly, however, in neither the rulemaking proceedings nor this litigation did the INS offer any evidence that compliance with that injunction caused any harm to juveniles or imposed any administrative burdens on the Agency.

The Agency's explanation for its new rule relied on four factual assertions. First, the rule "provides a single policy for juveniles in both deportation and exclusion proceedings." 53 Fed.Reg. 17449 (1988). It thus removed the basis for the outstanding injunction. Second, the INS had "witnessed a dramatic increase in the number of juvenile aliens it encounters," most of whom were "not accompanied by a parent, legal guardian, or other adult relative." *Ibid.* There is no mention, however, of either the actual or the approximate number of juveniles encountered, or the much smaller number that do not elect voluntary departure.[16] Third, the |₃₃₀Agency stated that "concern for the welfare of the juve-

---

11. See Deposition of Kim Carter Hedrick, *supra* n. 6, at 13.

12. See Declaration of Paul DeMuro, Consultant, U.S. Dept. of Justice, Office of Juvenile Justice and Delinquency Prevention (CD Cal., Apr. 11, 1987), p. 7. After inspecting a number of detention facilities, Mr. DeMuro declared:

"[I]t is clear as one approaches each facility that each facility is a locked, secure, detention facility. The Inglewood facility actually has two concentric perimeter fences in the part of the facility where children enter.

"The El Centro facility is a converted migrant farm workers' barracks which has been secured through the use of fences and barbed wire. The San Diego facility is the most jail-like. At this facility each barracks is secured through the use of fences, barbed wire, automatic locks, observation areas, etc. In addition the entire residential complex is secured through the use of a high security fence (16–18'), barbed wire, and supervised by uniformed guards." *Ibid.*

13. See *id.*, at 8.

14. See Defendants' Response to Requests for Admissions (CD Cal., Nov. 22, 1985), pp. 3–4.

15. The rule differs from the regional policy in three respects: (1) it applies to the entire country, rather than just the Western Region; (2) it applies to exclusion as well as deportation proceedings; and (3) it authorizes release to adult brothers, sisters, aunts, uncles, and grandparents as well as parents and legal guardians.

16. In its brief in this Court petitioners' attempt to describe the magnitude of the problem addressed by the rule is based on material that is not in the record—an independent study of a sample of juveniles detained in Texas in 1989, see Brief for Petitioners 8, n. 12, and the Court in turn relies on the assertions made in the brief for petitioners about the problem in 1990. See *ante*, at 2. Since all of those figures relate to a period well after the rule was proposed in 1987 and promulgated in 1988, they obviously tell us nothing about the "dramatic increase" mentioned by the INS. 53 Fed.Reg. 17449 (1988). Indeed, the study cited by the Government also has nothing to say about any *increase* in the number of encounters with juvenile aliens. In all events, the fact that both the Government and this Court deem it appropriate to rely on a *post hoc*, non-record exposition of the dimensions of the prob-

nile will not permit release to *just any adult." Ibid.* (emphasis added).[17] There is no mention, however, of the obvious distinction between "just any adult" and the broad spectrum of responsible parties that can assume care of these children, such as extended family members, godparents, friends, and private charitable organizations. Fourth, "the Service has neither the expertise nor the resources to conduct home studies for placement of each juvenile released." *Ibid.* Again, however, there is no explanation of why any more elaborate or expensive "home study" would be necessary to evaluate the qualifications of apparently responsible persons than had been conducted in the past. There is a strange irony in both the fact that the INS suddenly decided that temporary releases that had been made routinely to responsible persons in the past now must be

preceded by a "home study," and the fact that the scarcity of its "resources" provides the explanation for spending far more money on detention than would be necessary to perform its newly discovered home study obligation.[18]

|₃₃₁What the Agency failed to explain may be even more significant than what it did say. It made no comment at all on the uniform body of professional opinion that recognizes the harmful consequences of the detention of juveniles.[19] It made no comment on the period of detention that would be required for the completion of deportation proceedings, or the reasons why the rule places no limit on the duration of the detention. Moreover, there is no explanation for the absence of any specified procedure for either the consideration or the review of a request for release to an apparently responsible person.[20] It is difficult to understand why an

---

lem that supposedly led to a dramatic change in INS policy merely highlights the casual character of the Agency's deliberative process. One can only speculate about whether the "dramatic increase in the number of juvenile aliens it encounters," *ibid.*, or the District Court's injunction was the more important cause of the new rule.

17. This statement may be the source of the Court's similar comment that "the INS cannot simply send them off into the night on bond or recognizance." *Ante,* at 1443. There is, of course, no evidence that the INS had ever followed such an irresponsible practice, or that there was any danger that it would do so in the future.

18. The record indicates that the cost of detention may amount to as much as $100 per day per juvenile. Deposition of Robert J. Schmidt, Immigration and Naturalization Service (July 31, 1986), p. 76. Even the sort of elaborate home study that might be appropriate as a predicate to the adoption of a newborn baby should not cost as much as a few days of detention. Moreover, it is perfectly obvious that the qualifications of most responsible persons can readily be determined by a hearing officer, and that in any doubtful case release should be denied. The respondents have never argued that there is a duty to release juveniles to "just any adult." 53 Fed.Reg. 17449 (1988).

19. Consistent with the standards developed by the American Bar Association and other organizations and agencies, see n. 7, *supra,* the United

States Department of Justice's own Standards for the Administration of Juvenile Justice describe "the harsh impact that even brief detention may have on a juvenile, especially when he/she is placed in a secure facility, and the corresponding need to assure as quickly as possible that such detention is necessary." U.S. Dept. of Justice, Standards for the Administration of Juvenile Justice, *supra* n. 7, at 304.

20. As Judge Rymer pointed out in her separate opinion in the Court of Appeals: "Unlike the statutes at issue in *Schall v. Martin,* 467 U.S. 253 [104 S.Ct. 2403, 81 L.Ed.2d 207] ... (1984), and [*United States v.*] *Salerno,* [481 U.S. 739, 107 S.Ct. 2095, 95 L.Ed.2d 697 (1987),] which survived due process challenges, the INS regulations provide no opportunity for the reasoned consideration of an alien juvenile's release to the custody of a non-relative by a neutral hearing officer. Nor is there any provision for a prompt hearing on a § 242.24(b)(4) release. No findings or reasons are required. Nothing in the regulations provides the unaccompanied detainee any help, whether from counsel, a parent or guardian, or anyone else. Similarly, the regulation makes no provision for appointing a guardian if no family member or legal guardian comes forward. There is no analogue to a pretrial services report, however cursory. While the INS argues that it lacks resources to conduct home studies, there is no substantial indication that some investigation or opportunity for independent, albeit informal consideration of the juvenile's circumstances in relation to the adult's agreement to

|332agency purportedly motivated by the best interests of detained juveniles would have so little to say about obvious objections to its rule.

The promulgation of the nationwide rule did not, of course, put an end to the pending litigation. The District Court again enjoined its enforcement, this time on the ground that it deprived the members of the respondent class of their liberty without the due process of law required by the Fifth Amendment. For the period of over four years subsequent to the entry of that injunction, the INS presumably has continued to release juveniles to responsible persons in the Western Region without either performing any home studies or causing any harm to alien juveniles. If any evidence confirming the supposed need for the rule had developed in recent years, it is certain that petitioners would have called it to our attention, since the INS did not hesitate to provide us with off-the-record factual material on a less significant point. See n. 16, *supra.*

The fact that the rule appears to be an ill-considered response to an adverse court ruling, rather than the product of the kind of careful deliberation that should precede a policy change that has an undeniably impor-

tant impact on individual liberty, is not, I suppose, a sufficient reason for concluding that it is invalid.[21] It does, however, shed light|333on the question whether the INS has legitimately exercised the discretion that the relevant statute has granted to the Attorney General. In order to avoid the constitutional question, I believe we should first address that statutory issue. In the alternative, as I shall explain, I would hold that a rule providing for the wholesale detention of juveniles for an indeterminate period without individual hearings is unconstitutional.

II

Section 242(a) of the Immigration and Nationality Act provides that any "alien taken into custody may, in the discretion of the Attorney General and pending [a] final determination of deportability, (A) be continued in custody; or (B) be released under bond ... containing such conditions as the Attorney General may prescribe; or (C) be released on conditional parole." 8 U.S.C. § 1252(a)(1). Despite the exceedingly broad language of § 242(a), the Court has recognized that "once the tyranny of literalness is rejected, all relevant considerations for giving a rational content to the words become operative." *Unit-*

---

care for her is impractical or financially or administratively infeasible. Although not entirely clear where the burden of proof resides, it has not clearly been imposed on the government.· And there is no limit on when the deportation hearing must be held, or put another way, how long the minor may be detained. In short, there is no ordered structure for resolving custodial status when no relative steps up to the plate but an unrelated adult is able and willing to do so." *Flores v. Meese,* 942 F.2d, 1352, 1374–1375 (CA9 1991) (opinion concurring in judgment in part and dissenting in part) (footnotes omitted).

21. That fact may, however, support a claim that the INS' issuance of the regulation was arbitrary and capricious within the meaning of the Administrative Procedure Act (APA), 5 U.S.C. § 706. See *Motor Vehicle Mfrs. Assn. of United States, Inc. v. State Farm Mut. Automobile Ins. Co.,* 463 U.S. 29, 43, 103 S.Ct. 2856, 2867, 77 L.Ed.2d 443 (1983) ("[A]n agency rule would be arbitrary and capricious if the agency has relied on factors

which Congress has not intended it to consider, entirely failed to consider an important aspect of the problem, offered an explanation for its decision that runs counter to the evidence before the agency, or is so implausible that it could not be ascribed to a difference in view or the product of agency expertise"). Respondents brought such a claim in the District Court, but do not renew that line of argument in this Court. In any event, even if the INS has managed to stay within the bounds of the APA, there is nonetheless a disturbing parallel between the Court's ready conclusion that no individualized hearing need precede the deprivation of liberty of an undocumented alien so long as the conditions of institutional custody are "good enough," *ante,* at 1449, and similar *post hoc* justifications for discrimination that is more probably explained as nothing more than "the accidental byproduct of a traditional way of thinking about" the disfavored class, see *Califano v. Goldfarb,* 430 U.S. 199, 223, 97 S.Ct. 1021, 1035, 51 L.Ed.2d 270 (1977) (STEVENS, J., concurring in judgment).

ed States v. Witkovich, 353 |₃₃₄U.S. 194, 199, 77 S.Ct. 779, 782, 1 L.Ed.2d 765 (1957). See also *INS v. National Center for Immigrants' Rights, Inc.,* 502 U.S. 183, 112 S.Ct. 551, 116 L.Ed.2d 546 (1991) (*NCIR*).

Our cases interpreting § 242(a) suggest that two such "considerations" are paramount: indications of congressional policy, and the principle that "a restrictive meaning must be given if a broader meaning would generate constitutional doubts." *Witkovich,* 353 U.S., at 199, 77 S.Ct., at 782. Thus, in *Carlson v. Landon,* 342 U.S. 524, 72 S.Ct. 525, 96 L.Ed. 547 (1952), we upheld the Attorney General's detention of deportable members of the Communist Party, relying heavily on the fact that Congress had enacted legislation, the Internal Security Act of 1950, based on its judgment that Communist subversion threatened the Nation. *Id.,* at 538, 72 S.Ct., at 533. The Attorney General's discretionary decision to detain certain alien Communists was thus "wholly consistent with Congress' intent," *NCIR,* 502 U.S., at 194, 112 S.Ct., at 558 (summarizing Court's analysis in *Carlson*). Just last Term, we faced the question whether the Attorney General acted within his authority in requiring that release bonds issued pursuant to § 242(a) contain a condition forbidding unauthorized employment pending determination of deportability. See *NCIR, supra.* Relying on related statutes and the "often recognized" principle that "a primary purpose in restricting immigration is to preserve jobs for Amer-

ican workers," *id.,* at 194, and n. 8, 112 S.Ct., at 558, and n. 8 (internal quotation marks omitted), we held that the regulation was "wholly consistent with this established concern of immigration law and thus squarely within the scope of the Attorney General's statutory authority." *Ibid.* Finally, in *Witkovich,* the Court construed a provision of the Immigration and Nationality Act which made it a criminal offense for an alien subject to deportation to willfully fail to provide to the Attorney General " 'information . . . as to his nationality, circumstances, habits, associations, and activities, and such other information . . . as the Attorney General may deem fit and proper.' " 353 U.S., at 195, 77 S.Ct., at 780. Noting that "issues touching liberties that the Constitution safeguards, even for an alien 'person,' would fairly be |₃₃₅raised on the Government's [broad] view of the statute," we held that the statute merely authorized inquiries calculated to determine the continued availability for departure of aliens whose deportation was overdue. *Id.,* at 201–202, 77 S.Ct., at 783.

The majority holds that it was within the Attorney General's authority to determine that parents, guardians, and certain relatives are "presumptively appropriate custodians" for the juveniles that come into the INS' custody, *ante,* at 1451, and therefore to detain indefinitely those juveniles who are without one of the "approved" custodians.[22] In my view, however, the guiding principles ar-

22. While the regulation provides that release can be granted to a broader class of custodians in "unusual and compelling circumstances," the practice in the Western Region after the 1984 order, but before the issuance of the injunction, was to exercise that discretion only in the event of medical emergency. See Federal Defendants' Responses to Plaintiffs' Second Set of Interrogatories (CD Cal., Jan. 30, 1986), pp. 11–12. At oral argument, counsel for petitioners suggested that "extraordinary and compelling circumstances" might include the situation where a godfather has lived and cared for the child, has a kind of family relationship with the child, *and* is in the process of navigating the state bureaucracy in order to be appointed a guardian under

state law. Tr. of Oral Arg. 54. Regardless of the precise contours of the exception to the INS' sweeping ban on discretion, it seems fair to conclude that it is meant to be extremely narrow.

There is nothing at all "puzzling," *ante,* at 1452, n. 7, in respondents' objection to the INS' requirement that would-be custodians apply for and become guardians in order to assume temporary care of the juveniles in INS custody. Formal state guardianship proceedings, regardless of how appropriate they may be for determinations relating to *permanent* custody, would unnecessarily prolong the detention of these children. What *is* puzzling is that the Court acknowledges, see *ibid.,* but then ignores the fact that were these children in *state* custody, they

ticulated in *Carlson, NCIR,* and *Witkovich* compel the opposite conclusion.

Congress has spoken quite clearly on the question of the plight of juveniles that come into federal custody. As explained above, § 504 of the Juvenile Justice and Delinquency Prevention Act of 1974 demonstrates Congress' clear preference for release, as opposed to detention. See S.Rep. No. 93–1011, p. 56 (1974) U.S.Code Cong. & Admin.News p. 5283 ("[Section 504] establishes a presumption for release of the juvenile").[23] And, most significantly for this case, it demonstrates that Congress has rejected the very presumption that the INS has made in this case; for under the Act juveniles are not to be detained when there is a "responsible party," 18 U.S.C. § 5034, willing and able to assume care for the child.[24] It is no retort that § 504 is directed at citizens, whereas the INS' regulation is directed at aliens, *ante,* at 1448–1449, 1453, n. 8; Reply Brief for Petitioners 5, n. 4. As explained above, the INS justifies its policy as serving the best interests of the juveniles that come into its custody. In seeking to dismiss the force of the Juvenile Justice and Delinquency Act as a source of congressional policy, the INS

is reduced to the absurdity of contending that Congress has authorized the Attorney General to treat allegedly illegal aliens *better* than American citizens. In my view, Congress has spoken on the detention of juveniles, and has rejected the very presumption upon which the INS relies.

There is a deeper problem with the regulation, however, one that goes beyond the use of the *particular* presumption at issue in this case. Section 242(a) grants to the Attorney General the *discretion* to detain individuals pending deportation. As we explained in *Carlson,* a "purpose to injure [the United States] could not be imputed generally to all aliens subject to deportation, so discretion was placed by the 1950 Act in the Attorney General to detain aliens without bail...." 342 U.S., at 538, 72 S.Ct., at 533. In my view, Congress has not authorized the INS to rely on mere presumptions as a substitute for the exercise of that discretion.

The Court's analysis in *Carlson* makes that point clear. If ever there were a factual predicate for a "reasonable presumptio[n]," *ante,* at 1453, it was in that case, because Congress had expressly found that communism posed a "clear and present danger to

would be released to "other responsible adults" as a matter of course. See n. 7, *supra.*

23. As I have already noted, the 1938 Federal Juvenile Delinquency Act authorized the magistrate to release an arrested juvenile "upon his own recognizance or that of *some responsible person,*" § 5, 52 Stat. 765 (emphasis added). This language was retained in the 1948 Act, see 62 Stat. 858, and amended to its present form in 1974. The Senate Report on the 1974 bill stated that it "also amends the Federal Juvenile Delinquency Act, virtually unchanged for the past thirty-five years, to provide basic procedural rights for juveniles who come under Federal jurisdiction and to bring Federal procedures up to the standards set by various model acts, many state codes and court decisions." S.Rep. No. 93–1011, p. 19 (1974) U.S.Code Cong. & Admin.News pp. 5283, 5284. Juveniles arrested by the INS are, of course, within the category of "juveniles who come under Federal jurisdiction."

24. I find this evidence of congressional intent and congressional policy far more significant than the fact that Congress has made the unex-

ceptional determination that state human service agencies should play a role in the permanent resettlement of refugee children, *ante,* at 1453, n. 8 (citing 8 U.S.C. § 1522(d)(2)(B)), and orphans adopted abroad by United States citizens, *ante,* at 1453, n. 8 (citing 8 U.S.C. § 1154(d)). This case is not about the *permanent* settlement of alien children, or the establishment of *permanent* legal custody over alien children. It is about the *temporary detention* of children that come into federal custody, which is precisely the focus of § 504 of the Juvenile Justice and Delinquency Prevention Act of 1974.

Furthermore, the Court is simply wrong in asserting that the INS' policy is rooted in the "universally accepted presumptio[n] as to the custodial competence of parents and close relatives," *ante,* at 1453, n. 8. The flaw in the INS' policy is not that it prefers parents and close relatives over unrelated adults, but that it prefers government detention over release to responsible adults. It is that presumption—that detention is better or more appropriate for these children than release to unrelated responsible adults—that is contrary to congressional policy.

the security of the United States," and that mere membership in the Communist Party was a sufficient basis for deportation.[25] Yet, in affirming the Attorney |₃₃₈General's detention of four alien Communists, the Court was careful to note that the Attorney General had not merely relied on a presumption that alien Communists posed a risk to the United States, and that therefore they should be detained, but that the detention order was grounded in "evidence of membership *plus* personal activity in supporting and extending the Party's philosophy concerning violence," 342 U.S., at 541, 72 S.Ct., at 535 (emphasis added). In fact, the Court expressly noted that "[t]here is no evidence or contention that all persons arrested as deportable under the ... Internal Security Act for Communist membership are denied bail," and that bail is allowed "in the large majority of cases." *Id.*, at 541–542, 72 S.Ct., at 535.

25. The Internal Security Act of 1950 was based on explicit findings regarding the nature of the supposed threat posed by the worldwide Communist conspiracy. The Communist Party in the United States, Congress found, " 'is an organization numbering thousands of adherents, rigidly and ruthlessly disciplined ... [a]waiting the moment when the United States may be so far extended by foreign engagements, so far divided in counsel, or so far in industrial or financial straits, that overthrow of the Government of the United States by force and violence may seem possible of achievement....' " 342 U.S., at 535, n. 21, 72 S.Ct., at 531, n. 21 (quoting § 2(15) of the Internal Security Act of 1950).

26. Neither *NCIR*, 502 U.S. 183, 112 S.Ct. 551, 116 L.Ed.2d 546 (1991), nor *Heckler v. Campbell*, 461 U.S. 458, 467, 103 S.Ct. 1952, 1957, 76 L.Ed.2d 66 (1983), upon which the majority relies for the proposition that the INS can rely on "reasonable presumptions" and "generic rules," *ante*, at 1453, are to the contrary. The Court mentioned the word "presumption" in a footnote in the *NCIR* case, 502 U.S., at 196, n. 11, 112 S.Ct., at 559, n. 11, merely in noting that the regulation at issue—a broad rule requiring that all release bonds contain a condition forbidding unauthorized employment—seemed to presume that undocumented aliens taken into INS custody were not, in fact, authorized to work. We said that such a *de facto* presumption was reasonable

By the same reasoning, the Attorney General is not authorized, in my view, to rely on a presumption regarding the suitability of potential custodians as a substitute for determining whether there is, in fact, any reason that a *particular* juvenile should be detained. Just as a "purpose to injure could not be imputed generally to all aliens," *id.*, at 538, 72 S.Ct., at 533, the unsuitability of certain unrelated adults cannot be imputed generally to all adults so as to lengthen the detention to which these children are subjected. The particular circumstances facing these juveniles are too diverse, and the right to be free from government detention too precious, to permit the INS to base the crucial determinations regarding detention upon a mere presumption regarding "appropriate custodians," *ante*, at 1451. I do not believe that Congress intended to authorize such a policy.[26]

|₃₃₉And finally, even if it were not clear to me that the Attorney General has exceeded

because the vast majority of aliens that come into INS custody do not have such authorization, and because the presumption was easily rebutted. *Ibid.* To the extent that case has any bearing on the INS' use of presumptions, it merely says that the INS may use some easily rebuttable presumptions in identifying the class of individuals subject to its regulations—in that case, aliens lacking authorization to work. Once that class is properly identified, however, the issue becomes whether the INS can use mere presumptions as a basis for making fundamental decisions about detention and freedom. On *that* question, *NCIR* is silent; for the regulation at issue there was not based on a presumption at all. It simply provided that an alien who violates American law by engaging in unauthorized employment also violates the terms of his release from INS custody. *Id.*, at 185, 112 S.Ct., at 554.

Heckler v. Campbell, 461 U.S. 458, 103 S.Ct. 1952, 76 L.Ed.2d 66 (1983), presents a closer analog to what the INS has done in this case, but only as a matter of logic, for the factual differences between the governmental action approved in *Heckler* and the INS' policy in this case renders the former a woefully inadequate precedent to support the latter. In *Heckler*, the Court approved the use of pre-established medical-vocational guidelines for determining Social Security disability benefits, stating:

"The Court has recognized that even where an agency's enabling statute expressly requires it to hold a hearing, the agency may rely on its rule-

her authority under § 242(a), I would still hold that § 242(a) requires an individualized determination₃₄₀ as to whether detention is necessary when a juvenile does not have an INS-preferred custodian available to assume temporary custody. " 'When the validity of an act of the Congress is drawn in question, and even if a serious doubt of constitutionality is raised, it is a cardinal principle that this Court will first ascertain whether a construction of the statute is fairly possible by which the question may be avoided.' " *Witkovich,* 353 U.S., at 201–202, 77 S.Ct., at 783 (quoting *Crowell v. Benson,* 285 U.S. 22, 62, 52 S.Ct. 285, 296, 76 L.Ed. 598 (1932)). The detention of juveniles on the basis of a general presumption as to the suitability of particular custodians without an individualized determination as to whether that presumption bears any relationship at all to the facts of a particular case implicates an interest at the very core of the Due Process Clause, the constitutionally protected interest in freedom from bodily restraint. As such, it raises even more serious constitutional concerns than the INS policy invalidated in *Witkovich.* Legislative grants of discretionary authority should be construed to avoid constitutional issues and harsh consequences that were almost certainly not contemplated or intended by Congress. Unlike my colleagues, I would hold that the Attorney General's actions in this case are not authorized by § 242(a).

III

I agree with Justice O'CONNOR that respondents "have a constitutionally protected

interest in freedom from institutional confinement . . . [that] lies within the core of the Due Process Clause." *Ante,* at 1454 (concurring opinion). Indeed, we said as much just last Term. See *Foucha v. Louisiana,* 504 U.S. 71, 80, 112 S.Ct. 1780, 1785, 118 L.Ed.2d 437 (1992) ("Freedom from bodily restraint has always been at the core of liberty protected by the Due Process Clause from arbitrary governmental action"). *Ibid.* ₃₄₁("We have always been careful not to 'minimize the importance and fundamental nature' of the individual's right to liberty") (quoting *United States v. Salerno,* 481 U.S. 739, 750, 107 S.Ct. 2095, 2103, 95 L.Ed.2d 697 (1987)).

I am not as convinced as she, however, that "the Court today does not hold otherwise." *Ante,* at 1454 (concurring opinion). For the children at issue in this case *are* being confined in government-operated or government-selected institutions, their liberty *has been* curtailed, and yet the Court defines the right at issue as merely the "alleged right of a child who has no available parent, close relative, or legal guardian, and for whom the government is responsible, to be placed in the custody of a willing-and-able private custodian rather than of a government-operated or government-selected child-care institution." *Ante,* at 1447. Finding such a claimed constitutional right to be "nove[l]," *ante,* at 1447, and certainly not "fundamental," *ante,* at 1448, 1452, the Court concludes that these juveniles' alleged "right" to be released to "other responsible adults" is easily trumped by the government's interest

---

making authority to determine issues that do not require case-by-case consideration. A contrary holding would require the agency continually to relitigate issues that may be established fairly and efficiently in a single rulemaking." *Id.,* at 467, 103 S.Ct., at 1957 (citations omitted). Suffice it to say that the determination as to the suitability of a temporary guardian for a juvenile, unlike the determination as to the nature and type of jobs available for an injured worker, *is* an inquiry that requires case-by-case consideration, and *is not* one that may be established fairly and efficiently in a single rulemak-

ing. More importantly, the determination as to whether a child should be released to the custody of a friend, godparent, or cousin, as opposed to being detained in a government institution, implicates far more fundamental concerns than whether an individual will receive a particular government benefit. In my view, the Court's reliance on *Heckler v. Campbell* cuts that case from its administrative law moorings. I simply do not believe that Congress authorized the INS to determine, by rulemaking, that children are better off in government detention facilities than in the care of responsible friends, cousins, godparents, or other responsible parties.

in protecting the welfare of these children and, most significantly, by the INS' interest in avoiding the administrative inconvenience and expense of releasing them to a broader class of custodians. *Ante,* at 1448, 1452–1453.

In my view, the only "novelty" in this case is the Court's analysis. The right at stake in this case is not the right of detained juveniles to be *released* to one particular custodian rather than another, but the right not to be *detained* in the first place. "In our society liberty is the norm, and detention prior to trial or without trial is the carefully limited exception." *Salerno,* 481 U.S., at 755, 107 S.Ct., at 2105. It is the government's burden to prove that detention is necessary, not the

individual's burden to prove that release is justified. And, as Justice O'CONNOR explains, that burden is not easily met, for when government action infringes on this most fundamental of rights, we have scrutinized such conduct to ensure that the detention serves both "legitimate and compelling"₃₄₂ interests, *id.,* at 749, 107 S.Ct., at 2102, and, in addition, is implemented in a manner that is "carefully limited" and "narrowly focused." *Foucha,* 504 U.S., at 81, 112 S.Ct., at 1786.[27]

₃₄₃On its face, the INS' regulation at issue in this case cannot withstand such scrutiny.[28] The United States no doubt has a substantial and legitimate interest in protecting the welfare of juveniles that come into its custody.

---

27. A comparison of the detention regimes upheld in *Salerno* and struck down in *Foucha* is illustrative. In *Salerno,* we upheld against due process attack provisions of the Bail Reform Act of 1984 which allow a federal court to detain an arrestee before trial if the Government can demonstrate that no release conditions will " 'reasonably assure ... the safety of any other person and the community.' " *Salerno,* 481 U.S., at 741, 107 S.Ct., at 2098. As we explained in *Foucha:*

"The statute carefully limited the circumstances under which detention could be sought to those involving the most serious of crimes ..., and was narrowly focused on a particularly acute problem in which the government interests are overwhelming. In addition to first demonstrating probable cause, the Government was required, in a full-blown adversary hearing, to convince a neutral decisionmaker by clear and convincing evidence that no conditions of release can reasonably assure the safety of the community or any person.... Furthermore, the duration of confinement under the Act was strictly limited. The arrestee was entitled to a prompt detention hearing and the maximum length of pretrial detention was limited by the stringent limitations of the Speedy Trial Act." 504 U.S., at 81, 112 S.Ct., at 1786 (citations and internal quotation marks omitted).

By contrast, the detention statute we struck down in *Foucha* was anything but narrowly focused or carefully limited. Under Louisiana law, criminal defendants acquitted by reason of insanity were automatically committed to state psychiatric institutions, regardless of whether they were then insane, and held until they could prove that they were no longer dangerous. *Id.,* at 73, 112 S.Ct., at 1781–1782. We struck down the law as a violation of the substantive component

of the Due Process Clause of the Fourteenth Amendment:

"Unlike the sharply focused scheme at issue in *Salerno,* the Louisiana scheme of confinement is not carefully limited. Under the state statute, Foucha is not now entitled to an adversary hearing at which the State must prove by clear and convincing evidence that he is demonstrably dangerous to the community. Indeed, the State need prove nothing to justify continued detention, for the statute places the burden on the detainee to prove that he is not dangerous....

.   .   .   .   .

"It was emphasized in *Salerno* that the detention we found constitutionally permissible was strictly limited in duration. Here, in contrast, the State asserts that ... [Foucha] may be held indefinitely." *Id.,* at 81–82, 112 S.Ct., at 1786–1787.

As explained in the text, the INS' regulation at issue in this case falls well on the *Foucha* side of the *Salerno/Foucha* divide.

28. Because this is a facial challenge, the Court asserts that respondents cannot prevail unless there is " 'no set of circumstances ... under which the [regulation] would be valid.' " *Ante,* at 1446. This is a rather puzzling pronouncement. Would a facial challenge to a statute providing for imprisonment of all alien children without a hearing fail simply because there is a set of circumstances in which at least one such alien should be detained? Is the Court saying that this challenge fails because the categorical deprivation of liberty to the members of the respondent class may turn out to be beneficial to some? Whatever the Court's rhetoric may signify, it seems clear to me, as I explain in the text, that detention for an insufficient reason without adequate procedural safeguards is a deprivation of liberty without due process of law.

Schall v. Martin, 467 U.S. 253, 266, 104 S.Ct. 2403, 2410, 81 L.Ed.2d 207 (1984). However, a blanket rule that simply *presumes* that detention is more appropriate than release to responsible adults is not narrowly focused on serving that interest. Categorical distinctions between cousins and uncles, or between relatives and godparents or other responsible persons, are much too blunt instruments to justify wholesale deprivations of liberty. Due process demands more, far more.[29] If the Government is going to detain juveniles in order to protect their welfare, due process requires that it demonstrate, *on an individual basis,* that detention in fact serves that interest. That is the clear command of our cases. See, *e.g., Foucha,* 504 U.S., at 81, 112 S.Ct., at 1786 (finding due process violation when individual who is detained on grounds |₃₄₄of "dangerousness" is denied right to adversary hearing in "which the State must prove by clear and convincing evidence that he is demonstrably dangerous to the community"); *Salerno,* 481 U.S., at 742, 107 S.Ct., at 2098 (finding no due process violation when detention follows hearing to determine whether detention is necessary to prevent flight or danger to community); *Schall v. Martin,* 467 U.S., at 263, 104 S.Ct., at 2409 (same; hearing to determine whether there is "serious risk" that if released juvenile will commit a crime); *Gerstein v. Pugh,* 420 U.S.

103, 126, 95 S.Ct. 854, 869, 43 L.Ed.2d 54 (1975) (holding that Fourth Amendment requires judicial determination of probable cause as prerequisite to detention); *Greenwood v. United States,* 350 U.S. 366, 367, 76 S.Ct. 410, 411, 100 L.Ed. 412 (1956) (upholding statute in which individuals charged with or convicted of federal crimes may be committed to the custody of the Attorney General after judicial determination of incompetency); *Carlson v. Landon,* 342 U.S., at 541, 72 S.Ct., at 534 (approving Attorney General's discretionary decision to detain four alien Communists based on their membership and activity in Communist Party); *Ludecke v. Watkins,* 335 U.S. 160, 163, n. 5, 68 S.Ct. 1429, 1430, n. 5, 92 L.Ed. 1881 (1948) (upholding Attorney General's detention and deportation of alien under the Alien Enemy Act; finding of "dangerousness" based on evidence adduced at administrative hearings). See also *Stanley v. Illinois,* 405 U.S. 645, 657–658, 92 S.Ct. 1208, 1215–1216, 31 L.Ed.2d 551 (1972) (State cannot rely on presumption of unsuitability of unwed fathers; State must make individualized determinations of parental fitness); *Carrington v. Rash,* 380 U.S. 89, 95–96, 85 S.Ct. 775, 779–780, 13 L.Ed.2d 675 (1965) (striking down blanket exclusion depriving all servicemen stationed in State of right to vote when interest in limiting franchise to bona fide residents could have been achieved by assessing a serviceman's claim to residency on an individual basis).[30]

---

29. In objecting to this statement, see *ante,* at 1452, n. 6, the majority once again mischaracterizes the issue presented in this case. As explained above, see n. 24, *supra,* the INS can of course favor release of a juvenile to a parent or close relative over release to an unrelated adult. What the INS cannot do, in my view, is prefer *detention* over *release* to a responsible adult, a proposition that hardly "revolutionize[s]" our family law.

30. There is, of course, one notable exception to this long line of cases: *Korematsu v. United States,* 323 U.S. 214, 65 S.Ct. 193, 89 L.Ed. 194 (1944), in which the Court upheld the exclusion from particular "military areas" of all persons of Japanese ancestry without a determination as to whether any particular individual actually posed a threat of sabotage or espionage. *Id.,* at 215–

216, 65 S.Ct., at 193–194. The Court today does not cite that case, but the Court's holding in *Korematsu* obviously supports the majority's analysis, for the Court approved a serious infringement of individual liberty without requiring a case-by-case determination as to whether such an infringement was in fact necessary to effect the Government's compelling interest in national security. I understand the majority's reluctance to rely on *Korematsu.* The exigencies of war that were thought to justify that categorical deprivation of liberty are not, of course, implicated in this case. More importantly, the recent congressional decision to pay reparations to the Japanese–Americans who were detained during that period, see Restitution for World War II Internment of Japanese Americans and Aleuts, 102 Stat. 903, suggests that the Court should proceed with extreme caution when asked to permit the

⌐345If, in fact, the Due Process Clause establishes a powerful presumption against unnecessary official detention that is not based on an individualized evaluation of its justification, why has the INS refused to make such determinations? As emphasized above, the argument that detention is more appropriate for these children than release to responsible adults is utterly lacking in support, in either the history of this litigation, or expert opinion. Presumably because of the improbability of the INS' asserted justification for its policy, the Court does not rely on it as the basis for upholding the regulation. Instead, the Court holds that even if detention is not really *better* for these juveniles than release to responsible adults, so long as it is "good enough," *ante,* at 1449, the INS need not spend the time and money that would be necessary to actually serve the "best interests" of these children. *Ante,* at 1448–1449. In other words, so long as its cages are gilded, the INS need not expend its administrative resources on a program that would better serve its asserted interests and that would not need to employ cages at all.

The linchpin in the Court's analysis, of course, is its narrow reading of the right at stake in this case. By characterizing it as some insubstantial and nonfundamental right to be released₃₄₆ to an unrelated adult, the Court is able to escape the clear holding of our cases that "administrative convenience" is a thoroughly inadequate basis for the deprivation of core constitutional rights. *Ante,* at 1452 (citing, for comparison, *Stanley v. Illinois,* 405 U.S. 645, 92 S.Ct. 1208, 31 L.Ed.2d 551 (1972)). As explained above, however, the right at issue in this case is not the right to be released to an unrelated adult; it is the right to be free from Government confinement that is the very essence of the liberty protected by the Due Process Clause. It is a right that cannot be defeated by a claim of a lack of expertise or a lack of

resources. In my view, then, *Stanley v. Illinois* is not a case to look to for comparison, but one from which to derive controlling law. For in *Stanley,* we flatly rejected the premise underlying the Court's holding today.

In that case, we entertained a due process challenge to a statute under which children of unwed parents, upon the death of the mother, were declared wards of the State without any hearing as to the father's fitness for custody. In striking down the statute, we rejected the argument that a State's interest in conserving administrative resources was a sufficient basis for refusing to hold a hearing as to a father's fitness to care for his children:

"Procedure by presumption is always cheaper and easier than individualized determination. But when, as here, the procedure forecloses the determinative issues of competence and care, when it explicitly disdains present realities in deference to past formalities, it needlessly risks running roughshod over the important interests of both parent and child. It therefore cannot stand.

"*Bell v. Burson*[, 402 U.S. 535, 91 S.Ct. 1586, 29 L.Ed.2d 90 (1971),] held that the State could not, while purporting to be concerned with fault in suspending a driver's license, deprive a citizen of his license without a hearing that would assess fault. Absent fault, the State's declared interest was so attenuated that administrative convenience was insufficient to excuse a hearing where evidence of fault could be considered.₃₄₇ That drivers involved in accidents, as a statistical matter, might be very likely to have been wholly or partially at fault did not foreclose hearing and proof on specific cases before licenses were suspended.

"We think the Due Process Clause mandates a similar result here. The State's interest in caring for Stanley's children is *de minimis* if Stanley is shown to be a fit

---

detention of juveniles when the Government has failed to inquire whether, in any given case, detention actually serves the Government's inter-

est in protecting the interests of the children in its custody.

father. It insists on presuming rather than proving Stanley's unfitness solely because it is more convenient to presume than to prove. Under the Due Process Clause that advantage is insufficient to justify refusing a father a hearing when the issue at stake is the dismemberment of his family." *Id.*, at 656–658, 92 S.Ct., at 1215–1216.

Just as the State of Illinois could not rely on the administrative convenience derived from denying fathers a hearing, the INS may not rely on the fact that "other concerns ... compete for public funds and administrative attention," *ante*, at 1448, as an excuse to keep from doing what due process commands: determining, on an individual basis, whether the detention of a child in a government-operated or government-sponsored institution actually serves the INS' asserted interest in protecting the welfare of that child.[31]

Ultimately, the Court is simply wrong when it asserts that "freedom from physical restraint" is not at issue in this case. That is precisely what is at issue. The Court's assumption that the detention facilities used by the INS conform to the |348standards set forth in the partial settlement in this case has nothing to do with the fact that the juveniles who are not released to relatives or responsible adults are held in detention facilities. They do not have the "freedom from physical restraint" that those who are released do have. That is what this case is all about. That is why the respondent class continues to litigate. These juveniles do not want to be committed to institutions that the INS and the Court believe are "good enough" for aliens simply because they conform to standards that are adequate for the incarceration of juvenile delinquents. They want the same kind of liberty that the Con-

stitution guarantees similarly situated citizens. And as I read our precedents, the omission of any provision for individualized consideration of the best interests of the juvenile in a rule authorizing an indefinite period of detention of presumptively innocent and harmless children denies them precisely that liberty.

I respectfully dissent.

507 U.S. 349, 123 L.Ed.2d 47

|349SAUDI ARABIA, King Faisal
Specialist Hospital and
Royspec, Petitioners

v.

Scott NELSON et ux.

No. 91–522.

Argued Nov. 30, 1992.

Decided March 23, 1993.

American employee of Saudi hospital brought action against Kingdom of Saudi Arabia, hospital, and hospital's purchasing agent in United States, based on injuries arising from his alleged detention and torture by Saudi Government. The United States District Court for the Southern District of Florida, Lenore Carrero Nesbitt, J., dismissed action for lack of jurisdiction under the Foreign Sovereign Immunities Act, and plaintiff appealed. The Court of Appeals reversed, 923 F.2d 1528, and certiorari was granted. The Supreme Court, Justice Souter, held that action was not "based upon a commercial activity" within mean-

---

31. Of course, even as a factual matter the INS' reliance on its asserted inability to conduct home studies because of a lack of resources or expertise as a justification for its wholesale detention policy is unpersuasive. It is perfectly clear that the costs of detention far exceed the cost of the kinds of inquiry that are necessary or appropriate for temporary release determinations. See n.

18, *supra*. Moreover, it is nothing less than perverse that the Attorney General releases juvenile *citizens* to the custody of "other responsible adults" without the elaborate "home studies" allegedly necessary to safeguard the juvenile's interests but deems such studies necessary before releasing *noncitizens* to the custody of "other responsible adults."

Acknowledgments

Nafziger, James A.R. "Review of Visa Denials by Consular Officers," *Washington Law Review* 66 (1991): 1–38, 52–102. Reprinted with the permission of the Washington Law Review Association.

United States ex rel. *Knauff* v. *Shaughnessy*, 70 S.Ct. 309–17 (1950). Reprinted with the permission of the West Publishing Company.

Landon v. *Plasencia*, 103 S.Ct. 321–34 (1982). Reprinted with the permission of the West Publishing Company.

Shaugnessy v. *United States* ex rel. *Mezei*, 73 S.Ct. 625-37 (1953). Reprinted with the permission of the West Publishing Company.

Taylor, Margaret H. "Detained Aliens Challenging Conditions of Confinement and the Porous Border of the Plenary Power Doctrine," *Hastings Constitutional Law Quarterly* 22 (1995): 1087–1158. Reprinted by permission. Copyright by University of California, Hastings College of Law.

Osuna, Juan P., and Patricia Mariani. "Expedited Removal: Authorities, Implementation, and Ongoing Policy and Practice Issues," *Immigration Briefings* (1997): 1–15. Reprinted with the permission of Federal Publications, Inc.

Inspection by Immigration Officers, 8 U.S.C.A. Sects. 1125–1225. Reprinted with the permission of the West Publishing Company.

Benson, Lenni B. "The New World of Judicial Review of Removal Orders," *Georgetown Immigration Law Journal* 12 (1997): 233–64. Reprinted with the permission of the Georgetown University Law Center.

Yamataya v. *Fisher*, 23 S.Ct. 611-15 (1903).

Scaperlanda, Michael. "Are We That Far Gone?: Due Process and Secret Deportation Hearings," *Stanford Law and Policy Review* 7 (1996): 23–33. Reprinted with the permission of the Stanford law School.

Alien Terrorist Removal Procedudres, 8 U.S.C.A. Sects 1531–1537. Reprinted with the permission of the West Publishing Company.

INS v. *Lopez-Mendoza*, 104 S.Ct. 3479–95 (1984). Reprinted with the permission of the West Publishing Company.

Reno v. *Flores*, 113 S.Ct. 1439–71 (1993). Reprinted with the permission of the West Publishing Company.

350

Controversies in Constitutional Law

The Constitution and the Flag (1993)
Volume 1: The Flag Salute Cases
Volume 2: The Flag Burning Cases

Prayer in Public Schools and the Constitution 1961–1992 (1993)
Volume 1: Government-Sponsored Religious Activities
in Public Schools and the Constitution

Volume 2: Moments of Silence in Public Schools and the Constitution

Volume 3: Protecting Religious Speech in Public Schools:
The Establishment and Free Exercise Clauses in the Public Arena

Gun Control and the Constitution
Sources and Explorations on the Second Amendment (1993)

Volume 1: The Courts, Congress, and the Second Amendment
Volume 2: Advocates and Scholars: The Modern Debate on Gun Control
Volume 3: Special Topics on Gun Control

School Busing
Constitutional and Political Developments (1994)

Volume 1: The Development of School Busing as a Desegregation Remedy
Volume 2: The Public Debate Over Busing Attempts to Restrict Its Use

Abortion Law in the United States (1995)
Volume 1: From *Roe* v. *Wade* to the Present
Volume 2: Historical Development of Abortion Law
Volume 3: Modern Writings on Abortion

Hate Speech and the Constitution (1996)

Volume 1: The Development of the Hate Speech Debate:
From Group Libel to Campus Speech Codes

Volume 2: The Contemporary Debate:
Reconciling Freedom of Expression and Equality of Citizenship

Capital Punishment (1996)

Volume 1: The Philosophical, Moral, and Penological Debate Over Capital Punishment
Volume 2: Capital Punishment Jurisprudence
Volume 3: Litigating Capital Cases

Homosexuality and the Constitution (1997)

Volume 1: Homosexual Conduct and State Regulation
Volume 2: Homosexuals and the Military
Volume 3: Homosexuality, Politics, and Speech
Volume 4: Homosexuality and the Family

Environment, Property, and the Law (1997)

Federal and State Case Decisions & Journal Articles

Affirmative Action and the Constitution (1998)

Volume 1: Affirmative Action Before Constitutional Law, 1964–1977
Volume 2: The Supreme Court "Solves" the Affirmative Action Issue, 1978–1988
Volume 3: Judicial Reaction to Affirmative Action, 1989–1997

Domestic Violence:
From a Private Matter to a Federal Offense (1998)

Volume 1: Domestic Violence: Intimate Partner Abuse
Volume 2: The Crimes of Domestic Violence
Volume 3: The Civil Justice System's Response to Domestic Violence

Labor and the Constitution (1999)

Volume 1: The Constitutionality and the Purpose of the Federal Labor Laws
Volume 2: Labor and Property, Privacy, Discrimination, and International Relations

State Expansion of Federal Constitutional Liberties: Individual Rights in a Dual Constitutional System

(1999)

Volume 1: The Development of Independent State Constitutional Law
Volume 2: The Jurisprudential Crisis of State Constitutional Law

Privacy and the Constitution (1999)

Volume 1: Traditional Speech Rights
Volume 2: Electronic Speech Rights
Volume 3: Privacy Rights and the Body

Immigration and the Constitution (2000)

Volume 1: The Origins of Constitutional Immigration Law
Volume 2: Discrimination and Equality in Contemporary Immigration Law
Volume 3: Shark Infested Waters:
Procedural Due Process in Constitutional Immigration Law

www.ingramcontent.com/pod-product-compliance
Ingram Content Group UK Ltd.
Pitfield, Milton Keynes, MK11 3LW, UK
UKHW041106040325
455677UK00032B/38